GUIDE TO

Service-Learning

COLLEGES & UNIVERSITIES

Published by Kendall/Hunt Publishing Company
4050 Westmark Drive
P.O. Box 1840
Dubuque, IA 52004

Introduction material is based upon work supported by the Corporation for National and Community Service under Learn and Serve America Grant No. 05TAHCA005. Opinions or points of view expressed in this material are those of the authors and do not necessarily reflect the official position of the Corporation or the Learn and Serve America Program.

The National Service-Learning Clearinghouse (NSLC) produced this introductory material under Learn and Serve Grant No. 05TAHCA005. NSLC, as the copyright owner, has granted license to Student Horizons, Inc to use the material in this Guide.

For bulk sales to schools, colleges, and universities, please contact Student Horizons at info@studenthorizons.com or Kendall/Hunt Publishing Company at (800) 338-8290.

Printed in the United States of America
2008
10 9 8 7 6 5 4 3 2 1

Library of Congress Control Number: 2008932402

ISBN 9780980013214

Contents

Introduction

Making the Most of Your Life

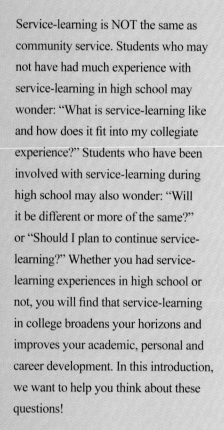

Introduction

You are about to make one of the biggest decisions of your life, and, for many students, choosing the right college isn't easy. There are questions about programs, size, student life, sports, location – and, of course, costs. Why should you now add "service-learning" to this already long list? Maybe you've already done a lot of community service. Maybe you did it precisely because you thought it would help you get into college. Or, maybe you did it because you really liked service activities. Why should you still be thinking about service *now, as you are busy preparing for transition to college?* What does service have to do with choosing a college? Isn't college about learning new things, getting good grades, preparing for a successful career (while at the same time having a little fun)? You might be surprised to learn service-learning is about these very same things – and a whole lot more!

This introductory material is based upon work supported by the Corporation for National and Community Service under Learn and Serve America Grant No. 05TAHCA005. Opinions or points of view expressed in this material are those of the authors and do not necessarily reflect the official position of the Corporation or the Learn and Serve America Program.

The National Service-Learning Clearinghouse (NSLC) produced this introductory material under Learn and Serve Grant No. 05TAHCA005. NSLC, as the copyright owner, has granted license to Student Horizons, Inc to use the material in this Guide.

Service-learning is NOT the same as community service. Students who may not have had much experience with service-learning in high school may wonder: "What is service-learning like and how does it fit into my collegiate experience?" Students who have been involved with service-learning during high school may also wonder: "Will it be different or more of the same?" or "Should I plan to continue service-learning?" Whether you had service-learning experiences in high school or not, you will find that service-learning in college broadens your horizons and improves your academic, personal and career development. In this introduction, we want to help you think about these questions!

In the best college service-learning programs, "learning" is as important as "serving," and students develop important new skills and ideas. Service-learning is active education; it is exciting, engaging, and challenging. And because of its dynamic nature, service-learning has great potential to transform your life. If, like the

Making the Most of Your Life

majority of today's students, you would like to add a "hands on" dimension to your college experience; if you're one of those people who like to know "*why?*" you're being asked to study something; or "how?" you would actually use classroom knowledge in real life; **if you don't like classes that are all lecture – then you owe it to yourself to learn a little about college service-learning programs.** This book will help you do just that!

Service-learning is concerned with many areas critical to what college can and does mean to your future. **As you know, education is not just about preparing for a career. It's also about engaging the world in a meaningful way.** Getting a college education is a privilege many people in our country, let alone the world, don't have, and with this privilege come respon-sibilities. Our society needs you,

as an educated person, to use your knowledge and skills to achieve public as well as private goals by being involved in your communities. Doing this is called "civic engagement."

Practicing the skills and experiencing the rewards of civic engagement has many benefits. It can help you clarify your values and empower yourself as both a student and a citizen. Some students see college primarily as the end of something – the last stage of their formal education. But college is also a bridge – a bridge that connects you to your future, and that spans the gap between what you already know and a wider world waiting to be explored. Some students spend their entire college career behind the walls of an 'ivory tower,' focused primarily on getting good grades. Clearly, good grades are important, but unless you learn to make a vital connection between the classroom and the community, your good grades may never help you bring knowledge to life.

In short, service-learning can have a significant impact on your academic success, your preparation for a career, and your understanding of what you can – and should – contribute to the rest of the world. Students involved in service-learning are able to see first-hand why a college education matters. They are able to bring their knowledge and skills to bear on a vast array of real world problems: literacy, environmental issues, education, political justice issues, homelessness, poverty, public health, and many more. **They learn – in an especially powerful way – what it means to make a difference.**

But perhaps the greatest benefit service-learning holds in store for you is that that it will help you get the experiences and develop the attitudes one expects of a leader. As your perspectives grow and your horizons broaden, you may be surprised to discover – regardless of your achievements thus far – just how much you have to learn, and to offer. Such self-knowledge and such-self confidence are themselves worth the price of a ticket!

Part 1: What is Service-Learning?

Service-learning: a teaching and learning strategy that integrates meaningful community service with instruction and reflection to enrich the learning experience, teach civic responsibility, and strengthen communities.

Service-learning brings together community service and academic learning in order to improve both the student and the community. **As you participate in service projects, you develop practical skills, critical thinking, self-esteem, and a sense of civic responsibility that can last a lifetime.**

The combination of rigorous study and community engagement is so powerful, service-learning can often promote learning to a depth and breadth that go beyond what happens in conventional classroom. Service-learning is knowledge in action!

Being involved with service-learning means being part of a rich tradition. Community service and civic engagement have a long history on American campuses: from the civil rights movement of the 1960s, and the formation of the Peace Corps, to Volunteers in Service to America (VISTA) which brought **a new passionate energy to education by engaging young people and giving them real opportunities to make a difference in the world**.

It was during this time period that the early pioneers of the service-learning movement began to emerge and attempted to combine 'service' to 'learning' in a direct and powerful way. **Today there is a push toward a fully-engaged university as a whole: active, vibrant partnerships of scholars,** as well as students and citizens who have the support and resources to achieve phenomenal things in education and in transforming communities nationwide. (For more information on the history of service-learning in higher education visit "http://www.servicelearning. org/what_is_service-learning/ history_hesl/index.php")

When you take a course that includes service-learning, the syllabus will offer you many different ways to explore the course's content; for example, lectures, class discussions, labs, readings and research papers. In the service-learning part of the course, you will be learning this content through activities that involve the off-campus community. This means you will often be learning from

5 Core Elements of Service-Learning

Preparation: Young people begin their research on the community problems of interest. They may conduct a needs assessment or other form of determination of community needs. Once they choose a need they would like to address, students conduct some form of research to document the extent and nature of the problem and establish a baseline for monitoring progress. At this stage, youth often identify the community partners with whom they will work. If the young people identify the area of interest based on the opportunities being provided by the community partner, the investigation typically involves documentation of the need.

Planning: In this component, sometimes called planning and sometimes called preparation, young people, often working with community partners, plan the ways in which they will meet the community need. Planning may include developing a common vision for success, deciding what to do, determining who will do what, creating timelines for completion, listing materials needed and costs, and including how funds will be procured.

Action: All participants implement their plans by engaging in the activities that will meet the community needs. This is the actual service portion of service-learning.

Reflection: At each stage, participants engage in some form of activity that allows them to think about the community need, their actions, their impacts, what worked and did not work, the ways in which their work contributes to the common good, and/or similar types of analytic thinking. Final reflections often include measures or other ways to gauge impact.

Demonstration/Celebration: These activities go hand in hand as young people show others, preferably in a public setting with those that have influence, what they have accomplished, what they have learned, and the impact of their work. Celebration of the learning and impact follows the demonstration.

Shelley Billig, RMC Research, 2008

people in that community as well as from your course instructor. Nevertheless, **whether you take a traditional test or work on a community-based project, you will be asked to demonstrate what you have learned.** Just providing service, no matter how valuable in itself, is not enough to earn academic credit.

One especially important feature of service-learning is its goal of helping every individual, group, and organization involved play the role of teacher as well as learner. **In other words, service-learning is reciprocal in nature, transforming both the recipient and the provider of the service.** That's why you'll find that when you are working with a community partner, you'll be learning from the people you work with – even if your job is tutoring or teaching them! This can make learning very exciting and encourage you to think about how the career you choose can also make a difference in communities.

Civic Responsibility **signifies an individual's commitment to be actively involved in his or her community.** Part of the idea of being an educated person is that knowledge empowers people to look beyond themselves to consider also the well-being of their community. As a service-learning college student, you will develop your own conception and understanding of civic responsibility and thus be better prepared to become an active citizen. Service-learning will show you new ways in which your knowledge and skills can contribute to the community – ways you may have never dreamed of! At the same time, it will allow you to do the kind of **hands-on exploring that makes it easier to decide what career is right for you.**

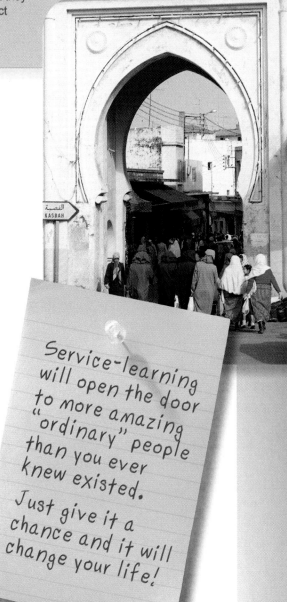

> Service-learning will open the door to more amazing "ordinary" people than you ever knew existed.
>
> Just give it a chance and it will change your life!

Partnerships

As you've probably guessed by now, partnerships are key to service-learning's effectiveness. Partnerships require professors and students to work with community groups in new ways. We said a little earlier that service-learning is reciprocal in nature. That implies that **those on the academic side learn from and with community partners, not just do things for them or give things to them. Such reciprocity requires extra time and effort, but it is well worth it.**

Often the difference between the deep learning and deep satisfaction students gain from a service-learning experience and **the short rush of good feeling they got from their high school community service experiences is a direct result** of taking the time to see that all the participants in a service-learning project are fully involved.

Whether your partner is an elementary or secondary schools, community service programs, government agencies, non-profit and faith-based school, a small local business, a neighborhood organization, or a particular population such as an immigrant or tribal communities, you'll be amazed how much that partner has to contribute to the service-learning process. By helping you access community leaders and people who have lived lives rich in experience, service-learning encourages you to learn to appreciate the value of such non-academic expertise.

Photo Courtesy Arizona State University

You probably already have people in your family and your home neighborhood from whom you have learned powerful lessons – even though those people have relatively little formal schooling. Service-learning will open the door to more amazing "ordinary" people than you ever knew existed.

Reflection

If Partnerships are key to service-learning's overall effectiveness, Reflection is *the* key to its effectiveness as a learning strategy. You can think of reflection as the space in which all service-learning participants – but particularly students – unpack the meaning of their experience, examining it from many different perspectives – personal, civic, academic, technical, social, etc. **Reflection is also the principal way in which service-learning promotes one of the most important goals of a college education: critical thinking.**

Reflection occurs in many forms: through reading, writing, discussion, performance – indeed, through any activity that allows someone to analyze and articulate their observations. It also occurs at multiple points throughout the service-learning

experience, marking the beginning and the end of the process as well as points of growth along the way.

Before the service activity even gets started, reflection will help you identify your attitudes and assumptions, making it possible for you to approach your project in an open-minded way.

Reflection that takes place *over the course of your service project* will not only make it more likely that both your serving and your learning will continue to go well but will also help you integrate your service–based learning with other course activities.

After you've completed your project, reflection will give you a chance to sort out what you've learned while it is still fresh in your mind. It will also give you a chance to evaluate your project, assess your own development, look for lessons to guide future decisions, and find 'new applications' for what you've learned."

But regardless of the form reflection takes and when it occurs, you'll find that it is reflection that connects the specifics of the community-based work with a wider world of theories, ideas, and concepts, and it is reflection that lets you see why those theories, ideas, and concepts are important in the first place.

Service-Learning is different from volunteering and community service

By this point you can probably see clearly why we've said service-learning is NOT the same as community service. Service-learning is different in the way you will interact with community organizations and community residents. In volunteering, you are doing something "for" someone else and there is no expectation that you will receive anything in return except warm thanks. **In service-learning you are doing things "with" people in the community in a collaborative manner; the community members you interact with will be influencing or even leading what you do, and they will be influencing your learning as well.**

As a student you should keep in mind that the learning in service-learning is as important as the service. Even if your professor requires a certain number of service hours, it is not those hours for which he/she will give you a grade. What finally counts towards your grade is the learning you've demonstrated through whatever papers, products, tests, reflections, and discussions your professor requires. **The service you do will help you complete these other kinds of assignments – it is part of what you do to demonstrate you've learned the course content.**

All this may be a far cry from the community service experiences you had in high school. Whether your high school called what you did "community service" or "service-learning," the key to college-level service-learning is THINKING about what you've done as an aspect of your LEARNING. So whether your professor says service-learning is a required or an optional assignment (usually in place of another assignment such as a test, a paper, or a case study), you won't earn academic credit simply for doing a good deed. **Service-learning is learning and exploring course content through action.**

Whether you were a high-achiever in high school or not, service-learning is a powerful item to put in your collegiate toolbox. Service-learning contributes to the development of learning skills, the discovery of your interests and abilities, the testing and choice of a career direction, a way to create positive relationships on campus and in the community, and can lead to greater academic success, a stronger resume, professional references, and a lifelong desire to learn and to be active in community life.

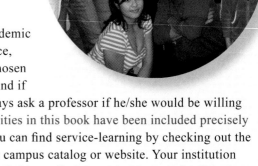

Service-Learning Across the Academic Disciplines

Service-learning can be a part of almost any course in any academic area, from dance to biology, anthropology to computer science, composition, economics, and philosophy. So, regardless of your chosen major, service-learning can be a part of your college experience. And if service-learning courses are not offered in your field, you can always ask a professor if he/she would be willing to let you do a community-based project. The colleges and universities in this book have been included precisely because they have a commitment to academic service-learning. You can find service-learning by checking out the details of a department's curriculum and course descriptions in the campus catalog or website. Your institution may also have a service-learning office or volunteer center that can help you find or create your service-learning experiences!

SERVICE-LEARNING IS **NOT** . . .

An **episodic** volunteer program

An **add-on** to an existing school or college curriculum

Logging a set number of community service hours in order to graduate

Compensatory service assigned as a form of punishment by the courts or by school administrators

Only for high school or college students

SERVICE-LEARNING **IS** . . .

Promotes learning through active participation in service experiences

Provides structured time for students to reflect by thinking, discussing and/or writing about their service experience

Provides an opportunity for students to use skills and knowledge in real-life situations

Extends learning beyond the classroom and into the community

Fosters a sense of civic engagement

*National Commission on Service-Learning

Federal Work Study: A Job that can really make a Difference

Did you know that there are ways you can even get paid for your service learning experiences?

By law colleges and universities are required to spend at least 7% of their Federal Work Study allocation on community service-jobs. Colleges and universities are also required to place Federal Work Study students in jobs that "...to the maximum extend practicable, complement and reinforce the educational program or vocational goals of each student..."[i] That means that instead of working in the campus cafeteria, you could be working for a community-based or non-profit organization **doing something that actually interests you**, and is making a difference to somebody!

For More Information, Check out: www.servicelearning.org/instant_info/hot_topics/work_study/

To help you get a better sense of just how many opportunities there are for service-learning, we provide here a few examples of possible service-learning projects in a variety of academic disciplines.

Students in a **Spanish** class might prepare Spanish language brochures for migrant farmers on health and safety, or provide translation services for an organization that helps new immigrants with their taxes—having the opportunity to use and practice the language skills they are using in class while addressing some need of the local Spanish-speaking community.

Computer Science students help a homeless shelter build a database to monitor client cases, and systems to manage their volunteers and budgets. The students also train staff and volunteers to use the new systems. After the service-learning course ends, some students continue to volunteer to help with updating.

Students in a **Chemistry** class might learn about the consequences of lead contamination to individuals and the environment and then prepare information flyers about the hazards of lead paint, distribute them door-to-door in a local neighborhood, and offer to test paint samples for lead content.

An introductory **Statistics** class might work with a nonprofit agency in need of statistical research for a program evaluation or community needs assessment by creating and administering surveys and analyzing the results.

By leading a reading group for teenagers at a local public library or high school, **English** students can help youth develop a love for reading and improve literacy, while reflecting and developing a deeper understanding of literature themselves.

In a **Women's Health** course, students might use what they've learned throughout the course by giving a presentation at a women's crisis center on a topic related to women's health. The students' own learning is enhanced as they teach their new knowledge to others.

Engineering students assess needs and design solutions that help disabled children participate in more activities at home or in school. These include mobility or communications devices, tools, toys, or games that can enhance a child's abilities.

Toole, J., & Toole, P. "Reflection as a tool for turning service experiences into learning experiences." In C. Kinsley & K. McPherson, Eds., Enriching the curriculum through service learning. Alexandria, VA: Association for Supervision and Curriculum Development, 1995.

Part 2: Success in College and Beyond

How Service-Learning Can Help You Succeed in College

Now that you have a pretty good understanding of college-level service-learning and can see just how many academic fields make use of it, let's go back to how it benefits you.

That it does benefit you – provided you give it a good shot – isn't really in doubt. We know about its outcomes not just through the testimony of countless students and professors (some of them included in this book), but also because dozens of scholars have demonstrated them through their research. As one of those scholars might put it: Service-learning can have a measurable impact on you personally, socially, and academically, allowing you to achieve goals and acquire skills that are important to your future. It has also been shown to improve students' satisfaction with their college or university experience as a whole, and increase their chances of graduating. Service-learning is not only a way for you to help your community; it is also a great way to help yourself!

Let's look at what we know in a little more detail.

Personal Outcomes

As you know, transitioning from 'teenager' to 'adult' is a major challenge. You are learning a lot about who you are as a person and what kind of person you want to become. Many studies have shown that participation in service-learning can have a very positive effect on your personal development.

Self-efficacy is the belief that you can succeed, affect change, and make a difference in your world. Service-learning has been shown to grow students' sense of self-efficacy because they can actually see the difference they are making through their service (Mullins, 2003; Yee et al., 2000). This results in greater self-esteem and a desire to continue providing service to others.

Service-learning also has a positive effect on students' *personal identity*, spiritual growth, and moral development (Astin & Sax, 1998). That's because it is a self-reflexive tool that tests your limits and encourages growth through the new challenges it asks you to face.

Service-learning helps you develop your interpersonal skills. The ability to communicate and work well with others is necessary for success both in school and in the workplace. Studies have shown that service-learning can help you develop these skills as you work with

Getting down to business: service-learning for business students

By Stan Dotson, Dean of LifeWorks, Mars Hill College

Business students today are finding ways to engage with the corporate world and serve the community through the core business practices of organizations large and small. Like fellow students who tutor in schools or work in homeless shelters, they are participating in activities which "count" for service.

Mars Hill College students, for example, work with UNC-Chapel Hill and micro-enterprise incubator Mountain BizWorks on the Appalachian Colleges Community Economic Development

Partnership – doing field research and consultation to help rural counties move from a tobacco-based economy to a viable economy with meaningful jobs in crafts, niche agriculture, and home construction.

Oberlin College students partner with their food service provider Bon Appétit Management Company and local farms to bring locally grown food into the cafeteria. Their "Farm to Fork" partnership trims food miles and brings more than a quarter of a million dollars of food spending to the local economy.

Miami University of Ohio partnered with rock star Bono's company, edun LIVE to create edun LIVE on Campus, a socially conscious t-shirt distribution company that uses for-profit practices to create financial independence for poor women in developing African countries.

Appalachian State University is working on a new community-based business enterprise aimed at creating alternative, clean energy sources, researching the potential of windmill technology developed in Belgium.

Stan Dotson, Dean of LifeWorks

A student's participation in service has positive effects on their –

Astin, Alexander W., Lori J. Vogelgesang, Elaine K. Ikeda, and Jennifer A. Yee. *How Service Learning Affects Students.* Los Angeles, CA: Higher Education Research Institute, University of California Los Angeles, 2000.

Grade point average
Writing skills
Critical thinking
Values
Leadership abilities
Interpersonal skills

This is the bottom line:

Whether or not you already know the field you're interested in, service-learning can help you better assess your options.

your classmates, professors, non-profit organizations, and diverse community members. And when you reflect back on those experiences and share them with others, your service-learning experiences can help build meaningful relationships as well as increase your leadership ability. After all, you will be intimately involved in the planning and carrying out of important real-world projects (Astin & Sax, 1998).

Finally, service-learning is an opportunity for career exploration

at Mars Hill College, calls it a sign that the service-learning movement is growing up when campuses across the country embrace a wider range of activities for students to serve the common good, including the business sector.

"After all," he says, "the real question shouldn't be about what sector or kind of organization a student works in but who is being served by that organization. Service-learning is about serving the interests and building the capacity of those parts of the community that have had less privilege, less advantage, less benefit. Businesses small and large can serve those interests."

and development. Maybe you're still not sure what you want to study or what career you want to pursue. If so, welcome to the club! Studies suggest that an increasing percentage of entering college students are unsure of exactly what they want to study or even what their options are. Enter service-learning. Because service-learning lets you actually do what people in a given field do, rather than just read about what they do, it can help you sort out what's really right for you. It can open your eyes to career opportunities that you may have never thought of or at least never seriously considered. Indeed, students often have such a powerful experience with a service-learning project that they find themselves considering a career in a service field.

But even if you already know what you want to major in and the kind of job you want – let's say nursing – why not start finding out from the get go what kind of nurse you're likely to be? While you won't be able to work as a nurse until you're well into your nursing program, you can find service-learning projects that bring you into contact with nurses and help you develop especially relevant skills – skills that will make your nursing practicum, when you're ready to take it, even more valuable and more enjoyable. ■

Some of the departments in which courses in service-learning are offered

Education
Sociology
English
Psychology
Accounting
Politics
Biology
Nursing
Foreign Language
History
Anthropology
Women's Studies
Natural Sciences
Computer Science
Physical Education
Religion
Philosophy
Economics
Music
Chemistry
Latino Studies
Engineering
Information Systems
Medical/Pre-Medical
Urban Studies
Law/Pre-Law
African-American Studies
American Studies
Architecture
Asian Studies
Physics
Native American Studies

Social Outcomes

Whether you go to a college or university just down the street from where you grew up or all the way across the country, you are going to encounter people who are different from you. **Colleges and universities are a great place to interact and learn from people with different economic, cultural, and religious backgrounds.** Service-learning offers additional opportunities to learn from others since it puts you in contact with members of the off-campus community you might not otherwise meet. Research shows that participation in service-learning has a positive effect on reducing negative stereotypes while it facilitates greater cultural and racial understanding (Grady, 1998; Vogelgesang & Astin, 2000).

Service-Learning can also help you discover and grow your sense of social responsibility, your commitment to take responsibility for the well-being of the community. This means not waiting around for someone else to solve public problems, but taking steps to make yourself part of the solution right now. Service-learning not only helps students understand this commitment; it also gives them a chance to turn that commitment into action. This kind of active commitment will probably push you to think of citizenship and democracy in new ways – ways that go beyond what you learned in high school. Citizenship does not mean just enjoying the rights and privileges guaranteed by our country's laws. It also means becoming an active contributor to that country on both the local and the national level.

Indeed, more and more, service-learning is helping students develop a sense of global citizenship as they serve and learn abroad and see firsthand how many contemporary problems do not recognize national borders. Furthermore, now that you are able (or close to being able) to vote, and have some say in what your country, state, and town does in your name, service-learning experiences can help you come to that deeper understanding of the issues that makes voting more than just a civic ritual. In short, service-learning is about learning to participate in democracy.

No wonder service-learning develops in many students a lifelong commitment to being involved. Studies show that students who participate in service-learning are more likely to stay civically engaged and to volunteer later in life. Indeed, you may yourself decide to join AmeriCorps or the Peace Corps after you graduate. You may later become one of your community's leaders, and after you retire, choose to join the SeniorCorps.

> Service-learning is about learning to participate in democracy.

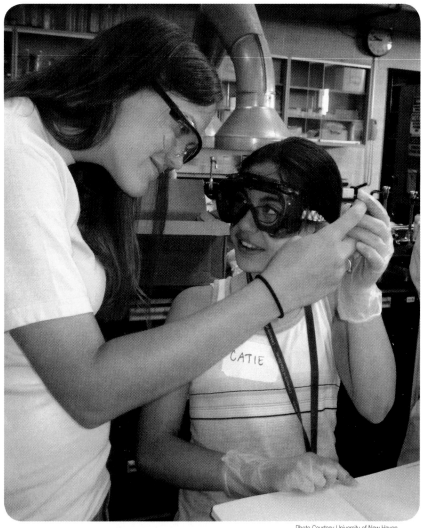

Photo Courtesy of Madonna University

Why Service-Learning?
By Kevin West, Director, Office of Service-Learning, Madonna University

Live a life of meaning and impact today.

Perhaps you have felt the following way at one time in your life, epitomized nicely one day by a student at my college whom I overheard recently one afternoon in the student lounge: "I am sooo bored in my classes. What do they have to do with anything anyway?" No? Well maybe you have uttered this one... "I just want this semester to be over." Don't feel guilty if you have. Many students in both high school and college fail to see the relevance of what they are learning to their lives and futures outside the classroom.

Service-learning practitioners understand this, and further, they understand *that students like you want to be fully engaged in the world right now.* Unfortunately, this desire is not often met in the traditional classroom setting, and it can eventually turn into a kind of anxiety. Why? Well, it's easy to become anxious if you believe that your "real life" will begin only *after* your schooling is over. This turns school into a kind of waiting room, where you are expected to fill time in an enjoyable yet personally productive way before you fulfill the real purpose of your presence, *your existence here on earth*, at some indeterminate point the future. That would make anyone anxious!

Service-learning addresses this source of anxiety by creating opportunities for students to fully engage in their studies and in the challenges faced in the larger world around them *right now.* Through high quality, appropriately structured service-learning opportunities, you can learn in a dynamic, constructive environment and gain a more sophisticated understanding of the world around you. At the same time, you will be contributing to a better world. Through partnerships with local and global organizations, you can work for social progress or to alleviate the suffering of people living in your local community or on distant continents. Either way, your contributions will be valued by others. You will be working for more than just yourself.

Ask yourself, "Am I looking to: See a stronger connection between goes on in my classes with what goes on outside?" "Know that my work has value to others?""Be fully engaged in the world right now?"

Then service-learning courses are probably right for you.

Prepare to lead tomorrow. Your need to live a meaningful and socially relevant life isn't the only need addressed by service-learning. Global trends are increasing the demand for leaders that are: *socially and culturally literate, morally and ethically grounded, and politically and technologically sophisticated.*

Most colleges and universities will attempt to address this demand by offering traditional courses on the increasingly global context of life and leadership in the 21st century. Fewer will recognize that service-learning is an effective strategy for training tomorrow's leaders today. In service-learning courses, you can meet business and community leaders and others that you would otherwise not get to know in traditional courses. You can get valuable experience using data collection strategies and instruments and computer technology "in the field" to help solve real-world problems. High quality service-learning also gives you the opportunity to discuss the moral and political issues that are associated with the service you provide. These are rich learning opportunities that will help you achieve the high level of sophistication that will be demanded from you if and when you assume a leadership role in your career.

Photo Courtesy of Madonna University

Reducing social disparities. Advances in computing, travel and communicative technology means that more and more people across the globe are learning about the lives of others around the world. Today, more people than ever before can access detailed information about the physical and social environment of people and places near and far. As a result, you have the ability to compare aspects of your world and the world of your friends and family to the lives and circumstances of others. For example, you can learn about poverty and disease rates, education levels, or water and air quality both in your own community and in far-flung places simultaneously. Two consequences can result from this increased ability to make social comparisons like this. First, you may be motivated to change something in your own community. Armed with the information you have collected, you can demand better planning, better services from your government or businesses, greater attention to pressing social issues, and more accountability from those in positions of power. Secondly, you may find that you can help others in different communities. You might, for example, start a drive to get school books or computers to schools that have few resources. You could help get medicines and blankets to places torn apart by war, strained by drought, or famine. In either case, service-learning assists you in acting to meet the various health, social and environmental challenges and problems confronting all communities.

Academic Outcomes

Engaged students are better students – it's almost as simple as that! **Because many students find that hands-on learning makes a course more interesting, service-learning helps many students become and stay academically connected.** In fact, not only can it make learning more interesting; it can also help students become better learners. Studies have shown that, all things being equal, service-learning students demonstrate more growth in their critical thinking abilities and greater complexity in their problem analysis than do their non-service-learning peers (Eyler, J. S. & Giles, D. E., Jr., 1999). **Other studies even suggest a correlation between service-learning participation and grade point average** (Astin & Sax, 1998; Strage, 2000; Vogelgesang & Astin, 2000; Yee et al, 2000).

So the benefits are quite concrete – even when it comes down to actually graduating and getting your degree! This is because service-learning has been shown to increase retention rates (the likelihood that you'll stay in school), especially for students who are the first in their family to attend college. Thus, in the end, service-learning students are more likely to graduate (Astin & Sax, 1998; Roose, Daphne, Miller, Norris, Peacock, White, & White, 1997). That's a sobering thought when you consider that, according to one study, the US national average for retention rates for first-time college freshmen returning their second year is only 73.6%. That means that over 25% of first-time freshmen don't make it back for a second year (NCHEMS Information Center, 2002)!

If you're going to college to graduate, you may want to stack the deck in your favor.

Satisfaction with Your Choice

It's no wonder that, given all these benefits, **students who take service-learning courses typically indicate more satisfaction with their course-work and with their overall college experience.** It is especially important for first-year students to know this because they can easily become overwhelmed with the amount of work expected of them. Add to that work the everyday strain of finding one's way in a new environment and, most likely, holding down some kind of part-time job, and it's easy to see how stress and dissatisfaction with college can quickly build up, especially during the first year.

Perhaps the best antidote to that stress and dissatisfaction is building strong new relationships. Service-learning can also help here because it often gives students additional opportunities to get to know each other as well as their professors.

Service-learning unites you with others working to make the changes necessary for enhancing the quality of life for people across the globe.

Service-learning is a movement.

Service-learning is not just a better way to learn. Specifically, it is a moral and strategic response to the problems and challenges we face across our communities. Service-learning uses the resources and expertise of our educational institutions to create healthier local communities; it unites students, faculty and community organizations for the purpose of making communities better. Do you want to make a difference? Do you want to

be ready to lead? Do you want to have impact? Join the movement. Choose service-learning. ∎

KEVIN J. WEST is the Director of the Office of Service-Learning at Madonna University in Livonia, Michigan, where he also teaches courses on community leadership and the global economy

Photo Courtesy Whittier College

For this reason it is not surprising that service-learning students tend to express greater satisfaction with their coursework and with their instructors than do their non service-learning counterparts. And since service-learning also helps students develop meaningful ties to members of the off-campus community, it provides still another way for students to begin to feel connected and at home. For many students, these human connections are what finally makes their college experience rich and fulfilling.

As you look through the institutional profiles that follow, you can feel confident that you've already made at least one excellent decision: You've decided to add service-learning to that list of factors you'll seriously take into account in making your college choice.

Good Luck!

REFERENCES

Astin, A. W., & Sax, L. J. (1998). How Undergraduates Are Affected by Service Participation. Journal of College Student Development, 39(3), 251-263.

Berson, J. S., & Younkin, W. F. (1998). Doing Well by Doing Good: A Study of the Effects of a Service-Learning Experience on Student Success. Paper presented at the American Society of Higher Education, Miami, FL.

Eyler, J. S. & Giles, D. E., Jr. (1999). Where's the Learning in Service-Learning? San Francisco, CA: Jossey-Bass, Inc.

Eyler, J. S., Giles, D. E., Jr., & Braxton, J. (1997). The Impact of Service-Learning on College Students. Michigan Journal of Community Service Learning, 4, 5-15.

Mullins, M.M. (2003). Impact of Service-Learning on Perceptions of Self-Efficacy. Dayton, OH: University of Dayton.

NCHEMS Information Center. (2002). "Retention Rates – First-Time College Freshmen Returning Their Second Year (ACT). http://www.higheredinfo.org/dbrowser/index.php?measure=67

Strage, A. (2000). Service-Learning: Enhancing Student Learning Outcomes in a College Level Lecture Course. Michigan Journal of Community Service Learning, 7, 5-13.

Vogelgesang, L. J., and Astin, A. W. (2000). Comparing the Effects of Service-Learning and Community Service. Michigan Journal of Community Service Learning, 7, 25- 34.

Williams, Rick, "The Impact of Field Education on Student Development: Research Findings," Journal of Cooperative Education, vol. 27, no. 2, pp. 29-45, Win 1991.

Yee, J.A., Ikeda, E.K., Vogelgesang, L.J., and Astin, A.W. (2000). How Service Learning Affects Students. Los Angeles, CA: Higher Education Research Institute.

SPOTLIGHT

College of William & Mary
helps one student turn a determination to serve into an international organization

In just a few short years, an idea inspired by one College of William & Mary student's trip to Uganda has evolved into an international organization which raises awareness and funds for educational projects serving vulnerable children in sub-Saharan Africa.

The evolution began in 2005 when George Srour visited the country as a United Nations intern and realized that there was a real and sustainable way to help the millions of children in the region. He returned to W&M eager to help the children he had met overseas.

Srour worked with W&M's Sam Sadler, Vice President for Student Affairs, and Drew Stelljes, Director of the Office of Student Volunteer Services, to establish a fund to collect $10,000 needed to build a new school and ensure its safe arrival in Uganda. In the December 2005 Christmas in Kampala campaign, W&M students managed to raise almost $45,000. By the next spring, Meeting Point Learning Center was complete.

Building Tomorrow was created as a continuation of the campaign to empower young people in the U.S. to make a difference in their global community and to provide millions of children with an opportunity to go to school and break the cycle of poverty. Srour was awarded a generous fellowship that allowed him to make building schools for the children in sub-Saharan Africa a full-time job. There are now chapters at more than 15 universities, and more than 10,000 undergraduate students have been involved in the work of the organization.

BT also launched a worldwide partnership with Key Club International, an organization of 250,000 high school students committed to service. Nearly $500,000 has been raised to support the organization and construct new schools in Uganda.

"As large as BT has become," says Stelljes, "the organization is representative of the entrepreneurial spirit the College of William & Mary fosters in the realm of civic engagement." ∎

"As large as Building Tomorrow has become, the organization is representative of the entrepreneurial spirit the College of William & Mary fosters in the realm of civic engagement."

- Drew Stelljes, Office of Student Volunteer Services

Articles and Spotlights

Part 1 Articles

What We've *Done* &
Where We're *Going*:

An interview with Amy Cohen
Director of Learn and Serve America

Learn and Serve America breathes life into service-learning at all levels. The largest service-learning funder and the only federal program devoted exclusively to service-learning, the organization was established in 1990 and made its first grants in 1992. A 1994 restructuring created today's Learn and Serve America and launched the national momentum for service-learning.

Learn and Serve America Director Amy Cohen spoke recently with Student Horizons about how Learn and Serve fosters service-learning and how she sees the program evolving in the future.

SH: What is unique about the role of Learn and Serve America?

COHEN: Learn and Serve's national support structure provides a sturdy foundation for service-learning in schools throughout the country. Because of the program's formula grants for K-12 school-based service-learning to every state education agency in the U.S., someone in each state Department of Education knows about and supports service-learning. State education agencies provide resources to help schools and school districts learn how to make service a part of education, and they provide funding to make service projects possible.

On top of this national structure, Learn and Serve makes competitive grants to nonprofits, colleges and universities to help drive new and innovative programs. These funds may also focus on a specific theme

such as improving literacy, building partnerships, or fighting drug abuse.

At the higher education level, Learn and Serve supports consortium grants to build service-learning through broad networks such as seed funding to help most of the state Campus Compacts which have evolved over the last 10 years strengthen and develop programming, as well as support for American Association for Community College's service-learning initiatives and Community-Campus Partnerships for Health which focuses on service-learning in the health professions. Grants

are also provided to individual schools and colleges to build strong, sustainable service-learning programs.

All of these programs are connected through email lists, an annual grantee meeting, and multiple conferences and meetings, resulting in a network of programs and people whose jobs include support for the growth of service-learning.

Learn and Serve America also supports the National Service-Learning Clearinghouse (www.servicelearning. org) – a free resource for finding anything related to service-learning.

The Clearinghouse has curriculum and project ideas, research, evaluation, and a calendar of events, and it supports email lists so people can share good ideas.

Through all of this, service-learning has grown – from nine percent of high schools offering service-learning in 1984 to nearly half of all high schools in 2004.

In higher education, **Campus Compact has grown from 5 schools in 1985 to over a thousand member colleges in 2008.** And nearly 60 percent of all community colleges support service-learning.

Another thing that helps us to have a common language is this definition of service-learning which is part of the legislation that created the Learn and Serve program:

Service-learning means a method—in which participants learn and develop through active participation in thoughtfully organized service that--

is conducted in and meets the needs of a community;

is coordinated with an elementary school, secondary school, institution of higher education, or community service program, and with the community;

and helps foster civic responsibility; and is integrated into and enhances the academic curriculum of the students, or the educational components of the community service program in which the participants are enrolled;

and provides structured time for participants to reflect on the service experience.

See Alan Melchior's article, Learn and Serve and the Growth of Service-Learning in America, in National Youth Leadership Council's The Generator, Special 15th Anniversary of Learn and Serve America Issue

SH: Has Learn and Serve's service-learning vision changed much as the field has evolved?

COHEN: Our first Learn and Serve America goal was to get service-learning on the map, to make it a reality in schools, afterschool programs and higher education institutions. **We wanted to ensure that service-learning programs built strong partnerships between schools or colleges and their surrounding communities to meet local community needs** and to ensure that we had the research to demonstrate which service-learning practices would lead to strong positive outcomes for students, schools and colleges, and communities.

We have achieved the basics, but we need to go much further. We continue to strive toward these goals and have made it our mission to make service-learning and civic engagement a standard feature of American education, both formal and informal. Our agency has set several strategic goals with respect to service-learning. **We are aiming to engage 5 million college students in service, up from approximately 2.8 million students.** And we intend to engage fully half of all K-12 public schools in service-learning, up from about a third of all schools today. These are substantial and aspirational goals.

We now have a great body of research, program experience that defines effective practices to lead to the strongest student and community outcomes, and strong programs and practitioners at every level.

Q&A

"It truly is a win, win, win."

SH: What kinds of challenges do you foresee in achieving your vision?

COHEN: We need to do a lot more to highlight the outstanding programs we have and the local and national impact of those programs. The National Learn and Serve Challenge is one resource and opportunity to do that. Led by the national nonprofit National Service-Learning Partnership, the Challenge is designed to help service-learning programs highlight their outstanding service-learning work more publicly. Tools and ideas for highlighting service and civic engagement projects are on the web at www.learnandservechallenge.org. The 2008 Challenge takes place October 6 to 12!

SH: More corporations and private foundations are getting involved in funding service-learning programs as they see the benefits of these strong programs on employment skills and civic engagement. How have you seen this development progressing? And does Learn and Serve play a role in facilitating these partnering activities?

SH: Does Learn and Serve encourage continuities between high-school and college service-learning programs?

COHEN: Partnerships between K-12 school and colleges are truly key to Learn and Serve programs.

COHEN: As they see the benefits service-learning brings to young people, schools, colleges, nonprofits and communities, increasing numbers of corporations and foundations are getting involved with service-learning. It truly is a win, win, win.

80 percent of young people prefer opportunities for real-world experiences

SH: How do high school service-learning programs influence students as they determine their college choices?

COHEN: I often hear from the people who run Learn and Serve programs that students on their campuses chose their school based on the opportunity for service. And there are many new tools to help students find a school that does service and civic engagement the way they want. Of course there is this guide!

And there are other tools too. Here in Learn and Serve America, we sponsor the President's Higher Education Community Service Honor Roll. Launched in 2006, the Honor Roll recognizes colleges and universities nationwide that support innovative and effective community service and service-learning programs. The Honor Roll's Presidential Award, given each year to only a handful of institutions, is the highest federal recognition a college or university can receive for its commitment to volunteering, service-learning, and civic engagement. The Honor Roll is a program of the Corporation for National and Community Service, and is sponsored by the President's Council on Service and Civic Participation, the USA Freedom Corps, and the U.S. Departments of Education and Housing and Urban Development. Find complete information at http://www.learnandserve.gov/about/programs/higher_ed_honorroll.asp.

SH: Retention is a big issue on many college campuses as schools fight to keep students enrolled. "Hands on" experiential programs such as service-learning appear to help with retention. What has Learn and Serve observed in this regard?

COHEN: Increasingly research demonstrates that service-learning is a key to helping young people stay engaged in school. Research with young people indicates that more than 80 percent would prefer opportunities for real-world experiences and that the connection between school and problem-solving in the real world would keep them in school.

When students get involved in service to the community, they become important assets in meeting community needs.

They become engaged with their academic work more intensively, in part because the academic relates more effectively to community needs. Students become connected citizens when they serve in their community. This effort frequently leads to stronger ties with other students as well as with community members. ■

See Bridgeland, J; DiIulio Jr., J; Wulsin, S; Engaged for Success: Service-Learning as a Tool for High School Dropout Prevention, A Report by Civic Enterprises in association with Peter D. Hart Research Associates for the National Conference on Citizenship (April 2008)

THE PRESIDENT'S HIGHER EDUCATION COMMUNITY SERVICE

Honor Roll

The President's Higher Education Community Service Honor Roll, launched in 2006, recognizes colleges and universities nationwide that support innovative and effective community service and service-learning programs. The Honor Roll's Presidential Award, given each year to only a handful of institutions, is the highest federal recognition a college or university can receive for its commitment to volunteering, service-learning, and civic engagement. The Honor Roll is a program of the Corporation for National and Community Service, and is sponsored by the President's Council on Service and Civic Participation, the USA Freedom Corps, and the U.S. Departments of Education and Housing and Urban Development.

2007 HONOR ROLL
WITH DISTINCTION

Alabama
Birmingham Southern College

California
Azusa Pacific University
California State University Monterey Bay
California State University Chico
California State University Los Angeles
California State University Fullerton
California State University Northridge
College of the Canyons
Dominican University of California
Humboldt State University
La Sierra University
Loyola Marymount University
Mills College
Occidental College
Saint Mary's College of California
San Francisco State University
Stanford University
University of California Santa Barbara
University of San Francisco

Delaware
University of Delaware

District of Columbia
American University
George Washington University
Georgetown University

Florida
Brevard Community College
Palm Beach Atlantic University Inc.
Rollins College
Stetson University
University of South Florida

Illinois
DePaul University
Illinois College
Midwestern University

Indiana
DePauw University
Franklin College
Indiana University East
Saint Mary's College
University of Notre Dame

Iowa
Central College
Wartburg College

Kentucky
Berea College
Western Kentucky University

Louisiana
Tulane University

Maine
Bates College

Maryland
Loyola College in Maryland
University of Maryland, Baltimore County

Massachusetts
Mount Wachusett Community College
Simmons College
Stonehill College
University of Massachusetts Amherst
Wentworth Institute of Technology

Michigan
Alma College
Kalamazoo College
Michigan State University
University of Michigan

Minnesota
Augsburg College
Hamline University
Macalester College
University of Minnesota

Mississippi
Rust College

Missouri
Missouri State University
Northwest Missouri State University
Rockhurst University
University of Missouri Kansas City

Montana
University of Montana

Nebraska
Creighton University
Hastings College
Union College

New Hampshire
Keene State College

New Jersey
College of New Jersey

New York
Cornell University
Hobart and William Smith Colleges
Le Moyne College
Nazareth College of Rochester
New York University
Niagara University
St. John Fisher College
State University of New York at Geneseo
State University of New York at Potsdam
Stony Brook University
University of Rochester
Wagner College

North Carolina
Appalachian State University
Duke University
Elon University
Guilford College
North Carolina Central University
North Carolina State University at Raleigh
Pfeiffer University

Ohio
Defiance College
Mount Union College
Oberlin College
Ohio State University
Wittenberg University

*Visit http://www.learnandserve.gov for more information
about the 2007 Honor Roll Members*

Oklahoma
Rose State College
Oregon
Portland State University
Pennsylvania
Cabrini College
Juniata College
Messiah College
Villanova University
Washington & Jefferson College
Waynesburg University
Widener University
Rhode Island
Bryant University
Johnson & Wales University
  Providence Campus
Roger Williams University
Salve Regina University
University of Rhode Island
South Carolina
Clemson University
Furman University
Presbyterian College
Tennessee
Crichton College
Lee University
Rhodes College
Tusculum College
Texas
Dallas Baptist University
Southwestern University
University of Texas at Arlington
Utah
Westminster College
Virginia
Bluefield College
College of William and Mary
James Madison University
University of Virginia
Virginia Polytechnic Institute
  and State University
Washington
Gonzaga University
University of Washington Seattle
Wisconsin
Marquette University
University of Wisconsin Eau Claire
University of Wisconsin Madison

• • • • • • • • • • • • • • • •

2007 HONOR ROLL

Alabama
Enterprise Ozark
  Community College
Judson College
University of Alabama
Arizona
Arizona Western College
Chandler Gilbert
  Community College
Mesa Community College
Arkansas
Arkansas State University Newport
Harding University
National Park Community College
Ouachita Baptist University
Southern Arkansas University
  Main Campus
California
Antioch University Los Angeles
Bakersfield College
California Polytechnic
  State University
California State University
  Long Beach
California State University
  Stanislaus
California State University
  San Bernardino
California State University
  San Marcos
Concordia University
MiraCosta College
San Jose State University
Santa Clara University
University of California Davis
University of California
  Los Angeles
University of San Diego
University of the Pacific
Western University of
  Health Sciences
Colorado
Colorado Christian University
Colorado State University
Johnson & Wales University
  Denver Campus
Mesa State College

United States Air Force Academy
University of Denver
Connecticut
Eastern Connecticut
  State University
Fairfield University
Saint Joseph College
Southern Connecticut
  State University
St. Vincent's College
University of Hartford
University of New Haven
Wesleyan University
Delaware
Wesley College
District of Columbia
Catholic University of America
Florida
Florida Community College
  at Jacksonville
Florida Gulf Coast University
Florida Institute of
  Technology Melbourne
Florida International University
Florida Southern College
Florida State University
Gulf Coast Community College
Hillsborough Community College
Johnson & Wales University
  Florida Campus
Miami Dade College
Ringling College of Art and Design
Saint Leo University
University of Central Florida
University of Florida
University of Tampa
Georgia
Albany Technical College
Atlanta Christian College
Columbus State University
Darton College
Georgia College and
  State University
Georgia Institute of Technology
  Main Campus
Oglethorpe University

Southeastern Technical College
University of Georgia
Wesleyan College
Guam
Guam Community College
Hawaii
Hawaii Technology Institute
Kapi'olani Community College
Maui Community College
Idaho
University of Idaho
Illinois
Aurora University
Benedictine University
Blackburn College
Bradley University
College of DuPage
Columbia College Chicago
Concordia University
Dominican University
Illinois Wesleyan University
John A. Logan College
McKendree University
Northern Illinois University

Roosevelt University

Saint Xavier University

Southern Illinois University
Carbondale

The Chicago School of
Professional Psychology

Trinity Christian College

Trinity International University

Indiana
Ball State University

Earlham College

Huntington University

Indiana State University

Ivy Tech Community
College Bloomington

Ivy Tech Community
College Kokomo

Manchester College

Purdue University North Central

Iowa
AIB College of Business

Ashford University

Cornell College

Iowa Western Community College

Loras College

Northwestern College

Simpson College

University of Dubuque

Upper Iowa University

Kansas
Butler County Community College

Emporia State University

Fort Hays State University

Pratt Community College

Southwestern College

University of Kansas
Main Campus

Kentucky
Louisville Technical Institute

Maysville Community and
Technical College

Morehead State University

Northern Kentucky University

Louisiana
Centenary College of Louisiana

Delgado Community College

Louisiana State University

Louisiana State University
at Eunice

Loyola University New Orleans

Nicholls State University

River Parishes Community College

Southern University and
A&M College

Xavier University

Maryland
Anne Arundel Community College

Carroll Community College

Frostburg State University

Howard Community College

Mount St. Mary's University

Towson University

University of Baltimore

University of Maryland
College Park

University of Maryland
Eastern Shore

Massachusetts
Babson College

Bentley College

Bridgewater State College

Bristol Community College

Bunker Hill Community College

Clark University

Emerson College

Endicott College

Lesley University

Massachusetts College of
Pharmacy and Health Sciences

Massachusetts Institute
of Technology

Middlesex Community College

North Shore Community College

Worcester State College

Michigan
Albion College

Central Michigan University

Davenport University

Eastern Michigan University

Hope College

Jackson Community College

Kirtland Community College

Madonna University

Marygrove College

Thomas M. Cooley Law School

University of Detroit Mercy

University of Michigan Flint

Wayne State University

Minnesota
Bethel University

Carleton College

Century College

Mesabi Range Community and
Technical College

Normandale Community College

Saint Mary's University
of Minnesota

Mississippi
Delta State University

Millsaps College

Mississippi Valley State University

Tougaloo College

University of Southern Mississippi

Missouri
A.T. Still University – Kirksville
College of Osteopathic Medicine

College of the Ozarks

Cottey College

Missouri Western State University

Park University

Saint Louis University

Washington University

Westminster College

Nebraska
Clarkson College

Doane College

Nebraska Methodist College

Nebraska Wesleyan University

University of Nebraska at Lincoln

University of Nebraska at Omaha

Nevada
Nevada State College
at Henderson

University of Nevada Las Vegas

New Hampshire
Antioch University New England

Dartmouth College

New Hampshire Community
Technical College Nashua

New Hampshire Technical Institute

Plymouth State University

Saint Anselm College

New Jersey
Felician College

Georgian Court University

Monmouth University

Rowan University

Rutgers University New
Brunswick/Piscataway

New York
Binghamton University

Buffalo State College

Daemen College

Dowling College

D'Youville College

Elmira College

Hudson Valley Community College

Ithaca College

Keuka College

Kingsborough Community College

Molloy College

Nyack College

Pace University New York

Saint Thomas Aquinas College

St. John's University New York

State University of New York
at Buffalo

State University of New York
at Canton

State University of New York
College at Old Westbury

State University of New York at
College of Environmental
Science and Forestry

State University of New York
at Cortland

State University of New York
at Delhi

State University of New York
at New Paltz

State University of New York
at Oswego

State University of New York
at Oneonta

Wells College

North Carolina
Cabarrus College of
Health Sciences

Campbell University

Central Piedmont
Community College

Davidson College

East Carolina University

Gardner Webb University

Greensboro College

Johnson & Wales University
Charlotte

Lenoir Rhyne College

Mars Hill College

Saint Augustine's College

Stanly Community College

University of North Carolina
at Charlotte

University of North Carolina
at Greensboro

University of North Carolina
   at Pembroke

University of North Carolina
Wilmington

Wake Forest University

Western Carolina University

Winston Salem State University

North Dakota
University of North Dakota

Ohio
Bowling Green State University

Cincinnati Christian University

Cuyahoga Community
   College District

Heidelberg College

John Carroll University

Kent State University
   Stark Campus

Kent State University

New Philadelphia Marietta College

Miami University

Mount Vernon Nazarene University

Notre Dame College

Sinclair Community College

University of Akron

University of Cincinnati

Urbana University

Wilmington College

Oklahoma
Community Care College

East Central University

Hillsdale Free Will Baptist College

Oklahoma City
   Community College

Oklahoma State University Oklahoma
City

Southeastern Oklahoma
   State University

University of Central Oklahoma

University of Tulsa

Oregon
National College of
   Natural Medicine

Portland Community College

Southern Oregon University

University of Portland

Western Oregon University

Willamette University

Pennsylvania
Alvernia College

Bloomsburg University of
   Pennsylvania

Career Training Academy

Carlow University

Carnegie Mellon University

Cedar Crest College

Drexel University

Duquesne University

Eastern University

Elizabethtown College

Franklin & Marshall College

Gannon University

Gettysburg College

Gwynedd Mercy College

King's College

La Salle University

Lake Erie College of
   Osteopathic Medicine

Lehigh University

Lock Haven University

Mercyhurst College

Millersville University
   of Pennsylvania

Misericordia University

Montgomery County
   Community College

Northampton Community College

Robert Morris University

Saint Joseph's University

Susquehanna University

University of Pittsburgh
   Greensburg

University of Scranton

Ursinus College

West Chester University
   of Pennsylvania

Westminster College

Puerto Rico
University of Puerto Rico
   Mayaguez

University of the Sacred Heart

Rhode Island
Providence College

South Carolina
Anderson University

Claflin University

Clinton Junior College

Converse College

Morris College

University of South Carolina Aiken

University of South Carolina
   Columbia

Winthrop University

South Dakota
Black Hills State University

Mount Marty College

Presentation College

University of Sioux Falls

University of South Dakota

Tennessee
Belmont University

East Tennessee State University

Free Will Baptist Bible College

LeMoyne Owen College

Lipscomb University

Maryville College

Northeast State Technical
   Community College

Union University

Texas
Abilene Christian University

Austin College

Blinn College

Brookhaven College

Collin County Community
   College District

Houston Baptist University

Howard Payne University

Kingwood College

LeTourneau University

North Harris Montgomery Community
College District

Rice University

San Antonio College

Southern Methodist University

St. Edward's University

St. Mary's University

Stephen F. Austin State University

Texas Tech University

Tyler Junior College

University of Houston Downtown

University of North Texas

University of Texas Pan American

Utah
Brigham Young University

Salt Lake Community College

Utah Valley

Weber State University

Vermont
Castleton State College

Norwich University

Saint Michael's College

University of Vermont

Virginia
Appalachian School of Law

Blue Ridge Community College

Hollins University

Mary Baldwin College

Norfolk State University

Old Dominion University

Piedmont Virginia
   Community College

Richard Bland College of The
   College of William & Mary

Virginia Commonwealth University

Washington
Cascadia Community College

Eastern Washington University

Heritage University

Seattle University

Spokane Community College

Tacoma Community College

University of Puget Sound

University of Washington Bothell

West Virginia
Concord University

Glenville State College

University of Charleston

West Virginia Northern
   Community College

West Virginia University

Wisconsin
Alverno College

Lawrence University

Milwaukee School of Engineering

Ripon College

University of Wisconsin Parkside

University of Wisconsin River Falls

Western Technical College

Wyoming
WyoTech

SPOTLIGHT

MSU students develop writing skills through active civic involvement

Photo Courtesy of Michigan State University

Projects for such groups as a Refugee Development Center and a racehorse rescue group offer unique service-learning opportunities to writing students at Michigan State University.

Along with a basic skill set and a diploma, MSU aims to send graduates into the world with an interest in becoming active participants in the work of democracy – a goal nurtured by the Center for Service-Learning and Civic Engagement, which placed more than 11,000 students in service assignments during a recent school year.

Still, reports David D. Cooper, professor in the department of Writing, Rhetoric and American Cultures, some students "slide through their

instruction, community-based service-learning and deliberative democracy. Some classes participate in smaller projects, but most undertake one large-scale community writing assignment resulting from a collaborative partnership through CSLCE or the interests of the instructor.

The racehorse rescue organization project, for example, was initiated by a faculty member interested in animal rescue efforts. His class developed a newsletter for CANTER: Communication Alliance to Network Thoroughbred Ex-Racehorses.

In another three-semester project, Cooper's students conducted research, developed policy briefs which were compiled into the handbook Generation Y

Photo Courtesy of Michigan State Universtiy

undergraduate careers with little understanding of academic civic involvement."

So Cooper established "the four seasons of deliberative learning" which includes a first year writing course, followed by a gateway course in professional writing, an elective junior seminar in the American Studies Program on Civic America, and a senior capstone course.

The process creates an active civic learning experience by uniting intellectual content, writing

Speaks Out: Public Policy Perspectives through Service-Learning, then presented the handbook to Michigan legislators in a public forum.

No longer teaching the course, Cooper remains heavily involved. He reports that the lessons learned through his experiences with the course have greatly affected his own academic career and his view of the University's threefold mission of teaching, research, and service. ■

> The process creates an active civic learning experience by uniting intellectual content, writing instruction, community-based service-learning and deliberative democracy

Students Feed Community Need With **APPLES**

Photo Courtesy of the University of North Carolina

Photo Courtesy of the University of North Carolina

At the University of North Carolina at Chapel Hill, students take service-learning into their own hands through an innovtive program called APPLES, or Assisting People in Planning Learning Experiences in Service. APPLES is unique in that it is led by UNC students, and is both a registered student organization as well as an academic program.

The mission of APPLES is to offer and facilitate service-learning programs and opportunities to students and faculty, and thereby build sustainable service-learning partnerships between students, faculty, communities, and beyond. Students are given ample opportunities to fulfill the mission of APPLES in a variety of ways. Some of the programs offered include service-learning internships, a global service-learning program, and alternative fall and spring breaks during which students participate in service-learning programs between semesters.

"Students participating in ... the APPLES program ... are living out what they learn in class, ... and helping communities both local and global in a sustainable and meaningful way."

The APPLES Global Service-Learning Program allows students to work with local immigrant communities, as well as with the communities of origin. Students travel to regions including South Africa and Mexico where local social, economic or political conditions are forcing residents to migrate to the United States. Students are able to work with and learn from these residents as they participate in service projects along with their academic studies. While abroad, students also study the culture, language and customs of the region while living with a local family.

Upon returning from the global experience, students enroll in a 1-credit "Connections" reflection seminar to discuss the differences and similarities of immigrants in the U.S. to those still living in their native countries. Students are able to share what they observed and learned during their experience. The seminar also addresses immigrant concerns such as social justice, and health and education needs. Returning students also engage in local service-learning with newly arrived immigrants. As mentors, they provide assistance with activities supporting school achievement and facilitation of bilingual fluency for middle or high school immigrant youth.

Students participating in service-learning opportunities through the APPLES program receive much more than an academic education can provide alone. They are living out what they learn in class, gaining experiences that they can take with them for the rest of their lives, creating lasting memories, and helping communities both local and global in a sustainable and meaningful way. ■

THE BONNER PROGRAM:

A Campus-Based Program Model for Impacting Students, Community, Curriculum, and Campus

"Being a Bonner is the best thing that has happened to me in college. I even got a chance to travel the world, see lots of new people and places, help build houses, plant gardens, teach kids, and put smiles on faces. But in this program, I'm not the only one so I know I'm not alone." ~ Kenisha Ellis, Berry College

Photo courtesy of Portland State University

Access to Education, An Opportunity to Serve

So, you believe that college students—and their campuses—can make a significant and meaningful impact in the lives of people and communities through the commitment of time, energy, and resources to community service and service-learning. We do too. The Bonner Foundation connects a network of colleges and universities that host the Bonner Scholars and Leaders Programs. The Bonner Scholars Program, currently at twenty-seven campuses, provides a service-based scholarship through which students participate in a four-year developmental service program, while also receiving scholarship assistance for college. Geared primarily at low-income and first generation college bound students, the program also underscores a commitment to providing "Access to Education, An Opportunity to Serve," while helping colleges and universities support the enrollment and service participation of often under-represented students.

The Bonner Leaders Program, established at nearly fifty campuses, likewise supports the intense, sustained involvement of students in community service and service-learning. Open to diverse students, the program engages students in at least a two-year commitment, often providing them financial support through Work Study, AmeriCorps Education Awards, and institutional aid. Yet Bonner is more than just a scholarship or aid program. The Scholars and Leaders Programs provide students with the opportunity to participate in a cohort and supportive community of students with similar interests in impacting communities, while also providing them with education and support to develop as engaged citizens and leaders.

> *"Because the Bonner Program has encouraged and assisted me in reflecting on my service work and reflecting on how my classes and service work interact, I see that my role in social justice should be helping the poor break the cycle."*
>
> – Jeremy Martinez, Maryville College

A Sustained, Multi-year Commitment to Service-Learning

Students in the Bonner Program make a serious commitment to community service, one that often connects to their academic study. Each week during the school year, Bonner Scholars and Leaders work 8-10 hours in community-based placements in schools and non-profit organizations. During the summer, they often work in full-time internships with non-profit organizations, locally, nationally, and even globally. Each month, they attend trainings, meetings, and even courses through which they develop knowledge and skills to apply in their community-based work. Because they are involved over multiple years, Bonners are able take on increasing leadership and responsibility in their community work. Often times, through structured service-learning courses, community-based research projects, and other innovative academic connections, these students also find ways to integrate their academic work with service in meaningful ways. In fact, at many participating institutions, there may be a major, minor, certificate or other course of study in civic engagement or a related area.

"The most important aspect that being a Bonner Scholar has brought into my life is the connection between my education and my life's work. I am a student, a scholar, a daughter, a sister, a wife, a leader, a community member; but if I cannot connect what I have gained through my education with my roles in life, then how has my education been improved? Without this connection I have only learned to serve myself and to ignore the world around me."

– Selena Hilemon, Mars Hill College
Selena now directs the Bonner Program at Lees-McRae College.

"Combining the Shepherd Program and the Bonner Leader Program took me inside classrooms at local schools, to a camp for grieving children in the Blue Ridge Mountains and within a group home for mentally ill homeless women in Washington, DC. It exposed me to domestic violence in Lexington, literacy issues around Rockbridge County, and childcare dilemmas for single parents. These explorations evoked tremendous emotions and supplied me with the passion and purpose behind my fight for social justice."
-Washington & Lee University student

on research, public policy, writing, and more. The Bonner Program engages six Common Commitments—community building, civic engagement, diversity, international perspective, spiritual exploration, and social justice—to support you as students to go beyond just doing the service to grapple with deeper issues, such as why a need exists or what may be long-term strategies for alleviating that need. Many of our campuses have created or are exploring sustained academic connections, moving beyond a one-semester service-learning course. These campuses are guided by a framework to examine

poverty and social inequity, public policy and political engagement, and global perspective. This is the type of work that draws students who are passionate and committed to making their education relevant to community building and problem solving. As the colleges integrate a developmental series of coursework, they provide students with a way to engage in a significant academically-connected internship and capstone-level project. For administrators and faculty who want to learn more about this model, you can obtain an upcoming publication by the American Association of Colleges and Universities, *Putting Civic Engagement at the Center: Building Democracy through Integrated Co-Curricular and Curricular Experiences* (April 2008, www. aacu.org). By combining a variety of academic connections, including course-based service-learning, community-based research, and even public policy research, we believe that our model can offer some interesting insights to institutions of higher education that are seeking to institutionalize a greater commitment to civic

A Student Development Framework

A core feature of the Bonner Program is the idea that students develop as leaders throughout their college experience, taking on significant leadership roles.

This happens through three primary ways: **(1)** as students, you are able to identify your passions, issue interests, and community interests and take on long-term projects and service placements; **(2)** by participating with a group of Bonners at your school in structured education, training, and reflection opportunities where you hone skills like project planning, critical thinking, public speaking, fundraising, and more; and **(3)** through intentional opportunities to connect your service work to the classroom and to other knowledge development opportunities, like working

Photo Courtesy of University of Pennsylvania

education and community-oriented problem solving within their curriculum. For those individual students who choose to make these significant a connection, their academic work and lives are often deeply impacted.

For Campuses and Students Interested in Joining the Bonner Network

We are honored to be a part of the Guide to Service-Learning Colleges and Universities. In fact, twenty-six of the 75 institutions with which we work are featured in this publication including:

Yet we know that the other forty-nine institutions in our network also have a commitment to civic engagement through the Bonner Program, and that many of them link their efforts to engage students in a sustained fashion in the community with academic coursework, service-learning, and other curricular connections.

For campuses who are interested in beginning a Bonner Leader Program, you may visit our website, www.bonner. org, where you can access start-up information, initiate contact with the Foundation, and sign up to attend an upcoming meeting. For high school (or college) students, you can find the full list of participating institutions, then contact their Admissions Offices or Bonner Programs directly.

Each school handles its own admissions and selection process. See our campus profiles at http://www.bonner. org/directories/bonnercampuscontacts. htm. Once you are in touch with the college or university's admissions office, obtain an application both to the school and find out how to apply to the Bonner Program. ■

Photo Courtesy of Portland State University

Photo Courtesy of Warren Wilson College

"We have learned to put others before ourselves. Being a Bonner Scholar is equivalent to a four-year course in empathy, human services, social services, and humility.

By helping others, we are making a positive impact on the community and being molded into the kind of people who will make a positive different in this area, state, country, and even world."

Carrie Bush, Waynesburg College

We are honored to be a part of the Guide to Service-Learning Colleges and Universities. In fact, twenty-six of the 75 institutions with which we work are featured in this publication including:

Berea College
Centre College
Concord University
Defiance College
Hamilton College
Hobart and William Smith
Johnson State College
Macalester College
Mars Hill College
Oberlin College
Pfeiffer University
Portland State University
Rider University
Ripon College
Saint Mary's of California
The College of New Jersey
Tougaloo College
Tusculum College
University of Alaska, Anchorage
University of New Mexico
Wagner College
Warren Wilson College
Washington & Lee University
West Chester University
Whitworth University
Widener University

Photo Courtesy of Tougaloo College

Bonner Community Scholar Corps Help Students Think Critically about Society

Photo Courtesy of College of New Jersey

The first year of college is often the best time to get involved, but it can also be the most overwhelming time for students as they struggle to determine just where and how to invest their time. At the College of New Jersey (TCNJ), all first-year students are involved almost immediately as they participate in service-learning experiences and projects, through an innovative approach: the students are led by 60 of their peers.

These 60 students, members of the Bonner Community Scholars Corps., develop their own civic engagement skills while mobilizing all 1300 first-year students during one academic year. The 1300 first-year students complete a minimum of an 8 hour community engaged learning experience as part of the College's required general education program. The College sees this as the first step

Photo Courtesy of College of New Jersey

towards ensuring that students think critically about their society and develop the skills and dispositions to advance not only themselves, but their communities.

The Bonner students begin their 4 year college career by participating in their own service-learning First-Year Seminar course, the Myths and Realities of Poverty. In addition to their course work, they spend 300 hours annually working with the community to address unmet needs such as homelessness, environmental issues, persons with disabilities, urban education, and more.

The Bonners begin the first-year student experience by organizing floor meetings on all 25 freshmen floors during Welcome Week in late August. By the end of these floor meetings, each floor is organized into three different issue groups and linked to a specific Community Engaged Learning (CEL) Day. On those days, 17-20 students from a floor come together to learn (via a brief program), serve (in a 5-7 hour project), and reflect (in a one hour session) together—under the direction of the Bonner Scholars.

The CEL days are organized by upper level Bonner students, usually juniors and seniors, in conjunction with campus staff and community partner organizations. Speakers are also featured during CEL days, focusing on relevant issues and topics related to the service experience about to take place. For example, an education professor might speak briefly to students before a day of working on literacy issues with local youth.

At the end of the day, Bonner students lead reflection sessions with the first-year students, allowing them to examine their experience. Additionally, opportunities are provided for first-year students to stay involved by becoming BVols (what is this? Should be full name) at one of the Bonner team sites.

CEL Days are one of two routes toward completion of the first-year service-learning graduation requirement, and over 400 students also engage in class-based CEL projects developed by their First Seminar Program (FSP) professors and Bonner Center staff. All first-year students participate in an FSP reading and writing intensive course designed by faculty around topics they are passionate about.

Together, the Bonners and first-year students, provide approximately 20,000 service-learning hours (a year?) to the local community. In 2008, TCNJ earned a place on the Corporation for National and Community Service's Honor Roll with Distinction. ■

> "College and university campuses are also uniquely placed to affect America's energy future..."
>
> *– Beth Blissman, PhD, Director, Bonner Center for Service & Learning, Oberlin College*

Cool Schools: Service-Learning and the Greening of Higher Education

Photo Courtesy of Oberlin College

Students who see global warming as the key challenge of their generation and a wake-up call for new perspectives about society, economics and religion are pleased to discover many colleges and universities in synch with this view.

Increasingly, institutions of higher education are not only creating service-learning opportunities aimed at ecological awareness and action, they're also taking steps to green their own campuses and communities.

A number of these schools have put their pledge for a greener society in writing. More than 350 university presidents and chancellors in over 40 countries have signed the Talloires Declaration promising to incorporate environmental literacy in teaching, research, operations and outreach. And 460 college and university presidents have signed a commitment with the Association for the Advancement of Sustainability in Higher Education (AASHE) – in collaboration with Second Nature and ecoAmerica - to

• Do a greenhouse gas inventory and then plan within 2 years to achieve climate neutrality
• Adopt select emission reduction measures
• Publicly report on plans and progress thru AASHE

One of the first colleges to sign the AASHE commitment was Oberlin College – named first among Sierra Club's list of America's Top 10 "Coolest" Schools in 2007.

Oberlin's culture of sustainability is evident in the many service-learning courses it offers, including independent studies, and in such accomplishments as getting more than one-third of the food served in dining halls from local producers and hosting Ohio's first car-sharing program. Students can get information about sustainability efforts from the school's new Office of Sustainability.

Oberlin student activity fees partially subsidize local public transportation, a monitoring system enables students to track real-time energy usage in 17 residence halls, and the school purchases much of its electricity from green sources.

Photo Courtesy of Oberlin College

Get the Scoop on Green

Students with intense interest in environmental issues will find many colleges, universities and other organizations who share their passion.

The Cool Schools piece mentions many such resources, including the following:

- The Talloires Declaration (http://www.ulsf.org/talloires_declaration.html)
- Association for Advancement of Sustainability in Higher Education (www.aashe.org)
- Sierra Club's Top 10 "Coolest" Schools in 2007 (http://www.sierraclub.org/sierra/200711/coolschools/)
- Oberlin College Office of Sustainability (http://www.oberlin.edu/sustainability/)

In addition, Beth Blissman, PhD, Director of Oberlin's Bonner Center for Service & Learning, offers these resources for those who want to nurture a green society:

- Want to become a Green College Administrator? The Campus Ecology program of the National Wildlife Federation (http://www.nwf.org/campusEcology/index.cfm) promotes climate leadership and sustainability among colleges and universities by providing resources and technical support, creating networking opportunities and organizing education events.

- Interested in international efforts for sustainability? International Institute for Sustainable Development (IISD) offers a Sustainable Development on Campus toolkit at http://www.iisd.org/educate/.

- Want to find out what's happening to green Historically Black Colleges and Universities (HBCU)? Contact Envirosource (http://www.theenvirosource.com/index.html), an Alabama-based company that proposes developing "The Carbon Footprint Awareness" programs within Historically Black Colleges and Universities.

- Looking for a Christian College? An article on integrating care of creation with academics as a growing movement on Christian campuses around the country can be found at http://www.christianitytoday.com/ct/2007/may/32.52.html. ■

Photos Courtesy of Oberlin College

Students can be work-study employees within many areas, or volunteer for such Student Groups Working for Sustainability as

- Environmental Policy Implementation Group advocating for and assisting with implementation of the school's policy
- Recycled Products Co-op collecting and distributing for reuse (for a donation) used office supplies
- Oberlin College Transportation Committee dealing with alternative transportation issues at the college

Beth Blissman, PhD, director of Oberlin's Bonner Center for Service & Learning, notes that young people today are in a better position than ever before to advance an inspiring new vision for the United States.

"College and university campuses are also uniquely placed to affect America's energy future," she says, "as they are centers of intellectual power, capable of leading experiments on new technologies and using these projects as teaching tools and research opportunities to better the education of the next generation of voters, consumers, politicians, and business leaders."

Rider program gives business students and local youth real-world marketplace insights

Photos Courtesy of Rider University

A rich community outreach program teaches important life and work skills to Rider University College of Business Administration students and the local youth they mentor.

Through Minding Our Business entrepreneurship education and mentoring program, established in 1997 by Dr. Sigfredo A. Hernandez, Rider students teach low-income Trenton (NJ) adolescents about starting and running a business. Since its inception, more than 1,300 middle school students have benefitted from the personal and vocational development provided by 250 Rider student mentors.

Each year, the MOB Service-Learning after-school program serves about 100 youth at partner middle schools. Three Rider students mentor groups of seven to twelve middle school students in team building, leadership, communication and entrepreneurship skills. Mentors receive 16 hours of intensive training and spend more than 30 additional hours leading the youth participants in 12 90-minute training sessions and a one-day community market fair. Student mentors earn three academic credits as part of the course.

Guided by their mentors, each student team develops an idea for a new business, then prepares and presents a business plan to the MOB Advisory Board. The board includes community and business leaders and grants loans of up to $200 to each student team, which executes its plan and manages the businesses at a community market fair. Student and mentors also visit successful local entrepreneurial firms, meeting with the CEOs to learn how their businesses were started and how they operate.

Mentors' reflections and end-of-program surveys provide evidence of a great learning experience and of the positive impact of MOB on their personal and vocational development. One Rider student explains, "The MOB program definitely prepared me for the world of work because it gave me confidence in myself." Another says, "I learned that I'm capable of helping others… that I have some things in common with all the children … I am definitely not the same person that I was at the beginning." ■

> "The MOB program definitely prepared me for the world of work because it gave me confidence in myself."
>
> *- Rider University MOB mentor*

Photo Courtesy of Rider University

Service-learning is part of the fabric at Defiance College

Community engagement is so woven into the experience at Defiance College – a school long recognized for its commitment to service-learning - that it's the norm for students, faculty and staff. "This is who we are. This is what we are about," says one student.

Beginning with Freshmen Seminar through advanced courses in academic majors, students regularly apply knowledge gained in the classroom to real-world settings to improve quality of life within their community. Located in rural Northwest Ohio, Defiance College is well-positioned to be a valued resource for local agencies and schools

The McMaster School for Advancing Humanity focuses and incubates efforts to link DC resources to community needs. Such opportunities as the Citizen Leader and Bonner Leader programs enable students to integrate community engagement with leadership development. Students also participate in AmericaReads, a program which provides supplemental academic support to local schools, as well as Big Brothers/Big Sisters, the local Volunteer Connection, and Good Samaritan School for children with developmental disabilities.

The First-Year Experience program introduces freshmen to service-learning concepts. The annual Freshmen Service Day ties community service to the classroom of Freshmen Seminars through such activities as ecological restoration projects for a local nature preserve or working with Bittersweet Farms, a local nonprofit nationally recognized for its innovative programs for young adults with autism.

The commitment continues throughout students' time at Defiance College. Faculty and students in social work courses address issues of homelessness and hunger - often less apparent in rural settings than in urban areas - by developing awareness and fundraising activities to benefit local shelters and food banks. Students conduct regular homelessness surveys to help local social service agencies understand area trends and address housing needs.

> **"... students regularly apply knowledge gained in the classroom to real-world settings to improve quality of life within their community."**

Business Department faculty integrates service-learning into courses for both traditional and non-traditional students through such projects as helping local organizations develop strategic and marketing plans. For one local town, students gained valuable professional experience when they created a downtown redevelopment plan which resulted in a grant request for government funds and saved the town thousands of dollars in design fees.

Students in the Sport Science program partner with a youth outreach organization to address childhood obesity issues. They provide physical fitness programming and games to rural and urban elementary schools, then, in the classroom, reflect on their fieldwork in the context of childhood obesity, fitness, and physical literacy.

The school's commitment to community service extends into its sports programs. Team members of

Photo Courtesy of Defiance College

men's and women's intercollegiate sports participate in service projects through the Office of Student Athlete Engagement. In August, football players spend their first day of training conducting service projects throughout the county.

The McMaster School also helps students apply their academic expertise and service interest to issues beyond the local community. Working with faculty to design community-based research projects, Defiance College students have helped partners in Belize, Cambodia and New Orleans address such issues as water quality, teacher training, basic health care outreach, violence toward women, and community restoration. ■

SPOTLIGHT

Professor and former U.S. Ambassador to South Africa talks about service

James A. Joseph is Professor of the Practice of Public Policy Studies at Duke University's Sanford Institute of Public Policy and Leader-in Residence at the Hart Leadership Program. A former U.S. Ambassador to South Africa, he now helps emerging leaders in southern Africa through a joint appointment at Duke University and the University of Cape Town. He also authored the books The Charitable Impulse and Remaking America and is currently working on a book focusing on ethics in public life.

Joseph offers these thoughts on service:

The highest praise that can be given anyone in South Africa is to say he or she has ubuntu, which means that they are generous, hospitable, friendly, caring and compassionate...You can, thus, understand why it would be both arrogant and wrong for anyone to approach voluntarism and civic engagement in places like South Africa as though it was a Western value rather than a shared value. The absence of a well-organized service movement does not necessarily mean the absence of a service ethic.

People around the world are agreeing that a good society depends as much on the goodness of individuals as it does on the soundness of government and the fairness of laws. They are reclaiming responsibility for their lives through neighborhood associations in squatter settlements, farming cooperatives in rural areas, micro-enterprises in urban areas, housing associations, mutual aid associations and various other forms of self-help groups to improve local conditions. What they need is not charity, but assisted self-reliance...

It is has been my experience that when neighbors help neighbors, and even when strangers help strangers, both are not only transformed, but they experience a new sense of connectedness. Getting involved in the needs of the neighbor provides a new perspective, a new way of seeing ourselves, a new understanding of the purpose of the human journey.

In other words, doing something for someone else is a powerful force in building community. The imperative of programs like the university's new DukeEngage initiative, for instance, is to help transform the laisez-faire notion of live and let live into the principle of live and help live.

Student consultants help local entrepreneurs improve operations and results

A Portland State University program recently helped one local entrepreneur overcome setbacks to build a thriving bakery business and provided real-world experience to the students who helped him.

Twenty-one year old Jake Wollner launched the vegan-organic wholesale Buddha Belly Bakery, then was stalled by several restructuring and relocation challenges. Connecting with PSU's Business Outreach Program provided him with the financial consulting he needed to secure loans that allowed the bakery to hire seven full-time staff and expand its product line.

Since its initiation in 1994, the Business Outreach Program has helped over 400 local small businesses like Wollner's by placing more than 1000 student consultants – who gain hands-on experience creating business plans, researching markets, developing human resource plans, and helping implement financial systems.

During the past four years alone, the program has donated some $750,000 in free consulting that has resulted in the creation of over 146 jobs. While providing small business owners and micro-entrepreneurs with knowledgeable and relevant mentoring and technical assistance, the program engages PSU students in community-based learning.

Most PSU students must take a Senior Capstone Course as the last phase of the school's required education program, and any student can enroll in the Business Outreach Capstone class. Through lectures, guest speakers, class discussions and an in-depth consulting project with a small business in the Portland metropolitan area, students work in teams to learn about the role of a small business consultant and how small business really works.

School of Business students who choose to become interns through the program are placed in local small businesses to provide assistance in marketing, finance, accounting, or general management. Most internships involve research plus hands-on assistance or leadership in implementing research recommendations. Interns work in diverse teams which include the business owner, a management counselor from the Business Outreach Program, firm employees, and, sometimes, other students. ■

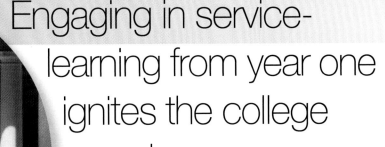

Engaging in service-learning from year one ignites the college experience

By Edward Zlotkowski

The most important things you bring to community service are your hands and your heart. In college you're also expected to bring your brain — which is why academic service-learning is so powerful... Students find new ways to learn but also connects their learning to the way things work in the larger world.

● ●

Because service-learning offers hands-on education in a real world framework, **some of the best service-learning programs in the country have made a special effort to see that students get to experience what college is all about beginning in their first year.**

First-year students can find service-learning programs in nearly any size, shape and flavor – from large one-day community plunges to service as part of a first-year seminar providing orientation and skill-building for new students to service embedded in courses in the general education curriculum or for a particular major.

At Montana State University, for example, a freshman seminar for business majors introduces service-learning in the "context of the stakeholder model that emphasizes the interconnectedness of businesses and legal, regulatory, sociological, and competitive environments." A panel of prominent businesspeople discuss their service commitment, then student teams undertake their own service project. Reflecting on this experience helps shape each student's "Personal Strategic Plan" as well as the team-created plan.

Montana State's program is typical of many first-year service-learning programs because the amount of service required is limited and the service students provide is familiar

– such as stocking shelves at a food bank, working with children at local schools, visiting shut-ins, building and repairing trails in a park.

What makes first-year programs different from similar high school service experiences is that they are not an end in themselves. The "service" in community service is its own reward. The "service" in service-learning is a fundamental part of a structured learning experience. That doesn't mean the service is somehow less important. **It means the service is important for educational as well as social reasons.**

Think of it this way: **The most important things you bring to community service are your hands and your heart. In college you're also expected to bring your brain – which is why academic service-learning is so powerful.** It not only helps students find new ways to learn but also connects their learning to the way things work in the larger world.

This connection is evident is programs like **Purdue's award-winning Engineering Projects in Community Service which invites first-year students to work with upper-class**

students. What better way for new students to develop motivation, teamwork, communication skills and a sense of professional responsibility right from the start than to design things real people really want?

Service-learning linked to courses in one's major may be a no-brainer, but it's just as valuable in the general education courses most schools require before students can begin their concentration. Many students find these introductory

Photo Courtesy of Purdue College

courses irrelevant to their interests and hence frustrating.

One group of experts sympathizes, noting: "First-year students enroll in many of their courses to meet curricular requirements, and they bring about as much enthusiasm to the task as we might expect from people doing something that someone else has decided will be good for them." ■

Service-learning can change the general education course experience in two ways.

● First it **MINIMIZES FRUSTRATION BY SHOWING HOW THE IDEAS YOU'RE STUDYING AND THE SKILLS YOU'RE GAINING PLAY OUT IN SITUATIONS THAT MATTER.** When sociology 101 introduces the concept of "social marginalization," it will cease to be just another academic term when you spend time with people who can't find a home, no matter how much they try.

● Second, **SERVICE-LEARNING CAN HELP STUDENTS GET THEIR EDUCATIONAL BEARINGS STRAIGHT — GIVING THEM A CHANCE AT HANDS-ON LEARNING, THE PREFERRED LEARNING STYLE OF MOST FIRST-YEAR STUDENTS.**

Finding a school that offers plenty of first-year service-learning opportunities could make for a very satisfying first year of college and eliminate boredom – which is the most frequently reported reason students give for leaving school.

In Portland State University's required Freshman Inquiry course, for example, each section of the course develops its own theme such as Constructing the Self: Me, Us and Them; Forbidden Knowledge: the Sacred and the Profane; Pathways to Sustainability and Justice; The Columbia Basin: Watershed of the Great Northwest; and Entering the Cyborg Millennium: Transformations in Technology and Human Society.

A growing majority of the sections include a service-learning component. For the Cyborg Millennium section, students made a map of surveillance cameras throughout the city of Portland and posted the map on a website.

Here's what one student wrote about this project: **"Through this project (the Portland Mapping Project) I was able to examine a problem and propose a solution. By analyzing multiple aspects I was able to determine problems that we, as a class, might run into. This led to the evaluation of how we should proceed collectively and how we could involve local organizations to assist us."**

It's hard to imagine this student being bored by this first-year experience! It's also hard to imagine anyone confusing this project with traditional community service!

Of course, it's important to note that while college-level service-learning should engage the head as well as the hands and the heart, sometimes it doesn't. As service-learning has become more popular on campuses around the country, more and more schools have rushed to claim they make it available.

"We must challenge ourselves to go Into the Streets, not just for a day, but for a lifetime."
– ITS Challenge Statement, 1991

Photo Courtesy of Stonehill College

Unfortunately, what some campuses call "service-learning" is, in fact, no different from high school community service. The activities are the same – which is not necessarily a problem; but there is no significant academic component – which is a major problem.

This is especially true of so-called "service-learning" experiences attached to orientation programs and one-credit first-year seminars. Sure, some specific community need is met. But you'll come back to campus with no special knowledge and no new skills. No one will have asked you to solve a problem that requires you to think. No one will have begun to help you learn to learn from real world experiences.

So if you find yourself doing "service-learning" that screams "been there, done that," don't get frustrated. Just look for another course, another instructor, or another program that will give you the real thing. This book gives you a heads-up on what to look for. ■

The rest is up to you!

Photo Courtesy of Portland State University

SPOTLIGHT

University of Dubuque Service-Learning Programs Aim "To Do Good Well"

Photo Courtesy of University of Dubuque

University of Dubuque students, faculty and staff thoroughly analyze every potential service-learning opportunity to ensure that the school engages in projects which truly serve specific, unmet community needs. This groundwork improves the school's aim "to do good well."

The process – which includes research, dialogue and discernment as well as cross-collaboration with academic affairs, student life, the library and athletics to determine need, talents and time – is illustrated in the course "World View Seminar Two" which is taken by all university sophomores and which includes planning and implementing a service project.

Students begin by discussing Better Together: Restoring the American Community by Robert Putnam and Lewis Feldstein, exploring library resources on various Dubuque service agencies and meeting with agency representatives. Their dialogue with agency directors and the clients they serve shapes the projects, helping students discern needs and what resources to use to address them.

Projects designed and implemented by Seminar students include

● Creating a work-out room center at a local homeless shelter.
● Teaching computer skills to immigrants at the city's Multicultural Center.
● Instituting a sexual assault awareness program on campus.
● Beginning a program in which the University's athletic teams teach skills sessions at the local Boys and Girls Club.
● Designing and coordinating a game night fund-raiser with local businesses.
● Organizing a sports day on campus for Big Brothers/Big Sisters
● Helping socialize abandoned or abused animals at the Dubuque Humane Society.

"Students' service-learning projects help them meet UD's call to "zeal for life-longlearning and service."

Each semester culminates in a Service-Learning Fair where students share their service work experiences with the University community. This event is a joyful, carnival-like street fair to celebrate the learning and service students have done and to inspire other attendees to think about how they might serve their communities.

Students' service-learning projects help them meet UD's call to "zeal for life-long learning and service." ∎

Photo Courtesy of Hobart and William Smith Colleges

Beyond the Classroom:
Moving forward to become engaged citizens
By Mark D. Gearan, President, Hobart and William Smith Colleges

A recent study reported the good news that Americans are "making more time to improve their communities through service." The better news is that hundreds of thousands of these individuals are college students.

According to the 2007 study conducted as part of Corporation for National and Community Service's annual assessment of Volunteering in America, 28.8 percent of the population volunteered throughout

the United States. Mark D. Gearan, President of Hobart and William Smith Colleges, believes this finding supports the strong ethic of community service and civic engagement which is a basic tenet in this country formed by the people, for the people.

Pointing to Thomas Jefferson, who wrote that every generation needs a new revolution, Gearan says, "For the generation of young men and women entering college in the 21st century, that revolution is one against apathy and indifference.

Now more than ever, young Americans are thinking about how they can make a difference, how they can engage their community."

Gearan explains that is the responsibility of higher education to integrate this revolution of service into the curriculum and to contextualize it within a rich, intellectual worldview. And he notes that public and private, four year and two year institutions have demonstrated their capacity to meet this challenge.

28.8%
of American's volunteered in 2007

Photo Courtesy of Hobart and William Smith Colleges

Photo Courtesy of Hobart and William Smith Colleges

While serving as President of the Peace Corps, President Gearan opened programs in South Africa, Jordan, Mozambique and Bangladesh and returned volunteers to Haiti after a five-year absence. He also created the successful Crisis Corps, which sends volunteers to crisis areas to help during emergencies.

Thomas Jefferson once wrote that every generation needs a new revolution. For the generation of young men and women entering college in the 21st century, that revolution is against apathy and indifference.

"Twenty five years ago," says Gearan, "Frank Newman - a strong voice for educational opportunity and active citizenship - observed the growing sense on many campuses that society emphasized advancing the private good over doing what is right for the public good. With the presidents of Stanford, Brown and Georgetown, Newman started an organization of college and university presidents committed to civic engagement, community service and service learning. Today, more than 1,100 presidents and chancellors are members of Campus Compact, headquartered at Brown.

Photo Courtesy of Hobart and William Smith Colleges

"As our students progress, the civic engagement skills that they develop here carry with them as they go on to be change agents in their own communities.

"We want to be able to say to our students that communities matter and that what they learn here should continue in their lives as they move forward to become engaged citizens."

"Six years ago, SUNY Geneseo President Chris Dahl and I started the New York State Campus Compact and became one of 31 states with an affiliate. Today, New York State has 70 active colleges and universities, making it the largest state organization in the network."

Increasingly, schools like Hobart and William Smith enrich community service and civic engagement with the reflective component of service-learning coursework. In a First-Year Seminar, for example, the study of the politics of disaster comes to life when HWS students travel to the Gulf Coast to speak with politicians and advocates and to gut Katrina-ravaged homes. In a new engagement known as the Geneva Partnership, the greater Geneva community and the school work together to enhance life for everyone who lives, works and studies in the community. HWS' new Center for Community Engagement and Service Learning bolsters the school's mission

and strategic plan to provide students with meaningful and thought-provoking service experiences.

"At Hobart and William Smith, we want to be able to say to our students that communities matter and that what they learn here should continue in their lives as they move forward to become engaged citizens," says Gearan. "As our students progress, the civic engagement skills that they develop here carry with them as they go on to be change agents in their own communities.

"Through service and engagement, and the subsequent lessons learned, our students integrate the revolution of service into their daily lives, develop an elevated sense of purpose, and go on to lead lives of consequence and meaning across the globe."

Photo Courtesy of Hobart and William Smith College

Preparing young artists for a lifetime of engagement

"We weave the academic, professional and community strands together to demonstrate to students that they can make their lives as artists out of whole cloth." – Kansas City Art Institute President Kathleen Collins

Photo Courtesy of Kansas City Art Institute

Students in Kansas City Art Institute's rigorous service-learning program gain historical context for the artist's role in society as well as practical instruction in working collaboratively with community groups and agencies.

The college, which had participated actively in community life for years, formally linked studio and classroom experiences in 2005 through its new Community Arts Service Learning (CASL) program. Today, the 15-hour CASL certificate program incorporates electives from all departments and includes an internship component.

"It is reasonable and responsible to introduce students to the many different aspects of the community and to provide them with meaningful opportunities for engagement."

- Collins

KCAI President Kathleen Collins explains that the school's efforts to instill "a broad understanding of the world helps them to find their own voices and ensures that the content of their work can have meaning beyond themselves. So it is reasonable and responsible to introduce students to the many different aspects of the community and to provide them with meaningful opportunities for engagement."

Collins' own background in social engagement taught her that early experiences can have a profound effect. "In my case," she says, "working with autistic children, patients in a state mental hospital and eventually working with Cuban refugees made their mark on my thinking about the world and how common citizens can make a difference."

CASL is housed in the school's Academic Resource Center as a part of Career Services. "We weave the academic, professional and community strands together to demonstrate to students that they can make their lives as artists out of whole cloth." Collins says.

In just three years, the burgeoning of diverse initiatives confirm faculty and student commitment to a vital civic life and healthy community. For example, in the class "Gashka: Art making and storytelling as cultural bridges. A course with the Osage," students learned about Native American traditions and camped on the Osage Reservation in Oklahoma as guests of an Osage scholar on her ancestral land. Drawing on the inspiration of their time exploring the uncultivated land, they created three-dimensional pieces for their sculpture class.

As part of a printmaking class, students met with a coalition of artists and educators who engage with homeless kids who drop in and out of local schools. Partnering with Chameleon youth development agency and Korean artist So Yeon Park, they helped

the children make drawings of their lives then scanned the drawings into a sewing program and made them into fabric squares which were assembled to make a quilt. "When it was completed, children, artists, art students and teachers came together," Collins says. "In a large circle with the quilt on their laps, they told their stories."

Each semester, faculty develop challenging and intense CASL electives that foster communication with different groups and communities. Together with students, they consider the challenges of collaboration and discuss the role of the artist and the dire need for creative solutions to society's most urgent problems.

Photo Courtesy of Kansas City Art Institute

"As a college of art and design, we have many resources to bring to bear on these problems," Collins notes. "It is exciting to see what we have begun together, and thrilling to think of all we can do in the years ahead." ■

Students and Residents Grow Together with the KCAI-Brush Creek Community Rain Garden

"To prepare students to build a garden that would not only be beautiful but also help the environment and educate the public, faculty gave students materials emphasizing the vital importance of ecological literacy, diversity, balance and interconnectedness for the future of the human species."

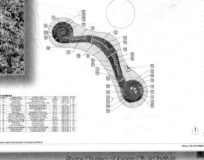

Photos Courtesy of Kansas City Art Institute

The Community Arts and Service Learning (CASL) program at the Kansas City Art Institute (KCAI) articulates an idea held by many of its faculty: one should not be teaching solely to students' individual, unique talents, but also to their capacity to grow into articulate and visionary citizens. To encourage student-community relationships, a category of elective known as "Community as Client" was incorporated into the CASL certificate program. Persuasive Ecology and Design, the rain garden class, was the first elective of this type.

In the course, students were to address a local ecological problem and design a small intervention that would contribute to building a solution. The faculty determined the class would respond to two factors: one was a growing local awareness of a surface-water run-off problem in Kansas City and the other was the proximity of KCAI to a waterway that demonstrates the reality of the problem.

Some months earlier, the mayor had addressed the situation by proposing the creation of Ten Thousand Rain Gardens as a community-based action that could contribute to solving the problem. KCAI took on the challenges of actually implementing such a program and, because of the

enthusiasm and youthful energy of the students, what began as collaboration between departments at KCAI grew to encompass a wide local community.

A rain garden is a working garden containing plants native to the local environment and climate. Plants native to the Kansas City area are heartier and have deeper, more substantial root systems than many non-native plants used in area gardens. Native plants capture and absorb heavy rainfall and alleviate run-off.

To prepare students to build a garden that would not only be beautiful but also help the environment and educate the public, faculty gave students materials emphasizing the vital importance of ecological literacy, diversity, balance and interconnectedness for the future of the human species. They also examined how artists and designers address ecological ideas in contemporary culture, and how urban life has disrupted natural hydrological cycles. Additionally, students studied and discussed local and global climate change in urban areas, the destruction of ground cover leading to erosion,

covering over of porous surfaces leading to run off, depletion of ground water, pollution of surface water, and various issues concerning the Kansas City metropolitan watersheds.

The class then undertook the design of an educational public rain garden-something that local people would relate to, learn from and become involved in. Brush Creek Community Partners, whose constituents range from neighborhood associations to universities, businesses and large corporations, became the class's "community client." Students made several design presentations, took suggestions from their client and offered the final design. Once the water run-off analysis and contour mapping were done, a landscape architect drew the final construction design.

Planting day emerged as a picture-perfect example of how the garden was conceived and how it would grow: under the caring hands of skilled artists, environmentalists and community members. ∎

NMU president tells how his school sets the stage for lifelong engagement

Photo Courtesy of Northern Michigan University

"I strongly believe that students end up living what they learn. That's why academic service-learning is so powerful."

When he hears people say that college students don't care about community, Northern Michigan University President Les Wong knows they're wrong – and can prove it by pointing to his own school.

"I know most students do care, and many actively work to make their communities better. The student who doesn't do something when asked is the exception."

The college's successful academic service-learning, volunteer initiatives and leadership and citizen programs are proof that students, faculty and staff are working to help others in the community and beyond, he says. Active participation in the greater community permeates the school's culture and is a valued part of an NMU education.

"I strongly believe that students end up living what they learn," says Wong. "That's why academic service-learning is so powerful. Rather than just reading and memorizing material, NMU instructors are teaching students how to put lessons into action."

Wong predicts that graduates who engaged in NMU service-learning opportunities will become leaders in their businesses and communities. "This is because they will already have hands-on, validated experience in being agents of change. They'll know that one or two people or a small group can make a difference, create miracles, and impact another person's life.

"They will know this can be done because they already will have done it. And that is the real test of learning." ∎

"My experience with service-learning taught me how to view events and people in their larger contexts. I learned to think of the bigger picture, work for systemic change and not settle for a 'band-aid' solution to a problem. For example, a homeless drunk man on the street was not someone to criticize and tell 'Sober up and get a job,' but someone suffering from a poor mental healthcare system and, maybe, a genetically increased risk for alcoholism.

"Additionally, this broad perspective took hold in the classroom. Academics were not just about memorizing facts and figures, school was about learning about myself— my strengths and weaknesses—and the world around me. I could then integrate that knowledge into my future career plans. Through service-learning I began to see my life as integrated and whole.

"Service-learning helped mold me into a poised and articulate young woman ready to make a difference in the world."

*Julie McClure, Student
North Carolina State University*

SPOTLIGHT

Geography service-learning students get their hands dirty (literally)

Photo Courtesy of Northern Michigan University

> "To be competitive in today's environmental job market or get accepted to graduate school, NMU students need hands-on, 'real-life' field experiences that pertain to their chosen discipline."
>
> - Professor Ron Sundell

Living in the pristine Upper Peninsula of Michigan, Northern Michigan University students are in an ideal setting for outdoor service-learning experiences like Professor Ron Sundell's "Environmental Restoration and Management" course.

This experience was created by Sundell, who is also director of the school's environmental science program, in cooperation with the United States Forest Service, Hiawatha National Forest, The Nature Conservancy's Marquette regional office and the Superior Watershed Partnership.

Course objectives – to provide each student with direct field experience in habitat assessment, restoration activities, stream monitoring techniques, and resources management strategies – were built around enabling students to engage in "hands-on" environmental and conservation resources practices, techniques and procedures commonly used in both private and public (state and federal) sectors.

"To be competitive in today's environmental job market or get accepted to graduate school, NMU students need hands-on, 'real-life' field experiences that pertain to their chosen discipline," Sundell says. "The Environmental Restoration and Management course provides students with valuable field experience that directly relates to their class work in the environmental science, geography and biology/ecology curriculums and ultimately their chosen profession."

Students gained practical benefits from the service-learning provided by the "Environmental Restoration and Management" course. "The aspect of this class that I think will end up being most valuable was the connections we made with

> "I would have to say the best part of the class was being able to do the actual work we are preparing to do by giving back to the world and actively engaging in something that makes a good impact on the earth." -NMU student Michael Rotter

the organizations that we worked with," says NMU student Dan Fisher. "I feel that I can now call these people and ask for help or advice on my future career search or possibly have a better shot at getting an internship." Other students appreciated the informal learning that occurred during the 40-mile van ride to and from sites in the Hiawatha National Forest.

Jennifer Riley offers her assessment of the experience: "I think this class should be required for all conservation students." ■

Inside-Out Prison Exchange *Opens* Minds

Photo Courtesy of Temple University

> ## *"We don't live from the eyebrows up. So why do we think we can best learn from the eyebrows up?"*
>
> *- Lori Pompa, Founder and Director of The Inside-Out Prison Exchange Program at Temple University*

Attending class in prison, alongside women and men who are incarcerated, Temple University students view issues of social significance through a sort of "prism of prison."

Through the Inside-Out Prison Exchange program, undergraduate and graduate students together with those who are incarcerated explore issues of crime, justice, inequality, freedom, and other social concerns.

"What the class does is open up minds," said Paul, who said his involvement in Inside-Out and the Graterford Prison Think Tank assures him that he won't be remembered only for his crime. "I don't want to die with that type of label on me," he said. "On so many levels, Inside-Out transforms you, empowers you." Students agree.

Tricia, a senior criminal justice major in the honors program, calls Inside-Out one of the most talked-about courses among Temple students. She says,

"Before I took the class, I had never engaged in a discussion with incarcerated individuals. It's very intense. You're bombarded by ideas. I can now look back at my reflection papers and see a progression, a growth in how I view things."

Founder and Director Lori Pompa says Inside-Out is "radically different" from other education and training received by students pursuing careers in law, corrections or criminal justice. "In much of that training, there is a strong emphasis on holding yourself apart from those who have been accused and convicted of crimes, on not connecting with them on an especially human level or on a level of equality, of seeing them as 'other'."

Inside-Out is now a national movement, driven by students, incarcerated women and men, and college and university instructors trained to design and teach Inside-Out courses in multiple subject areas.

Pompa says, "Hopefully, through this experience, perspectives of all kinds are challenged and changed...perspectives of both 'outside' students and 'inside' students. This, to me, is how we make change in the world, one person at a time. And then it multiplies." ■

SPOTLIGHT

Leadership Development

The Student Leader Fellowship Program:

Preparing the Community Leaders of the Future

Northern Michigan University's Student Leader Fellowship Program has a great track record in sparking students' long-term commitment to civic engagement: More than 80 percent of SLFP graduates report that they are now playing active roles within their communities.

Learning through service is a hallmark of the two-year SLFP program, which was established in 1991 to promote "leadership at the community level." First year students learn about leadership and their own abilities through an annual fall retreat, two-credit leadership theory and practice course, Skill Builder! workshops, and special occasions with visiting leaders. Each student fellow is matched with a community member who serves as a leadership mentor. The second year, students work individually or with teams to plan and organize internships which involve three-four hours weekly in unpaid community service, include leadership content and are supervised by a community member.

Through their internships, NMU student fellows engage with Big Brothers/Big Sisters, daycare facilities, classrooms, Girl Scouts, the Upper Peninsula Children's Museum, youth councils, middle school and high school bands, theater productions and athletic teams. They serve as mentors for those involved in the court system and also champion environmental causes and assist with environmental education. And they help provide health care for the uninsured through the Medical Care Access Coalition and work with non-profit organizations like the Alzheimer's Foundation and Home Hospice.

Reflection is a key theme for interns, especially during monthly fellowship meetings where community service projects become service-learning experiences as student fellows consider pivotal questions:
How can opportunities at my site be extended to larger numbers of people?
How can difficult social issues be resolved, eliminating the need for the service I am providing?

What is my role as a leader in moving the process forward at my site?
How are my views changing as a result of my experience?
What am I learning about myself?
What am I learning about how communities operate and how positive change is achieved?

Since the program's inception, 613 NMU students have completed the two-year commitment, donating 68,656 hours of leadership and service at 283 community service internship sites. The entire community has partnered in this enterprise, and 507 community members have already volunteered to act as student mentors - many more than once - providing guidance, support, and insight into community needs and processes.

Profiles completed before and after students engage in the program show substantial growth and development in leadership ability, confidence, knowledge of community processes, and commitment to be actively involved in these processes. ■

"My community service internship affected me on a whole new level. I would have never done something like that had I not been in the SLFP...I have experienced many different leadership roles throughout the program and have become more comfortable with myself in general. I can confidently say that I am leaving the program a better and more well-rounded person."

- Skyla Vandervest, Student Leader Fellowship Program Participant

Photo Courtesy of Northern Michigan University

SPARC Ignites Rollins College Student Engagement

"Rollins students have had a tremendous impact on our organization. Their involvement will have a positive effect on our staff and programs for months to come." - Shannon Lacek, Director of Marketing & Development, Enzian Theater/Florida Film Festival

Rollins College students are fired-up about community involvement! Their journey of community engagement begins even before they open their first book as college freshman – with in a day of education, service and action called SPARC: Service Philanthropy Activism Rollins College.

During Fall Orientation, incoming students join faculty and staff to engage with more than 25 community partners and agencies throughout Central Florida for this special event - the only State of Florida program that includes a community service component which continues throughout the first-year experience in academic service-learning courses, projects and reflections.

SPARC facilitates participation in thousands of hours of community involvement, creating meaningful campus and community partnerships that meet the academic goals of several first-year experience courses. Because of SPARC many students are empowered to enroll in service-learning courses, join and create service-projects, and continue to engage with community agencies and partners throughout their college experience.

"Rollins students have had a tremendous impact on our organization. Their involvement will have a positive effect on our staff and programs for months to come," says Shannon Lacek, director of marketing & development for the Enzian Theater/Florida Film Festival.

"We love our continued relationship with Rollins," says Holly Vanture, community and mentor coordinator at Fern Creek Elementary. "For our kids, interacting with college students allows them to understand that one day they could go to college."

And Maia Ryan, a Rollins freshman who participated in a landscaping project at Fern Creek Elementary School calls SPARC "an awesome experience. I am already getting to know the community around me. It is definitely a great feeling." ■

Photo Courtesy of Rollins College

"I can't believe how much this opportunity opened my eyes to the world and our community. I feel like I had no clue about any of this…I have really grown and now understand that I have the ability to create meaningful change."
--Rollins College, Class of 2010, SPARC Participant

Photo Courtesy of Rollins College

Service-learning nurtures future community leaders

At Bentley College in metropolitan Boston (MA), service-learning programs facilitated by the Bentley Service-Learning Center challenge students to use critical thinking and self-examination to become socially responsible, engaged, and aware leaders. Four Bentley students - Manuel Carneiro, Danielle Boczar, William Quinn and Ashley Stevens – rose to the challenge and gained significant leadership experience.

They share their thoughts about the leadership skills which can be built by students who seize service-learning opportunities:

Many high school students are pushed to do "the right thing" and participate in community service activities. However, there is often no thought as to what the service will accomplish, other than it will help someone.

Service-learning takes the idea of community service and makes serving a learning opportunity through the classroom, educating students through their service. The community work service-learning students do helps them relate to class material in a new way and to grow through experiential learning. As students become more involved with programs and take on more responsibility, they grow as leaders.

As Project Managers, students oversee other student volunteers who attend the service sessions. Project managers are responsible for communicating with the partner organization, the students who work with them, and the supervisor. In addition to managing multi-faceted projects, project managers are responsible for planning and leading reflection sessions.

Experienced project managers may become Program Coordinator – a competitive position and limited to one or two senior students. Much like the President in other school organizations, the Program Coordinator trains and oversees all project managers and works with staff to ensure all programs are running smoothly.

Some colleges and universities offer Staff positions to students completing bachelor's or master's programs. In these part-time positions, students with in-depth service-learning knowledge and experience are responsible for completing specific projects.

Service-learning students learn to be leaders in the community by heading-up community-based projects, managing their fellow students, dealing with logistics, resolving conflicts, and handling other managerial issues and duties. Because of their skills and the relationships they develop, these students are often sought out by for-profit and non-profit organizations.

Service-learning takes the idea of community service and makes serving a learning opportunity through the classroom, educating students through their service. ∎

Photo Courtesy of Bentley College

Colgate Program Enables Students to be *"Heroes on Call"*

Colgate University student Kyle Spitzfaden finished the take-home final at 3:00 a.m. and went to bed. It would be a short night.

When his pager beeped 30 minutes later, he pulled on the clothes he'd set out "just in case" and raced to answer an emergency call at the Southern Madison County Ambulance Corps (SOMAC) station house - as he had done for the past four years.

Spitzfaden is one of a dedicated group of students, faculty, and staff volunteers for fire departments and ambulance corps in Hamilton, NY, where the school is located, and in surrounding communities. Their efforts are organized by Colgate's Center for Outreach, Volunteerism, and Education (COVE).

"It's one of the most serious volunteer jobs you can do," he says. Training includes at least 113 hours of classes on fighting fires, handling hazardous materials, and meeting health and safety standards, plus weekly training sessions at the station for all firefighters, and additional optional classes.

> "By integrating meaningful service-learning experiences... nursing educators... connect coursework with future professional practice."

New recruit Danielle Mercado explains, "It takes the majority of your first semester, meeting twice a week for three-hour lectures each time, and five Saturdays for eight to ten hours each. On the last Saturday they put us in a burning building. The testing certifies us to wear an Air-Pak. And then there's yearly training to keep up."

The ready resource of student reinforcements makes Hamilton the envy of other small communities, says Hamilton Fire Department Chief Ross Hoham.

Emergency services are just one way Colgate students can participate in service experiences. COVE supports volunteer organizations, service-learning classes, internship programs, residential life initiatives, and more to help students affect direct change within surrounding communities. Students gain an appreciation of service, an understanding of the social and economic issues of Central New York, and become passionate, engaged, and globally-minded citizens. ∎

New Center is a Conduit for Students to Meet Essential Community Needs

Photo Courtesy of University of Scranton

Through a new free health clinic at University of Scranton, students in occupational therapy, physical therapy, counseling and allied health fields are meeting pressing community needs.

Opened late 2007, the Edward R. Leahy Jr. Center Clinic for the Uninsured: A Cooperative Project at the University of Scranton provides non-emergency health care to Lackawanna County (PA) residents who can't afford private health insurance and don't qualify for public health insurance. At the Center, located in the university's Leahy Community Health and Family Center, students supervised by faculty and doctors treat fevers, influenza, respiratory infections and other conditions usually addressed by primary care physicians.

University of Scranton President Rev. Scott R. Pilarz, S.J. explains the Center "fits well with the University's Jesuit mission by combining learning with service and by engaging our resources, faculty and the exuberant energy of our students with professional collaborators to meet a pressing community need.

"The clinic offers new opportunities for faculty and student teaching, learning research and service in the fields of health, human services and education."

Alumnus and benefactor Edward R. Leahy, after whose son the clinic is named, sees service-learning as a critical component of the education provided by a university. "It is more important than ever to put our teaching to the practical test; to implement our learning within our community for the wellbeing of all," he says.

"A university today that does not engage with its community is like the plant that, no matter how beautiful, is in danger of withering. Its knowledge comes only from within and, therefore, tends to be secondhand, repetitive and usually one-dimensional."

Senior nursing student Lauren Whymeyer says, "The Leahy Clinic not only gave me a chance to improve on previous learned skills, but also provided interaction with multifarious nationalities and cultures. It offered a wealth of information and experience that could not be obtained from classroom or hospital learning." ∎

SPOTLIGHT

Program immerses students in Lakota Nation culture for service, academic credit

South Dakota State University student Beth shares these thoughts about her Lakota Nation Program Experience:

The most difficult experiences are those that remove you from your context and alter that reality, either shattering it or expanding it. These experiences are also the most rewarding.

To say the least, living on the Standing Rock reservation changed my life. Through living with an elder Hunkpapa woman and working at a children's center, I came to understand the grace and travesty of the situation on the rez. I came to question my own values and my own fears while listening to stories of a way of life in tumult.

What I learned there did not occur in the stale confines of a university classroom, but in the gestures and moments and traditions of the everyday. I learned how little I really know and how an education is a life-long process.

This program transcends the typical college experience. In its richness, its depth, and its knowledge, it gives participants what schooling has taken away.

Just one program in the United States places students on South Dakota Indian Reservations to earn academic service-learning credit: The International Partnership for Service-Learning and Leadership' Lakota Nation Program.

South Dakota State University is ISPL's affiliate, providing supervision and teaching and issuing academic credit for learning related to American Indian issues, history and culture. Primarily designed for a full semester with 15 academic credits, other shorter sessions offer fewer credits.

Placement is oriented to students' interests and academic majors.

The semester program includes two weeks of intense orientation including classroom and cultural instruction as well as extensive field trips to reservations and significant historic sites such as Wounded Knee and Pipestone quarries.

Photo Courtesy of South Dakota State University

Students then spend 10 weeks living with a Native family on a reservation while engaged in service-learning at a nearby tribal agency. Service locations include offices for tribal historic preservation, a tribal radio station, Boys & Girls Clubs, schools and other facilities. When service is completed, a final week of reflection, writing and a formal presentation on the experience concludes the program.

While Lakota Nation service-learning program's strong academic emphasis is sustained throughout the program, the experience also becomes deeply personal as students become part of their host family and local community.

Dr. Allen Branum, Director for Diversity Enhancement at South Dakota State University explains, "The issues and concerns of American Indian Reservations become personal concerns, and family trials and challenges are felt directly.

"At the same time, the joys and fulfillment of participation in a compassionate and rich culture that lies within, yet outside, the boundaries of mainstream America bring new insights regarding both culture and personal actualization. Students usually develop lifelong relationships, returning to the reservations in later years to visit families and friends or perhaps pursue employment in a reservation environment where their skills are needed and appreciated."

ISPL places students for academic credit service-learning at sites around the globe. ∎

Photos Courtesy of Truman State University

Service-Learning at
Truman State University
Yields Real-World Results

"Students participating in these projects obtain hands-on experiences and develop key professional skills which are of great value to employers."

From its founding in 1867 to the present day, Truman State University has fostered a tradition of service. In the past, emphasis was placed on teachers to fulfill the call to serve in the emerging state school system. Today that tradition continues with the school's mission to produce graduates equipped to better society through leadership in both their professional and personal lives. Service at TSU finds expression in a myriad of volunteer activities, course-embedded service-learning offerings, and a special program that takes advantage of an exceptionally vibrant student organization culture.

Students can also participate in service-learning projects through classes in which service-learning is a core component of the course. The service-learning program is supported by an AmeriCorps*VISTA Member who assists faculty with their service-learning goals. Current courses with significant service-learning components emphasize projects relating to economic development, rural Latino population needs, assistance for rural non-profit organizations, environmental awareness, youth outreach, and health-care matters.

A program unique to Truman State University is the Service-Learning Advantage program, which provides a second opportunity for students to engage in co-curricular service-learning through involvement in student organizations. The program is designed to support student organizations as they create and incorporate service-learning projects that address university-wide learning objectives. These learning objectives have been publicly agreed upon by the institution and are a central component of its mission.

Another unique aspect benefiting students participating in a Service-Learning Advantage Project is that students are able to document their participation on the Co-Curricular Record that the University sponsors. The Co-Curricular Record is an internal tracking system that allows students to document all activities, events, organizations, and leadership roles that they participate in during their college careers. Real-world experience through service-learning projects and internships carry significant weight with employers, who oftentimes consider a student's entire college background during the hiring process. Like the academic transcript which records course grades, the co-curricular record is a permanent register that can be issued to future employers or programs of study as official documentation of a student's accomplishments at Truman State University.

The power of a co-curricular service-learning experience is evident in the leadership skills that students develop throughout the project's duration. Students spearhead the projects and assume full responsibility—they do not have an instructor directing the venture and are in charge of keeping the project moving forward.

Students participating in these projects obtain hands-on experiences and develop key professional skills which are of great value to employers. Students are expected to learn and use skills such as delegation, planning, resourcefulness, and program development.

These real-world skills not only make campus service-learning projects successful, they also equip students to be successful in their communities and workplaces upon graduation. ■

At Syracuse University, public scholarship is a catalyst for community problem-solving

Syracuse University Chancellor Nancy Cantor envisions a Scholarship in Action which expands the content and scope of discovery, learning, and public engagement. Service-learning provides the foundational framework for this vision and allows faculty and students to consider their goals and values in context of the larger community.

Service-learning programs are facilitated by SU's Mary Ann Shaw Center for Public & Community service as part of Academic Affairs. Founded in 1994, CPCS, **a "learning laboratory," interacts daily with students, faculty, staff and community.** The Center collaborates with community partners – who play significant roles in all areas of the school's community based service-learning/research agenda and provide knowledge and wisdom which enhance learning outcomes – and connects them with appropriate University areas.

Syracuse University Community Based Service-Learning Program works with every school and college at the University, placing students at some 100 community sites every year. CPCS staff work with faculty and community partners to develop courses such as

- *Art in the Community* - helps students understand recent practices in community art;

- *Boundaries in Syracuse* - teaches students about the boundaries at work in city residents' lives inhibiting/enabling mobility;

- *Sociology of Childhood* - gives students a clear idea of the social nature of childhood and significant issues facing children today.

Syracuse Community Geographer works with local nonprofit agencies and community members using Geographic Information Systems to map and analyze community challenges. Supported by local foundations,

Photo Courtesy of Syracuse University

> Community partners play significant roles in all areas of the school's community based service-learning/ research agenda and provide knowledge and wisdom which enhance learning outcomes.

the Chancellor's Office, the Geography Department in Maxwell, and CPCS, **the Community Geographer serves as a resource for community and neighborhood groups** and works with faculty and students in several different courses.

The Southside Innovation Center - located in a former carpet showroom on the city's South Side, and overseen by the Falcone Center for Entrepreneurship in SU's Martin J. Whitman School of Management - spurs economic growth at a grassroots level on the city's South Side. SSIC functions as an incubator for local businesses with WSM faculty and students providing support in developing business plans, professional office space and financial consultation.

Upstate Institute in the School of Architecture supports Dean Mark Robbins' philosophy that urban renewal is more than just fixing up rundown buildings and adding parks. **He believes it is about "...changing the way a city and a region function through more innovative and smarter design."** The Upstate Institute is a center for collaboration between the region and the School of Architecture supporting lectures, conferences, symposia, and faculty/student design studios in partnership with community residents. ■

Penn service-learning programs benefit thousands of students and community members

Photo Courtesy of University of Pennsylvania

Every year, thousands of University of Pennsylvania students regularly engage in comprehensive and mutually beneficial community-school-university initiatives in West Philadelphia, Penn's local community.

Penn's commitment to innovative service-learning has grown steadily over more than two decades and was reinforced in President Amy Gutmann's 2004 inaugural address which introduced the Penn Compact and its focus on increasing access, integrating knowledge, and engaging locally and globally.

More than 2,000 students engage annually with the community through fifty-plus student organizations which address a broad range of issues including housing and food security, health, education, arts and culture, and the environment. These groups work in partnership with local schools and community-based organizations to support ongoing efforts to improve the quality of life for constituents.

Civic House is Penn's central hub for student-led community service and social

advocacy, and Civic House's Service and Advocacy Education Series helps students improve the effectiveness of their work. Through this series – facilitated by students, faculty, staff, and community partners - students address fundamental issues raised by community work and learn skills essential to their efforts.

"More than 2,000 students engage annually with the community through fifty-plus student organizations which address a broad range of issues including housing and food security, health, education, arts and culture, and the environment."

Recognizing students' growing commitment to careers in the public interest, Civic House provides Public Interest Internship Fund stipends and introduces students to alumni involved in these careers. The new Civic Scholars Program provides close faculty mentorships, courses, summer internships, and capstone research projects aimed at public policy recommendations to undergraduates who commit to a four-year experience in civic service and scholarship. A mentoring program launched by Penn's Fox Leadership Program and Big Brothers Big Sisters Southeastern Pennsylvania recently matched 295 student mentors with West Philadelphia youth. More than 170 School of Nursing students are engaged in the Living Independently for Elders program, which helps frail elderly remain in their homes. And through Penn's School of

Engineering and Applied Sciences, the student-driven nonprofit CommuniTech has established computer labs in West Philadelphia classrooms and taught technology skills to hundreds of community youth and adults.

Many students, faculty, and staff engaged in these programs also work through Penn's Barbara and Edward Netter Center for Community Partnerships, which supports a variety of academically-based community service (ABCS) courses that engage students in real-world problem-solving. The courses aim to strengthen public schools, neighborhood economic development, and community organizations and emphasize student and faculty reflection on the service experience. Each year, more than 1500 Penn students (professional, graduate and undergraduate) and 50 faculty members from a wide range of Penn schools and departments are engaged in West Philadelphia through these courses.

A major component of Netter Center's current strategy focuses on transforming existing public schools into university-assisted community schools designed to educate, engage, activate, and serve all members of the school's community. The Penn-Sayre High School partnership is the Center's most intensive of these school development sites. Sayre youth and residents are empowered in their own education through learning activities geared to improving the quality of life for the entire community. Hundreds of Penn faculty, staff, and students participate in new and existing academic courses, internships, federal work-study, and volunteer opportunities at Sayre.

The Penn-Sayre university-assisted community school model is comprised of four integrated initiatives - school day, after school, community, and health center – which serve the community's educational, social service, health, and professional needs.

Through Sayre's School Day Program, Penn faculty, staff and students from such disciplines as Medicine, Nursing, Dentistry, Education, Social Work, Law, and Arts & Sciences partner with the high school on core curriculum topics. In the Pipeline Program, for example, students link with Sayre science instructors to teach the basics of Neuroscience - neuroanatomy, neurotransmission, and basic pathologies. A select group of Sayre students go to Penn for weekly lessons on the brain taught by medical students, residents, and neurologists. In partnership with Penn Nursing, the program includes a Cardiology/Chemistry partnership.

The Moelis Access Science Program aims to improve math and science curriculum through hands-on labs and teacher professional development.

Penn student fellows help Sayre teachers make the best use of their current resources and introduce variety of supplemental resources to create engaging labs, lessons, and experiential activities. For example, Penn Nursing students in a Crime Scene Investigation course create mock crime scenes at Sayre and teach high school students in a Chemistry class on forensic science basics.

Sayre's After School Program provides a safe space and academic and recreational activities daily for students from Sayre plus 65 students from Sayre's feeder elementary schools. The program also hosts field trips, parent meetings, and student showcases. Many activities are staffed by Penn students who volunteer through ABCS courses or are paid through work-study programs. The Summer Program (K-12) implements a literacy and service-learning curriculum for 180 K-8 students while more than 20 high school students work as Junior Servant Leaders alongside college-aged Servant Leaders.

The High School After School Program combines academic supports, mentoring that focuses on college and career access, real-world job experience, and extracurricular and youth development activities. College and Career Pathway activities, part of a four-year plan, offer school day coordination, mentorship, test preparation, and other supports.

Throughout the year, more than 150 high school students participate in paid internship opportunities that incorporate academic support and mentoring, including Nutrition's Most Wanted program for which students host healthy cooking classes and cater nutritious meals for community events; The Stay Safe Crew – a group of peer health educators who promote healthy sexuality and positive decision-making to teens; and Health System Internships, which enable students to work in cardiology, diet and nutrition, finance, patient education, physical therapy, and radiation.

● **Sayre's Community Wide Programming includes Family Fitness Nights at Sayre High School.** Open to community members of all ages, sessions range from adult computer literacy to arts and crafts and free health screenings from Penn's Schools of Medicine, Nursing and Dentistry. Parents and community members volunteer for the Safe Corridors Program, which combats neighborhood violence by securing the surrounding blocks before and immediately after school. Penn students coach teams and conduct tutoring and

youth development sessions as part of the Penn West Philly Basketball League, started by an undergraduate.

● **REACH Anti-Truancy Initiative offers workshops and skill-building classes on Saturdays for students with unexcused school absences and their parents.** Behavioral health, employment and food assistance are provided to community members through the program's social worker.

The federally funded and federally qualified Sayre Health Center provides students and community members both clinical as well as educational/ health promotion services and hands-on opportunities for Sayre students interested in health careers.
The Penn-Sayre Partnership has resulted in significant accomplishments. Sayre was one of three school recipients of the 2007 Coalition for Community Schools' National Award for Excellence and one of only a handful of schools which attained all Pennsylvania System of School Assessment test targets.

With Penn undergraduates as the core tutoring staff, the after school program's adult-to-student ratio is approximately 1:5. Attendance at monthly parent meetings is better than 90 percent. In 2006-07, 200-plus Sayre students received free vision screening from Penn practitioners; free dental screenings and follow-up were provided for 133 Sayre students. And of the 150 community member participants in twice-weekly Family Fitness Nights, more than 90 percent report that they are eating healthier and exercising more.

The Netter Center envisions the Sayre initiative to be a national model of how to link K-16 curriculum to solving locally identified, real world, community problems as well as how to create collaborative, sustainable programs which improve the health and education of community, school, and university partners. ■

Photo Courtesy of University of Pennsylvania

SPOTLIGHT

Education and Service:
Building a Bridge to the Community

Photo Courtesy of Emmanuel College

One goal of service-learning is to build life-long connections between students, institutions and communities. At Emmanuel College, the success of that relationship is evidenced in one of the college's graduates, Maura M. Bradley. Not only did Ms. Bradley participate in service-learning while a student at Emmanuel College, but she worked with Our Lady of the Perpetual Help Mission Grammar School in the heart of the city of Boston, the very same school of which she is now principal. Ms. Bradley spoke with Emmanuel Magazine about her role as an administrator in an urban Catholic school and the tremendous success of the school's collaboration with Emmanuel College.

EM: How did Emmanuel prepare you for this role? How has your Emmanuel education shaped your career?

MB: Emmanuel cultivates in people that security to live your faith, to be active in your faith, and to be proud of it. The College creates a forum to grow as a young person. There is also an expectation as an Emmanuel graduate that you will take your talents and your gifts and use them where they are most necessary, and through that you will be fulfilled through giving of yourself.

As a student I participated in service activities, but more importantly, I was introduced to the Mission Hill community as an Emmanuel student. At the time, Mission Main was a run-down housing project infested with criminal activity, neglected property, and no safe play space. The first time I worked in Mission Hill, during my pre-practicum, was at the Tobin School. I was invited to learn about the community and to meet the people living and working here for years and years. It was a broken, but wonderful community, there was such a desire to get involved.

When I left Emmanuel, I had a great handle on not only the craft of teaching, but also on the discipline for learning. In the Education Department, we were encouraged to learn what we were most passionate about, and then go out into the world and apply it.

EM: How have Emmanuel and Mission collaborated?

MB: Firstly, I have such great pride in what Mission Grammar and Emmanuel College have in common. We share the same mission of educating urban students in the Catholic tradition, and feel a true sense of community ownership. The collaboration with Emmanuel itself has been essential. It has provided resources and opportunities that have helped the entire Mission Grammar family, including scholars, faculty and families.

One example of collaboration is that students in [Associate Professor of Management] Diana Stork's service learning course, **Management Research for Positive Change,** provided us with great data for our marketing efforts. We have developed a wonderful relationship with these students, who are able to use their classroom knowledge in a real-world situation. Dr. Stork sparked interest in other faculty, who are developing other service learning courses in psychology and art. They will provide essential resources for our students and excellent opportunities for Emmanuel students.

Through the Carolyn A. Lynch Institute, Emmanuel's Education Department has developed early math intervention training and provided quality graduate-level professional development for faculty. The Institute also provides us with all the necessary materials to implement these math strategies in the classroom.

Campus Ministry sponsored a service day in the fall, and we had about 40 students here who painted, washed the walls and made bulletin boards in preparation for our students' return. I would say that on an average day, there is a minimum of five students here tutoring, in work study positions, student teaching, or doing field work for class. Through the **ECSTATIC [Emmanuel College Students Taking Action to Initiate Change]** program, students conducted an eight-week art enrichment program here at Mission, coming in once a week to do art classes with the children.

We also have a great connection with the Black Student Union [BSU], who invited us to the Martin Luther King, Jr. talk and the evening with Prince Cedza Dlamini, which were wonderful opportunities for our middle schools students. BSU President Jeff Joseph is a natural mentor of our students and he takes a real interest in them. Our students are also invited to come to dinner and to basketball games on campus.

EM: How important is your connection with Emmanuel today?

MB: The collaboration is essential to success – we could not do what we do without Emmanuel College. The relationship shows our students, many of whom have really tough lives, that someone important cares. When they are invited to the Emmanuel campus and have relationships with college students, it provides an opportunity they would not normally have, and they are able to experience and articulate what it means to go to college and how to get there. ■

Student philanthropy at Northern Kentucky raises funds, awareness

Photo Courtesy of Northern Kentucky University

While each class works a little differently, the basic principles that have guided this program for the past seven years are the same.

● Students identify a community need and select nonprofits that work to meet this need.

● Within each class, students form community boards or small work groups to begin collecting information, researching nonprofits and eventually advocating for funding for their agency.

● As a part of this process, students interact with people in the nonprofit sector (through interviews, site visits, in-class presentations by nonprofit representatives, etc.).

● As a class, students present and evaluate Requests for Funding Proposals.

● Students engage in a deliberative group decision-making process to select successful applicants and award $3-4000 to the community.

In just a few short years, student philanthropic projects at Northern Kentucky University have provided a powerful teaching and learning tool and delivered nearly $300,000 in funding to hundreds of nonprofit agencies.

NKU first introduced student philanthropy in 2000 following a series of discussions between faculty members, university president Dr. Jim Votruba, and local foundation leader Dr. Neal Mayerson. Today, the Mayerson Student Philanthropy program offers every student and every class the opportunity to learn and contribute.

No one NKU discipline owns philanthropy. Faculty members find innovative ways to integrate student philanthropy into such diverse classes as African American Studies, Art, Criminal Justice, Marketing, Public Administration, and Theatre, among others. Students learn course content such as writing, public speaking, persuasion strategies, history and theory through giving to the local community.

During a celebration event each semester, students award checks to the selected agencies. Last year an Honors Freshman Composition class donated $2000 to Little Brothers-Friends of the Elderly and a Sales Management class donated $1000 each to a local humane society, The Friars Club and The Center for Peace Education. These are just a few examples of the classes and organizations involved – during 2007 students in the Mayerson Student Philanthropy Classes presented a total of $23,570 to the community.

In addition to allowing students to give through this direct model, NKU recently began working with Citi to develop an indirect giving model, through which university students help review funding requests from the local Community Impact Board and then make funding recommendations. Both models allow students to learn about the process of fundraising and fund giving.

Many students report that the insights they've gained about the nonprofit world have led them to increase their own time and money donations and to explore career opportunities in nonprofits. ■

A list of programs that have hosted a Mayerson Student Philanthropy Course

African American Studies	Philosophy
Anthropology	Political Science
Art	Public Administration
Criminal Justice	Public Relations
Education	Religion
English	Speech
Honors	Social Work
Human Services	Sociology
Management	Theatre
Marketing	Women's Studies
Nursing	

A sample of Mayerson Student Philanthropy Classes and funds given in 2007

Spring 2007

MKT 306-001: Sales Management

Starfire Council of Greater Cincinnati Inc.	$1,000.00
Clermont County Humane Society	$1,000.00
The Friars Club	$1,000.00
The Center for Peace Education	$1,000.00

SPE 340-001: Strategies of Persuasion

National Underground Railroad Freedom Center

$1,320.00

ENG 151-003: Honors Freshman Composition

Ronald McDonald House of Greater Cincinnati	$1,500.00
Little Brothers—Friends of the Elderly	$2,000.00

SWK 408-002: Field Instruction III

AD Owens Elementary and Campbell County Family Literacy	$1,000.00
Peaslee Neighborhood Center	$1,000.00
Shelterhouse Volunteer Group (The Drop Inn Center)	$1,750.00

HNR 302-003: Investing in the Community

Community Christian Academy	$2,000.00
Total Spring Awards	$14,570.00

Fall 2007

HNR 308-001: The Arts for Social Change

Elementz	$1,500.00
The Frank Duveneck Arts & Cultural Center	$1,500.00
Children's Performing Arts of Lakota, Inc	$1,500.00

MKT 306-001: Sales Management

Fernside	$1,000.00
Lighthouse Youth Services	$1,000.00
Cinderella's Closet	$1,500.00

Total Awards to the Community	**$23,570.00***

I really enjoyed my experience with the Mayerson Project in my class. The best part of the class was ... that actually meant something more than taking notes and tests. I feel like I actually made a positive impact on the community and the project made me care about class and doing well in it. It was a great way to teach course concepts using real life situations. I would definitely recommend the class to anyone."

– Mayerson Student

SPOTLIGHT

Part 7 Articles

Service-Learning Semester Provides Students with *Deep, Life-Changing Experiences*

(The program) "increased my awareness of the global community and has greatly strengthened my relationship with the local Hispanic community."

– Chris Hartmann, Xavier University senior Biology major

Students juggle classes, trips and service in the poorest areas of Managua as participants in Xavier University's Academic Service-Learning Semester in Nicaragua.

Initiated in 1995 by professors who made an Ignatian pilgrimage to Nicaragua and El Salvador, the program combines classes in Service-Learning, Central American Culture and Society, Liberation Theology and Spanish with another class – usually history or literature – in the faculty trip leader's field.

Living with families in working-class neighborhoods, students work at child nutrition projects, at the children's hospital, with street children and at a home for children with mental and physical challenges.

Speakers complement course readings and service, and students travel on weekends to learn about other parts of Nicaragua, do weekly reflections and write final integration papers.

The coordinator of one of the child nutrition projects says Xavier's program is different from other groups that come for a visit and then leave: "Xavier students are with us for a whole semester, sweating with us in the kitchen, sharing our experience."

Dr. Irene Hodgson, five-time faculty trip leader, says: "This program has totally changed the way I teach and relate to students. It is the best example of integrated learning I have ever seen…The students come to see the United States and the world differently and also grow as people."

Senior Biology major Chris Hartmann, who worked at La Mascota Children's Hospital, says the program "increased my awareness of the global community and has greatly strengthened my relationship with the local Hispanic community." This experience has encouraged him to study Latin American rural and agricultural issues in grad school.

Senior Business major Kari Huske says that the experience "allowed me to realize the impact that I have on the community and my potential to make positive change in the world." Huske is working with Xavier's business school to start a service-learning certificate to "provide opportunities for business students to use what they've learned in their majors ….to benefit the community."

Academic Service-Learning Semesters have also been offered in India, Ghana and inner-city Cincinnati. ∎

Photos Courtesy of Xavier University, Ohio

Service and Learning Merge in Providence College's Major and Minor Programs

The Feinstein Institute for Public Service and Department of Public and Community Service Studies

A deeply integrated program combining community service with academic study is nothing new for students of Providence College. Through the first such program in the nation, the Rhode Island school has offered the opportunity to major or minor in Public and Communities Service Studies since 1993.

Providence's innovative academic program to educate caring community leaders came to life that year when a grant enabled it to create the Feinstein Institute for Public Service. Thirteen years later, the program became a full department within the Feinstein Institute. The department currently has 50 majors, 20 minors, and numerous other students taking courses as electives.

Department of Public and Community Service Studies courses are developed by faculty from various disciplines who engage students and community partners. Built on the pedagogical model of service-learning, courses cover central themes in community, democracy, and service. Students typically serve at least 2-4 hours weekly in such diverse activities as direct service, community organizing, community development, and public policy. Similar to a text, the service is "read" for its insights and forms the basis for a significant part of the course discussion and reflection.

The department partners with organizations that are deeply imbedded in the community and have a strong interest in facilitating students' learning. Students work with partners such as Times² Academy, Smith Hill Library, Southside Community Land Trust, Providence After School Alliance, Chad Brown Health Center, and the Providence Housing Authority with various responsibilities including tutoring, facilitating after school programs, teaching English, urban gardening, and providing diabetes health education.

Community partner representatives join faculty from the department to bring a range of perspectives to the classroom. Additionally, juniors and seniors sometimes co-teach the Public Service 101 course, which enhances their teaching

Photo Courtesy of Providence College

> "The Feinstein Institute for Public Service engages multiple voices to weave a rich and dynamic texture into the service-learning experience."

skills and provides students with a peer leadership voice.

The curriculum for the major and minor begins with an Introduction to Service in Democratic Communities and includes courses on organizational systems and community organizing, diversity, Catholic social thought, an internship requiring 120 service hours, independent study, practicum and a capstone. Students choose an academic track with at least three courses that enhance their learning on a particular topic (i.e. nonprofit management; humanities; policy analysis).

During the pivotal two-semester practicum, students develop leadership, management, facilitation, and grant writing skills. Serving as prime liaison between the Institute and a community partner, these Community Assistants volunteer 6-10 hours weekly with increased organizational responsibilities including coordinating and managing experiences for other service learners.

The Feinstein Institute for Public Service engages multiple voices to weave a rich and dynamic texture into the service-learning experience. Its Town Meetings each semester and annual retreat enable students, faculty, staff, community partners and alumni to share ideas and concerns. Through a grassroots initiative called the Community Congress, the Institute partners with nearby neighborhood organizations in beautification and advocacy activities. It hosts Justice Talks, a dynamic series of civic reflections for all AmeriCorps members throughout the state. The Institute also maintains ties with alumni to nurture a social and professional network of people interested in service and social change. ■

Majors, Minors and Certificate Programs

Assumption College: Minor on Service-Learning

Bentley College: Service-Learning Certificate

Bryant University: Major and a minor in service-learning and sociology

California State University Dominguez Hills: Post-Master of Arts Degree Graduate Certificate in Conflict Analysis & Resolution

California State University Monterey Bay: Service-Learning Leadership Minor

College of St. Catherine: Minor in Civic Engagement

Colorado School of Mines: Offers two undergraduate minors and an area of special interest in humanitarian engineering.

Colorado State University: Service-Learning Graduate Teaching Certificate Program.

Concord University: Civic Engagement Minor

DePaul University: Community Service Studies Minor

Emory and Henry College: Public Policy and Community Service Major and Minor

Humboldt State University: Leadership Studies Minor

Kansas City Art Institute: Certificate in Community Arts

Murray State University: Service Learning Scholars (recognized at graduation, at the institutional "Honors" day, and receive a special designation on their transcripts)

Northern Michigan University: Superior Edge initiative - Student Enrichment Transcript

Northwestern University: Certificate in Service Learning

Portland State University: Minor in Civic Leadership

Providence College: Public and Community Service Studies

Saint Louis University: Service Leadership Certificate Program

Salt Lake Community College: Service Learning Scholars Program (receive recognition from the college in the form of a service-learning cord at commencement, notations in the commencement program, and designation on their official transcript as Service Learning Scholars)

San Jose State University: Service-Learning minor

Slippery Rock University: Minor in Community Service and Service-Learning

State University of New York Stony Brook: Living/Learning Center Interdisciplinary Minor in Community Service Learning

University of Alaska Anchorage: Civic Engagement Certificate

University of California, Los Angeles: Civic Engagement Minor

University of Kansas: Certification in Service Learning

University of Massachusetts Boston College of Public and Community Service: Offers a variety of undergraduate majors and concentrations—leading to a Bachelor of Arts degree, and graduate degrees in Dispute Resolution and Human Services. The focus of the College of Public and Community Service is education for students who are interested in working towards social change.

University of Missouri: Minor in Leadership and Public Service

University of New Hampshire: Associates of Applied Science Degree in Community Leadership

University of North Carolina (Chapel Hill): Public Service Scholars Program

University of San Francisco: Honors minor in public service, a public service minor, and public service certificate program

For more listings please visit:
http://www.servicelearning.org/instant_info/fact _sheets/he_facts/minors__certs_he/

Photo Courtesy of University of Montana

Service-Learning Opportunity at The University of Montana (UM) Builds Nonprofit Administration Skills

When UM students perform a 300-hour internship with a nonprofit community organization, they fulfill part of the requirements to earn a Minor in Nonprofit Administration and/or National Certification in Nonprofit Management from American Humanics. American Humanics is a national alliance of colleges, universities, and nonprofits whose mission is to educate, prepare, and certify professionals to strengthen and lead nonprofit organizations.

These internships enable students to continually utilize classroom knowledge in ongoing community engagement activities. Students work alongside nonprofit staff, service recipients and other governmental and nonprofit community representatives to solve problems, provide services, and create programming while meeting critical community needs.

Examples of The University of Montana's student internship sites include Missoula's Biomimicry Institute, the Missoula Art Museum, the United Way of Missoula County, the Missoula Urban Demonstration project, and the Curry Health Center on the UM campus. ■

SPOTLIGHT

College of St. Catherine Inspires Students to be Change Agents

At the College of St. Catherine, where civic participation and community activism motivate students to achieve, citizenship is considered a verb.

Founded in 1905 by the Sisters of St. Joseph of Carondelet, this St. Paul (MN) school is committed to the liberal arts, Catholic Social Teaching, and professional programs which teach women to lead and influence. Today St. Kate's continues to develop innovative ways to fulfill its mission and to educate and inspire students.

Photos Courtesy of College of Saint Catherine's

> *"St, Kate's prepares graduates to be ready, willing and able to create and implement initiatives for justice at home and across the globe."*

In 2006, the school launched a minor in Civic Engagement. Developed in partnership with its Center of Excellence for Women, Economic Justice and Public Policy (one of four Centers of Excellence at the College), the minor propels students to effect and promote positive change in their communities. Its foundational course "Challenging Oppressions: Civic Engagement and Change" and such interdisciplinary electives as "Social and Political Activist Art" provide students with the tools and resources necessary to combat inequality and create systemic social change.

Deep Shikha, Ph.D., who chairs the College's Economics Department and who played an instrumental role in creating the minor in Civic Engagement, believes the minor engenders "the active citizenship that students need to be change agents."

Believing that engagement implies action, St, Kate's prepares graduates to be ready, willing and able to create and implement initiatives for justice at home and across the globe. Through projects which focus on such issues as domestic violence, women's rights, women's health, among others, students learn to think critically and compassionately about their communities.

One student explains, "I often suspected that my feminist views and my Catholic faith tradition were at odds with each other." But, she says, instructors like Professor Shikha taught her that feminism and faith can work together. ■

Integrating Service-Learning into General Education Programs

Cabrini College, Tulane University, California State University Monterey Bay

It's rare to find a college today without some type of service-learning initiative on its campus or a university which hasn't explored how to integrate service-learning into the collegiate experience. But only a few schools have fully institutionalized service-learning so that it provides the underlying structure for the entire educational enterprise.

At these schools, the various constituencies - students, staff, faculty, and administrators – share an understanding of the importance of service-learning to the achievement of the institution's mission and vision, and service learning is prominent within the educational environment and integrated into general education programs.

At Cabrini College, for example, service-learning is the central unifying concept and experience within each student's general education program. For each of their four years at this Catholic residential college in suburban Philadelphia, students enroll in courses that develop a deepening understanding of social justice and a deepening experience of service-learning.

Cabrini students move from observation and reflection, to participation and reflection, to research and advocacy with a community partner – toward graduation as fully engaged citizens and professionals. In year one, they engage in local projects that introduce them to community involvement and community partners. In year two, they expand their understanding of how change-makers impact the world as they commit to weekly, direct service with a community partner. In year three, students learn the skills for national, regional, and local engagement by partnering with community agencies to conduct community-based research and advocacy. In year four, they complete a capstone in the major that integrates the

knowledge and experience of civic engagement with their professional development in the field.

To illustrate, representatives from Laurel House, which works with victims of domestic violence, met recently with Cabrini administrators to hear the results of a study conducted for this organization as part of third-year Cabrini students' community-based research course. As they discussed the methodology, data gathered and conclusions, the students

Photo Courtesy of Cabrini College

> "...students move from observation and reflection, to participation and reflection, to research and advocacy with a community partner – toward graduation as fully engaged citizens and professionals."

also demonstrated their passion about the work.

"Students were engaged with the process as much as they were with the product," says Charlie McCormick, Dean of Academic Affairs at Cabrini College. "In short, their work mattered to them, and the responses from the Laurel House representatives indicated that the students' work mattered to them, too. This is the benefit of service-learning and sophisticated models of service-learning like community-based research. Students cannot be blasé about their educational experience; they are energized and engaged because it matters."

Tulane University is another school with service-learning as its infrastructure. Utilizing a developmental approach to teaching civic engagement, this New

Orleans institution requires undergraduates to participate in a least one service-learning course before their third year.

Advanced students then engage in one of a series of offerings designed to deepen their involvement and strengthen the connection between service and scholarship. Opportunities include service-learning courses, internships, research projects, honors thesis projects, international study abroad programs, and capstone experiences, all in the context of public service.

Tulane's Center for Public Service supports the graduation requirement that unites academics and action, classrooms and communities. Founded in 2006 as part of the university's renewal plan following Hurricane Katrina, the Center reflects Tulane's revitalized sense of purpose within a city and region rising from devastation. Through the integration of service-learning in the general education program, students, faculty and community partners dedicate themselves to transforming civic life - helping Tulane build on its rich history of civic and research activities and address urgent and

Photos Courtesy of Tulane University

long-term social challenges in their region and beyond.

Institutionalization of service-learning takes an evolutionary next step at California State University Monterey Bay, a school founded in 1995 with service-learning as a core value, as reflected in its vision statement which asserts that undergraduates will have "the social responsibility and skills to be community builders." Service-learning in the general education program and majors compels all students to develop the knowledge, skills and attitudes to participate sensi-

> *"...service-learning serves as a unifying experience for students – connecting courses across the curriculum and integrating general education with the disciplines while fulfilling its traditional role of bringing together the theoretical and intellectual with the practical and experiential."*

tively in multicultural communities and to work effectively to address deep-seated social inequalities.

CSUMB's two-tiered service-learning requirement begins with the general education program. In the context of participating in multicultural communities, students provide direct services while examining issues related to diversity, social power, privilege, and oppression. This work prepares the students to examine the stereotypes that they hold as well as the systemic injustices that perpetuate inequality. Building on this foundation, students then enter into upper-

division service-learning courses in their majors, addressing social justice issues relevant to their field.

As one example, CSUMB computer science students provide technology support to community organizations while examining issues of the digital divide. This engagement helps them develop heightened awareness of their role as future technology professionals in overcoming economic and social marginalization.

At Cabrini, Tulane and CSUMB, institutionalization of service-learning serves as a unifying experience for students – connecting courses across the curriculum and integrating general education with the disciplines while fulfilling

its traditional role of bringing together the theoretical and intellectual with the practical and experiential.

"This is not to suggest that every college or university can or should institutionalize service-learning," says McCormick. "But when it is the organizing element of the educational experience, an institution's various components 'fit' and the reasons for this 'fit' are transparent.

"Students understand why they are at college and what they are learning. And the institution understands how the educational experiences it offers come together to meet the needs of students, local partners, and the global community." ■

Community Service is 'at the heart' of Slippery Rock University

Photo Courtesy of Slippery Rock University

Charity Bradley, an SRU community counseling graduate student who grew up in New Castle and who works with children at the I CARE House, explains, "I like giving back to the community. A lot of these kids are from low-income families. When they come into the house, I assist with homework and read to them."

"We're training people who will make contributions in their academic field. We're also training people who are going to make contributions in the everyday lives of communities, their families and in schools," Kaiser-Drobney says.

Slippery Rock University's I CARE House helps more than 100 disadvantaged children accomplish everyday victories each month.

This New Castle (PA) community center is just one of SRU's many service programs which engage more than 1100 student volunteers every year.

Alice Kaiser-Drobney, director of the Institute for Community, Service-Learning and Nonprofit Leadership which oversees SRU service projects, says community service is much more than a food drive or recycling project at this public residential university where commitment to service-learning, social justice and equality are core interdisciplinary values.

Kaiser-Drobney likes the school's understanding of the importance of developing civic-minded, socially responsible people. "That's at the heart of what we do here," she says.

Students show leadership by volunteering in on and off campus programs to tutor children, providing relief in cities nationwide, working with the homeless, leading environmental cleanups, heading after-school programs, and working with hospitalized veterans, and individuals with physical and mental disabilities.

"We do that by developing this ethic of service. When people are no longer engaged, democracy is in jeopardy."

"It's a critical component of being a citizen of the world, especially in today's global environment. We teach students how to use their minds. When you do that, you can help others improve their quality of life." ■

"We're training people who will make contributions in their academic field. We're also training people who are going to make contributions in the everyday lives of communities, their families and in schools. We do that by developing this ethic of service. When people are no longer engaged, democracy is in jeopardy."

– Alice Kaiser-Drobney, Director, Institute for Community Service-Learning and Nonprofit Leadership, Slippery Rock University

Students Earn Emotional Dividends Helping Community Residents Discover Tax Refunds

> "It is such a great feeling to know that I can use my tax knowledge and interest in the field to help benefit other people. Being a part of this program not only gives me experience with tax preparation, but really exposes me to the real world and is aligned with the Jesuit tradition here at Fairfield."
>
> *– Fairfield University student Beth Grossman*

Two Fairfield University accounting majors found unexpected personal rewards when they provided free tax services at the local Volunteer Income Tax Assistance site.

Beth Grossman and Kylin Wentz worked four hours weekly from February to mid-April to fulfill the service-learning component of their elective Federal Income Taxation

Photo Courtesy of Fairfield University

II course in the Fairfield, CT, university's Charles F. Dolan School of Business. At Hall Neighborhood house in nearby Bridgeport, the two seniors helped mostly lower-income single mothers and working families prepare income tax forms and discover tax credits which often resulted in significant refunds.

The experience also paid big emotional dividends to the students. Wentz found that participating in the program translated her classroom education into a "real world" experience.

"This program is yet another example of our University's success at integrating our education with the Fairfield mission to share with its neighbors its resources and special expertise for the betterment of the community," Wentz says.

Grossman added that preparing returns provided practical experience in identifying taxpayer filing status and dependents, determining applicable tax credits that may be taken, and much more.

"It is such a great feeling to know that I can use my tax

knowledge and interest in the field to benefit other people," says Grossman. "Being a part of this program not only gives me experience with tax preparation, but also exposes me to the real world and is aligned with the Jesuit tradition here at Fairfield."

Dr. Kathy Weiden, assistant professor of accounting says, "The Office of Service Learning was key in helping me understand the notion of how to develop this course so it doesn't turn into an internship for the students. There's a big difference between a service learning course and an internship [program]. Service learning courses cultivate the value of being responsible community members. [OSL] helped me shape it into something that is both strong academically and strong in the areas of reflection and civic-mindedness. The students can think back on everyone they helped prepare taxes for, and know that they brought economic benefits to these individuals, these families. One student told me that the course was valuable to her career - and life. It was a win-win situation." ■

Photo Courtesy of Fairfield University

Princeton Students Engage in Community-based Research

Photo by: John Jameson, Princeton Office of Communications

In collaboration with the New Jersey Audubon Society, Princeton students and faculty monitored the impact of sprawl and land use on the health of a local lake.

"Instead of writing a traditional academic research paper, I got to write about trends that are shaping communities as we speak."

Princeton University students are working with local organizations on such meaningful projects as helping families avoid home foreclosure and exploring the vulnerability of nuclear reactors to terrorist attack. The tool they're using to make a difference in their community is community-based research.

Community-based research (CBR) is a dynamic form of service-learning in which students use academic skills and knowledge for important community issues such as education, the environment, homelessness, safety, inequality, and affordable housing. CBR is community-driven and action-oriented: organizations determine what they need to know to advance their work and then, empowered with the information, decide what action steps they should take.

For last spring's foreclosure project, students in an urban poverty class gathered data on home foreclosures in Trenton, plotting foreclosures and documenting the scope of the problem for each neighborhood in the New Jersey city. Their nonprofit partner used the information they collected to create and run programs designed to help families keep their homes.

For the nuclear reactor project, research conducted by students in a Princeton class on science, technology and public policy helped lead to a Federal policy change which broadens the radius for crucial medicine distribution in the event of a nuclear emergency.

A practical way for students to apply the research and writing required in college, community-based research projects can happen in courses throughout the curriculum, from architecture to anthropology and psychology to lab science, or through independent or honors research.

For example, at University of Notre Dame, chemistry students test older homes in low-income neighborhoods for disinte-

A practical way for students to apply the research and writing required in college, community-based research projects can happen in courses throughout the curriculum

grating lead paint which can pose risks to the developing brains of young children and can have lifelong effects. Students work with families and a local community center to test homes and yards and to educate families about lead mitigation and health interventions. They have helped more than 39 families.

Students in a University of New Mexico class on city and regional planning partnered with Albuquerque's Santa Barbara-Martineztown Neighborhood Association on a proposal for a new water pumping station. Studying engineering documents from the 1940s for the original water pumping system, analyzing water flow in the area, gathering information from the Army Corps of Engineers, and synthesizing the data for a presentation to the Zoning and Planning Board, they developed a proposal which eventually garnered a $46 million grant to build the system.

As part of a North Carolina's Appalachian State University junior seminar that teaches research methods and how to design a research project, students do a community-

Photo by: Denise Applewhite, Princeton Office of Communications

An internship with Mount Carmel Guild's Emergency Assistance Program led to a community-based research project on the availability of health-care for low-income people in Trenton, New Jersey. This senior thesis in Sociology won a prize.

based research project with the Blue Ridge Parkway, a 469 mile long national park in the Blue Ridge Mountains of North Carolina and Virginia. Currently they are studying trail use conflicts and possible interventions. The following year, for their senior thesis, they can undertake a community-based research project with a partner of their choice. At many of these schools, community-based research has been able to develop and thrive because of the support provided by Learn and Serve America, a program of the Corporation for National and Community Service.

CBR has opened new doors for students at Princeton. One notes, "Instead of writing a traditional academic research

paper, I got to write about trends that are shaping communities as we speak." According to another student, "Knowing that my work will matter to real people and learning about my community sparked my interest in this topic." **And a third student says, "The work completed is important not only for me, but also for another audience, making the obligation to produce a quality body of work greater.** I found the tangible aspect of the academic work rewarding, and I thoroughly enjoyed gaining a better understanding of the inner-workings of a nonprofit." ■

Trisha Thorme is the Assistant Director of the Community-Based Learning Initiative at Princeton University, a position she has held since 2000. She facilitates the collaboration of students, faculty, and community partners on community-driven research projects and works with faculty to integrate such projects into courses throughout the curriculum.

By the Numbers:

39: The number of families helped by student work to educate about lead mitigation and health interventions

$46 million: The size of the grant students earned to build a new water pumping system for a neighborhood

Over **100** college and universities have received funding (as subgrantees) from Learn and Serve to establish or deepen community-based research on their campuses

DePaul builds a socially-engaged learning program in an urban setting

Proximity generates opportunity for students in DePaul University's comprehensive service-learning program. The school is in the middle of Chicago where, according to Howard Rosing, "Many different ways to serve are close to home."

Rosing is Executive Director of DePaul's Steans Center for Community-based Service Learning and Community Service Studies, repeatedly recognized as one of the nation's top service-learning programs by *U.S. News & World Report*. The Center creates educational opportunities which unite students and faculty with residents from communities throughout this large metropolitan area to share knowledge and promote better understanding and positive change. In sync with DePaul's Vincentian mission of service and preferential option for the poor, the Center focuses on access to resources for underserved communities and service to low-income, exploited and oppressed groups.

"Our work facilitates the mission by directly integrating service into DePaul's curriculum," Rosing explains. "By applying theory to practice through creative service opportunities directly linked to course learning goals

and objectives, we create experiential and values-based learning that distinguishes DePaul as one of the most socially-engaged universities in the country."

The Office for Community-based Service Learning was established in 1998 to support development of service-learning throughout DePaul's curriculum. In 2001, it was renamed the Irwin W. Steans Center for Community-based Service Learning following a generous endowment by the Steans family. During 2006-07 the Center supported 176 courses with a service-learning component.

Rosing says that the University can be "a kind of a bubble where students can opt to attend class and not work on issues in the community." DePaul has no mandatory service-learning requirement. But many students do participate in service-learning because it's embedded in the university's curriculum." In fact, last year, 2831 students engaged with more than 100 community organizations in Chicago and

internationally through DePaul service-learning programs

"Chicago is dealing with significant structural changes related to gentrification," he explains. "Like many cities, it faces such issues as educational access, literacy for both adults and children, affordable housing, homelessness, healthcare access, immigration, labor rights issues, access to technology (the digital divide), and such emerging concerns as environmental justice. We're an urban university, and we're in the middle of it."

DePaul addresses these urban challenges through a broad range of service-learning programs, including:

● Students learn language in the context of weekly conversations with community residents through Intercambio Spanish Service Learning program. According to Dr. Susana Martinez, who teaches courses in the sequence that makes up this program, the experience helps students "build on the basics for class." At the end of class, students and participants engage in discussion about issues facing Latinos in the U.S.

Photo Courtesy of DePaul University

The North Lawndale Initiative links students with leaders in organizations and schools in this Chicago neighborhood for projects including physicals and health education, provided by DePaul nursing students, nurse practitioners and faculty; a teen violence prevention program, and an oral history project.

Community change and preservation are the focus of DePaul's geography service-learning program in the Pilsen neighborhood. Guided by urban geography professors Euan Hague and Winifred Curran, a growing number of students combine continuing study with service-learning in an approach which encourages understanding and discussion to study how neighborhoods develop and how gentrification works.

Through the support of the McCormick Tribune Foundation, some of DePaul's "best and brightest" who demonstrate a commitment to community service and academic excellence participate in advanced, paid internships which enable them to apply knowledge and skills to benefit an organization while they also gain valuable work experience.

The Black Metropolis Project – a collaborative effort of Steans Center and Sociology professor Dr. Ted Manley – was designed around a year-long course sequence that connected undergraduates and Chicago Public School students in projects involving research, writing and photography to capture the history of Bronzeville, Chicago's original "Black Belt" and an area where residents face displacement due to redevelopment.

Students in Dr. Ann Marie Klingenhagen's Money and Banking Course may choose to participate in a service-learning opportunity directed at low-income families facing financial challenges. By facilitating workshops which explain how to balance a checkbook, use a debit card and other basics, students help participants build financial literacy and learn about alternatives to high-cost non-bank providers.

DePaul is a Catholic university with access to many Catholic schools in the city. Through its mission-driven Catholic Schools Initiative, a paid community service program, DePaul students who are Federal Work Study eligible to work in selected K-12 urban Catholic schools provide tutoring, mentoring, and supplemental enrichment activities. In turn, students are enrolled in a course in Catholic Social Teaching.

Professor Laura Washington, a veteran journalist and contributing columnist for several Chicago newspapers, led her Investigative Journalism students outside the classroom in a service-learning project that enabled them to pursue stories in the Logan Square neighborhood. "What I love about Steans projects," she says, "is that they force students to…meet people they wouldn't normally meet."

Through this national AmeriCorps Jumpstart program, students are trained to deliver an innovative early education program by developing one-on-one relationships with preschool children in low-income communities. Participants work for at least 300 hours over a year to help children develop language, literacy, social and initiative skills. With 60 students at six community preschools during 2006-07, DePaul supports the largest Jumpstart program in the city and one of the largest in the U.S.

For students interested in learning how global issues affect local communities outside the U.S., the Steans Center collaborates with DePaul's International Programs Office and Study Abroad to offer a variety of international service-learning opportunities that engage students in critical issues that are relevant across borders. The Center supports programs in Mexico, El Salvador, Puerto Rico, Kenya, Rome, and Hungary.

Community Partners Internships help DePaul students gain work experience that combines professional development and community involvement. Those eligible for Federal Work Study employment are paid to work 15 hours each week for the full school year to provide a consistent level of assistance to some of the school's strongest community partners.

Photo Courtesy of DePaul University

Maintaining consistency is a challenge for most schools on the quarter system. As often as possible, says Rosing, DePaul's programs "try to mitigate that revolving door by placing students for an entire academic year."

Students who want to develop what Alexandra G. Murphy, Communications professor and Faculty Director of Community Service Studies, calls "a deeper understanding and practice of community service either as a prelude to a career after graduation or to enhance their personal sense of social justices as they enter the world of work" may choose the CSS minor. This interdisciplinary minor consists of three core courses addressing historical and contemporary perspectives on community service, nonprofit management and a community internship, plus electives from across disciplines or among

such recently created concentrations as community service and the arts, women's and gender studies, or others.

DePaul's robust service-learning program is driven by the large numbers of courses and students it has and by the quantity of organizations nearby. But Rosing explains, "We must think strategically about where to focus our resources. " The school's strongest relationships are with about 120 organizations who have the capacity to develop collaborations that target specific areas of the city and who are amenable to working with students.

Proximity and numbers aren't the only reasons for DePaul's large, strong service-learning program. "Significant institutional commitment is critical," says Rosing. "Faculty is at the core of development of any service-learning program. DePaul encourages faculty to explore service learning as a pedagogy for what it can add to their course goals and objectives and what they and their students can contribute to the community."

Steans Center supports faculty through one-on-one consulting and through quarterly peer education in Faculty Development Workshops, initiated by Rosing, where faculty share their best practices and explain how they integrate service-learning in the classroom.

The Center also offers periodic Community Development Workshops, which bring community organizations to campus to learn how they can better

> DePaul's robust service-learning program is driven by the large numbers of courses and students it has and by the quantity of organizations nearby.

utilize and maximize the relationship with DePaul, as well as logistical support for the organizations, reflection sessions for students, and evaluations of student learning and community impact.

DePaul's strong service-learning program has a positive effect on participants at all levels. Among countless success stories is that of the Money and Banking course financial literacy workshops. Dr. Klingenhagen, whose students' efforts targeted "underbanked" members of the community, notes that the program provides "more of an opportunity to learn about the impact of financial realities on communities." Mercy Housing Lakefront's Cleora M. Murff reports that the program "really helped the participants become more economically aware." And service-learner Jeanne Valenta, a student who is living the mission of the school and the Steans Center, says the experience enhanced what she was learning in the class about the financial lives of low-income people in this country. ■

Photo Courtesy of DePaul University

American University and Facilitating Leadership in Youth (FLY)

Students at American University have formed a unique bond with young people and the their community in Southeast Washington, DC. In a program which goes far beyond traditional tutoring models, both students and local youth gain rich learning experiences.

In 1999, three AU students – aware of the tough public education challenges facing the District of Columbia, where dropout rates surpass most US urban settings – became involved in the citywide DC Reads program and got to know young people from the Barry Farms public housing community in the distressed Anacostia neighborhood. After graduation, they created an organization that would continue to address the educational needs and other socio-economic concerns of these youth.

Facilitating Leadership in Youth (FLY), the only long-term, free, youth-led development organization in Southeast DC, was incorporated as a nonprofit 2002. Engaging youth in consistent year-round programs for six to ten years, FLY concentrates on academic achievement, youth development, and leadership. The elementary school students who started with FLY are now applying for college scholarships, getting fellowships, and engaging their peers in youth organizing. Forty youth, ranging from nine to 18 years old, enrolled by older siblings who participated in the program, now attend FLY sessions three to six days weekly during the school year and five days a week in summer.

The FLY-AU partnership takes different forms throughout the year. About 45 AU students work annually for all four years through the Community Service Center's DC READS program to provide one-on-one tutoring to each FLY participant during the school year. Some students stay on as counselors and workshop leaders for a six-week summer camp and teen leadership program. The program is held on the campus of the University, which offers space at no charge. The camp curriculum offers innovative ways to learn, such as Spoken Word and Fashion design classes that incorporate writing, literacy, and math skills.

The close campus-community connection is maintained by the FLY Student Club advisory board. Some AU students link their

Molly Norris, a recent graduate of American University who tutored and also worked at the summer camp, describes her experience:

"The walls of my classrooms blurred to include the entire city when I started to volunteer with FLY."

Photo Courtesy of American University

FLY service to a class in service-learning projects with the Anthropology Department's American Dreams, American Lives course or the School of Education's Schools and Society course. Students working within the School of Communications help design FLY publications such as "Guns Killin' Youngins: The Youth of Southeast Washington DC Want Answers." That publication, created by FLY's Youth Leadership Council to help young people understand the violence in their community, was supported by student-conducted research among parents of children murdered by gun violence, a juvenile justice organizer, a gun-law advocate, a police sergeant and the owner of a gun dealership. Students in the Young Women's Leadership Program work with young women to co-lead excursions and workshops designed to help them develop various skills and long-term goals. ∎

Going Native for Engagement

When Dr. Gary Welborn seized the opportunity to help his community rebound from years of decline, he also opened the door to new service-learning opportunities for his students at Buffalo State College (SUNY).

The school where Welborn works as a faculty member in the Sociology Department is located on Buffalo's West Side, an old Italian "ethnic village" where he has lived with his family for more than 25 years. This area is the most diverse in Western New York - just under half the population is white, and there are sizable Hispanic, African-American and Native-American communities as well as immigrants and refugees from such places as Somalia, Sudan, Burma, Liberia, among others – and is home to the city's international grade school and international high school.

The West Side was especially hard hit when Buffalo was devastated by deindustrialization beginning in the 1970s. Steel production, once a pillar of Buffalo economy, is nonexistent now, and only a shell remains of the formerly robust auto industry. Manufacturing has also declined precipitously, and the city's population has followed. As affluent residents moved, both out of Western New York and out of the city to the suburbs and rural areas, population dropped from 600,000 in 1950 to under 300,000 in 2000. In an injured economy with living-wage jobs hard to find and a badly deteriorated tax base, social problems increased, and there was less money for services to address them.

1992 was a particularly difficult year for the city which faced growing street violence, mostly connected with drug trade, and murder rates. It was a shooting that summer just outside Welborn's door which sparked neighborhood discussions of how to address the problems. That fall, the Welborns (who had helped organize improvement efforts throughout their time in the community) and their neighbors formed the Massachusetts Avenue Project (MAP), a grassroots movement dedicated to bringing the area's diverse residents together to improve the quality of life, especially for children and youth.

MAP's first project in June 1994 gathered 600 volunteers who worked together for five days at the local Boys and Girls Club to build a state-of-the-art playground with new murals, sidewalks and green space. Dr. Welborn likens the effort to "an

Photo Courtesy of Buffalo State College (SUNY)

old-fashioned barn-raising. It didn't matter what your race, religion, gender or age were – if you cared about the kids, you could contribute." By that time, he had joined the Buffalo State faculty, and he encouraged a few students to do their internships at the Boys and Girls Club and help with the playground project. "This was a sign of things to come," says Welborn.

In the years since the playground was constructed, building bridges between the students, faculty and staff of Buffalo State College and the vibrant grassroots movements on the city's West Side has become a calling for Dr. Welborn. He continues his involvement in many community projects, serves on the boards of several area organizations and, on campus, is Faculty Coordinator for the Volunteer and Service Learning Center (VSLC). "To build successful community-college partnerships, you have to know what's going on in both places," he explains. "Each side has to know what the other side is thinking and doing. Then you can develop partnerships that meet real community needs at the same time that they address the academic objectives of the college."

Recently, with encouragement from Dr. Welborn, the college adopted Asarese-Matters Community Center. Located on

Photo Courtesy of Buffalo State College (SUNY)

the western border of the campus in a neighborhood that faces many challenges, Asarese is dramatically under

funded and has only two staff to cover all programs and daily facility maintenance. Although Asarese has been open since 1989, the college had no connection with it until VSLC reached out to it in 2003. Since then, a partnership has grown swiftly. During spring 2007, more than 50 students in classes from the Sociology, Social Work, Geography, Creative Studies and Interior Design departments were involved in service-learning projects at Asarese.

As one example, advanced Interior Design students worked with the youth at Asarese to create a more colorful and livelier vision of the Center. Five groups of students worked on designs for the gym, recreation room, computer room, a "girls room", and the main foyer entrance. They came up with color schemes, furniture choices, and wall and floor applications, and they researched materials and prices to develop realistic cost elements. At a mid-semester presentation on their project, students were eager to know if any of their ideas were "really going to happen" or if this was just an "academic exercise." Dr. Welborn was able to respond, "Some version of what you have put together IS going to happen." In spring 2008, the Center will see a new computer room and new gym floor, both based on the students' designs.

The partnership between Asarese-Matters and Buffalo State is having a positive effect on the Center in many significant ways. "Even more importantly," says Welborn, "it is having an effect on the youth who go to the Center, many of whom come from very difficult circumstances. And it is also having an important effect on Buffalo State students who find it rewarding being involved in real projects that make a real difference in the community." ■

Macalester College's Lake Street Project:

Collaboration among Macalester College, the Minnesota Historical Society, In the Heart of the Beast Theatre, and Lake Street Communities

History came to life in a service-learning project at Minneapolis' Macalester College where students engaged in a multifaceted civic partnership with the Minnesota Historical Society, In the Heart of the Beast Theatre, and other members of the community.

Over the past two years, students in history, theatre and dance, political science, and environmental studies, and other departments collaborated with

Photo Courtesy of Macalester College

More than 80 Macalester students were involved in the exhibit, and the research of 45 students is reflected in the exhibit or interactive website or both. Class projects took shape in historic displays, photography, documentary film, maps, dance performances, art pieces, and essays. Methodologies including oral interviews, ethnographic research, Geographic Information Systems mapping and archival research were matched to academic disciplines, course learning

Photo Courtesy of Macalester College

community partners to create small-scale public projects documenting and sharing the history of Lake Street, a six-mile corridor linking Minneapolis and St. Paul. Today, diverse cultures, ethnicities, classes and religions in 14 neighborhoods and an important commercial district intersect in this stretch, which has been a destination for more than a century for immigrants and refugees - first from Western and Central Europe and, more recently, from East Africa and Latin America.

In fall 2007, the projects – developed in conjunction with the historical society, the theatre and the Lake Street Council - culminated in a major six-month exhibition at the acclaimed MN History Center. Titled "Right on Lake Street," it reflected the diversity of Lake Street and showcased Macalester student research and design along with their experiences engaging Lake Street communities.

> "Presenting scholarly research in an interactive, accessible and informative way enabled Macalester College to demonstrate how its students connect academic knowledge with community engagement."

goals, and community needs. Each project was designed in conjunction with the community to make sure it would meet community needs and communicate Lake Street history to a broad public audience including children, families and adults from diverse backgrounds.

Individual classes included a "Lake Street component" as a requirement for all students or an option for final student projects. In most cases, students completed two both a research paper demonstrating deep academic knowledge and the ability to research the topic among wider literature, guided by a professor who evaluated according to strict scholarly standards, and a public history project which adapted research paper content for a broad public, guided by community leaders and professionals from the Minnesota Historical Society. Presenting scholarly research in an interactive, accessible and informative way enabled Macalester College to demonstrate how its students connect academic

knowledge with community engagement.

When the exhibit closed, the museum retained key artifacts for its collection and donated the rest back to the Lake Street community, where they will be displayed at Midtown Global Market. ∎

Photo Courtesy of Macalester College

SPOTLIGHT

Service-Learning at Tufts University:
Learn, Think, Do

Before students at Tufts University engage in university sponsored service-learning programs, they study the history of the community where they'll be working and the issues they'll likely confront there.

According to Jean Wu, Senior Lecturer in the American Studies Program at this Medford, Massachusetts school, "If students are to develop skills they can bring to the kinds of community involvements they want to engage in throughout their lives and be able to make a difference, they need to know how to approach and understand unfamiliar situations and institutional structures that shape communities."

This preparation is completed, for example, by students who serve as interns with organizations in Boston's Chinatown. As part of the service-learning course Active Citizenship in an Urban Community: Race, Culture, Power and Politics, about 12 students work with – and are supervised by - housing groups or local public schools or legal service agencies. Co-sponsored by the Jonathan M. Tisch College of Citizenship and Public Service and Tufts' American Studies Department, the year-long course requires students to participate in a weekly seminar on campus while they work at a nonprofit organization.

"Many times, students work with people without understanding the community's history and contemporary issues. This can be quite detrimental to both the students' development and the communities involved," notes Wu. "Since communities give a great deal of time and resources when they work with students, it's important that anyone who goes into any community setting has some deep knowl-

edge about it."

Tufts' "Learn. Think. Do." approach begins with preparatory coursework which provides students with the foundation they'll need for everything that follows. Students learn first, then reflect on that new knowledge, then apply the knowledge at their community sites.

> "… it's important that anyone who goes into any community setting has some deep knowledge about it."

In addition to learning about the history of the community and the issues it faces, students reflect on the community they come from, the values and beliefs they bring to their work because of that community. In journals which chronicle their community-based learning, students record what they're doing—how they may or may not fit in with the organization, how to make sense of that, and how to respond. Assessments by site supervisors provide direct and honest feedback that lets students know how they're doing from the community's point of view.

While community involvement can strengthen students' skills by providing practical experience, service-learning as practiced at Tufts is not about building resumes, Wu explains, "The focus is on learning about systems of inequality and the ways these operate in our society, and about our own positions and roles in these systems. If students are to make a difference, they need to learn what roles they can play and what skills will help them do that." ∎

Photos Courtesy of Tufts University

Photo Courtesy of Tufts University

Concordia University Chicago
Builds on its Fundamental Commitment to Service

Photo Courtesy of Concordia University Chicago

Concordia University Chicago has been listed in the *"President's Higher Education Community Service Honor Roll"* since it began bestowing this honor, in 2006, to universities committed to providing meaningful service in the community. Students at CUC can provide service in multiple ways, be it volunteer work, community service, or Academic Service Learning.

Among the partnerships with CUC two stand out because of their flexibility and variety. They provide students with multiple service options and are easily accessible via the Chicago system of public transportation; so students need not worry about having a car!

The first partnership is "Vital Bridges", a wrap around social services organization serving people impacted by HIV/AIDS in the Chicago and metropolitan area. Two branches of this agency are easy to get to from the CUC campus, via the CTA trains. This agency provides services so their clients can improve their health and build self-sufficiency. It provides food, case and nutrition management, and prevention services.

Students who serve at "Vital Bridges" can help out with light office work, or assist as a receptionist, help clients with grocery lists, stock shelves, unload trucks, bag groceries for clients and "shop" at the food pantries for the clients. CUC students can also teach basic computer skills such as Windows, Microsoft WORD, Internet and Email for clients. They can also serve as literacy volunteers, working one-on-one with a client, helping the client establish and maintain education goals. This tutoring takes place at the Learning Center or at a public off-site facility

"The school's fundamental commitment to service has allowed its Service-Learning Program to grow quickly and will ensure its continued growth."

– Alannah Ari Hernandez, Director, CUC Academic Service-Learning Center

at the discretion of both tutor and client (i.e. libraries, coffee shops, etc.)

"I worked at the food pantry, getting food items for people struggling with AIDS who are too sick to work and are trying to make ends meet. After getting the food items I had the opportunity to talk to the clients for a while. I learned that people with AIDS are really no different from anyone else." Colleen Weems, Concordia University student and Vital Bridges volunteer

The other partnership that stands out is the program, "For the Love of Reading". This opportunity allows the CUC students to read aloud to third, fourth and fifth graders at Melrose Park Elementary School. It helps children from low income families develop a positive attitude towards reading for pleasure, while increasing their vocabulary. The goal of this program is to help increase language development, so the children's reading scores on the ISAT increase. Most children in this partnership are Hispanic/Latino children, with first generation, Spanish speaking immigrant parents in the community. Their exposure to English is limited to school only, which affects their reading and comprehension scores.

All students can add Service Learning to any class, even if the class doesn't have it. They need to notify their professor about adding an independent Service Learning project to their class; then they're placed by the Service Learning Center into a service location where they pursue their passion.

CUC offers official Service Transcripts to students engaging in Service Learning, and other civic activities. When students graduate, or apply for employment, an official Service Transcript is issued, to be included with the student's job application, to showcase their experience.

Students with a year, or more, of Service Learning can attend local or national conferences that address every aspect of community service, and present a paper –if they wish- based on their reflection journals from their Service experiences. ∎

Service-Learning in Rural Settings

Dr. Paul Roodin, Director of Experience Based Education
SUNY College at Oswego

Creating service-learning opportunities can be a challenge for rural colleges and universities. State University of New York at Oswego has risen to the challenge by focusing on the isolation and loneliness of older adults in its upstate New York county of about 125,000 people.

About ten years ago, the Office of Aging reported more than 50 percent of older adults in Oswego County were living in social isolation. Friends and family members had moved far away or died. Occasional phone calls from friends no longer able to drive were poor substitutes for face-to-face visits, and families living nearby stopped by infrequently because they were busy with jobs and children.

Sometimes the only contact for elders living alone in the homes, trailers, or remote farms where they raised their own families came from meal or health care providers. Most rural counties don't have the resources to provide individual transportation for elders to get to Senior Centers or other organizations, especially if older adults have other limitations. This lack of mobility can send seniors into a cycle where they become homebound, then - dependent only on a family member, neighbor or health care professional for social stimulation - they lose the motivation to engage socially and this often leads to depression.

Some older adults become socially isolated and lonely after moving to apartments, assisted living facilities, or nursing homes far from their former homes, churches and friends. Other seniors experienced social isolation after vision and hearing losses and chronic diseases made it difficult to develop new friendships or participate in group activities or meals.

These were the older people targeted by SUNY Oswego's service-learning program that connected socially isolated older adults with college students. Students engaged in friendly visiting and provided companionship and friendship. One component of the program called Adopt-a-Grandparent, encouraged students to spend time with residents in area nursing homes or assisted living facilities who eagerly anticipate their visits and the opportunity to interact with young people who are genuinely interested in them. Students are often amazed at how easily the older adults share their life stories and how quickly friendships develop.

Photo Courtesy of SUNY Oswego

"Older adults who participate in SUNY Oswego's service-learning programs report enhanced life satisfaction, self-esteem, and health."

SUNY Oswego's service-learning program is designed to reach out to elders wherever they live. Partnering with organizations that serve rural county residents helps service-learning participants address transportation and other issues. Some students are paired with social service professionals to check on the welfare of older adults living in isolation and make sure they have enough food and heat and are taking care of themselves. When Visiting Nurses take service-learning students on home visits and teach them to help monitor senior's health status, the nurses are able to increase the number of weekly visits they can make to others in need. Students also help arrange for Meals-on-Wheels delivery to Seniors, help staff Senior Nutrition Centers, work with other agencies to provide transportation to appointments or activities, and assist in YMCA water aerobics classes for seniors with arthritis, and osteoporosis prevention programs.

Older adults who participate in SUNY Oswego's service-learning programs report enhanced life satisfaction, self-esteem, and health. They enjoy sharing their joys, disappointments and unique personal histories with younger people and find the social relationship with college students emotionally rewarding and satisfying.

One challenge of service-learning in rural environments is to work with agencies, organizations, and residents to identify basic needs. A second challenge is to recognize that some programs must be delivered to many people in larger communities (cities, towns, villages) while those in smaller venues reach a much smaller number in settings such as village churches, local YMCAs, libraries, and public schools. The needs of all seniors are recognized, regardless of where they live.

SUNY Oswego students may enroll for one additional credit in a Service-Learning course that requires 20 hours of service during the semester, written papers, journals, and discussion participation. In such courses as Introduction to Gerontology, they may write academic assignments and complete journals based on their experiences with the elderly. Other classes require students to submit papers addressing key issues illustrated through their service and use their service in classroom discussions.

Up to six credits can be earned for service-learning, and many students who earn the additional credit for their service are often compelled look for additional opportunities to combine classroom learning with service. Working with older adults also helps students realize the growing opportunities in this area and leads many to explore careers in gerontology, social work, psychology, health care administration, business, marketing, recreation, nursing, public policy, law, activities directors, and the allied health professions. Their service-learning experiences help them establish relationships with mentors in the field.

SUNY Oswego believes strongly in the joy of giving to others and learning from the experience as the foundation of service-learning. Research shows clearly that students engaged in service-learning enjoy long-term rewards. In addition to encouraging students to dig deeper into their academic subjects, service-learning teaches them how to make a difference to others, when to take action, and why it is important to participate in their communities – not just during their college years but for the rest of their lives. ■

Photo Courtesy of SUNY Oswego

A few area students – especially those without grandparents nearby - maintain these friendships after college and even extend them by bringing their own children to share regular visits with the "adopted" grandparent. Establishing intergenerational bonds is a consistent dimension of SUNY Oswego's service-learning program and one which benefits all participants.

The Adopt-a-Grandparent program also provides special evening activities for residents of assisted living facilities including an annual Senior Ball on the SUNY campus. Transportation is provided for older adults, and students are happy to be with the seniors who appreciate the night out and the opportunity to share a dinner, listen to music and teach students old dance steps.

Service-Learning in a Rural Setting:
Making a Real Difference in the Community

By Amy Brenner-Fricke

Students at Eastern Connecticut State University and residents of rural Willimantic, CT, are joining forces in a win-win initiative that is providing meaningful service-learning opportunities for students and an economic jump-start for the community.

Lacking a significant industrial base, Willimantic has struggled to create jobs and other economic opportunities. But this small northeastern Connecticut town's rich natural resources make it an ideal candidate for development that emphasizes the Willimantic River and surrounding woodlands, rolling hills and farms, and the rural charm of Connecticut's "Quiet Corner."

In 2002, a grassroots movement to revitalize the riverfront's pastoral beauty, re-energize the downtown area, and serve as a catalyst for economic development began to form. Today, the nonprofit Willimantic Whitewater Partnership — which includes local, state, regional and national organizations — is working on a variety of projects that include a multi-use hiking trail along the river through downtown Willimantic, a recreational park, and a whitewater park with fish and kayak passage.

These three projects will create new jobs while preserving the region's economy and recreational traditions — and offering myriad service-learning opportunities for Eastern students to develop leadership skills and a commitment to social responsibility.

From the start, Eastern faculty and students from several different disciplines have been instrumental in helping the WWP propel its agenda forward. Under the direction of business administration professor and WWP board member Eric Martin, Eastern and the partnership have found many ways to connect. "The interdisciplinary component is key — real community needs don't fit well into any one academic discipline. We all need to work together to begin to address the opportunities before us," says Martin.

Photo Courtesy of Eastern Connecticut State University

Architectural drawings showing the Bridge Street trailhead park were unveiled at an August 2007 ground-breaking ceremony to announce purchase of the land on which the park will be built.

In spring 2006, students in Professor Miriam Chirico's Business Writing class wrote research papers about various partnership components. Their projects, on such topics as safety issues associated with whitewater parks and the economic benefits provided by similar parks in other rural communities around the country, have been used as background research for WWP grants and promotional work.

For her work in updating the group's web site, computer science major Sarah Hemenway '07 received the WWP "Volunteer of the Year Award." Students in Professor June Bisantz's Eastern Design Group contributed their creative vision and graphic design skills to create a logo and promotional brochures for the WWP.

Videos and news segments produced by students in Communication Professor Denise Matthews' course provided positive publicity when they aired on the University's news channel and other local television stations. "When Jake Williams, the producer of one of the

> "Students are applying their skills and talents in a real-world environment, gaining valuable work experience while learning that their efforts make a difference to the community in which they live."

videos, showed it at the WWP's annual meeting in June 2007, the audience reacted so favorably that Jake realized in that moment the impact of his work," says Matthews. "It was not just the fulfillment of a graded assignment. Connecting and contributing to the community in such a tangible way is one of the most powerful learning experiences a student can have. Jake could clearly see how his classroom learning was leading to positive changes in the community."

Service-learning connections between Eastern and the WWP are benefiting all participants. Faculty can focus instruction on authentic local issues that resonate with students. Students are applying their skills and talents in a real-world environment, gaining valuable work experience while learning that their efforts make a difference to the community in which they live. The WWP enjoys students' creative input and energy, which advances the project's purpose without generating additional costs. Within Willimantic's small town setting, relationships between Town Hall, nonprofit agencies, the University, and other participating organizations have blossomed. And the vision of the WWP — protecting and enriching the area's natural resources — serves as a guiding principle.

"It gets the students more dedicated to Willimantic, with the result that they are more invested in the community. It helps break down the barriers between the town and the university," says Chirico.

As one Eastern student described the service-learning experience: "I got the feeling that I was a part of something bigger than just a classroom setting. Our work carried out into the town — and it made me feel like we were making a difference." ■

NMU
SERVICE-LEARNING OPPORTUNITIES

Photo Courtesy of Northern Michigan University

Northern Michigan University students can choose among three different levels of service-learning: **through traditional courses, as part of the service internship requirement in NMU's nationally recognized Student Leader Fellowship Program, or as a component of the new Superior Edge program.**

The recent Upper Peninsula 200 Sled Dog Championship provided a course-based service-learning opportunity. Students in Northern's College of Business earned one credit by applying concepts learned in a prerequisite management course to work in the field managing aspects of the race, which is a premier qualifier for the Iditarod, draws 15,000-plus spectators and relies on help from 500 volunteers. Students complete at least 12 hours of service, attend mandatory pre- and post-race class meetings, and write a paper reflecting how they applied lessons from the management course to their race teamwork activities.

Race organizers have been pleased with students' efforts "and have even made job offers to some students," said Professor Carol Steinhaus, who reports that the students do everything from crowd control to administrative work to helping stopped teams get back on track. Students in an NMU feature-writing course also put their notebook computers to use in a real-world application by researching and producing stories for the U.P. 200 Web site.

Fifty students are selected each fall for NMU's Student Leader Fellowship Program. Fellows meet regularly with community leaders, who act as role models, advisers and teachers, and engage in a leadership theory and practice course, skill-building workshops, and a one-year community service internship.

"The internships allow students to put into practice what they learned the first year," said Dave Bonsall, director of the Center for Student Enrichment. "Students provide leadership to a project or service of their choice, often

> *"...students realize that they are the resource to make things happen."*

Photo Courtesy of Northern Michigan University

working with area youth, gaining a flavor of how things operate in a community rather than a university where there's more built-in support. The students realize that they are the resource to make things happen.

"Reaction from students who complete the program says it all: They are more self-confident, capable of accomplishing goals, and realize they could do it again in their own communities in the future."

Northern's new Superior Edge program

is the only program in the country to combine leadership with citizenship, diversity and real-world experience. Self-designed to match students' interests and schedules, the program involves 100 hours beyond normal degree requirements for each "edge".

Students may complete any or all of the edges, and results are reflected on students' enrichment transcripts. Those who put in the full 400 hours graduate with special honors for achieving the Superior Edge. Superior Edge participants demonstrate and document their commitment to making a difference - which helps prospective employers and grad school admissions counselors distinguish between multiple applicants.

Northern's service-learning programs offer a range of options. "Students who are already heavily involved will be able to package that to their advantage," said Rachel Harris, associate director of the Center for Student Enrichment. "Those involved to a lesser degree may have an incentive to do a little more. And students not doing much of anything outside of class might decide to change that. It's up to the students how much they're willing or able to invest, and they can finish at their own pace." ■

Taking Animals Seriously:
From Service-Learning Course to Interdisciplinary Minor

Photo Courtesy of University of Redlands

> *"To my knowledge...ours is the first interdisciplinary Human-Animal Studies minor in the country."*
>
> *– Kathie Jenni, Philosophy Professor University of Redlands*

University of Redlands Philosophy Professor Kathie Jenni's rewarding involvement with service-learning began 10 years ago when she was asked to identify an opportunity for students who wanted to work with animals.

Jenni knew immediately that she wanted to help - to assist students seeking "an avenue for their ardent desire to help animals and to fulfill a longstanding dream to incorporate service into my academic life."

Recently acquainted with Best Friends Animal Sanctuary, the nation's largest no-kill sanctuary for abandoned and abused companion animals, Jenni traveled to Southern Utah to investigate. She was impressed with the organization's thoughtful expertise and delighted to discover their Humane Education Department sponsored animal care internships. "Our University's one-month May Term seemed ideally suited to the opportunity."

The internship soon evolved into a Community Service-Learning program through which students could interweave study of human-animal ethics with hands-on animal care.

Later invited to join a scholarly Human-Animal Studies group, Jenni learned about creation of majors and minors in this burgeoning area. She knew students with a wide array of majors and career aims were strongly interested in human-animal relationships. Combined with her institution's high regard for interdisciplinary collaboration, experiential learning, and curricular innovation and what Jenni calls the selfless and thoughtful support of University Community Service-Learning Director Tony Mueller, "We were well-positioned to create an interdisciplinary minor."

Through colleagues in Environmental Studies, Biology, Psychology, English Literature, and Philosophy, Jenni found sufficient existing courses across the curriculum to serve a minor in Human-Animal Studies, healthy interest on the part of students and faculty in the subject; and colleagues who would help make the Minor a reality. With foundational and elective courses plus a practicum, the Minor was unanimously approved by College of Arts and Sciences faculty in fall 2007.

"To my knowledge," says Jenni, "ours is the first interdisciplinary Human-Animal Studies minor in the country."

Underground Railroad Service-Learning Project
Connects the Past and the Present

> "...the North Star Service-Learning project was a means to "take the academy into the streets of our cities, towns and communities to effectively link what we can do as students and professors to learn from and share with the community in a manner that empowers all participants."

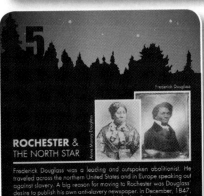

**ROCHESTER &
THE NORTH STAR**

Frederick Douglass was a leading and outspoken abolitionist. He traveled across the northern United States and in Europe speaking out against slavery. A big reason for moving to Rochester was Douglass' desire to publish his own anti-slavery newspaper. In December, 1847, the first issue of the North Star was published in Rochester. Later, the name was changed to Frederick Douglass' Paper, and in 1859 it was called Frederick Douglass' Monthly.

Frederick Douglass was often away from Rochester speaking against slavery, so his wife, Anna Douglass, not only took care of the children and the household, but she also met the needs of fugitive slaves who came to their home. She was helped to run the Underground Railroad station by Shields Green. Green had escaped from Charleston, South Carolina, and made it all the way to Canada. However, in 1858, he was at the Douglass' home doing this important work.

[The Frederick Douglass Papers at the Library of Congress.]

Rochester, New York's connection with the struggle for freedom by enslaved African-Americans and the city's rich history with the Underground Railroad came to life recently during an 18-month project by an interdisciplinary team of Nazareth College students, faculty and staff.

For the Underground Railroad North Star Service-Learning Project, Nazareth sociology, history, art history, and art education faculty and students worked with Freedom Trail Commission Chairman and local historian Dr. David Anderson as well as faculty and students from Monroe Community College to produce a portable interactive public display tracing Rochester's role in the fight for freedom for enslaved men, women and children.

Faculty members and students compiled data from newspapers, history journals, and local historical archives. Coordinated by the Center for Service-Learning's director, Dr. Marie Watkins, the foundational work by students in Dr. Tim Kneeland's African-American Experience history course led to the second phase of the project, during which Drs. Kneeland, Doot Bokleman, Shannon Elliot, and adjunct faculty member Tim Weider with students from Nazareth and Monroe created museum quality public history panels. According to Dr. Bokelman, "Bringing faculty, community groups and students together through service-learning is of greater benefit to all members of the partnership. If it is not mutually beneficial, it is not much of a learning experience for anyone. I have seen great growth in my students as researchers, writers, and members of the larger community as a result of service-learning."

Dr. Tim Kneeland states the North Star Service-Learning project was a means to "take the academy into the streets of our cities, towns and communities to effectively link what we can do as students and professors to learn from and share with the community in a manner that empowers all participants."

Historical documentation was synthesized into a story board that evolved into 10 full-color, portable panels showing the path of the UGRR from Georgia through Rochester to Canada. The panels were presented at the 2007 International Underground Railroad Conference and the 2008 Capitol Hill Undergraduate Research Conference.

Additional activities created and implemented by over 200 Freshman Seminar and Community Youth Development students are designed to teach local school-aged youth about Rochester's historical roots in abolitionism, social justice, and the Underground Railroad.

Since the project's inception in Fall 2006, 13 undergraduate classes and one graduate class have incorporated the Underground Railroad North Star Service-Learning Project into their course activities. ■

Meeting the Needs of Millennials:
Faith, Academics and Service-Learning

Photo Courtesy of Azusa Pacific University

*Judy Hutchinson, Ph.D. Director,
Center for Academic Service-Learning
and Research, Azusa Pacific University*

*Debra Fetterly, M.A. Coordinator
for Service-Learning Research and
Development, Azusa Pacific University*

Are you a high school student?

If so, then you are a Millennial – a member of what many predict will be the next "Greatest Generation." And like other Millennials who yearn to participate in changing their world, you may be seeking an educational experience at a college or university with a strong commitment to service-learning.

For Millennials who want to live a life of meaning, relationship and purpose and who also want their college years to provide opportunities for spiritual as well as academic development, the holistic education offered by a faith-based school may be a good option. At these six schools – Catholic, Protestant and Jewish, rural and urban, across the country – education is thoroughly integrated with real life.

Sometimes location provides unique challenges and opportunities for faith-based schools, as in the case of Xavier University where the devastation wrought by Hurricane Katrina ignited students' passions to serve.

Many Xavier students experienced significant storm-related losses, and Kimberly Reese, assistant dean of students and a New Orleans native, observes a changed student body:

"They're more intense, more thoughtful, and more committed than they've ever been to this city…What goes on in this city matters to us."

Xavier is establishing service-learning academies which will provide ways to help in the recovery while offering lessons in community involvement for students in the Orleans Parish school system. In one service-learning project, business students with a minor in entrepreneurship work with local high school students to create business plans - one of which has already been put into action resulting in a thriving lawn care business.

At the University of San Diego (USD), near the northern border of Mexico, there is a strong connection among academics,

"They [Millennials] want to be able to live their lives and to offer them, if necessary, for something worthy of sacrifice and service; and they want to live so as to leave the world a better place than the mess that they have inherited."

- Peter Gomes, Harvard University College Pastor

faith, and the human and community dilemmas of immigration. Elaine Elliott, director of Community Service-Learning, reinforces the importance of faith in supporting service-learning opportunities at USD. "From my point of view, one of the ways that we are most exemplifying Catholic Social Thought (CST) is in the issue of immigration." Elliott explains that service-learning courses in various disciplines offer students the opportunity to see the human side of a very complex issue while working at various community centers and foster-care centers, all founded and operated by Catholic organizations.

On the serene campus of semi-rural Messiah College in Pennsylvania, students are not isolated from the local and global needs, challenges and opportunities of an ever-changing world.

Dr. John Eby, a founder of service-learning at Messiah, explains how service-learning provides a significant setting for faith development and spiritual growth. "The act of service itself is a key expression of faith. Many service-learning projects also include group activities that, in addition to providing training in skills needed for service, include Bible study, prayer and other spiritual disciplines."

Messiah engages students in outreach through many different discipline-based courses. According to Chad Frey, Agape Center Director, "Service-learning students in math, engineering and business seek to foster justice, empower the poor, reconcile adversaries, and care for the earth, in the context of academic engagement in the disciplines of each school." Sometimes this takes Messiah students far away to assess water access issues and water and sanitation facilities for disabled and elderly persons in communities served by World Vision Mali.

Messiah also brings the world to its campus. Each year the Agape Center for Service and Learning coordinates one of the largest service days in Pennsylvania, mobilizing nearly 1,500 college volunteers to serve the Capitol area community. During Service Day the campus hosts the Area M Special Olympic Games, and hundreds of enthusiastic students wake up early to volunteer as "buddies" to participating athletes.

Tennessee's Lee University prepares students to "make a profound and lasting difference in their world" through service-learning which draws upon the school's rich spiritual foundation and traditions to meet local community needs.

Students in Lee's Language Acquisition course learn while serving in the Developmental Inclusion Classroom. Working with autistic and developmentally challenged children, they begin to understand not only the complex process of language acquisition but also the difficulties faced by some individuals.

Other ways students extend the foundational tenets of their faith to social responsibility include organizing and marketing a local, student-run food bank; working on a Habitat for Humanity project as part of an Industrial/Organizational Psychology class; traveling to the Amazon River Basin and performing a series of concerts in churches and villages with Lee University's Symphonic Band; and serving through academic training at Esperanza de Vida in a Central Guatemalan mountaintop community.

American Jewish University is committed to integrating longstanding faith traditions and values into service-learning which makes a difference in its Los Angeles community.

Dr. Gabe Goldman, Director of Experiential Education, links service-learning to ancient Biblical texts. Drawing from thousands of years of

Photo Courtesy of American Jewish University

(CHAMP) program which introduces 700 local fourth graders, mostly from Spanish-speaking immigrant homes, to college life. Through career search activities, training about college applications and funding, and a field trip to explore college facilities, university participants and the fourth graders prepare for a highly anticipated graduation ceremony which draws hundreds of family members to

"We decided to go in as learners, not as teachers. We did not want to be looked at as having all the answers, because, quite honestly, I had no idea how to answer some of the questions these kids were asking."

Jewish history, he teaches "what the Israelites learned was that with freedom came the responsibility to take care of those in need; to protect natural resources, to sit by the side of the sick; to perform acts of gemilut chasidim–random acts of loving kindness; and to do whatever one can to bring about tikun olam--a healing of the world. Despite what must have been an overwhelming experience for them, these ancient Israelites listened and then responded 'Na-aseh v'nishmah--We will do these things, [and through the doing of them] we will understand.' "

All AJU sophomores participate In a weeklong service-learning immersion experience which focuses on service and earth stewardship. Students work an organic farm, sharing their bounty with local food pantries and soup kitchens. Others provide support to such Jewish social service agencies as addiction treatment and adult day care centers for clients with dementia and Alzheimer's.

Azusa Pacific University students make their disciplines count in their local Los Angeles community. In one of many service-learning courses across the curriculum, students in the senior level education course "Diversity in the Classroom" participate in the 10-week College Headed and Mighty Proud

Photo Courtesy of Abilene Christian University

campus, many for their first experience at an institution of higher education. This program is one of APU's most effective and natural bridges to faith integration through intercultural competence.

Statistics and Marketing students earned certificates of appreciation from the Azusa City Council for their help in revitalizing the city by conducting critical surveys to help recruit new business into what had

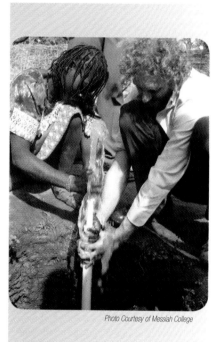

Photo Courtesy of Messiah College

been a very depressed area.

Students in Principles and Practice of Community Engagement, a core course of APU's South Africa Semester, facilitate community development processes in some of the world's most challenging circumstances. One student reflected on her experience with a classroom of young children: "We decided to go in as learners, not as teachers. We did not want to be looked at as having all the answers, because, quite honestly, I had no idea how to answer some of the questions these kids were asking. They have been through so much in their lives, things I had never even thought of as being possible. Therefore, we really decided to make a conscious effort to just facilitate, not teach. Within the community of children, we were looking for the answers because we knew that these children could arrive at the answers all by themselves."

Students in an APU Biblical Studies class - challenged to understand the historical context and spiritual implications of the Passover – planned and shared in a Passover Seder with the members of a local senior center. The mostly Evangelical Christian and Catholic students gained new insights and commented, "I helped serve others the way Christ served others during the Last Supper," and "I now understand more of the tradition and where I come from."

Students at USD, in a course on "Islamic Faith and Practice" were charged to find elements of Islamic principles while working with a middle-school violence-prevention program "Circle of Peace" founded by a Muslim-American whose teenaged son was killed. Director Elliot notes, "The example of this father working together with the grandfather of the young man who killed his son provided a powerful example of forgiveness and of compassionate confrontation, both core values of the organization and linked to Islamic principles in student reflection papers."

Notre Dame's profound faith heritage frames current efforts to proactively integrate Catholic Social Thought with programs and courses, using experiential learning to enhance service and social awareness experiences.

The school's Center for Social Concerns, whose mission is to enable students to recognize and respond to a responsibility in our global community, initiated the International Summer Service-Learning Program which expands the Notre Dame experience to include a theology course

that sends students to Mexico, El Salvador, Honduras, Brazil, Ecuador, Ghana, Malawi, Uganda, Cambodia, Thailand, and India. Their service-learning relates to their own fields of study ranging from research, evaluation of programs and writing funding reports, to assisting in medical clinics and conducting public health seminars; from teaching computer skills, English, math and science, to working in schools, orphanages and community centers.

For students at all these schools and others not mentioned, faith-based service-learning lends spiritual relevance to the educational process.

The words of one Notre Dame student,

who served in Ghana, bring his faith-based service-learning experience to life. Telling about the impact of leaving behind a boy who had given him a small token so he would always remember the village and the people he had met, the student said,

"In this moment, the poverty and injustice I had been observing firsthand and reading [about] for years took a human face…I now have Dickson's silence and tears indelibly imprinted on my memory. They will affect everything I say and do for the rest of my life." ∎

Photo Courtesy of Notre Dame University

Learning, Leadership and Service in the Jesuit Tradition

Photo Courtesy of Rockhurst University

For students who want to take their service experiences to the next step, service-learning at Jesuit colleges and universities combines academic learning with disciplined reflection and spiritual development in the pursuit of social justice.

Twenty-eight colleges and universities in the United States are based in the 450-year-old Jesuit tradition of transformative education which prepares students to be future leaders with the vision and commitment needed to shape and change the world around them.

Three elements distinguish a Jesuit approach to service-learning: action/reflection, leadership and global perspective.

The element of action/reflection helps students learn that the decisions they make have economic and moral implications and that service helps them put their unique gifts and talents into action to transform the world. Service-learning enables students to engage in service experiences, followed by opportunities to reflect on those experiences and to let their

reflection lead to more action. With the benefit of newly learned knowledge, skills and insights, the service-learning cycle is continuous and the process engages students' bodies, minds and spirits.

Creighton University strives to educate the whole person through such flagship programs as Cortina Community – a sophomore living-learning community dedicated to community, service, faith and justice. Through Creighton's Office of Interprofessional Scholarship, Service, and Education, health professional students gain real world experiences while making a difference in underserved communities.

At Rockhurst University, students may choose from a variety of course-based service-learning opportunities in over half of its academic departments. Service is also woven throughout the fabric of the university – students in sororities and fraternities serve together and Christian Living Communities encourage a combination of service and faith.

Fr Kevin Cullen, S.J., Rockhurst's Vice President of Mission and Ministry, Rockhurst, explains "As a Catholic, Jesuit education institution, Rockhurst University engages both its student body and its faculty in transforming lives and forming leaders in the Jesuit tradition. When our

faith traditions are put into action, we live as women and men in service of others through learning, leadership, service, and the pursuit of justice."

Canisius College students learn about themselves, their faith and the interconnectedness of all people through such service-learning programs as Mothers in Literature and Film, which enables students to volunteer at service sites that provide aid to mothers and children.

This cycle of action and reflection places students on a leadership path where they can act on their commitments and values through service to others, one of the main purposes of a Jesuit education.

Peter-Hans Kolvenbach, S.J., Superior General of the Society of Jesus, says "our purpose in education is to form men and women 'for others.' The Society of Jesus has always sought to imbue students with values that transcend the goals of money, fame and success. We want graduates who will be leaders concerned about society and the world in which they live. We want our graduates to be leaders in service."

Saint Joseph's University focuses on freshmen through innovative year-long courses which build a sense of community through classroom learning

SPOTLIGHT

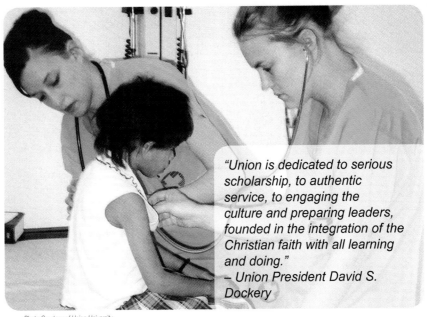

Photo Courtesy of Rockhurst University

and service experiences.

The courses introduce students to service scholarship and opportunities to work as peer leaders in service-learning courses by facilitating classroom discussions, reading and responding to students' volunteer journals and addressing placement concerns.

Service-learning at Holy Cross has a special Worcester focus which helps students engage in a critical dialogue with the world around them to see systemic needs and offers them opportunities to participate in collaborative research projects to address local problems and issues of concern.

To prepare students to live and lead in an increasingly global world, Jesuit institutions offer such opportunities as Gonzaga University's month-long service-learning program in Zambia to promote community development and cultural growth. Marquette University's South Africa Service-Learning Program includes a semester of classes in Cape Town and work for non-governmental organizations. Through Creighton's Encuentro Dominicano, undergraduate students balance traditional coursework, cultural experiences, service work and retreats during a cross-cultural immersion in the Dominican Republic. Rockhurst regularly offers spring break service trips to Guatemala, Honduras, Mexico and Belize.

Creighton and Gonzaga also offer extensive service opportunities in Native American communities. Holy Cross, Saint Joseph's and Rockhurst provide special service-learning opportunities with Spanish-speaking communities. ■

Rigorous academics and Christian commitment align in service-learning programs at Union University

Photo Courtesy of Union University

"Union is dedicated to serious scholarship, to authentic service, to engaging the culture and preparing leaders, founded in the integration of the Christian faith with all learning and doing."
– Union President David S. Dockery

Union University is committed to service learning as an invaluable approach to real life learning. Service learning advances Union's Christ-centered approach to higher education and promotes excellence and character development in service to church and society.

Union President David S. Dockery explains that Union provides "an education characterized by rigorous academic pursuit and authentic Christian commitment—an education involving head, heart and hands.

"You will be challenged to think creatively and critically – and, most of all, Christianly," says Dockery. "Union is dedicated to serious scholarship, to authentic service, to engaging the culture and preparing leaders, founded in the integration of the Christian faith with all learning and doing."

Provost Carla Sanderson leads the way in encouraging service-learning as a significant learning initiative. Melinda Clarke -- a service-learning fellow who gained recognition for developing a new model which measures the community impact of service initiatives -- provides day-to-day support and leadership for service-learning initiatives planned by individual faculty, by academic departments or as university-wide projects. Service initiatives are tailored to a specific discipline and are evaluated for their outcome and impact on the community served and on student learning.

An ongoing international service-learning project through Union's engineering department involves education, training, development and relief with non-governmental organizations in North Africa. Students and professors demonstrate how science can improve daily life by using wind power, solar and biodiesel as sources of renewable energy and by helping local farmers learn how to perform soil tests.

For another project, advanced Spanish grammar students partnered with the local school system to translate important academic and school information being sent to Hispanic homes. Students learned to give careful attention to the meaning and intent of words and saw that their efforts had real purpose. Today one of those students is a full-time professional Spanish translator. ■

Service-learning helps ACU educate the next generation of Christian leaders

Service means more than civic responsibility at **Abilene Christian University**. With the mission to educate students for Christian service and leadership throughout the world, ACU teaches students about the connections between academics, service, and leadership and helps them understand that leadership is service as modeled by Jesus.

Through these courses, students read to children, build a house, develop educational materials about diseases, give meals to people on the street, write annual reports for a nonprofit agency, teach Junior Achievement modules in elementary schools, and analyze communication

According to one student, "Through this experience [service-learning course], I have realized that there are a lot of things in my life that I need to change—getting out of my comfort zone to see how God can use me."

Another student says, "The community service [service-learning] has opened my eyes to a whole new world, a world without hate and segregation but with unity and love for one God."

Photo Courtesy of Abilene Christian University

ACU faculty, staff and students actively and thoughtfully engage in local and global issues through service-learning components in a wide range of courses including management, biology, Spanish, English (writing), education, Bible, missions, psychology, political science, communications, honors social science, and freshman seminar. Professors link service experiences with course material and engage students in conversations which help them understand their service from a Christian perspective.

systems within an organization, among other projects.

ACU believes it is in a unique position to educate the next generation of Christian leaders and explains, "In a Christian context, service is about giving back to God in thanks for what he has given us. It also means extending the love of Jesus, being his 'hands and feet' in a world of need. We seek talented Christian students from across the nation and around the

world who believe faith is about personal commitment as well as community."

Those who engage in required service through service-learning are challenged to express their experiences and thoughts through guided reflection processes and to consider how they can make a difference through service as a lifestyle. ∎

SPOTLIGHT

Faith-based service-learning teaches students to recognize and repair injustice

John Carroll University is perfectly positioned to live out its Jesuit tradition of integrating faith and learning. Located in Cleveland – rated both the most livable city and the poorest city in the U.S in 2006 – the school finds many opportunities to be "Men and Women for Others" and includes this Jesuit commitment as an essential part of the educational process.

Service-learning helps students explore the connection between theory and practice. In the Cultivating Community course, for example, they focus on Cleveland neighborhoods' history and governing systems and meet with residents. The class culminates in a day-long service project which engages 250 John Carroll students, faculty, staff and alumni.

Community-based research is another important element of John Carroll's service-learning program. During one semester in 2007, students in the Poverty and Social Welfare class interviewed participants in programs of the Thea Bowman Center and assessed programs against stated goals. Their efforts met a real community need and demonstrated how theory and practice inform one another.

Photo Courtesy of John Carroll University

John Carroll University maintains that creating a just world means exposing students to the world's injustices and engaging them in productive ways to facilitate change. Through service that is fully integrated in academic courses, the school takes students out of the safe walls of the classroom and gives them an experience in worlds they never knew existed.

JCU's liberal arts foundation creates a robust intellectual life that exposes students to everyday reality and the hidden worlds around them, encourages them to question and act upon inequalities, and supports them in creating service programs which meet greater community needs, including:

- **Circle K.** Through more than 100 service projects each year, students do crafts at the Cleveland Clinic Children's Hospital, play bingo with seniors at retirement centers, and serve dinners at Ronald McDonald House.

- **Labre Project.** Every Friday night students venture under bridges, down alleys and along city streets to provide food and companionship to Cleveland's homeless. They've never missed a week since the program launched in October 2004, and there is a waiting list to participate.

- **Seeds of Hope.** This mentorship program helps at-risk middle school children avoid violence and gang activity.

- **Relay for Life.** Named the top relay event for its enrollment bracket by American Cancer Society, this event raised $100,000 for ACS. ∎

Service-learning is part of Jesuit mission for transformative education

Photo Courtesy of Marquette University

Marquette University students serve and learn in community shelters and meal programs, in jail and prisons predominantly populated by the poor, and with immigrant populations facing unemployment and other concerns. Their service-learning is based in a Theology course on Dorothy Day and the Catholic Worker Movement she founded.

During the Great Depression, Day and a French peasant named Peter Maurin created a newspaper for poor immigrant workers in New York City. The Catholic Worker sold for a penny a copy and addressed such concerns as housing, health care, education, homelessness, workers' rights, labor issues, children, and war and peace. Its content elaborated on Catholic Social Teaching and the social Gospel.

Soon after the first issue hit the streets on May 1, 1933, readers began coming to the door of the apartment where the paper was produced, many looking for food. Hundreds more sent donations to keep the paper going. The Catholic Worker Movement was born as a hospitality center and place offering inspiration for people on the margins of society. The Movement continues today in more than 200 Catholic Worker houses of hospitality in such US cities as New York, Chicago, Houston, Los Angeles, Washington DC, Detroit, Cleveland and Milwaukee.

Offered annually at Marquette University, the home of the Dorothy Day Archives, the Dorothy Day Course concretely puts the Jesuit mission of Marquette and the power of service-learning into action. Through this course, for example, students go out in below-zero temperatures to offer soup and hot beverages to homeless and financially challenged men, women and children. Afterward, they reflect that - while they can soon return to warm residence halls or apartments - the people they serve walk the streets day in and day out.

> Transformative education may begin with charity but leads to passion about justice and advocacy, and change and improvement for the lives of many.

Students who see the connections between local situations of injustice and global implications evolve into leaders in business, medicine, public service, social work, health care, and scores of other fields dedicated to bringing about a more just society through their attitudes, behaviors, actions and public policy.

Susan M. Mountin, Ph.D., a member of Marquette's Theology Department and Director of the Manresa Project explains, "The students' experiential learning is visceral and heart-rending. The charitable act they perform in this setting, or in scores of other service learning settings, is the starting place for an education that strives to prepare 'men and women for and with others'." ■

SPOTLIGHT

Service-learning experiences at Loyola University Chicago are transformative

"Here we are learning through experience how to develop compassion, consideration, and appreciation of others. This can not be instilled in us from reading or from a professor speaking about it. We have to obtain it in the real world as we develop our character."

— Loyola University Chicago student Christiana Ansong

Photo Courtesy of Loyola University Chicago

Biology major Christiana Ansong knew that her Seminar in Organizational Change and Community Leadership at Loyola University Chicago would require a service internship. But she didn't know the experience would transform her view on the world.

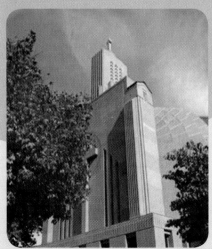

Photo Courtesy of Loyola University Chicago

By working through the Center for Experiential Learning at Loyola University Chicago, Ansong works with Make-A-Wish Foundation, calling families of children with life-threatening illnesses to help grant their wishes.

"Before taking this service internship," she explains, "I had few people skills. Make-A-Wish Foundation has helped me get better people skills because of the many phone conversations I have during the day. The more I speak with others the more I improve my communication skills."

Ansong's service-learning experience did more than build her professional skills. She reflects, "Here we are learning through experience how to develop compassion, consideration, and appreciation of others. This cannot be instilled in us from reading or from a professor speaking about it. We have to obtain it in the real world as we develop our character. I believe that at Make-A-Wish Foundation I am learning the true meaning of being a good person to go out in the world and succeed."

Loyola University Chicago - the largest Jesuit, Catholic University and the largest Catholic Research (high) institution in the nation – is committed to "preparing people to lead extraordinary lives."

More than 25 Loyola service-learning courses offered each semester enable students to engage in real-world experiences which enhance their course learning and prepare them for their careers and for lives as global citizens.

Students may also participate in nearly 20 local, national, and international immersion trips with faculty or staff advisors, including trips to the Appalachian region, Washington, D.C., New Orleans, or Latin America, or engage with the community through service-learning, academic internships, or undergraduate research with a faculty mentor. ■

Spirituality gives an added dimension to service-learning at Christian colleges

Photo Courtesy of Messiah College

During recent Messiah service-learning opportunities, students in various disciplines worked:

- in a hospital in Central America

- in community health in rural Central America and Belize

- to install solar power in West Africa

- to teach English in China

- in peacemaking in Ireland, Israel and Palestine

- in mentoring and youth recreation programs in Camden, Pittsburg, Chicago and Los Angeles

Today's college and university student are increasingly interested in spirituality. Christian colleges and universities like Pennsylvania's Messiah College are uniquely equipped to respond to this growing interest through service-learning which intentionally connects spirituality and faith with service.

A UCLA Higher Education Research Institute survey shows 80 percent of students entering college – both schools with a Christian identity and those without - report some or a great extent of interest in spirituality and 47 percent say seeking out opportunities to grow spiritually is very important or essential.

At Christian colleges where faith development is a specific goal, service-learning links moral commitment with intellectual and civic concern. Messiah College's course Foundations of Service, Mission and Social Change, for example, combines study of Sociology, Anthropology, Theology, Literature, and Economics with service during the summer at a development, service and social change agency.In the fall, students meet to reflect together on their experiences and to read and write about issues they encountered.

Messiah's course shares the academic rigor and innovative pedagogy of service-learning anywhere, but an added dimension makes service-learning at Christian colleges unique. Many projects are set in a context that reflects a holistic strategy of loving God and neighbor because students serve with local churches and contribute to their long-term ministry. Academic analysis and theory are explored within a theological perspective. The act of service is a spiritual discipline and provides opportunity for students to reflect on their own faith commitments and grow spiritually. ■

EMU Student *Tells How Cross-Cultural Study and Service Changed His* World View

Photo Courtesy of Eastern Mennonite University

Cross-cultural study is a requirement for all students at Virginia's Eastern Mennonite University. In fact, this small liberal arts college dedicated to Anabaptist and Mennonite values of peacebuilding and service was one of the first schools to make this requirement more than 30 years ago.

Beyond study abroad, EMU explains, cross-cultural is "a unique chance to change your outlook and grow in your faith. It's an opportunity to learn about yourself and the broader world, developing character and values while building relationships." Student Chris Lehman tells how his 15-week cross-cultural study trip in Guatemala and Mexico did all this...and more.

> *"...I felt a connection much more alive and compelling than I could have ever hoped to experience. My eyes were opened to the realities of people, not just in Guatemala but all across the globe..."*

In the remote Guatemalan village of Chitap, my two roommates and I nodded, smiling in the wavering candlelight and repeating "Bantiox, bantiox, bantiox." Although we gringos could barely see his face, we knew our host father Pedro was beaming, as always, as he repeated "Us, us, us."

Back and forth we exchanged these words, which tasted as strange to us as the corn-mush beverage we gulped down as we recovered from our half hour hike through green tangles along a steep mountain trail to reach our host family's home. Bowls of steaming soup were placed in front of us and more tortillas than all three of us could eat in a week.

The door to our one-room hut was politely closed, allowing us freedom to discuss our new experiences, although we could count as many as five pairs of curious eyes peeking through openings in the walls. Despite the giggles and whispers on the other side of the boards, my two companions and I did not even know where to start discussing what new things we had seen and heard and tasted and felt.

I still feel a lack of sufficient words to describe the depth and emotion of my experiences during my fifteen week cross-cultural trip in Guatemala and Mexico. Especially living and working with people in rural regions where stable electricity and running water were only dreams, I felt a connection much more alive and compelling than I could have ever hoped to experience. My eyes were opened to the realities of people, not just in Guatemala but all across the globe, as I lived with this family of Q'eqchi Indians and worked under the sun with them in my feeble attempt to "serve" them.

I did not enter the week of our service trip with an air of superiority or arrogance of any kind, but was expecting to give much more than I would receive. I realized this group of indigenous Guatemalans would have little, especially compared to the wealth of my middle-class family in the United States. And of course I understood that these families, with dirt floors and boards for beds, could still be very happy. "Of course you know all these things," I asked myself, "But do you believe them?"

In Chitap I realized a source of the Q'eqchi people's happiness: Even though the families had so little, they were so completely generous - freely offering us their best of food, beds, blankets, and anything else, and beaming brighter than the blazing Guatemalan sun while they did it Throughout that week and since I've returned, I've often thought, "How could those people so freely offer everything they had? Is it possible or even feasible for me to aspire to that? What would it take for me to reach that level of freedom from possessions, combined with such a caring and loving attitude for others?"

During all fifteen weeks of my cross-cultural, I was challenged and stretched through new experiences and in new ways of thinking, but no week had a greater impact on my life than that short week in the beautifully rustic Guatemalan highlands, far from the world's chaos and materialistic lifestyles. It was there in our dirty one-room hut that I was challenged by those who seemed so willing to give all they had to traveling strangers. ■

Photo Courtesy of Tulane University

Katrina's Aftermath:

Universities Participate in Rebuilding the Gulf Coast

While the world watched and wondered what to do about the devastation caused by Hurricane Katrina, university students took action. Their efforts during the past two years – from housing evacuees to gutting flooded homes to committing long-term to help restore the area – have been rare bright spots in the halting Gulf Coast recovery. And colleges and universities have embraced this opportunity to challenge their ideas of community commitment and to reform educational service experiences. Like communities which are thinking about a rebuilding process which is more than simply remaking what was there before Katrina, universities are re-imagining their role and purpose in the communities around them.

Tulane University opened the door to substantial growth through initiatives developed in the wake of Katrina. When its New Orleans campuses suffered hundreds of millions of dollars in storm damage, the school closed for the entire fall semester and began crafting a Renewal Plan to enable students and faculty to return in January 2006. The Plan forced many difficult decisions and program reductions, but it also instituted a new two-tiered public service graduation requirement for all incoming undergrads. Within a few years, Tulane would send more than 1800 students into the community every semester to complete service projects that met unfilled area needs and enhanced students' educational experience.

No stranger to service-learning, Tulane already had a decade-long commitment to community service when it created the Office of Service Learning in 1998. OSL staff and committed faculty members guided service-learning into diverse departments through spring 2005, resulting in 40 service-learning classes and a public service internship program.

With the Renewal Plan's new graduation requirement came the need for additional university resources, and the Center for Public Service was created from OSL and other Tulane service programs. CPS became an entryway for public service opportunities at Tulane and center for the community to engage the university. Today it supports more than 70 service-learning courses plus 75 public service interns every semester and sponsors programs, including an AmeriCorps*VISTA program, to build community partners' capacity.

Along with direct work in the city, Tulane facilitates partnerships between non-profit and community groups and universities around the US. It runs HelpNOLA, a clearinghouse for colleges and universities interested in service ranging from one-week alternative break programs to courses for students and faculty who are extremely committed to the area's recovery, connecting participants with community partners and helping them find housing. And through Tulane's one-month Semester in NOLA program, students from other universities work with New Orleans community agencies and participate in weekly seminars with Tulane faculty to earn six credit hours and contribute more than 120 hours of service.

New Orleans' Delgado Community College has also worked to institutionalize service-learning on its campus in the past two years. Dean Warren Punecky explains that the disaster changed the conscience of the college and motivated the school's administration to provide more support for service-learning courses and involve more faculty members. Delgado is leaving an imprint on the city's green space as faculty members teaching horticulture work with neighborhood groups and city departments to landscape public spaces and design community gardens.

Responding to increased community need for engaged education, Xavier University of Louisiana solidified and expanded its service-learning programs over the past two years by recruiting colleges offering alternative breaks in New Orleans and hosting more than 1000 student volunteers. A service-learning course in Xavier's communications department oversaw writing and recording of public service recruitment messages that were sent to historically black colleges and universities across the country.

More than a million volunteers have aided in Gulf Coast recovery – many of them college students whose experiences may translate into increased volunteerism, demands for stronger institutional commitment to service-learning, and dedication to the communities surrounding their universities. Faculty members and administrators using this student participation can argue in their home cities for further expansion of service-learning programs which help their institutions reach out to marginalized groups, utilize knowledge and share resources to build stronger communities for students and long-term residents. ∎

"Those of us that had the good fortune of participating in the ACRON Housing/University Collaborative are in awe of the extraordinary commitment residents, citizen organizations, like ACORN, and local institutions, such as Tulane and the University of New Orleans, have made to advance recovery in the city's most distressed neighborhoods. Our small consortium remains committed to supporting resident led recovery efforts in the 9th Ward as long as our assistance is desired by local leaders."
-Ken Reardon, associate professor in city and regional planning at Cornell University

Photos Courtesy of Tulane University

Schools outside the area pitch in

In the months following Katrina, many urban planners worldwide recommended that some New Orleans neighborhoods be leveled and replaced with green space. When the well-defined city center century-old community of Broadmoor was targeted, residents enlisted their own urban planners to counteract plans presented to the city and found a partner in Harvard and the Kennedy School of Government. Through a collaboration which began in 2006 and continues today, Harvard faculty members and students with area residents designed and began to implement the first complete neighborhood recovery plan in the city, turning the tide against possible large scale buyouts that would have left Broadmoor as green space.

Cornell University and the University of Illinois have also worked to design neighborhood recovery plans. Partnering with the Association of Communities for Reform Now (ACORN), an activist group with constituencies across many neighborhoods, the schools developed a strategy for an entire district covering much of New Orleans' Ninth Ward. The planning they facilitated challenged a city-sponsored process which ACORN believed left many residents without proper representation, produced a document that was added to the city's recovery blueprint for the area, and bridged differences between the city and ACORN members. ∎

TSU community makes a real difference for Katrina victims

> **"This was a huge collaborative in which TSU and our North Nashville community partners combined heart and hands, specific skills and good old warm-hearted generosity."**
>
> – Deena Sue Fuller, Director, TSU Center for Service-Learning and Civic Engagement, on a special event planned for victims of Hurricane Katrina

Photos Courtesy of Tennessee State University

Members of the Tennessee State University community turned their concern for victims of Hurricane Katrina into action by helping the thousands of evacuees who sought shelter in Nashville.

TSU faculty, staff and students responded in force to American Red Cross requests to meet evacuees at the airport, work at shelters, sort donations, and assist with other needs. Later, the organization asked the school to host an on-campus event to connect evacuees with services in Nashville.

During the one-day Open Arms, Open Hearts: Service and Information Fair for Victims of the Hurricanes, students from 16 organizations plus 61 faculty and staff offered information on legal aid, mental health, housing, dental care, health screenings and other services and helped assess evacuees' needs. Children's games, science experiments, arts and crafts, books, toys, winter clothing, and more were provided. Musical entertainment and

food added to the festive atmosphere and encouraged friendly socializing.

According to Deena Sue Fuller, Director of TSU's Center for Service-Learning and Civic Engagement, "This was a huge collaborative in which TSU and our North Nashville community partners combined heart and hands, specific skills and good old warm-hearted generosity."

Prompted by these experiences to seek other ways to help, TSU seized the US Department of Housing and Urban Development's offer of a Universities Rebuilding America Grant to establish a free 4-week summer day camp offering high quality learning

activities, emotional counseling,

mentoring, and fun in an engaging environment to young hurricane victims transitioning back into their communities.

"We called it 'Supercharge Summer Camp' because we hoped the children would be 'supercharged' for the new school year and more prepared to cope with the continuing challenges of their lives," says Fuller.

Located on the Loyola University campus near central New Orleans, the camp served 250 children. Twenty-nine TSU students and three faculty worked closely with certified teachers to lead, instruct, and mentor Supercharge campers. ■

Oklahoma City University composition students personalize the consequences of violence

"The service-learning partnership with the Oklahoma City National Bombing Memorial has given students a tremendous learning experience."

– H. Brooke Hessler, English professor, Oklahoma City University

Photos Courtesy of Oklahoma State University

Through profiles of individuals directly affected by the 1995 Murrah Federal Building bombing and other meaningful projects, Oklahoma City University honors composition students are illustrating the consequences of violence.

Students are collaborating with curators at the Oklahoma City National Bombing Memorial, survivors and others to research and create digital exhibits for the museum's virtual archives kiosk and to create "teaching trunks" that are sent to elementary schools nationwide.

According to OCU English professor H. Brooke Hessler, who co-founded the service-learning partnership in 2002 with Memorial curators, "Students typically produce a profile of someone killed in the bombing, someone who survived, or a first-responder. The profiled person or their family shares objects, photos and other artifacts for the exhibits."

Students also have developed exhibits on unique artifacts donated to the museum, such as a massive quilt pieced together by people from around the world, and on such symbols of hope as the Memorial's Survivor Tree and the Fence which is lined with messages and mementoes from visitors.

Current service-learning projects at the memorial include designing a full-scale exhibit about the fence itself entitled "Messages from the Fence." Students in honors composition I and II work on museum projects.

"Most of the students working on Messages from the Fence also worked on digital exhibits last fall, giving them a deep knowledge of the archives," Hessler explained. "They have spent hours there documenting artifacts."

Hessler says, "The service-learning partnership with the museum has given students a tremendous learning experience.

"The students do amazing work. This project has been wonderfully rewarding in so many ways." ■

Historically Black Colleges and Universities:

A Rich Tradition of

Service & Civic Engagement

*Deena Sue Fuller, Director of Service-Learning
and Civic Engagement, Tennessee State University*

Photos Courtesy of Tennessee State Univeristy

African Americans who eagerly pursued opportunities for higher education after the Civil War were denied admission by most established colleges. Black churches and committed individuals stepped in to fill this growing need by establishing their own colleges. **In 1890, the federal Morrill Act made provision for establishment of public colleges for Blacks.** These schools – which were expanded to provide educational opportunities for all students – are collectively termed Historically Black Colleges and Universities (HBCUs).

More than simply rich repositories of African American culture, **HBCUs have produced prominent leaders in all fields including medicine, science, law, education, entertainment, politics and literature.** George Washington Carver, activist/writer/poet Nikki Giovanni, Supreme Court Justice Thurgood Marshall, former Atlanta Mayor Maynard Jackson, and Oprah Winfrey are just a few of the many individuals well-known for their leadership and service who are products of HBCUs.

Service to the local community is one of the important pillars of HBCUs where students are encouraged to become actively involved. During the civil rights movement, HBCUs and black churches took the lead by mobilizing volunteers, raising money, and participating in demonstrations.

In 1960, students from Tennessee State University, Fisk University, Meharry Medical College, and American Baptist Theological Seminary led the movement to desegregate downtown Nashville, TN. These students organized and conducted three months of sit-ins and other nonviolent protests against unfair practices. On May 10, 1960, Nashville became the first major city to begin desegregating its public facilities - a direct result of the students' persistent efforts. **The students' principles of direct nonviolent protest and consistent rules of conduct became models for later protests in the South.** And the service and civic engagement central to the missions of HBCUs further established them as valuable community resources.

In the wake of desegregation, many HBCUs turned their attention and funding to the research and teaching missions that allowed them to be competitive with white institutions. **Active engagement with the community often received less attention as the schools became more comprehensive,** expanded their academic curriculum and built challenging research agendas.

Recently, however, as part of the revived focus on civic engagement and community, HBCUs are among those leading the trend to move colleges and universities out of the "ivory tower"

In 1890, the federal Morrill Act made provision for establishment of public colleges for Blacks. These schools – which were expanded to provide educational opportunities for all students – are collectively termed Historically Black Colleges and Universities

mentality and toward collaboration with communities, government and corporate structures to create a more just and humane society.

Many HBCUs have reinvigorated their strong service traditions by integrating civic engagement initiatives into the curriculum.

Students can choose from an increasingly wide range of service-learning opportunities such as

tutoring and mentoring in high needs schools; working on fundraising initiatives for local nonprofits; advocating for social justice; developing health promotion programs in low income communities, or teaching community members about environmental issues that affect quality of life. Other options include developing business or marketing plans for non-profits; working with politicians to develop more equitable laws; teaching computer skills; developing needs assessments, or working in violence and drug prevention programs in local schools. **"Every field of study can include service opportunities that help students connect theory with practice,"** explains Deena Sue Fuller, Director of Service-Learning and Civic Engagement at Tennessee State University. **"What better way to learn how to solve the world's problems than to actually be engaged in addressing real world problems as a part of the**

college curriculum?"

HBCUs who intentionally integrate service and civic engagement into academic programs that prepare students for productive careers also inspire them to live lives of purpose.

Through service-learning opportunities, says Fuller, **"HBCUs are equiping students to apply academic knowledge and skills to the improvement of our neighborhoods, our cities, and the world."** ■

> "Every field of study can include service opportunities that help students connect theory with practice,"

Networking for Mutual Reinforcement:

Tougaloo College & the HBCU Faculty Development Network

Photo Courtesy of Tougaloo College

Building on its strong foundation in social commitment, **Tougaloo College supports two important initiatives to help enhance their community service skills** and knowledge of HBCU faculty and to ensure the sharing of best practices among institutions. Through the HBCU Faculty Development Network and the Tougaloo College Center for Civic Engagement, this private, historically black, liberal arts institution - located in Jackson, Mississippi, and founded in 1869 – continues to open new doors in community outreach.

Tougaloo College's rich tradition includes its key role in partnering with the African-American community and with white civil rights volunteers in the struggle to end racial segregation during the 1960s when it was known as the "cradle of

motto is "Where history meets the future."

During the 1990s, the school's focus on community outreach was sharpened when faculty members voted to **establish a 60-hour community service requirement for graduation, which led to student placements in a wide variety of service-learning opportunities** including discipline-specific internships, faculty engaging students in projects that help them apply skills and knowledge to service to the community, and growing interaction with community representatives who conduct classroom sessions and participate in campus forums on community issues.

In 1991, Tougaloo College received a faculty development grant from the Bush Foundation of St Paul, Minnesota, and became eligible for travel scholarships to semi-annual faculty development

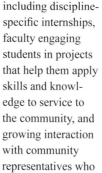

> Tougaloo College's rich tradition includes its key role in partnering with the African-American community and with white civil rights volunteers in the struggle to end racial segregation during the 1960s

the Mississippi civil rights movement." The school's historic Woodworth Chapel was the site of rallies led by Dr. Martin Luther King, Jr., Medgar Evers, Fannie Lou Hamer and other movement leaders. Growing community outreach is an important emphasis at the school whose

conferences of the Collaboration for the Advancement of College Teaching and Learning. Participation at these events helped Dr. **Stephen Rozman and other Tougaloo faculty identify a need for more sharing opportunities,** particularly in the Southeastern United States, and they asked for permission to use part of the Bush grant to fund an HBCU faculty development conference in Jackson. Permission was granted, and faculty from five other HBCUs was invited to help plan the event under the name HBCU Faculty Development Network.

When the first HBCU Faculty Development Symposium was held to favorable review, support was ignited for institutionalizing the HBCU Faculty

Development Network and making the HBCU Faculty Development Symposium an annual event. The HBCU Faculty Development Network was formally founded in 1994; Dr. Rozman and Dr. Phyllis Worthy Dawkins, of Johnson C. Smith University, became Network co-directors and remain in these positions today. Planning is now underway for the Fifteenth National HBCU Faculty Development Symposium in Washington, DC, in October 2008. The Bush Foundation continues to be the major funder of the Network.

The Network's goals and objectives flow from its vision statement which focuses on empowering faculty **"to promote effective teaching and learning practices that will enable students to become engaged lifelong learners in an ever-changing society."** Its two overriding goals - to use HBCUs' collective experience to enhance the teaching and learning process and to provide leadership and coordination in collaborative efforts among HBCUs – are advanced through the annual HBCU Faculty Development Symposium, recruiting members into the Network and enhancing participation at the symposium, collaboration and partnership agreements, marketing, and regional workshops or institutes.

Ten years after the HBCU Faculty Development Network was founded, Tougaloo College created the Center for Civic Engagement & Social Responsibility and appointed Dr. Rozman as director. The Center is charged with engaging **"in activities designed to empower citizens so that they become active participants in the life of their communities** by providing a forum for the sharing of ideas, expression of diverse views, and the formulation of opinions and actions that serve the common good."

Its objectives include the following:

- **Engaging students in research on important policy issues in classes across the curriculum**
- **Conducting student-led forums to share research findings**
- **Directing student community service projects**
- **Directing service-learning projects**
- **Sponsoring forums and films**
- **Hosting workshops, symposia, and conferences**

Networking with other organizations Since its establishment in 2004, the Center for Civic Engagement & Social Responsibility has become another important partner for the HBCU Faculty

. . . designed to empower citizens so that they become active participants in the life of their communities. . .

Development Network. Activities initiated by the Network are promoted by the Center, and activities initiated by the Center are promoted by the Network, sometimes in the capacity of co-sponsor.

During their initial collaboration in 2005, with the Jackson, Mississippi, summer institute on "Civic Engagement and Social Justice," **the Center used its growing community ties to engage leaders of several community organizations as well as public officials.** In 2006, when the Gulf-South Summit on Service-Learning was compelled to cancel its conference because of hurricane damage, the Center took the lead and hosted a symposium on "Response to Community Crisis: Lessons from Recent Hurricanes."

Photo Courtesy of Tougaloo College

A new challenge for the Center for Civic Engagement, the HBCU Faculty Development Network, and HBCUs in general has been to document HBCU community involvement. **Historically black colleges and universities have lengthy records of community outreach and service,** but they have traditionally not undertaken the systematic research necessary to document their initiatives.

In planning the 2006 summer symposium on "Response to Community Crisis: Lessons from Recent Hurricanes," the Center invited presentations on established research projects related to community crisis and also encouraged presenters to undertake scholarly research related to this topic following the symposium. With the symposium as a springboard for community-based research on community crisis, the Center earned a small grant from the

National Science Foundation.

Participating in a summit conference of civic engagement leaders in February 2006 at Wingspread (in Racine, Wisconsin) at which the umbrella organization Higher Education Network for Community Engagement was formed, Dr. Rozman was invited to assemble a representative group of HBCU faculty for a proposed training intensive in community-based participatory research with HBCUs at Michigan State University. **In September 2006, the Center received a small grant from the Bonner Foundation to participate in a workshop on community-based research in Princeton, New Jersey. Tougaloo College was the only HBCU participant.**

The synergy of HBCU Faculty Development Network, Tougaloo College's strong role in the Network, and the school's Center for Civic Engagement & Social Responsibility encourages the flow of such opportunities. His leadership roles in these infrastructures, has helped Dr. Rozman develop a growing network of personal relationships, increase his awareness of these opportunities, and enabled him to take advantage of these opportunities. Gloria Roberts (Brown), whose initial part-time role with the Network was expanded to full-time thanks to funding from the Bush and

Ford Foundations, assists in the work of the Center and contributes to the network of personal relationships through contacts she has established.

Recently, the perceptions of faculty developers at HBCUs were compared with those at non-HBCUs affiliated with POD (institutions with predominantly non-minority populations). Asked to identify the most important issues for faculty development at their respective institutions, faculty developers at HBCUs ranked "community service learning" significantly higher than those at non-HBCUs. **They also indicated that courses in community service learning were more prevalent at HBCUs than at non-HBCUs.**

Asked recently to identify new challenges and pressures on institutions which affect faculty work - both in terms of how important they think it is to address those issues through faculty development and the extent to which their institutions are already responding - faculty developers at HBCUs gave significantly greater importance to "community-based research," "outreach/service activities," and "commitment to civic life/the public good" than those at non-HBCUs. **The former group also indicated a greater response to these challenges and pressures on the part of their institutions than the latter group in all three of these areas.**

How will the community benefit from these developments? According to Dr. Rozman, "If, as the data reveal, HBCUs lend greater importance to community outreach and community-based research than non-HBCUs and have taken more steps to develop courses in these areas, their surrounding communities may expect to reap greater benefits than communities adjacent to non-HBCUs. The benefits would be enhanced if HBCUs feel relatively greater challenges and pressures to engage in community-based research and outreach." ■

Faculty developers at HBCUs ranked "community service learning" significantly higher than those at non-HBCUs.

A **Glimpse** *of* **Service** *at* Benedict College

Photos Courtesy of Benedict College

The Benedict College Leadership Development Institute (LDI) is designed to provide students with a foundation for developing or furthering their potential as leaders. Students are chosen for participation in LDI based upon the scoring of the application packet. LDI trains a cadre of students to be more than leaders. **It is not enough for leaders to simply mobilize individuals or groups, they must now have knowledge of how to develop, facilitate, and implement change in their respective environment.** At Benedict College, LDI provides students with tangible tools and skills that will enable them to fully realize their potential and "become powers for good in society."

> **"Yes, it is time consuming, but the reward is great!"**

The principles of the Leadership Development Institute - service, reflection and leadership- model the service-learning framework of preparation, action, reflection, and celebration. Education activist Marion Wright Edelman once said,

"Service is the rent we pay for being. It is the very purpose of life, and not something you do in your spare time." Service is intentionally woven throughout the fabric of Benedict College. Examples that document the service ethic of the Institution include the following: the College's mission statement which details Benedict's commitment to teaching research, and service; the catalog where the college-wide service-learning graduation requirement is outlined and detailed; and administrative divisions such as Student Affairs and Community Development, which works directly with community residents and city officials to improve conditions.

The service activities completed by Leadership Development Institute participants are in addition to the service-learning projects that all students must complete as a graduation requirement. Students are assisted in the service-learning experiences by the College's Service-Learning Program staff in collaboration with college instructors. The staff members are full time employees whose primary purpose is to provide students with viable service projects that are academically sound and positively impact the lives of both the service provider and service recipient.

As students interact in their service experiences, elements of the traditional African philosophy Ubunto can be found throughout the Institute. Ubunto, when translated, means that there are common bonds that connect us all; **through our interaction with others, we discover our own human qualities.** In an effort to build these bonds with their peers, LDI participants serve as peer mentors to freshman students who need assistance making the transition from high school to college. They also help new students to effectively manage collegiate life, both in and outside the classroom, to ensure a successful first year experience.

The Service-Learning Program staff understands the importance of continuously providing Institute participants with the tools needed to ensure that these current college leaders will be prepared to take on their future roles as world leaders when the time arrives. For this reason, LDI participants meet regularly with identified staff to engage in leadership training, design service projects and activities, and reflect on their overall experiences. One student participant noted in a program survey: *"This is one of the best programs at Benedict. Yes, it is time consuming, but the reward is great!"* ■

"Should Service-Learning be **FORCED** Or *Encouraged*?"

Recently Norfolk State University asked incoming freshmen and graduating seniors to share their opinions of mandatory versus voluntary service-learning programs.

The question was an appropriate one for this Historically Black University located in urban Norfolk, Virginia. According to Dr. Lymon Brooks, the first president of NSU, **the school "was developed on the principle that community service was important to the purpose and progress of the college. Faculty members would become better teachers as a result of involvement in constructive community involvement**....During the early 1950s, NSU was the major place where the people of the community met, discussed and planned the strategy and implementation of integration."

NSU's study built on previous surveys, including one conducted by Campus Compact, a national coalition of more than 900 colleges and universities. Completed by students in some 400 institutions of higher education, the Campus Compact survey found that **Minority Serving Institutions (MSIs) are more likely than other schools to require service and service-learning for graduation, provide support structure for engaging activities, and establish partnerships with K-12 and faith-based organizations.**

Those findings were no surprise, explains NSU Coordinator of Service-Learning and Civic Engagement, Amelia Ross-Hammond, Ph.D., "because faith-based organizations play a major

Photos Courtesy of Eastern Mennonite University

role in the socio-cultural lives and values of MSIs. Service to the community is taught early in the process.

"Historically, the churches served multi-purposes and were the anchor for African American families," she says. "Community leaders and churches played a significant role in advocating for institutions to enable young African Americans to attain a college degree and become more economically empowered. The heritage and traditions of community service inherited from their faith-based activities resulted in the natural desire of our students and faculty to 'give back' to the community."

Norfolk State's open-ended essay format study was administered by the Office of Institutional Effectiveness and Assessment with the assistance of Associate Director Alexei Matveev. Results were compared to two annual national surveys conducted

around the same time: The Beginning College Student Survey (BCSS), and the National Survey of Student Engagement (NSSE).

According to the 2004 BCSS, 47% of incoming freshmen volunteered or did community service often during the last year of high school, and 39% of incoming freshmen expected to participate in a school-sponsored community service project during the first year. In the 2005 NSSE, only 18% of freshmen reported that they often participated in a community-based project as part of a regular course during their first year and 59% never participated. **NSU's survey found that 45% of freshmen planned on doing community service or volunteer work before graduation.**

Among graduating seniors, the 2005 NSSE found that less 29% had participated in a community-based project as part of a regular course, although 71% of them agreed that courses offered opportunities to participate in internships and community service. In contrast, 46.5% of NSU graduating students reported being involved in structured volunteer work, community service, and/ or civic activities while at the school.

Four general themes emerged from NSU's survey:

● **Service-learning as a component of the course should be voluntary.**

● **Service-learning is an enriching experience and should be a mandatory component of the college curriculum.**

● **Commitment service needs to, and can be, taught.**

● **Steps needed to be taken to implement a successful program at NSU.**

Photo courtesy of Xavier University

Students' recommendations were implemented by NSU's Service-Learning Taskforce Committee into a successful program which has expanded to include a Civic Engagement component. Freshmen are introduced to the concept and best practices of service-learning through mandatory service-learning activities as part of general education courses.

Activities are sustained on a voluntary basis by administrators, faculty members and students interested in curricula and co-curricular activities, and the program is strongly supported by new University president Dr. Carolyn Winstead Meyers. Additionally, student organizations, coordinated by the Office of Student Activities and the Student Government Association, participate in campus-wide community service, service-learning, and civic engagement.

Most compelling are the students' own reflections on their service-learning experiences, including the following comments:

"The service-learning program has helped me remember the importance of serving others. It has also helped refresh basic concepts

and various techniques that I would have otherwise forgotten. Additionally, I was able to develop fun and creative ways to teach the students assigned to me."

"Every action a person learns is taught to them. That is why I believe that if a

---

46.5% of NSU graduating students reported being involved in structured volunteer work, community service, and/or civic activities while at school.

• •

person is taught to do positive things in the community, he or she will replicate these ideas when the opportunity is presented."

"Reflecting on this course, I realized how influential my quest played to make my community a better place in the service I chose to do…By my involvement in Adopt-a-Highway, food banks, and mentoring, I too intend to provoke change. My change may not come as large scale as a revolution, but it starts with my community. "

"By participating in this activity, I have gained skills and abilities that will help enrich my undergraduate course and give more meaning to my classroom studies.

"I know that I could spend a lifetime helping others because there will always be a need and reason to give back to the community."

Dr. Ross-Hammond agrees. She says, "The expansion of community based scholarship integrated with academic learning allows our students, faculty, and staff, to address important needs of our community and expand collaborative partnerships with private and public, civic and faith-based organizations in the Hampton Roads region. This tradition is one of the most valued practices of Historically Black Colleges and Universities." ∎

Students at Hispanic-Serving Institutions Learn "Values in Action"

Original material contributed by Margarita Lenk,
Associate Professor of Accounting and Computer Information Systems,
Colorado State University

Photos Courtesy of Colorado State University

Programas de aprendizaje-servicio desarrollan líderes para el futuro con procesos que conectan a estudiantes con sus comunidades y sus valores de solidaridad. En forma activa, estudiantes integran conocimientos del currículo académico en proyectos que directamente resuelvan necesidades reales de familia, salud, educación, e injusticias en sus comunidades. El ayudar a otros miembros de la sociedad tener más esperanza y posibilidades es muy importante en la comunidad y la cultura Hispana. Los estudiantes también practican como colaborar con instituciones sociales y sus clientes. Investigaciones han demostrado que esta forma de enseñanza resulta in mejor y más profundo conocimiento que otras formas de instrucción.

Service-learning programs develop future leaders by connecting students to their communities and their solidarity values. In an active mode, students integrate academic curricular knowledge with projects that directly help resolve real family, health, education and injustice needs in their communities. Helping other members of society have more hope and possibilities is very important to the Hispanic community and culture. Students also practice collaboration skills with community institutions and their clients. Research has shown that this form of teaching results in better and deeper learning than other forms of teaching.

Recognizing that their students are members of their local communities who want to learn how to build the resources in your community as part of your life goals. Hispanic-Serving Institutions have created some of the most progressive community-based programs in the United States.

Hispanic-Serving Institutions (HSIs) are those with at least 25 percent of students from Hispanic cultures. As Margarita Lenk, Associate Professor of Accounting and Computer Information Systems at Colorado State University, explains, "These schools are dedicated to providing Hispanic students with an experience that helps grow awareness, understanding and respect for their own cultural heritage and the heritage of others, to improve the social and economic well-being of their communities, and to develop future leaders for those communities and for the larger world."

Hispanic-Serving Institutions are different from traditional colleges and universities in several significant ways:

● First, they have worked hard to blur the boundary lines and "ivory tower" walls that separate them from their communities to focus on building their communities. HSIs' commitment to outreach is visible, with structures that invite community members to discuss their needs and work with the college to address those needs. Partnership grants with local organizations help build sustainable improvements to the local community. Administrators focus on creating collaborations with a variety of groups (including alumni, recruiters, elected officials, and foundations) to build the economic capacity of their regions. Input from students and community members is encouraged. Funded academic programs and financial aid facilitate a quality college experience and help students begin successful careers in areas of demand and need in local communities.

● Second, HSI faculties have self-selected to work at these community-engaged institutions and are active members of their communities, leading and participating in boards, task forces, and councils. Many have integrated their work in the community into their courses, student advising, research, and activism. They create mentoring opportunities to help students develop as "whole citizens" with their own community service values and habits. They create academic opportunities to brainstorm community issues while developing collaboration, leadership, follow-through, and communication skills, and they invite local organizations and their boards of directors to support student projects.

SPOTLIGHT

"These schools are dedicated to providing Hispanic students with an experience that helps grow awareness, understanding and respect for their own cultural heritage and the heritage of others, to improve the social and economic well-being of their communities, and to develop future leaders for those communities and for the larger world."

– Margarita Lenk, Associate Professor of Accounting and Computer Information Systems, Colorado State University

Students at HSIs are typically from nearby communities and want to remain in the area after college. Many of these students have already started families of their own, are working, and are committed to playing a greater role in their communities. Service-learning projects that value social justice and that help residents - children and teenagers, young parents, and the elderly - live more comfortably and securely help students empower their communities while helping them learn valuable workplace and leadership skills.

A wide portfolio of both curricular and co-curricular programs that may last a day or throughout students' entire program are offered. Students are encouraged to identify, participate in, organize, and lead a wide range of programs - such as designing community celebrations to promote local cultural awareness – which develop sustainable organizational leadership and collaboration skills that promote active democracy, social progress, family support, and economic development.

Service-learning programs at Hispanic-Serving Institutions are plentiful, and these schools speak with great pride about their programs. Our Lady of the Lake, in San Antonio, Texas, for example, currently engages college and high school students in joint programs designed to reduce teenage pregnancy. The university has also developed service-learning programs to help reduce hunger among the elderly and to encourage opportunities to buy and sell local arts and products. Local leaders are invited to campus as "Barrio Professors" to provide detailed community knowledge and to serve as role models for the students.

Other HSIs have launched similar programs. Some have created child-care, pre-school and charter school programs to provide community children with a good educational start and to help students who are already parents complete their degrees. These are just a few examples of how Hispanic-Serving Institutions act on their commitment to grow competent citizen leaders and communities with promising futures. ■

For a complete list of Hispanic-Serving Institutions in the United States, visit

http://www.hacu.net

and click on the "members" tab.

University of South Carolina
Provides Spanish Translation for Healthcare Professionals

In the last two decades, South Carolina's Latino population has increased 22% (U.S. Census Bureau). This increased Latino presence in South Carolina has made the need for services to Spanish speakers more noticeable and significant. Recognizing this community need, two students from the South Carolina Honors College (funded by a university undergraduate research grant) conducted research on Latin-American immigrant women in South Carolina. Their research spanned one year and focused on linguistic and social factors inhibiting communication in medical environments between Spanish-speaking patients and their healthcare providers. Their collaborative research efforts with community members, health providers, and outreach organizations identified a great need that has gone unnoticed in South Carolina.

With the desire to use this research as a tool for creating and sustaining effective change, these two students and a faculty member created a service-learning course, Spanish for Healthcare Professionals. In partnership with local Hispanic/Latino health advocacy groups, students enrolled in this course utilize their Spanish speaking skills by translating and interpreting necessary medical information to patients in the Columbia, South Carolina community. Students have an active, hands-on-learning experience that develops enhanced communication skills in areas of specialization, increased awareness of professional ethics, rules and protocol, as well as the cultural demands of dealing with Hispanic clients in a variety of contexts. Students increase their Spanish-speaking skills while engaging in academic work that explores the ethical and cultural aspects of interpretation.

This service-learning project is a model for others to use in engaging undergraduate students in community-based research. ■

Spanish Students Help Hispanic Neighbors with Healthcare Issues

Texas Christian University students can engage in service-learning – largely geared to neighboring Hispanic communities - as soon as they hit the campus.

Known as the Horned Frogs, TCU students are first introduced to service opportunities at freshman orientation programs like Frog Camp. Further connections to service throughout the city are made via the school's Center for Community Involvement and Service-Learning – which coordinates co-curricular service activities and also offers incentive grants and technical support to help faculty members develop or strengthen service-learning courses.

Because Hispanic communities comprise nearly one-third of the population of Fort Worth (where TCU is located), linking students to these citizens through such courses as Dr. Mary McKinney's Spanish in the Workplace: Spanish for Healthcare is a natural. Each semester, the service-learning project students conduct with such partners as the county hospital, children's hospital and an advocacy agency enhances the academic material being studied.

"Language and cultural barriers can be difficult to overcome in any situation," explains Dr. McKinney, "especially when health is involved. Therefore, one goal of the service-learning projects is to ease the situation of the Hispanic patient while providing language practice and culture study for the TCU student."

While partnering with the hospitals, students employ newly acquired Spanish vocabulary and language skills to talk with patients and their families within the confines of strict privacy laws. This interaction also enables students to observe firsthand the cultural norms discussed in class.

Photos Courtesy of Texas Christian University

One student project with the advocacy agency focused on the uninsured and under-insured Hispanic patients which made up 37 percent of the patients at one hospital. Many of these patients were eligible for grant monies which would help them pay their healthcare bills, but faced communication and cultural barriers which prevented them from applying for the grants. Students designed and produced a brochure the agency could give to patients to help them surmount the obstacles and successfully complete grant applications.

McKinney says, "The brochure helped the agents better connect with the patients, provided access to much needed resources for the patients, and exposed students to cultural and social aspects of the Fort Worth community about which they were previously unaware."

Students in another of Dr. McKinney's classes wrote and designed an activity book geared to young patients in hospital waiting rooms. The story and games in the book were bilingual, and students collected items to include in a first aid kit which was packaged with the book. Students then spoke with young patients, read the story, played

"One goal of the service-learning projects is to ease the situation of the Hispanic patient while providing language practice and culture study for the TCU student."

– Texas Christian University Professor Dr. Mary McKinney

Photos Courtesy of Texas Christian University

the games with them, and explained some first aid concepts in Spanish.

Enabling students to earn academic credit while providing service is an approach which aligns with Texas Christian University's mission "to educate individuals to think and act as ethical leaders and responsible citizens in the global community." The success of the projects described has prompted Dr. McKinney to incorporate service-learning into other Spanish courses. ■

SPOTLIGHT

Service-Learning Provides Experience Greater than the Sum of Its Parts

International service-learning programs offer Kansas State University students opportunities which transcend either classroom or study abroad experience and allow them to apply academic and life skills to real needs identified by communities.

In Izamal, Mexico, for example, K-State students organized a day camp. For more than 13 years, students followed up on the work of their predecessors, ensuring continuity and enhancing impact.

The office of Civic Leadership, part of the university's Leadership Studies and Programs, is home to these and other service-learning and community service activities:

- Academic Mentoring Program
- International Teams
- Kansas Campus Compact
- WaterLINK
- American Humanics
- AmeriCorps
- Alternative Breaks
- K-State Volunteer Center of Manhattan.

For 20 years, students have served in international communities in more than 20 countries, creating plans and projects to address health, education, environmental, and other concerns. Host communities are identified through relationships with faculty, community members, K-State alumni, and past students, and the university

Photos Courtesy of Kansas State University

looks for partners interested in long-term relationships. Interdisciplinary teams of three to six K-State students – usually juniors or seniors with

> *"Unlike volunteer experiences or mission trips, the students apply their academic skills to community problems."*

outstanding academic and service records and, often, foreign language proficiency - are selected in a competitive process during the fall semester. Truman, Marshall, and Rhodes scholars, leaders in student government and campus organizations, and top scholars from many academic disciplines have been among student participants.

Living within the community and working daily with community members, students enhance problem-solving skills, gain leadership experience, and develop an appreciation for other cultures and perspectives.

Civic Leadership Associate Director Mary Hale Tolar explains, "Unlike volunteer experiences or mission trips, the students apply their academic skills to community problems.

Unlike academic structures, the students must adapt to constantly changing plans, people, and activities."

Following the service experience, students participate in a structured reflection which helps them recognize important underlying social and community issues and understand the role of citizens in effectively addressing these issues. ■

For more information:
Mary Hale Tolar
Associate Director, Civic Leadership
Leadership Studies and Programs
Kansas State University
2323 Anderson Ave., Ste. 125
Manhattan, KS 66502
Tel: 785-532-3651
Fax: 785-532-0671
e-mail: mtolar@ksu.edu

SPOTLIGHT

Creighton Students Embrace Invitation to Serve in the *Dominican Republic*

Photos Courtesy of Creighton University

Creighton University's Institute for Latin American Concern (ILAC) has a 35 year relationship with Centro de Educacion para la Salud Integral (CESI) in the Dominican Republic (DR). It provides service-learning and immersion experiences for those with a heart to serve, and emphasizes the importance of global vision and understanding in the process of educating well-rounded men and women for and with others.

Photos Courtesy of Creighton University

> *"Each program is a collaboration between the volunteers and those who are served so that both parties can benefit from working together and learning from each other. In essence, it is an exchange of gifts."*

Creighton exists to educate students with a view to their intellectual expansion, social awareness, physical development, aesthetic appreciation and spiritual enrichment. The school's core values include service to others, the importance of family life, the inalienable worth of the individual, and appreciation of ethnic and cultural diversity.

Creighton ILAC Center's relationship with CESI began in 1975 and has flourished ever since. ILAC is an international, Christian, Ignatian-inspired collaborative health care and educational organization that exists to promote the integral well-being and spiritual growth of all participants.

Creighton's ILAC programs offer unmatched opportunities

to learn, serve and be served in the developing world. ILAC participants include dental, medical, nursing, pharmacy, law, physical therapy and occupational therapy, undergraduate and high school students, as well as faculty-led groups, medical/surgical teams and students from other colleges/universities. The ILAC/CESI Center in the Dominican Republic also provides training in cooking and nutrition, agriculture and small business opportunities, an undergraduate campus for students from Creighton University, and many other programs.

"Each program is a collaboration between the volunteers and those who are served so that both parties can benefit from working together and learning from each other," says Creighton. "In essence, it is an exchange of gifts."

Housed at La Mision, ILAC/CESI Center's eight-building campus provides numerous opportunities for students and professionals to grow personally, professionally and spiritually. ∎

SPOTLIGHT

Early service-learning initiatives lay groundwork for long-term benefits and opportunities

Service-learning programs at the University of Kentucky in Lexington are helping students become more active and reflective learners and providing them with creative outlets which help them meet identified needs of children and adults in the community.

Almost 10 years ago, new assistant professor Kristine Jolivette learned about the possibilities of service-learning and applied for funding from the UK Experiential Education program to include it in her coursework. Although she has since moved on from UK, her initiative launched a journey which has been continued by colleagues in the department and college.

Dr. Jolivette's class Survey of Exceptional Learners – in the College of Education Department of Special Education and Rehabilitation Counseling - focused on creating interactive disability awareness bulletin boards to meet the needs of faculty, students, family members and other segments of the university community. Students were charged with making each bulletin board accessible to individuals with disabilities and interactive so that users could be active participants in achieving content objectives. Feedback from the university community and students was extremely positive, and students enjoyed the project's collaborative and creative aspects.

Dr. Linda Gassaway, also an instructor in the Department of Special Education and Rehabilitation Counseling, leads students in two service-learning activities. The first supports activities at the Blue Grass Technology Center, a local consumer-driven, nonprofit grassroots organization which helps individuals with disabilities, their families, and service providers connect with various technologies and services to support greater independence, productivity, and quality of life. Participating students worked with chil-

"I learned how even small choices for teachers and families of individuals with disabilities take time and must be deliberate and thoughtful."

– Student participant in a service-learning project led by Dr. Gassaway

Photo Courtesy of University of Kentucky

dren with disabilities and their parents to evaluate toys sent by toy manufacturers to determine whether children liked the toys and if the toys they liked could be adapted for children with disabilities. The second service-learning project partners students with adolescents and adults with disabilities to organize a community dance.

Students' comments illustrate how much they enjoy working with and for their neighbors with disabilities through these service-learning experiences. One student notes, "I learned how even small choices for teachers and families of individuals with disabilities take time and must be deliberate and thoughtful." Another says, "I began to realize what I take and have taken for granted in my own life."

Other comments like this one demonstrate a renewed recognition that the student has chosen the right career path: "Upon completion of this service-learning project, I have realized that teaching children in special education is where my heart truly lies."

Students also appreciate how these service-learning opportunities provide a sense of the connection between knowl-

edge and application which is so important in learning to be a good teacher. They note, "I never put my knowledge and the information I had together to realize some of the little things in life that do not come easily for children with disabilities" and "my eyes were opened to new ways of helping others."

Dr. Gassaway finds this student reflection especially meaningful, "I am a firm believer that everything has a purpose, and my purpose for this service-learning project was to figure out what really drives me to go through college and what I really want to accomplish. I am so lucky to have found my passion this early in life, and simply cannot wait to start solving the mystery."

UK's Experiential Education and Career Services at the James W. Stuckert Career Center continues the mini-grant program which launched these efforts and, to date, has funded more than 30 faculty and graduate students in using service-learning in local and international communities within coursework across a wide range of departments and programs. ■

Two Community Colleges: Both Engaged

SALT LAKE COMMUNITY COLLEGE

Photo Courtesy of Salt Lake Community College

Civic engagement initiatives and a strong service-learning program connect students among Salt Lake Community College's 14 different locations with each other and with the school's focus on educating students to become good citizens.

Nearly 4000 of this commuter school's population -- largely non-traditional, working and part-time students -- participate each year in programs which fulfill SLCC's mission to encourage "respectful and vigorous dialogue that nourishes active participation and service in a healthy democracy." Supportive administrators and faculty, the campus-wide presence of the Thayne Center for Service & Learning established in 1994, and innovative programs created specifically for students, faculty, and community partners all contribute to the success of service-learning at the school.

More than 120 sections of designated service-learning courses offered annually by the college, including many general education classes which encourage civic involvement early in students' college careers. Professional and vocational classes in such areas as nursing, occupational therapy assisting, cosmetology, and pre-teacher certification also include service-learning.

To illustrate, students can enroll in the Civically-Engaged Scholar program which enables them to apply academic knowledge to community concerns. Scholars who complete a variety of service-learning classes, 300 hours of co-curricular service, monthly reflections, and a capstone project graduate with special recognition and a Civically-Engaged Scholar distinction on their transcripts.

Faculty initiatives include a grant program that supports the development of new service-learning courses; a faculty mentor who works with other professors college-wide; a service-learning faculty consulting corps; a comprehensive service-learning handbook and troubleshooting guide; and discipline-specific service-learning toolkits.

More than 200 community partners have registered with Salt Lake Community College's on-line database. "Partners in Service & Learning," a collaboration among local agencies and all four institutions of higher education in Salt Lake City, holds training events twice a year to bring together community partners and faculty.

Salt Lake Community College has received national attention for its strong service-learning program and currently serves is one of four colleges in the nation selected by the American Association of Community Colleges for the "Community Colleges Broadening Horizons through Service Learning" project.

KAPI'OLANI COMMUNITY COLLEGE

Photos Courtesy of Kapi'olani Community College

Kapi'olani Community College takes more than its name from Hawai'i's penultimate female monarch. This two-year urban institution's service-learning program is inspired by Queen Julia Kapi'olani's deep commitment to the health, education and well-being of Hawai'i's people.

One of 10 public colleges in the University of Hawai'i system, the college used funding from the American Association of Community Colleges and the Corporation for National Service to initiate an intercultural and intergenerational service-learning program in 1995. Since then, more than 7000 students have engaged in service-learning -- addressing educational, environmental, health and human service challenges in Honolulu's diverse ethnic communities and learning to understand and celebrate Hawai'i's multicultural traditions of service and social responsibility.

For example, native Hawaiians' rich traditions of environmental and familial service – and concepts of mālama (to care for) and kūleana (special responsibility to the community) -- intersect with the college's environmental service-learning program. Land nurtures the people, and the people nurture the land in a reciprocal, sustainable relationship.

Collaborating with colleagues at the University of Hawai'i at Mānoa, Kapi'olani faculty and students address early literacy, digital divide, and health and environment issues in Palolo Valley, a multi-ethnic, low-income community near both campuses. For more than 10 years, collaborations among institutions and community partners have received significant national recognition from

Campus Compact, Carnegie Foundation, AAC&U and external funding from Corporation for National and Community Service, Kellogg Foundation, and HUD.

Service-learning has played a critical role in redefining and articulating Kapi'olani Community College's larger public and civic purposes. Robert Franco, Professor of Anthropology, and Service-Learning Outreach Coordinator Ku'ulani Miyashiro explain, "Intentionally building the social and intellectual capital of the faculty has created a 'multiplier effect' whereby thousands of students better understand community issues and work for the social, economic, and environmental betterment of the communities we serve.

"As we act upon Queen Kapi'olani's motto

'Kūlia i ka nu'u' (to strive for the highest), our communities are experiencing troubled times like those that shaped her life and legacy. We draw inspiration and imagination from the Queen so that this College's mission of equity, access, success, and engagement will shape a new generation of Hawai'i's people." ■

Service-learning opportunities add up to new perceptions for accounting students

At **Bentley College (MA)**, service-learning is opening accounting students' eyes and helping them to realize that business is about more than the bottom line and shareholder returns.

Opportunities which focus on corporate social responsibility as an integral part of the future of a successful business help students in accounting recognize that there are multiple stakeholders to consider in the communities where businesses are located. Service-learning helps students begin to critically analyze the ideas behind corporate social responsibility and understand the returns that are associated with companies' investments in the larger community.

Service-learning also illustrates the complex issues underlying social problems – such as the fact that car manufacturers moving their production processes to China is the leading cause of job loss and poverty in Michigan. Through their community-based experiences, students learn that, although basic financial assistance may offer short-term help to laid-off workers, long-term solutions must include education and retraining that help people prepare for and find new, more highly skilled jobs.

As Karen Osterheld, Senior Lecturer in Accounting, and Manuel Carneiros, Graduate Student in Accounting, explain, "Accounting students who take part in service-learning courses and learn to appreciate the ways in which corporate social responsibility can benefit all stakeholders truly have a better understanding of business and the ways in which it needs to function." ■

> *"Accounting students who take part in service-learning courses and learn to appreciate the ways in which corporate social responsibility can benefit all stakeholders truly have a better understanding of business and the ways in which it needs to function."*
>
> *- Karen Osterheld, Senior Lecturer in Accounting, and Manuel Carneiros, Graduate Student in Accounting, Bentley College*

Clemson architecture students build on strong service-learning foundation

Clemson University's School of Architecture has provided rich and varied service-learning opportunities from the start. Under its first dean Harlan McClure, students worked on projects varying in scale from furniture to seaports, including facilitating the development of Hilton Head Island's Shelter Cove Harbor and the Waterfront Park in Beaufort, SC.

Today, the school's "Fluid Campus" concept offers even more service-learning opportunities through ongoing programs in Italy and Spain and closer to its South Carolina home. Its new association with Clemson's Community Research and Design Center will bring many future interdisciplinary opportunities for students, faculty and citizens to improve built environments.

Clemson Architecture Center in Charleston has won numerous awards, including National Council of Architectural Registration Boards recognition for integrating practice into the classroom. Initiatives with the South Carolina Design Arts Partnership link the College of Architecture, Arts & Humanities and Public Service Extension to leadership groups across the state. Joining the ranks of students in Auburn University's Rural Studio and University of Kansas' Studio 804, Clemson students are taking service-learning to new levels via design-build projects, constructing projects they've designed.

Through the Pendleton Foundation for Black History and Culture, Clemson Studio South students and faculty worked with community members to design and build a new public space and rehabilitate a community center. Working all day nearly every day for most of a semester to create a meaningful public space, students gained powerful learning experiences, especially as they grew to know many of the neighborhood's older African American residents.

Studio South student Kelley Hubbard describes her experience: "When I first approached the project, I just kind of joked about how, as a group of mostly white, middle/upper class graduate students, we didn't exactly fit into the community, and the thought of collaborating with them was somewhat intimidating. Now I feel like we are all friends…like this experience has prepared me for working with different groups of people in the future. I would never have had any of these experiences as part of a traditional studio…now I feel like I have learned so much as part of a "design-build" studio and the opportunity to work with a group of clients that became my community." ■

Photo Courtesy of Clemson University

> *"I would never have had any of these experiences as part of a traditional studio…now I feel like I have learned so much as part of a "design-build" studio, and also was given the opportunity to work with a group of clients that became my community."*
>
> *– Clemson architecture student Kelley*

Meeting real-world communications challenges through service-learning

Providing video production and advertising services for community organizations gives hands-on, meaningful experience to Alvernia College communications students.

"We have the ideal situation for our students," says Dr. Jodi Radosh, associate professor of communication and associate director for Community Based Learning for the Reading, PA, college's Center for Community Engagement: "Community service that has real value to both the organization being served and to the student serving is true service learning at its best."

Advertising Workshop students worked on two projects: an advertising campaign – including web site design, print ads and public relations – for an eye doctor and, to boost the professional image of the Reading-Berks Literacy Council, a new web site, brochures, letterhead, and logo.

Such applied service opportunities lend relevance and meaning to Alvernia students' education, connecting them to the school's motto "To live, to love, to serve." ■

Dr. Radosh's Video Production and Broadcasting and Electronic Media courses at a local community television station have offered up a range of interesting service-learning projects:

• A video for women newly diagnosed with ovarian cancer. In this project for Lehigh Valley Hospital, students interviewed cancer survivors, physicians, and nurses. The hospital plans to put it on their website and also recently submitted to a gynecology conference.

• Documentaries of Skate America, one of Central Pennsylvania's largest fundraisers, including behind-the-scenes interviews with well-known ice skaters.

• Taped Seniors College classes so audiences, especially elderly shut-ins, could watch lectures on Berks Community Television. This project was funded by a grant through the Office of Aging and a Pennsylvania State Senator.

• A training video for new producers at Berks Community Television.

• Videography and promotional videos for such campus groups such as Sigma Delta Tau English honor society, intramural sporting events, the International Club, First-Year Seminar, the College Bookstore, and for BCTV.

Service-learning students share engineering skills with community

Engineering service-learning students at Purdue University are harnessing new technologies to address community needs and to help not-for-profits enhance services and operations.

Purdue's Engineering Projects in Community Service (EPICS) program draws from 30 majors and engages student design teams in defining, developing and delivering projects over time periods ranging from one semester for less complicated projects to several years for large and complex projects.

Students leverage their skills to help human services agencies improve computer and operational efficiencies, to design and built devices, programs and systems that improve learning and increase access for people with disabilities, and to address energy efficiencies and environmental impacts. Through the combined efforts of students, their professors and their mentors, organizations gain access to technologies, products and expertise they could otherwise not afford.

EPICS works with local not-for-profits, educational institutions, and governmental agencies to create long-term partnerships so those that are fielded can be supported after deployment, existing projects can be upgraded, and community partners can come to understand better the projects they have helped develop.

Participation in engineering-related service-learning experiences goes beyond those who think of themselves as future engineers, explains William Oakes, Associate Professor of Engineering Education at Purdue. He says, "In many engineering programs, multidisciplinary teams are required, and projects need, in addition to those with technical expertise,

Photo Courtesy of Purdue

"The concept of service-learning in engineering has the potential not only to bring resources to traditionally underserved communities but also to improve the pipeline of those interested in making engineering their life's work."

- Oakes

Oakes also notes that the service-learning approach to engineering is drawing a significantly more diverse population – both by gender and ethnicity – than do more traditional approaches. "Thus," he notes, "the concept of service-learning in engineering has the potential not only to bring resources to traditionally underserved communities but also to improve the pipeline of those interested in making engineering their life's work." ■

students who think of the people first and can react and evaluate as a user not familiar with technology."

Students apply project management skills to engineer organization's relocation

Photo Courtesy of Western Carolina University

Planning and executing an organization's major move to a new facility recently provided engineering students at Western Carolina University with an opportunity to put the problem-solving, leadership and planning skills gained in the classroom to work on a project benefitting the community.

This assignment, through Dr. Phil Sanger's course Project Management for Engineers, gave students a sampling of the kinds of challenges they might face in their professional careers as project managers.

The students worked on behalf of Foothills Industries, Inc., of Marion, NC, a small nonprofit corporation that employs and trains people with disabilities and prepares them to enter the workforce. Foothills had outgrown its original space scattered in multiple buildings and, with support from the community, built a new, much larger facility.

In consultation with the organization's executive officer, the 22 student participants broke down the move into manageable pieces and plotted the sequence of tasks and priorities.

"Then," says Sanger, "they rolled up their sleeves to get the job done over two weekends."

Exceeding expectations, the students finished the project ahead of schedule and satisfied the client.

"The class was delighted and proud to make a difference in the lives of the people of this wonderful organization," Sanger says. ∎

Students connect study of French literature with contemporary issues and needs

"Through reading, reflection, writing and service, students better understand the history and social dynamics that warrant imprisonment and the plight of those unjustly incarcerated, all the while weighing the value of human goodness and community support to those in need."
— Pamela Gay, Associate Professor of French, Alabama State University

Service-learning enables Alabama State University students to apply their study of literature written in France in the 1800s to contemporary community issues.

In an intermediate-advanced readings course concentrating on Victor Hugo's Les Miserables, students compare crime, rural poverty, incarceration, and other 19th century social issues with 21st century crime, increasing rates of incarceration, and reentry into society.

Students read selected themes of Les Miserables, exploring concepts of freedom and incarceration on both the physical and moral levels. Combining that learning with the study of newsletter accounts from the Alabama Department of Corrections and related service activities helps students understand the precariousness of imprisonment and freedom and the difficulties faced by those attempting to reintegrate into society.

Students also perform 15 hours in service to individuals preparing to reenter society and their families - as reading tutors with individuals headed for reentry and tutoring the children of reentering individuals in daycare facilities administered by one of several Montgomery (AL) housing sites. Working at Renaissance House, a newly established residence in Montgomery, students hear firsthand accounts about the hardships of reentry and its effects on the wider community.

Keeping journals also helps improve students' understanding of incarceration and release in both Les Miserables and in modern society as well as the redemptive spirit present in service. According to Pamela Gay, Associate Professor of French at Alabama State University, the journals help students "ponder the relationship between service to the community and the justices and injustices present in the current legal structure that pushes the poor to commit crimes to survive.

"Through reading, reflection, writing and service," says Gay, "students better understand the history and social dynamics that warrant imprisonment and the plight of those unjustly incarcerated, all the while weighing the value of human goodness and community support to those in need." ∎

Down-to-earth service-learning at Tennessee State

> "Community-based learning gives my students an opportunity to make significant contributions to the community while learning broadly applicable course content."

Students in several geography service-learning courses at Tennessee State University help at-risk students learn valuable skills and make important contributions to their community.

As part of a recent Urban Geography course taught by David A. Padgett, PhD, students partnered with grassroots and non-profit organizations to train the youth in geographic information systems (GIS) and global positioning systems (GPS) methods necessary to create "community asset maps." This project, funded by a State Farm Good Neighbor Service Learning Grant, will facilitate production of community-based "emergency response" maps.

Students also assisted partner organizations in writing small grant proposals. Two grants were funded, and the funds will go to help the organizations improve technological capacity.

The State Farm grant was initiated by a student enrolled in Padgett's Cartography course. The student co-authored a "My Community, My Earth" proposal that was funded and used as the basis for the larger grant.

Taking the State Farm project to the next level, students in his Weather & Climate course focused on improving emergency preparedness and response during weather-related hazards for low-income, inner-city residents. And his next Urban Geography course will focus on developing GPS best practices for mapping Nashville's homeless population and helping local 4-H students work on GIS-based environmental projects.

Padgett says, "Community-based learning gives my students an opportunity to make significant contributions to the community while learning broadly applicable course content." ■

Interior Design service-learning students turn housing into a real home

Connecting with an organization which provides housing to homeless single mothers, Interior Design students at Louisville Technical Institute used their skills to help one family make a new home.

Through Project Women, which helps women get the housing and education they need to break the cycle of poverty for themselves and their children, the students learned about Cedric and his family - who had recently moved into housing provided by the not-for-profit and had little furniture. Cedric, the oldest of three boys, slept on the floor and had no place to store clothes.

Students worked with instructors Terri George, Nancy Menz and Carla Wallace to improve the family's living space. Because they couldn't afford to buy all the supplies needed, they sought out donations of furniture, curtains, paint, carpet and much more from local businesses. And when they couldn't find a donor, they organized fundraisers involving the entire college community.

Their efforts resulted in a space in which Cedric could feel at home. Other spaces, the entry hall, the master bedroom and the bedroom shared by his two younger brothers, also benefited from the students' design work.

"This project is what Interior Design is all about!" says student Tina Lair. "It is not about glamour or money. It is about the joy you can bring into another person's life. We aren't doctors so we can't heal the sick. But

> "This project is what Interior Design is all about! It is not about glamour or money. It is about the joy you can bring into another person's life. We aren't doctors so we can't heal the sick. But by using our design talents, we can make the world a better place one home at a time."
>
> – Tina Lair, Interior Design student, Louisville Technical Institute

by using our design talents, we can make the world a better place one home at a time."

Jenny Cotton, another student participant, agrees. "We were able to help out a truly needy young man and his family, use all the things we've been learning in a classroom setting and apply them in a real situation. As future designers, we gained the experience of a real world project with budgets, deadlines and mishaps. We got to experience the joy of seeing our work really make a difference in someone's life. I am a different and better person for having done this project."

A similar focus on service-learning is embedded in all programs of this 600-student career college. ■

Photo Courtesy of Louisville Technical Institute

119

Students' efforts to build a sustainable community garden produce great results

Cal Poly Pomona landscape design students' efforts to create a native garden at a local school blossomed into new interests and skills for community youth as well as American Society of Landscape Architects' Award of Excellence in Community Service.

The MathMagical Landscape Project paired seven students in Professor Gerald Taylor's Advanced Landscape Design Studio with teachers and students of Lassalette Middle School.

George Urena, who teaches sixth grade at Lassalette, suggested partnering with the university on the project. About 30 middle school students volunteered for the afterschool program, which aimed at improving math skills and was funded by an $8,000 Edison International grant. "It was heterogeneous education," he says.

> **"High performing and low performing kids worked together and learned from each other."**

Students researched the project and created lesson plans – based upon California math content standards - related to the design, development and construction of the garden, visiting Lassalette twice a week to present lessons. Hands-on participation was the main method of instruction and included exercises in determining area of geometric shapes, percentage of slope, volume of materials, and using architecture and engineering scales to make dimensioned drawings of buildings, plants and other landscape elements.

Taylor notes the thought and time students gave to the project and the enthusiasm of the youth and their families. "When it came to planting the garden, we

Photo Courtesy of CAL Poly Pomona

had 60 people helping us. I have never seen so many people get so much finished in one day."

Prominently located at the school entrance, the garden features a small wooden bridge, pathway and amphitheatre. Plants are all native and drought-tolerant, and a dry stream bed is designed to catch runoff.

Lassalette Principal Christina Sanchez reports remarkable changes in program participants and says, "I didn't anticipate the pride they would take in the project. Some really found their niche." ■

SUNY landscape architecture service-learning students break ground on many levels

Landscape architecture students at the State University of New York's College of Environmental Science and Forestry (SUNY-ESF) put classroom learning to work to design a public garden space that tells the story of Vietnamese immigrants living in a local Syracuse neighborhood.

Working at the request of the city of Syracuse, seven students joined forces with community partners and a local landscape architecture firm to transform space formerly filled by abandoned houses into a physically attractive and spiritually meaningful gathering place for residents.

The "Freedom Garden" features vegetation similar in texture, structure and color to that found in Southeast Asia. Student Heather Washburn explains, "We used elements that would be found in Vietnamese landscapes such as arbors.

"It was a good opportunity to go out into a real community while still in school and get a feeling for how our work will affect communities like this," she says.

According to student Nicole Formoso, "It was something we took seriously because we knew it would be something that would affect this community. It was also the first time in my design career at school that we focused on a real life scenario. This was something that was actually going to break ground."

During the 2007-08 academic year, SUNY ESF students devoted 65,000 service hours through 53 service-learning courses in a variety of academic fields. ESF's service-learning program was named to the 2007 President's Higher Education Community Service Honor Roll.

"We do service-learning because, first and foremost, it's good education. It allows our students to put into action the things they are learning in the classroom," says Leah Flynn, director of student activities. ■

Photo Courtesy of SUNY ESF

Law students demystify legal information for Habitat for Humanity homeowners

> "The volunteer and outreach components of the course...push students to 'humanize' contracts and consider practical applications of legal concepts and theories."
>
> —University of Colorado Law School Professor Amy Schmitz

As part of a unique service-learning seminar, University of Colorado law students have helped new Habitat for Humanity homeowners understand vital legal information.

Professor Amy Schmitz's Humanizing Contracts seminar is different from the law school's other seminars, courses and clinics because it combines rigorous academic study with outreach volunteer work. "Students traditionally learn theory and practice in this area in a more doctrinal manner," explains Schmitz.

This seminar helps expand students' understanding and analysis of contract law beyond the basic concepts they learn in the first-year Contracts course.

"Through course work, students explore and question concepts and theories that underlie contract law," says Schmitz. "The volunteer and outreach components of the course then push students to 'humanize' contracts and consider practical applications of legal concepts and theories."

As part of the workshop, students give presentations on various contracting and consumer protection issues — ranging from consumer protection laws, credit and payday lending and alternative dispute resolution, to homeowners' associations, Internet transactions, and bankruptcy — while the class works with Habitat for Humanity volunteers to provide free childcare and snacks.

Creating, developing and presenting the workshop is the key project for the seminar, but this has led to students' also volunteering with Schmitz at the Habitat for Humanity thrift store and on a Habitat build.

In discussing a skills seminar, Schmitz reported, "The students all did a wonderful job explaining tough concepts in a very straight-forward and informative manner." "The participants asked good questions, and seemed to learn quite a bit. Participants also left with gift bags with various coupons, treats, and other "goodies" for their children to thank them for their participation as well as colored booklets and brochures expanding on the information discussed in the presentations."

Professor Schmitz is now expanding service learning at the law school through her new Consumer Empowerment seminar. Students again analyze and discuss legal theory in class, and write rigorous academic papers. However, they see this theory in action through their creation of published materials on consumer issues and their presentation of a consumer skills seminar. They are working with the Boulder Community Housing Authority to teach the "Be a Savvy Consumer" class to a large group of consumers. These projects are a lot of work for students, but well worth it for both students and the community!

Service-learning + mathematical sciences = an elegant equation

Service-learning can be used in connection with a surprising number of mathematical science courses – and not just in tutoring younger students in mathematics courses. According to Charles R. Hadley, Professor of Mathematical Sciences at Bentley College (MA), math-related service-learning projects typically fall into one of three categories:

- using mathematical modeling to improve an organization's or government agency's operational capabilities or expense structure
- statistical analyses
- educational initiatives

He cites three successful service-learning modeling examples - one using graph theory and combinatorial mathematics to design improved snowplow routes for an upper Midwest municipality, another involving detailed analysis of fire department

"The students...see their own subject matter in a new light, get a chance to practice it in a real-world environment, and develop an enhanced sense of its value and importance."

- Charles R. Hadlock, Professor of Mathematical Sciences, Bentley College

overtime expenses to find alternative scheduling methods for a major city, and a third involving a quantitative risk assessment of hazardous materials transportation through a city.

Statistical analysis opportunities range from elementary tasks suitable for beginning statistics students to advanced applications of statistical inference. "One social service agency simply lacked the personnel and resources to compile and prepare descriptive statistics on data they had collected from their service population," he notes. "In other cases, statistics classes have been involved in the development of survey instruments, including appropriate advanced testing, as well as in the administration of the surveys and the statistical analysis of the results."

Service-learning projects can also help preservice teachers understand the challenges associated with mathematics education through programs targeting younger students and, in some cases, their parents.

Math-related service-learning projects offer benefits to all participants. Hadley says, "Certainly the client organization or the population being served gets a valuable benefit from the activity. "At the same time, especially under the supervision of an effective teacher, the students...see their own subject matter in a new light, get a chance to practice it in a real-world environment, and develop an enhanced sense of its value and importance." ■

Students learn more than tenets in psychology service-learning course

Community Psychology Capstone students at Portland State University (OR) work with local health, education, corrections, and welfare agencies to apply their studies to real life.

The Community Psychology course addresses how individuals' thoughts, feelings and actions are influenced by other people and by social institutions and partners with such organizations as STARS - an agency which teaches healthy sexuality programs in nearby middle and high schools. To help STARS reach and educate parents of teens, Capstone students helped identify key issues and used the findings to create a high-quality video. The video was written using teens' voices and became the centerpiece of STARS' parent education program.

Senior Capstone Courses -- the final stage of PSU's

Service experiences humanize bioethical issues explored in class

Community-based service experiences enable St. Joseph's University (PA) students to put a human face on concerns they study in their Medical Issues in Christian Ethics service-learning course.

This course teaches the ethical, theological and philosophical theories and principles which are the foundation of independent research in Christian Bioethics. Students develop ethical skills and then – through course assignments including case studies - learn how to articulate their own informed positions on such issues as abortion, stem cell research, reproductive technologies, euthanasia, human experimentation, and organ transplantation.

Theory and learning come to life during community-based service experiences. SJU students volunteer weekly at diverse placements within the local community where they can work with people affected by the complexities of health care and bioethical issues. Their focus is on building relationships with the people and the sites rather than on performing specific sets of tasks.

For example, students may converse during activities periods with men and women facing terminal cancer, play with medically fragile children in foster care, help adults at a local health clinic gain access to needed medications, or spend time with men and women living with HIV and AIDS.

"It is the students' time spent in the community which enhances what is taught in classes by extending student learning beyond the classroom to personalize and humanize the bioethical issues."

"Furthermore the service experiences serve as an additional text for their coursework as students form and articulate their positions on complex bioethical cases including HIV/AIDS, human cloning, stem cell research, euthanasia and more."

> "It is the students' time spent in the community which enhances what is taught in classes by extending student learning beyond the classroom to personalize and humanize the bioethical issues."
>
> *– Quote from Fr. Peter Clark' syllabus*

Over the 30-year history of the course, students have

- developed training and recruitment videos
- researched the usefulness of treatment programs nationwide
- made recommendations for the adoption of new programs
- assessed the PSU campus climate to determine the need for new services
- created scientific literature reviews
- conducted community focus groups to better understand high school students' needs
- provided consulting groups with final reports detailing findings and recommendations.

four-year, required general education program – all involve cross-disciplinary collaborative teams in a community-based setting. Along with strategies for positive team participation and enhancing team performance, students learn how to analyze community agency needs around particular projects, organize meetings, develop project timelines, carry out tasks, and address group process. Through close supervision students improve their technical writing skills and group presentation skills.

In addition to STARS, Community Psychology Capstone students have engaged recently in similar service-learning efforts with local Women's Resource Centers, the Sexual Assault Resource Center, Tryon Community Farm, and the African Refugee Support Group. ■

Florida Southern students find innovative service applications for computer skills

Photo Courtesy of Florida Southern College

A t Florida Southern College in Lakeland, students can apply their Computer Science coursework and skills to engage in unique service-learning programs.

Students Alan George and Laura Quintana worked with faculty mentors Dr. Ken Anderson and Dr. Gwen Walton in the Summer 2007 research project "Explorations with Robotics Software" to develop software to control small robots. The students designed and developed educational modules that use robots and robotics applications to enhance the mathematics curriculum and help students understand object-oriented software development and a variety of mathematical concepts.

Project results were presented to a group of high school AP students at the College's FIAT LUX Undergraduate Research Symposium and, also, at the Florida Chapter Meeting of the Mathematics Association of America. The results of the students' work will enhance FSC's computer science and mathematics curricula and have potential applications in other areas of the curriculum. The effort was part of the FSC Student/Faculty Collaborative Research and Creative Activities Program.

Another of Dr. Walton's courses, "Database Analysis and Design," includes a major service-learning component involving design and implementation of a database to assist researchers in a non-profit organization. For the Fall 2007 project, students worked with Dr. Ernest Esteves, Director of the Center for Coastal Ecology at Sarasota's Mote Marine Laboratory.

The Laboratory houses records from the Bass Biological Laboratory, which operated on the west coast of Florida during the 1930s. Species Lists from the Bass data describe the fauna and flora of Lemon Bay and the Gulf of Mexico. The Lemon Bay is particularly important in terms of the diversity of marine life and terrestrial wildlife that inhabit the bay and its watershed. Indeed, Bass records may represent the most complete account of peninsular Florida's shallow-water biodiversity prior to World War II.

To meet the Laboratory's needs for an electronic system to store and support queries of the data, Walton's students designed and implemented a relational database, a data entry program with validation procedures, and full documentation including a user manual to explain how to use the data entry program and how to query the database.

Using photocopies of the original data, the students demonstrated their final product by entering data from a representative sample of the Bass records into the database system, validating the data input, and running sample queries. ∎

Service-learning in the sciences provides direct community benefits

M any Wesleyan University science classes have a laboratory component. For service-learning courses in the sciences, that laboratory component has a benefit to the community.

Service-learning opportunities integrated into courses throughout the sciences deepen students' understanding of the subject and fill community needs. The commitment ranges from two to three hours per week in a non-major Biology course to a complete environmental analysis in Earth & Environmental Sciences that requires more work than any two other courses.

The course Biology - Aging and the Elderly, for example, addresses the biological processes and mechanisms associated with normal aging and diseases more likely to affect the elderly. These diseases include arthritis, atherosclerosis, cancer, dementia, diabetes, and osteoporosis. To learn how these diseases affect quality of life of the elderly, students work with individuals at area senior centers assisted living residences and nursing homes. They reflect and report upon their interactions in the context of biological processes and quality of life issues.

Students in Wesleyan's Computer Science - Computer Programming course use their new proficiency to help not-for-profit organizations, which lack funds, to upgrade or individualize their software.

Earth & Environmental Sciences – Introduction to Geographic Information Systems (GIS) students recognize that local towns and community groups often need – but can't afford – GIS surveys. So they collaborate with local environmental and governmental groups to complete GIS projects, such as an analysis of which land areas need to be preserved as open space in order to enhance biological diversity. Results are presented through written reports, web pages, data repositories, and community meetings.

"When students learn that their analyses and reports will be used to inform a community decision, there's a more important reason than a grade to get the work right." – Suzanne O'Connell, Wesleyan University "There are career benefits as well. Service-learning science projects help students develop professional skills, can be included on

Photo Courtesy of Wesleyan University

a resume, and may even result in a job offer or reference for a job." ∎

Students and community meet on common ground of service-learning

In a partnership between Kansas State University and Flint Hills Job Corps, students are finding common ground.

Students in Dr. Laura Kanost's Advanced Spanish Conversation course are engaging in experiential learning about language and community as they connect with FHJC students.

Participants identify the goals for their collaboration during an initial session, then meet each week at a selected location in the community. The project varies each semester but always connects to four overarching objectives for participants:

- **learning from each other**
- **improving self-esteem**
- **deepening their roots in the Manhattan community**
- **having fun together**

During recent outings, students hiked the Konza prairie, bowled at the K-State Student Union, and enjoyed a picnic of homemade empanadas at the local zoo.

The program enables Kanost's students to accelerate their development of oral proficiency and gain confidence through real-life conversation with native speakers. For many, this is their first extended opportunity to use Spanish outside they classroom, and the thrill of this interaction inspires them to continue their studies and pursue future immersion experiences.

Job Corps participants who have struggled in conventional educational settings are empowered by the opportunity to use their expertise to help the K-State Spanish students.

Members of both groups enjoy the opportunities to improve their social skills, serve as positive peer role models, and become more integrated in the greater community.

The K-State students keep weekly journals to reflect on their progress, and a few weeks into the project, one student wrote, "Antes de este proyecto, no pensé en las culturas diferentes que están aquí, y no participé en las comunidades. Ahora, me doy cuenta que necesito extender mi perspectiva." ("Before this project, I didn't think about the different cultures that are here, and I didn't participate in the community. Now, I realize that I need to broaden my perspective.") ∎

"Antes de este proyecto, no pensé en las culturas diferentes que están aquí, y no participé en las comunidades. Ahora, me doy cuenta que necesito extender mi perspectiva." ("Before this project, I didn't think about the different cultures that are here, and I didn't participate in the community. Now, I realize that I need to broaden my perspective.")
– KSU Student

Photo Courtesy of Kansas State University

Business service-learning students help shape a city's economy

Seizing a unique opportunity to influence the future of their city, Azusa Pacific University students recently merged business course work with several real-world economic development research projects.

Photo Courtesy of Azusa Pacific University

APU is located in Azusa (CA), an area with an expanding manufacturing base. However, most retail firms had moved away, no commercial facilities had been built for more than 40 years, and the city's housing was considered inadequate.

During the past decade, local leaders addressed these issues by planning seven major real estate developments, including the overhaul of four major shopping areas and a new 1100-home development. But the city lacked tenants to fill the newly expanded retail space and turned to APU's School of Business for help.

Service-learning research projects to analyze the city's retail situation were set up within Applied Statistics and Marketing Research courses. Some classes were held at the Chamber of Commerce or City Hall or consisted of field trips to development sites. Analyzing residents' expenditure habits, students estimated that over $63 million retail dollars were being spent outside the city and that much of another $23 million spent by the university

community - students, staff and faculty – went to businesses outside Azusa.

Presenting their findings to the mayor, city council, city staff, and Chamber of Commerce members during a public meeting, students concluded that city leaders should target businesses that were underrepresented in the retail landscape including garden centers, full-service restaurants, and stores selling clothing, toys, books, offices supplies, pets, jewelry, and shoes.

Using the research results to show national retail firms that Azusa offered a largely untapped market, leaders were successful in recruiting numerous high quality retailers. – including Target, Fresh-n-Easy grocery, Jamba Juice and Panda Express.

"Through these projects," says Hutchinson, "students connected their classroom experience with real world experience and made an important contribution to the improvement of their local city." ∎

Sharing technology expertise enhances WIT students' educational experiences

Students at Wentworth Institute of Technology are changing the landscape of their Boston community – building bridges across the digital divide by sharing their technology expertise with local not-for-profits and the residents they serve. The incubator for these efforts is WIT's Center for Community & Learning Partnerships.

By creating programs which address community needs while enhancing the educational experience of Wentworth students, The Center centralizes community service, service-learning, and community outreach initiatives. The Center focuses on students' capabilities in technology, management, design and youth/family outreach to advance the school and community relationship, while providing students with hands-on learning experiences which benefit the community. According to the Center's Director Sean Bender, "This hands-on approach to service-learning adds a valuable dimension to the students' learning experience."

Among the school's diverse and extensive service activities, there are five key issue areas where critical community needs intersect with WIT's strengths as an institute of technology:

- Digital Divide: Computer & Information Technology
- Sustainable Development: Design/Build
- Social Enterprise & Management
- Adaptive & Green Technology: Engineering & Design
- College Access & Success

Wentworth's core capabilities have aligned with community interests in such programs as Camp Tech, launched in the early 1990s, which matched faculty and students with local residents to introduce youth to technology and technology-related fields. In Technology Goes Home, children and parents learned computer skills and earned a free computer, and the summer Youth@Art Tech program taught technology skills for art applications. And WIT students in database and software design courses provided specialized database development. All of these programs have led to new efforts in technology education and mentoring through WIT's support of youth and family service agencies and programs on campus and in the community.

With the establishment of the Center for Community & Learning Partnerships in 2003, Wentworth's commitment to issues of the digital divide has broadened and deepened. The Center's "Technology Team" tackles a broad range of technology issues. Composed of faculty, co-op, community work study, and student volunteers, the team primarily focuses on technology assessment, capacity building, program development, and research.

Bender explains, "Efforts have moved from a traditional notion of the digital divide as households without computers to focus increasingly on working with not-for-profit community organizations, public agencies, small businesses, and schools. While the Center and its technology team work in projects and partnerships on an intimate scale, the overall focus is on not simply bridging but eliminating the digital divide in our communities.

"As the Technology Team's experience and track record grows, so will the breadth and depth of its impact - in Boston and beyond." ■

For one Boston youth, Wentworth Institute of Technology service-learning programs have provided a steady progression of educational opportunities and fueled an interest in community service.

Elvin Diaz-Bock was introduced to technology at Wentworth's Camp Tech. That involvement led to his participation as a youth leader in the Technology Goes Home program. And he went on to become a student at Wentworth, on full scholarship through a program for local residents.

Now a Junior in Management at WIT, Elvin's leadership is stronger than ever. He plays key roles in the Center's Volunteer Income Tax Assistance program and in Students in Free Enterprise, an active group which engages in such diverse community learning projects as a market research study for a local business district and a Red Sox Sports Management program for area high school students. In addition, Elvin is currently a project manager with the Mission Hill Main Streets through the community co-op program.

"We believe that Elvin's story is a fantastic example of the intersection of service-learning and college access/success," says the Center's Director Sean Bender.

Service-learning inspires students to share the magic and power of art

Columbia College Chicago blends a huge range of arts programming with service-learning to give new perspective and inspiration to students.

The mission of Columbia College – one of the nation's largest arts, media and communications colleges – mandates active community involvement and empowers undergraduates to leave studio confines to explore how their artistic practice might transform society. In 1998 the school formalized its commitment to college and community by establishing the Center for Community Arts Partnerships.

CCAP's first initiative, Urban Missions, is a model for linking the college with community-based arts organizations to provide an array of programming in theater, film and television, fiction writing, audio arts and acoustics, graphic arts and design, dance, and music for youth in low-income urban communities. Through jointly-designed arts projects that draw on the unique strengths of both partners, Urban Missions has served over 5,000 Columbia College undergraduates and school-age youth from elementary through high school.

About six service-learning courses are collaboratively designed each year by college faculty and staff and artists from the organizations. Ideas are shared openly and across disciplines, and professors, artists, administrators and students are encouraged to learn from each other. When courses are approved, undergraduates receive training in how to work effectively with the organizations, and community youth are recruited to participate.

Key learning shared by Columbia College students and youth through Urban Missions includes:

- firsthand understanding of various art forms and how they are practiced professionally
- how to set challenging artistic goals and develop thoughtful plans to meet them
- how to use imagination to solve problems and create unique works of art
- appreciation of different cultures and their perspectives on life

CCAP Executive Director David Flatley explains, "Because of their immediacy and authenticity, service-learning experiences in the field are much more likely to have a deeper impact socially, emotionally, and cognitively." ■

Photos Courtesy of Columbia College Chicago

Art students' service-learning project helps refugees navigate their new home

Connecting art course learning with community service, SUNY College at Buffalo students made a significant contribution to members of their community and developed new awareness of the value of civic engagement.

Freshmen in the course Essentials of Visual Art who were also participants in a school learning community partnered with Journey's End Refugee Services – an organization supporting Somali refugees. The idea was born to create Life Activity Teaching Guides to help the refugees (who spoke little English) carry out everyday activities and acclimate to urban living.

The process began when instructor Phyllis I. Thompson, Ph.D., met with Volunteer and Service Learning staff to identify a need which could be addressed by a visual art class. Students visited Journey's End Refugee Services to visit with refugee families and learn about the conditions that contributed to Somalis fleeing their homeland.

The art class explored expressive forms of relief printmaking and bookmaking processes as powerful literacy and visual communication supports.

"I gained a better understanding of what these refugees have to endure when coming into America, and how American citizens can help them through it. I also learned about how important community service is in order to help many people in need."

Students decided the guides would use visual images with few words and cover such topics as bus travel, using laundromats, grocery shopping, and seasonal dress. Each team selected a topic and used direct drawing, printmaking, collage, bookmaking, photography, and computer software programs to complete its guide, which was critiqued and then presented to the organization.

Students' reflections reveal the meaning behind their service-learning experience. One explained, "I gained a better understanding of what these refugees have to endure when coming into America, and how American citizens can help them through it. I also learned about how important community service is in order to help many people in need." Another said, "I learned that I would really like to work with cultures and ethnic groups other than my own. I learned a lot about how to express ideas without using words." ■

Service-learning is relevant for students in engineering, business and music, too

University of Texas at Arlington students in disciplines as widely varied as engineering, business and music are practicing service-learning to meet a broad range of community needs.

The Mechanical and Aerospace Engineering Senior Capstone courses engage teams of 3 to 6 students, who select a project suggested by faculty or outside industries or agencies. The intent is to conceive, analyze, and design a product or system the first semester and to build or verify it the second semester. The teams operate as an engineering company and write a proposal, make several oral presentations to a client during the semester, write a final report, and give a formal oral presentation to the public at the end of the semester. In addition to the project activity, the weekly class meetings present subjects ranging from professionalism, ethics, organization and management, design procedures, patent law, product liability, finance, and other subjects of interest to their upcoming professional life.

Recent engineering service-learning projects include the design and fabrication of a large, automated swing for high school students with severe physical challenges, as well as the design and testing of electronic-assisted hearing protection devices, an electronic remotely-controlled bone extender for young people with deformed limbs, a bar to correct clubfoot in infants, and a neck brace for spine stabilization.

Photo Courtesy of University of Texas, Arlington

Students in business operations management classes help non-profits improve operational efficiency. For one organization struggling with attendance increases, in tandem with insufficient staff to provide transportation services and to deliver programs to the kids, students reviewed demand, capacity constraints and transportation needs to develop recommended changes. Their transportation study and data analysis enabled the organizations to obtain more than $125,000 in additional funding from the North Texas Tollway Authority.

Participants in UT Arlington's African/Brazilian Music Ensemble spend significant class time discussing the culture and customs of West Africa, especially Ghana. These musicians give six performances each year at area middle schools, local elementary schools, libraries, churches and clubs wearing traditional Ghanaian attire. Ten ensemble members also took part in a four-week, twenty-eight hours a week, service learning study abroad project in Ghana.

The Innocence Project of Texas is a consortium of independent projects from Texas Tech University, Texas Wesleyan, University of St. Thomas, University of Texas at Arlington, and the Southern Methodist University Dedman School of Law. The projects' student volunteers devote their time to investigating inmates' claims of actual innocence and to working toward freedom processes for the wrongfully-convicted who would otherwise become lost in the criminal justice system.

Students involved in the Innocence Project at UT Arlington study the law and procedure of exonerations, the reasons citizens are wrongfully convicted, and how to investigate claims. The students then put this education into practice by investigating claims of incarcerated inmates that have been wrongfully convicted. Within the past two years, the students have investigated cases involving murder, sexual assault, aggravated robbery, and sudden infant death. Currently, students are involved in the examination of pending requests for DNA testing in Dallas County. ■

Service transforms lives from the inside out

Kelly Dotson learned the joy of serving others as a freshman at Wartburg College (IA). Four years later, she and three friends began a year-long journey that would change their lives and intorduce others to the transforming experience of service.

Dotson's spring 2000 enrollment at Wartburg

Kelly Dotson reads to a child at a low-income after-school program in Los Angeles, one of 50 service projects she completed during a year of travel with Latreia, a group she helped found as a college senior.

coincided with her decision to get involved in Habitat for Humanity where she developed relationships with other volunteers and found working with Habitat families to be extremely rewarding.

"I began to understand for the first time what an impact I could make on others' lives, even as a college student," she says. "Service changes you from the inside out and teaches you to evaluate the world from a new lens, a lens with a greater worldview." Her Habitat experience led Dotson to other campus service activities in Haiti, Texas and Alaska.

Forty-five high school students from Nebraska traveled to Minnesota for one of six Urban Plunge experiences organized and hosted by Latreia in Minneapolis-St. Paul during the summer of 2007. Latreia employs college students to administer the trips alongside the founders.

On a trip during her senior year, Dotson and three other service trip veterans saw how the experience transformed the group's first-time participants and thought "Wouldn't it be cool if we could travel the United States and volunteer for one week in each of the 50 states?"

They mapped a 12-month itinerary including all 48 contiguous states, plus Prince Edward Island, Canada, and Imuris, Mexico, and incorporated an organization they named Latreia - a Greek word from the New Testament that describes service as an act of worship. By August, they raised enough money to begin a year of travel in a van the college sold Latreia for $1, and they continued to receive donations as they traveled from state to state, speaking in churches about their service. Their trip ended a year later with enough surplus funds to create a sustaining ministry, and Latreia settled in Minneapolis, MN.

Dotson is now the program director for Latreia, which partners with local nonprofits to provide year-round adult and youth volunteers. In addition, Latreia's Urban Plunge creates awareness about urban challenges and triumphs in Minneapolis, which has the largest U.S. population of four immigrant ethnic groups. ∎

Utah's Bryce Canyon is symbolic of the expanded horizons created by the founders of Latreia for themselves and others. After a year of travel and service throughout the United States, they established a permanent location in Minneapolis, Minn., where they help introduce others to the transforming experience of service. Latreia founders, clockwise from center, are Jesse Henkle, Stephanie Fisk, Kelly Dotson and Laura Nielsen.

Photo Courtesy of Wartburg College

Connecting with local youth teaches Wartburg student how to be a leader

Wartburg College (IA) student Jenny Breitbach believes that guiding youth is one of the most important types of leadership. Through her Interdisciplinary Studies class Leadership Theories and Practices and a project with the school's Community Builders program - which connects local youth, Wartburg students and members of the community - she learned how to do it.

She shares her thoughts about this experience:

Through Community Builders, we interacted with sixth graders. We learned how to be effective communicators, critical thinkers, rational teachers and problem-solvers with young people - all building blocks to becoming a good leader.

Communicating with young adolescents is much different than communicating with adults. We needed to put things in their terms and relate to their situations to know what to say and how to say it. It became clear through the communication back to me what the students were learning.

Critical thinking skills helped us analyze each situation to come up with the best plan possible. It was necessary to critically think about how we were going to tie a connection from the project to service-learning in such a way that the kids would relate. I discovered that I was learning how to analyze a situation and make good decisions.

Rational thinking was used to strategize lesson plans that were within reason for the kids to achieve. Analytical reasoning made me realize what we could and couldn't do with the kids.

We had to problem-solve as troubles arose - to evaluate the meeting, think on our feet and make decisions based on how things were going.

On the surface the program seems to help only the children, but Community Builders is not just education for the students. It is a program that offers opportunities for the leaders to learn too. I feel that now I am an effective leader for today's youth.

OH! The People I've Met

Photo Courtesy of Montclair State University

When I first began my service experience at Van Dyk Manor, a rehabilitation center and nursing home for older adults, I knew I wanted a career working with the elderly. I began my service assisting the physical therapy staff, and slowly began to understand the many challenges facing the elderly as they work to recover from various illnesses and accidents. This experience made it possible for me to learn on-site as well as in the classroom.

I became so comfortable with the residents, their families, and the staff at Van Dyk Manor that at the end of my semester-long service-learning experience I decided to do my internship there as well. Here are just a couple of stories about some of the residents I've met and the fascinating lives they've led.

"Mary" is a friendly 99 year old resident who loves to be around people. Don't let her age fool you though, she has no problem seeing or hearing, and although she can't walk on her own, she tries to be as independent as possible. Mary is an avid participant in activities including Bingo, weekly coffee gatherings, and religious services. As a child, Mary loved to dance. When she turned ten, her mother enrolled her in a dancing school in New York City. She was so passionate about dance that when she turned 15, she auditioned for a spot with the Radio City Rockettes. Mary said that to be a Rockette, dancers had to meet two requirements: they had to be 5 '5" tall and weigh 110 lbs. Mary got her dream job and for five years performed on stage at Radio City Music Hall as a Rockette. At the age of 20, she fell in love, got married and moved down south. At age 99, even though she can't walk unaided, she can still bend over and touch her toes!

"Frank" is 80 years old and one of the few male residents at Van Dyk Manor. Looking at him, you would never guess that he has met and worked with many well known people in his life. Frank graduated from New York University with a degree in journalism. His first job was in the mailroom at CBS studios in New York City where he was eventually promoted to copy boy. He was later promoted to assistant director to Don Hughet, the director of the TV show 60 Minutes. During his career, Frank traveled to various political conventions where he met Dan Rather, and suggested that Dan be the next host of 60 Minutes. After years of experience, Frank was promoted to Director and worked with CBS for 25 years. Although his career was very demanding, Frank found the time to go on a blind date with the woman who would later became his wife. Frank's wife visits daily and together they recall the many famous people he met while working at CBS Studios.

"Martha" is 88 years old and is sharp as a tack, but she cannot see, has trouble breathing, and cannot walk, bathe, dress, eat food or take medication without assistance. Although Martha complains a lot, it is primarily because she has to depend on others to do almost everything. Martha has regular visits from family and friends, keeps up with the news by listening to the radio, has a good relationship with the staff, and has recently become more involved in various activities. Martha began her career as a secretary in a local municipality and worked her way up to tax assessor, the position from which she eventually retired. Martha became a tax assessor at a time when women did not hold such positions, and I was amazed to learn that she was the first female tax assessor in her county. Martha was a pioneer of women's rights without even knowing it! She did not marry until she was in her 50s, and married a widower who was the tax assessor in a nearby town. At the time, municipal employees had to live in the town in which they worked. So, in order for them to wed, the governor of the state of New Jersey passed "the Love Bill", allowing an exception to the residency requirement so that Martha could keep her job when she moved into her husband's home.

Through these experiences, I realized that it was not just the work I did, but the people I met that made my job so interesting and rewarding. Taking a service-learning course was an amazing experience for me and it can be for you. ■

DukeEngage makes service-learning a worldwide endeavor

Because two Duke University students were in the right place with the right skills at the perfect time, New Orleans city officials met an important deadline to receive a $300 million grant for ongoing rebuilding and recovery efforts.

As part of a pilot program called DukeEngage, the students were helping companies assemble road damage reports to assist with repairs when they learned the city was scrambling to complete an application for FEMA funding. The students' knowledge of statistics and public policy and the critical thinking and writing skills they brought to the process were pivotal in helping the city receive funds to repair nearly 1500 miles of mostly neighborhood streets.

The North Carolina university's newest co-curricular program for undergraduates, DukeEngage – announced in 2007 - enables students to translate knowledge into service to society in unprecedented numbers and ways. Under the auspices of the new Duke Center for Civic Engagement and funded by a $15 million grant each from the Duke Endowment and the Bill & Melinda Gates Foundation, DukeEngage is already changing lives both on-campus and off.

> "While many forms of civic engagement can further a student's educational goals, we've learned that the most robust learning occurs when students are immersed in their field work for a sustained period."
>
> *- Eric Mlyn, Ph.D., Director of the Duke Center for Civic Engagement*

DukeEngage funds undergraduates in meaningful civic engagement projects. Some 360 Duke undergraduates planned to tackle various endeavors during summer 2008, nearly 300 of them outside the United States - which dovetails well with one of Duke's other strategic initiatives for the increased internationalization of all parts of the university and undergraduate curriculum.

Eric Mlyn, Ph.D., Director of the Duke Center for Civic Engagement, explains, "While many forms of civic engagement can further a student's educational goals, we've learned that the most robust learning occurs when students are immersed in their field work for a sustained period; thus DukeEngage experiences last at least eight weeks."

Students can get involved in a faculty-led program, work with a partner agency identified by DukeEngage, or customize their own individual projects. Fully-funded by DukeEngage, the experience is comparable to an internship and doesn't award academic credit.

Faculty and staff with deep connections to communities around the world have built most of the 20 international programs for students in 2008. Under their guidance, students will pursue such projects as:

Photo Courtesy of Duke University

- **Working with children of migrant workers who have moved from rural areas in China to Beijing**

- **Training staff in partner hospitals in Northern Tanzania to use idled equiment and interviewing them to learn their healthcare technology needs**

- **Installing clean-burning stoves and ceramic water filtration systems in a village in Peru**

- **Serving as social entrepreneurial consultants for businesses and nonprofits in Antigua, Guatemala**

- **Assisting African refugees who have been relocated to Dublin, Ireland**

"Students at Duke who wish to become involved with DukeEngage, hear this charge: 'Challenge yourself. Change your world.' The possibilities, for us and for our students, are nearly limitless." *- Mlyn*

Photo Courtesy of Duke University

The program doesn't overlook neighbors closer to home. "Our largest DukeEngage program in the summer of 2008," explains Mlyn, "will be focused in neighborhoods in Durham, North Carolina, with more than 40 students invested in civic engagement initiatives not far from campus. We also are sending students back to New Orleans to continue the rebuilding efforts and are establishing new programs with NGOs in Seattle and on immigration issues in Tucson."

All students who receive DukeEngage funding participate in workshops to prepare for the cultural differences they will encounter as they explore the world and the ethical issues they will no doubt face as they attempt to serve communities with respect and mutuality. And all DukeEngage programs—whether individual projects or group endeavors—must focus on needs that come from the communities themselves.

"Never before has there been this kind of opportunity to make an immediate and indelible impact throughout the world, and few institutions have the capacity to implement or manage such broad-based efforts," says Mlyn. "This makes Duke distinctive and a leader in civic engagement both nationally and internationally.

"Students at Duke who wish to become involved with DukeEngage, hear this charge: 'Challenge yourself. Change your world.' The possibilities, for us and for our students, are nearly limitless." ■

Thank you
to all the institutions who helped fund our
National Free Book Distribution program!

Look for us!

This blue box tells you that this Contributing Institution is featured with a Full-page College Profile!

Get an in-depth look at service-learning at these colleges and universities across the nation and Canada!

Many selected institutions submitted contributions to help further educate students, parents, and mentors on the role college service-learning opportunities play in improving student academic, personal, and career and leadership development. Because of their generous donations, many libraries, schools, and community organizations have been able to provide students access to this valuable resource.

About the program

From the conception of this program, our goal has been to provide college resources for all strata of the college-bound community. To do this, we partnered with many institutions around the country, and worked with various sources including Learn & Serve America to distribute 50,000 copies of the book to selected community organizations. The success of this program is due to the generosity of all those involved, and we sincerely thank you.

GUIDE TO

Service-Learning

COLLEGES & UNIVERSITIES

Directory

Directory

Criteria for inclusion

The colleges and universities profiled here do not reflect each and every—or the only—schools that integrate service-learning as a hands-on learning opportunity into their courses. Still, the colleges and universities that are included exemplify the many schools committed to service-learning, civic engagement, and community-based research in order to enhance the academic experience. The schools in this section are profiled in light of the programs and opportunities they present for students of all academic areas.

The blue box designates colleges with a separate page profile due to their generous contributions to our national free book distribution program to low-income schools, libraries, and community organizations.

Colleges were nominated or referred by numerous organizations and persons that work closely with colleges and universities to develop these programs. This included a national independent advisory board comprised of leaders within the service-learning landscape in government organizations and private and public colleges and universities. Colleges themselves were also able to submit self-nominations and asked to give details on their focus and commitment with service-learning, as well as the breadth and depth of opportunities they offer. These nominations were reviewed by the Beyond the Books staff and its advisory board to determine inclusion. Participating colleges confirmed their selection with Beyond the Books, and helped to develop their profiles, listings, and feature articles within the Guide.

ALABAMA

Alabama State University

PROFILE PAGE 174

http://www.alasu.edu
Four Year, Public, Urban, Founded in 1857
Affiliation: Historically Black College and University, Nondenominational
Student Profile: Undergraduate students (40.3% male, 59.7% female); 40 states and territories, 10 countries; 2% minority, 3% international.
Faculty Profile: 239 full-time faculty. 65% hold a terminal degree in their field. 15:1 student/faculty ratio. Average class size is 25.
Cost and Aid: 2007–2008: $11,968 comprehensive. 94% of students receive financial aid.
Admissions
admissions@alasu.edu
Service-Learning
Pamela Gay, Ph.D.Chair,
Standing Committee on Service-Learning
Phone: 334-229-5618
pgay@alasu.edu
Douglas Strout, Ph.D.
Standing Committee on Service-Learning
Phone: 334-229-4718
dstrout@alasu.edu

Birmingham-Southern College

PROFILE PAGE 175

http://www.bsc.edu
Four Year, Public, Founded in 1856
Affiliation: United Methodist
Student Profile: 1,339 undergraduate students; 29 states and territories, 8 countries.
Faculty Profile: 109 full-time faculty; 96% hold a terminal degree in their field. 12:1 student/faculty ratio. Average class size is 17.
Costs and Aid: 2007–2008: $33,000 (approximate) comprehensive ($23,600 tuition). 98% of students receive financial aid.
Admissions
Phone: 205-226-4696 or 800-523-5793
admitme@bsc.edu
Service-Learning
Bunting Center for Engaged Study and
  Community Action
Kristin Harper, Director
Phone: 205-226-4720
kharper@bsc.edu

Gadsden State Community College

http://www.gadsdenstate.edu
Two Year, Public, Founded in 1985
Student Profile: 2,437 part-time undergraduate

students and 3,080 full-time students (44.7% male, 55.3 % female); 17 states and territories, 58 countries; 26.5% minority.
Faculty Profile: 146 full-time faculty. Average class size is 30.
Costs and Aid: 2007-2008: $8,624 in-state comprehensive; $10,754 out-of-state comprehensive; $90 per semester hour in-state; $161 per hour out-of-state tuition. 56.3% of students receive financial aid.
Admissions
P.O. Box 227
1001 George Wallace Drive
Gadsden, AL 35902
Phone: 256-549-8259
Service-Learning
Center for Civic Engagement and Service
Beryl Odom, Coordinator
Phone: 256-549-8386
bodom@gadsdenstate.edu

Spring Hill College

PROFILE PAGE 176

http://www.shc.edu
Four Year, Private, Suburban, Founded in 1830
Affiliation: Catholic
Student Profile: 1,100 undergraduate students (34% male, 66% female); 23 states and territories, 3 countries; 31 % minority.
Faculty Profile: 84 full-time faculty; 14:1 student/faculty ratio. Average class size is 23.
Costs and Aid: 2007–2008: $ 23,100 comprehensive ($21,686 tuition). 90% of students receive financial aid.
Admissions
Phone: 251-380-3030, or 866-362-3645
admit@shc.edu
Service-Learning
Albert S. Foley, S.J. Community Service Center
Kathleen Orange, Director
Phone: 251-380-3499
orange@shc.edu or foleycenter@shc.edu2

ALASKA

University of Alaska Anchorage

http://www.uaa.alaska.edu
Four Year, Public, Urban, Founded in 1954
Student Profile: 16,547 undergraduate students (40% male, 60% female); 50 states and territories, 41 countries; 33% minority, 2% international.
Faculty Profile: 575 full-time faculty. 17:1 student/faculty ratio. Average class size is 21.
Costs and Aid: 2007-2008: $11,570 in-state comprehensive ($3,840 tuition); $20,540 out-of-state comprehensive ($12,810 tuition).
Admissions
Phone: 907-786-1480
enroll@uaa.alaska.edu
Service-Learning
Center for Community Engagement & Learning
Nancy Andes, Professor and Director
Phone: 907-786-4062
engage@uaa.alaska.edu

ARIZONA

Arizona State University

PROFILE PAGE 177

http://www.asu.edu
Four Year, Public, Urban, Founded in 1885
Student Profile: 38,984 undergraduate students (49% male, 51% female); 36% out-of-state.
Faculty Profile: 1,778 full-time faculty. 23:1 student/faculty ratio. Most frequent class size is 20-29.
Costs and Aid: 2007-2008: $5,063 in-state tuition; $17,697 out-of-state.
Admissions
Phone: 480-965-7788
Service-Learning
Service-Learning Programs
Phone: 480-727-6382
servicelearning@asu.edu
Deborah Ball, Director
Phone: 480-965-8092
Deborah.Ball@asu.edu

Chandler-Gilbert Community College

http://www.cgc.maricopa.edu
Two Year, Public, Suburban, Founded in 1992
Student Profile: 9,420 undergraduate students (43% male, 54% female); 16 states and territories; 26% minority, 1% international.
Faculty Profile: 251 full-time faculty. 18.5:1 student/faculty ratio. Average class size is 22.
Costs and Aid: 2007-2008: $65 per credit in-county/state tuition; $90 per credit out-of-county/state tuition. 22% of students receive financial aid.
Admissions
2626 E. Pecos Road
Chandler, AZ 85225-2499
Phone: 480-732-7000
Service-Learning
Mike Greene
mike.greene@cgcmail.maricopa.edu

Mesa Community College

http://www.mc.maricopa.edu
Two Year, Public, Suburban, Founded in 1963
Student Profile: 25,000 undergraduate students (46% male, 54% female); 50 states and territories, 100 countries; 30% minority, 1% international.
Faculty Profile: 350 full-time faculty. Average class size is 30.
Costs and Aid: 2007-2008: $1,560 yearly tuition. 27% of students receive federal financial aid.
Admissions
1833 W. Southern Avenue
Mesa, AZ 85202
Phone: 480-461-7000
Service-Learning
Phone:480-461-7393

Directory

CALIFORNIA

American Jewish University

PROFILE PAGE 178

http://www.ajula.edu
Four Year, Private, Suburban
Affiliation: Jewish
Student Profile: 115 undergraduate students (45% male, 55% female); 25 states and territories, 5 countries; 6% minority, 5% international.
Faculty Profile: 15 full-time faculty; 100% hold a terminal degree in their field. 7:1 student/faculty ratio. Average class size is 6 - 8.
Costs and Aid: 2007–2008: $33,568 comprehensive ($21,408 tuition). 80% of students receive financial aid.
Admissions
Phone: 310-440-1247
admissions@ajula.edu
Service-Learning
Sid B. Levine Service Learning Program

Azusa Pacific University

PROFILE PAGE 179

http://www.apu.edu
Four Year, Private, Suburban
Affiliation: Christian (Nondenominational)
Student Profile: 4,027 traditional undergraduate students; 61% women and 39% men; 24% minority; 49 states; 72 countries.
Faculty Profile: 376 full-time faculty; 73% hold terminal degrees; 15:1 student/faculty ratio.
Costs and Aid: 2008-2009 $33,398 comprehensive ($12,920 semester tuition); 89% of students receive
Admissions
Phone: 626-812-3016 or 1-800-TALK-APU
admissions@apu.edu
Service-Learning
Center for Academic Service-Learning and Research
Judy Hutchinson, Ph.D. Director
Phone: 626-815-6000 Ext: 2823
jhutchinson@apu.edu

California State Polytechnic University, Pomona

PROFILE PAGE 180

http://www.csupomona.edu
Four Year, Public, Urban, Founded in 1938
Student Profile: 19,615 undergraduate students (56% male, 44% female); 2% states and territories, 60% minority, 6% international.
Faculty Profile: 603 full-time faculty; 75% hold a terminal degree in their field. 22.5:1 student/faculty ratio. Average class size is 26.
Costs and Aid: 2007–2008: $16,194 comprehensive ($3,288 tuition). 76% of students receive financial aid.
Admissions
Phone: 909-869-3210
Service-Learning
Center for Community Service-Learning
Phone: 909-869-4269

California College of the Arts

http://www.cca.edu
Four Year, Private, Urban, Founded in 1907
Student Profile: 1,360 undergraduate students, 310 graduate students (41% male, 59% female); 7% international, 35% out of state.
Faculty Profile: 3.7:1 student/faculty ratio.
Costs and Aid: 2007-2008 $35,970 comprehensive ($29,280 tuition). 76% of students receive financial aid.
Admissions
Phone: 1-800-447-1ART
enroll@cca.edu
Service-Learning
Art In Education Teaching Institute
Center For Art & Public Life
Ann Wettrich
Phone: 510-594-3769
AWettrich@cca.edu

California State University, Channel Islands

PROFILE PAGE 181

http://www.csuci.edu
Four Year, Public, Suburban
Student Profile: 3,123 undergraduate students (37.7% male, 62.3% female).
Faculty Profile: 82 full-time faculty, 200 full and part-time lecturers (100% hold a terminal degree in their field); average class size is 18.5.
Costs and Aid: 2007–2008: $22,000 (tuition); 98% of students receive financial aid, including scholarships, grants and loans; average financial award is $17,500.
Admissions
Phone: 805-437-8500
admissions@csuci.edu
Service-Learning

Center for Community Engagement
Pilar Pacheco, M.A., Assistant Director
Phone: 805-437-8851
pilar.pacheco@csuci.edu

California State University, Chico

PROFILE PAGE 182

http://www.csuchico.edu
Four Year, Public, Suburban, Founded in 1887
Student Profile: 15,527 undergraduate students (47% male, 53% female); 47 states and territories, 51 countries; 22.2 % minority, 4.3% are out-of-state or international.
Faculty Profile: 555 full-time faculty. 80% hold a terminal degree in their field. 22:1 student/faculty ratio. Average class size is 27.
Costs and Aid: 2007-2008: $3,690 in-state comprehensive ($1,845 tuition). Non-resident tuition $399 per unit, in addition to fees.
Admissions
Phone: 800-542-4426 or 530-898-4428
INFO@csuchico.edu
Service-Learning
Office of Civic Engagement
Deanna Berg, Director of Civic Engagement
Phone: 530-898-5486
dberg@csuchico.edu

California State University, Fresno

PROFILE PAGE 183

http://www.csufresno.edu
Four Year, Public, Founded in 1911
Student Profile: 18,951 undergraduate students, (59.3% women, 40.7% men); 2,177 graduate students; 970 post-baccalaureate; 56% minority; 29 countries.
Faculty Profile: 710 full-time faculty. Average class size is 20-29.
Costs and Aid: 2007-2008: $3,298 per academic year; 57% of students receive some form of institutional, need-based financial aid.
Admissions
Phone: 559-278-2261
Service-Learning
Jan and Bud Richter Center for Community Engagement and Service-Learning
Mr. Chris Fiorentino, Director
Phone: 559-278-7079
chrisf@csufresno.edu

California State University, Fullerton

PROFILE PAGE 184

http://www.fullerton.edu/CISL
Four Year, Public, Urban, Founded in 1957
Student Profile: 30,606 undergraduate students (42% male, 58% female); 64.6% minority, 3.7% international.
Faculty Profile: 881 full-time faculty; 76% hold a terminal degree in their field. 22.26 student/faculty ratio. Average class size is 30.2.
Costs and Aid: 2007–2008: $1,651 in-state comprehensive ($1,306-1,707 tuition). 43% of students receive financial aid.
Admissions
Phone: 714-278-2011
admissions@fullerton.edu
Service-Learning
Center for Internships & Community Engagement
Jeannie Kim-Han, Director
800 N. State College Blvd., LH 209
Fullerton, CA 92831
Phone: 714-278-3746

California State University, Long Beach

http://www.csulb.edu
Four Year, Public, Urban, Founded in 1949
Student Profile: 36,868 undergraduate students (39.6% male, 60.4% female); 48 states and territories, 103 foreign countries; 63% minority, 3.4% international.
Faculty Profile: 1,033 full-time faculty. 20:1 student/faculty ratio. Average class size is 30.
Costs and Aid: 2007-2008: $11,334 in-state comprehensive ($3,394 tuition); $19,470 out-of-state comprehensive ($11,530 tuition). 50% of undergraduate students receive financial aid (49% of all students).
Admissions
1250 Bellflower Boulevard
Long Beach CA 90840
Phone: 562-985-5471
Service-Learning
Center for Community Engagement
Phone: 562-985-7131
cce@csulb.edu

California State University, Monterey Bay

PROFILE PAGE 185

http://www.csumb.edu
Four Year, Public, Founded in 1924
Student Profile: 3,864 undergraduate students (43% male, 57% female; 95% in-state; 3% out-of-state; 2% international)
Faculty Profile: 323 faculty (includes lecturers); 21:1 student/faculty ratio. Average class size is 25.
Costs and Aid: 2007–2008: $10,175 in-state comprehensive ($3,055 tuition); $20,345 out-of-state comprehensive ($10,170 tuition). 90% of students

receive some financial aid.
Admissions
Phone: 831-582-3738
admissions@csumb.edu
Service-Learning
Service Learning Institute
Phone: 831-582-3644
service_learning@csumb.edu

California State University, San Bernardino

PROFILE PAGE 186

http://www.csusb.edu
Four Year, Public, Urban, Founded in 1965
Student Profile: 13,311 undergraduate students (35% male, 65% female), 68% minority, 2% international. 88% of students are from either San Bernardino or Riverside counties in California.
Faculty Profile: 467 full-time faculty. 23:1 student/faculty ratio.
Costs and Aid: 2007-2008: $3,452.50 in-state comprehensive, $11,588 out-of-state comprehensive. 73% of students receive financial aid.
Admissions
Phone: 909-537-5188
Service-Learning
Community-University Partnerships
Diane Podolske, Ph.D., Director
Phone: 909-537-7483

California State University, San Marcos

PROFILE PAGE 187

http://www.csusm.edu
Four-Year, Public, Suburban, Founded in 1988
Student Profile: 9,159 undergraduate students (37% male, 63% female); 38% minority, 2.7% international.
Faculty Profile: 230 full-time faculty; 99.9% hold a terminal degree in their field. 1:26.5 student/faculty ratio. Average class size is 30.7.
Costs and Aid: $17,630 in-state comprehensive, $27,820 out-of-state comprehensive; 49% of students receive financial aid. Average award is $7,400.
Admissions
Phone: 760-750-4848
apply@csusm.edu
Service-Learning
Office of Community Service Learning
Darci L. Strother, Ph.D. Director
Phone: 760-750-4160
strother@csusm.edu

College of the Canyons

http://www.canyons.edu
Two Year, Public, Suburban, Founded in 1969
Student Profile: 19,115 undergraduate students (58.7% male, 41.3% female); 50% minority, 06% international.
Faculty Profile: 183 full-time faculty. 27:1 student/faculty ratio. Average class size is 25.
Costs and Aid: 2007–2008: 22% of students receive financial aid.
Admissions
26455 Rockwell Canyon Road,
Santa Clarita, CA 91355
Service-Learning
Service-Learning Center
Dr. Jennifer Hauss
Phone: 661-362-3422

Humboldt State University

http://www.humboldt.edu
Four Year, Public, Rural, Founded in 1913
Student Profile: 7,500 undergraduate students (45% male, 55% female).
Faculty Profile: 381 full-time faculty. 18:1 student/faculty ratio. Average class size is 24.
Costs and Aid: 2007-2008: $3,840 in-state tuition, $11,979 out-of-state tuition.
Admissions
1 Harpst St.
Arcata, CA 95521
Phone: 866-850-9556
Service-Learning
Annie Bolick-Floss
Phone: 707-826-4965
amb2@humboldt.edu

Los Angeles Valley College

http://www.lavc.edu
Community College, Public, Suburban, Founded 1949
Student Profile: 16,736 undergraduate students (40% male, 60% female); 66% minority, 1% international.
Faculty Profile: 500 full-time faculty. 33:1 student/faculty ratio. Average class size is 35.
Costs and Aid: 2007-2008: $480 in-state tuition; $4,824 out-of-state; $5,064 out-of-country tuition. 39% of students receive financial aid.
Admissions
5800 Fulton Ave.
Valley Glen, CA 91401
Phone: 818- 947-2600
Service-Learning
Los Angeles Valley Service Learning Program
Richard Brossman
Phone: 818-947-2642

Occidental College

http://www.oxy.edu
Four Year, Private, Urban, Founded in 1887
Student Profile: 1,877 undergraduate students (44% male, 56% female); 45 states and territories, 22 countries; 36.1% minority, 2.1% international.
Faculty Profile: 156 full-time faculty. 10:1 student/faculty ratio. Average class size is 21.
Costs and Aid: 2007-2008: $44,873 comprehensive. 81% of students receive financial aid.
Admissions
600 Campus Rd.

Los Angeles, CA 90041
Phone: 323-259-2904
Service-Learning
Center for Community Based Learning
Maria Avila
Phone: 323-259-2904
mavila@oxy.edu

Saint Mary's College of California
http://www.stmarys-ca.edu
Four Year, Private, Suburban, Founded in 1863
Affiliation: Christian Brothers
Student Profile: 2,489 undergraduate students (36% male, 64% female); 44.1% minority, 1% international.
Faculty Profile: 193 full-time faculty. 14:1 student/faculty ratio. Average class size is 20.
Costs and Aid: 2007-2008: 39,616 comprehensive ($29,050 tuition). 73 % of students receive financial aid (20% of the College's FWS is dedicated to community service engagement.)
Admissions
1928 St. Mary's Road
Moraga, CA 94556
Phone: 925-631-4000
Service-Learning
Catholic Institute for Lasallian Social Action (CILSA)
Phone: 925-631-4975

Santa Clara University
http://www.scu.edu
Four Year, Private, Suburban, Founded in 1851
Affiliation: Jesuit
Student Profile: 5,038 undergraduate students (44% male, 56% female); 36 % minority, 2.8% international.
Faculty Profile: 488 full-time faculty. 12:1 student/faculty ratio. Average class size is 24.
Costs and Aid: 2007–2008: $43,500 comprehensive ($33,000 tuition). 71 % of students receive financial aid.
Admissions
500 El Camino Real,
Santa Clara, CA 95053
Phone: 408-554-4000
Service-Learning
Ignatian Center for Jesuit Education/Arrupe Partnerships for Community-based Learning
Phone: 408-554-6917
arrupe@scu.edu

University of California, Berkeley
http://www.berkeley.edu
Four Year, Public, Urban, Founded in 1868
Student Profile: 24,636 undergraduate students (46% male, 54% female); 85% in-state, 15% out-of-state; 100 countries represented; 58% minority (includes 42% Asian American/Pacific Islander), 3% international.
Faculty Profile: 1,723 full-time faculty. 15.3:1 student/faculty ratio.
Costs and Aid: 2007-2008: $25,308 in-state comprehensive ($8384 tuition); $44,928 out-of-state comprehensive ($19,620 tuition & fees). 49% of students receive financial aid.
Admissions
110 Sproul Hall #5800
Berkeley, CA 94720-5800

Phone: 510-642-3175
Service-Learning
Cal Corps Public Service Center
505 Eshleman Hall #4550
Megan Voorhees, Director
Phone: 510-642-3916
ccorps@berkeley.edu

University of Redlands

PROFILE PAGE 188

http://www.redlands.edu
Four Year, Private, Town, Founded in 1907
Student Profile: 2,400 undergraduate students (45% male, 55% female); 45 states represented with 61% from California.
Faculty Profile: 163 full-time faculty; 11:1 student/faculty ratio.
Costs and Aid: 85% of students at Redlands receive financial aid with the average package at $19,000. Full comprehensive tuition runs just under $42,000.
Admissions
Phone: 800-455-5064 or 909-748-8074
Service-Learning
Office of Community Service Learning
Tony Mueller, Director
Phone: 909-748-8288

Westmont College

PROFILE PAGE 189

http://www.westmont.edu
Four Year, Private
Student Profile: 1,336 undergraduate students (61% female, 39% male); 24% minority; 41 states; 8 countries.
Faculty Profile: 93 full-time faculty, 89% hold terminal degrees; 12:1 student/faculty ratio.
Costs and Aid: 2008-2009: $32,150 annual tuition; 85% of students receive financial aid.
Admissions
Phone: 800-777-9011
admissions@westmont.edu
Service-Learning
Ray Rosentrater, Ph.D.Professor of Mathematics
Phone: 805-565-6185
rosentr@westmont.edu

Whittier College

PROFILE PAGE 190

http://www.whittier.edu
Four Year, Private, Suburban, Founded in 1887
Affiliation: Formerly Quaker
Student Profile: Undergraduate students (44% male,

56% female); 40 states and territories, 25 countries; 43% minority, 5% international.
Faculty Profile: 88 full-time faculty. 12:1 student/faculty ratio. Average class size is 19.
Costs and Aid: 2007-2008: $38,480 comprehensive ($29,860 tuition). 87% of students receive financial aid.
Admissions
Phone: 562-907-4238
admission@whittier.edu
Service-Learning
Sally Cardenas, Director of Internships and Community-Based Learning
Phone: 562-464-4533
scardenas@whittier.edu

COLORADO

Colorado State University

PROFILE PAGE 191

http://www.colostate.edu
Four Year, Public, Suburban, Founded in 1870
Student Profile: 24,670 undergraduate students (48% male, 52% female). 20% out-of-state (sister-states: California, Texas, Illinois, Minnesota & Alaska), 1,200 foreign students from 90 countries; 12.6% minority.
Faculty Profile: 1,400 full-time faculty. 99% hold a terminal degree in their field. 18:1 student/faculty ratio. Average class size is 46 students; average class size in science labs: 22 students.
Costs and Aid: 2007–2008: $13,288 in-state comprehensive ($5,388 tuition).
Admissions
Phone: 970-491-6909
admissions@colostate.edu
Service-Learning
The Institute for Learning and Teaching
Clayton Hurd, Director of Service-Learning
Phone: 970-491-2032
clayton.hurd@colostate.edu

Fort Lewis College

PROFILE PAGE 192

http://www.fortlewis.edu
Four Year, Public, Rural, Founded in 1911
Student Profile: 53% male, 47% female; 48 states and territories, 10 countries; 34% minority.
Faculty Profile: 240 faculty members (including part-time); 18:1 student/faculty ratio. Average class size is 25.
Costs and Aid: 2007–2008: $14,063 in-state comprehensive ($2,648 tuition). $22,593 out of state comprehensive ($13,848 tuition). 43% of students receive financial aid, and Native American students receive a tuition waiver.
Admissions

Phone: 877-FLC-COLO
admission@fortlewis.edu
Service-Learning
Center for Civic Engagement
Kalin Grigg, Director
grigg_k@fortlewis.edu
Phone: 970-247-7641

Regis University

PROFILE PAGE 193

http://www.regis.edu
Four Year, Private, Urban, Founded in 1877
Affiliation: Catholic Jesuit
Student Profile: 1,670 undergraduate students (46% male, 54% female); 41 states and territories; 24% minority, 1.3% international.
Faculty Profile: 93 full-time faculty. 92% hold a terminal degree in their field. 14:1 student/faculty ratio. Average class size is 20 students or less.
Costs and Aid: 2007–2008: $37,682 comprehensive ($28,700 tuition). 90% of students receive financial aid, 60% of which is need-based.
Admissions
Phone: 800-388-2366 Ext: 4900
regisadm@regis.edu
Service-Learning
Ignatian Collaborative for Service & Justice Center for Service & Community-Based Learning
Melissa Nix, M.A., Coordinator of Curriculum & Intercultural Programming
Phone: 303-458-4217

University of Colorado-Boulder

PROFILE PAGE 194

http://www.colorado.edu
Four Year, Public, Urban, Founded in 1876
Student Profile: 25,495 undergraduate students (53% male, 47% female); 14% minority, 4% international. 32% out of state.
Faculty Profile: 1177 full-time faculty. 71% phds. 16:1 student/faculty ratio. Average class size is 20-29.
Costs and Aid: 2007–2008: $5,418 tuition. $23,580 out of state.
Admissions
Phone: 303-492-6301
Service-Learning
Martin Bickman, Director
Phone: 303-492-8945
SERVICEL@colorado.edu

University of Denver

PROFILE PAGE 195

http://www.du.edu
Four Year, Private, Urban, Founded in 1864
Student Profile: 5,311 undergraduate students (45% male, 55% female).
Faculty Profile: 500 full-time faculty. 93% hold either doctoral or the highest degree appropriate to their discipline. 10:1 student/faculty ratio. Average class size is 20 students.
Costs and Aid: 2007–2008: $40,929 comprehensive ($31,428 tuition). 77% of students receive financial aid.
Admissions
Phone: 800-525-9495
admission@du.edu
Service-Learning
Center for Community Engagement & Service-Learning
Phone: 303-871-3706
engage@du.edu

CONNECTICUT

Eastern Connecticut State University

PROFILE PAGE 196

http://www.easternct.edu
Four Year, Public, Rural, Founded in 1889
Student Profile: 4,826 undergraduate students (45% male, 55% female); 26 states and territories, 34 countries; 16% minority, 3% international.
Faculty Profile: 71% full-time faculty. 95% hold a terminal degree in their field. 16:1 student/faculty ratio. Average class size is 24.
Costs and Aid: 2007-2008: $16,641 in-state comprehensive ($3,346 tuition). $24,126 out-of-state comprehensive ($10,831 tuition). 81% of students receive financial aid.
Admissions
Phone: 860-465-5286
admissions@easternct.edu
Service-Learning
Center for Educational Excellence
Phone: 860-465-4567
dubinad@easternct.edu

Fairfield University

PROFILE PAGE 197

http://www.fairfield.edu
Four Year, Private, Urban, Founded in 1942
Affiliation: Jesuit, Catholic
Student Profile: Undergraduate students (42% male,

58% female); 26 states and territories, 17 countries; 13% minority, 1% international.
Faculty Profile: 239 full-time faculty. 94% hold a terminal degree in their field. 13:1 student/faculty ratio.
Costs and Aid: 2007–2008: $ 44,000 comprehensive ($33,340 tuition). 67% of students receive financial aid.
Admissions
Phone: 203-254-4100
admis@mail.fairfield.edu
Service-Learning
Melissa Quan, Coordinator for Service Learning
Phone: 203-254-4000 Ext: 3455
mquan@mail.fairfield.edu

Quinnipiac University

PROFILE PAGE 198

http://www.quinnipiac.edu
Four Year, Private, Suburban, Founded in 1929
Student Profile: 5,400 undergraduate students (61% male, 39% female); 25 states and territories, 8 countries; 11% minority. In all, 80% of freshmen come from outside of Connecticut and 95% of all freshmen live on campus.
Faculty Profile: 290 full-time faculty, 85% hold a terminal degree in their field. 15:1 student/faculty ratio. Average class size is 22.
Costs and Aid: 2007–2008: $39,200 comprehensive ($28,720 tuition and fees). 70% of students receive financial aid.
Admissions
Phone: 203-582-8600 or 1-800-462-1944
admissions@quinnipiac.edu
Service-Learning
Professor Gregory P. Garvey,
Phone: 203-582-8389
greg.garvey@quinnipiac.edu

Sacred Heart University

PROFILE PAGE 199

http://www.sacredheart.edu
Four Year, Private, Town, Founded in 1963
Student Profile: 3,500 undergraduate students (40% male, 60% female); 31 states and territories, 42 countries; 15% minority, 68% out of state.
Faculty Profile: 189 full-time faculty. 76% hold a terminal degree in their field. 13:1 student/faculty ratio. Average class size is 22.
Costs and Aid: 2006–2007: $25,400 tuition; 66% of students receive financial aid. Average award is $16,025.
Admissions
Phone: 203-371-7880
enroll@sacredheart.edu
Service-Learning
Office of Service-Learning and Volunteer Programs
Phyllis Machledt, Director
Phone: 203-365-7622
machledtp@sacredheart.edu

Trinity College

http://www.trincoll.edu
Four Year, Private, Urban, Founded in 1823
Student Profile: Undergraduate students (51% male, 49% female); 45 states and territories, 24 countries; 21% minority, 3% international.
Faculty Profile: 172 full-time faculty. 11:1 student/faculty ratio. Average class size is 20.
Costs and Aid: 2007-2008: $53,950 comprehensive ($35,110 tuition). 42 % of students receive financial aid
Admissions
300 Summit St.
Hartford CT 06106
Phone: 860-297-4275
Service-Learning
Community Learning Initiative
Elinor Jacobson
elinor.jacobson@trincoll.edu

University of New Haven

PROFILE
PAGE
200

http://www.newhaven.edu
Four Year, Private, Suburban, Founded in 1920
Student Profile: 3,011 undergraduate students (51.9% male, 48.1% female); 40.4% of students are out-of-state; 20.2% minority, 1.8% international.
Faculty Profile: 182 full-time faculty, 80% of whom have a doctoral or other terminal degree in their field. 14:1 student/faculty ratio. Average class size is 21.
Costs and Aid: 2007–2008: $ 38,926 comprehensive ($26,168 tuition). 75.3% of students receive some financial aid.
Admissions
Phone: 203-932-7319 or 1-800-342-5864 Ext. 7319
adminfo@newhaven.edu
Service-Learning
Experiential Education Office
Sally Anastos, Academic Service Learning Specialist
Phone: 203-479-4588
sanastos@newhaven.edu

Wesleyan University

PROFILE
PAGE
201

http://www.wesleyan.edu
Four Year, Private, Urban, Founded in 1831
Affiliation: Nondenominational
Student Profile: Undergraduate students (50% male, 50% female); 51 states and territories, 44 countries; 6% international, 26% students of color (7% Black or African American, 11% Asian or Asian American, 8% Latino or Hispanic, 1% Native American).
Faculty Profile: 399 full-time faculty. 99% hold a terminal degree in their field. 9:1 student/faculty ratio.
Costs and Aid: 2007–2008: $46,646 comprehensive (tuition, room and board). 43% of students receive financial aid.

Admissions
admissions@wesleyan.edu
Service-Learning
Office of Community Partnerships
Suzanne O'Connell, Ph.D.
Director, Service-Learning Center
Phone: 680-685-2262
soconnell@wesleyan.edu

DELAWARE

University of Delaware

http://www.udel.edu
Four Year, Public, Suburban, Founded in 1743
Student Profile: 15,318 undergraduate students (41% male, 58% female); 50 states and territories, 100 countries; 15% minority, 1% international.
Faculty Profile: 1,167 full-time faculty. 12:1 student/faculty ratio. Average class size is 35.
Costs and Aid: 2007-2008: $15,288 in-state comprehensive ($7,340 tuition); $26,538 out-of-state comprehensive ($18,590 tuition). 55% of students receive financial aid.
Admissions
Newark, DE 19716
Phone: 302-831-8125
Service-Learning
Phone: 302-831-3188

DISTRICT OF COLUMBIA

American University

PROFILE
PAGE
202

http://www.american.edu
Four Year, Private, Suburban, Founded in 1905
Student Profile: 5,922 undergraduate students (35% male, 65% female); 19% minority, 7% international.
Faculty Profile: 594 full-time faculty, 428 adjunct. 97% hold a terminal degree in their field. 14:1 student/faculty ratio. Average class size is 23.
Costs and Aid: 2007–2008: $40,219 comprehensive ($30,958 tuition). 67% of students receive financial aid.
Admissions
Phone: 202-885-6000
Service-Learning
Community Service Center
Marcy Fink Campos, Director
Phone: 202-885-7378
mfcampos@american.edu

Georgetown University

http://www.georgetown.edu
Four Year, Private, Urban, Founded in 1789
Student Profile: 6,630 undergraduate students (46% male, 54% female); 22% minority, 7% international.

Faculty Profile: 1,166 full-time faculty. 11:1 student/faculty ratio. Average class size is 26.
Costs and Aid: 2007-2008: $53,800 comprehensive ($35,536 tuition). 40% of students receive financial aid.
Admissions
Room 103,
White Gravenor Hall
37th and O Streets, NW
Washington, D.C. 20057-1002
Phone: 202-687-3600
Service-Learning
Center for Social Justice
Kathleen Maas Weigert, Executive Director

FLORIDA

Bethune-Cookman University

PROFILE
PAGE
203

http://www.bethune.cookman.edu
Four Year, Private, Founded in 1904
Affiliation: Methodist
Student Profile: 3,093 undergraduate students (42% male, 58% female); 30% out-of-state, 3% international.
Faculty Profile: 150 full time faculty, 17:1 student/faculty ratio. Most frequent class size is 10-19.
Costs and Aid: 2007-2008: $11,792 tuition; 87% of undergraduates receive financial aid.
Admissions
Phone: 386-481-2600
Service-Learning
Claudette McFadden
Phone: 386-299-3065
mcfaddec@cookman.edu

Florida Gulf Coast University

PROFILE
PAGE
204

http://www.fgcu.edu
Four Year, Public, Urban, Founded in 1997
Student Profile: Undergraduate students (40% male, 60% female); 47 states and territories, 87 countries; 18% minority, 1% international.
Faculty Profile: 304 full-time faculty. 79% hold a terminal degree in their field. 18:1 student/faculty ratio. Average class size is 32.
Costs and Aid: 2007–2008: $3,647 in-state comprehensive ($2,211 tuition). 58% of students receive some financial aid.
Admissions
Phone: 239-590-7878
admissions@fgcu.edu
Service-Learning
Center for Civic Engagement
Linda Summers, Director
Phone: 239-590-7016
lsummers@fgcu.edu

Florida Institute of Technology

PROFILE PAGE 205

http://www.fit.edu
Four Year, Private, Suburban, Founded in 1958
Student Profile: 2,594 undergraduate students (70% male, 30% female); 48 states and territories, 81 countries; 11% minority, 21% international.
Faculty Profile: 208 full-time faculty. 89% hold a terminal degree in their field. 9:1 student/faculty ratio. Average class size is 20.
Costs and Aid: 2007-2008: $36,690 comprehensive ($28,920 tuition). 89% of students receive financial aid.
Admissions
Phone: 800-888-4348
admission@fit.edu
Service-Learning
Civic Engagement Initiative
Student Life Office
Phone: 321-674-8080
civic@fit.edu

Florida International University

http://www.fiu.edu
Four Year, Public, Urban, Founded in 1965
Student Profile: 38,614 undergraduate students (43.5% male, 56.4% female); 129 countries; 76% minority, 6% international.
Faculty Profile: 1,000 full-time faculty. 24:1 student/faculty ratio.
Costs and Aid: 2007-2008: $18,031 in-state comprehensive ($3,571 tuition); $30,430.80 in-state comprehensive ($15,970 tuition).
Admissions
PO Box 659003
Miami, FL 33265-9003
Phone: 305-348-2363
Service-Learning
Center for Leadership & Service
Patricia T Lopez-Guerrero, Associate Director
Phone: 305-348-6995

cls@fiu.edu

Florida Southern College

PROFILE PAGE 206

http://www.flsouthern.edu
Four Year, Private, Suburban, Founded in 1883
Affiliation: Methodist
Student Profile: 1,710 undergraduate students (40% male, 60% female); 29% out of state, 4% international.
Faculty Profile: 109 full-time faculty; 13:1 student/faculty ratio. Most frequent class size is 10-19.
Costs and Aid: 2007-2008: $27,380 tuition. 96% of students receive financial aid.
Admissions
Phone: 863-680-4131

Service-Learning
Center for Service-Learning
Dr. Marcia Posey
Phone: 863-680-4315
mposey@flsouthern.edu

Rollins College

PROFILE PAGE 207

http://www.rollins.edu
Four-Year, Private, Suburban, Founded in 1855
Student Profile: 1,778 undergraduate students (42% male, 58% female); 42 states, 32 countries; 22% minority, 4% international.
Faculty Profile: 168 full-time faculty; 93% hold a terminal degree in their field; 10:1 student/faculty ratio; average class size is 17.
Costs and Aid: 2007–2008: $42,840 comprehensive ($32,640 tuition); 75% of students receive financial aid.
Admissions
Phone: 407-646-2161
admission@rollins.edu
Service-Learning
Office of Community Engagement
Micki P. Meyer, Director
Phone: 407-691-1250
mmeyer@rollins.edu

Stetson University

http://www.stetson.edu
Four Year, Private, Founded in 1883
Student Profile: 2,235 undergraduate students (42% male, 58% female); 20% out-of-state, 3% international.
Faculty Profile: 231 full-time faculty; 11:1 student/faculty ratio. Most frequent class size is 10-19.
Costs and Aid: $27,100 tuition (room and board $7,968). 53% of students receive financial aid.
Admissions
421 N.Woodland Blvd.
Unit 8378
DeLand, FL 32723
Phone: 386-822-7100
Service-Learning
Marchman Program for Civic and Social Responsibility
Phone: 386-822-7200

GEORGIA

Mercer University

PROFILE PAGE 208

http://www.mercer.edu
Four Year, Private, Urban, Founded in 1833
Student Profile: 2,268 undergraduate students (47% male, 53% female); 50 states and territories; 41%

minority, 2% international.
Faculty Profile: 352 full-time faculty; 88% hold a terminal degree in their field. 13:1 student/faculty ratio; average class size is 21.
Costs and Aid: 2007–2008: $34,775 comprehensive ($26,760 tuition). 97% of students receive financial aid.
Admissions
Phone: 800-840-8577 or 478-3201-2650
admissions@mercer.edu
Service-Learning
Mary Alice Morgan
Chair, Women and Gender Studies
Phone: 478-301-2571
morgan_ma@mercer.edu

Oxford College of Emory University

http://www.emory.edu/OXFORD/
Two Year, Private, Suburban, Founded in 1836
Student Profile: 700 undergraduate students (44% male, 56% female); 33 states and territories, 8 countries; 47% minority, 4% international.
Faculty Profile: 53 full-time faculty. 10:1 student/faculty ratio. Average class size is 17.
Costs and Aid: 2007-2008: $37,616 comprehensive ($27,000 tuition). 86 % of students receive financial aid.
Admissions
100 Hamill St.,
Oxford, GA 30054
770-784-8456
Service-Learning
Theory Practice Service Learning
Crystal McLaughlin
Phone: 770-784-8456
Crystal.mclaughlin@emory.edu

HAWAII

Chaminade University of Honolulu

PROFILE PAGE 209

http://www.chaminade.edu
Affiliation: Catholic Marianist
Student Profile: 1,112 undergraduate students. (31% male, 69% female); 51% come from outside of Hawaii.
Faculty Profile: 16:1 student/faculty ratio. Average class size is 20.
Costs and Aid: 2007-2008: 74% of undergraduates receive financial aid. Average freshman need based gift is $8,258.
Admissions
Phone: 808-735-4735 or 1-800-735-3733
admissions@chaminade.edu
Service-Learning
Candice Sakuda,
Director of Service-Learning
Phone: 808-735-4895
csakuda@chaminade.edu

Directory

Hawaii Pacific University

http://www.hpu.edu
Four Year, Private, Urban
Founded in 1965
Student Profile: 8,200 undergraduate students (40% male, 60% female); 50 states and territories, more than 100 countries, 33% international.
Faculty Profile: 500 full-time faculty. 18:1 student/faculty ratio. Average class size is under 25.
Costs and Aid: 2007-2008: $26,764 comprehensive ($13,900 tuition).
Admissions
1188 Fort Street Mall,
Honolulu, HI 96813
Phone: 808-544-0238
Service-Learning
HPU Service Learning Program
Dr. Valentina M. Abordonado

Kapi'olani Community College

http://www.kapiolani.hawaii.edu
Two Year, Public, Urban, Founded in 1964
Student Profile: 7,272 undergraduate students (47% male, 53% female).
Faculty Profile: 225 full-time faculty. 15:1 student/faculty ratio.
Costs and Aid: 2007-2008: $63 per credit hour in-state, $320 per credit hour out-of-state.
Admissions
Kekaulike Information & Service Center 4303
Phone: 808-734-9555
kapinfo@hawaii.edu
Service-Learning
Ku'ulani Miyashiro, Service-Learning Coordinator
Phone: 808-734-9353
kccserve@hawaii.edu

Maui Community College

http://www.maui.Hawaii.edu
Two Year, Public, Suburban/Rural, Founded in 1931
Student Profile: 2,841 undergraduate students (33% male, 67% female); 2.1% US Mainland states; 71.3% minority, 1.9% international.
Faculty Profile: 76 full-time faculty. 21:1 student/faculty ratio. Average class size is 22.
Costs and Aid: 2007-2008: $63/cr resident; $320/cr out-of-state tuition.
Admissions
310 W. Kaahumanu Avenue,
Kahului, HI 96832
Phone: 808-984-3500
Service-Learning
Molli Fleming, mollif@hawaii.edu

ILLINOIS

College of DuPage

http://www.cod.edu
Community College, Public, Suburban, Founded 1967
Student Profile: 28,767 undergraduate students (44% male, 56% female); 32% minority from 44 communities within District 502; 91% in-district; 8% out-of-district; 1% international.
Faculty Profile: 305 full-time faculty and 922 part-time faculty. 97% of faculty hold doctorate or master's degrees. 19:1 student/faculty ratio.
Costs and Aid: 2006-2007: $96 per semester credit hour for in-district tuition. Total tuition for full-time student in-district (32 semester hours) is $3,072; out-of-district tuition per year is $8,000; out-of-state tuition per year is $9,824. Total expenses for full-time dependent student (residing with parents): $9,697; independent student (living away from home): $14,698.
Admissions
Phone: 630-942-2482
protis@cod.edu
Service-Learning
Service Learning Program
Steven Gustis, Coordinator
Phone: 630-942-2655
gustis@cod.edu

Columbia College Chicago

http://www.colum.edu
Four Year, Private, Urban, Founded in 1890
Student Profile: 10,671 undergraduate students (49% male, 51% female); 50 states and territories, 46 countries.
Faculty Profile: 1,497 full-time faculty. Average class size is under 20 students.
Costs and Aid: 2007-2008: $17,588 tuition.
Admissions
Phone: 312-344-7130
Service-Learning
Center for Community Arts Partnerships
Paul Teruel, Director
Phone: 312-344-8871
pteruel@colum.edu

Concordia University Chicago

http://www.cuchicago.edu
Four Year, Private, Suburban, Founded in 1864
Affiliation: The Lutheran Church
Student Profile: 1,121 undergraduate students (38% male, 62% female). 30% out-of-state.
Faculty Profile: 17:1 student/faculty ratio. Average class size is 20.
Costs and Aid: $21,950 tuition; 78% of undergraduate students receive financial aid.
Admissions
Phone: 1-877-262-4422
Service-Learning
Academic Service Learning
Alannah Ari Hernandez, Director
Phone: 708-209-3633
alannah.hernandez@cuchicago.edu, or service@cuchicago.edu

DePaul University

http://www.depaul.edu
Four Year, Private, Urban, Founded in 1898
Student Profile: 15,024 undergraduate students (44% male, 56% female).
Faculty Profile: 850 full-time faculty; 85% hold terminal degrees; 16:1 student/faculty ratio; 68% of all classes have fewer than 30 students.
Costs and Aid: 2008-2009: $25,490 tuition for most programs. About 68% of undergraduate students receive financial aid.
Admissions
Phone: 312-362-8300 or 1-800-4-DEPAUL
Service-Learning
Steans Center for Community-Based Service
Howard Rosing, Ph.D., Executive Director
Phone: 773-325-7463
Learninghrosing@depaul.edu

Elmhurst College

http://www.elmhurst.edu
Two Year, Private, Suburban, Founded in 1871
Student Profile: 2,600 undergraduate students (36% male, 64% female); 30 states and territories, 36 countries; 17 % minority, 1% international.
Faculty Profile: 127 full-time faculty. 13:1 student/faculty ratio. Average class size is 19.
Costs and Aid: 2007-2008: $33,500 comprehensive ($26,000 tuition). 93% of students receive financial aid.
Admissions
Phone: 630-617-3500
admit@elmhurst.edu
Service-Learning
Dr. Michael Savage, Ph.D.
Director of Service-Learning
Phone: 630-617-6488

Harold Washington College

http://www.hwashington.ccc.edu/
Community, Public, Urban, Founded in 1962
Student Profile: 7,284 undergraduate students (40% male, 60% female); 80% minority, 7% international.
Faculty Profile: 42% full-time faculty. 20:1 student/faculty ratio. Average class size is 25.1.
Costs and Aid: 2007-2008: $72 per credit hour tuition.
Admissions
30 E. Lake St.,
Chicago, IL 60601
Phone: 312-553-5600
Service Learning
Tim Donahue, Assistant Professor of English & Service Learning Coordinator
Phone: 312-553-5887
tdonahue@ccc.edu

Illinois College

http://www.ic.edu
Four Year, Private, Rural, Founded in 1929
Affiliation: Congregational Church and Presbyterian
Student Profile: 1,014 undergraduate students (48.1% male, 51.9% female); 23 states and territories, 14 countries; 7.4% minority, 2.4% international.
Faculty Profile: 71 full-time faculty. 13:1 student/faculty ratio. Average class size is 16.
Costs and Aid: 2007-2008: $25,770 comprehensive ($18,600 tuition). Students receive a total of $6.4 million in financial aid.
Admissions
1101 West College Avenue,
Jacksonville, Ill. 62650
Phone: 217-245-3000
Service-Learning
IC Connections – First Year Experience
Karen Homolka
Assistant Dean of Students/Director of Student Activities
Phone: 217-245-3094
khomolk@ic.edu

Loyola University Chicago

PROFILE PAGE 215

http:// www.luc.edu
Four Year, Private, Urban, Founded in 1870
Student Profile: 9,729 undergraduate students; 33% minority; 15,545 total enrollment from 50 states and territories and 82 countries.
Faculty Profile: 1,100 full-time faculty; 96% hold a terminal degree in their field. 13:1 student/faculty ratio.
Costs and Aid: 2007-2008: $42,846 comprehensive ($28,700 tuition). 91% of students receive financial aid.
Admissions
Phone: 800-262-2373
admission@luc.edu
Service-Learning
Center for Experiential Learning
Patrick M. Green, Ed.D., Director,
Phone: 773-508-3366
experiential@luc.edu

Rockford College

http://www.rockford.edu
Four Year, Private, Suburban, Founded in 1947
Student Profile: Undergraduate students (35% male, 65% female); 14% minority, 1% international.
Faculty Profile: 62 full-time faculty. 11:1 student/faculty ratio. Average class size is 13.
Costs and Aid: 2007-2008: $29,700 comprehensive ($22,950 tuition). 98% of students receive financial aid.
Admissions
5050 E State St.
Rockford, IL 61108
Phone: 800-892-2984 or 815-226-4050
Service-Learning
Community Based Learning Program
Dr. Rufus Cadigan
Phone: 815-226-4108
rcadigan@rockford.edu

Roosevelt University

PROFILE PAGE 216

http://roosevelt.edu
Four Year, Private, Urban, Founded in 1945
Student Profile: 3,973 undergraduate students (32% male, 68% female); 48 states and territories, 26 countries; 35% minority, 4% international.
Faculty Profile: 216 full-time faculty; 84% hold a terminal degree in their field. 13:1 student/faculty ratio. Average class size is 19.
Costs and Aid: $16,680 tuition. 85% of students receive financial aid.
Admissions
Phone: 312-341-3500
applyRU@roosevelt.edu
Service-Learning
Pamela Robert, PhD
Associate Professor of Sociology
Phone: 312-341-3737
probert@roosevelt.edu

INDIANA

Ball State University

http://www.bsu.edu
Two Year, Public, Suburban, Founded in 1918
Student Profile: 15,513 undergraduate students (45% male, 55% female; 48 states and 2 territories, 80 countries; 9% minority, >2% international).
Faculty Profile: 915 full-time faculty. 17:1 student/faculty ratio. Average class size is 31.
Costs and Aid: 2007-2008: $14,522 in-state comprehensive ($6,672 tuition); $25,590 out-of-state comprehensive ($17,740 tuition). 75% of students receive financial aid.
Admissions
2000 University Avenue,
Muncie, IN 47306
Phone: 765-289-1241
Service-Learning
Office of Student Life, Student Center
Kathy L. Smith, Associate Director
Phone: 765-285-3476

Butler University

http://www.butler.edu
Four Year, Private, Urban, Founded in 1855
Student Profile: 3,829 undergraduate students (37% male, 63% female); 50 states and territories, 36 countries; 9% minority, 2% international.
Faculty Profile: 291 full-time faculty. 12:1 student/faculty ratio. Average class size is 20.
Costs and Aid: 2007-2008: $35,546 comprehensive ($26,070 tuition). 85% of students receive financial aid.
Admissions
4600 Sunset Avenue,
Indianapolis, IN 46208
Phone: 888-940-8100
Service-Learning
Center for Citizenship and Community
Donald Braid, Ph.D.
Phone: 317-940-8353
dbraid@butler.edu

Franklin College

PROFILE PAGE 217

http://www.franklincollege.edu
Four Year, Private, Suburban, Founded in 1834
Student Profile: Undergraduate students (50% male, 50% female); 14 states and territories, 3 countries.
Faculty Profile: 65 full-time faculty. 12:1 student/faculty ratio. Average class size is 15.
Costs and Aid: 2007-2008: $27,540 comprehensive ($21,150 tuition). 97% of students receive financial aid.
Admissions
Phone: 317-738-8062 or 800-852-0232
admissions@franklincollege.edu
Service-Learning
Ruth Lilly Leadership Center
Doug Grant, Service Learning Coordinator
Phone: 317-738-8762
dgrant@franklincollege.edu

Goshen College

PROFILE PAGE 218

http://www.goshen.edu
Four Year, Private, Founded in 1894
Affiliation: Christian
Student Profile: 947 undergraduate students (45% male, 55% female); 3.6% African American, 81.3% Caucasian, 6% Hispanic, 6% international.
Faculty Profile: 64 full-time faculty, 13:1 student/faculty ratio. Average class size is 20.
Costs and Aid: 2008-2009: $22,300 tuition, 7500 room and board, 98% of students receive financial aid.
Admissions
Phone: 1-800-348-7422
admission@goshen.edu

Indiana State University

http://www.indstate.edu
Four Year, Public, Town, Founded in 1865
Student Profile: 8,493 undergraduate students; 2,050 graduate students; 17% international. Indiana State hosts students from all 92 Indiana counties, 53 states and U.S. territories and 65 countries.
Faculty Profile: 446 full-time faculty, 17.4:1 student/faculty ratio.
Costs and Aid: ISU recognizes academic excellence by awarding over $1 million each year in merit-based scholarships to deserving students. These renewable scholarships range from $1,100 a year to the full costs of in-state tuition, housing, and books.
Admissions
Phone: 800-GO-TO-ISU
admissions@indstate.edu
Service-Learning
Center for Public
Service and Community Engagement
Nancy Brattain Rogers, Director
Phone: 812-237-2334
cpsce@indstate.edu

Indiana University-Purdue University Indianapolis

http://www.iupui.edu
Four Year, Public, Urban, Founded 1969
Student Profile: 21,202 undergraduate students (42% male, 58% female); 50 states and territories, 122 countries (undergraduate); 15% minority, 4% international.
Faculty Profile: 2,205 full-time faculty. 90% hold a terminal degree in their field. 10:1 student/faculty ratio.
Costs and Aid: $6,850 tuition. $8,904 out-of-state tuition. 72% of students receive financial aid. Average award is $7,664.
Admissions
Phone: 317-274-4591
Service-Learning
Center for Service and Learning
Dr. Steven G. Jones, Coordinator
Phone: 317-278-2539
jonessg@iupui.edu

University of Notre Dame
http://www.nd.edu
Four Year, Private, Urban, Founded in 1842
Student Profile: 8,300 undergraduate students (53% male, 47% female); 50 states and territories, 100 countries; 20.7% minority, 3.3% international.
Faculty Profile: 758 full-time faculty. Average class size is 16.
Costs and Aid: 2007-2008: $44,000 comprehensive

($34,680 tuition). 79% of students receive financial aid.
Admissions
220 Main Building
Notre Dame, IN, 46556-5602
Phone: 574-631-7505
admissions@nd.edu
Service-Learning
Center for Social Concerns
Paul Horn
Phone: 574-631-3209
phorn@nd.edu

Purdue University

http://www.purdue.edu
Four Year, Public, Urban, Founded in 1869
Student Profile: Undergraduate students (58.1% male, 41.9% female); 13.4% minority, 6.5% international. 50 states and 3 territories represented.
Faculty Profile: 97.5% of faculty are full-time, part-time faculty 2.5%. 100% of faculty hold a terminal degree in their field.
Costs and Aid: $18,800 in-state comprehensive, $23,224 out-of-state comprehensive. 79.2% of students receive financial aid.
Admissions
Schleman Hall of Student Services
475 Stadium Mall Drive
West Lafayette, IN 47907-0544
Phone: 765-494-1776
admissions@purdue.edu
Service-Learning
Center for Instructional Excellence
Marne Helgesen, Ph.D., Director
Phone: 765-496-6424
helgesen@purdue.edu

IOWA

Central College
http://www.central.edu
Four Year, Private, Rural. Founded in 1853
Affiliation: Reformed Church in America
Student Profile: 1,605 undergraduate students (46% male, 54% female); 38 states and territories, 15 countries; 4.17% minority, 1.80% international.
Faculty Profile: 89 full-time faculty. 14:1 student/faculty ratio. Average class size is 20.
Costs and Aid: 2007-2008: $30,134 comprehensive ($22,230 tuition). More than 98% of students receive financial aid.
Admissions
812 University St.,
Pella, IA 50219
Phone: 641-628-5332
Service-Learning
Community-based Learning
Cheri Doane
Phone: 641-628-5424
Doanec@central.edu

Iowa Western Community College
http://www.iwcc.edu
Two Year, Public, Urban, Founded in 1966
Student Profile: 5,300 undergraduate students (44% male, 56% female); 30 states and territories, 45 countries; 18% minority, 4% international.
Faculty Profile: 120 full-time faculty. 14:1 student/faculty ratio. Average class size is 25.
Costs and Aid: 2007-2008: $12,130 in-state comprehensive ($3,480 tuition). $13,630 out-of-state comprehensive ($4,980 tuition). 70% of students receive financial aid.
Admissions
Phone: 800-432-5852 Ext: 3277
admissions@iwcc.edu
Service-Learning
Service-Learning Initiatives
Corrine Grace, Service-Learning Coordinator
Phone: 800-432-5852 Ext: 6539 or 712-256-6539

Mount Mercy College
http://www.mtmercy.edu
Four Year, Private, Urban, Founded in 1928
Affiliation: Catholic
Student Profile: 1,506 undergraduate students (28.4% male, 71.6% female); 16 states, 7 countries.
Faculty Profile: 76 full-time faculty. 13:1 student/faculty ratio. Average class size is 20.
Costs and Aid: 2007-2008: $26,340 comprehensive ($20,070 tuition). 92% of students receive financial aid.
Admissions
1330 Elmhurst Drive NE,
Cedar Rapids, IA 52402
Phone: 319-363-8213
Service-Learning
Office of Volunteerism and Service Learning
Susan Davidson, Coordinator
Phone: 319-363-1323 Ext: 1399
sdavid@mtmercy.edu

Simpson College
http://www.simpson.edu
Four Year, Private, Suburban, Founded in 1860
Student Profile: 2,040 undergraduate students (41.7% male, 58.3% female); 19 states and territories, 11 countries; 6.1% minority, .7% international.
Faculty Profile: 97 full-time faculty. 16:1 student/faculty ratio. Average class size is 22.
Costs and Aid: 2007-2008: $30,251 comprehensive ($23,956 tuition). 99% of students receive financial aid.
Admissions
701 North C St.
Indianola, IA 50125
Phone: 515-961-1624 or 800- 362-2454
admiss@simpson.edu
Service-Learning
Service Hub
Jim Hayes, Director
Phone: 515-961-1281
jim.hayes@simpson.edu

University of Dubuque

http://www.dbq.edu
Four Year, Private, Urban, Founded in 1852
Affiliation: Presbyterian
Student Profile: 1,285 undergraduate students (56% male, 44% female); 35 states and territories, 20 countries; 18% minority, 3% international.
Faculty Profile: 70 full-time faculty. 70% hold a terminal degree in their field. 13:1 student/faculty ratio. Average class size is 20.
Costs and Aid: 2007-2008: $26,810 comprehensive ($19,600 tuition). 95% of students receive financial aid.
Admissions
Phone: 563-589-3000 or 800-722-5583
admssns@dbq.edu
Service-Learning
Office of Service-Learning
Mark Smith, Coordinator
Phone: 563-589-3127
mwsmith@dbq.edu

Wartburg College

http://www.wartburg.edu
Four Year, Private, Rural, Founded in 1852
Affiliation: Evangelical Lutheran Church in America (ELCA)
Student Profile: 1,810 students (48% male, 52% female); 24 states and territories represented.
Faculty Profile: 107 full-time faculty; 12:1 student/faculty ratio.
Costs and Aid: 2007-2008: $33,415 comprehensive ($25,360 tuition). 99% of students receive financial aid.
Admissions
Phone: 800-772-2085
Service-Learning
Center for Community Engagement
Phone: 319-352-8701
cce@wartburg.edu

KANSAS

Fort Hays State University

http://www.fhsu.edu
Four Year, Public, Rural, Founded in 1902
Student Profile: 9,588 undergraduate and graduate students (42% male, 58% female); 50 states and territories; 7.5% minority, 27% international.
Faculty Profile: 295 full-time faculty; 17:1 student/faculty ratio.
Costs and Aid: 2007–2008: $10,206 in-state comprehensive ($ 3,355 tuition); $17,394.50 out-of-state comprehensive ($10,543 tuition); 52% of students receive financial aid.
Admissions
Phone: 800-628-FHSU
admissions@fhsu.edu
Service-Learning
Center for Civic Leadership
Jill Arensdorf
Phone: 785-628-5592 or 800-628-FHSU
ccl@fhsu.edu

Kansas State University

http://www.k-state.edu
Four Year, Public, Suburban, Founded in 1863
Student Profile: 18,545 undergraduate students (50% male, 50% female); 50 states, 109 countries; 12% minority, 5.2% international.
Faculty Profile: 1,242 full-time faculty. 12:1 student/faculty ratio. Average undergraduate class size ranges from 26-28.
Costs and Aid: 2007–2008: $16,568 in-state comprehensive ($6,036tuition). $25,654 out-of state comprehensive ($15,122 tuition). 73% of students receive financial aid. Average award: $10,925.
Admissions
Phone: 800-432-8270 or 785-532-6250
k-state@k-state.edu
Service-Learning
Civic Leadership
Mary Hale Tolar, Associate Director, Leadership Studies and Programs
Phone: 785-532-5701
mtolar@k-state.edu

Southwestern College

http://www.sckans.edu
Four Year, Private, Suburban, Founded in 1885
Affiliation: United Methodist
Student Profile: 567 undergraduate students (44% male, 56% female); 24 states and territories, 12 countries; 17% minority, 4% international.
Faculty Profile: 48 full-time faculty. 58% hold a terminal degree in their field. 12:1 student/faculty ratio.
Costs and Aid: 2007-2008: $23,442 comprehensive ($17,720 tuition). 99% of students receive financial aid.
Admissions
Phone: 620-229-6236
scadmit@sckans.edu
Service-Learning
Dr. Cheryl Rude, Director of Leadership Southwestern
Cheryl.Rude@sckans.edu

University of Kansas

http://www.ku.edu
Four Year, Public, Founded in 1866
Student Profile: 20,298 undergraduate students (49% male, 51% female); 69% in-state; 50 states and territories, 110 countries; 13% multicultural, 6% international.
Faculty Profile: 2,201 full-time faculty. 96% of full-time faculty with Ph.D. or equivalent in their fields. 19:1 student/faculty ratio.
Costs and Aid: 2007-2008: $12,620 in-state comprehensive ($6,390 tuition); $23,030 out-of-state comprehensive ($16,800 tuition). Approximately 60% of KU undergraduate students received financial aid in the 2006-07 academic year for a total of more than $100 million.
Admissions
Phone: 785-864-3911
adm@ku.edu
Service-Learning
Center for Service Learning
Phone: 785-864-0960
csl@ku.edu

KENTUCKY

Berea College

http://www.berea.edu
Four Year, Private, Rural, Founded in 1855
Student Profile: 1,514 undergraduate (40% male, 60% female); 40 states and territories, 71 countries; 22% minority, 7% international.
Faculty Profile: 131 full-time faculty. 91% hold a terminal degree in their field.10:1 student/faculty ratio. Average class size is 16.
Costs and Aid: 2007–2008: $6,282 comprehensive ($0 tuition). 100% of students receive financial aid. Average award: the equivalent of a four year scholarship, up to $85,000.
Admissions
Phone: 859-985-3500 or 800-326-5948
askadmissions@berea.edu
Service-Learning
Center for Excellence in Learning Through Service
Meta Mendel-Reyes, Ph.D., Director
Phone: 859-985-3940

Centre College

http://www.centre.edu
Four Year, Private, Rural, Founded in 1819
Student Profile: 1,189 undergraduate students (45% male, 55% female); 38 states and territories, 11 countries; 1% minority.
Faculty Profile: 102 full-time faculty. 11:1 student/faculty ratio. Average class size is 18.
Costs and Aid: 2007-2008: $35,000 comprehensive. 85% of students receive financial aid.
Admissions
Phone: 800-423-6236
admission@centre.edu
Service-Learning
Office of Volunteer Service and The Bonner Program
Patrick Noltemeyer, Director
Phone: 859-238-8752
Patrick.Noltemeyer@centre.edu

Louisville Technical Institute

http://www.louisvilletech.edu
Two/Four Year, Private, Urban, Founded in 1961
Student Profile: 580 undergraduate students (59.5% male, 40.5% female); 100% from states and territories. 18.6% minority.
Faculty Profile: 29 full-time faculty. 8:1 student/faculty ratio (includes adjuncts). Average class size is 8.
Costs and Aid: 2007-2008: $17,755 comprehensive ($13,435 tuition). 86% of students receive financial aid. There is no difference in tuition for in-state or out-of-state students.
Admissions
3901 Atkinson Square Drive
Louisville, KY 40218
Phone: 502-456-6509
Service-Learning
Dr. Sheree P. Koppel, Academic Dean
Phone: 502-456-6509
skoppel@louisvilletech.edu

Northern Kentucky University

PROFILE PAGE 228

http://www.nku.edu
Four Year, Public, Suburban
Student Profile: 12,647 undergraduate students (42.3% male, 57.7% female); 42 states and territories, 91 countries; 11.6% minority, 1.4% international; 1,970 graduate and professional students
Faculty Profile: 608 full-time faculty. 75% hold a terminal degree in their field. 14:1 student/faculty ratio. Average class size is 24.
Costs and Aid: 2007–2008: $2,976 per semester (in-state); $5388 per semester (out-of-state). 73% of students receive financial aid. Average award is $8,010.
Admissions
Phone: 859-572-5220 or 1-800-637-9948
admitnku@nku.edu
Service-Learning
Scripps Howard Center for Civic Engagement
Phone: 859-572-1448
civicengage@nku.edu

Transylvania University

http://www.transy.edu/
Four Year, Private, City, Founded in 1780
Student Profile: 1,116 students (44% male, 56% female); 33 states, 3 countries; 6% minority, <1% international.
Faculty Profile: 79 full-time faculty. 95% hold a terminal degree in their field. 13:1 student/faculty ratio. Average class size is 18.
Costs and Aid: 2007–2008: $29,430 comprehensive ($22,300 tuition). 85% of students receive financial aid.
Admissions
Phone: 800-872-6798
admissions@transy.edu
Service-Learning
Karen Anderson, Coordinator of Community Service and Civic Engagement
Phone: 859-233-8182
smelia@assumption.edu

University of Kentucky

PROFILE PAGE 229

http://www.uky.edu
Four Year, Public, Urban, Founded in 1865
Student Profile: Undergraduate students (48% male, 52% female); 50 states and territories, 117 countries; 9.1% minority, 5.1% international.
Faculty Profile: 2,028 full-time faculty.
Costs and Aid: 2007–2008: $3,651 tuition per semester (resident); $7,547 tuition per semester (out-of-state; non-resident).
Admissions
100 W.D. Funkhouser Bldg.
Lexington, KY 40506-0054
Phone: 859-257-2000
Service-Learning
James W. Stuckert Career Center
Esther Livingston, Assistant Director, Experiential Education and Career Services
Phone: (859) 257-1564
ELivingston@uky.edu

Western Kentucky University

PROFILE PAGE 230

http://www.wku.edu
Four Year, Public, Suburban, Founded in 1906
Student Profile: 16,508 undergraduate students (43% male, 57% female); 17% out-of-state, 3% international.
Faculty Profile: 726 full-time faculty; 18:1 student/faculty ratio. Most frequent class size is 20-29.
Costs and Aid: $12,056 comprehensive in-state ($6,416 tuition). $21,220 comprehensive out-of-state ($15,470 tuition).
Admissions
Phone: 270-745-2551
Service-Learning
ALIVE Center for Community Partnerships

Cheryl Kirby-Stokes, Service-Learning & Volunteer Coordinator
Phone: 626-782-0020

LOUISIANA

Louisiana State University

http://www.bgtplan.lsu.edu
Four Year, Public, Urban, Founded in 1860
Student Profile: 23,397 undergraduate students (49% male, 51% female); 50 states and territories, 111 countries; 15.6% minority, 2% international.
Faculty Profile: 1,267 full-time faculty. 20:1 student/faculty ratio. Average class size is 39.
Costs and Aid: 2007-2008: $11,395 resident undergraduate comprehensive ($4,543 tuition). $19,695 non-resident undergraduate comprehensive ($12,843 tuition). 79.7% of undergraduate students receive financial aid.
Admissions
1146 Pleasant Hall
Baton Rouge, LA 70803
Phone: 225-578-1175
Service-Learning
Center for Community Engagement, Learning, and Leadership
Jan Shoemaker
Phone: 225-578-9264
ccell@lsu.edu

Nicholls State University

PROFILE PAGE 231

http://www.nicholls.edu
Four Year, Public, Rural, Founded in 1948
Student Profile: Undergraduate students (37.8% male, 62.2% female); 33 states and territories, 40 countries; 24.4% minority, 1.3% international.
Faculty Profile: 54.9% of full-time faculty hold a terminal degree in their field. 19.7:1 student/faculty ratio. Average class size is 22.
Costs and Aid: 2007-2008: $3,623 in-state comprehensive ($2,231 tuition); $9,071 out-of-state comprehensive ($7,679 tuition).
Admissions
Phone: 1-877-Nicholls
Service-Learning
Laynie Barrilleaux, Ph.D., Vice President for Academic Affairs
Phone: 985-448-4174
laynie@nicholls.edu

Our Lady of the Lake College

http://www.ololcollege.edu
Four Year, Private, Suburban, Founded in 1923
Student Profile: 2,000 undergraduate students (14% male, 86% female); 99.6% from Louisiana states and territories; 29 % minority.
Faculty Profile: 81 full-time faculty, 75 adjunct faculty. 12:1 student/faculty ratio. Average class size is 17.
Costs and Aid: 2007-2008: $260 per credit, (no dorms or on campus living). 85% of students receive financial aid.
Admissions
7434 Perkins Road,
Baton Rouge, LA 70808
Phone: 225-768-1719 or 877-242-3509
Service-Learning
Dr. Phyllis Simpson
Phone: 225-768-1700

Tulane University

PROFILE PAGE 232

http://www2.tulane.edu
Four Year, Private, City, Founded in 1834
Student Profile: 6,533 undergraduate students; 46 states and territories, 21 countries.
Faculty Profile: 1,112 full-time faculty. 97% hold a terminal degree in their field. 9:1student/faculty ratio. Average class size is 22 students with 25% of classes under 10 students.
Costs and Aid: 2007–2008: $45,550 comprehensive ($36,610 tuition). 79% of students receive financial aid. Average award is $25,224.
Admissions
Phone: 800-873-9283
undergrad.admission@tulane.edu
Service-Learning
Center for Public Service
Phone: 504-862-8060

Xavier University of Louisiana

PROFILE PAGE 233

http://www.xula.edu
Four Year, Private, Urban, Founded in 1925
Affiliation: Roman Catholic
Student Profile: 3,100 undergraduate students (27.7% male, 72.3% female); 56.5% in-state, 38.2% out-of-state. 72% African American.
Faculty Profile: 132 full-time faculty. 15:1 student/faculty ratio.
Costs and Aid: 2007–2008: $13,700 tuition. 75% of students receive financial aid.
Admissions
Phone: 504-520-7388 or 1-877-XavierU
apply@xula.edu
Service-Learning
Nedra J. Alcorn, Associate Vice-President,

Student Services/Dean of Students
Phone: 504-520-7357
nalcorn@xula.edu;
Typhanie J. Butler
Service-Learning Site Coordinator
Phone: 504-520-5133
ttjasper@xula.edu

MAINE

Bates College

http://www.bates.edu
Four Year, Private, Founded in 1855
Student Profile: 1,744 undergraduate students (834 male, 910 female); 45 states and territories, 78 countries; 9% minority, 5% international.
Faculty Profile: 193 full-time faculty. 10:1 student/faculty ratio.
Costs and Aid: 2007-2008: $46,800 comprehensive. 44 % of students receive financial aid.
Admissions
2 Andrews Road,
Lewiston, ME 04240
Phone: 207-786-6255
Service-Learning
Harward Center for Community Partnerships
David Scobey, Director
Phone: 207-786-6443

Colby College

http://www.colby.edu
Four Year, Private, Urban, Founded in 1813
Student Profile: 1,865 undergraduate students (46.3% male, 53.7% female); 45 states and territories, 68 countries; 12.5% minority, 6.8% international.
Faculty Profile: 161 full-time faculty. 10:1 student/faculty ratio. Average class size is 17.
Costs and Aid: 2007-2008: $44,080 comprehensive. 38% of students receive financial aid.
Admissions
5313 Mayflower Hill Drive,
Waterville, ME 04901,
Phone: 207-859-5313
Service-Learning
The Goldfarb Center for Public Affairs and Civic Engagement
Alice D. Elliott, Assistant Director
Phone: 207-859-5313
aelliott@colby.edu

Unity College

PROFILE PAGE 234

http://www.unity.edu
Four Year, Private, Rural, Founded in 1965
Student Profile: 550 undergraduate students (1.5:1 male/female ratio); 70% of students live on campus; 30 states represented.
Faculty Profile: 31 full-time faculty; 68% hold terminal degrees; 14:1 student/faculty ratio.

Cost and Aid: 2007-2008: $26,950 comprehensive ($18,630 tuition); 66% of students receive need-based institutional aid.
Admissions
Phone: 800-624-1024 or 207-948-3131
Service-Learning
Jennifer Olin
Community Service-Learning Coordinator
Phone: 207-948-3131 Ext: 273
jolin@unity.edu

MARYLAND

Anne Arundel Community College

http://www.aacc.edu
Two Year, Public, Suburban, Founded in 1961
Student Profile: 14,699 undergraduate students (38.1% male, 61.9% female); 31 states and territories, 20 countries; 24.7% minority.
Faculty Profile: 250 full-time faculty. 17:1 student/faculty ratio. Average class size is 20.
Costs and Aid: 2007-2008: $2,860 comprehensive. 21.8% of students receive financial aid.
Admissions
101 College Parkway,
Arnold, MD 21012
Phone: 410-777-2366
Service-Learning
Center for Learning Through Service
Sam Weiner
smweiner@aacc.edu

College of Southern Maryland

http://www.csmd.edu
Community College, Public, Suburban. Founded 1958
Student Profile: 10,000 undergraduate students (34% male, 66% female).
Faculty Profile: 440 full-time faculty. 336 part-time faculty. 20:1 student/faculty ratio. Average class size is 20.
Costs and Aid: 2007-2008: $94 per credit (in county rate), $164 per credit (out of county), $209 per credit (out of state tuition).
Admissions
8730 Mitchell Rd.
La Plata, MD 20646
Phone: 301-934-7790
Service-Learning
Center for Civic Engagement and Service-Learning
Sarah Merranko, Director
sarahm@csmd.edu
Phone: 301-934-2251 Ext: 7367

MASSACHUSETTS

Assumption College

PROFILE PAGE 235

http://www.assumption.edu
Four Year, Private, Urban, Founded in 1904
Affiliation: Catholic
Student Profile: 2,125 undergraduate students (40% male, 60% female); 25 states and territories, 8 countries; 6% minority & international.
Faculty Profile: 143 full-time faculty. 91% hold a terminal degree in their field. 12:1 student/faculty ratio. Average class size is 20.
Costs and Aid: 2007–2008: $ 36,977 comprehensive ($27,320 tuition). 96% of students receive financial aid. Merit Scholarships up to $20,000 per year.
Admissions
Phone: 866-477-7776
admiss@assumption.edu
Service-Learning
Community Service Learning Program
Susan Perschbacher Melia, Ph.D., Director,
smelia@assumption.edu

Babson College

PROFILE PAGE 236

http://www.babson.edu
Four Year, Private, Suburban, Founded in 1919
Student Profile: 1,799 undergraduate students (59% male, 41% female); 43 states and territories, 59 countries; 25% minority, 18% international.
Faculty Profile: 157 full-time faculty. 90% hold a terminal degree in their field. 14:1 student/faculty ratio. Average class size is 29.
Costs and Aid: 2007-2008: $45,782 comprehensive ($34,112 tuition). 48% of students receive financial aid.
Admissions
Phone: 781-239-5522 or 800-488-3696
ugradadmission@babson.edu
Service-Learning
Lisa Hellmuth, Coordinator
Volunteer Programs
Phone: 781-239-5354
thomasl@babson.edu

Bentley College

PROFILE PAGE 237

http://www.bentley.edu
Four Year, Private, Suburban, Founded in 1917
Affiliation: Non-denominational
Student Profile: 4,241 undergraduate students (60% male, 40% female); 42 states and territories, 71 countries; 27% minority, 8% international.
Faculty Profile: 271 full-time faculty. 12:1 student/faculty ratio. Average class size is 23.88.
Costs and Aid: 2007-2008: $43,900 comprehensive ($31.450 tuition). 73% of students receive financial aid.
Admissions
Phone: 781-891-2244
Service-Learning
Bentley Service-Learning Center
Phone: 781-891-2170
service-learning@bentley.edu

Bridgewater State College

http://www.bridgew.edu
Four Year, Public, Suburban, Founded in 1840
Student Profile: 7,825 undergraduate students (38% male, 62% female); 8% minority, 1% international.
Faculty Profile: 292 full-time faculty. 19.7:1 student/faculty ratio.
Costs and Aid: 2007-2008: $12, 718 comprehensive ($5866 tuition). 44 % of students receive financial aid.
Admissions
Bridgewater, MA 02325
Phone: 508-531-1237
admission@bridgew.edu
Service-Learning
Service-Learning Initiative in the Community
Service Center
Dr. Jonathan White
jonathan.white@bridgew.edu

Bristol Community College

PROFILE PAGE 238

http://www.bristolcc.edu
Two Year, Public, Urban, Founded in 1965
Student Profile: 9,680 undergraduate students (36.9% male, 63.1% female); 5 states and territories, 37 countries, 12% minority, 0.5% international.
Faculty Profile: 102 full-time faculty with 17 Doctorates, 81 Master's, and 4 Bachelor's degrees. 17:1 student/faculty ratio. Average class size is 18.
Costs and Aid: 2007-2008: Annual in-state tuition $3,120. Annual out-of-state tuition $8,064; 40.44% of students receive financial aid.
Admissions
Room G 128777 Elsbree Street
Fall River, MA 02720
Phone: 508-678-2811 ext. 2177
rodney.clark@bristolcc.edu

Service-Learning
Mary Zahm, Ph.D.
Director of Civic Engagement
Phone: 508-678-2811 ext. 2579
mary.zahm@bristolcc.edu

College of the Holy Cross

PROFILE PAGE 239

http://www.holycross.edu
Four Year, Private, Urban, Founded in 1843
Affiliation: Catholic
Student Profile: 2,790 undergraduate students (45% male, 55% female); 46 states and territories, 13 countries; 62 % out of state, 15% minority.
Faculty Profile: 239 full-time faculty. 95% hold a terminal degree in their field. 1:11 student/faculty ratio.
Costs and Aid: 2007–2008: $42,893 comprehensive ($32,820 tuition); 59% of students receive financial aid.
Admissions
Phone: 800-442-2421 or 508-793-2443
admission@holycross.edu
Service-Learning
Donelan Office of Community-based Learning
Margaret A. Post
Phone: 508-793-3009
mapost@holycross.edu

Emerson College

http://www.emerson.edu
Four Year, Private, Suburban, Founded in 1880
Student Profile: 3,000 undergraduate students (45% male, 55% female); 42 states and territories, 40 countries; 15% minority, 2.4% international.
Faculty Profile: 159 full-time faculty. 14:1 student/faculty ratio. Average class size is 25.
Costs and Aid: 2007-2008: $38,256 comprehensive ($26,880 tuition). 65% of students receive financial aid.
Admissions
120 Boylston Street,
Boston, MA 02116
Phone: 617-824-8500
admission@emerson.edu
Service-Learning
Office of Service Learning & Community Action
Jennifer Greer-Morrissey
Phone: 617-824-8266

Emmanuel College

PROFILE PAGE 240

http://www.emmanuel.edu
Four Year, Private, Urban Founded in1919
Affiliation: Catholic
Student Profile: 1,750 undergraduate students (30% male, 70% female); 32 states and territories, 24 countries; 33% minority, 3% international.

Faculty Profile: 86 full-time faculty; 79% hold a terminal degree in their field. 15:1 student/faculty ratio. Average class size is 20.
Costs and Aid: 2007–2008: $40,000 comprehensive ($28,200 tuition).
Admissions
Phone: 617-735-9715
enroll@emmanuel.edu
Service-Learning
Community Service and Service Learning
Deirdre Bradley-Turner, Associate Director
Phone: 617-735-9753

Northshore Community College
http://www.northshore.edu
Two Year, Public, Urban/Suburban
Founded in 1965
Student Profile: 7,107 undergraduate students (39% male, 61% female); 28% minority, less than 1% international.
Faculty Profile: 134 full-time faculty. 20:1 student/faculty ratio. Average class size is 19.
Costs and Aid: 2007-2008: $3,630 comprehensive, no board ($750 tuition only). 45% of students receive financial aid.
Admissions
1 Ferncroft Road,
P.O. Box 3340,
Danvers, MA 01923
Phone: 978-762-4000
Service-Learning
Center for Teaching, Learning, and Assessment
Cate Kaluzny
Service-Learning Program Coordinator
Phone: 978-739-5571 or 781-477-2148

Pine Manor College

PROFILE PAGE 241

http://www.pmc.edu
Four Year, Private, Urban, Founded in 1911
Student Profile: 500 undergraduate students (100% female); 24% out-of-state, 62% minority, 31 countries.
Faculty Profile: 30 full-time faculty; 10:1 student/faculty ratio. Most frequent class size 14.
Costs and Aid: 2007-2008: $30,072 comprehensive ($18,957 tuition).
Admissions
400 Heath St.
Chestnut Hill, MA 02467
Phone: (800) PMC-1357
Service-Learning
The Center for Inclusive Leadership and Social Responsibility
Whitney Retallic, Director
Phone: 617-731-7620
inclusive@pmc.edu

Simmons College

PROFILE PAGE 242

http://www.simmons.edu
Four Year, Private, Urban, Founded in 1899
Student Profile: 2,072 undergraduate students (0% male, 100% female); 40 states and territories, 39 countries; 23% minority, 6% international.
Faculty Profile: 236 full-time faculty. 12:1 student/faculty ratio.
Costs and Aid: 2007-2008: $38,606 comprehensive ($27,468 tuition). 80% of students receive financial aid.
Admissions
Phone: 617-521-2051
Service-Learning
Scott/Ross Center for Community Service
Dr. Stephen London, Director
Phone: 617-521-2590
stephen.london@simmons.edu

Stonehill College

PROFILE PAGE 243

http://www.stonehill.edu
Four Year, Private, Suburban, Founded in 1948
Student Profile: 2,440 undergraduate students (40% male, 60% female).
Faculty Profile: 145 full-time faculty; 81% faculty hold a terminal degree in their field. 13:1 student/faculty ratio. Average class size is 19.8.
Cost and Aid: 2007-2008: $28,440 (tuition); $11,430 (room and board); no comprehensive fees. 87.5% of students receive financial aid.
Admissions
Phone: 508-565-1373
admissions@stonehill.edu
Service-Learning
Office of Community Service & Volunteerism
Nuala Boyle
Phone: 508-565-1067
nboyle@stonehill.edu

Suffolk University

PROFILE PAGE 244

http://www.suffolk.edu
Four-Year, Private, Urban, Founded in 1906
Student Profile: 5,196 undergraduate; 2,016 graduate; 1,546 degrees conferred annually; 948 international students from 95 countries.
Faculty Profile: 91% hold Ph.D. degrees; 12:1 student/faculty ratio (undergraduate); 21:1 student/faculty ratio (law school).
Costs and Aid: 2007-2008: $24,170 (undergraduate) $35,948 (law school); $54,673,740 financial aid available for

the College of Arts & Sciences and Sawyer Business School (awarded to 50% of students); $50,020,842 financial aid for Suffolk Law School (awarded to 88% of students).
Admissions
Phone: 617-573-8460 or 1-800-6SUFFOL(k)
admission@suffolk.edu
Service-Learning
Carolina Garcia
Director of Service Learning
Phone: 617-305-6306
Cgarcia@suffolk.edu

Tufts University

PROFILE PAGE 245

http://www.tufts.edu
Four Year, Private, Suburban, Founded in 1852
Student Profile: 4,997 undergraduate students (49% male, 51% female); 53 states and territories, 67 countries; 45 % minority, 6.0 % international.
Faculty Profile: 411 full-time faculty (229 part-time).100% hold a terminal degree in their field.
Costs and Aid: 2007–2008: $51,400 comprehensive ($38,840 tuition). 49% of students receive some financial aid.
Service-Learning
Jonathan M. Tisch College of Citizenship & Public Service
Nancy E. Wilson
Director & Associate Dean
Phone: 617-627-3453
Nancy.wilson@tufts.edu

University of Massachusetts Amherst
http://www.umass.edu
Four Year, Public, Suburban, Founded in 1863
Student Profile: 19,823 undergraduate students; 52 states and territories, 70 countries; 17% minority, .01% international.
Faculty Profile: 1,168 full-time faculty. 17.6:1 student/faculty ratio. Average class size is 40.
Costs and Aid: 2007-2008: $17,399 in-state comprehensive ($9,921 tuition). $27,977 out-of-state comprehensive ($20,499 tuition). 71% of students receive financial aid.
Admissions
Phone: 413-545-0222
mail@admissions.umass.edu
Service-Learning
UMass Office of Community Learning at Commonwealth College
Phone: 413-545-2015
servelearn@acad.umass.edu

University of Massachusetts Lowell

PROFILE PAGE 246

http://www.uml.edu
Four Year, Public, Urban, Founded in 1890
Student Profile: 8,879 undergraduate students -
6,063 FTEs - (59.8 % male, 40.2 % female); 7.5%
out-of-state, 19% minority, 1% international. 2,756
graduate students - 1,660 FTEs - (52.5% male,
47.5% female); 32.6% out of state, 11.9% minority,
15.3% international.
Faculty Profile: 684 faculty; 94% hold a terminal
degree in their field. 14:1 student/faculty ratio. 56% of
classes have fewer than 20 students; 4% of classes
have 50 or more students.
Costs and Aid: 2007–2008: $15,709 in-state
comprehensive ($8,731 tuition & fees); $27,362 out-
of-state comprehensive ($20,384 tuition & fees). 73%
of students receive financial aid. UML awarded more
than $50 million in aid.
Admissions
Phone: 978-934-3931
Service-Learning
Linda Barrington
Engineering S-L Coordinator
Phone: 978-934-2627
Linda_Barrington@uml.edu

Wentworth Institute of Technology

PROFILE PAGE 247

http://www.wit.edu
Four Year, Private, Urban, Founded in 1904
Student Profile: 3,412 undergraduate students
(80% male, 20% female); 37 states and territories, 50
countries; 15% minority, 5% international.
Faculty Profile: 15:1 student/faculty ratio.
Costs and Aid: $20,150 tuition; 75% of students
receive financial aid.
Admissions
Phone: 800-556-0610 or 617-989-4000
admissions@wit.edu web
Service-Learning
Center for Community & Learning Partnerships
Sean P. Bender
Phone: 617-989-4985
Directorbenders@wit.edu.edu

MICHIGAN

Central Michigan University

PROFILE PAGE 248

http://www.cmich.edu
Four Year, Public, Suburban, Founded in 1892
Student Profile: 20,078 undergraduate students (44%
male, 56% female); 16% minority, 3% international.
Faculty Profile: 704 full-time faculty, 82% hold a
terminal degree in their field. 22:1 student/faculty
ratio. Average class size is 20-29 students.
Costs and Aid: 2007–2008: $9,120 in-state
comprehensive ($7,343 tuition); $21,210 out-of-state
comprehensive ($17,078 tuition). 80% of students
receive financial aid.
Admissions
Phone: 888-292-5366 or 989-774-3076
cmuadmit@cmich.edu
Service-Learning
Faculty Center for Innovative Teaching
Todd Zakrajsek, Ph.D. Director
zakra1t@cmich.edu
Shawna K. Ross
Coordinator of Volunteer Center
ross1sk@cmich.edu

Madonna University

PROFILE PAGE 249

http://www.madonna.edu
Affiliation: Catholic
Four Year, Private, Suburban, Founded in 1937
Student Profile: 3,264 undergraduate students
(22.4% male, 77.6% female); 38 states and territories,
45 countries; 17.4% minority, 1% international.
Faculty Profile: 108 full-time faculty. 53% hold a
Ph.D. in their field. 13:1 student/faculty ratio. Average
class size is 15.
Costs and Aid: 2007–2008: $ 6,092 comprehensive
($2,700 tuition). 74% of students receive financial aid.
Admissions
Phone: 734-432-5341 or 800-852-4951 ext. 5341
Service-Learning
Office of Service-Learning
Kevin West, Director
Phone: 734-432-5704
kwest@madonna.edu.

Michigan State University

PROFILE PAGE 250

http://www.msu.edu
Four Year, Public, Suburban, Founded in 1855
Student Profile: 35,821 undergraduate students
(45% male, 55% female); 50 states, 150 countries;
18% minority, 7.5% international.
Faculty Profile: 4,148 full-time faculty. 14:1 student/
faculty ratio. Average class size is 34-47.
Costs and Aid: 2007–2008: $18,876 in-state
comprehensive ($8,672 tuition). $32,678 out-of state
comprehensive ($22,474 tuition). 73% of students
receive financial aid. Average award is $10,925.
Admissions
250 Hannah Administration Building
Phone: 517-355-8332
Service-Learning
Center for Service Learning and Civic Engagement
Phone: 517-353-4400
www.servicelearning.msu.edu

Northern Michigan University

PROFILE PAGE 251

http://www.nmu.edu
Four Year, Public, Small Town, Founded in 1899
Student Profile: 8,488 undergraduate students
(47% male, 53% female); 48 states and territories, 19
countries; 7% minority, 1% international.
Faculty Profile: 322 full-time faculty. 23:1 student/
faculty ratio. Average class size is 28.
Costs and Aid: 2007-2008: $13,704 comprehensive
($6,144 tuition). 80% of students receive financial aid.
Admissions
Phone: 906-227-2650
Service-Learning
Center for Student Enrichment
Dave Bonsall, Director
Phone: 906-227-2439
dbonsall@nmu.edu

University of Michigan

http://www.umich.edu
Four Year, Public, Suburban
Founded in 1817
Student Profile: 24,000 undergraduate students
(49% male, 51% female); 50 states and territories;
23% minority, 6% international.
Faculty Profile: 2,500 full-time faculty. 16:1 student/
faculty ratio. Average class size is 28.
Costs and Aid: 2007-2008: $18,700 in-state
comprehensive ($10,200 tuition); $39,600 out-of-state
comprehensive ($31,300 tuition). 70% of students
receive financial aid.
Admissions
Ann Arbor, MI 48109
Phone: 734-764-7433
Service-Learning
Ginsberg Center
734-647-7402

MINNESOTA

Augsburg College

PROFILE PAGE 252

http://www.augsburg.edu
Four Year, Private, Urban, Founded in 1869
Affiliation: The Evangelical Lutheran Church in America
Student Profile: 1911 undergraduate students (50% male, 50% female); 42 states, 40 countries; 21.7% students of color, 72 international students.
Faculty Profile: 185 full-time faculty, 15:1 student/faculty ratio. Average class size is 13-17.
Costs and Aid: 2007-2008: $24,046 comprehensive tuition. More than 80% of students receive financial aid.
Admissions
Phone: 800-788-5676
admissons@augsburg.edu
Service-Learning
Center for Service, Work, and Learning
Phone: 612-330-1148
careers@augsburg.edu

Century College

PROFILE PAGE 253

http://www.century.edu
Student Profile: 8,288 students, 43% male, 57% female, 24% minority.
Faculty Profile: 169 full-time faculty., 24:1 student/faculty ratio.
Costs and Aid: 2007-2008: Tuition and fees is $146.99/credit. A full-time student taking 15 credits Fall and Spring (30 credits per year) would be charged $4,409.70
Admissions
Phone: 651-773-1700 or 800-228-1978 ext. 1700
admissions@century.edu
Service-Learning
Tracey Wyman
Director of Service Learning and Global Education
Phone: 651-748-2602
tracey.wyman@century.edu

College of Saint Benedict and Saint John's University

PROFILE PAGE 254

http://www.csbsju.edu
Four Year, Private, Rural
Student Profile: 3,928 undergraduate (52% female, 48% male). 3.8% international, 38 countries, 127 international students.
Faculty Profile: 294 full-time faculty. 13:1 student/faculty ratio; average class size is 21.
Costs and Aid: 2007-2008: $28,668 tuition and fees, $7,959 room and board.
Admissions
Phone: 800-544-1489
Service-Learning
Marah Jacobson-Schulte
Service-Learning Coordinator
Phone: 320-363-5117
mjacobsonsc@csbsju.edu

College of St. Catherine

PROFILE PAGE 255

http://www.stkate.edu
Four Year, Private, Suburban, Founded in 1905
Student Profile: 3,811 undergraduate students (96.6% female, 3.4% male); 37 states, 38 countries; 23.3% minority/international.
Faculty Profile: 261 full-time faculty. 11:1 student/faculty ratio. 82% hold a terminal degree in their field. Average class size is 13.
Costs and Aid: 2007–2008: $25,942 comprehensive ($802 per credit tuition). 90% of students receive financial aid. Average award is $8,800.
Admissions
Phone: 800-690-8850 or 800-656-KATE
admissions@stkate.edu
Service-Learning
Community Work and Learning
Phone: 651-690-6842
communitywork@stkate.edu

Macalester College

PROFILE PAGE 256

http://www.macalester.edu
Four Year, Private, Urban, Founded in 1874
Affiliation: Presbyterian, Nonsectarian
Student Profile: 1,920 undergraduate students (42% male, 58% female); 48 states and territories, 75 countries; 18% minority, 12% international.
Faculty Profile: 157 full-time faculty; 94% hold a terminal degree in their field. 10:1 student/faculty ratio. Average class size is 17.
Costs and Aid: 2007–2008: $41,914 comprehensive ($33,694 tuition). 66% of students receive financial aid. Average first year need based award is $28,298.
Admissions
Phone: 651-696-6357 or 800-231-7974
admissions@macalester.edu
Service-Learning
Community-Based Learning
Karin Trail-Johnson
Associate Dean, Institute for Global Citizenship
Director, Civic Engagement Center
Phone: 651-696-6040
trailjohnson@macalester.edu
Department Email: cec@macalester.edu

Normandale Community College

http://www.normandale.edu
Two Year, Public, Suburban, Founded in 1968
Student Profile: 9,239 undergraduate students (43% male, 55% female); 20 states and territories, 52 countries; 22% minority, 1% international.
Faculty Profile: 186 full-time faculty. 28:1 student/faculty ratio. Average class size is 22.
Costs and Aid: 2007-2008: $150.40 per credit for tuition and fees for both in-state and out-of-state (no on campus student housing). 40% of students receive financial aid.
Admissions
Main Phone: 952-487-8200
Rick Smith, Director of Admissions
Phone: 952-487-8494
rick.smith@normandale.edu
Service-Learning
Center for Service-Learning
Wanda Kanwischer, Director
Phone: 952-487-8123
wanda.kanwischer@normandale.edu

University of St. Thomas

http://www.stthomas.edu
Student Profile: 5,682 undergraduate students (50% female, 50% male); 21% out-of-state; 1% international.
Faculty Profile: 400 full-time faculty. Most frequent class size is between 10 and 19.
Costs and Aid: $33,586 comprehensive. 55% of undergraduates receive financial aid; average freshman aid is $11,411.
Admissions
Mail 32F
2115 Summit Avenue
St. Paul, MN 55105-1096
651-962-6150
Service-Learning
Barbara Baker, Service-Learning Program Manager
Phone: 651-962-5380
servicelearn@stthomas.edu

Metropolitan State University

http://www.metrostate.edu

Four Year, Public, Urban, Founded in 1971

Student Profile: 8,943 undergraduate students (39.8% male, 60.2% female); 31.6 average age of students; 2.4% out-of-state students; 26.3% minority, 2.6% international.

Faculty Profile: 132 full-time faculty. 17:1 student/faculty ratio. Average class size is 22.

Costs and Aid: 2007-2008: $5,293 tuition (no dormitories). 55% of students receive financial aid.

Admissions

Monir Johnson, Director of Admissions

Phone: 651-793-1300

Monir.johnson@metrostate.edu

Service-Learning

Center for Community-Based Learning

Susan Shumer, Director

Phone: 651-793-1292

susan.shumer@metrostate.edu

Winona State University

PROFILE PAGE 257

http://www.winona.edu

Four-Year, Public, Rural, Founded in 1858

Student Profile: 7,693 undergraduate students (40% male, 60% female); 34 states and territories, 54 countries; 5% minority, 25% international.

Faculty Profile: 382 full-time faculty; 70% hold a terminal degree in their field; 21:1 student/faculty ratio; average class size is 27.

Costs and Aid: 2007–2008: $12,710 comprehensive ($5,600 tuition); $17,180 out-of-state comprehensive ($10,070 tuition; 70% of students receive financial aid.

Admissions

Phone: 800-DIAL-WSU Ext: 5100 or 507-457-5100

Admissions@winona.edu

Service-Learning

Center for Engaged Teaching and Scholarship

Joan Francioni, Ph.D., Director

Phone: 507-457-2336

jfrancioni@winona.edu

MISSISSIPPI

Jackson State University

http://www.jsums.edu

Four Year, Public, Urban, Founded in 1877

Student Profile: 6,509 undergraduate students (38% male, 62% female); 18% out-of-state, 1% international.

Faculty Profile: 335 full-time faculty; 18:1 student/faculty ratio. 71% of full/part time faculty hold Ph.D.'s.

Costs and Aid: $185 per credit hour in-state; $231 per credit hour out-of-state.

Admissions

1400 J. R. Lynch Street

P. O. Box 17330

Jackson, MS, 39217

Phone: 601-979-2100

Service-Learning

The Community Service/Service Learning Center

Phone: 601-979-1240

Tougaloo College

PROFILE PAGE 258

http://www.tougaloo.edu

Four Year, Private, Urban, Founded in 1869

Affiliation: United Church of Christ and the Disciples of Christ

Student Profile: 913 undergraduate students (31% male, 69% female), 24 states, 2 foreign countries; 99% African-American; less than 1% international.

Faculty Profile: 77 full-time faculty; 60% hold a terminal degree in their field. 1:12 student/faculty ratio.

Costs and Aid: $16,525 comprehensive ($9,900 tuition). 97% of students receive financial aid. Average award is $7,000.

Admissions

Phone: 601-977-7772

jjacobs@tougaloo.edu

Service-Learning

Center for Civic Engagement & Social Responsibility

Stephen L. Rozman, Director

Phone: 601-977-4460

srozman@tougaloo.edu

MISSOURI

Cottey College

http://www.cottey.edu

Two Year, Private, Rural, Founded in 1884

Student Profile: 321 undergraduate students (0% male 100% female); 44 states and territories, 11 countries; 20% minority, 7% international.

Faculty Profile: 32 full-time faculty. 10:1 student/faculty ratio. Average class size is 9.

Costs and Aid: 2007-2008: $19,360 comprehensive ($13,200 tuition). 97% of students receive financial aid.

Admissions

Richard R. Eber

Dean of Enrollment Management

Phone: 417-667-8181 Ext: 2238

reber@cottey.edu

Service-Learning

Service Learning/Academic Career Center

Linda Platt, Service-Learning Advisor

Phone: 417-667-8181 Ext. 2184

lplatt@cottey.edu

Kansas City Art Institute

PROFILE PAGE 259

http://www.kcai.edu

Four Year, Private, Urban, Founded in 1885

Student Profile: 676 undergraduate students (49% male, 51% female); 26 states and territories, 8 countries; 15% minority, 2% international.

Faculty Profile: 50 full-time faculty. 15:1 student/faculty ratio. Average class size is 15.

Costs and Aid: 2007-2008: $25,680 tuition. 99% of students receive financial aid.

Admissions

4415 Warwick,

Kansas City, MO 64111

Phone: 816-802-3300

Service-Learning

Community Arts and Service Learning Program (CASL)

Julie Metzler, Director

Phone: 816-802-3357

Missouri State University

PROFILE PAGE 260

http://www.missouristate.edu

Four Year, Public, Urban, Founded in 1905

Student Profile: 14,709 undergraduate students (56% female; 44% male); 81 countries.

Faculty Profile: 718 full-time faculty.

Costs and Aid: 2008–2009: $11,922 in-state comprehensive ($6,256 tuition); $17,200 out-of-state comprehensive ($11,536 tuition); 58% of students receive financial aid.

Admissions
Phone: 417-836-5517
Admissions@missouristate.edu
Service-Learning
Citizenship & Service-Learning
Elizabeth Carmichael Burton, Associate Director
Phone: 417-836-5774
ServiceLearning@missouristate.edu

Rockhurst University

PROFILE PAGE 261

http://www.rockhurst.edu
Four Year, Private, Urban, Founded in 1910
Student Profile: 1,528 undergraduate students (41% male, 59% female); 26 states and 1 territory, 8 countries; 16% minority, 1% international.
Faculty Profile: 125 full-time faculty. 11:1 student/faculty ratio. Average class size is 21. 87% hold a terminal degree in their field.
Costs and Aid: 2007–2008: $22,000 tuition. 98% of students receive financial aid including scholarship, grants and loans. Average award is $17,500.
Admissions
Phone: 816-501-4100 or 800-842-8776
admission@rockhurst.edu
Service-Learning
Center for Service Learning
Julia Vargas, Director
Julia.Vargas@rockhurst.edu
Phone: 816-501-4545

St. Louis Community College at Meramec

http://www.stlcc.edu
Two, Public, Suburban, Founded in 1965
Student Profile: 23,425 undergraduate students (37% male, 63% female); 2% out-of-state; 44% minority.
Faculty Profile: 435 full-time faculty. 20:1 student/faculty ratio. Average class size is 20.
Costs and Aid: 2007–2008: $81 per credit hour, $148 out-of-state. 31% of students receive financial aid.
Admissions
11333 Big Bend Blvd.
St. Louis, MO 63122
Phone: 314-984-7608
Service-Learning
Office of Service-Learning and Civic Engagement
Donna Halsband
Phone: 314-984-7893

Truman State University

PROFILE PAGE 262

http://www.truman.edu
Four Year, Public, Rural: Founded 1867
Student Profile: 5,608 undergraduates (43% male, 57% female); 9.8% minority, 4.2% international.

Faculty Profile: 344 full-time faculty, 83% hold a terminal degree in their field. 16:1 student/faculty ratio.
Costs and Aid: 2007–2008: $12,247 in-state comprehensive ($6,210 in-state tuition); $16,857 out-of-state comprehensive ($10,820 out-of-state tuition). 96% of students receive some financial aid.
Admissions
Phone: (800) 892-7792
Email: admissions@truman.edu
Service-Learning
The Center for Teaching and Learning
Julie Lochbaum, Ph.D.
Director
Phone: (660) 785-4391
Email: ctl@truman.edu

Westminster College

http://www.westminster-mo.edu
Four Year, Private, Rural, Founded in 1851
Student Profile: 960 undergraduate students (57% male, 43% female); 9% minority, 14% international.
Faculty Profile: 55 full-time faculty. 14:1 student/faculty ratio. Average class size is 16.
Costs and Aid: 2007-2008: $21,920 comprehensive ($15,500 tuition). 98% of students receive financial aid.
Admissions
501 Westminster Ave,
Fulton, MO 65251-1299
Phone: 1-800-475-3361
Service-Learning
Office of Community Action & Service-Learning/
Emerson Center for Leadership & Service
Courtney Swan
Phone: 573-592-6045
courtney.swan@westminster-mo.edu

William & Jewell College

PROFILE PAGE 263

http://www.jewell.edu
Four-Year, Private, Suburban Founded in 1849
Student Profile: 1,329 undergraduate students (40% male, 60% female); 10.8% minority.
Faculty Profile: 78 full-time faculty; 84.5% hold a terminal degree in their field; 14:1 student/faculty ratio; average class size is 19.
Costs and Aid: 2007–2008: $27,240 comprehensive ($21,400 tuition). 99% of students receive financial aid.
Admissions
Phone: 816-415-7511 or 888-2-JEWELL
admission@william.jewell.edu
Service-Learning
Phone: 816-415-7504
servicelearning@william.jewell.edu

MONTANA

University of Montana Missoula

PROFILE PAGE 264

http://www.umt.edu
Four Year, Public, Mid-town campus with a rural backyard, Founded in 1893
Student Profile: 11,841 undergraduate students (46% male, 54% female); 68% in-state, 32% out of state.
Faculty Profile: 588 full-time faculty (73%), 221 part-time (27%);19:1 student-faculty ratio.
Costs and Aid: 2007–2008: $5,849 in-state comprehensive ($2,494 tuition); $10,602 out-of-state comprehensive ($7,247 tuition). 67% of students receive financial aid.
Admissions
Enrollment Services
Phone: 406-243-6266
admiss@umontana.edu
Service-Learning
Office for Civic Engagement
Andrea Vernon, Ed D.
Phone: 406-243-5159
andrea.vernon@mso.umt.edu

NEBRASKA

College of Saint Mary

http://www.csm.edu
Four Year, Private, Urban, Founded in 1955
Affiliation: Catholic
Student Profile: 818 undergraduate students (0% male, 100% female); 22 states and territories, 4 countries; 21% minority, 1% international.
Faculty Profile: 55 full-time faculty. 11:1 student/faculty ratio. Average class size is 14.
Costs and Aid: 2007-2008: $26,436 comprehensive ($19,800 tuition). 81% of students receive financial aid.
Admissions
7000 Mercy Road
Omaha, NE 68106
Phone: 402-399-2400
Service-Learning
Jennifer Reed-Bouley Ph.D.
Jreed-bouley@csm.edu

Directory

Directory

Creighton University

PROFILE PAGE 265

http://www.creighton.edu
Four Year, Private, Founded in 1878
Student Profile: 4,104 undergraduate students (40% male, 60% female); 49 states and 2 territories, 33 countries; 15.5% minority, 1.8% international.
Faculty Profile: 501 full-time faculty. 87% hold a terminal degree in their field. 12:1 student/faculty ratio. Average class size is 22.
Costs and Aid: 2008–2009: $28,542 comprehensive ($27,282 tuition).
Admissions
Phone: 402-280-2703 or 800-282-5835
admissions@creighton.edu
Service-Learning
Office for Academic Excellence and Assessment
Mary Ann Danielson Ph.D., Director
Phone: 402- 280-2535
maddam@creighton.edu

Hastings College

http://www.hastings.edu
Four Year, Private, Rural, Founded in 1882
Student Profile: 1,091 undergraduate students (54% male, 46% female); 29 states and territories, 3 countries; 6% minority, 0.5% international.
Faculty Profile: 87 full-time faculty. 12:1 student/faculty ratio. Average class size is 18.
Costs and Aid: 2007-2008: $25,036 comprehensive ($18,822 tuition). 98 % of students receive financial aid.
Admissions
710 N. Turner Ave.,
Hastings, NE 68901
Phone: 402-463-2402
Service-Learning
Vocation and Values
Jheriot@hastings.edu

University of Nebraska at Kearney

PROFILE PAGE 266

http://www.unk.edu
Four Year, Public, Suburban, Founded in 1905
Student Profile: 5,400 undergraduate students; 44 states and territories, 54 countries.
Faculty Profile: 17:1 student/faculty ratio.
Costs and Aid: $129.50/credit hour for residents; $265.25 for non-residents. More than two-thirds of UNK students receive some form of financial assistance through scholarships, grants, loans, and work-study programs.
Admissions
905 West 25th Street
Kearney, NE 68849
Phone: 308-865-8702 or 1-800-KEARNEY

Service-Learning
Geraldine Stirtz, Director
B185 College of Education
Phone: 308-865-8957
stirtzg@unk.edu

University of Nebraska at Omaha

PROFILE PAGE 267

http://www.unomaha.edu
Four Year, Public, Urban, Founded in 1908
Student Profile: 11,929 undergraduate students (50.1% male, 49.9% female); 91% in-state, 111 countries; 13% of all students are minority or international students.
Faculty Profile: 499 full-time faculty. 18:1 student/faculty ratio. 63% of classes are under 30 students.
Costs and Aid: 2007–2008: Resident: $10,620 w/parent; $15,200 - $15,230 (tuition/fees $4,430.) Non-resident: $17,680 w/parent; $22,260 - $22,290 (tuition/fees $11,490.) About 70% of students receive financial aid. Average award is $1,500 (estimated per semester for undergraduate State of Nebraska residents.)
Admissions
dcicotello@mail.unomaha.edu
Service-Learning
Service-Learning Academy
Paul Sather, Director of Service-Learning Academy & American Humanics
Phone: 402-554-3196
psather@mail.unomaha.edu

NEW HAMPSHIRE

Saint Anselm College

http://www.anselm.edu
Four Year, Private, Suburban, Founded in 1889
Affiliation: Catholic, Order of Saint Benedict
Student Profile: 1,928 undergraduate students (43% male, 57% female); 28 states and territories, 21 countries.
Faculty Profile: 170 full-time faculty. 13:1 student/faculty ratio. Average class size is 18.
Costs and Aid: 2007-2008: $37,160 comprehensive ($26,960 tuition). 85% of students receive financial aid.
Admissions
100 Saint Anselm Drive,
Manchester, NH 03102
Phone: 603-641-7500
Service-Learning
Meelia Center for Community Service
Dan Forbes

NEW JERSEY

Montclair State University

PROFILE PAGE 268

http://www.montclair.edu
Four Year, Public, Founded in 1908
Student Profile: 12,190 undergraduate students (40% male, 60% female); 2% out-of-state, .3% international
Faculty Profile: 465 full-time faculty. 17:1 student/faculty profile, most frequent class size is 20-29.
Costs and Aid: $3,028 in-state tuition, $11,382 out-of-state tuition. 50% of undergraduates receive financial aid.
Admissions
Phone: 973-655-4444
Service-Learning
Center for Community Based Learning
Dr. Freyda Lazarus, Director
Phone: 973- 655-7202

Princeton University

www.princeton.edu
Four Year, Private, Suburban, Founded in 1746
Student Profile: 4,760 undergraduate students (51% male, 49% female); 50 countries; 30% minority, 9% international.
Faculty Profile: 850 full-time faculty. 5:1 student/faculty ratio.
Costs and Aid: 2007-2008: $47,375 comprehensive ($33,000 tuition). 54% of students receive financial aid.
Admissions
Phone: 609-258-3060
uaoffice@princeton.edu
Service-Learning
Community-Based Learning Initiative (CBLI)
Phone: 609-258-6986
cbli@princeton.edu

Raritan Valley Community College

http://www.raritanval.edu
Two Year, Public, Suburban, Founded in 1965
Student Profile: 6,408 undergraduate students (43% male, 57% female; 24% minority, 1.1% international.
Faculty Profile: 103 full-time faculty. 18:1 student/faculty ratio. Average class size is 19.4.
Costs and Aid: 2007-2008: $87 per credit. 23% of students receive financial aid.
Admissions
P.O. Box 3300,
Somerville, NJ 08876
Phone: 908-526-1200 Ext: 8284
Service-Learning
Service Learning Office
Lori Moog
www.raritanval.edu/servicelearning

The Richard Stockton College of New Jersey
http:// www.stockton.edu
Four Year, Public, Suburban
Founded in 1969
Student Profile: 6,766 undergraduate students (41% male, 59% female); 2.3% out-of-state, 19 countries; 20% minority, less than .05% international.
Faculty Profile: 259 full-time faculty. 18:1 student/faculty ratio. Average class size is 26.6.
Costs and Aid: 2007-2008: $18,952 in-state comprehensive ($9,697 tuition); $23,853 out-of-state comprehensive ($14,597 tuition). 77% of students receive financial aid.
Admissions
PO Box 195
Pomona, NJ 08240-0195
John Iacovelli, Dean of Enrollment Management
Phone: 609-652-4833
john.iacovelli@stockton.edu
Service-Learning
Office of Service-Learning
Tara N. Ronda, Service-Learning Coordinator

Rider University

PROFILE PAGE 269

http://www.rider.edu
Four Year, Private, Suburban, Founded in 1865
Student Profile: 4,733 undergraduate students (40% male, 60% female); 35 states, 50 countries; 17% minority, 3% international, 23% out-of-state.
Faculty Profile: 244 full-time faculty, 301 part-time faculty; 96.3% of full-time faculty have terminal degrees. 13.5:1 student/faculty ratio. Average class size is 27.
Costs and Aid: 2007-2008: $25,650 tuition; $5,640 room, $4,140 board, $580 fees. 63.8% of students receive financial aid.
Admissions
Phone: 609-896-50402 or 800-257-9026
admissions@rider.edu
Service-Learning
Bart Luedeke Center, Student Affairs
Phone: 609-896-5247

Rutgers, Newark
http://www.newark.rutgers.edu
Four Year, Public, Urban, Chartered in 1766
Student Profile: 10,553 undergraduate students (48% male, 52% female); 34 states and territories, 90 countries; 62% minorities, 31% underrepresented minorities, 6 % international.
Faculty Profile: 465 full-time faculty. 13:1 student/faculty ratio. Average class size for undergraduate is 33, graduate is 36.
Costs and Aid: 2007-2008: $20,091 in-state comprehensive ($8,541 tuition), $29,265 out of state comprehensive ($17,710 tuition). 53% of students receive financial aid (average award is $13,741).
Admissions
Provost Office, 123 Washington Street, Room 590, Newark, NJ 07102

Phone: 973-353-5541
Service-Learning
Tom Hopkins, Director
thopkins@newark.rutgers.edu
Honors Program
John Gunkel, Director
jgunkel@newark.rutgers.edu

Rutgers, New Brunswick
http://www.nb.rutgers.edu
Four Year, Public, Urban, Founded in 1766
Student Profile: 36,888 university-wide undergraduate students (48.2% male, 51.8% female); 92% in-state residency; 8% out-of-state students; 33.8% minority, 1.7% international.
Faculty Profile: 2,636 full-time faculty. 14:1 student/faculty ratio.
Costs and Aid: 2007-2008: $20,096 in-state comprehensive ($8,541 tuition). $29,265 out-of-state comprehensive ($17,710 tuition). 82% of students receive financial aid.
Admissions
Deborah Epting, Associate VP, Enrollment Management
epting@ugadm.rutgers.edu
Service-Learning
Civic Engagement and Service Education Partnerships Program (CESEP)
Amy Michael, Senior Program Administrator
civic@rci.rutgers.edu

Seton Hall University

PROFILE PAGE 270

http://www.shu.edu
Four Year, Private, Suburban, Founded in 1856
Affiliation: Catholic
Student Profile: 8,400 undergraduate students (46% male, 54% female).
Faculty Profile: 860 full-time faculty. 14:1 student/faculty ratio. Average class size is 25.
Costs and Aid: 2007-2008: $37,860 comprehensive ($28,150tuition). 90% of students receive financial aid.
Admissions
Phone: 973-761-9000
Service-Learning
Center for Community Research and Engagement
Phone: 973-275-5882

The College of New Jersey

PROFILE PAGE 271

http://www.tcnj.edu
Four Year, Public, Suburban, Founded in 1855
Student Profile: Undergraduate students (42% male, 58% female); 19 states and territories, 12 countries; 22% minority, 4% international.

Faculty Profile: 335 full-time faculty; 88% hold a terminal degree in their field; student/faculty ratio is 13:1. Average class size is 21.
Costs and Aid: 2007–2008: $20,549 in-state comprehensive ($8,072 tuition); $27,772 out-of-state comprehensive ($15,295 tuition). 56% of students receive financial aid.
Admissions
Phone: 609-771-2131
Service-Learning
Bonner Center for Civic & Community Engagement
Patrick Donohue, Director
Phone: 609-771-2548
service@tcnj.edu

NEW MEXICO

University of New Mexico
http://www.unm.edu
Four Year, Public, Urban, Founded in 1889
Student Profile: 18,199 undergraduate students (43% male, 57% female); 49% minority, 1% international.
Faculty Profile: 1,048 full-time faculty. 19:1 student/faculty ratio. Average class size is 30.
Costs and Aid: 2007-2008: $16,656 in-state comprehensive ($4,570 tuition); $622.60 per credit out of state. 85 % of students receive financial aid.
Admissions
Albuquerque, NM 87131
Phone: 505-277-2447 or 1-800-CALL UNM
apply@unm.edu
Service-Learning
Research Service Learning Program
Marilyn Davis
Phone: 505-277-8282

NEW YORK

Binghamton University
http://www.binghamton.edu
Four Year, Public, Suburban, Founded in 1946
Student Profile: 11,515 undergraduate students (52% male, 48% female); 41 states and territories, 66 countries; 12% minority, 8% international.
Faculty Profile: 575 full-time faculty. 20:1 student/faculty ratio. Average class size is 24.
Costs and Aid: 2007-2008: $13,538 in-state comprehensive ($4,350 tuition); $19,798 out-of-state comprehensive ($10,610 tuition). 68% of students receive financial aid.
Admissions
Box 6000
Binghamton NY, 13902
Phone: 607-777-2171
Service-Learning
Discovery
Elizabeth Carter, Director
Phone: 607-777-5985

Directory

Buffalo State College

http://www.buffalostate.edu
Four Year, Public, Urban, Founded in 1871
Student Profile: 9,314 undergraduate students (41% male, 59% female); 20% minorities. 30 states are represented at BSC with .01% international students.
Faculty Profile: 416 full-time faculty, 339 part-time faculty. 44% hold terminal degrees, 16:1 student/faculty ratio.
Costs and Aid: $8,700 in-state tuition ($21,220 comprehensive). 69% of students receive financial aid.
Admissions
Phone: 716-878-4017
admissions@buffalostate.edu
Service-Learning
Volunteer and Service-Learning Center
Phone: 716-878-5811
vslc@buffalostate.edu

Canisius College

http://www.canisius.edu
Four Year, Private, Urban
Affiliation: Catholic
Founded in 1870
Student Profile: 3,233 undergraduate students (45.6% male, 55.4% female).
Faculty Profile: 215 full-time faculty (more than 95% hold a terminal degree in their field). Student/faculty ratio is 12:1. Average class size is 17.
Costs and Aid: 2007-2008: $25,370 annual tuition. 98% of students in the class of 2011 receive financial aid.
Admissions
Phone: 716-888-2200 or 1-800-843-1517
admissions@canisius.edu
Service-learning
Sr. Patricia Brady, SSMN
Director of Service-Learning
Phone: 716-888-2177
bradyp@canisius.edu

Colgate University

http://www.colgate.edu
Four Year, Private, Rural Founded in 1819
Student Profile: 2,800 undergraduate students (48% male, 52% female); 35 countries; 22% identify themselves as students of color.
Faculty Profile: 277 full-time faculty. 96% hold a terminal degree in their field. 10:1 student/faculty

ratio. Average class size is 18.
Costs and Aid: 2007–2008: $ 46,830 tuition and fees. 39% of students receive financial aid.
Admissions
Phone: 315-228-7401
admission@colgate.edu
Service-Learning
Upstate Institute
Ellen Kraly, Director
ekraly@colgate.edu
Phone: 315-228-6623
The Center for Outreach, Volunteerism, and Education (COVE)
Ingrid Hale
Directorihale@colgate.edu
Phone: 315-228-6880

Cornell University

http://www.cornell.edu
Four Year, Private, Rural, Founded in 1865
Student Profile: 13,562 undergraduate students (51% male, 49% female); 29% minority.
Faculty Profile: 1,526 full-time faculty. 9:1 student/faculty ratio. Most frequent class size is 20-29.
Costs and Aid: 2007-2008: $50,384 comprehensive ($36,504 tuition). 60% of students receive financial aid.
Admissions
Ithaca, NY 14853
Phone: 607-254-4636
Service-Learning
Public Service Center
Phone: 607-255-1148
cupsc@cornell.edu

Daemen College

http://www.daemen.edu
Four Year, Private, Suburban, Founded in 1947
Affiliation: Nondenominational
Student Profile: 1,705 undergraduate students (24% male, 76% female); 3% out-of-state.
Faculty Profile: 102 full-time faculty. 15:1 student/faculty ratio. Most frequent class size is 10-19.
Costs and Aid: 2007–2008: $18,750 comprehensive ($18,300tuition). 96% of students receive financial aid.
Admissions
Phone: 716-839-8225
Service-Learning
The Center for Sustainable Communitites and Civic Engagement
Phone: 716-839-8489

Fordham University

http://www.fordham.edu
Four Year, Private, Urban, Founded in 1841
Affiliation: Jesuit
Student Profile: 8,477 undergraduate students (40% male, 60% female); 53 states and territories, 46 countries; 24.6% minority.
Faculty Profile: 704 full-time faculty. 12:1 student/faculty ratio. Average class size is 22.
Costs and Aid: 2007-2008: $45,000 comprehensive ($31,800 tuition). 80% of students receive financial aid.
Admissions
Phone: 718-817-4000
Service-Learning
Service Learning Program
Sandra Lobo Jost
Community Service Program Director
lobo@fordham.edu
Phone: 718-817-4510

Hobart and William Smith Colleges

http://www.hws.edu
Four Year, Private, Rural. Hobart - Founded in 1822, William Smith - Founded in 1908
Affiliation: Episcopal/ Nondenominational
Student Profile:Student Profile: undergraduate students (47% male, 53% female); 39 states and territories, 20 countries.
Faculty Profile: 207 full-time faculty. 96% hold a terminal degree in their field. 11:1student/faculty ratio. Average class size is 18.
Costs and Aid: 2007–2008: $47,768 comprehensive ($36,718 tuition). 77% of students receive financial aid.
Admissions
Phone: 800-852-2256
admissions@hws.edu
Service-Learning
Center for Community Engagement and Servce-Learning
W. Averell H. Bauder, Director
Phone: 315-781-3825
bauder@hws.edu

Houghton College

http://www.houghton.edu
Four Year, Private, Rural, Founded in 1883
Affiliation: Wesleyan
Student Profile: 1,160 undergraduate students; 40states and territories, 20 countries.
Faculty Profile: 87 full-time faculty. 13:1 student/faculty ratio. Average class size is 22.
Costs and Aid: 2007-2008: $28,480 comprehensive ($21,620 tuition). 90% of students receive financial aid.
Admissions

PO Box 128
Houghton, NY 14744
Phone: 800-777-2556
Service-Learning
Office of Service-Learning
Matthew Dougherty
Director of Service Learning
585-567-9674
Matthew.dougherty@houghton.edu

Nazareth College

PROFILE PAGE 278

http://www.naz.edu
Four Year, Private, Suburban, Founded in 1924
Student Profile: 2,167 undergraduate students (25% male, 75% female); 24 states and territories; 10% minority, 1.6% international.
Faculty Profile: 24 full-time faculty; 90.1% hold a terminal degree in their field. 12:1 student/faculty ratio.
Costs and Aid: 2007–2008: $35,412 comprehensive ($23,046 tuition). 96% of students receive financial aid.
Admissions
4245 East Avenue
Rochester, NY 14618-3790
Phone: 585-389-2860 or 1-800-462-3944
admissions@naz.edu
Service-Learning
Center for Service-Learning
Dr. Marie Watkins, Ph.D., M.S.W., M.S.
Associate Professor; Director, Center for Service-Learning; Director, Community-Based Youth Development Minor
Phone: 585-389-2748
mwatkin2@naz.edu

Niagara University

PROFILE PAGE 279

http://www.niagara.edu
Four Year, Private, Suburban, Founded in 1856
Affiliation: Catholic
Student Profile: 2,800 undergraduate students (40% male, 60% female); 31 states and territories, 8% minority, 12% international.
Faculty Profile: 150 full-time faculty; 92% hold a terminal degree in their field.14:1 student/faculty ratio. Average class size is 25.
Costs and Aid: 2007–2008: $ 30,700 comprehensive ($ 21,000 tuition). 98% of students receive financial aid.
Admissions
Phone: 716-286-8700
Service-Learning
Marilynn P. Fleckenstein,
Associate Vice President for Academic Affairs
Phone: 716-286-8750

Onondaga Community College
http://www.sunyocc.edu
Community, Public, Suburban, Founded in 1961
Student Profile: 10,637 undergraduate students (49.2% male, 50.8% female); 14 states and territories; 12.1% minority, 0.4% international.
Faculty Profile: 163 full-time faculty. Average class size is 18.83.
Costs and Aid: 2007-2008: $12,146 in-state comprehensive ($3,280 tuition). $15,426 out-of-state comprehensive ($6,560 tuition). 86.4% of students receive financial aid.
Admissions
4585 W. Seneca Turnpike,
Syracuse, NY 13215-4585
Phone: 315-498-2000
studentcentral@sunyocc.edu
Service-Learning
Center for Service-Learning and Volunteering
Phone: 315-498-7207
volunteer@sunyocc.edu

Pace University
http://www.pace.edu
Four Year, Private, Urban NYC Campus, Suburban Westchester Campus; Founded in 1906
Student Profile: 7,716 undergraduate students (40% male, 60% female); 54 states and territories, 123 countries; 30% minority, 5% international.
Faculty Profile: 438 full-time faculty. 13:1 student/faculty ratio. Average class size is 20.
Costs and Aid: 2007-2008: $40,428 comprehensive ($29,454 tuition). 61% of students receive financial aid.
Admissions
Pace University
New York City and Westchester, NY
Phone: 800-874-PACE
Service-Learning
Center for Community Outreach at Dyson College & Project Pericles at Pace University
Dr. Mary Ann Murphy, Director
Phone: 212-346-1767
mmurphy@pace.edu

Skidmore College
http://www.skidmore.edu
Four-year, Private, Founded in 1903
Student Profile: 2,300 undergraduate students (41% male, 59% female); 17% minority, 2.2% international. 32.5% in-state, 67.5% out-of-state/country.
Faculty Profile: 241 full-time faculty; 82% hold a terminal degree in their field; 9:1 student/faculty ratio.
Costs and Aid: 2007–2008: $46,696 comprehensive, $36,126 tuition. Skidmore awards 27 million dollars in financial aid. 41% of students receive need-based grant assistance; 55% receive financial aid; 50% are given the opportunity to work on campus. The average first-year financial aid package is $33,000.
Admissions
815 North Broadway
Saratoga Springs, NY 12866-1632
Phone: 800-867-6007
admissions@skidmore.edu

Service-Learning
Office of Community Service Programs
Michelle Hubbs, Director
Phone: 518-580-5784
mhubbs@skidmore.edu

State University of New York- College of Environmental Science and Forestry

PROFILE PAGE 280

http://www.esf.edu
Four Year, Public, Urban, Founded in 1911
Student Profile: Undergraduate students (60% male, 40% female); 24 states and territories, 7 countries; 9% minority, 1% international.
Faculty Profile: 136 full-time faculty; 90% hold a terminal degree in their field; 12:1 student/faculty ratio. Average class size is 20.
Costs and Aid: 2007–2008: $18,670 in-state comprehensive ($4,350 tuition); $24,930 out-of-state comprehensive ($10,610 tuition). 85% of students receive financial aid.
Admissions
Phone: 315-470-6600 or 800-777-7373
esfinfo@esf.edu
Service-Learning
Associate Dean for Student Life and Experiential Learning
Phone: 315-470-6658

State University of New York at Oswego

PROFILE PAGE 281

http://www.oswego.edu
Four Year, Public, Small-city, Founded in 1861
Student Profile: 6,669 undergraduate students (47% male, 53% female); 18 states and territories, 30 countries; 12% minority, 2% international.
Faculty Profile: 326 full-time faculty. 83% hold a terminal degree in their field. 18:1 student/faculty ratio. Average class size is 24.
Costs and Aid: 2007–2008: $14,904 in-state comprehensive ($4,350 tuition); $20,080 out-of-state comprehensive ($10,610 tuition). 64% of students receive financial aid. Average award is $8,596.
Admissions
Phone: 315-312-2250
admiss@oswego.edu
Service-Learning
Center for Service Learning and Community Service
Phone: 315-312-2505
service@oswego.edu

Syracuse University

PROFILE PAGE 282

http://www.syr.edu
Four Year, Private, Urban, Founded in 1870
Affiliation: Nondenominational
Student Profile: 12,491 undergraduate students
(44% male, 56% female); 50 states and territories,
115 countries, 29% minority, 4% international.
Faculty Profile: 909 full-time faculty, 106 part-time,
447 adjunct. 88% of full-time faculty have earned
Ph.D or professional degrees.
Costs and Aid: 2007-2008: $30,470 tuition. 64%
of undergraduate students receive need-based
financial aid.
Admissions
Phone: 315-443-1870
Service-Learning
Mary Ann Shaw Center for Public & Community
Service (CPCS)
Pamela Kirwin Heintz, Director
Phone: 315-443-3051
pkheintz@syr.edu

University of Rochester

PROFILE PAGE 283

http://www.rochester.edu
Four Year, Private, Suburban, Founded in 1850
Student Profile: Undergraduates (49% male, 51%
female); 50 states, 52 countries; 44% undergraduates
Out-of-state, 8% international.
Faculty Profile: 515 full-time faculty; 88% hold a
terminal degree in their field. 9:1 student/faculty ratio.
Average class size is 30.
Costs and Aid: 2007-2008: $45,830 comprehensive
($34,380 tuition). 87% of students receive financial aid.
Admissions
Phone: 585-275-3221 or 888-822-2256
admit@admissions.rochester.edu
Service-Learning
Rochester Center for Community Leadership
Phone: 585-276-3278
csn@ur.rochester.edu

NORTH CAROLINA

Appalachian State University

PROFILE PAGE 284

http://www.web.appstate.edu
Four Year, Public, Rural, Founded in 1899
Student Profile: 13,997 undergraduate students
(52.7% male, 47.3% female); 9% out-of-state; 10%
minority.
Faculty Profile: 17:1 student/faculty ratio. Average
class size is fewer than 25 students.
Costs and Aid: 2007-2008: $9,894 in-state
comprehensive ($4,534 tuition), $19,954 out-of-state
comprehensive ($14,594 tuition). 59% of students
receive financial aid.
Admission
Phone: 828-262-2000
Service-Learning
University College/ACT Program
Shari Galiardi
Phone: 828-262-2193

Asheville-Buncombe Technical Community College

http://abtech.edu
Two Year, Public, Urban, Founded in 1959
Student Profile: 6,626 undergraduate students
(43.1% male, 56.9% female); 42 states and territories;
9.4% minority, 0.1% international.
Faculty Profile: 160 full-time faculty. Average class
size is 15.6.
Costs and Aid: 2007-2008: $1,264 tuition in-state,
$7,024 tuition out of state. 76% of students receive
financial aid.
Admissions
340 Victoria Rd.
Asheville, NC 28801
Phone: 828-254-1921 Ext: 202
Service-Learning
Service-Learning Center
Lloyd Weinberg
Phone: 828-254-1921 Ext: 7573
Lweinberg@abtech.edu

Central Piedmont Community College

http://www1.cpcc.edu/
Four Year, Public, Urban, Founded in 1963
Student Profile: 14,811 undergraduate students
(48% male, 52% female); 5% out-of-state.
Faculty Profile: 21:1 student/faculty ratio.
Cost and Aid: $42 per credit in-state, $233.30 per
credit out-of-state.

Admissions
PO Box 35009
Charlotte, NC 28235
Phone: 704-330-CPCC (2722)
Service-Learning
Service Learning Center
Phone: 704-330-6445
service.learning@cpcc.edu

Duke University

PROFILE PAGE 285

http://www.duke.edu
Four Year, Private, Founded in 1924
Student Profile: 6,197 undergraduate students (51%
male, 49% female); 85% out of state; 46% minority,
6% international.
Faculty Profile: 787 full-time faculty. 8:1 student/
faculty ration. Average class size is 22.
Costs and Aid: 2007-2008: $45,091 comprehensive
($35,856 tuition). 40% of students receive financial
aid.
Admissions
Phone: 919-684-3214
Service-Learning
Duke Center for Civic Engagement/DukeEngage
Phone: 919-668-1724

Elon University

http://www.elon.edu
Four Year, Private, Suburban
Affiliation: United Church of Christ
Founded in 1889
Student Profile: 4,939 undergraduate students (41%
male, 59% female); 46 states and DC, 45 countries;
10% minority, 2% international.
Faculty Profile: 310 full-time faculty. 14:1 student/
faculty ratio. Average class size is 22.
Costs and Aid: 2007-2008: $29,462 comprehensive
($21,886 tuition). 61% of students receive financial aid.
Admissions
100 Campus Drive
Elon, NC 27244
Phone: 336-278-2000
Service-Learning:
John R. Kernodle, Jr. Center for Service Learning
Phone: 336-278-7250

Mars Hill College

PROFILE PAGE 286

http://www.mhc.edu
Four Year, Private, Rural, Founded in 1856
Affiliation: Baptist
Student Profile: Undergraduate students (51% male, 49% female); 34 states and territories, 21 countries; 22% minority.
Faculty Profile: 81 full-time faculty. 14:1 student/ faculty ratio. Average class size is 15-22.
Costs and Aid: 2007-2008: $26,785 comprehensive ($19,984 tuition). 96% of students receive financial aid.
Admissions
Phone: 866-642-4968
Service-Learning
Stan Dotson
Dean of Life Works
Phone: 828-689-1161
sdotson@mhc.edu

North Carolina State University

PROFILE PAGE 287

http://www.ncsu.edu
Four Year, Public, Urban, Founded in 1887
Student Profile: 21,438 undergraduate students (57% male, 43% female); 7% out-of-state, 1% international.
Faculty Profile: 1,638 full-time faculty. 16:1 student/ faculty ratio.
Costs and Aid: $3,760 in-state tuition, $15,958 out-of-state tuition. 39% of students receive financial aid.
Admissions
hone: 919-515-5039
Service-Learning
Phone: 919-515-3276
http://cnr.ncsu.edu/prtm/extension/service.html

University of North Carolina at Chapel Hill

PROFILE PAGE 288

http://www.unc.edu
Four Year, Public, Suburban, Founded in 1789
Student Profile: 49 states and territories, over 100 countries; 28.18% minority, 3.9% international.
Faculty Profile: 3,200 full-time faculty. 14:1 student/ faculty ratio. Average class size is 30.
Costs and Aid: 2007-2008: $15,796 comprehensive ($3,705 tuition).
Admissions
Phone: 919-966-3621
Service-Learning
APPLES Service-Learning Program
Phone: 919-962-0902
apples@unc.edu

University of North Carolina at Greensboro

http://www.uncg.edu
Four, Public, Urban, Founded in 1891
Student Profile: 13,154 undergraduate students (32% male, 68% female); 7% out of state; 24% minority, 1% international.
Faculty Profile: 790 full-time faculty, 211 part-time. 17:1 student/faculty ratio.
Costs and Aid: 2007-2008: $10,100 comprehensive ($4,029 tuition). 65 % of students receive financial aid.
Admissions
P. O. Box 26170
Greensboro, NC 27402
Phone: 336-334-5000
Service-Learning
Office of Leadership and Service-Learning
Dr. Cathy H. Hamilton, Director
chhamilt@uncg.edu

Warren Wilson College

PROFILE PAGE 289

http://www.warren-wilson.edu
Four Year, Private, Rural, Founded 1894
Student Profile: 868 students (38% male, 62% female); 44 states and territories; 5% minority, 4% international.
Faculty Profile: 62 full-time faculty. 12:1 student/ faculty ratio. Average class size is 16.
Costs and Aid: 2007–2008: $25,384 comprehensive ($21,384 tuition). 90% of students receive some financial aid. Average award: $12,374.
Admissions
Phone: 800-934-3536 or 828-771-2073
admit@warren-wilson.edu
Service-Learning
Carolyn Wallace
Dean of Service-Learning
Phone: 828-771-3015
service@warren-wilson.edu

Western Carolina University

PROFILE PAGE 290

http://www.wcu.edu
Four Year, Public, Rural, Founded 1889
Student Profile: 8,665 total; 7,403 undergraduate; 1,263 graduate students 46% male, 54% female; 46 states and territories, 39 countries;13.3% minority, 3.6% international
Faculty Profile: 457 full-time faculty; 74% hold terminal degrees in their fields; 14:1 student/faculty ratio; average freshman class size is 23.
Costs and Aid: $13,630 in-state comprehensive ($4,871 tuition); $23,767 out-of-state comprehensive ($14,454 tuition); 74% of students receive some financial aid; average award is $7,500.
Admissions
Phone: 828-227-7317 or 877-WCU-4YOU

admiss@wcu.edu
Service-Learning
Center for Service-Learning
Glenn Bowen, Ph.D.
Phone: 828-227-2643
gbowen@email.wcu.edu

NORTH DAKOTA

University of North Dakota

http://www.und.edu
Four Year, Public, Founded in 1883
Student Profile: 10,376 undergraduate students (54% male, 46% female); 2% international.
Faculty Profile: 593 full-time faculty; 18:1 student/ faculty ratio; average class size is 20-29.
Costs and Aid: 2007-2008: $5,025 in-state tuition, $13,418 out-of-state tuition. 59% of students receive financial aid.
Admissions
205 Twamley Hall 264
Grand Forks, ND 5820
Phone: 800-225-5863
Service-Learning
Center for Community Engagement
Lana Rakow , Director
Phone: 701-777-2287
lanarakow@mail.und.nodak.edu

OHIO

Bowling Green State University

http://www.bgsu.edu
Four Year, Public, Rural, Founded in 1910
Student Profile: 17,657 undergraduate students (45% male, 54% female); 51 states and territories, 81 countries; 19% minority.
Faculty Profile: 921 full-time faculty. 19:1 student/ faculty ratio. Average class size is 25.
Costs and Aid: 2008-2009: $16,360 in-state comprehensive ($8,220 tuition); $23,668 out-of-state comprehensive ($11,874 tuition). 69 percent of all BGSU undergraduate students receive financial aid.
Admissions
110 McFall Center
Bowling Green, OH, 43403
Phone: 1-866-CHOOSEBGSU
Service-Learning
Office of Service-Learning
Phone: 419-372-9287
slbgsu@bgsu.edu

Defiance College

PROFILE PAGE 291

http://www.defiance.edu
Four year, Private, Suburban, Founded in 1850
Student Profile: 1,000 undergraduate and graduate students (50% women, 50% men); 66% of traditional students live on campus.
Faculty Profile: 12:1 student/faculty ratio. Average class size is 15.
Costs and Aid: 2007-2008: $10,655 tuition per semester. 99% of full-time students receive financial aid.
Admissions
Phone: 419-783-2359 or 800-520-GODC (4632)
admissions@defiance.edu
Service-Learning
Dr. Laurie Worrall
Dean, McMaster School for Advancing Humanity
Phone: 419-783-2553
lworrall@defiance.edu

John Carroll University

PROFILE PAGE 292

http://www.jcu.edu
Four Year, Private, Suburban, Founded in 1886
Affiliation: Jesuit, Catholic
Costs and Aid: 2007–2008: $34,934 comprehensive ($26,144 tuition). 98% of students receive financial aid
Admissions
Phone: 216-397-4294 or 888-335-6800
admission@jcu.eduwww.jcu.edu
Service-Learning
Center for Service and Social Action
Dr. Peggy Finucane, Interim Director
Phone: 216-397-1780
mfinucane@jcu.edu

Kent State University

http://www.kent.edu
Four Year, Public, Suburban, Founded in 1910
Student Profile: 29,227 undergraduate students (39% male, 61% female); 50 states and territories, 10.3% minority.
Faculty Profile: 570 full-time faculty. 18:1 student/faculty ratio.
Costs and Aid: 2007-2008: $16,770 comprehensive ($8,430 tuition). $23, 992 out-of-state comprehensive ($15,862 tuition). 75% of students receive financial aid.
Admissions
161 Michael Schwartz Center
Kent, OH 44242
Phone: 330-672-2444 or 800-988-5368
Service-Learning
Center for Student Involvement
Megan O'Dell-Scott
modellsc@kent.edu

Oberlin College

PROFILE PAGE 293

http://www.oberlin.edu
Four Year, Private, Rural, Founded in 1833
Student Profile: 2,800 undergraduate students (45% male, 55% female); 19% minority, 6% international, 9% in-state, 85% out-of-state, 6% from abroad.
Faculty Profile: 274 full-time faculty, 95% hold a terminal degree in their field. The student-faculty ratio in the College of Arts and Sciences is 11:1 and in the Conservatory of Music the ratio is 8:1. Average class size is 18.
Costs and Aid: 2008–2009: $48,150 comprehensive ($38,012 tuition). 70% of students receive financial aid. Average award is $25,000.
Admissions
Phone: 800-622-6243 or 440-775-8411
college.admissions@oberlin.edu
Service-Learning
Bonner Center for Service & Learning
Beth Blissman, Ph.D., Director
Phone: 440-775-8055
beth.blissman@oberlin.edu

Otterbein College

PROFILE PAGE 294

http://www.otterbein.edu
Four Year, Private, Suburban, Founded in 1847
Affiliation: United Methodist
Student Profile: 2,715 undergraduate students (35% male, 65% female); 35 states and territories, 11 countries; 10% minority, 1% international.
Faculty Profile: 162 full-time faculty; 91% hold a terminal degree in their field. 13:1 student/faculty ratio.
Costs and Aid: 2007–2008: $25,065 tuition. 95% of students receive financial aid.
Admissions
Phone: 614-890-3000
Service-Learning
Center for Community Engagement
Melissa Kesler Gilbert
Phone: 614 -823-1251

Sinclair Community College

http://www.sinclair.edu
Two Year, Public, Urban, Founded in 1887
Student Profile: 22,555 undergraduate students (41% male, 59% female); 19.8% minority, .5% international.
Faculty Profile: 434 full-time faculty. Average class size is 17.84.
Costs and Aid: 2007-2008: $2,025 tuition. 37% of students receive financial aid.
Admissions
444 West Third Street,
Dayton, OH 45402
Phone: 937-512-3000
Service-Learning

Service Learning Office
Marilyn Rodney,
Service Learning Coordinator
Phone: 937-512-5040
marilyn.rodney@sinclair.edu

Xavier University, Ohio

PROFILE PAGE 295

http://www.xavier.edu
Four Year, Private, Urban Founded in 1831
Affiliation: Catholic, Jesuit
Student Profile: Undergraduate students (46% male, 54% female); 30 states and territories, 38 countries; 18% students of color, inclusive of both minority and international.
Faculty Profile: 289 full-time faculty. 90% hold a terminal degree in their field. 13:1 student/faculty ratio. Average class size is 22.
Costs and Aid: 2007-2008: $34,000 comprehensive ($24,000 tuition). 95% of students receive financial aid.
Admissions
Phone: 513-745-3301 or 800-344-GOXU
xuadmit@xavier.edu
Service-Learning
Academic Service Learning Semester Programs
Irene B. Hodgson, Ph.D., Interim Director
Phone: 513-745-3541
hodgson@xavier.edu

OKLAHOMA

Oklahoma City University

PROFILE PAGE 296

http://www.okcu.edu
Four Year, Private , Founded in 1904
Affiliation: United Methodist
Student Profile: 1,726 undergraduate students (45% male, 55% female); 46 states, 56 countries; 17% minority, 27% international.
Faculty Profile: 156 full-time faculty and 142 part-time faculty; More than 79% hold a terminal degree in their field. 14:1 student/faculty ratio. Average class size for freshmen is17; average class size for upperclassmen is 13.
Costs and Aid: 2007–2008: $30,900 comprehensive ($19,600 tuition per year). 96% of freshmen receive financial aid.
Admissions
uadmissions@okcu.edu
Service-Learning
Wimberly School of Religion
Mark Davies, Ph.D., Dean
Phone: 405-208-5284
mdavies@okcu.edu

Rose State College
http://www.rose.edu
Two Year, Public, Suburban, Founded in 1970
Student Profile: 7,500 undergraduate students (39% male, 61% female); 32% minority, .3% international.
Faculty Profile: 121 full-time faculty. 1:18 student/faculty ratio. Average class size is 21.
Costs and Aid: 2007-2008: $1,798 resident tuition; $6,256 non-resident. 58.6% of students receive financial aid.
Admissions
Mechelle Aitson-Roessler
Phone: 405-733-6203
maitson-roessler@rose.edu
Service-Learning
Service-Learning Office
Sherri Mussatto
Phone: 405-733-7503
smussatto@rose.edu

The University of Science and Arts of Oklahoma
http://www.usao.edu
Four Year, Public, Suburban, Founded in 1908
Student Profile: 1,195 undergraduate students (45% male, 65% female); 6% out-of-state students.
Faculty Profile: 47 full-time faculty, 18:1 student/faculty ratio. Most frequent class size is 10-19.
Costs and Aid: 65% of students receive financial aid.
Admissions
1727 West Alabama
Chickasha, OK, 73018
Phone: 405-574-1357

OREGON

Portland Community College
http://www.pcc.edu
Two Year, Public, Urban, Founded in 1961
Student Profile: 24,000 undergraduate students (44.4% male, 55.6% female); 25% minority, 3% international.
Faculty Profile: 415 full-time faculty. 58:1 student/faculty ratio. Average class size is 21.
Costs and Aid: 2007-2008: $2,664 tuition; 33% of students receive financial aid.
Admissions
PO Box 19000
Portland, OR 97280
Phone: 503-977-8888
Service-Learning
Jennifer Alkezweeny
Phone: 503-977-4419
jennifer.alkezweeny@pcc.edu

Portland State University

PROFILE PAGE 297
http://www.pdx.edu
Four Year, Public, Founded in 1946
Student Profile: 16,980 undergraduate students (46.8% male, 53.1% female); 82.1% in-state, 17.9% out-of-state; 24 % minority, 3.9 % international.
Faculty Profile: 648 full-time faculty; 563 hold a terminal degree in their field; 23:1 student/faculty ratio. Average class size is 23.
Costs and Aid: 2007–2008: $18,777 comprehensive in-state ($3,528 tuition); $30,630 comprehensive out-of-state ($16,617 tuition). 52.99% of students receive financial aid.
Admissions
Phone: 503-725-3511 or 800-547-8887 Ext: 5-3511
Service-Learning
Office of Community-University Partnerships
Amy Spring, Assistant Director
Phone: 503-725-5642

University of Portland

PROFILE PAGE 298
http://www.up.edu
Four Year, Founded in 1901
Affiliation: Catholic, Congregation of Holy Cross
Student Profile: 2,849 undergraduate students (37% male, 63% female); 40 states and territories; 15% minority, 1% international.
Faculty Profile: 197 full-time faculty, 119 part-time faculty. 12:1 student/faculty ratio. Average class size is 25.
Costs and Aid: 2007–2008: $35,800 comprehensive ($27,500 tuition). Nearly 94% of students receive financial aid.
Admissions
5000 N. Willamette Blvd.
Portland, OR 97203
Phone: 503-943-7147
Service-Learning
Moreau Center for Service and Leadership
Phone: 503- 943-7132
moreaucenter@up.edu

PENNSYLVANIA

Allegheny College
http://www.allegheny.edu
Four Year, Private, Urban, Founded in 1788
Affiliation: Methodist
Student Profile: 2,100 undergraduate students (47% male, 53% female); 33 states and territories, 27 countries; 5% minority, 3% international.
Faculty Profile: 135 full-time faculty. 14:1 student/faculty ratio. Average class size is 15-22.
Costs and Aid: 2007-2008: $35,300 comprehensive ($28,300 tuition). 68 % of students receive financial aid.
Admissions
520 North Main Street
Meadville PA 16335
Phone: 814-332-3100
Service-Learning
Community Service and Service-Learning, ACCEL
David Roncolato, Ph.D.
Phone: 814-332-5318
droncola@allegheny.edu

Alvernia College

PROFILE PAGE 299
http://www.alvernia.edu
Four Year, Private, Suburban, Founded in 1958
Affiliation: Catholic
Student Profile: 2,038 undergraduate students (31% male, 69% female); 11 states and territories 16 countries; 19% minority, 1% international.
Faculty Profile: 81 full-time faculty. 62% hold a terminal degree in their field. 15:1 student/faculty ratio.
Costs and Aid: 2007–2008: $33,656 comprehensive ($21,400 tuition). 98% of students receive financial aid.
Admissions
Phone: 1-888-ALVERNIA (1-888-258-3764)
admissions@alvernia.edu
Service-Learning
Ginny Hand, Director,
Center for Community Engagement
ginny.hand@alvernia.edu

Cabrini College

PROFILE PAGE 300
http://www.cabrini.edu
Four Year, Private, Suburban, Founded in 1957
Student Profile: 1,600 undergraduate students, 37% out-of-state.
Faculty Profile: 66 full-time faculty, 16:1 student/faculty ratio. Average class size is 18.
Costs and Aid: 2007–2008: $38,530 comprehensive ($27,200 tuition). 97% of students receive financial aid.
Admissions
Phone: 610-902-8100
Service-Learning
David Chiles, Coordinator of Service-Learning
Phone: 610-902-8408
David.chiles@cabrini.edu

Dickinson College

http://www.dickinson.edu
Four Year, Private, Small Town, Founded in 1783
Student Profile: 2,381 undergraduate students
(45% male, 55% female); 41states and territories, 46
countries; 14% minority, 6% international.
Faculty Profile: 188 full-time faculty. 11:1 student/
faculty ratio. Average class size is 17.
Costs and Aid: 2007-2008: $47,834 comprehensive
($37,900 tuition). 61% of students receive financial aid.
Admissions
PO Box 1773,
Carlisle, PA 17013
Phone: 717-243-5121
Service-Learning
Shalom D. Staub, Ph.D., Assistant Provost for
Academic Affairs
staubs@dickinson.edu

Eastern University

http://www.eastern.edu
Four Year, Private, Suburban, Founded in 1925
Affiliation: Christian
Student Profile: 1,700 undergraduate students (38%
male, 62% female); 17% minority, 1% international.
Faculty Profile: 15:1 student/faculty ratio.
Costs and Aid: 2007-2008: $29,700 comprehensive
($21,000 tuition). 94% of students receive financial aid.
Admissions
1300 Eagle Rd,
St. Davids, PA 19087
Phone: 610-341-5800
Service-Learning
Service Learning and Campus Ministries
Andrew Horvath
Phone: 610-341-1830

Elizabethtown College

http://www.etown.edu
Four Year, Private, Suburban, Founded in 1899
Student Profile: 2,000 undergraduate students (35%
male, 65% female); 61% in-state, 38% out of state;
5% minority, 2% international.
Faculty Profile: 130 full-time faculty. 11:1 student/
faculty ratio. Average class size is 25.
Costs and Aid: 2007-2008: $36,600 comprehensive
($29,000 tuition). 90% of students receive financial aid.
Admissions
One Alpha Drive,
Elizabethtown, PA 17022
Phone: 717-361-1400
Service-Learning
Office of Service-Learning and Civic Programs
Nancy Valkenburg, Director
Phone: 717-361-1108
valkenburgn@etown.edu

Gettysburg College

http://www.gettysburg.edu
Four Year, Private, Rural, Founded in 1832
Student Profile: 2,659 with 2,459 on-campus
undergraduate students (49% male, 51% female);
40 states and territories, 29 countries; 8% minority,
1.5% international.
Faculty Profile: 194 full-time faculty. 11:1 student/
faculty ratio. Average class size is 18.

Costs and Aid: 2007-2008: $44,620 comprehensive
($35,640 tuition). 77% of students receive financial aid.
Admissions
300 N. Washington Street,
Gettysburg, PA 17325
Phone: 800-431-0803 or 717-337-6100
Service-Learning
Center for Public Service
Phone: 717-337-6490
serve@gettysburg.edu

Juniata College

http://www.juniata.edu
Four Year, Private, Rural, Founded in 1876
Student Profile: 1,410 undergraduate students
(47% male, 53% female); 30 states and territories, 36
countries; 5% minority, 7% international.
Faculty Profile: 109 full-time faculty. 13:1 student/
faculty ratio. Average class size is 14.
Costs and Aid: 2007-2008: $36,290 comprehensive
($28,250 tuition). 99.6% of students receive financial aid.
Admissions
1700 Moore Street,
Huntingdon, PA 16652
Phone: 877-JUNIATA
Service-Learning
Career & Community Services
Phone: 814-641-3365

King's College

http://www.kings.edu
Four Year, Private, Urban, Founded in 1946
Student Profile: 1,942 undergraduate students
(52.9% male, 47.1% female); 18 states and territories,
6 countries; 15% minority, .2% international.
Faculty Profile: 125 full-time faculty. 15.5:1 student/
faculty ratio. Average class size is 17.7.
Costs and Aid: 2007-2008: $32,650 comprehensive
($23,450 tuition). 79.5% of students receive financial aid.
Admissions
Phone: 570-208-5900
admissions@kings.edu
Service-Learning
Shoval Center for Community Engagement and
Learning
William P. Bolan, Ph.D.
Phone: 570-208-5900 Ext. 5608
williambolan@kings.edu

Mercyhurst College

http://www.mercyhurst.edu
Two and Four Year, Urban, Founded in 1926
Affiliation: Catholic, Sisters of Mercy
Student Profile: 3,856 undergraduate students
(42% male, 58% female); 44 states and territories, 32
countries; 5% minority, 5% international.
Faculty Profile: 171 full-time faculty. 17:1 student/
faculty ratio. Average class size is 25.
Costs and Aid: 2007-2008: $29,676 comprehensive
($20,370 tuition). 91% of students receive financial aid.
Admissions
501 East 38th St
Erie, PA 16546
Phone: 814-824-2471
Service-Learning
Office of Service Learning

Sr. Michele Schroeck, RSM
mschroeck@mercyhurst.edu
Phone: 814-824-2471

Messiah College

PROFILE PAGE 301

http://www.messiah.edu
Four Year, Private Suburban, Founded in 1909
Affiliation: Brethren In Christ
Student Profile: 2,837 undergraduate students
(36% male, 64% female); 46% out-of-state, 37
states and territories, 23 countries; 6.5 % minority,
1.8 % international.
Faculty Profile: 172 full-time faculty. 79% hold a
terminal degree in their field. 3:1 student/faculty ratio.
Costs and Aid: 2007–2008: $ 31,760
comprehensive ($23,710 tuition). 97% of students
receive financial aid.
Admissions
Phone: 717-691-6000
admiss@messiah.edu
Service-Learning
Agape Center for Service and Learning
Chad Frey, Director
Phone: 717-796-1800 Ext. 7255

Muhlenberg College

http://www.muhlenberg.edu
Four Year, Private, Urban, Founded in 1848
Affiliation: Lutheran Church
Student Profile: 2,150 undergraduate students (42%
male, 58% female); 38 states and territories; 11%
minority, less than 1% international.
Faculty Profile: 161 full-time faculty. 12:1 student/
faculty ratio. Average class size is 19.
Costs and Aid: 2007-2008: $40,880
comprehensive ($33,090 tuition). 70% of students
receive financial aid.
Admissions
2400 W. Chew St,
Allentown, PA 18104
Phone: 484-664-3100
Service-Learning
Office of Community Service and Civic Engagement
Beth Halpern, Director
Phone: 484-664-3657

Northampton Community College

http://www.northampton.edu
Two Year, Public, Suburban, Founded in 1967
Student Profile: 9,488 undergraduate students
(62% male, 38% female); 28 states and territories, 43
countries; 24% minority, .01% international.
Faculty Profile: 134 full-time faculty. 20:1 student/
faculty ratio. Average class size is 20.
Costs and Aid: 2007-2008: $4,236 comprehensive
($100 per credit tuition). 34 % of students receive
financial aid.
Admissions
3835 Green Pond Rd.
Bethlehem, PA 18020

Phone: 610-861-5061
Service-Learning
NCC Service Learning Office
Debra Bohr, Service Learning Administrator
dbohr@northampton.edu
www.northampton.edu/committee/servicelearning

Rosemont College

PROFILE PAGE 302

http://www.rosemont.edu
Four Year, Private, Suburban, Founded in 1921
Affiliation: Catholic
Student Profile: 371 undergraduate students (100% female), 13 states and territories, 8 countries; 51% minority, 3.1% international.
Faculty Profile: 31 full-time faculty. 90% hold a terminal degree in their field. 8:1 student/faculty ratio. Average class size is 12.
Costs and Aid: 2007–2008: $31,735 comprehensive ($21,630 tuition). 79% of students receive financial aid.
Admissions
Phone: 610-526-2966
admissions@rosemont.edu
Service-Learning
Lezlie McCabe, Coordinator of Experiential Learning
Phone: 610-527-0200 Ext: 2389
lmccabe@rosemont.edu

Saint Joseph's University

PROFILE PAGE 303

http://www.sju.edu
Four Year, Private, Urban, Founded in 1851
Student Profile: 4,150 undergraduate students (49% male, 51% female); 36 states and territories, 40 countries; 8.6% minority.
Faculty Profile: 281 full-time faculty, 381 part-time faculty. 98% hold a terminal degree in their field. 1:15 student/faculty ratio.
Costs and Aid: 2007–2008: $41,400 comprehensive ($30,850 tuition). 85% of students receive financial aid.
Admissions
Phone: 610-660-1300 or 1-888-BE-A-HAWK
admit@sju.edu
Service-Learning
The Faith-Justice Institute
Ann Marie Jursca, MSW, Assistant Director
Phone: 610-660-1337
ajursca@sju.edu

Slippery Rock University

PROFILE PAGE 304

http://www.sru.edu
Four Year, Public, Rural, Founded in 1889
Student Profile: 8,325 undergraduate students; 481 in-state, 7,628 out-of-state, 607 international.
Faculty Profile: 331 full-time faculty, 39 part-time faculty. 90% hold a terminal degree or Ph.D.; 20:1 student/faculty ratio.
Costs and Aid: 2007–2008: $5,178 in-state tuition, $7,766 out-of-state tuition. Students receiving need-based aid whose need was fully met: 46%.
Admissions
Phone: 1-800-929-4778
Service-Learning
The Institute for Community, Service-Learning, and Nonprofit Leadership
Alice Kaiser-Drobney, Director
Phone: 724.738.CARE
theinstitute@sru.edu

Swarthmore College
http://www.swarthmore.edu
Four Year, Private, Suburban, Founded in 1864
Student Profile: 1,491 undergraduate students (48% male, 52% female); 46 states and territories, 35 countries; 37% minority, 6.6% international.
Faculty Profile: 165 full-time faculty. Full-time faculty holding highest degree is 99%. 8:1 student/faculty ratio. Average class size is 15.
Costs and Aid: 2007–2008: $45,700 comprehensive ($34,564 tuition). 49% of students receive financial aid.
Admissions
Swarthmore College
500 College Avenue
Swarthmore, PA 19081
Phone: 610-328-8300
Service-Learning
The Lang Center for Civic and Social Responsibility
Phone: 610-328-5742

Temple University
http://www.temple.edu
Four Year, Public, Founded in 1884
Student Profile: 24,070 undergraduate students (45% male, 55% female); 28% out-of-state, 3% international.
Faculty Profile: 1,206 full-time faculty; 17:1 student faculty ratio. Most frequent class size is 20-29.
Costs and Aid: $10,252 in-state tuition; $18,770 out-of-state tuition. 63% of undergraduates receive financial aid.
Admissions
1801 North Broad Street
Philadelphia, PA, 19122-6096
Phone: 215-204-7200
Service-Learning
Community Based Learning
Eli Goldblatt
eligold@temple.edu

University of Pennsylvania
http://www.upenn.edu
Four Year, Private, Urban, Founded in 1740
Student Profile: 9,730 undergraduate students (50% male, 50% female); 81% out-of-state, 9% international.
Faculty Profile: 1,400 full-time faculty; 7:1 student faculty ratio. Most frequent class size is 10-19.
Costs and Aid: 2007-2008: $30,598 tuition. 44% of undergraduate students receive financial aid.
Admissions
3451 Walnut Street,
Philadelphia, PA 19104
Phone: 215-898-5000
Service-Learning
Barbara and Edward Netter Center for Community Partnerships
Phone: 215-898-5351

University of Scranton

PROFILE PAGE 305

http://www.scranton.edu
Four Year, Private, Urban, Founded in 1888
Affiliation: Catholic, Jesuit University
Student Profile: 4,083 undergraduate students (43% male, 57% female); 25 states and territories, 18 countries; 9% minority, 1% international.
Faculty Profile: 267 full-time faculty; 82% hold a terminal degree in their field. 14:1 student/faculty ratio. Average class size is 23.
Costs and Aid: 2007–2008: $37,782 comprehensive ($28,458 tuition). 82% of students receive financial aid.
Admissions
Phone: 1-888-SCRANTON or 570-941-7540
Service-Learning
Community Outreach Office
Phone: 570-941-7429

Washington & Jefferson College
http://www.washjeff.edu
Four Year, Private, Urban, Founded in 1781
Affiliation: Nondenominational
Student Profile: 1,531 undergraduate students (53% male, 47% female); 34 states and territories, 5 countries; 6% minority, 1% international.
Faculty Profile: 109 full-time faculty. 12:1 student/faculty ratio. Average class size is 16.
Costs and Aid: 2007-2008: $37,162 comprehensive ($29,132 tuition). 96% of students receive financial aid.
Admissions
60 South Lincoln Street
Washington, PA 15301
Phone: 724-503-1001
Service-Learning
Office of Volunteer Services
Phone: 724-503-1001 Ext: 3086
www.washjeff.edu/volunteerservices

Directory

163

Waynesburg University

http://www.waynesburg.edu
Four Year, Private, Rural, Founded in 1849
Student Profile: 1,800 undergraduate students (35% male,65% female); 25 states and territories, 3 countries; 3% minority, 0.3% international.
Faculty Profile: 65 full-time faculty. 14:1 student/faculty ratio. Average class size is 20.
Costs and Aid: 2007-2008: $$24,130comprehensive ($16,730 tuition). 82% of students receive financial aid.
Admissions
51 W. College St.
Waynesburg, PA 15370
Robin L. King
Phone: 724-852-3333
Service-Learning
Center for Service Leadership
Dave Calvario
Phone: 724-852-3318

West Chester University

http://www.wcupa.edu
Four Year, Public, Suburban, Founded in 1871
Student Profile: 10,821 undergraduate students (38.43% male, 61.57% female); 19 states and territories, 24 countries; 14.04% minority, 0.27% international.
Faculty Profile: 570 full-time faculty. 17:1 student/faculty ratio. Average class size is 25.6.
Costs and Aid: 2007-2008: $11,767 comprehensive ($5,177 tuition). 72% of students receive financial aid.
Admissions
Emil H. Messikomer Hall
100 W. Rosedale Ave.,
West Chester, PA 19383
Service-Learning
Office of Service-Learning & Volunteer Programs
Margaret Tripp, Director
Phone: 610-436-3379

Westminster College

http://www.westminster.edu
Four Year, Private, Rural, Founded in 1852
Student Profile: 1,385 undergraduate students (40% male, 60% female); 71% in-state; 2% minority, 1% international.
Faculty Profile: 103 full-time faculty. 12.3:1 student/faculty ratio.
Costs and Aid: 2007-2008: $33,295 comprehensive ($24,430 tuition). 78% of students receive financial aid.
Admissions
Bradley P. Tokar
Dean of Admissions
Phone: 724-946-8761
Service-Learning
Drinko Center for Excellence in Teaching and Learning
Virginia M. Tomlinson
Phone: 724-946-6097
tomlinvm@westminster.edu

Widener University

http://www.widener.edu
Four Year, Private, Suburban, Founded in 1821
Student Profile: 3,410 undergraduate students (43% male, 57% female); 26 states and territories, 12 countries; 30% minority, 2% international.
Faculty Profile: 309 full-time faculty. 12:1 student/faculty ratio. Average undergraduate class size is 16.
Costs and Aid: 2007-2008: $38,420 comprehensive ($26,180 tuition). 87% of students receive financial aid.
Admissions
One University Place,
Chester PA 19013
Phone: 1-888-WIDENER
Service-Learning
Office of Community Engagement & Diversity Initiatives
Dr. Marcine Pickron-Davis
Phone: 610-499-4566

RHODE ISLAND

Providence College

PROFILE PAGE 306

http://www.providence.edu
Four Year, Private, Urban, Founded in 1917
Student Profile: 3,850 undergraduate students (43% male, 57% female); 42 states and territories, 17 countries; 9% minority, 2% international.
Faculty Profile: 295 full-time faculty. 91% hold a terminal degree in their field. 12:1 student/faculty ratio. Average class size is 22.
Costs and Aid: 2007–2008: $39,255 comprehensive ($28,920 tuition). 59% of students receive financial aid. Average award is $20,470.
Admissions
Phone: 401-865-2535
pcadmiss@providence.edu
Service-Learning
Feinstein Institute for Public Service
Phone: 401-865-2786
fips@providence.edu

Salve Regina University

http://www.salve.edu
Four Year, Private, Suburban, Founded in 1947
Affiliation: Catholic
Student Profile: 2,000 undergraduate students (35% male, 65% female); 38 states and territories, 16 countries; 7% minority, 17% international.
Faculty Profile: 130 full-time faculty. 13:1 student/faculty ratio. Average class size is 19.
Costs and Aid: 2007-2008: $37,150 comprehensive ($26,950 tuition). 75 % of students receive financial aid.
Admissions
100 Ochre Point Avenue
Newport, RI 02840
Phone: 401-341-2908
Service-Learning

Office of Community Service
Sarah.B. Kelly
Community Service Coordinator
Phone: 401-847-2440
sarahb.Kelly@salve.edu

SOUTH CAROLINA

Benedict College

PROFILE PAGE 307

http://www.benedict.edu
Four Year, Private Urban, Founded in 1870
Affiliation: Baptist
Student Profile: 2,587 full-time undergraduate students (50% male, 50% female).
Faculty Profile: 117 full-time faculty. 65% hold a terminal degree in their field. 19:1 student/faculty ratio.
Costs and Aid: 2007–2008: $20,454 comprehensive ($12,516 tuition). 95% of students receive financial aid.
Admissions
Phone: 803-705-4491 or 800-868-6598
Service-Learning
Tondaleya Green Jackson,
M.Ed. Director of Service-Learning
Phone: 803-705-4726
jacksont@benedict.edu

Clemson University

PROFILE PAGE 308

http://www.clemson.edu
Four Year, Public, Suburban, Founded in 1855
Student Profile: 14,069 undergraduate students (54% male, 46% female); 50 states and territories, 53 countries (undergraduate); 10% minority, .5% international.
Faculty Profile: 1,246 full-time faculty. 86% hold a terminal degree in their field. 14:1 student/faculty ratio. Average class size is 31.
Costs and Aid: $16,592 in-state comprehensive ($9,870 tuition). $28,522 out-of-state comprehensive ($21,800 tuition). 72% of students receive financial aid. Average award is $11,123.
Admissions
105 Sikes Hall Box 345124
Clemson, SC 29634-5124
Service-Learning
Community Engagement and Service-learning Education
Kathy Woodard, Director
Phone: 864-656-0205
ckathy@clemson.edu

University of South Carolina

PROFILE PAGE 309

http://www.sc.edu
Four Year, Public, Urban, Founded in 1801
Student Profile: 18,827 undergraduate students (45% male, 55% female); 17.75% minority.
Faculty Profile: 88.46% of faculty hold a Ph.D.
Costs and Aid: 2007-2008: $7,946 in-state, $21,232 out-of-state. Room and board for the academic year is approximately $6,946. 94% of new freshmen receive financial aid.
Admissions
Phone: 803-777-7700 or 800-868-5872
admissions-ugrad@sc.edu
Service-Learning
Jimmie Gahagan
Assistant Vice Provost for Student Engagement
Phone: 803-777-1445
gahagan@sc.edu

Wofford College

PROFILE PAGE 310

http://www.wofford.edu
Four Year, Private, Suburban, Founded in 1854
Affiliation: Methodist
Student Profile: 1,260 undergraduate students (52% male, 48% female); 32 states and territories, 10 countries; 11% minority, less than 1% international.
Faculty Profile: 98 full-time faculty. 92% hold a terminal degree in their field. 1:11 student/faculty ratio. Average class size is 13.
Costs and Aid: 2007–2008: $35,535 comprehensive ($27,830 tuition). 86.9% of students receive some financial aid. Average award: $22,889
Admissions
429 North Church Street
Spartanburg, SC 29303-3663
Phone: 864-597-4130
admissions@wofford.edu
Service-Learning
Corella Bonner Service Learning Center
Lyn Pace, MDIV Director
Phone: 864-597-4402
pacepl@wofford.edu

SOUTH DAKOTA

South Dakota State University

PROFILE PAGE 311

http://www3.sdstate.edu/
Four Year, Public, Rural, Founded in 1881
Student Profile: 10,332 undergraduate students (47% male, 53% female); 50 states and territories, 47 countries; 6% minority, 3% international.
Faculty Profile: 522 full-time faculty; 77% hold a terminal degree in their field; 17:1 student/faculty ratio, average class size is 25-30.
Costs and Aid: 2007-2008: $11,126 in-state comprehensive ($1,328 tuition); $12,438 out-of-state comprehensive ($1,984 tuition). 87% of students receive financial aid.
Admissions
Phone: 605-688-4121 or 800-952-3541
SDSU.Admissions@sdstate.edu
Service-Learning
Office for Diversity Enhancement
Dianne Nagy
Phone: 605-688-6004

University of South Dakota

http://www.usd.edu
Four Year, Public, Rural, Founded in 1862
Student Profile: 5,984 undergraduate students (39% male, 61% female); 43 states and territories, 17 countries; 14% minority, 1% international.
Faculty Profile: 377 full-time faculty. 14:1 student/faculty ratio. Average class size is 24.
Costs and Aid: 2007-2008: $11,211.60 in-state comprehensive ($2643.20 tuition); $12,531.60 out-of-state comprehensive ($3963.20 tuition). 90% of students receive financial aid.
Admissions
The University of South Dakota
414 E Clark Street,
Vermillion, SD 57069
Phone: 1-800-COYOTES
Service-Learning
Center for Academic Engagement
Phone: 605-677-6338
engage@usd.edu

TENNESSEE

East Tennessee State University

PROFILE PAGE 312

http://www.etsu.edu
Four Year, Public, Suburban, Founded in 1911
Student Profile: 13,300 undergraduate students (42% male, 58% female); 50 states, 60 countries; 1% international.
Faculty Profile: 476 full-time faculty. 18:1 student/faculty ratio. Average class size is 20-29.
Costs and Aid: 2007–2008: $16,929 in state comprehensive ($4,887 tuition); $27,205 out of state comprehensive ($4,887 tuition); 74% of students receive some financial aid; average award: $10,907.
Admissions
Phone: 423-439-4213 or 1-800-GO2-ETSU
GO2ETSU@etsu.edu
Service-Learning
Teresa Brooks Taylor
Assistant Director
Phone: 423-439-5675
taylort@etsu.edu

Lee University

PROFILE PAGE 313

http://www.leeuniversity.edu
Four Year, Private Suburban, Founded in 1918
Affiliation: Church of God
Student Profile: 3,789 undergraduate students (43.6% male, 56.4% female); 48 states and territories, 41 countries; 13% minority, 5.4% international.
Faculty Profile: 167 full-time faculty, 79% hold a terminal degree in their field; 16:1 student/faculty ratio. Average class size is 22.
Costs and Aid: 2007–2008: $16,460 tuition; 85.5% of students receive financial aid.
Admissions
Phone: 800-533-9930 or 423-614-8500
admissions@leeuniversity.edu
Service-Learning
Mike Hayes, Ed.D.
Assistant Vice President for Student Life
Phone: 423-614-8406
mhayes@leeuniversity.edu

Directory

Lipscomb University

PROFILE PAGE 314

http://www.lipscomb.edu
Four Year, Public, Founded in 1891
Affiliation: Church of Christ
Student Profile: undergraduate students (47% male, 53% female); 43 states and territories, 18 countries; 13% minority, 8% international.
Faculty Profile: 43 full-time faculty. 83% hold a terminal degree in their field. 14:1 student/faculty ratio. Average class size is 22.
Costs and Aid: 2007–2008: $24,457 comprehensive ($15,986 tuition). 97% of students receive financial aid.
Admissions
Phone: 877-LU-BISON (582-4766)
www.golipscomb.com
Service-Learning
The SALT Center
Christin Shatzer, MPA, Director of Service-Learning
Phone: 615-966-7225
christin.shatzer@lipscomb.edu

Tennessee State University

PROFILE PAGE 315

http://www.tnstate.edu
Four-Year, Public, Urban, Founded in 1912
Student Profile: 7,132 undergraduate students (36% male, 64% female); 42 states and territories, 78% minority, 1% international.
Faculty Profile: 421 full-time faculty; 80% hold a terminal degree in their field. 22:1 student/faculty ratio. Average class size is 19.
Costs and Aid: 2007–2008: $4,886 in-state comprehensive ($2,243 tuition); $15,162 out-of-state comprehensive ($7,581 tuition).
Admissions
PO Box 96093500
John A. Merritt Blvd.
Nashville, TN. 37209-1561
Phone: 615-963-5105 or 1-888-463-6878
Service-Learning
Center for Service Learning and Civic Engagement
Deena Sue Fuller, Ph.D., Director of Service Learning
Phone: 615-963-5383

Union University

PROFILE PAGE 316

http://www.uu.edu
Four Year, Private, Suburban, Founded in 1823
Affiliation: Southern Baptist Convention
Student Profile: 2,383 undergraduate students (40% male, 60% female); 41 states and territories; 15% minority, 1% international.
Faculty Profile: 178 full-time faculty. 83% hold a terminal degree in their field. 11:1 student/faculty ratio.
Costs and Aid: 2008-2009: $26,870 comprehensive ($18,980 tuition). More than 90% of students receive financial aid.
Admissions
Phone: 1-800-33-UNION
info@uu.edu
Service-Learning
Center for Educational Practice
Melinda Clarke, Ed.D., Director
Phone: 731-661-5379
mclarke@uu.edu

TEXAS

Abilene Christian University

PROFILE PAGE 317

http://www.acu.edu
Four-Year, Private, Suburban, Founded in 1906
Affiliation: Churches of Christ
Student Profile: About 4,700 undergraduate students (45% male, 55% female); 50 states and territories, 60 countries; 16% minority, 4% international.
Faculty Profile: More than 200 full-time faculty. 95% hold a terminal degree in their field. 17:1 student/faculty ratio. Average class size is 17.
Costs and Aid: 2007–2008: $25,265 for tuition, fees, room and board, plus approximately $800 for textbooks and supplies. 90% of students receive financial aid.
Admissions
Phone: 325-674-2650 or 800-460-6228
info@admissions.acu.edu
Service-Learning
Volunteer and Service-Learning Center
Nancy Coburn, Director
Phone: 325-674-2932
vslc@acu.edu

Austin Community College

http://www.austincc.edu/
Public, Urban, Founded in 1972
Student Profile: 33,508 undergraduate students (43.1% male, 56.9% female).
Faculty Profile: 445 full-time faculty; 1,224 adjunct faculty. 22:1 student/faculty ratio. Average class size is 21.3.
Costs and Aid: 2007-2008: $39/credit hour (in-district); $110/credit hour (out-of-district). 30% of students receive financial aid.
Admissions
5930 Middle Fiskville Rd.
Austin, TX 78752
Phone: 512-223-7000
Service-Learning
Phone: 512-223-4767
servlrng@austincc.edu

Blinn College

http://www.blinn.edu/
Two Year, Public, Suburban/Rural, Founded in 1883
Student Profile: 13,000 undergraduate students (49% male, 51% female); 24% minority, 1% international.
Faculty Profile: 758 full-time faculty. 23:1 student/faculty ratio. Average class size is 25.
Costs and Aid: 2007-2008: $3,000 comprehensive ($1,380 tuition). 33% of students receive financial aid.
Admissions
902 College Ave
Brenham, TX 77833
Phone: 979-830-4000
Service-Learning
Blinn College Service Learning Program
Dr. Gregory W. Phillips, Service Learning Director
Phone: 979-830-4294

Collin County Community College

http://www.ccccd.edu
Two Year, Public, Suburban, Founded in 1985
Student Profile: 20,143 undergraduate students (43.8% male, 56.2% female); 33.1% minority, 1.6% international.
Faculty Profile: 274 full-time faculty; 21.7:1 student/faculty ratio. Average class size is 20.7.
Costs and Aid: 2007-2008: $6,922 in-county comprehensive ($810 tuition); $6,978 in-state out-of-county comprehensive ($1,170 tuition); $8,598 out-of-state comprehensive ($2,790 tuition) 15.5 % of students receive financial aid
Admissions
2800 E. Spring Creek Parkway
Plano, TX 75074
Phone: 972-881-5900
Service-Learning
Service-Learning Program
Regina M. Hughes, Director
Phone: 972-881-5900
rhughes@ccccd.edu

Southern Methodist University
http://www.smu.edu
Four Year, Private, Urban, Founded in 1911
Student Profile: 6,176 undergraduate students
(53.9% male, 46.1% female); 51 states and territories,
82 countries; 21% minority, 7% international.
Faculty Profile: 600 full-time faculty. 12:1 student/
faculty ratio. Average class size is 25-30.
Costs and Aid: 2007-2008: $41,705 comprehensive
($27,400 tuition). 70% of students receive financial aid.
Admissions
Phone: 1-800-323-0672
ugadmission@smu.edu
Service-Learning
Leadership and Community Involvement
Phone: 214-768-4403
lci@smu.edu

Texas Christian University

PROFILE
PAGE
318

http://www.tcu.edu
Four Year, Private, Urban, Founded in 1873
Affiliation: Christian Church (Disciples of Christ)
Student Profile: Undergraduate students (42% male,
58% female); 15% minority, 5% international. 85
countries represented.
Faculty Profile: 465 full-time faculty. 90% hold a
terminal degree in their field. 14:1 student/faculty
ratio. Average class size is 27.
Costs and Aid: 2007–2008: $33,918 comprehensive
($24,868 tuition). 70% of students receive financial aid.
Admissions
Phone: 817-257-7490
Service-Learning
Center for Community Involvement and Service-
Learning
Rosangela Boyd, Ph.D., Director
r.boyd@tcu.edu
Phone: 817-257-5356

Texas Tech University
http://www.ttu.edu
Four Year, Public, Urban, Founded in 1923
Student Profile: 22,851 undergraduate students
(55% male, 45% female); 51 states and territories;
18.38% minority, 5.04% international.
Faculty Profile: 1,165 full-time faculty. 18:1 student/
faculty ratio. Average class size is 36.
Costs and Aid: 2007-2008: $14,242.84
comprehensive ($6,783.10 tuition). 51% of students
receive financial aid.
Admissions
2500 Broadway,
Lubbock, TX 79409
Service-Learning
Service Learning Program/Teaching, Learning and
Technology Center
Phone: 806-742-0133

University of Texas at Arlington

PROFILE
PAGE
319

http://www.uta.edu
Four Year, Public, Metropolis, Founded in 1895
Student Profile: Undergraduate students (48% male,
52% female); 48 states and territories; 130 countries;
32.85% minority, 10.8% international.
Faculty Profile: 1,100 full-time faculty; 85% hold
a terminal degree in their field. 20:1 student/faculty
ratio; average class size is 25.
Costs and Aid: 55% of students receive financial aid.
Admissions
Phone: 817-272-6287
beamaverick@uta.edu
Service-Learning
Center for Community Service Learning
Shirley Theriot, Ph.D. Director
Phone: 817-272-2124
theriot@uta.edu

The University of Texas at Austin
http://www.utexas.edu
Four Year, Public, Urban, Founded in 1883
Student Profile: 39,000 undergraduate students
(49% male, 51% female); 50 states and territories, 30
countries; 44% minority, 9.2% international.
Faculty Profile: 2,300 full-time faculty. 19:1 student/
faculty ratio.
Costs and Aid: 2007-2008: $22,000 comprehensive
($8,000 tuition). 70% of students receive financial aid.
Admissions
1 University Station A6300
Austin, TX 78713-8058
Phone: 512-471-6161
Service-Learning
Volunteer and Service Learning Center
Phone: 512-471-6161
gbaumgart@mail.utexas.edu

UTAH

Salt Lake Community College

PROFILE
PAGE
320

http://www.slcc.edu
Community College, Public, Urban, Founded in 1948
Student Profile: 23,822 students in credit-seeking
programs (51% male, 49% female); 50 countries;
14% minority, 1% international.
Faculty Profile: 352 full-time faculty. 20:1 student/
faculty ratio. Average class size is 18.
Costs and Aid: 2007—2008: $2,534 in-state tuition
(12-18 credits); $7,954 out-of-state tuition (12-18
credits). 65% of students receive some financial aid.
Average award is $2,990.

Admissions
Phone: 801-957-4298
futurestudents@slcc.edu
Service-Learning
Thayne Center for Service & Learning
Betsy Ward, Director
Phone: 801-957-4689
betsy.ward@slcc.edu
Gail Jessen, Service-Learning Coordinator
Phone: 801-957-4688
gail.jessen@slcc.edu

Weber State University
http://www.weber.edu
Four Year, Public, Urban, Founded in 1889
Student Profile: 18,081 undergraduate students
(49% male, 51% female); 50 states and 3 territories,
35 countries; 9% minority, 1% international.
Faculty Profile: 497 full-time faculty. 22:1 student/
faculty ratio. Average class size is 17.6.
Costs and Aid: 2007-2008: $7,762 in-state
comprehensive ($3,662 tuition & fees); $15,233 out-
of-state comprehensive ($11,133 tuition & fees). 53%
of students receive financial aid.
Admissions
Student Service Center, Room 101
Christopher C. Rivera, Director
Janet Shaner
Phone: 801-626-6005
Service-Learning
Community Involvement Center
Phone: 801-626-7737
cic@weber.edu

VERMONT

Green Mountain College
http://www.greenmtn.edu
Four Year, Private, Rural, Founded in 1834
Affiliation: Methodist
Student Profile: 750 undergraduate students (51%
male, 49% female); 35 states and territories, 11
countries; 14.4% minority, 1% international.
Faculty Profile: 42 full-time faculty. 14:1 student/
faculty ratio. Average class size is 19.
Costs and Aid: 2007-2008: $32,138 comprehensive
($23,772 tuition). 90% of students receive financial aid.
Admissions
One College Circle,
Poultney, VT 05764
Phone: 802-287-8000
Service-Learning
Service-Learning & Sustainability Office
Jesse Pyles, Coordinator
Phone: 802-287-8379
pylesj@greenmtn.edu

Johnson State College

PROFILE PAGE 321

http://www.jsc.edu
Four Year, Public, Rural
Student Profile: 1,934 total students (1,554 undergraduate, 201 graduate, 179 non-degree); 50% male, 50% female; 25 states and territories; 67% in-State; 33% out-of-state.
Faculty Profile: 54 full-time faculty; 83 part-time faculty; 17:1 student/faculty ratio. Average class size is 17.
Costs and Aid: 2007–2008: $14,464 in-state comprehensive ($7,056 tuition); $22,648 out-of-state comprehensive ($15,240 tuition). 80% of students receive financial aid.
Admissions
337 College Hill
Johnson, Vermont 05656
Phone: 802-635-1219 or 1-800-635-2356
Service-Learning
Career Center Experiential Education and Community Partnerships
Ellen Hill, Co-Director
Phone: 802-635-1257
Ellen.Hill@jsc.edu

Norwich University

http://www.norwich.edu
Four Year, Private, Rural, Founded in 1819
Student Profile: 2,016 undergraduate students (71.3% male, 28.7% female); 44 states and territories, 7 countries; 12.7% minority, 2% international.
Faculty Profile: 128 full-time faculty. 14:1 student/faculty ratio. Average class size is 18.
Costs and Aid: 2007-2008: $33,478 comprehensive ($22,314 tuition). 95% of students receive financial aid.
Admissions
158 Harmon Drive,
Northfield, VT 05663
Phone: 802-485-2889
Service-Learning
Norwich University Service-Learning (NUSL) Program
Michelle Barber, Service-Learning Coordinator
Phone: 802-485-2889
mbarber@norwich.edu

Southern Vermont College

PROFILE PAGE 322

http://www.svc.edu
Four-year, Private, Rural, Founded in 1926
Student Profile: 450 undergraduate students (36% male, 64% female); 22 states and territories, 5 countries; 9% minority.
Faculty Profile: 19 full-time faculty; 16% hold a terminal degree in their field. 16:1 student/faculty ratio. Average class size is 13.
Costs and Aid: 2007–2008: $26,460 comprehensive

($17,960 tuition). 75% of students receive financial aid.
Admissions
Phone: 800-378-2782 or 802-447-6304
admiss@svc.edu
Service-Learning
Daniel Cantor Yalowitz, Ed.D., Associate Dean for Special Projects
Phone: 802-447-6351
dyalowitz@svc.edu

University of Vermont

http://www.uvm.edu
Four Year, Public, Urban, Founded in 1791
Student Profile: 9,450 undergraduate students (45% male, 55% female); 6.8% minority, .5% international. 65% out-of-state, 48 states, 20 countries.
Faculty Profile: 1,059 full-time faculty. 16:1 student/faculty ratio. Average class size is 26.
Costs and Aid: 2007-2008: $20,078 in-state comprehensive ($10,422 tuition); $35,962 out-of-state comprehensive ($26,306 tuition). 58% of students receive financial aid.
Admissions
Phone: 802-656-3370
admissions@uvm.edu
Service-Learning
Community-University Partnerships and Service-Learning (CUPS)
partnerships@uvm.edu
Community Service Programs, Student Life/Volunteers in Action
service@uvm.edu

VIRGINIA

Eastern Mennonite University

PROFILE PAGE 323

http://www.emu.edu
Four Year, Private, Suburban, Founded in 1917
Student Profile: 916 undergraduate students (40% male, 60% female); 19.9% ethnic/international enrollment.
Faculty Profile: 60 full-time faculty. 12:1 student/faculty ratio.
Costs and Aid: 2007–2008: $21,860 tuition and fees. 97% of students receive some financial aid.
Admissions
Phone: 540-432-2665 or 800-EMU-COOL
admiss@emu.edu
Service-Learning
EMU Community Learning
Phone: 540-432-4912

James Madison University

http://www.jmu.edu
Four Year, Public, Rural, Founded in 1908
Student Profile: 15,653 undergraduate students (39% male, 61% female); 46 states and territories, 42 countries (optional); 11% minority, 1% international.
Faculty Profile: 831 full-time faculty. 16:1 student/faculty ratio. Average class size is 29.
Costs and Aid: 2007-2008: $10,256 [in-state, 14 meal] $20,976 [out-of-state, 14 meal] comprehensive ($3,420 [in state] $14,140 [out of state] tuition). These costs do not include fees of $3,246. Estimated 60% of students receive financial aid.
Admissions
800 South Main St.,
Harrisonburg, VA 22807
Phone: 540-568-6211
Service-Learning
Community Service-Learning
Phone: 540-568-2373

Lynchburg College

http://www.lynchburg.edu
Four Year, Private, Urban, Founded in 1903
Affiliation: Disciples of Christ
Student Profile: 2,113 undergraduate students (41% male, 59% female); 37 states and territories, 8 countries.
Faculty Profile: 157 full-time faculty, 13:1 student/faculty ratio. Average class size is 23.
Costs and Aid: $13,180 per semester tuition. 98% of undergraduates receive financial aid.
Admissions
1501 Lakeside Drive
Lynchburg, VA, 24501
Phone: 434-544-8300
Service-Learning
Center for Community Development and Social Justice
www.lynchburg.edu/centers

Mary Baldwin College

PROFILE PAGE 324

http://www.mbc.edu
Four Year, Private, Founded in 1842
Affiliation: Presbyterian
Student Profile: 100% female; 35 states and territories, 4 countries; 33% minority, 2% international.
Faculty Profile: 97% of faculty hold a terminal degree in their field. 1:10 student/faculty ratio. Average class size is 16.8.
Costs and Aid: 2007–2008: $29,200 comprehensive ($22,530 tuition). 98% of students receive financial aid.
Admissions
Phone: 540-887-7019 or 800-468-2262
admit@mbc.edu
Service-Learning
Julie Shepherd
Director of Civic Engagement
Phone: 540-887-7181
civicengagement@mbc.edu

Norfolk State University

PROFILE PAGE 325

http://www.nsu.edu
Four Year, Public, Urban, Founded in 1935
Student Profile: 6,250 total, including graduate (38% male, 62% female). 31% out-of-state, 1% international, 92% African American.
Faculty Profile: 314 full-time faculty; 16:1 student/faculty ratio. Most frequent class size is 10-19. 46% of faculty have the Ph.D's
Costs and Aid: 2007-2009: $1,658 in-state tuition, $10,065 out-of-state tuition, $5,588 room and board. 64% of students receive some financial aid.
Admissions
Phone: 757-823-8396
Service-Learning
Service-Learning and Civic Engagement Program
Dr. Amelia Ross-Hammond
Phone: 757-823-8568

The College of William and Mary

PROFILE PAGE 326

http://www.wm.edu
Four Year, Public, Suburban, Founded in 1693
Student Profile: 5,703 undergraduate students (46% male, 54% female); 52 states and territories, 43 countries; 35% minority.
Faculty Profile: 596 full-time faculty. 12:1 student/faculty ratio.
Costs and Aid: 2007-2008: $4,582 in-state comprehensive ($2,774 tuition); $13,467 out-of-state comprehensive ($11,555 tuition). 85% of students receive financial aid.
Admissions
Phone: 757-221-4223
admission@wm.edu
Service-Learning
Sharpe Community Scholars Program
Monica Griffin, Ph.D., Director
Phone: 757- 221-2669
mdgrif@wm.edu

Washington and Lee University

http://www.wlu.edu
Four Year, Private, Suburban, Founded in 1749
Student Profile: 1,783 undergraduate students (50% male, 50% female); 48 (plus DC) states and territories, 41 countries; 13.6% minority, 4.5% international.
Faculty Profile: 173 full-time faculty. 10:1 student/faculty ratio. Average class size is 16.
Costs and Aid: 2007-2008: $44,170 comprehensive ($34,650 tuition). 52% of students receive financial aid.
Admissions
204 West Washington Street,
Lexington VA 24450
Phone: 540-458-8710
admissions@wlu.edu

Service-Learning
Shepherd Program for the Interdisciplinary Study of Poverty and Human Capability
Phone: 540-458-8131

WASHINGTON

Antioch University Seattle

http://www.antiochsea.edu
Four Year, Private, Urban, Founded in 1852
Student Profile: 210 undergraduate students; 8% African American, 3% Asian American or Pacific Islander, 3% Hispanic American, 4% Native American; 1% international.
Faculty Profile: (BA Program) 19 full-time faculty; 42% are full-time. 10:1 student/faculty ratio.
Costs and Aid: 2007-2008: $16,020 full-time, $445 per credit part-time. No Housing is available. 83% of students receive financial aid. Average percent of need met is 75%; average financial aid package is $6,681.
Admissions
Phone: 206-441-5325 or 888-268-4477
admissions@antiochseattle.edu
Service-Learning
Antioch University Seattle
Phone: 206-441-5352

Gonzaga University

PROFILE PAGE 327

http://www.gonzaga.edu
Four Year, Private, **Affiliation:** Jesuit Catholic
Student Profile: 4,385 undergraduate students (46% male, 54% female).
Faculty Profile: 325 full-time faculty. 11:1 student/faculty ratio; average class size 22.
Costs and Aid: $27,820 tuition; room & board $7,600 (double occupancy with Gold Meal Plan). 98% of students receive financial aid.
Admissions
Phone: 509-323-6572 or 1-800-322-2584
mcculloh@gu.gonzaga.edu
Service-Learning
Center for Community Action and Service-Learning
Sima Thorpe, Director
Phone: 509-323-6856 Ext: 6856
thorpe@gu.gonzaga.edu

Seattle University

http://www.seattleu.edu
Four Year, Private, Urban, Founded in 1891
Student Profile: Undergraduate students (39% male, 61% female); 55% out-of-state. 34.6% minority, 8% international.
Faculty Profile: 426 full-time faculty. 13:1 student/faculty ratio.
Costs and Aid: 2007-2008: $36,600 comprehensive ($28,260 tuition). 78.1% of students receive financial aid.
Admissions
Seattle, WA 98122-1090

Phone: 206-296-2000 or 800-426-7123
admissions@seattleu.edu
Service-Learning
Center for Service and Community Engagement
www.seattleu.edu/csce

Whitworth University

http://www.whitworth.edu
Four Year, Private, Suburban, Founded in 1890
Student Profile: 2,331 undergraduate students (44% male, 56% female). 30 states and territories, 18 countries; 13% minority, 1% international.
Faculty Profile: 127 full-time faculty. 12:1 student/faculty ratio. 82% of classes have fewer than 30 students.
Costs and Aid: 2007-2008: $35,120 comprehensive ($27,100 tuition). 91% of students receive financial aid.
Admissions
Phone: 800-533-4668
admissions@whitworth.edu
Service-Learning
Center for Service-Learning and Community Engagement
Jacob Spaun, Assistant Director of Service-Learning
Phone: 509-777-4673
jspaun@whitworth.edu

WEST VIRGINIA

Bethany College

PROFILE PAGE 328

http://www.bethanywv.edu
Four Year, Private, Rural, Founded in 1840
Affiliation: Disciples of Christ
Student Profile: 887 undergraduate students (49% female, 51% male); 74% out-of-state, 4% international.
Faculty Profile: 66 full-time faculty; 12:1 student/faculty ratio. Most frequent class size is 10-19.
Costs and Aid: $15,750 tuition; 88% of students receive financial aid.
Admissions
Bethany, WV, 26032
Phone: 304-829-7611

West Virginia University

http://www.wvu.edu
Four Year, Public, Suburban, Founded in 1867
Student Profile: 21,145 undergraduate students (54% male, 46% female); 50 states and territories, 91 countries; 7% minority, 42% out-of-state.
Faculty Profile: 1,870 full-time faculty. 22:1 student/faculty ratio.
Costs and Aid: 2007-2008: $11,548 in-state comprehensive ($4,722 tuition); $21,426 out-of-state comprehensive ($14,600 tuition). 70% of students receive financial aid.
Admissions
Phone: 304-293-0111 or 800-344-WVU1
go2wvu@mail.wvu.edu

Directory

Service-Learning
Center for Civic Engagement
Phone: 304-293-8761
cce@mail.wvu.edu

WISCONSIN

Lawrence University
http://www.lawrence.edu
Four Year, Private, Urban, Founded in 1847
Student Profile: 1,480 undergraduate students
(43% male, 57% female); 45 states and territories, 51
countries; 3% minority, 11% international.
Faculty Profile: 150 full-time faculty. 9:1 student/
faculty ratio. Average class size is 15.
Costs and Aid: 2007-2008: $37,536 comprehensive
($30,846 tuition). 93% of students receive financial aid.
Admissions
PO Box 599,
Appleton, WI 54912-0599
Phone: 800-227-0982
Service-Learning
Career Center
excel@lawrence.edu

Marquette University

PROFILE PAGE 329

http://www.marquette.edu
Four Year, Private, Urban, Founded in 1881
Student Profile: 7,923 undergraduate students;
11,470 total students (including dental, graduate and
law schools); all states and more than 80 countries
represented in student population; more than 200
student organizations.
Faculty Profile: 15:1 student/faculty ratio; average
lower-division class size is 31; average upper-division
class size is 25.
Costs and Aid: 2007-2008: $26,270 (tuition), $8,590
(typical room and Board).
Admissions
Phone: 414-288-7302
admissions@marquette.edu
Service-Learning
Service Learning Program
Bobbi Timberlake, Director
Phone: 414-288-3261
bobbi.timberlake@marquette.edu

Ripon College

PROFILE PAGE 330

http://www.ripon.edu
Four Year, Private, Rural, Founded in 1851
Student Profile: 1,000 undergraduate students
(52% male, 48% female); 34 states and territories, 14
countries; 9% minority, 2% international.
Faculty Profile: 81 full-time faculty. 97% hold a
terminal degree in their field. 15:1 student/faculty
ratio. Average class size is 20.
Costs and Aid: 2007-2008: $29,733 comprehensive
($23,048 tuition). 90% of students receive financial aid.
Admissions
Phone: 920-748-8114 or 800-947-4766
adminfo@ripon.edu
Service-Learning
Office of Community Engagement
Deano Pape, Director
Phone: 920-748-8152
paped@ripon.edu

University of Wisconsin- Eau Claire

PROFILE PAGE 331

http://www.uwec.edu
Four Year, Public
Student Profile: 10,096 undergraduates (59% women,
41% men); 5.7% international students; 43 countries.
Faculty Profile: 412 full-time faculty; 84% hold
Ph.D. or other terminal degree; 19:1 student/faculty
ratio (undergraduate).
Costs and Aid: 2007-2008: $10,465 in-state
comprehensive ($5,845 tuition); 10,859 reciprocity
with Minnesota ($6,239 tuition); $18,038 out-of-state
comprehensive ($7,842 tuition). 65% of students
receive financial aid including grants, loans,
scholarships and/or on-campus employment.
Admissions
Phone: 715-836-5415
admissions@uwec.edu
Service-Learning
Center for Service Learning
Donald Mowry, Ph.D.,
Director, Human Sciences & Services
Phone: 715-836-4649
dmowry@uwec.edu

University of Wisconsin-Madison
http://www.wisc.edu
Four Year, Public, Urban, Founded in 1848
Student Profile: Undergraduate students (47% male,
53% female); 50 states and territories, 134 countries;
12% minority, 10% international.
Faculty Profile: 2,054 full-time faculty.
Costs and Aid: 2007-2008: $18,200 comprehensive
($7,188 tuition). 60% of students receive financial aid.
Admissions
Red Gym
716 Langdon Street
Madison, WI 53706
Phone: 608-262-3961
Service-Learning
Morgridge Center for Public Service
Phone: 608-263-2432

University of Wisconsin – Parkside
http://www.uwp.edu
Four Year, Public, Suburban, Founded in 1968

Student Profile: 4,893 undergraduate students
(45% male, 55% female); 9% from out of state, 10
countries; 21.9% minority, 1% international.
Faculty Profile: 174 full-time faculty. 20:1 student/
faculty ratio. Average class size is 22.
Costs and Aid: 2007-2008: $10,998 in-state
comprehensive ($5,388 tuition); $18,472 out-of-state
($12,862 tuition). 60% of students receive financial aid.
Admissions
900 Wood Road,
Kenosha, WI 53141-2000
Phone: 262-595-2345
Service-Learning
Center for Community Partnerships
Thomas Schnaubelt, Dean for Community
Engagement and Civic Learning
Phone: 262-595-3340

CANADA

University of British Columbia
http://www.ubc.ca
Four Year, Public, Urban, Founded in 1908
Student Profile: 39,000 undergraduate students;
7,800 graduate students; 12% international.
Faculty Profile: 4,500 full-time faculty. 15:1 student/
faculty ratio.
Costs and Aid: 2007-2008: $2,295 tuition.
Admissions
2329 West Mall, Vancouver,
British Columbia, V6T 1Z4

University of Ottawa

PROFILE PAGE 332

http://www.uottawa.ca
Four-Year, Public, Suburban, Founded in 1848
Student Profile: 30,283 undergraduate students
(39.4% male, 60.6% female).
Faculty Profile: 1,063 full-time faculty.
Costs and Aid: 2006-2007: (non-exempt International
Students) $13,701 to $21,702 (undergraduate tuition
and fees). 2006-2007: (Canadian citizens, permanent
residents, exempted international students) $4,770
to $9,089 (undergraduate tuition and fees). 35.8% of
students receive financial aid.
Admissions
Tabaret Hall
75 Laurier Av. E.
Ottawa, ON, Canada
K1N 6N5
Toll-free: 1-877-868-8292
infoserv@uOttawa.ca
Service-Learning
Experiential Learning Service
Professor Jeff Keshen, Manager
PhoneL 613-562-5800 ext. 1287
keshen@uOttawa.ca

GUIDE TO **Service-Learning** COLLEGES & UNIVERSITIES

Selected **Profiles**

In the following pages, you'll find a snapshot of colleges and universities throughout North America with a commitment to providing hands-on service-learning opportunities. These colleges are profiled due to their generous contributions to our national free book distribution program to low-income schools, libraries, and community organizations.

If a college is not profiled here, check the directory for all selected colleges and universities. Or, contact an institution individually to learn about their service-learning opportunities and how you can be involved during your college years.

Photographs in this section were submitted and approved by each individual college or university.

Explaining the College Profile

The information and data represented in the college profiles were developed by the Beyond the Books staff in collaboration with and approved by the schools themselves. Because of this close editorial process, we believe the information presented in the profiles to be accurate and up-to-date. If you want more information or have questions, we encourage you to check with the college or university of interest.

Organization

This section is organized by state, with schools presented alphabetically within each state. The state is noted on the bottom right-hand side. Students, parents, counselors, and others are encouraged to continue their research and to connect with the colleges and universities profiled here.

Profiles have been arranged to allow for an overview of each school's offerings, with special attention being paid to service-learning programs. Additionally, academics and basic college facts and statistics are included.

Overview

Each profile begins with the institution's name, a picture, and a statement encapsulating the overall spirit of the school. Following this, the school's Flagship Programs are highlighted, often with a service-learning overview statement. It is in this section that you will find a wonderful variety of service-learning programs and projects, and discover how students at these institutions are involved in both classes and community, and how you can be too.

The Course Snapshot

provides a look at how service-learning is being integrated into specific classes, such as language or math courses, and how it can apply to every major and across the disciplines.

The Academics section

includes a statement about service-learning's role in academics, as well as a list of areas that incorporate these experiences. A web address is also included so you can see a complete list of majors and programs.

Under the Awards and Recognitions section

you will find each institution's notable accomplishments and awards in the areas of both academics and service. In addition to providing basic information, the Fast Facts section will also provide you with a glimpse of the school's student body, faculty, athletics programs, and costs and aid.

Admissions and Service-Learning contact

information is provided for further communication with the school(s) of your choice.

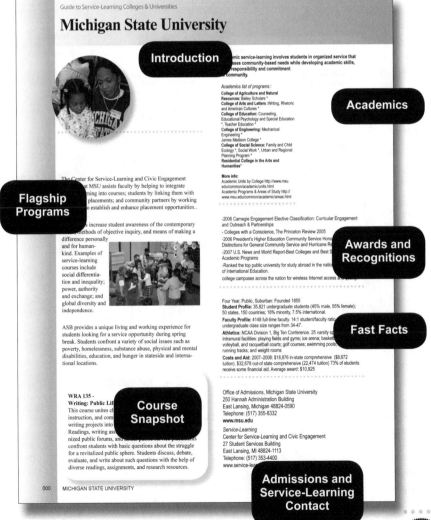

This logo indicates inclusion in The President's Higher Education Community Service Honor Roll

Alabama State University

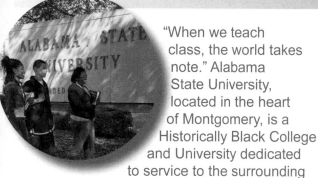

"When we teach class, the world takes note." Alabama State University, located in the heart of Montgomery, is a Historically Black College and University dedicated to service to the surrounding Montgomery community.

Flagship Programs

Focus First at ASU

ASU students taking courses in Biology 127 and 128 Honors collaborate with universities across the state under Focus First, an initiative sponsored by the University of Alabama, Tuscaloosa, to provide a cost-effective direct response to the vision problems of underprivileged children. Students, under the direction of a member of The University of Alabama faculty and/or staff, learn about the anatomy of the eye and how visual information is processed, through providing invaluable eye-care service to the poor of Alabama's Black Belt.

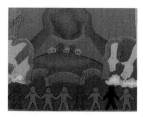

Art Impacts Local Community

Students of Dr. Chris Greenman's class in graphic design create mural designs for Habitat for Humanity. The design chosen from Art 416 for a mural in a neighborhood designated as "a challenge" shows two hands holding the world against a blue background. Beneath the design, people of all cultures hold hands. On one side, two hands plant seedlings, while on the other, two hands (black and white) clasp a candle.

Course Snapshot

PTH 654: Development and Management of Pediatric Patient

In Physical Therapy 654, "The Development and Management of the Pediatric Patient," students travel to nearby rural communities to work with children with disabilities in underserved school communities. This course emphasizes child and adolescent development through clinical examinations and therapy interventions to assist in providing movement activities under supervision of a licensed physical therapist, that are standard tools for physical therapy practice. The experience comprises reflection on community needs and awareness, allowing students to solve issues related to community needs. Through visits to designated schools, students engage in hands-on experiences while enhancing the future of the university community through addressing its community health needs.

Academics

Service Learning Is Changing Education:

S.L.I.C.E., the service-learning initiative at Alabama State University, encompasses the breadth of its history while directing its future. Students incorporate hands-on giving back to the community through the classroom experience, while academic learning supports community needs. As the classroom merges with the world outside, students experience and reflect on their role as citizens of tomorrow. Through service-learning courses that enjoin teaching methodologies to civic responsibility, ASU students develop a lifetime commitment to service and gain a disposition that will serve them well.

Art
Biology
Business
Chemistry
Communications
Education
English
Foreign Language
History
Physical Therapy
Social Work
Sociology
Theater

"I knew we were appreciated when people in the community came by and said 'thank you' for brightening up our area, making a difference, and caring."

—*Graphic Design Major, Richard Lott*

Check out all majors at: www.alasu.edu/academics/

Awards and Recognition

Service-Learning
• Gulf South Summit on Service-Learning, March 2007, New Orleans.
• Montgomery Advertiser, November 16, 2006. "Community Service: A Learning Experience."

Academics
• ASU offers more than 50 areas of undergraduate study, 23 master's degrees, and 3 doctorates.
• Collaboration with Southern University, Baton Rouge: Overseas study and Service-Learning program in Senegal.
• Recipient of U.S. Department of Education Title VI Grant (2007) for development of program in International Business.

College Fast Facts

Four Year, Public, Urban, Year Founded: 1857

Web site: www.alasu.edu

Affiliation: Historically Black College and University, Non denominational

Student Profile: Undergraduate students (40.3% male, 59.7% female); 40 states and territories, 10 countries; 2% minority, 3% international.

Faculty Profile: 239 full-time faculty. 65% hold a terminal degree in their field. 15 :1 student/faculty ratio. Average class size is 25.

Athletics: NCAA Division I, SWAC Conference. 14 varsity sports.

Cost and Aid: 2007-2008: $11,968 comprehensive. 94% of students receive some financial aid.

Admissions

Alabama State University
Office of Undergraduate Admissions
P.O. Box 271
Montgomery, Alabama 36104-0271
Email: admissions@alasu.edu

Service-Learning

Pamela Gay, Ph.D.
Chair, Standing Committee on Service-Learning
Phone: (334) 229-5618; Email: pgay@alasu.edu

Douglas Strout, Ph.D.
Standing Committee on Service-Learning
Phone: (334) 229-4718; Email: dstrout@alasu.edu

Birmingham-Southern College

For 150 years, Birmingham-Southern College has been providing young men and women with a high-quality liberal arts education. It's an experience that has produced leaders in all fields who have literally helped change the world in which we live.

Flagship Programs

Service-Learning Interim Term Projects

The month-long January Interim Term encourages students to develop their potential for creative activity and independent study by exploring one topic. Since 1987, Service-Learning Interims have taken teams to communities all over the world. Whether building a school in a foreign country or painting a house down the street, students are able to engage with the world around them, put their classroom knowledge to practical use, and cultivate an empirical understanding of social problems and their solutions.

Ongoing Community Projects

Ongoing projects are student-initiated and student-coordinated activities which occur on a regular basis throughout the school year. These projects allow our students to develop real relationships with organizations they work with while fostering and strengthening BSC's partnerships with the surrounding community. Projects include First Light Women's Shelter, Woodrow Wilson Elementary School, Urban Kids after school program, and International Tutoring.

Course Snapshot

EH 200: Literature and the Social Experience

In Dr. John Tatter's class, students read essays and short stories about race, class and gender. They are also required to participate regularly in a community project throughout the semester, working with either an after school tutoring program for urban kids, a downtown homeless shelter for women, or a local soup kitchen. Students submit weekly journal entries in which they draw connections between their experiences in the community and the texts they are reading.

Academics

The Bunting Center for Engaged Study and Community Action is the home of service-learning at BSC. Since the proper end of liberal arts education is to foster informed, responsible citizenship, the Bunting Center promotes community service outside the curriculum but emphasizes service that is integrally connected to academic course content.

Through service-learning courses, BSC students develop a lifetime commitment to service that makes a difference locally, nationally and internationally.

Economics
English
Environmental Studies
Human Rights
Music
Philosophy
Psychology
Spanish
Leadership Studies

"Taking a service-learning course during my first semester has not only shaped the rest of my college career, but also the way I think about social issues and how to react to them."

~ Mary Page Wilson, Class of 2008

Check out all majors at: www.bsc.edu/academics

Awards and Recognition

Service-Learning
• President's Higher Education Community Service Honor Roll with Distinction.
• One of 40 Colleges That Change Lives by former *New York Times* education editor Loren Pope.
• The John Templeton Foundation's Honor Roll for Character-Building Colleges.

Academics
• Phi Beta Kappa Designation.
• One of 26 private institutions in the nation named a Best Buy for the "quality of the academic offerings in relation to the cost of attendance," designated by *Fiske Guide to Colleges*.
• A Best Value College, designated by The Princeton Review.

More at www.bsc.edu/communications/accolades.htm

College Fast Facts

Four Year, Public, Founded: 1856

Affiliation: United Methodist

Web site: www.bsc.edu

Student Profile: 1,339 undergraduate students; 29 states and territories, 8 countries.

Faculty Profile: 109 full-time faculty. 96% hold a terminal degree in their field. 12:1 student/faculty ratio. Average class size is 17.

Athletics: Birmingham-Southern is a member of the NCAA Division III and the Southern Collegiate Athletic Conference and competes in 21 varsity sports for men and women, including newly added football, men's and women's indoor and outdoor track and field, and men's and women's lacrosse.

Costs and Aid: 2007-2008: $33,000 (approximate) comprehensive ($23,600 tuition). 98% of students receive some financial aid.

Admissions
Birmingham-Southern College
Office of Admissions
Box 549008
Birmingham, Alabama 35254
Phone: (205) 226-4696
(800) 523-5793
Email: admitme@bsc.edu

Service-Learning
Kristin Harper
Director of the
Bunting Center for Engaged
Study and Community Action
Phone: (205) 226-4720
Email: kharper@bsc.edu

Spring Hill College

Rooted in its Catholic heritage and Jesuit tradition of educational excellence, Spring Hill College prepares students to become responsible leaders in service to others.

Flagship Programs

Tutoring Inner-City Children

Spring Hill College students tutor at 12 inner-city public schools: 9 elementary and 3 middle schools. Two freshman English courses, American Government, and Introduction to Sociology place their students at these schools to help children with basis literacy and provide mentoring. They then discuss in class ideas about the structure of opportunity in America and compare it with their tutoring experience.

English as a Second Language classes (ESL)

Spring Hill College offers free English classes staffed by our students for immigrants and refugees. These teachers are participating in our service scholarship program. Many of them are Hispanic and thus are able to give back to their own community.

Stories from Immigrant Families

Students in a Latino Immigrant Literature class taught by Dr. Margaret Davis interview immigrant families, write their narratives, and then publish a book with the stories and pictures of the families.

Course Snapshot

POL 112: American Democracy and Citizenship

The College has developed a service-learning class, American Democracy and Citizenship. It does not just present the technical aspect of American government to students, but focuses on what it takes to be an effective citizen.

As a part of their study of citizenship, students engage in different service activities through the Foley Center – tutoring, visiting senior citizen centers, or helping at the Boys and Girls Club.

Academics

Spring Hill College helps students learn to lead and make a difference in the world through service to others.

Philosophy
Literature
Political Science
Sociology
Communication Arts
Mathematics
Teacher Education
Accounting

Check out all majors at:
www.shc.edu/academics/

The service learning approach to teaching helps "students make important real-world connections to their learning."

–Catherine Swender, Ph.D. Assistant Professor, Languages & Literature Division

Awards and Recognition

• *U.S. News & World Report* ranks Spring Hill College 11th among the best Southern Colleges and Universities.

• Spring Hill College is the first Catholic college in the Southeast, the third oldest Jesuit college and the fifth oldest Catholic college in the United States.

• Spring Hill is ranked 8th among only 15 schools listed in the South's "Great Schools, Great Values" category, campuses that offer quality academic programs, affordable tuition and significant financial aid.

• Spring Hill students represent numerous religious denominations and cultural backgrounds and come from 37 states and 10 countries.

• Spring Hill has the highest graduation rate of any college or university in the region and the highest freshman-to-sophomore retention rate.

• According to the National Survey of Student Engagement (NSSE), Spring Hill students are more satisfied with their college on the whole than the national average.

• Spring Hill gives more than $16.5 million a year in scholarships and grants.

College Fast Facts

Four Year, Private Suburban, Founded: 1830

Affiliation: Catholic

Web site: www.shc.edu

Student Profile: 1,100 undergraduate students (34% male, 66% female); 23 states and territories, 3 countries; 31 % minority.

Faculty Profile: 84 full-time faculty; 14:1 student/faculty ratio. Average class size is 23.

Athletics: NAIA Division, GCAC Conference.13 varsity sports.

Costs and Aid: 2007–2008: $23,100 comprehensive ($21,686 tuition). 90% of students receives some financial aid.

Admissions

Spring Hill College
Office of Admissions
4000 Dauphin Street
Mobile, Alabama 36608
Phone: (251) 380-3030; toll free (866) 362-3645
Email: admit@shc.edu

Service-Learning

Albert S. Foley, S.J. Community Service Center
Kathleen Orange, Director
Phone: (251) 380-3499
Email: orange@shc.edu or foleycenter@shc.edu

Arizona State University

ASU, a University dedicated to superior instruction; to excellent student performance; to original research, creative endeavor, and scholarly achievement; and to outstanding public service and economic development activities.

Flagship Programs

Service Learning Program Internships

SLP conducts unique "stand-alone" service-learning internships in which cohorts of students become academic tutors and mentors to children living in low-income areas. Students are paired with kindergarten through eighth grade children. Internships supervised by SLP staff.

Youth in Transition

YIT students provide adolescents exiting the Arizona Department of Juvenile Corrections support and guidance as they transition back into the community. Students help the incarcerated youth to develop reentry plans in an effort to reduce recidivism and increase successful engagement in school, work, and community life.

Environmental Sustainability

ASU students lead children in fun, interactive activities focused on environmental sustainability. The emphasis pertains to water, energy, and materials used at their school and in their community. Students assist the children in conducting service projects designed to reduce resource use.

Course Snapshot

**UNI 402 After-School Tutoring &
ENG 102 English Composition**

In the After-School Service-Learning Internship, students work one-on-one with up to three children for an entire semester. The students correlate academic curriculum with fun, hands-on activities to increase the children's academic skills, self-esteem, high school graduation rates and college-going expectations. The students also register for a special section of ENG 102 which focuses on diverse contemporary American society. Students use their community experiences for their ENG writing assignments.

Academics

The Service Learning Program at ASU provides opportunities for students to engage in service projects while enhancing curriculum, knowledge and "real-life" experiences. Reflections and structured discussions provide personal and professional development as well as a deep understanding of social justice facing our local Phoenix communities. Service-learning strives to meet our university standard of "Social Embeddedness" encompassing community capacity building, teaching and learning, economic and social development and research.

Biology
Geology
Physical Geography
English
Mathematics
Microbiology
School of Material Science
-and Engineering
Physical Science
Plant Biology
Sociology (SOC 294)
Spanish (SPA 294)
University (UNI 402) Literacy Tutoring
University (UNI 484) Art
University (UNI 484) Environmental -Sustainability
University (UNI 494) Leadership

"Our goal is to provide as many opportunities for students that encourage life-long civic engagement while enhancing the education and experiences of our students."

*–Deborah Ball, Administrator
The Service Learning Program*

* In addition to these stand-alone service-learning courses, faculty from other departments often add a service-learning component to various courses.

For Details, Go To: www.uc.asu.edu/servicelearning

Awards and Recognition

• Excellence in Nonprofit Collaboration, Volunteer Center of Maricopa County –2006

• President's Award for Social Embeddedness, Arizona State University - 2004

• Mayor's Partnership Award for Educational Partnership, City of Phoenix - 2003

• Best Practices in Education: Gold Star Award, Arizona Commission for post-secondary education – 2003

• President's Award for Innovation, Arizona State University - 2002

• Mayor's Partnership Award for Neighborhood and Community Involvement, City of Phoenix – 2002

• Mayor's Partnership Award for Mentoring, City of Phoenix - 1999

Service-Learning
The Service Learning Program
PO Box 873801
Tempe, AZ 85287-3801
Phone: (480) 727-6382
Email: servicelearning@asu.edu

Deborah Ball, Director
Service-Learning Programs
Phone: (480) 965-8092
Email: Deborah.Ball@asu.edu

American Jewish University

Sid B. Levine Service-Learning Program

American Jewish University is a dynamic institution whose approaches to undergraduate education have garnered the respect and praise of academics across the nation.

Flagship Programs

Psychology of Prejudice

Upper division students learn to translate prejudice reduction theory into practice when they run the Prejudice Awareness Summit where 250 Los Angeles middle school students increase their understanding of prejudice and develop skills to reduce prejudice at their schools (recognized by the City Council of Los Angeles).

Of the Students - By the Student - For the People

This semester-long program is entirely student-led with students deciding the course curriculum, community service projects, logistical planning and evaluation strategies. Students work with a faculty member who serves as an advisor and program resource. This is one of our students' favorite programs.

International Service Opportunity (Brand new for 2008!)

Students learn for a semester about a disadvantaged Jewish community in the world. At the end of the semester, students travel to that community where they spend two weeks working on a site-based project.

Course Snapshot

Sophomore Service-Learning Experience

Students learn the power of living and working in a community during their Sophomore Service-Learning Experience. Students live at our 3,000 acre Brandeis Bardin Campus and Conference Center for the week of

their program. During this time, they perform community service, work in Gan Eitan (an organic garden whose produce is donated to area soup kitchens), learn about the relationship between environmental and social health through hikes in the "outback," and develop lasting friendships.

Contact: Gabe Goldman; primskills@yahoo.com.

Academics

Na-aseh v'Nishmah: Learning through Doing

Service-learning at AJU is an evolving process that reflects changing social conditions; our better understanding of how to address social needs; and the passion of our students and teachers to achieve social equality. Working together as a community, our students realize their inner strengths and the power of collective purpose.

The AJU service-learning program develops "whole people" through experiences that gently challenge them emotionally, intellectually, physically, socially and spiritually.

Courses Include:
Bioethics and Natural Sciences
Mathematics
Business
Communication Arts and Advocacy
Hebrew Language and Literature
Jewish Studies
Jewish and World Civilizations
Liberal Studies
Philosophy
Political Science
Psychology
Sociology

Check out all majors at:
http://academics.ajula.edu.

"After participating in the service-learning project, many of us have truly been affected and left with life altering perceptions in correspondence to the paths we want to embark upon, and the marks we hope to leave in this world."

~ Nicole Keller, Service-Learning 2007

Awards and Recognition

• AJU ranks #1 in the country according to *U.S. News & World Report* in highest proportion of classes with under 20 students per class. An average class at American Jewish University ranges from 6-10 students

College Fast Facts

Four Year, Private, Suburban

Web site: http://academics.ajula.edu

Affiliation: Jewish

Student Profile: 115 undergraduate students (45% male, 55% female); 25 states and territories, 5 countries; 6% minority, 5% international.

Faculty Profile: 15 full-time faculty; 100% hold a terminal degree in their field. 7:1 student/faculty ratio. Average class size is 6 - 8 .

Costs and Aid: 2007-2008: Comprehensive $33,568 (includes tuition, double-occupancy residence hall room, meal ticket and fees). Tuition: $21,408. 80% of students receive some form of financial aid.

Admissions

American Jewish University
admissions@ajula.edu.
Contact: Matt Davidson
mdavidson@ajula.edu
310-440-1247

Azusa Pacific University

Azusa Pacific University is a comprehensive, Christian, evangelical university, committed to God First and excellence in higher

Service-Learning Focus

Service-learning at Azusa Pacific University puts classroom theory into the kind of practice that transforms both student and community. Experiences and classroom reflection promote growth in compassion, personal faith, an expanded worldview, and intercultural competence.

Flagship Programs

C.H.A.M.P. (College Headed and Mighty Proud)
The C.H.A.M.P. program, the service-learning component of the undergraduate upper-division education course Diversity in the Classroom, facilitates college and career exploration with 600-700 fourth graders from six local majority Hispanic elementary schools each year.

Art at Azusa on Wheels
APU students taking courses in 2-Dimensional Design, Multicultural Art, Sculptural Objects and Functional Art, and Special Topics: Mixed Media bring art to the community by teaching different art forms to local elementary children and youth in foster homes.

Azusa Conservatory of Music
APU music students serve as instrumental and choral instructors for local elementary, middle, and high school students who could not otherwise afford formal music instruction. Instrument donations enable the most financially challenged families to participate.

Course Snapshot

MKTG 363: Marketing Research

A student reflected: *"The greatest value of this project was getting out into the community and enhancing the future of Azusa by providing information to help recruit businesses to the area."* Undergraduate marketing majors from the School of Business and Management received a certificate of appreciation from the Azusa City Council for the retail analysis they designed and administered as their service-learning project for this course.

Academics

Through service-learning courses APU students develop a lifetime commitment to service that makes a difference locally, nationally and internationally. Some of these courses include:

Art
Business
Communications
Education
English
History
Journalism
Math and Physics
Music
Nursing
Physical Education
Psychology
Social Work
Sociology
Spanish
Theater
Undergrad Bible

"Through their actual teaching experiences, students learned about classroom management, classroom structure/ organization and student motivation."

– Professor Sharon Lehman
(P.E. 451 Methods in P.E. 7-12)

Check out all majors at: http://apu.edu/academics

Awards and Recognition

Service-Learning
• *U.S.News & World Report* - APU named 1 of 42 Best Academic Programs for Service-Learning.
• President's Higher Education Community Service Honor Roll with Distinction for both 2007 and 2008.

Academics
•APU offers more than 60 areas of undergraduate study, 26 master's degree programs and 7 doctorates to a total student population of more than 8,100.
• In 2007, APU secured a coveted place in the most prestigious category of national universities in *U.S.News & World Report's America's Best Colleges* 2008.
• For the fourth consecutive year, The Princeton Review designated APU as 1 of 124 colleges in the 2008 Best in the West category.
• *Diversity Issues in Higher Education recognized APU as one of the nation's top schools in awarding degrees to minority students.*
• In 2005, Intel Corporation ranked APU among the top 50 most unwired college campuses across the nation for wireless Internet access and quality.

College Fast Facts

Web site: www.apu.edu
Service-Learning Facts: 125 service-learning classes offered in 2007-2008 with over 2,800 students participating. 95% of all departments offer service-learning courses. *Service-learning courses and credit-earning experiences are also integrated into:* General education and/or core curriculum, Senior capstones or other culminating experience, Undergraduate research programs, Independent study, International study.

Student Profile: 4,027 traditional undergraduate students; 61% women and 39% men; 24% minority; 49 states; 72 countries.

Faculty Profile: 376 full-time faculty; 73% hold terminal degrees; 15:1 student/faculty ratio.

Athletics: NAIA Division I, 14 intercollegiate sports. APU holds 25 national titles and three consecutive wins of the Directors' Cup.

Costs and Aid: 2008-09 $33,398 comprehensive ($12,920 semester tuition); 89% of students receive some form of institutional, need-based, and other financial aid.

Admissions

Azusa Pacific University, Office of Undergraduate Admissions
PO Box 7000 Azusa, CA 91702-7000
Phone: (626) 812-3016; (800) TALK-APU
Email: admissions@apu.edu

Service-Learning

Center for Academic Service-Learning and Research
Judy Hutchinson, Ph.D., Director
Phone: (626) 815-6000, ext. 2823
Email: jhutchinson@apu.edu

California State Polytechnic University, Pomona

Service-learning is a way of using Cal Poly Pomona's "learn-by-doing" philosophy to make a difference in the world around us.

Flagship Programs

First Year, First Step Experience Residential Community

Ethnic and Women's Studies (EWS) 280S "Community Service-Learning" is linked to a residence hall where students gain understanding of multicultural issues and develop leadership skills by doing service activities and taking part in multicultural programs.

The Cal Poly Pomona Downtown Center

Located in the heart of Pomona, the Center allows the University to bring art, education and applied knowledge to the downtown area, contributing to the economic revitalization of the city. This collaborative university-community partnership fosters a spirit of creativity, experimentation, diversity, and lifelong learning.

Department of Urban and Regional Planning

Students are introduced to service-learning through small projects, many of which are connected. Their involvement in local communities progressively increases, culminating in related, in-depth service-learning projects that allow them to synthesize knowledge and apply skills to specific issues that they have followed throughout their education.

Course Snapshot

Externship in Animal Health Science 442S: Pet Therapy

Approximately 40 students each quarter are involved in professor Michele Rash's pet-assisted therapy program at Cal Poly Pomona. Once a month, these students bring their pets — iguanas, cats, dogs, turtles, snakes, birds and rabbits — to interact with patients at El Encanto Healthcare and Habilitation Center in the City of Industry. During these visits, students aspiring to work in the veterinary field learn about the healing effects that pets can bring to patients. Through the experience, students learn compassion, real-world skills and the importance of community service.

Academics

Service-learning at Cal Poly Pomona enhances the academic experience of students by relating academic content and course objectives to issues in the community.

Accounting
Animal Health Sciences
Anthropology
Behavioral Health Sciences
Biological Sciences
Business
Communication
Computer Information Systems
E-Business
Economics
Electrical and Civil Engineering
Engineering Technology
English
Ethnic and Women's Studies*
Food Science and Technology
Foods and Nutrition
Geography

Graduate Business Administration
Hospitality and Restaurant Management
Interdisciplinary General Education
International Business Marketing
Kinesiology and Health Promotion
Landscape Architecture
Liberal Studies
Management and Human Resources
Music
Philosophy
Psychology
Public Administration*
Spanish
Teacher Education
Theatre
Urban and Regional Planning*

* Majors with a required service-learning component.

Check out all majors at:
www.csupomona.edu/college_school_dept_index.php

"We've been trying to blur the line where the campus ends and the community begins. With the help of service-learning classes and activities, it's been possible."

~ Dr. J. Michael Ortiz, Cal Poly Pomona President

Awards and Recognition

Service-Learning
• Service-learning projects have been funded by the U.S. Department of Housing and Urban Development, the National Endowment for the Arts, and the Corporation for National and Community Service.
General
• Cal Poly Pomona is tied for 6th overall in the category of Top Public Schools in the West Region according to the *U.S. News & World Report* 2008 College Rankings: Universities-Master's category.
• Cal Poly Pomona is 3rd overall in the West for campus diversity amongst all private and public schools, according to the *U.S. News & World Report* 2008 College Rankings: Universities-Master's category.

College Fast Facts

Four Year, Public, Urban, Founded: 1938

Web site: www.csupomona.edu

Student Profile: 19,615 undergraduate students. 56% male, 44% female; 60% minority, 6% international.

Faculty Profile: 603 full-time faculty, 75% hold a terminal degree in their field. 22.5:1 student/faculty ratio. Average class size is 26.

Athletics: NCAA Division II Conference. 12 varsity sports.

Costs and Aid: 2007-2008: $16,194 comprehensive ($3,288 tuition). 76% of students receive some financial aid.

Admissions

Office of Admissions and Outreach
California State Polytechnic University, Pomona
3801 W. Temple Avenue
Pomona, CA 91768
Phone: (909) 869-3210
http://dsa.csupomona.edu/admissions/

Service-Learning

Center for Community Service-Learning
California State Polytechnic University, Pomona
3801 W. Temple Avenue
Pomona, CA 91768
Phone: (909) 869-4269
http://www.csupomona.edu/servicelearning

California State University, Channel Islands

CSU Channel Islands (CSUCI) is a student-centered university committed to providing experiential learning based on interdisciplinary, multicultural, and international perspectives.

Flagship Programs

Post Katrina Environmental Impact
This course in Environmental Science and Resource Management empha-sizes community service wherein students travel to New Orleans, Louisiana to examine drivers of wetland loss and policy failures, conduct post-Hurricane Katrina environmental impact assessments, and rebuild homes.

Sociology/English 331: Narratives of the Working Class
Students enrolled in this course captured oral histories of farm-worker families who recently moved into brand new housing as a result of a civil court case. These oral histories became a traveling exhibit; shared on campus and in the community in celebration of Cesar Chavez Day of Service and Learning.

Engaging the Environmental Learner in Mexico
Cal State University Channel Islands students taking UNIV 392: Mexican Mangroves and Wildlife Experience/Service Learning course, travel to La Manzanilla, Mexico to understand issues facing Mexican conservation. Working with researchers students help collect data that is used to inform local restoration and educational activities.

Course Snapshot

Liberal Studies 499: Family Literacy

A student reflected:

"I would strongly recommend service learning courses. I gained experience and learned so much about myself. I will always remember the children; not only did they learn from me but I learned from them too!" CSUCI students enrolled in this course work with 4th grade students to improve their reading skills. Students also work with the children's parents to provide various reading strategies to help their child at home.

Academics
Through service learning courses CSUCI students have the opportunity to engage with local and global communities in preparation for their role as socially responsible citizens.

Business
Chicano/a Studies*
Communication
Early Childhood Studies*
Education*
Environmental Science and Resource Management*
History
Liberal Studies*
Psychology
Political Science*
Sociology*
* indicates required service component

Check out all majors at:
www.csuci.edu/academics

"Through service learning my students, most of whom plan to become teachers, have learned strategies for teaching and working with children. It has also deepened their appreciation for the teaching profession."
-Dr. Claudia Reder

Awards and Recognition
Awards
• Maximus Award honors outstanding members of the campus community who give their time and effort into making the University a better place.
• Outstanding Experiential and Service Learning Award recognizes a faculty member, community partner and student for their dedication and commitment to the community.

Scholarships
• The University offers numerous academic scholarships including:
• President's Scholars Program, a four-year, full fees scholarship for outstanding high school seniors
• Business & Technology Partnership scholarships for local community college transfer students in business, math or science
• CSUCI Foundation provides funds for general scholarships for qualified students.

College Fast Facts
Four Year, Public, Suburban, Year Founded: 2002

Web site: www.csuci.edu

Student Profile: 3,123 undergraduate students (37.7% male, 62.3% female).

Faculty Profile: 82 full-time faculty. 200 full and part-time lecturers. Average class size is 18.5. 100% hold a terminal degree in their field.

Cost and Aid: $13,232 in-state comprehensive ($3,432 tuition); $30,140 out-of-state comprehensive ($8,776 tuition)

Campus activities: Student programs, intramuralsports, health and fitness, 30 student organizations,waterfront programs (sailing and kayaking), outdoor adventures, honor societies.

Admissions
California State University Channel Islands
Admissions & Recruitment
One University Drive
Sage Hall, Room 144
Camarillo, CA 93012
Phone: (805) 437-8500
Fax: (805) 437-8509
Email: admissions@csuci.edu
Monday - Thursday 8:30a - 5:30p
Friday 8:30a - 5:00p

Service Learning
Center for Community Engagement Pilar Pacheco, MA
Assistant Director
Phone: (805) 437-8851
Email: pilar.pacheco@csuci.edu

California State University, Chico

California State University, Chico, founded in 1887, is one of the oldest post-secondary institutions in the state and among the most highly ranked public universities in the West. Above the doors of the campus administration building is the inscription "Today Decides Tomorrow." We take these words to heart as we focus with optimism and hope on the future, while building on the best of our past.

Flagship Programs

Community Action Volunteers in Education (CAVE) is the largest student-run organization and has been serving the Chico community since 1966. CAVE offers over 20 volunteer and service-learning programs, including work with children, the elderly, special populations, as well as state parks, national forests, and state institutions throughout Northern California. Each year, the 80 student leaders who run CAVE recruit, screen, place, and supervise over 2,500 volunteers who then serve 30,000 clients and complete approximately 80,000 hours of service. This all results in an estimated economic impact of $1.28 million in the region.

The Community Legal Information Center (CLIC) established in 1970 as the Public Law Internship Program, is a collection of student-run projects which serve the community by providing free legal information, referrals, seminars, workshops, and informational media to North State residents. Student paralegal interns staff CLIC and provide both free legal information and representation to clients in administrative law forums. To effectively dispense information and ensure greater expertise in a particular area of law, CLIC is divided into 12 specialized programs including (but not limited to) Family Law, Traffic Law, Disabled and the Law, Environmental Advocates, Chico Consumer Protection Agency, County Jail Law Project, and Workers Rights. During 2006-07, over 200 students contributed free services to over 12,000 low-income and incarcerated individuals through CLIC.

Course Snapshot

HCSV 369: Health Education Techniques

In Professor Mike Mann's HCSV 369: Health Education Techniques service-learning course, students worked with Four Winds Indian Education Center to plan, develop, conduct, and evaluate the REALGirls health education and promotion program. REALGirls was targeted to meet the health needs and concerns of adolescent girls attending the school and provided CSU, Chico students an opportunity to gain experience and practice in all of the main skills associated with providing effective health education.

Academics

Students are engaged in service-learning at CSU, Chico as a way to increase their awareness of the world's problems and the public policies that are needed to make positive, long-lasting changes for our local and global communities. Some departments with a special emphasis on service-learning include:

Agriculture
Biological Sciences
Child Development
Communication Arts & Sciences
Education
English
Geography & Planning
Health & Community Services
Kinesiology
Math & Statistics
Nursing
Nutrition & Food Sciences
Political Science
Professional Studies in Education
Psychology
School of Social Work
Recreation & Parks Management
Sociology

"I think, honestly, that this has been the best class that I have ever taken because it allowed me to get to know somebody from a different generation and break the stereotype. I definitely think that it had an impact on my life and if I had another service-learning class, I would be really excited."

~ Student in RECR 260: Introduction to Therapeutic and Inclusive Recreation

Check out all majors at: www.csuchico.edu/colleges_departments.shtml

Awards and Recognition

Service-Learning
• 2007 Community Engagement Classification, Carnegie Foundation for the Advancement of Teaching.
• 2007 President's Higher Education Community Service Honor Roll with Distinction.
• 2006 President's Higher Education Community Service Honor Roll Finalist for Excellence in General Community Service.
• In both 2006 and 2007, CSU, Chico was the top collegiate fund-raiser for St. Jude Children's Research Hospital in Memphis, Tenn., raising over $180K each year.

Academics
• Ranked fourth among master's level public universities in the western United States in the 2007 America's Best Colleges from *U.S.News & World Report* magazine. The University was fourth in 2006 and 2003 and ranked third in 2005, 2004, and 2002.
• CSU, Chico offers more than 100 undergraduate majors and options, and maintains one of the highest graduation rates in the CSU system.
• CSU, Chico is one of 19 CSU campuses named as "Publisher's Picks" by *Hispanic Outlook in Higher Education*, an annual national list of colleges and universities that the publication sees as having solid records in recruiting, enabling, and graduating Hispanic students.

College Fast Facts

Web site: www.csuchico.edu

Student Profile: 17,034 undergraduate students (47% male,53% female);47 states and territories, 51 countries; 22.2 % minority, 96% of total student population comes from California, 4.3% are out-of-state or international.

Faculty Profile: 555 full-time faculty. 80% hold a terminal degree in their field. 22:1 student/faculty ratio. Average class size is 27.

Costs and Aid: 2007-2008: $3,690 in state comprehensive/semester ($1,845 tuition). Non-resident tuition $399 per unit, in addition to fees. Residence Hall rates: $5,760-$8,466 (meal plan may or may not be included, depending on choice of plans and location).

Admissions
California State University, Chico
400 West First Street
Chico, CA 95929
Office of Admissions
Zip 0722
Phone: (800) 542-4426
(530) 898-4428
http://em.csuchico.edu/admissions/

Service-Learning
Office of Civic Engagement
Deanna Berg
Director of Civic Engagement
Phone: (530) 898-5486
Email: dberg@csuchico.edu
Zip 0110

California State University, Fresno

Fresno State is one of the 23 campuses of the California State University, the largest system of higher education in the world.

Flagship Programs

Jumpstart Fresno

This program pairs college students with disadvantaged preschool children with the intent of improving language, literacy and social skills. Jumpstart's mission is to ensure that every child in America enters school ready to succeed. Now in its sixth year, Jumpstart Fresno has 109 tutors.

American Humanics

This certificate program offers students specialized training in nonprofit management, and offers a chance for participants to forge careers in youth and human services. The American Humanics Program has an outstanding record of placing graduates in jobs with nonprofit organizations.

Mediator Mentors

A university-public school partnership in which future teachers, counselors, social workers and school psychologists support the development of conflict resolution skills in children. Fresno State students have trained and mentored youngsters to resolve disputes with their peers at 50 Central Valley schools.

Course Snapshot

Marketing 100S

Each year, more than 600 Fresno State students in Marketing 100S – "Marketing Concepts" – apply marketing theories and strategies to help meet critical needs in the community. Through this service-learning course, more than 10,000 hours of marketing assistance is provided to area nonprofits, making this class a win-win-win experience for the students, the agencies and their clients. Said one student: "The service-learning experience made this material come alive. I've never learned so much in a class before!"

Academics

There are about 150 courses that involve students on a daily basis in meaningful community service. Service-learning classes take place in 28 different academic departments and in seven of the eight schools and colleges. They include:

Agricultural Sciences and Technology
Arts and Humanities
Craig School of Business
Kremen School of Education and Human Development
Health and Human Services
Science and Mathematics
Social Sciences

For a list of undergraduate degrees, visit:
www.csufresno.edu/academics/degrees_programs/degrees/undergrad.shtml

"The opportunity to serve the community enriched my life far more than I imagined." ~ Mitchell Casados, Fresno State Student

Awards and Recognition
Service-Learning
• In 2006-07, 6,300 Fresno State students participated in some form of organized service. They logged 485,300 hours, providing an economic benefit estimated at more than $10.4 million.
• The university has set a goal of providing 1 million of hours of service annually by its Centennial in 2011.
• 2008 President's Honor Roll Special Achievement Award from the Corporation for National and Community Service.
• One of the first colleges in the nation to earn the prestigious Carnegie Foundation's Community Engagement classification in 2007.
Academics
• *Princeton Review* 2007, Craig School of Business among "Best 290 Business Schools."
• *Entrepreneur* magazine rates Fresno State one of the Top 100 Entrepreneurial Colleges and Universities in the United States.
• Henry Madden Library will be the largest in the CSU system when it is completed in 2009.
• Fresno State has the only commercial winery at any university in the country.

College Fast Facts
Web site: www.csufresno.edu

Student Profile: 18,951 undergraduate students, 2,177 graduate students, 970 postbaccalaureate; 59.3% women and 40.7% men; 56% minority; 29 countries.

Faculty Profile: 710 full-time faculty.

Athletics: NCAA Division I, Western Athletic Conference, 14 intercollegiate sports.

Costs and Aid: 2007-2008: $3,298 per academic year; 57% of students receive some form of institutional, need-based financial aid.

Admissions
California State University, Fresno
Admissions, Records and Evaluations
5150 N. Maple Ave. M/S JA57
Fresno, CA 93740-8026
www.fresnostate.edu/are/home/index.shtml
Phone: (559) 278-2261

Service-Learning
Mr. Chris Fiorentino
Director, Jan and Bud Richter Center for Community Engagement and Service-Learning
chrisf@csufresno.edu
Phone: (559) 278-7079
www.csufresno.edu/cesl

California State University, Fullerton

Orange County's Cal State Fullerton is a comprehensive regional university celebrating its 50th anniversary of educational excellence and service 2007-08.

Flagship Programs

Project SHINE

TESOL students help immigrants and refugees learn language, history and civics knowledge required to pass the U.S. citizenship exam. The program was honored in January 2008, with the U.S. President's Volunteer Service Award.

Jumpstart

At CSUF, this national program offers Child & Adolescent Studies majors opportunities to earn upper and lower division course credit while working with children in local Head Start and low-income preschool programs to improve their literacy, language, and social development.

The Communications major offers a Public Relations concentration that is one of the hallmarks of the University. In the capstone course, Public Relations Management, student teams research nonprofit agencies and develop full Community Relations projects responding to their needs.

Course Snapshot

BUAD 301: Advanced Business Communication student teams competed to produce a brand logo and tagline for the City of Stanton's Community Services Center. The winning team was acknowledged by the Stanton City Council for creating a brand

that appeals to a diverse community. One of the students reflected, "I learned the greatest lesson in life. When you work for something with all your heart, you get it if you think of the end receiver. We always tried to look at the people of Stanton when branding a logo, and we did [win]."

Academics

CSUF provides high-quality programs that meet the evolving needs of our students, community, and region through community-centered programs and activities. Some courses that include service-learning are:

American Studies	Electrical Engineering
Anthropology	Engineering (Engineering Science)
Art	English
Biochemistry	Ethnic Studies
Biological Science	European Studies
Business Administration	French
Chemistry	Geography
Child and Adolescent Development	Geology
Civil Engineering	German
Communications*	Health Science
Communicative Disorders	History
Comparative Literature	Human Services
Computer Engineering	International Business
Computer Science	Interpersonal Communications
Criminal Justice	
Dance	
Economics	

Check out all majors at:
www.fullerton.edu/catalog/Academic_Programs/degree_listing/index.asp

"This community engagement project helped me understand what's important in life. It is important to have goals, missions, and visions, but to obtain them in a way that is helpful. Perhaps it can be said that life is powered by the willingness and want to donate your time to people who need it."

~ Sara Castro, Advanced Business Communication student

Awards and Recognition

Service-Learning
• 2007 President's Higher Education Community Service Honor Roll with Distinction.

Academics
• *U.S.News & World Report* - ranked 8 among the nation's Top Public Universities-Master's institutions in the West.
• *Diverse Issues in Higher Education* – ranked 8 in the nation in terms of baccalaureate degrees awarded to minority students (June 2006 for '04-'05).
• *Hispanic Outlook in Higher Education* – ranked 2 (CA) and 6 (US) among top 100 colleges and universities awarding bachelor's degrees to Hispanics.
• *The Templeton Guide: Colleges That Encourage Character Development*: A Resource for Parents, Students and Educators lists CSUF's Student Leadership Institute among the guide's "Exemplary Programs" in the student leadership category.

College Fast Facts

Web site: www.fullerton.edu/CISL

Student Profile: 30,606 undergraduate students (42% male, 58% female); 64.6% minority, 3.7% international.

Faculty Profile: 881 full-time faculty; 76% hold a terminal degree in their field. 22.26 student/faculty ratio. Average class size is 30.2.

Athletics: NCAA Division 1, Big West Conference. 13 varsity sports.

Costs and Aid: 2007–2008: in-state comprehensive $1,651 FT undergraduate; $1,873 FT credential; $1,972 FT graduate; ($1,306-1,707 tuition); 12 units out-of-state comprehensive $5,719 undergraduate; $5,941 credential; $6,040 ($4,068 tuition). 43% of students receive some financial aid. Average award: $4,780 (first-time freshmen, 2005-2006).

Admissions

California State University, Fullerton
P.O. Box 34080
Fullerton, CA 92834-9480
Phone: (714) 278-2011
Email: admissions@fullerton.edu

Service-Learning

Jeannie Kim-Han, Director
Center for Internships
& Community Engagement
800 N. State College Blvd., LH 209
Fullerton, CA 92831
Phone: (714) 278-3746
Fax: (714) 278-1217
www.fullerton.edu/cisl

California State University, Monterey Bay

Committed to the success of every student, CSUMB uses small classes and talented faculty to help students achieve big things.

Flagship Programs

Student Leadership in Service Learning
Service learning at CSUMB is student led. Student leaders support CSUMB's service learning program in the classroom and the community. Student leaders serve as co-teachers

with faculty and site liaisons in the community, and graduate with a Minor in Service Learning Leadership.

Watershed Institute
The Watershed Institute's Return of the Natives Project is an environmental education program that involves students in habitat restoration with the goals of protecting local waters and bringing people and nature together through restoration and garden projects in local watersheds.

Chinatown Renewal Project
Students from a variety of majors – including business and humanities – are helping to revitalize a blighted inner-city neighborhood. CSUMB is helping to bring the cultural richness back to a forgotten community, while providing a sanctuary for the homeless and marginalized.

Course Snapshot

TAT 399S: Teledramatic Arts and Technology in the Community
In Professor Steven Levinson's service-learning course, students improve their media production skills and deepen their understanding of community needs by creating media projects for local community organizations. The organization helps the students learn the issues and then the students develop such projects as TV/radio public service announcements, volunteer training videos and publicity or fundraising videos. Students also study the impact and community service potential of media.

Academics
Though service-learning courses, students learn about their roles as community members and future professionals in fostering positive social change.
Academics list of programs:

Biology
Business
Collaborative Health & Human Services
Environmental Science and Policy
Global Studies
Human Communication
Integrated Studies
Kinesiology
Liberal Studies
Math
Music and Performing Arts
Psychology
Social and Behavioral Sciences
Telecommunications, Multimedia and Applied Computing
Teledramatic Arts & Technology
Visual & Public Art
World Languages and Cultures

Check out all majors at: http://csumb.edu/academics

Awards and Recognition
Service-Learning

• *U.S.News & World Report* – Best Academic Programs for Service Learning (2003-2007);
• Recipient of the inaugural White House President's Award for Excellence in Community Service (2006)
• Princeton Review – lists CSUMB as one of the best schools for fostering social responsibility and public service
• Carnegie Classification for Community Engagement (2006)
• Learn and Serve grant recipient (1997, 2000, 2004)

College Fast Facts
Web site: www.csumb.edu

Affiliation: Public, one of the 23 campuses of the California State University system

Student Profile: 3,864 undergraduate students (43% male, 57% female; 95 percent of students come from California; three percent from other states; two percent from other countries)

Faculty Profile: 323 faculty (includes lecturers): student/faculty ratio 21-to-1. Average class size is 25.

Athletics: Division II NCAA (California Collegiate Athletic Association). 13 varsity sports. An extensive recreation program, capitalizing on the area's beaches and hiking trails, is also offered.

Costs and Aid: 2007–2008: $ 10,175 in-state comprehensive ($3,055 tuition); $20,345 out-of-state comprehensive ($10,170 tuition). 90% of students receive some financial aid.

Admissions
Admissions & Recruitment
California State University, Monterey Bay
100 Campus Center, Bldg. 47
Seaside, CA 93955-8001
Phone: (831) 582-3738
Email: admissions@csumb.edu

Service-Learning
Service Learning Institute
100 Campus Center, Bldg. 45
Seaside, CA 93955-8001
Phone: (831) 582-3644
Email: service_learning@csumb.edu

California State University, San Bernardino

Come here…go anywhere. A world of possibilities.

Flagship Programs

DisAbility Sports Festival

More than 60 athletes of all ages with a variety of disabilities participated in CSUSB's inaugural DisAbility Sports Festival. The festival incorporates a new service-learning class in which kinesiology students plan and participate in the event.

Coyote Conservatory for the Arts

Multiple service learning courses take place at CSUSB's Coyote Conservatory, including creative drama, puppetry and acting classes. Students taking "Puppetry in the Classroom" collaborate with neighborhood children and community members to create performances on local history.

Gear Up Inland Empire (GUIE)

GUIE creates a "college-going culture" among ethnic minority middle/high school students of low socio-economic status, who have parents who did not graduate from high school, have low academic status and have attendance issues. Service-learning students provide tutoring, mentoring, individual and group counseling and college preparation seminars.

Course Snapshot

Accounting 575 & 595: Volunteer Income Tax Assistance (VITA)

Students in the VITA program prepare tax returns for low-income residents. In 2007, the program significantly expanded to serve seven sites in four cities. Students filed 2,523 returns totaling more than $23 million in adjusted gross income. Participating residents received more than $1.29 million in tax refunds, thanks to the students' 8,754 service hours. The tax refunds not only benefit the low-income residents, but also the local economy through dollars that are spent in the Inland Empire.

Academics

CSUSB students partner with the community through service-learning to address community-identified needs and promote educational, social, economic and cultural advancement.

Accounting
Anthropology
Art
Chemistry
Communication Studies
Dance
Educational Psychology and Counseling*
Language, Literacy and Culture
English
Science, Math and Technology Education
Geological Sciences
Health Science and Human Ecology

History
Humanities
Kinesiology
Management
Psychology
Social Work
Sociology
Spanish
Theater Arts

* Majors with a required service-learning component.

Click through all CSUSB majors and programs at:
www.csusb.edu/majorsDegrees/

"…there is no better way I could learn this much in a 10-week quarter…" ~ *Brian Carlson, senior, computer systems*

Awards and Recognition

Service-Learning
• President's Higher Education Community Service Honor Roll 2006, 2007.
Academics
• *Hispanic Outlook in Higher Education* named CSUSB as one of its "Publisher's Picks."
• CSUSB was re-accredited by WASC, the Western Association of Schools and Colleges, for the maximum 10 years in 2004.
• CSUSB was ranked among the top 60 colleges and universities that received the "Best in the West" designation by the *Princeton Review*.
• Students recognized CSUSB as the most beautiful campus in the 23-campus California State University system.
• *U.S.News & World Report* ranked CSUSB among the best universities offering master's degrees in the West in its annual "America's Best Colleges Guide."
• CSUSB's graduate-level entrepreneurship program was ranked No. 4 in the nation in 2006, according to *The Princeton Review* and *Entrepreneur* magazine.

College Fast Facts

Four Year, Public, Urban, Founded: 1965

Web site: www.csusb.edu

Student Profile: 13,311 undergraduate students (35% male, 65% female), 68% minority, 2% international. 88% of students are from either San Bernardino or Riverside counties in California.

Faculty Profile: 467 full-time faculty. 23:1 student/faculty ratio.

Athletics: NCAA Division II Conference: California Collegiate Athletic Association. 11 varsity sports. 53 student athletes earned All-California Collegiate Athletic Association academic honors for grade point averages of 3.4 or higher during 2006-2007.

Costs and Aid: 2007-2008: $3452.50 in-state comprehensive, $11,588 out-of-state comprehensive. 73% of students receive financial aid awards, averaging approximately $6,945 per year. Of those students, 57% are funded entirely through grants and never have to pay a single penny for fees.

Admissions

Office of Admissions & Student Recruitment
California State University
San Bernardino
5500 University Parkway
San Bernardino, CA 92407
Phone: (909) 537-5188
www.csumentor.edu
Email: moreinfo@mail.csusb.edu

Service-Learning

Diane Podolske, Ph.D.
Director
Community-University Partnerships
Phone: (909) 537-7483
Email: dpodolsk@csusb.edu

California State University, San Marcos

Cal State San Marcos offers the ambiance of a small, personal campus with the unequaled value of the California State University.

Flagship Programs

College of Business/Senior Experience
The Senior Experience Program, required of all Business Administration undergraduates, utilizes a consulting approach. Teams of four or five students are matched with projects submitted by non-profit organizations and local businesses. Students work on real-world projects that require teamwork and application of classroom knowledge.

Human Development
The Human Development Program offers real-world experiences that make its students competitive applicants for professional jobs in human services fields. Field Experience in Human Development (HD495) is one of several courses that require service-learning experience in human services fields.

EDUC 364

Future teachers enrolled in EDUC 364 tutor foster care youth in a highly successful service learning program called, "The Tutor Connection." Twenty hours of tutoring can boost these youths' reading, spelling, and basic math skills two grade levels! The Tutor Connection was recognized as a finalist in the Jimmy and Rosalynn Carter Partnerships Foundation, JRCPF-National 2008.

Course Snapshot

SPAN 399: Internship/Field Work in Community and University Service

SPAN 399, a required course for Spanish majors and popular elective for many others, gets students into the local Hispanic community where they can make a difference while actively using their Spanish. Students serve the community by tutoring school children, interpreting in hospitals, working with residents in community housing developments, providing adult education and computer literacy courses, and much more! Students put their "book Spanish" to the test in this course, and discover that knowing Spanish opens many doors.

Academics

Students who participate in service-learning courses at CSUSM gain experience in applying what they learn in the classroom to "real life" issues.
Programs of Study include:

Anthropology
Business
Communication
Computer Science
Education
Human Development
Ethnic Studies
Kinesiology
Liberal Studies

Literature and Writing
Nursing
Political Science
Psychology
Sociology
Spanish
Visual Arts
Visual Performing Arts

Check out all majors at: www.csusm.edu/academicprograms.htm

"If the world isn't up to our standards, then we should strive to make a permanent change for the sake of ourselves and for those who live after us." ~ Billy Eggert, SOC major

Awards and Recognition
Service-Learning

• Carnegie Classification of Community Engagement 2006-07 (CSUSM was classified in both Curricular Engagement and Outreach & Partnerships categories).

• California State University San Marcos won the RecycleMania's "Grand Champion" title, in 2005, 2006, 2007, and 2008.

• CSUSM's Barahona Center for the Study of Books in Spanish for Children and Adolescents is the first and only center in the world to collect books published worldwide in Spanish for children and adolescents.

Academics

• CSUSM has been recognized for the second consecutive year on the President's Higher Education Community Service Honor Roll, a national distinction that celebrates CSUSM's leadership in helping build a culture of service and civic engagement, and for supporting innovative and effective community service and service-learning programs.

• CSUSM was recognized as a "Publisher's Pick" and listed in *Hispanic Outlook* magazine as one of 100 top schools in the United States graduating Hispanic students.

• *U.S.News & World Report: Best Colleges in 2007* ranked CSUSM as #37 among western U.S. master's granting institutions with the most student ethnic diversity.

College Fast Facts

Four-Year, Public, Suburban: Founded 1988

Web site: www.csusm.edu

Student Profile: 9,159 students (37% male, 63% female); 37% minority, 2.6% international.

Faculty Profile: 230 full-time faculty; 99.9% hold a terminal degree in their field. 58.3% part time faculty; 1:26.5 student/faculty ratio. Average class size is 30.7.

Athletics: NAIA Conference: (no affiliation region): Far West Region II Men's and Women's Golf, Cross Country, Track and Field, Soccer, Softball, Baseball. (See www.csusm.edu/athletics for more information.)

Costs and Aid: $17,630 in-state comprehensive (living on/off campus including $3,374 tuition and fees), $27,820 out-of-state comprehensive living on/off campus; 49% of students receive some financial aid. Average award: $7,400.

Admissions
Office of Admissions & Recruitment
California State University
Cougar Central
San Marcos, CA 92096-0001
Phone: (760) 750.4848
Email: apply@csusm.edu

Service-Learning
Office of Community Service Learning
Darci L. Strother, Ph.D., Director
strother@csusm.edu
Phone: (760) 750-4160
www.csusm.edu/ocsl

University of Redlands

The University of Redlands continues to be a nationally- ranked liberal arts institution whose mission statement is specific in addressing a commitment to educating the head and the heart.

Flagship Programs

Service and Study Abroad

Our faculty-led service study abroad courses are highly popular with students and integrate service into travel during our month-long May Term. Service learning in countries such as China, Ecuador, Japan, Uruguay, Mexico, Chile, Costa Rica and elsewhere captures the essence of an international travel experience while embracing the spirit of service-learning.

Jasper's Corner Homework Club

Staffed completely by undergraduate tutors, this homework club meets the growing need our local families have for individual children struggling with academics. Jasper's Corner partners college tutors with local children who need an extra hand with homework and subject matter at no cost to families.

Big Buddies

Big Buddies is a mentoring program for elementary, middle and high school students which brings local children to campus weekly for arts and crafts, concerts, tours, homework help, and other activities. This program has been matching college mentors with children since 1987 and is fully funded by the Associated Student Body and Redlands' Town and Gown.

Course Snapshot

Freshman Seminar #4 -- Environmental Stewardship; Taking the Next Step in Environmental Activism and Service

This course asks first year students to become active stewards while learning about sustainable communities and environmental non-profit agencies. Service takes place at Joshua Tree National Forest, Catalina Island, San Bernardino National Parks and in our local neighborhoods and orange groves in Southern California.

Academics

Several departments have built academic service components into the structure of their courses. Programs of study include:

Accounting
Business
Environmental Studies
Philisophy
Race and Ethnic Relations
Religious Studies
Sociology
Women's Studies

Check out all majors at:
www.redlands.edu

"Serving the community has expanded my college experience by giving me an opportunity to make a difference in local children's lives."

– Lauren Brewer, Senior Liberal Studies Major, U of R

Awards and Recognition
Service-Learning

• The University of Redlands was elected as one of three institutions nationally as a Presidential Award winner from the Corporation for National and Community Service for exceptional accomplishments in Service to Youth from Disadvantaged Circumstances in the 2007 President's Higher Education Community Service Honor Roll.

• The University of Redlands was recognized by the Carnegie Foundation for the Advancement of Teaching in both Curricular Engagement and Community Partnerships.

• Redlands was named to the President's Higher Education Community Service Honor Roll with Distinction for contributions to the Gulf Coast hurricane recovery effort in 2006.

The University of Redlands Bulldog Football Team received the Jostens Award for single service project for service in New Orleans in helping to clean up and rebuild after Hurricane Katrina.

College Fast Facts
Web site: www.redlands.edu

Service-Learning Facts: 700 hundred students per year enroll in service learning or community service courses in multiple disciplines. One hundred percent of students participate in service learning or community outreach by graduation. Redlands students served over 100,000 hours of service in 2007 in agencies around the world.

Student Profile: 2,400 undergraduate students; 45 states represented with 61% from California; 55% women, 45% men; average academic GPA over 3.5. 39% of entering freshman had been recognized with academic honors; 25% students of color, 14% first-generation college enrollees.

Athletics: NCAA Division III and 21 athletic teams with first-rate facilities and multiple national championships and Southern California All-Sports Trophy in 2006-2007.

Costs and Aid: 85% of students at Redlands receive financial aid with the average package at $19,000. Full comprehensive tuition runs just under $42,000.

Admissions
University of Redlands Office of Admissions
1200 E. Colton Avenue
P.O. Box 3080
Redlands, CA 92373-0999
Phone: 800-455-5064 or
(909) 748-8074

Service-Learning
Office of Community Service Learning
Tony Mueller, Director
Phone: (909) 748-8288

Westmont College

Westmont is a Christian liberal arts college committed to developing students' intellectual competence, healthy personal development and strong Christian commitments.

Flagship Programs

Spring Break in the City

Student-led service projects to Los Angeles and San Francisco which also educate Westmont's campus community about urban issues. Students live, worship and work alongside inner city families and organizations, cultivating relationships and sensitivities that bridge social and cultural differences.

Potter's Clay

This student-run program works with local Mexican pastors to build housing, promote health and support Bible teaching among children and adults in Ensenada, Mexico. Begun in 1978, Potter's Clay involves some 200 students plus about 50 professionals.

Emmaus Road

A student-led organization serving the global Church by sending four missions teams to selected countries each summer, while making the global Church a reality to Westmont students by inviting Christian speakers on global issues to campus throughout the school year.

Course Snapshot

COM 133 - Conflict Transformation and Reconciliation

How might human communication enable peacemaking both internationally and interpersonally? Special attention paid to theories of dialogue and conflict resolution, as well as differing conceptions of justice as  precursor to peace. Opportunity to spend five weeks in Ireland studying conflict resolution between Catholics and Protestants while helping facilitate peaceful communication between the two groups. Professor Dunn: "We want students to see first-hand the dedication and commitment of peacemakers as well as the complex resistance and turmoil that accompany peacemaking efforts."

Academics

Service-learning at Westmont provides students opportunities to bring academic learning to bear on concerns in the local community. They enable them to read and think about issues of justice, reconciliation, and restoration and to think critically about what it means to be a Christian in a fallen world. Courses fulfilling Westmont's 'Serving Society, Enacting Justice' graduation requirement encourage students to exercise charity and compassion.

List of Programs Offering Service-Learning Courses:

Anthropology	Kinesiology
Biology	Mathematics
Computer Science	Political Science
Economics/Business	Psychology
Education	Religious Studies
English	Sociology
History	Spanish

"The 'Serving Society/Enacting Justice' requirement may be a component of a standard course or a stand-alone internship."

Check out all majors at:
www.westmont.edu/admissions/majors-programs.html

Awards and Recognition
Academics

• Ranked in the top tier of national liberal arts colleges for 2007 by *U.S.News & World Report.*

• Named a 2008 Best College in the Western Region by *The Princeton Review.*

• Westmont offers 26 majors of study and 10 pre-professional programs.

• Westmont is a member of the Council of Christian Colleges and Universities.

• The Templeton Foundation consistently recognizes Westmont as among the nation's top 100 colleges committed to character development.

College Fast Facts

Web site: www.westmont.edu

Student Profile: 1,336 undergraduate students; 61% women and 39% men; 24% minority; 41 states; 8 countries.

Faculty Profile: 93 full-time faculty, 89% hold terminal degrees; 12:1 student/faculty ratio.

Athletics: NAIA Division I, Golden State Athletic Conference (GSAC), 12 intercollegiate sports, Westmont holds 7 NAIA national titles.

Costs and Aid: 2008-2009; $32,150 annual tuition; 85% of students receive financial aid.

Admissions

Westmont College
Office of Admission
955 La Paz Road
Santa Barbara, California 93108-1089
Phone: 800-777-9011
Email: admissions@westmont.edu

Service-Learning

Ray Rosentrater, Ph.D.
Professor of Mathematics
Phone: 805-565-6185
Email: rosentr@westmont.edu

Guide to Service-Learning Colleges & Universities

Guide to Service-Learning Colleges & Universities

Whittier College

Whittier College is a four year, residential, liberal arts college in the Quaker tradition committed to community-building, hands-on, interdisciplinary learning.

Flagship Programs

The Fifth Dimension

Partnered with the Boys & Girls Club of Whittier, Whittier students provide an after-school program for community children aged 7-14 to provide mentoring and engage kids in reading, writing, math, and other school subjects through computer-based projects.

Students in Free Enterprise (SIFE)

A nationally-affiliated group, SIFE's Whittier College chapter is dedicated to creating economic opportunities in the Whittier area through various outreaches, such as educating local high school students in success skills and financial literacy, and holding food drives and fund raisers for local homeless shelters.

Helping Hands Day

Every year, many Whittier students, faculty, staff, and societies (local fraternities and sororities) hold a day of service to the community, participating in such activities as gardening, street cleaning, and working with the homeless or elderly.

Course Snapshot

The Broadoaks Children's School

Whittier College undergraduates studying in subjects such as Education, Child Development, and Psychology, or graduate students pursuing a Master's in Education, have the opportunity to work with students at The Broadoaks Children's School, a preschool through sixth grade school located right on the Whittier campus.

Qualified students in specific departments can also work in special programs such as the Broadoaks Music and Theatre Academy, which introduces students to the performing arts and has even produced original plays like Don Quixote.

Academics

Students are given opportunities across the curriculum to engage with and improve the Whittier community through service learning. Whittier offers 30 majors and 30 minors in 23 disciplines; the following programs include service-learning components.

Business Administration
Child Development
Education
History
Music
Psychology
Social Work
Theatre
Whittier Scholars Program

"Being at Whittier has opened my eyes to just how much is out there, and it makes me want to work harder to benefit myself and my community."

~ Eric Shane, Class of '07

Check out our departments and programs at:
www.whittier.edu/Academics/

Awards and Recognition

Service-Learning

• California Campus Compact member, receiving grants for service learning initiatives.

Academics

• National Survey of Student Engagement, ranked top ten percent in four out of five Benchmarks of Success by graduating seniors.

• *U.S. News & World Report, America's Best Colleges*, consistently ranking high in diversity, #1 for Hispanic population.

• Nationally recognized Hispanic Serving Institution.

• Wabash National Study of Liberal Arts Education, participating institution.

• *Templeton Guide of Colleges*, listed Whittier as encouraging Character Development.

• Whittier professors have included Fulbright Scholars, Grammy Award Winners, the 2006 California Professor of the Year (named by the Council for the Advancement and Support of Education and The Carnegie Foundation for the Advancement of Teaching), and received grants and fellowships from the National Science Foundation, National Endowment for the Arts, and National Endowment for the Humanities.

Awards such as: four Rhodes Scholarships and several Pickering Fellowships have been granted to Whittier students.

College Fast Facts

Four Year, Private, Suburban, Founded: 1887

Affiliation: Formerly Quaker

Web site: www.whittier.edu

Student Profile: Undergraduate students (44% male, 56% female); 40 states and territories, 25 countries; 43% minority, 5% international.

Faculty Profile: 88 full-time faculty. 12:1 student/faculty ratio. Average class size is 19.

Athletics: NCAA Division III, SCIAC Conference. 21 varsity sports.

Costs and Aid: 2007-2008: $38,480 comprehensive ($29,860 tuition). 87% of students receive some form of financial aid.

Admissions

Whittier College Office of Admission
13406 E. Philadelphia St.
PO Box 634
Whittier, CA 90608
Phone: (562) 907-4238
Fax: (562) 907-4870
Email: admission@whittier.edu

Service-Learning

Sally Cardenas
Director of Internships and Community-Based Learning
Phone: (562) 464-4533
Email: scardenas@whittier.edu

Colorado State University

Colorado State University is committed to setting the standard for public research universities in teaching, research, and service for the benefit of the citizens of Colorado, the United States, and the world.

Service-Learning Focus

Colorado State promotes excellence in service-learning by supporting the development of meaningful, active and hands-on learning experiences that promote academic excellence while serving genuine community needs.

Flagship Programs

The Key Service Living Learning Community is a first-year learning community of students living together and co-enrolling in linked academic courses. The program is a social community with an academic focus that values community service, civic engagement, academic achievement, and diversity.

The Alternative Spring Break program immerses students in different cultural, environmental and socioeconomic communities both in the US and abroad. The trips are primarily student led, and student leaders spend a full academic year in "Site Leader School" training to prepare themselves and their groups for the trip.

Praxis-Social Action Projects
PRAXIS supports students interested in developing community service or action projects that are innovative, creative, and change oriented. PRAXIS provides resources, training, support, and grant funds to help students develop their ideas and implement their projects.

Course Snapshot

MC576 Sustainable Technology in the Built Environment

This construction management course connects students with an emerging local or regional public works project and requires them to collaborate with project stakeholders to research, recommend, and present potential solutions.

Academics

Service-learning at CSU creates partnerships of mutual benefit in which student interests, academic course objectives, and the needs of community groups are balanced and reciprocally supportive.

Programs of study with service-learning courses include:

College and Applied Human Sciences: Departments of Education, Social Work, Occupational Therapy, Human Development and Family Studies, Food and Human Nutrition, Apparel and Merchandising, Interior Design, Health and Exercise Science, Construction Management, Restaurant and Resort Management

College of Liberal Arts: Departments of Art, Ethnic Studies, Sociology, Anthropology, Journalism, Political Science, English, Foreign Languages and Literatures, Philosophy, Sociology, Speech Communication, Music

College of Agricultural Sciences: Departments of Soil and Crop Sciences, Horticultural and Landscape Architecture, Agriculture and Resources Economics

College of Business: Marketing, Accounting, Computer Information Systems, Global Sustainable Enterprise

College of Natural Resources: Departments of Human Dimensions of Natural Resources, Fish Wildlife and Conservation Biology

College of Engineering: Departments of Civil Engineering, Mechanical Engineering, Engineering Science

College of Veterinarian Medicine and Biological Sciences: Departments of Microbiology and Environmental Health

President's Leadership Program, Key Living/Learning Communities, Women's Studies and Programs

Check out all majors and programs of study at:
http://admissions.colostate.edu

Awards and Recognition
Service-Learning
• 2007 President's Higher Education Community Service Honor Roll with Distinction.

• Recipient of Learn and Service grant providing over 300 AmeriCorps Educational Awards annually to CSU studetns involved in community service.

Academics
• *U.S.News & World Report's* "America's Best Colleges" 2007 edition ranked Colorado State among the top national universities.

• *The Princeton Review* included Colorado State among its 2008 "Best 366 Colleges."

• *Kiplinger's Personal Finance Magazine* named CSU one of the top public universities in the United States in terms of educational quality and affordability.

• Colorado State University has named among the nation's Top Character Building Institutions by the Templeton Foundation.

College Fast Facts
Four-Year, Public, Suburban; Founded 1870
Web site: www.colostate.edu
Student Profile: 24,670 undergraduate students (48% male, 52% female). 20% out-of-state (sister-states: California, Texas, Illinois, Minnesota & Alaska), 1,200 foreign students from 90 countries; 12.6% minority.
Faculty Profile: 1,400 full-time faculty. 99% hold a terminal degree in their field. 18 :1 student/faculty ratio. Average class size: 46 students and in Sciences Labs: 22 students

Athletics: NCAA Division I, Conference. Mountain West Conference, 16 varsity sports.

Costs and Aid: 2007-2008: $13,288 in-state comprehensive ($5,388 tuition) $26,748 out-of-state comprehensive ($18,828 tuition).

Admissions
Office of Admissions
Colorado State University
Fort Collins, CO 80523-1062
(970) 491-6909 or admissions@colostate.edu

Service-Learning
Clayton Hurd, Director of Service-Learning
The Institute for Learning and Teaching (TILT)
Fort Collins, CO 80523-1052
(970) 491-2032 or clayton.hurd@colostate.edu
http://tilt.colostate.edu/sl/

Fort Lewis College

Fort Lewis College offers accessible, high quality, baccalaureate liberal arts education to a diverse student population, preparing citizens for the common good in an increasingly complex world.

Flagship Programs

School of Business Administration

All School of Business Administration students take a course with significant community-based learning and research engagements for nonprofit, government, or small business clients. Courses include Management Consulting, Marketing Research, Systems Analysis, Strategic Management, and Economic Impact Studies.

Engineers Without Borders

Engineers Without Borders is a national organization designed to help developing areas worldwide with their engineering needs while engaging and training internationally-responsible engineering students. Recently, FLC EWB students constructed a water system for a village in Ecuador and provided health assessment and health education to village residents.

Environmental Education

Environmental Studies works closely with the FLC Environmental Center. The EC leads the way in addressing many environmental issues in our local community and region. Students in environmentally focused classes play prominent hands-on and research roles in local environmental efforts.

Course Snapshot

Sociology Block Program

The Sociology Block and Mexico programs integrate 16 credits of academic course work with an intensive, 15-20 hour/week community placement in a regional human service agency or grassroots community organization. Students in the program choose to remain either in the Four Corners region or live for the trimester in rural communities in the State of Chihuahua, Mexico. Both programs provide an educational experience in which the academic study is integrated around, and driven by, a community-based service internship.

Academics

For Fort Lewis College students, scholarly service and informed civic engagement are the bridge uniting learning and social responsibility.

A sampling of academic programs at Fort Lewis that incorporate service learning into their curriculum include:

Accounting	Gender and Women's Studies
Adventure Education	Geosciences
Agricultural Science	Humanities
American Indian Studies	Mathematics
Art	Modern Languages
Biology	Music
Business Administration	Philosophy
Computer Science	Psychology
Economics	Sociology
English	Southwest Studies
Environmental Studies	Teacher Education
Exercise Science	Theatre

Check out all majors and programs of study at:
http://explore.fortlewis.edu/prospective/mmm/index.asp

"Tying the civic engagement component to what I was studying gave me a tangible way to act on what I was learning." - Fort Lewis College Sociology graduate

Awards and Recognition

Service-Learning

• FLC Center for Civic Engagement Director, Kalin Grigg, appointed by Colorado Governor Roy Romer to serve on the Governor's Commission on National and Community Service and was 1999 finalist for the Ehrlich Faculty award.

• One of 8 colleges/universities modeled in the 2000 Campus Compact publication, Benchmarks for Campus/Community Partnerships.

• FLC students among the selected group of students from 27 colleges and universities to participate in the 2001 Wingspread Summit on Student Engagement.

Academics

• The FLC School of Business Administration is one of 551 business schools/colleges accredited by the Association to Advance Collegiate Schools of Business (AACSB) International – only 10% of business schools/colleges in the world are so accredited.

• The School of Business Administration received "effective management practice" designation for integration of community-based learning and research course engagements and extensive international experience programs during last maintenance of accreditation visit in 2005-06.

College Fast Facts

Four Year, Public, Rural: Founded 1911

Student Profile: 53% male, 47% female; 48 states and territories, 10 countries; 34% minority.

Faculty Profile: 240 (including part-time); 18:1 student/faculty ratio. Average class size is 25.

Athletics: NCAA Division II, Rocky Mountain Athletic Conference. 10 varsity sports.

Costs and Aid: 2007–2008: $14,063 in-state comprehensive ($2,648 tuition). $22,593 out of state comprehensive ($13,848 tuition). 43% of students receives some financial aid and Native American students receive a tuition waiver.

Admissions

Fort Lewis College
Office of Admission
1000 Rim Drive
Durango, CO 81301
Phone: (877) FLC-COLO
Email: admission@fortlewis.edu

Service-Learning

Center for Civic Engagement
Kalin Grigg, Director
grigg_k@fortlewis.edu (970) 247-7641

Michelle Bonanno
Program Coordinator for
Community-Based
Learning and Research
Phone: (970) 247-7183
bonanno_m@fortlewis.edu

Jennifer Stark
Community Outreach
Phone: (970) 247-7026
stark_j@fortlewis.edu

Regis University

Regis is a four-year, co-educational, liberal arts/preprofessional, Catholic Jesuit university where students learn to answer the question "How ought we to live?" and prepare themselves to face the world.

Flagship Programs

Tinansa Intercultural Service-Learning Program
Tinansa offers a balanced academic and experiential opportunity to explore the connections between West African history and heritage and African American social thought and experience. The program involves three phases: classroom instruction, field experience in Ghana, Africa, and community outreach in Denver. Through this year-long program, students practice serving as positive agents of social change for global justice.

Community-Based Spanish English Exchange Program
This program connects the assets and knowledge of two different cultural communities: Regis College students and Latino immigrant families with children studying at 2 local dual language elementary schools. College Spanish and Education students are hosted by local Denver families. In groups of 3, the students visit the families two hours a week and communicate in Spanish. Students participate in the family's daily activities and discuss issues of importance to immigrant families living in the U.S.

Health Fairs & Health Education
Regis students and faculty collaborate with the 9Health Fair to provide an annual health fair on the Regis campus for over 300 adults from the local community and to provide preventative health education in several K-12 classrooms throughout the Denver metro area and beyond (Wind River Indian Reservation, Nicaragua, and the Dominican Republic).

Course Snapshot

"For **BA 420, Marketing,** we worked directly with refugee women from Baghdad and Darfur to help them create a business plan for their jewelry coop, A Little Something. We worked with the women to determine their product, pricing, placement, and promotion. Through this project, I actually applied the knowledge I had been learning in class and leveraged that knowledge to the benefit of others. I had more of a desire to actually learn the class material and not just to memorize it, as I knew it mattered to the lives of others." ~ Regis student Pete Johnston

Academics
Through community-based learning classes at Regis, students develop a critical consciousness, transform themselves and gain the tools through which to challenge and change the inequitable systems and structures in society.

Anthropology
Biology
Business
Chemistry
Communication
Core Seminars
Education
English Language & Literature
Environmental Studies
Fine Arts

History & Politics
Leadership Development Program
Mathematics
Modern & Classical Language & Literature
Nursing
Peace & Justice Studies
Psychology
Religious Studies
Sociology
Women's Studies

Check out all majors at: www.regis.edu

"I want Regis students to be critical thinkers who question everything for the sake of making choices that promote nonviolence, human dignity, justice, and the common good."
~ Dr. Byron Plumley, Director, Peace & Justice Studies

Awards and Recognition
• For the 13th consecutive year, Regis has been ranked as a Top Tier Western University by *U.S.News & World Report*.

• The annual National Survey of Student Engagement consistently shows that Regis ranks high in factors such as level of academic challenge and student/faculty interaction.

• Regis is one of 102 schools from 32 states on the John Templeton Foundation Honor Roll for Character-Building Universities and Colleges.

• Regis University has been ranked by *U.S.News & World Report* as the 5th best university in the western U.S. for the highest proportion of classes with 20 students or less.

• Regis University has been successful in bringing in $1 million in student service scholarships through the UCAN Serve AmeriCorps program, benefitting over 700 Regis University students who have dedicated their professional lives to Careers in the Common Good.

College Fast Facts
Four Year, Private, Urban, Founded: 1877
Affiliation: Catholic Jesuit
Web site: www.regis.edu
Student Profile: 1670 undergraduate students (46% male, 54% female); 41 states and territories, 19% minority, 1% international.
Faculty Profile: 93 full-time faculty, 92% hold a terminal degree in their field; 14/1 student/faculty ratio. Average class size is 20 students or less.
Athletics: NCAA Division II, Rocky Mountain Athletic Conference. 5 men's and 7 women's varsity sports. Regis offers an active athletic program at the varsity, club, and intramural levels.
Costs and Aid: 2007-2008: $37,682 comprehensive ($28,700 tuition/fees and $8,982 room/board). 90% of students receive some form of financial aid, 60% of which is need-based.

Admissions
Regis College Office of Admissions
3333 Regis Boulevard, A-12
Denver, CO 80221-1099
Phone: 1(800) 388-2366 ext. 4900 or (303) 458-4900
Email: regisadm@regis.edu

Service-Learning
Ignatian Collaborative for Service & Justice
Center for Service & Community-Based Learning
Melissa Nix, M.A.
Coordinator of Curriculum & Intercultural Programming
Phone: 1(800) 388-2366 ext. 4217 or (303) 458-4217
www.regis.edu/collegeservice

The University of Colorado-Boulder

The University of Colorado-Boulder offers a rich tradition of excellence, nationally recognized academics, outstanding faculty, and a multitude of unique learning opportunities.

Flagship Programs

Engineering for Developing Communities (EDC)
The EDC program, available to students in the College of Engineering and Applied Science, educates globally responsible engineering students and professionals who can offer sustainable and appropriate solutions to the endemic problems faced by developing communities worldwide.

The Puksta Scholars Program
Puksta Scholars is an exemplary non-academic program which provides substantial scholarships and support to approximately twenty students per year who develop and implement intensive year-long civic engagement projects.

INVST Community Studies
programs develop engaged citizens and leaders who work for the benefit of humanity and the environment. Programs include a comprehensive two-year Community Leadership Program, Community Studies Electives, and Youth Council for Public Policy.

Course Snapshot

College of Architecture and Planning "Engaging the Community in Design: "Participatory Community Planning: Designing Outdoor School Environments with Children and Youth"- This course will provide undergraduate students the necessary skills and experience in design and planning processes with the community. This will be accomplished through a special topics studio/seminar in which enrolled students will have the opportunity to learn about the theoretical and practical aspects of participatory planning and gain hands-on experience facilitating a participatory process in the design and implementation of an outdoor classroom with students at Horizons Alternative School, a K-8 school in Boulder.

Academics

Service-learning courses at CU transcend the notion that the university is a detached, self-contained unit by discovering and creating vibrant relations with the world outside of it. Service-learning combines community service with academic instruction focusing on critical thinking, problem solving, social and personal development, and civic responsibility.

Colleges and Schools
College of Architecture and Planning
College of Arts and Sciences
School of Education
College of Engineering and Applied Science
Graduate School
School of Journalism and Mass Communications
School of Law
Leeds School of Business
College of Music

"At CU, service-learning is an integral component of academics, reaching into all sectors campus-wide."

Sample List of Courses Offering Service-Learning
The Literature of Education, ENGL 4038.
Humanizing Contracts, LAWS 8011.
Technical Communication and Design, WRTG 3035.
Teaching and Learning Physics, PHYS 4810/7810.
Introduction to Women's Literature: Coming of Age In the U.S., ENGL 1260.
Queer Rhetorics, WRTG 3020

Check out all majors at: www.colorado.edu/academics/majors.html

Awards and Recognition
Service-Learning
• CU-Boulder was named a 2007 Presidential Award winner by the federal Corporation for National and Community Service, the President's Council on Service and Civic Participation, the USA Freedom Corps and the U.S. Departments of Education and Housing and Urban Development as one of the top three universities in the nation in general community service.

• CU-Boulder was named as the third best university in the nation for current graduates serving in the Peace Corps and the best per capita in the country.

• CU-Boulder was selected as one of the 81 best community service universities in the country in the book *Colleges with a Conscience*.

Academics
• CU-Boulder was one of only 19 public universities ranked as a "Best Buy" in the 2008 edition of *The Fiske Guide to Colleges*.

• Two undergraduate specialty programs were ranked nationally in the top 20 among universities offering doctoral programs in *U.S.News & World Report*'s *2008 America's Best Colleges* issue. They are business entrepreneurship (16th) and aerospace engineering (16th).

• Two undergraduate academic programs were ranked in the top 40 universities offering doctoral programs in *U.S.News & World Report's 2008 America's Best Colleges* issue. They are engineering (33rd) and business (41st).

• CU-Boulder is the only research institution in the world to have designed and built space instruments for NASA that have been launched to every planet in the solar system.

College Fast Facts
Four Year, Public, Urban, Founded: 1876
Web site: www.colorado.edu
Student Profile: 25,495 undergraduate students (53% male, 47% female); 14% minority, 4% international. 32% out of state.
Faculty Profile: 1,177 full-time faculty. 71% phds. 16:1 student/faculty ratio. Average class size is 20-29.
Athletics: NCAA Division 1, big 12 Conference.
Costs and Aid: 2007-2008: Comprehensive ($5,418 tuition). $23,580 out of state.

Admissions
552 UCB
Boulder, CO 80309-0552
Phone: (303) 492-6301
Email: apply@colorado.edu

Service-Learning
Martin Bickman
Professor of English
Director, Service Learning
Phone: 303-492-8945
Email: Martin.Bickman@colorado.edu

University of Denver

At the University of Denver, students join a community committed to pioneering excellence. Our programs are characterized by innovative curriculum, an emphasis on community engagement, and a commitment to academic integrity.

Flagship Programs

Public Achievement (PA) is a youth initiative that engages young people by empowering them with the public skills to become problem-solvers in their school or community. DU students from all majors and backgrounds work with K-12 students as "coaches" to tackle a community issues that the students identify.

Project Homeless Connect

DU is the first university in the nation to host Project Homeless Connect, a one-day event to help people overcome barriers to self-sufficiency by offering a full array of services in one location. Over 1000 DU volunteers and over 525 homeless individuals come together annually to help people access on-site services such as: housing, legal, employment, medical, dental, veteran and child care.

Immersion Programs

Programs as close as downtown Denver and as far away as Nicaragua and India, there is no shortage of opportunities for transformative life experiences. Our Nicaragua program focuses on a variety of issues around the Fair Trade movement, and the history and politics of Nicaragua. Our Denver Urban Immersion program focuses on the Denver metropolitan area, where students serve and learn in the issues of education, homelessness, economic development and immigration.

Course Snapshot

CUI 3995: Urban Education

"It is impossible to think clearly about urban schools, curriculum, and teaching without looking deeply into the contexts within which teaching occurs. To be aware of the social and moral universe we inhabit and share, aware too of what has yet to be achieved in terms of human possi-

bility, is to be a teacher who is capable of being a critic and a public person."
– Dr. Nick Cutforth

Academics

Service-Learning is a part of every college and virtually every department at the University of Denver. Some of the key departments or classes are listed here:

Anthropology
Business
Chemistry
Education
English
Gender and Women Studies
Geography
Humanities
International Studies
Management
Marketing

Mass Communication
Music
Natural Science
Political Science
Psychology
Religious Studies
Social Work
Sociology
Spanish
Writing

Comprehensive list of our programs can be found at:
www.du.edu/engage

"The University of Denver undergraduate experience allows students to achieve an educational balance built on knowledge acquired through classroom research and discussion, and knowledge gained through exploration."

Awards and Recognition
Academics

• *U.S.News & World Report's* annual 2007 college rankings for undergraduate education place the University of Denver 85th among national doctoral universities. DU ranked high for its freshman retention rate (87%); its acceptance rate (73%), its number of full-time faculty (73%), and its graduation rate (72%).

• More than 40 specialized research centers and institutes in a wide range of disciplines are housed at the University of Denver. The University annually receives about $13 million in sponsored research support in multiple areas.

• DU has an outstanding study abroad program. 70% of our students study abroad in more than 45 countries, which ranks us 2nd nationally among doctoral and research institutions for percentage of students participating.

• In 2007 the *Princeton Review* recognized the University of Denver as one of 123 colleges in the Best in the West category.

Service-Learning

•2007 President's Higher Education Community Service Honor Roll

College Fast Facts

Four Year, Private, Urban, Founded: 1864

Web site: www.du.edu

Student Profile: 5,311 undergraduate students (45% male, 55% female)

Faculty Profile: 500 full-time faculty, DU also employs 41 part-time faculty and 473 adjunct faculty; 93% hold either doctoral or the highest degree appropriate to their discipline. 10:1 student/faculty ratio. Average class size is 20 students.

Athletics: 17 athletic teams at the University of Denver compete in the NCAA Division I Conference.

Costs and Aid: 2007-2008: $40,929 comprehensive ($31,428 tuition). 77% of students receive some form of financial aid.

Admissions

Office of Admission
University of Denver
2197 S University Blvd.
Denver, CO 80208
Phone: (800) 525-9495
Fax: (303) 871-3331
Email: admission@du.edu

Service-Learning

Center for Community Engagement & Service-Learning
University of Denver
2050 E. Evans Avenue
Driscoll Center South, Suite 22
Denver, CO 80208
Phone: (303) 871-3706
Fax: (303) 871-3110
Email: engage@du.edu
Web site: www.du.edu/engage

Eastern Connecticut State University

Eastern Connecticut State University is Connecticut's public liberal arts university, and provides an outstanding undergraduate education on a residential campus.

Flagship Programs

American Humanics

This national program prepares and certifies students for leadership positions in nonprofit organizations. The program includes a 300-hour internship. Eastern is the only college in New England with the program, and our student chapter coordinates a number of volunteer programs in the community.

Digital Art and Design Major

The Senior Design Group works on pro-bono design projects for public agencies and nonprofit organizations. In the past, clients have ranged from an historical museum to a community street festival, local food cooperative, and the Juvenile Court.

Willimantic Whitewater Partnership

Eastern students and faculty are very involved in this project, which is bringing whitewater rafting and other recreational and commercial activities to Willimantic. Eastern students have developed the WWP website, created a promotional video, and volunteered other time and expertise.

Course Snapshot

"Thinking Globally and Acting Locally: Perspectives on Development" uses Professor Eric Martin's work in Poland and Bosnia, as well as field work in the local Willimantic community, to explore environmental advocacy and collaboration, post-conflict recovery, transition to a free market economy, and infrastructure redevelopment. "With all the change going on in Willimantic, we can use our local community as a large learning lab at the same time the students gain a sense of social responsibility." -Professor Eric Martin

Academics

Service-learning reinforces classroom learning at Eastern as students work with nonprofits and community organizations in the vibrant, multicultural Willimantic area. The following majors have courses with a service-learning component:

Accounting
Biology
Biochemistry
Business Administration
Business Information Systems
Communication
Computer Science
Digital Art and Design
Economics
Education
English
Environmental Earth Science

Environmental Management and Policy (BGS)
Health and Physical Education
History
Mathematics
Performing Arts (Theatre, Music)
Political Science
Psychology
Sociology (includes anthropology)
Social Work
Spanish
Sports and Leisure Management
Sustainable Energy Studies

Check out all majors at: www.easternct.edu/majors.htm

"I believe that engaging service is part of the civil society America was founded on." ~ Carter Lennon '07

Awards and Recognition
Service-Learning
• 2007 President's Higher Education Community Service Honor Roll
• American Marketing Association students won national community service award the past two years.
• American Humanics Club received Community Service Award from Connecticut Department of Higher Education.
• Sarah Hemenway '07 named Volunteer of the Year by Willimantic Whitewater Partnership.
• Katarina Russo '08 received $4,500 stipend from American Humanics for paid Red Cross internship.
• Kevin Douglas named 2007 Connecticut Social Work Student of the Year.

Academics
• 33 majors; 55 minors; selected graduate programs.
• One of top Northeast Colleges (Princeton Review).
• "One of New England's most active Honors Programs," Peterson's Guide
• Three Fulbright awards in two years.
• Named to Colleges of Distinction.

College Fast Facts
Four Year, Public, Rural, Founded:1889
Web site: www.easternct.edu
Student Profile: 4,826 undergraduate students (45% male, 55% female); 26 states and territories, 34 countries; 16% minority, 3% international.
Faculty Profile: 71% full-time faculty. 95% hold a terminal degree in their field. 16/1 student/faculty ratio. Average class size is 24.
Athletics: Eastern's 17 varsity teams play in the NCAA Division III Little East Conference, and have won nine national championships.
Costs and Aid: 2007-2008 (In-State): $16,641 comprehensive ($3,346 tuition). (Out of State): $24,126 comprehensive ($10,831 tuition). 81% of students receives some financial aid.

Admissions
Eastern Connecticut State University
Office of Undergraduate Admissions
83 Windham Street
Willimantic, CT 06226
Phone: (860) 465-5286
Email: admissions@easternct.edu

Service-Learning
Center for Educational Excellence
dubinad@easternct.edu
Phone: (860) 465-4567

Fairfield University

A Fairfield University education prepares individuals for success in life measured by how deeply they challenge themselves and how they influence the world for the better. We believe that education has a practical, tangible value – that it should reach out, embrace the world, serve human needs, work for the common good.

Flagship Programs

Adrienne Kirby Family Literacy Project

Students are involved in preventive intervention that helps low-income preschoolers and their parents in language and reading, while learning about child development and cognition. Students have opportunities to engage with the project through service-learning courses and internships in psychology, and through volunteer opportunities for students in all majors.

The Greater Bridgeport Family Economic Security Coalition and VITA (Volunteer Income Tax Assistance)

Students work as income tax preparers, helping hundreds of qualifying community members file their income taxes while also learning about the impact of tax policy on citizens across socioeconomic levels. Students can participate through a service-learning course – Federal Income Taxation II or as volunteers.

Bridgeport Health Promotion Center

Nursing students provide health education, screening, referral, and follow-up services to underserved populations. Students gain professional experience while providing needed healthcare and education. Additionally, the HPC provides service-learning opportunities for students in a variety of disciplines.

Course Snapshot

Accounting 345. Federal Income Taxation II

Student Kylin Wentz said, "This program is yet another example of Fairfield's success at integrating our education with the University's mission to share with its neighbors its resources and special expertise for the betterment of the community."

Student Beth Grossman reflects on the fact that some families were not aware of the tax credits that they were entitled to. "Telling our clients about the credits was so rewarding because we were able to really help our clients claim what they deserve."

Academics

The Office of Service-Learning in the Center for Faith and Public Life animates the Fairfield University mission and facilitates the integration of living and learning as participants explore the interconnections of knowledge, experience, reflection, and action through academically-rigorous service-learning courses.

Charles F. Dolan School of Business
Accounting
Finance
Management
Information Systems & Operations Management
College of Arts and Sciences
Biology
Communication
Economics
English
History
International Studies
Peace and Justice Studies

Philosophy
Politics
Psychology
Religious Studies
Sociology & Anthropology
Women's Studies
Graduate School of Education
- and Allied Professions
Curriculum and Instruction
Marriage and Family Counseling
School of Engineering
School of Nursing
University College

Check out all majors at: www.fairfield.edu/aca_majors.html

"Service-learning encompasses the tenets of Ignatian Pedagogy, which is a signature methodology at Jesuit institutions. Through service-learning, students not only put into practice what they learn in the classroom, but they also encounter a disadvantaged population, learn about injustice, and develop a response to it."

~ Winston Tellis Ph. D., Stephen & Camille Schramm

Awards and Recognition

Service-Learning
• President's Higher Education Community Service Honor Roll 2007 and 2008.
• Recognized for 8 consecutive years at the CT Higher Education Community Service Awards.
• Member of Campus Compact since 2003.
• Home of CT State Campus Compact since 2008.

Academics
• Fairfield offers 34 undergraduate majors, 16 interdisciplinary minors and 34 graduate programs.
• 44 Fulbright scholars in the past 15 years.
• Chapters of Phi Beta Kappa and 20 honor societies.
• Ranked #2 in its category by *U.S.News & World Report's America's Best Colleges 2008*.
• Among Princeton Review's *Best 282 Business Schools* for 2007.
• Received major awards from the National Student Campaign against Hunger and Homelessness.

College Fast Facts

Comprehensive, Private, Urban, Founded: 1942

Affiliation: Jesuit, Catholic

Web site: www.fairfield.edu

Student Profile: Undergraduate students (42% male, 58% female); 26 states and territories, 17 countries; 13% minority, 1% international.

Faculty Profile: 239 full-time faculty. 94% hold a terminal degree in their field. 13 to 1 student/faculty ratio.

Athletics: NCAA Division 1, Metro Atlantic Athletic Conference. 20 varsity sports.

Costs and Aid: 2007-2008: $44,000 comprehensive ($33,340 tuition). 67% of students receive some financial aid. Total financial aid provided: $30 million.

Admissions
Office of Undergraduate Admission
Fairfield University
1073 N. Benson Road
Fairfield, CT 06824
Phone: 203.254.4100
Email: admis@mail.fairfield.edu

Service-Learning
Melissa Quan, asst. dir.,
Center for Faith and Public Life
and Office of Service Learning
Phone: 203.254.4000 ext. 3455
Email: mquan@mail.fairfield.edu
www.fairfield.edu/servicelearning

Quinnipiac University

Quinnipiac University is centered on three values: excellence in academic programs, a student-centered campus and a spirit of community. Internships, study abroad opportunities and service learning all play a role in the educational development of each student.

Flagship Programs

Albert Schweitzer Institute

The Albert Schweitzer Institute sponsors international trips for Quinnipiac faculty and students to fulfill the institute's mission of encouraging young adults to expand their horizons to a global perspective in the areas of humanitarian values, health care and peace.

Presidential Public Service Fellowship

The Presidential Public Service Fellowship program offers Quinnipiac students the opportunity to learn about public service by working in local government departments that match their interests and majors. Department heads mentor fellows while they work on significant community projects.

Alternative Spring Break

During spring break, Quinnipiac students have dedicated their week off to travel across the country to build houses for Habitat for Humanity and to travel to Barbados and Nicaragua for humanitarian missions.

Course Snapshot

PRR 495B - Public Relations Campaigns

In this service-learning course, students have a unique opportunity to create public relations campaigns for a non-profit client. Students recently developed creative public relations campaigns for non-profits located in New Orleans. Reaching out to non-profits in New Orleans provided student the chance to help with the on-going rebuilding efforts. The non-profits included Goodwill of New Orleans, Limitless Vistas, Replant New Orleans, The Priestley School of Architecture & Engineering and KIDsmART. Final presentations were delivered via conference call and students mailed a hard copy of public relations campaigns to the respective client, allowing the client to utilize their favorite aspects of the campaign.

Academics

Service-Learning at Quinnipiac blends the academic classroom performance with a caring attitude and real experiences that give a practical focus and human face to a subject or discipline.

Through service-learning courses Quinnipiac students develop a lifetime commitment to service that makes a difference locally, nationally and internationally. Some courses include:

DR 305:　Theater for Young Audience
IB 313:　International Marketing Research
MG222:　Ventures in Social Enterprise
MG 490:　Field Projects
OT 212:　Group Leadership.
PL 220:　Ethics and Human Values
PL 320:　Life and Thought of Albert Schweitzer
PO 315:　Democratic Theory and Practice
PO 331:　Human Rights
PRR495:　Public Relations Campaigns

"Service-Learning courses integrate meaningful community service with instruction and reflection to enrich the learning experience."

– Gregory P. Garvey, professor, computer science & interactive digital design

To learn more about Quinnipiac's majors and minors, visit: www.quinnipiac.edu/x160.xml

Awards and Recognition

• *U.S.News & World Report* – consistently in the top 12 of the top tier of Master's level Colleges in the North.

• Featured in Princeton Review's *Best 366 Colleges and Universities*.

• Quinnipiac offers over 50 undergraduate and 19 graduate degrees through the School of Business, Communications, Education, Health Sciences and the College of Arts and Sciences.

• Featured in Peterson's *Guide to Competitive Colleges*.

• Quinnipiac is ranked number 9 in PC magazine's 2007 "Most Wired Colleges."

• Featured in Princeton Review's 2008 *Best Business Schools*.

College Fast Facts

Four Year, Private Suburban, Founded: 1929

Web site: www.quinnipiac.edu

Student Profile: 5,400 undergraduate students (61% male, 39% female); 25 states and territories, 8 countries; 11% minority, 1% international. In all, 80% of freshmen come from outside of Connecticut and 95% of all freshmen live on campus.

Faculty Profile: 290 full-time faculty, 88% hold a terminal degree in their field. 15:1 student/faculty ratio. Average class size is 22.

Athletics: NCAA Division I, NEC in all major sports plus ECAC (Men's and Women's Ice Hockey) Conference. 21 varsity sports. The "Bobcats" compete in 21 sports. Basketball and Ice Hockey compete in the 3500 seat twin arenas at the TD Banknorth Sport Center (opened Jan 2007).

Costs and Aid: 2007-2008: $39,200 comprehensive ($28,720 tuition and fees). 70% of students receive some financial aid.

Admissions

Quinnipiac University, Office of Undergraduate Admissions
275 Mount Carmel Avenue
Hamden, CT 06518
Phone: (203) 582-8600 or 1 (800) 462-1944
Email: admissions@quinnipiac.edu

Service-Learning

Professor Gregory P. Garvey
Phone: (203) 582-8389
Email: greg.garvey@quinnipiac.edu

Sacred Heart University

Sacred Heart University is a leading comprehensive Catholic university in the Northeast, offering over 40 undergraduate, masters, and doctoral programs.

Service-learning at Sacred Heart University offers students the opportunity to engage in service experiences that are integrated into the University's academic curriculum. Through service-learning, students develop academic and leadership skills in real-life situations, while embracing social responsibility and a sense of caring about others.

Flagship Programs

The Sacred Heart University-St. Charles Church Health and Wellness Center is a collaborative initiative designed to meet the health and wellness needs of parishioners while providing students with clinical service-learning experiences in Nursing, Physical Therapy, Occupational Therapy, and related disciplines.

Bridgeport Rescue Mission & Merton Center

Students in Psychology's Drug Use and Abuse course complete service-learning at the Bridgeport Rescue Mission and Merton Center, both valuable community programs catering to individuals recovering from addictions.

Educational Psychology/Education in the U.S.

Students in these introductory Education courses are required to complete 16 hours minimum of service learning in nearby Bridgeport K-8 schools. Students generally work for two hours per week as a classroom assistant or tutor, helping educate a diverse urban population.

Course Snapshot

SIFE (Students in Free Enterprise)

Sacred Heart University sponsors a highly active chapter of SIFE, a competitive, global collegiate program with a one-credit course option that offers opportunities to build communication, teamwork, problem-solving, and leadership skills while students develop and implement community outreach programs emphasizing free enterprise.

In a recent project, the SHU SIFE team partnered with Century21 Access America in a six-month community sweep to bring back the American dream for families who were previously unable to afford homes.

Academics

Service-learning fosters students' academic and personal growth while enabling them to positively impact the lives of those less fortunate.

A few examples are:
Art (AR)
Biology (BI)
Business (BU)
Criminal Justice (CJ)
Economics (EC)
Education (ED)*
English (EN)
ESL (ES)*
Exercise Science (EX)*
Finance (FN)
Media Studies (MS)
Nursing (NU)*
Psychology (PS)*
Social Work (SW)*
Sociology (SO)

*courses have a required service-learning component

Note: these can be designated as service-learning courses, or they can have a strong service-learning component.

View all academic programs at:
www.sacredheart.edu/academics.cfm

Educational Psychology: ED 101: *"Through service-learning in local schools I applied my coursework to real-life situations working with students."* ~ Allyson Conca, student, Class of '07

Awards and Recognition
Service Awards
• SHU's Habitat for Humanity chapter named among the top five collegiate chapters in the nation, receiving the "Habitat Collegiate Chapter of the Year Honorable Mention" award, 2007.
• Connecticut Department of Higher Education Service Award (twelve of past fourteen years).
• In Spring 2008, SHU finished third in the nation in the ONE Campus Challenge campaign that seeks to raise public awareness about the issues of global poverty, hunger, disease and efforts to fight such problems in developing countries.

Academic Recognitions
• The Princeton Review Best 366 Colleges: 2008 Edition.
• The Princeton Review Best 290 Business Schools: 2008 Edition.
• U.S. News & World Report America's Best Colleges: Top Tier Institution, Master's North Category, 2005-present.
• The Princeton Review Best Northeastern Colleges, 2005-present.
• Member of Colleges of Distinction, 2007-present.
• John F. Welch College of Business AACSB-Accreditation, 2006.
• Association of American Colleges & Universities Core Commitments Leadership Consortium, 2007-present.
• Ranked #11 on Intel's latest edition of Most Unwired Colleges, 2005.

College Fast Facts
An independent liberal arts university founded in 1963
Web site: www.sacredheart.edu
Student Profile: 3,500 undergraduate students (40% male, 60% female); 31 states and territories, 42 countries; 15% minority, 68% out of state.
Faculty Profile: 199 full-time faculty. 80% hold a terminal degree in their field. 13:1 student/faculty ratio. Average class size is 22.
Athletics: NCAA Division I - Northeast Conference; 32 varsity sports.
Costs and Aid: 2007-2008: $27,150; 66% of students receive some financial aid. Average award: $16,266.

Admissions
Sacred Heart University
Office of Undergraduate
 Admissions
5151 Park Avenue
Fairfield, CT 06825
Phone: (203) 371-7880
Email: enroll@sacredheart.edu

Service-Learning
Office of Service-Learning and
Volunteer Programs
Phyllis Machledt, Director
Phone: (203) 365-7622
Email: machledtp@sacredheart.edu

University of New Haven

The University of New Haven engages its students in discovery-based learning across the curriculum to expand intellectual curiosity, enhance personal growth, and advance professional development.

Flagship Programs

The President's Public Service Fellowship

University of New Haven students are placed in a nonprofit or public service work environment during the summer. While students gain awareness of community assets and needs, they also gain valuable work experience, teambuilding, and leadership skills. The program fosters positive relationships in our community.

In-Kind Interior Design 599 Independent Study

Interior design students impact our community in meaningful ways by applying their design skills in the nonprofit sector. Using a worthwhile collaborative effort, students serve our local veteran's hospital by creating space which nurtures and celebrates the patients, visitors, and staff.

Volunteer Income Tax Assistance Program

The Volunteer Income Tax Assistance (VITA) program provides students with a hands-on learning opportunity to assist in the preparation of tax returns for low and moderate income community members at no cost. The program is sponsored by the IRS.

Course Snapshot

Dental Hygiene 462:
Senior Internship Global Journeys in Dental Health

Students are engaged locally, nationally, and globally offering oral health care services and education to underserved populations; in some instances abroad, providing individuals with their first toothbrush. A student reflected, "Now that I have had experience with oral health care in other cultures I know that I would do it again in a heart beat. I wouldn't mind where, just as long as I can do a service to those in need." This is an example of a program which transforms clinical field experiences into meaningful service-learning opportunities.

Academics

Academic service-learning at the University of New Haven provides opportunities for students and faculty to work in partnership with the Greater New Haven region and beyond for the purpose of exchanging knowledge and resources to strengthen our global society.

The following programs offer service-learning courses:
Accounting
Chemistry
Criminal Justice
Dental Hygiene
Environmental Science
Fire Science
General Engineering
Interior Design
Legal Studies
Management
Management of Sports
Industries

"Working with community-based clients, interior design students improve living environments through creative design solutions."

~ Christy Somerville, Assistant Professor, ID 599

Check out all majors at: www.newhaven.edu/academics/10836/

Awards and Recognition

Service-Learning
• President's Higher Education Community Service Honor Roll.

Academics
• University of New Haven is the Northeast Campus for the National Society Experiential Education's Academy.

• As the Northeast Regional Campus for the National Society for Experiential Education, the University of New Haven has more than 20 faculty and staff certified in Experiential Education, more than any other institution in the U.S.

• University of New Haven President Steven Kaplan named 2008 Businessperson of the Year by *Business New Haven.*

College Fast Facts

Four Year, Private, Suburban, Founded: 1920

Web site: www.newhaven.edu

Student Profile: 3,011 undergraduate students (51.9% male, 48.1% female); 40.4% of students from out-of-state; 20.2% minority, 1.8% international.

Faculty Profile: 182 full-time faculty 80% of whom have doctoral or other terminal degrees in their fields. 14:1 student/faculty ratio. Average class size is 21.

Athletics: NCAA Division II, Northeast - 10 Conference. 18 varsity sports. The University of New Haven Chargers represent a comprehensive and successful varsity athletics program.

Costs and Aid: 2008-2009: $39,856.00 comprehensive ($27,000 tuition). 75.3% of student receive some financial aid.

Admissions

University of New Haven
Office of Undergraduate Admissions
300 Boston Post Road
West Haven, CT 06516
Phone: (800) 342-5864 ext. 7319 or (203) 932-7319
Email: adminfo@newhaven.edu

Service-Learning

Sally Anastos
Academic Service-Learning Specialist
Experiential Education Office
University of New Haven
300 Boston Post Road
West Haven, CT 06516
Phone: (203) 479-4588
Email: sanastos@newhaven.edu

Wesleyan University

Founded in 1831, Wesleyan University is a nonsectarian liberal arts and sciences institution distinguished by its commitment to academic excellence in an atmosphere of freedom and intellectual rigor.

Flagship Programs

Psychology of Reading

Wesleyan students taking the Psychology of Reading learn about many aspects of human cognition from sensation and perception to compre- hension and reasoning. They spend two hours a week at an elementary school as reading tutors and conduct a book drive to provide reading material for the students' homes.

The Health of Communities

In the Service-Learning component of this course, students serve as research assistants for projects being conducted by Middletown's Community Health Center. These include investigations such as school-based efforts to reduce the risk of obesity and the health needs of homeless persons.

Activism and Outreach Through Theater

Theater can be a means for social change. In this class, social activism is put into practice through the staging of theatrical events in unconventional settings (prisons, senior centers, schools). Students work collectively to devise informal presentations and workshops that include the participation of their audiences.

Course Snapshot

Environmental Geochemistry

Geochemistry provides a tool to analyze the environment, be it toxic waste, water quality, gas leaks, or past environments. Students in this class work collectively to analyze multiple characteristics of a specific environment in order to understand its biogeochemistry. Results from these studies are used by community groups to plan remediation or further development. For example, in Middletown, Conn., an abandoned landfill sits adjacent to extensive wetlands. Students analyzed soils, water, and gases. Methane (CH_4), a green house gas and potential energy source, is seeping from the landfill. Now developers are investi- gating the site to determine the feasibility of using the methane to heat a community center that may be located at the site.

Academics

Service-Learning seeks to broaden students' understanding of course content through activities which are of service to the community. Through structured reflection, students are able to test and deepen their understanding of theoretical approaches in virtually any discipline.

Anthropology
Art Studio
Biology
Computer Science
Dance
Earth and Environmental Sciences
History
Less Commonly Taught Languages
Music
Psychology
Religion
Sociology
Spanish
Theater

"Understanding health care issues from both a practical and academic standpoint has given me a passion to devote my life to health policy for the uninsured."

— Beth Newell '04

Check out all majors at: www.wesleyan.edu/acaf/dept.html

Awards and Recognition

Service-Learning
• President's Higher Education Community Service Honor Roll

Academics
• Wesleyan University offers majors in almost 50 areas of undergraduate study, 10 master's degrees, and 6 doctorates.
• As of 2008, 86 Wesleyan students have been awarded the prestigious Watson Fellowship, which sponsors one year of independent study abroad.
• Wesleyan ranks first among its liberal arts peers in federal science grants, according to the National Science Foundation.

College Fast Facts

Four Year, Private, Urban, Founded: 1831

Affiliation: Nondenominational

Web site: www.wesleyan.edu

Student Profile: Undergraduate students (50% male, 50% female); 51 states and territories, 44 countries; 6% international; 26% students of color (7% Black or African American; 11% Asian or Asian American; 8% Latino or Hispanic, 1% Native American).

Faculty Profile: 399 full-time faculty. 99% hold a terminal degree in their field. 9:1 student/faculty ratio.

Athletics: NCAA Division III, New England Small College Athletic Conference. 29 varsity teams; 11 club sports teams; 9 intramural sports. About 700 students participate in intercollegiate sports each year.

Costs and Aid: 2007-2008: $46,646 comprehensive (tuition, room, and board). 43% of students receive some form of financial aid. Most students live in campus facilities.

Admissions

Office of Admission
Wesleyan University
70 Wyllys Ave.
Middletown, CT 06459-0265
Email: admissions@wesleyan.edu

Service-Learning

Suzanne O'Connell, Ph.D.
Director
Service-Learning Center
Office of Community Partnerships
Phone: (680) 685-2262
Email: soconnell@wesleyan.edu

American University

American University is a distinctive academic community that embraces five core principles: Internationalism, Diversity, Ethics, Action and Service Ideas.

Through service-learning at American University, students have the opportunity to practice, reexamine and deepen their classroom learning, while responding to the significant needs of the D.C. metropolitan area.

Flagship Programs

Community Service-Learning Program
Students, faculty and community partners work together in devising a community-based learning project that combines classroom study with support for the nonprofit sector. Students receive an additional credit linked to a course after completing 40 hours of service work.

Washington Initiative, Kogod School of Business
This course offers undergraduates practical, hands-on experience. In the fall, students work on a fundraising event for a local nonprofit group. During the second semester, they assist low-income D.C. residents complete their tax forms. Typically students offer 500 hours of free income tax assistance, serving hundreds of taxpayers who receive over $1.5 million in returns.

Alternative Break Trips
Through the Alternative Break program, students can lead or participate in domestic and international trips centered on social justice issues during their summer, winter or spring breaks. This experiential learning opportunity, typically including a service component, addresses systems of inequality and human rights.

Course Snapshot

Laboratory in Leadership Development
This course for freshmen in the School of Public Affairs (SPA) Leadership Program is designed to introduce students to various contemporary social issues and obliges students to engage meaningfully with members of the community. Students are encouraged to reflect on the relevance and political importance of service to the community and to take action by choosing an issue, partnering with a community-based organization, independently researching the policies, laws, major players and politics of the issue and designing and executing a practical project with group members.

Academics

Courses that incorporate service-learning encourage students to develop both a fuller understanding of topics discussed in class and a stronger commitment to the community. Programs of study include:

College of Arts and Sciences
  Passport to Service-Learning (School of Education)*
  Anthropology
  Biology
  Economics
  Education, Teaching and Health
  Health and Fitness
  History
  Language/Foreign studies
  Literature
  Performing Arts
  Sociology
  Women and Gender Studies
Kogod School of Business
  Washington Initiative*
  Kogod Leadership and Applied Business
School of Public Affairs
  Leadership Program*
  Government
  Justice Law and Society
  Washington Semester*
School of Communication
  Film and Media Arts
  Public Communication
School of International Service
  Leadership Gateway*

"Having students work in the Washington, D.C. area with the elderly, Latino immigrant communities and homeless people was a significant step in their linking economic, political and social stratification issues to everyday challenges for residents of the nation's capital."

-Sociology Professor, Salvador Vidal-Ortiz

*Courses with a required service-learning component.
View all majors: www.american.edu/academics/

Awards and Recognition

Service-Learning
• President's Higher Education Community Service Honor Roll in 2006, 2007.
• In 2007, The Princeton Review named American University the 6th most politically active campus in America.

Academics
• In 2007, AU was ranked 85th among the top national universities by *U.S.News & World Report*.
• *The Princeton Review* has cited AU as one of its best-value colleges.
• The National Survey of Student Engagement rates AU as one of the top doctoral/extensive research-level schools in the country.
• *The 2006 Fiske Guide to Colleges* selected AU as a "Best Buy" college in the United States.

College Fast Facts

Four Year, Private, Surban, Founded: 1905

Web site: www.american.edu

Student Profile: 5,922 undergraduate students (35% male, 65% female); 19% minority, 7% international.

Faculty Profile: 594 full-time faculty, 428 adjunct, 97% hold a terminal degree in their field. Student/faculty ratio: 14 to 1, Average class size: 23.

Athletics: NCAA Division I, Patriot League, 11 varsity sports.

Costs and Aid: 2007–2008: $40,219 comprehensive ($30,958 tuition). 67% of students receiving some financial aid.

Admissions
American University
Admissions
4400 Massachusetts Ave. NW,
Washington D.C. 20016-8001
Phone: 202-885-6000
Fax: 202-885-1025

Service-Learning
Marcy Fink Campos
Director, Community Service Center
Mary Graydon Center 273
Phone: 202-885-7378
Email: mfcampos@american.edu

Bethune-Cookman University

Bethune-Cookman University is an historically Black university, with deep roots in the history of America and continues to provide services to the broader community through a focus on service learning and civic engagement.

Flagship Programs

Global Civic Engagement

In partnership with Covenant United Methodist Church's Kenya Mission, BCU focuses on two issues facing our global community today: environmental pollution and poverty. Faculty, staff and students collect printer cartridges and recycle them for funds that will be used to purchase school supplies for children in Gaitu Primary School in Meru, Kenya-Africa. These children come from very poor homes and most of them cannot afford to buy even a pencil.

Rosa Parks Commemoration

Project Pericles & The Young Pericleans initiated and provided leadership for the 50th Year Commemoration of Rosa Parks. The main focus was "1,000 Votes for Rosa Parks," a major voter registration and Election Day voter turnout initiative. The goal was to end Election Day with 1,000 or more students having voted.

Gale Leramand School of Nursing and the Odessa

Chambliss Wellness Center

In December, 2007, the Odessa Chambliss Wellness Center was dedicated. This 35,000 square foot state-of-the-art facility will help meet the health care needs of Daytona's uninsured and homeless residents. The wellness center will provide both students and faculty -- some of whom are nurse-practitioners -- with a venue for helping these two citizen groups that are routinely marginalized.

Academics

The motto of the university "Enter to learn; depart to serve" has become the mantra of the approximately 13,000-plus alumni, who now live and serve their communities all over the world.

The mission is to serve in the Christian tradition the diverse educational, social, and cultural needs of its students and to develop in them the desire and capacity for continuous intellectual and professional growth, leadership and service to others.

Bethune-Cookman University accomplishes its mission by providing quality instruction in an intellectually stimulating environment that nurtures the mind (intellect), the heart (transformative leadership) and the hand (service learning).

View information about our Freshman College at:
http://www4.cookman.edu/freshmancollege/

Awards and Recognition

• AmeriCorps Program Director and members received special recognition from the city of Daytona Beach Leisure Services Department for volunteer services within the community.

• The AmeriCorps program has work diligently for the last three years networking and serving as community mentor for events such as the Fall Kids Festival, the Charles Cherry Festival, MLK march, the annual Easter Beach Run, and several field days at Turtie Small Elementary and Campbell Middle Schools.

• President's Community Service Honor Roll, 2006

Fast Facts
Four Year, Private, Urban; Founded 1904

Web site: www.bethune.cookman.edu

Student Profile: 3,433 undergraduate students (58% female, 42% male); 30% out-of-state, 3% international, 91% African-American.

Faculty Profile: 170 full-time faculty. 80% hold a terminal degree in their field. 17:1 student/faculty ratio. Average class size is 10-19.

Athletics: NCAA Division I. 16 varsity sports.

Costs and Aid: 2008–2009: $11,792 tuition. 97% of students receive some financial aid.

Admissions
640 Dr. Mary McLeod Bethune Boulevard
Daytona Beach, FL 32114
Phone: (386) 481-2000
Email: admissions@cookman.edu

Civic Engagement
Project Pericles
Dr. Claudette McFadden, Director
Phone: (386) 481-2753
Email: mcfaddec@cookman.edu

Florida Gulf Coast University

Florida Gulf Coast University is a young, vibrant, state university with a mission and guiding principles that feature civic engagement and environmental sustainability.

Service-Learning Focus

FGCU has a service graduation requirement fulfilled through independent service-learning projects and/or through course requirements. Service-learning is a reflective activity designed to increase knowledge and skills, provide an enriched learning experience, and facilitate civic engagement and responsibility through reciprocal learning and sensitivity to cultural, economic, and social differences.

Flagship Programs

University Colloquium

All FGCU students take Colloquium, an upper-level course which joins service-learning, environmental sustainability, and the FGCU accreditation quality enhancement plan. Extensive readings, classroom work, and hands on experiences build a local and global sense of responsibility in students.

Wings of Hope

Wings of Hope, a premier service-learning experience, is integrated into Environmental Humanities, allowing college students to develop and present age-appropriate environmental programming to elementary school children. Children come to campus for fun-filled lessons about Florida panthers, water conservation, and other pertinent Southwest Florida environmental issues.

American Democracy Project (ADP)

The ADP fosters scholarship and activities that promote a collaborative and democratic community. The project supports reflections and discussion of the concepts and questions surrounding our shared public existence and provides institutional scaffolding to facilitate rich, thoughtful engagements.

Academics

FGCU forges broad community partnerships; and working with these partnerships, students are enriched now and provided connections for lifetime commitments. Service-Learning can be a part of every academic discipline, some examples are:

College of Arts and Sciences
• Music
• Chemistry
• Communications
Lutgert College of Business
• Accounting
• Computer Science
• Marketing
U.A. Whitaker School of Engineering
• Bioengineering
• Environmental Engineering
• Civil Engineering

College of Education
• Early Childhood Education
• Elementary Education
• Secondary Education
College of Health Professions
• Health Science
• Physical Therapy
• Community Health
College of Professional Studies
• Legal Studies
• Social Work
• Public Administration

Check out service-learning opportunities at our EaglesConnect website at:
www.fgcu.edu/connect/

"...more effective to learn in an experiential way than to read from a book and memorize information for a test."

~ Student in Nonprofit Public Relations, spring 2007

Awards and Recognition
Service-Learning
• Learn and Serve Grantee
• Recipient of two Florida Campus Compact Grants
• President's Higher Education Community Service Honor Roll , 2007
• Florida Campus Compact "Most Engaged Campus" Award (State University – 2007).

Academics
• *U.S.News & World Report: America's Best Colleges 2008*
• On a national survey (National Survey of Student Engagement), FGCU students rated the quality of their undergraduate learning experience in the 85th- 99th percentile.
• The Lutgert College of Business' success was noted in the 2007 edition of *The Princeton Review's "Best 282 Business Schools."*

College Fast Facts
Four Year, Public, Urban, Founded: 1997
Web site: www.fgcu.edu
Student Profile: Undergraduate students (40% male, 60% female); 47 states and territories, 87 countries; 18% minority, 1% international.
Faculty Profile: 304 full-time faculty. 79% hold a terminal degree in their field. 18:1 student/faculty ratio. Average class size is 32.
Athletics: NCAA Division I, Atlantic Sun Conference. 14 varsity sports. Additional intramural sports; Women's Basketball second nationally in 2007.
Costs and Aid: 2007–2008: $3,647 in-state comprehensive ($2,211 tuition). 58% of students receive some financial aid.

Admissions
Florida Gulf Coast University
Admissions
10501 FGCU Blvd.
Fort Myers, Florida 33965
Phone: (239) 590-7878
Email: admissions@fgcu.edu

Service-Learning
Center for Civic Engagement
Linda Summers
Director
Phone: (239) 590-7016
Email: lsummers@fgcu.edu

Florida Institute of Technology

Florida Institute of Technology provides hands-on, research-based undergraduate education in engineering, the sciences, aeronautics, psychology and business.

Flagship Programs

Civic Engagement Initiative

Through the Civic Engagement Initiative, students are given the opportunity to make significant contributions to the community through service at campus events, in cooperation with local organizations, and in projects of their own creation (Civic Engagement Initiative Brochure, 2006). Both academic and non-academic service-learning is designed to benefit both the students and the community.

University Park Elementary School

In 2000, Florida Tech "adopted" University Park Elementary School (UPES). For course projects, students have developed a public relations campaign, and proposals for school security and landscaping for UPES. Other annual activities include: campus tours for UPES students; faculty presentations on both sites; activities by Athletics staff; a Giving Tree event in which university groups gather materials to restock UPES teachers' supplies; and a UPES float in the university's Homecoming Parade. This relationship serves as a rich context for community service and service-learning... a good example of "high tech with a human touch."

Course Snapshot

The Methods for Citizenship and Environmental Responsibility course, focuses on the role of education in preparing citizens for greater environmental responsibility, and is designed to complement coursework on governmental responsibility for environmental policy, planning, and management. Students are exposed to theory, research, and guidelines associated with citizen action, service learning, and other relevant pedagogical strategies from social studies, science, and environmental education. To bring this material to life, students plan, carry out, and eventually report on an environmental service/action project of their own choosing, either alone or in small teams.

Academics

Service learning courses and community projects are an integral part of our academic mission. At Florida Institute of Technology, the scientists and engineers of tomorrow provide insight and elbow grease toward solving today's problems in their communities. Florida Tech's students use their unique talents to improve the lives of the less fortunate and, in the process, grow into caring, compassionate adults.

College of Engineering
College of Science
College of Aeronautics
College of Business
College of Psychology and Liberal Arts

Check out all majors at:
www.fit.edu/ugrad/majors.htm

"Through the Civic Engagement Initiative, we are building a culture of service, citizenship, and responsibility that will last for decades to come. You can be part of the gathering momentum of acts of kindness and decency that are changing Florida Tech, one heart and one soul at a time".

~ Anthony James Catanese, Ph.D., FAICP, University President

Awards and Recognition

• Named to President's Honor Roll for Higher Education Community Service.
• Listed among America's top doctoral universities by *U.S.News & World Report*.
• Listed as *Baron's Best Buy in Higher Education*.
• Listed as one of America's top Institutes of Technology by the *Fiske Guide to Colleges*.
• Listed as a top southeastern university by the Princeton Review.
• Listed as Florida's top private university by Washington Monthly.

College Fast Facts

Four Year, Private, Suburban, Founded: 1958

Web site: www.fit.edu

Student Profile: 2594 undergraduate students (70% male, 30% female); 48 states and territories, 81 countries; 11% minority, 21% international.
Faculty Profile: 208 full-time faculty. 89% hold a terminal degree in their field. 9:1 undergraduate student/faculty ratio. Average class size is 20.

Athletics: NCAA Division 2, Sunshine State Conference. 15 varsity sports. Panther teams have earned regional titles and Sunshine State Conference championships.

Costs and Aid: 2007-2008: $36,690 comprehensive ($28,920 tuition). 89% of students receive some financial aid.

Admissions

Florida Institute of Technology,
Office of Undergraduate Admission
150 W University Blvd.
Melbourne, 32901-6975
Phone: (800) 888-4348
Email: admission@fit.edu

Service-Learning

Civic Engagement Initiative
Student Life Office
150 W University Blvd.
Melbourne, 32901-6975
(321) 674-8080
Phone:civic@fit.edu

Florida Southern College

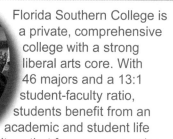

Florida Southern College is a private, comprehensive college with a strong liberal arts core. With 46 majors and a 13:1 student-faculty ratio, students benefit from an academic and student life culture that focuses on service learning, student-faculty collaborative research and performance, study abroad, and internships.

Flagship Programs

Wellness Education

Students in the undergraduate nursing capstone course work with community-based health organizations to promote wellness education. One of the many projects included the development of a Pandemic Flu and Infectious Diseases Plan in collaboration with local schools and the Polk County Health Department.

Preserving an Architectural Legacy

Florida Southern has the largest collection of Frank Lloyd Wright architecture in the world. Honors College students researched and catalogued photos, drawings, and correspondence relating to Wright's work at the College from 1939-1958 and created a corresponding web site for use by students, Wright scholars and the public.

Promoting Intercultural Understanding

A service learning project at the Archives of Temple Emanuel, conducted as part of a service learning research and writing course, provided students with new perspectives on Judaism while preserving the historical heritage of the city's Jewish community. The students prepared an exhibit that is on display at Roux Library.

Course Snapshot

Sustainability

FSC biology students participated in a wetlands restoration project that is helping the City of Lakeland remove pollution from storm runoff from beautiful Lake Hollingsworth next to the campus. In addition to the environmental benefits of the project, the recreated wetland now has boardwalks and displays on the plants and wildlife there for public education and enjoyment. Biology students continue to monitor the success of the project in their Biological Survey Methods course.

Academics

Providing students with meaningful service learning experiences is central to the College's mission to prepare students to make positive and consequential contributions to society. The faculty has collectively designed an innovative, cross-curricular program that promotes a culture of service learning called "SAGA," or Student Awareness Generates Action.

Service-Learning can be integrated in any course. Some courses that have a required service-learning component are:

Athletic Training
Biology
Information Technology Management
International Business
Computer Science/Mathematics
Educational Studies
Elementary Education
English
Horticultural Science
Landscape Horticulture Design or Production
Recreational Turf Grass Management
Music Education
Nursing
Physical Education
Psychology
Religion
Sport Management

"We are proud of our rich tradition of service learning that inspires leadership and changes lives," says FSC president Dr. Anne Kerr.

"Our students are truly passionate about what they do and are having a profound impact on our community."

Check out all majors at: www.flsouthern.edu/academics

Awards and Recognition
Academics
• Top 5 Best Baccalaureate Colleges in the South—*U.S.News & World Report*
• #4 Best Value—*U.S.News & World Report*
• One of the "Best 366 Colleges"—*The Princeton Review*
• A Best Value College—*The Princeton Review*
• A Best Buy in College Education—*Barron's*
Service-Learning
• President's Higher Education Community Service Honor Roll with Distinction
• FSC has a vibrant service-learning culture that integrates academic learning with community service. Sixty percent of undergraduates volunteer in the community, logging 10,000 hours of service annually through the Center for Service Learning and Center for Community Service.

College Fast Facts
Four Year, Private, Suburban, Founded: 1883

Web site: www.flsouthern.edu

Affiliation: Methodist

Student Profile: 1,710 undergraduate students (40% male, 60% female); 42 states and 2 territories; 31 countries; 14% minority, 4% international.

Faculty Profile: 106 full-time faculty. 88% hold a terminal degree in their field. 13:1 student/faculty ratio.

Athletics: NCAA Division II, Sunshine State Conference. 18 varsity sports. FSC's athletic program boasts 26 NCAA II National Championships: men's and women's golf, baseball, softball, and basketball.

Costs and Aid: 2007–2008: $27,380 comprehensive ($20,690 tuition). 96% of students receive some financial aid.

Admissions
Florida Southern College
111 Lake Hollingsworth Drive
Lakeland, FL 33801
Phone: 1 (800) 274-4131

Service-Learning
Marcia Miller Posey, Ed.D., MSN, APRN
Chair of the FSC Council on Diversity, Civic Engagement and Social Awareness
Phone: (863) 680-4315
Email: mposey@flsouthern.edu

Rollins College

Rollins College educates students for global citizenship and responsible leadership, empowering graduates to pursue meaningful lives and productive careers.

Flagship Programs

SPARC (Service, Philanthropy, Activism, Rollins College)

SPARC, the service-learning component of the Rollins Explorations Program, engages new students in igniting a life of service. SPARC pairs first-year seminar courses with over 26 agencies across Central Florida. Faculty and students co-engage in projects that bring course curriculum to life by connecting academic passion with community.

Youth Mentoring and Engagement

Rollins students engage with economically underserved populations across Central Florida through a number of service-learning courses from Biology and Chemistry to Psychology and Sociology in partnership with the West Winter Park Community Center, Fern Creek Elementary School, Boys and Girls Club, CEP-Community Educational Partnership, and internationally in Costa Rica, Dominican Republic, and Ecuador.

Life-Legacy Project

At Rollins, service-learning courses in history, communication, philosophy, anthropology, and career and life-planning engage students in intergenerational dialogue with senior citizens. Students and seniors together discuss everything from the "meaning of life" to careers and loneliness through oral histories, cultural events, and one-to-one dialogue.

Course Snapshot

SPN 302: Spanish for Advanced Communication

In Professor Gabriel Barreneche's SPN 302: Spanish for Advanced Communication course, students put their language skills into practice by partnering with Junior Achievement (JA) to teach the JA curriculum at local elementary schools in Spanish. Service-learning students must translate all of their materials and lesson plans into Spanish, teach in Spanish, and write their service-learning reflections in the target language.

Academics

Service-learning brings curriculum to life at Rollins by empowering students to become actively engaged in issues and challenges that face the global community.

"Service-learning at Rollins transforms our students' lives by allowing them to dig deeper…creating a sense of ownership and passion for a life of engagement."

- *Micki P. Meyer, Director of Community*

Programs of Study include:

Anthropology
Art and Art History
Art Studio
Biochemistry/Molecular Biology
Biology
Chemistry
Classical Studies
Computer Science
Critical Media and Cultural Studies
Economics
Education
English
Environmental Studies
Film
German
History

Honors Degree Program
International Business
International Relations
Latin American and Caribbean Studies
Marine Biology
Mathematics
Music
Philosophy and Religion
Physics
Political Science
Psychology
Sociology
Spanish
Theatre

Check out all majors at:

www.rollins.edu/admission/academic_programs/futurestudents/majors.html

Awards and Recognition

Service-Learning

• 2007 President's Higher Education Community Service Honor Roll with Distinction

• 2007 Engaged Campus Award for Independent Schools and Overall State Award Top Recipient, Florida Campus Compact

• Colleges with a Conscience, Campus Compact and *Princeton Review*.

Academics

• From 2006-2008, Rollins College ranked #1 among 120 Southern master's-level universities in the annual rankings of "America's Best Colleges," released by *U.S. News & World Report*.

• The Princeton Review lists Rollins among the nation's top schools in The *2007 Best 366 Colleges Guide*.

• Rollins was recognized as "The Best Education Under the Sun" by the Colleges of Distinction.

College Fast Facts

Four-Year, Private, Suburban: Founded 1855
Web site: www.rollins.edu

Student Profile: 1,778 undergraduate students (42% male, 58% female); 42 states, 32 countries; 22% minority, 4% international.

Faculty Profile: 168 full-time faculty; 93% hold a terminal degree in their field;10:1 student/faculty ratio; Average class size is 17.

Athletics: NCAA Division II, Sunshine State Conference; 23 varsity sports.

Costs and Aid: 2007–2008: $42,840 comprehensive ($32,640 tuition); 75% of students receive some financial aid.

Admissions

Rollins College
Office of Admission
1000 Holt Ave. Box 2720
Winter Park, FL 32789
Phone: (407) 646-2161
Fax: (407) 646-1502
Email: admission@rollins.edu

Service-Learning

Rollins College
Office of Community Engagement
Micki P. Meyer, Director
1000 Holt Ave. Box 2789
Winter Park, FL 32789
Phone: (407) 691-1250
Email: mmeyer@rollins.edu
www.rollins.edu/communityengagement

Mercer University

With 11 schools and colleges, Mercer University is recognized as one of the South's top private universities for both outstanding quality and value.

Flagship Programs

Mercer on Mission

Mercer On Mission is a unique blend of study abroad and service-learning that provides life-transforming experiences for students through academic instruction, cultural immersion, meaningful service, and spiritual reflection. Students and faculty work together on various service and assistance projects in foreign countries.

Women's and Gender Studies Program

Students are involved in bettering the lives of women by partnering with diverse community and international organizations. Among their many activities, they work and collect supplies for local shelters, raise relief funds for the women of Darfur, and sponsor productions to raise awareness of violence against women.

Joshua House

Joshua House is the after-school program of Out & Up, a faith-based organization that works within low-income neighborhoods in the Macon area. Along with Mercer, a number of partners help Joshua House to perform its mission of providing after-school tutoring and a summer enrichment camp for elementary-aged students.

Course Snapshot

Program in Leadership and Community Service (PLS)

The goals of this major:

• To deepen the students' understanding of and commitment to personal, cultural and ultimate values,

• To help students develop the skills and values necessary for effective servant leadership roles,

• To promote the common good both here and abroad,

• To help meet unmet human needs in diverse communities,

• To bridge the gap between traditional academic disciplines, the liberal arts, and public and community service.

Academics

No matter what major or career interest a Mercer student is pursuing, there is a service-learning class that can make the learning more relevant and the results more valuable.

College of Liberal Arts
Stetson School of Business and Economics
School of Engineering
Tift College of Education
Townsend School of Music
First Year Seminar Experiential (FYS/X)
Program in Leadership and Community Service
Mercer Service Scholars

Service Learning Courses include:
Environmental Injustice (EES)
Intro to Political Science Research (POL)
Advanced Reporting (JRN)
Editing and Design (JRN)
Spanish Composition & Conversation (SPN)
Honors Colloquim (HON)
Fighting Violence Against Women (WGS)

"Through service-learning in WGS, we work to heal the wounds of oppression, and in effect, we heal ourselves."

~ Jacqueline Johnson '09

Check out all majors at:
Mercer.edu/admissions

Awards and Recognition
Service-Learning

• Jimmy and Rosalynn Carter Campus-Community Award.

• Community Outreach Partnership Center, U.S. Department of Housing and Urban Development.

• National Award of Merit, Boys & Girls Clubs of America.

• "Exemplary Campus-Community Partnerships." Campus Compact.

• *Colleges with a Conscience, Princeton Review.*

• Charter Award, Congress for the New Urbanism.

• Top 25 Good Neighbor Universities, New England Board of Higher Education.

• President's Higher Education Community Service Honor Roll

Academics

• "A Best 366 College" *The Princeton Review.*

• Academic excellence continues to place Mercer University among America's best institutions of higher education in the latest *U.S.News & World Report* college guide.

College Fast Facts

Four Year, Private, Urban, Founded: 1833

Web site: www.mercer.edu

Student Profile: 2268 undergraduate students (47% male, 53% female); 50 states and territories; 27% minority, 2% international.

Faculty Profile: 352 full-time faculty. 88% hold a terminal degree in their field. 13:1 student/faculty ratio. Average class size is 21.

Athletics: NCAA Division 1, Atlantic Sun Conference. 15 varsity sports.

Costs and Aid: 2007-2008: $34,775 comprehensive ($26,760 tuition). 97% of students receives some financial aid.

Admissions

Mercer University
Office of Undergraduate Admissions
1400 Coleman Ave. Macon, GA 31207
Phone: (800) 840-8577; (478) 301-2650
Email: admissions@mercer.edu

Service-Learning

Mary Alice Morgan
Chair, Women and Gender Studies
Phone: (478) 301-2571
Email: morgan_ma@mercer.edu

Chaminade University of Honolulu

Chaminade University offers its students an education in a collaborative learning environment, preparing them for life, work and service.

Flagship Programs

The Palolo Pipeline

Students from all majors serve in this collection of creative tutoring projects in our neighborhood. Our higher education partnerships create a "pipeline" of educational support that shepherds children from low-income and immigrant families through school transitions, inspiring college goals.

VITA and FAFSA: Financial Assistance Enabling Success

Accounting students do budget-planning & help homeless and "working-poor" families obtain federal and state income tax credits. To prepare for this, students in Accounting, Business, and Marketing students work to obtain financial assistance, creating new college-bound students at partner schools.

SHINE Tutorial Program: Support for Citizenship Across Generations and Cultures

Through almost any major, students can learn to help older immigrants with English and citizenship. This community-/ student-led program strives to empower all stakeholders, building civic engagement, cross-cultural/intergenerational skills, & understanding of diversity. Opportunities for leadership and continued involvement abound.

Course Snapshot

Peggy Friedman's Marketing Strategy, and Richard Kido's Intermediate Accounting

"As we learned course material each day, our FAFSA Project brought it to life," said one marketing student. "We were responsible to our partner Accounting class, and to the community. We also leave a legacy for the next class to learn and build upon." Marketing students provide community outreach, bringing the Accounting Class' FAFSA assistance to low-income and immigrant communities. Each class is a consultant for the other. Accounting students mentor families and complete financial paperwork, honing their professional skills.

Academics

Service-learning brings students the skills and knowledge for defining their roles in bringing about positive change in the world.

Accounting
Anthropology
Biology
Business
Communications
Computer Science
Criminal Justice
Economics
Education

English
Environmental Studies
Interior Design
Marketing
Math
Philosophy
Psychology
Religion
Sociology

Check out all majors at: http://chaminade.edu/admissions

"My personal and professional skills have really developed through these pathways of service-learning courses."

Awards and Recognition
Service-Learning
• One of six institutions nationwide chosen for the "Presidential Award," of the President's Higher Education Community Service Honor Roll – February 2008
• Honoree for partnerships with area schools, Hawaii State Board of Education and Department of Education 2007
• Everyday Environmental Hero Award, City and County of Honolulu, 2007
• Community Impact Student Awards - Campus Compact: Chelcy Reyes, Crystal Weseman, 2007
• Faculty Teaching Excellence Award, International Society of Business Disciplines, Wayne Tanna, for service-learning and community engaged scholarship, 2007
• Network of Volunteer Leaders Award, Candice Sakuda, 2005

Academics
• Communication students Rand Wilson and Krista Catian were named to the American Advertising Federation's list of Most Promising Minority Students, 2008
• Biology student Charissa Kahue was invited to present by the Council for Undergraduate Research, Posters on the Hill competition, 2007

College Fast Facts
Affiliation: Catholic Marianist
Web site: www.chaminade.edu
Student Profile: 1,112 undergraduate students. (31% male, 69% female); 51% come from outside of Hawaii.
Faculty Profile: 16:1 student/faculty ratio. Average class size is 20.
Costs and Aid: 2007-2008: 74% of undergraduates receive financial aid. Average freshman need based gift is $8,258.

Admissions
Phone: (808) 735-4735
Toll Free: 1 (800) 735-3733
Fax: 808-739-4647
Email: admissions@chaminade.edu
http://chaminade.edu/admissions

Service-Learning
Candice Sakuda
Director of Service-Learning
Phone: (808) 735-4895
Email: csakuda@chaminade.edu

Kapi'olani Community College

Perpetuating Queen Kapi'olani's legacy, "Kūlia i ka Nu'u," to strive for the highest.

Flagship Programs

Adopt an Ahupua'a: Environmental Sustainability Pathway

Students in Botany or Anthropology can learn about environmental sustainability, traditional land use, and Native Hawaiian cultural stewardship by actively participating in weekend activities in an ahupua'a (traditional land division from mountain to the sea).

Palolo Pipeline Program: Education Pathway

Students entering a Family Resources course, especially those planning to major in Education, can gain hands-on experience tutoring, mentoring, and teaching younger children from grades K-12 in the neighboring

low-income housing in the communities of Palolo Valley and Kaimuki. The program aims to address literacy issues while bridging a "pipeline" of education from Headstart to higher education.

Course Snapshot

SOC 257: Sociology of Aging
This course provides an overview of the significant sociological perspectives, social issues and empirical social science research pertaining to the phenomenon of aging in society. Students in SOC 257 participate in community-based service-learning projects within the Bridging Generations Service-Learning Pathway, where they are able to interact with seniors one-on-one through conducting oral histories, facilitating art projects, providing companionship and light household chores and errands, and assisting elders in fitness classes and training centers in the community. Through their participation in these projects, students gain an appreciation and understanding of elders and aging issues, they see elders in the respected Hawaiian sense as kūpuna – contributing, valuable members of the community, while learning from elders and experiencing significant personal and intellectual transformation.

Academics

Service-learning has played a critical role in helping the College redefine and articulate its larger public and civic purposes. By intentionally building the social and intellectual capital of the faculty, we have created a "multiplier effect" whereby thousands of students better understand community issues and work for the social, economic, and environmental betterment of the communities we serve.

Kapi'olani Community College is recognized as a national leader in service-learning and community engagement. Our Service-Learning "pathway" model creates a bridge from the classroom to the community, and provides students a real world experience where they can become civically engaged while reducing the severity of social issues.

Check out **Kapi'olani Community College's programs of study** at: www.kcc.hawaii.edu/page/programs

Awards and Recognition
• 2007 President's Higher Education Community Service Honor Roll

• Carnegie Foundation for the Advancement of Teaching for Promoting Civic and Moral Responsibility in Higher Education, 2000 and 2006.

• American Council of Education for Promising Practices in Intercultural and International Education, 2001 and 2004.

• Association of American Colleges and Universities Greater Expectations Initiative, 2004.

• National Association of Foreign Student Advisors for Engaging Diverse Communities, 2003.

• Campus Compact for Service-Learning and Civic Engagement, 2004.

• Blood Bank of Hawaii, 2007.

College Fast Facts

Two Year, Public, Urban, Founded: 1964

Web site: www.kapiolani.hawaii.edu

Student Profile: 7,272 undergraduate students (47% male, 53% female).

Faculty Profile: 225 full-time faculty. 15:1 student/faculty ratio.

Costs and Aid: 2007-2008: $63 per credit hour in-state, $320 per credit hour out-of-state.

Admissions
Kekaulike Information & Service Center
4303 Diamond Head Road Ilima 102
Honolulu, HI 96816
Phone: (808) 734-9555
Fax: (808) 734-9896
Email: kapinfo@hawaii.edu

Service-Learning
4303 Diamond Head Rd Naio 214
Honolulu, HI 96816
Contact: S-L Coordinator
Phone: (808) 734-9353 Fax: (808) 734-9287
Email: kccserve@hawaii.edu
www.kcc.hawaii.edu/object/servicelearning.html

College of DuPage

Though it is the fourth-largest community college in the nation, College of DuPage remains a close-knit academic community where students benefit and thrive.

Flagship Programs

Reap What You Sow

A multiple-disciplined service learning project, students work in the C.O.D. Community Garden where they obtain hands-on experience and learn socio-economical, anthropological and biological concepts. Students sow, tend, and harvest the vegetables which are donated to a local food pantry.

Decision 2006: Rhetoric and Reason

This course was a team-taught course involving Political Science, English and Speech. Students participated in the excitement and drama of the election process and studied the role of rhetoric through involvement with the 2006 election campaigns.

It's What's Inside that Counts

In the Fundamentals of Medical Imaging course, faculty stress to students that medical imaging involves people as well as technology. Students

develop skills and apply course content by volunteering at local organizations where they can experience care-giving to different populations.

Course Snapshot

Biology 1110: Environmental Biology

A course in environmental science should go beyond the classroom to take advantage of the learning only nature can provide. Students in this course gain a clear understanding of how environmental issues intertwine with the fabric of people's lives. Seeing the effects of human exploitation and carelessness on the environment, as well as helping to reverse this complicated problem one step at a time, transforms a student's perception on whether he or she can make a difference. Such experiences help to engender critical and reflective thinking as well as promote civic responsibility.

Academics

Through service-learning, students master course content and develop marketable skills, while making a real difference in their community.

Accounting
Anthropology
Biology
Business
Criminal Justice
Diagnostic Medical Imaging
Radiography
Early Childhood Education
Education
English
Fashion Merchandising and Design
Geography
Health Sciences
Human Services
Humanities
Philosophy
Political Science
Psychology
Sociology
Spanish
Speech Communication
College of Nursing
College of Osteopathic Medicine
College of Social Science
College of Veterinary Medicine
Honors College
Residential College in the Arts and Humanities

"By working with real clients on real projects, students can apply the knowledge and skills that are critical to their use of basic technical writing concepts."

-- Linda Elaine, English Faculty

College of DuPage offers 46 pre-baccalaureate areas of study and more than 90 certificates and degrees for occupational and technical careers.

View all academic majors at:
www.cod.edu/academic

Awards and Recognition

Service-Learning

• Howard R. Swearer Student Humanitarian Award Winner, Richard Rodriguez 2003.

• Nominated for a Jimmy and Rosalyn Carter Partnership award in 2006 Grantee American Association of Community College Bridges to Healthy Communities.

Academic

• Established the Multicultural Student Center which targets at-risk, underrepresented students – 2004.

• Secured funding for Planting the Seeds of Success project to promote hi-tech majors and careers to underserved and underrepresented youth -- 2006.

College Fast Facts

Community College, Public, Suburban: Founded 1967

Web site: www.cod.edu

Student Profile: 28,767 undergraduate students (44% male, 56% female); 32% minority; from 44 communities within District 502; 91% in-district; 8% are out-of-district; 1% international.

Faculty Profile: 305 full-time faculty and 922 part-time faculty. Ninety-seven percent of faculty hold doctorate or master's degrees. 19 to 1 student/full-time faculty ratio.

Athletics: NCAA Division III, National Junior College Athletic Association (NJCAA) Conference.

Costs and Aid: 2006-2007: $96 per semester credit hour for in-district tuition. Total tuition for full-time student in-district (32 semester hours): $3,072; out-of-district tuition per year: $8,000; out-of-state tuition per year: $9,824. Total expenses for full-time dependent student (residing with parents): $9,697; independent student (living away from home): $14,698. 45% of students receive some financial aid. Average award: $1,310.

Admissions

College of DuPage
Office of Admissions
425 Fawell Blvd
Glen Ellyn, IL 60137
Phone: (630) 942-2482
Email: protis@cod.edu

Service-Learning

Steven Gustis
Coordinator, Service Learning Program
Phone: (630) 942-2655
Email: gustis@cod.edu
www.cod.edu/servicelearning

Columbia College Chicago

Columbia College is known for its extensive diversity and experiential approach to arts and media education with a progressive social agenda.

Flagship Programs

Theater Dept. Teaching Practicum

This course combines the expertise of faculty from Association House and the Theater Department and places college students' learning in a vital community-based organization. Columbia College students receive valuable experience in teaching youth under the direct supervision of teaching and theatrical professionals.

Television Dept. Production, Directing the Special Project

CCC students venture out of the classroom and into the community to fulfill their course requirements and to receive real world experience with a community based arts organization. Two faculty members and one community-teaching artist lead the course to ensure the reciprocity.

Teaching Practicum

The Teaching Practicum, run by the Theater Department, students work in teaching teams, exploring how to plan lessons and deliver content within an actual classroom setting. The Teaching Practicum course is held jointly at Columbia College and a Community Based Organization, with meetings at Columbia designed to prepare students for their teaching practice sessions, and to examine teaching theater as it relates to artistic discipline. This course is designed to provide Theater students with a practical outlet to develop their teaching skills.

Course Snapshot

Teaching Praticum, Theater Department
Student Reflection:
I am enjoying my time at Free Street very much. The style of teaching is a bit similar to Columbia and the people there are very warm, energetic and love what they do.

I am learning so much about live street performance and teaching. I am having a lot of fun.

Academics

Columbia College Chicago (CCC) is one of the largest arts and media colleges in the country. We have applied a "service-learning in the arts" approach throughout the college. CCC applies classroom theory with community arts and arts in public schools for the purposes of mutual learning, transformation, and reflection.

Art & Design
Arts, Entertainment & Media Management
Audio Arts & Acoustics
Cultural Studies
Dance
Early Childhood Education
Educational Studies
Fiction Writing
Film & Video
Interactive Arts & Media

Interdisciplinary Arts
Journalism
Liberal Education
Marketing Communication Department
Music Department
Photography Department
Radio
Television
Theater Department

Check out all majors at: www.colum.edu/Academics/

"Our partnership with Columbia provides us with a powerful sounding board for exchanging new ideas about community-based work, inspiring emerging artists about this field, and integrating best practices that endure."

Awards and Recognition
Service-Learning
• 2007 President's Higher Education Community Service Honor Roll with Distinction.
• 2006 Coming Up Taller: Certificate of Excellence.

College Fast Facts

Four Year, Private, Urban

Affiliation: Nondenominational

Web site: www.colum.edu

Student Profile: Undergraduate students (49% male, 51% female); 50 states and territories, 46 countries.

Faculty Profile: 1,497 full-time faculty. Average class size is under 20 students.

Costs and Aid: 2007: 17,588.00 tuition.

Admissions

Columbia College Chicago
Office of Undergraduate Admissions
Phone: 312-344-7130
Fax: 312-344-8024
Email: admissions@colum.edu

Service-Learning

Center for Community Arts Partnerships
Paul Teruel
Director of Community Partnerships
Columbia College Chicago
600 S Michigan Ave.
Chicago IL 60605
Phone: (312) 344-8871
Fax: (312) 344-8015
Email: pteruel@colum.edu
www.colum.edu/ccap

Concordia University Chicago

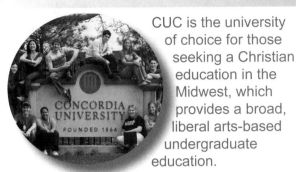

CUC is the university of choice for those seeking a Christian education in the Midwest, which provides a broad, liberal arts-based undergraduate education.

Flagship Programs

CUC students serve at Vital Bridges helping individuals in the Chicago area impacted by HIV/AIDS by providing food, nutrition and case management, housing assistance and other social services. Students also provide administrative assistance, multi-task in food pantries and serve as literacy volunteers.

CUC students serve Melrose Park Elementary School children through "For the Love of Reading." Most of the children are Hispanic/Latino, whose parents are Spanish-speaking immigrants. Currently, this Academic Service Learning option can be added to 22 courses offered at Concordia University Chicago.

Serving With Habitat for Humanity® in Hungary

CUC students served with faculty and staff on two trips to Szarvas, Hungary. Teams completed construction on new homes–complete with indoor plumbing–a feature the new homeowners previously did not have.

Course Snapshot

IDS-1970 Freedom and Responsibility: First Year Experience

There are 11 sections of Freedom and Responsibility, the First Year Experience course for all incoming freshmen. Each section is connected with a different partnership in the community. Concordia students can work with children and teenagers in literacy, mentoring, tutoring, enrichment services, and at the juvenile detention center; they also provide diverse services to senior citizens, the disabled, other ethnic groups, people suffering with HIV/AIDS, hunger relief, homelessness issues, non-profit organizations, elementary schools, health services clinics and the forest preserve.

Academics

CUC students engaging in Service Learning serve diverse populations, acquiring valuable life and job skills transferable to their future careers. Concordia University Chicago offers Service Learning components in three forms:

A. **Curricular:** as an integral part of a specific course required of all the students in that class.
B. **Co-curricular:** as a component that the student can add to any of the classes in his/her major.
C. **Independent:** where students can add any type of Service project to any class, with the help of the Service Learning Director and their professor.

Independent Service Learning allows students to explore those areas of Service where their hearts lie, as well as allowing them to explore areas outside their majors, as a way of exploring career choices.

Students can choose their location of Service when they do co-curricular and independent Service Learning, if they desire. Curricular Service locations are determined by the professor in relation to the course content.

"Vital Bridges opened my eyes to the hardships other people face. I'm happy I had the chance to help!"

~ *Colleen Weems, CUC Class of 2011*

Check out all CUC majors at: www.cuchicago.edu/academics/

Awards and Recognition

Service-Learning
• 2008 - President's Higher Education Community Service Honor Roll for second consecutive year.
• Recipient of 2008-2009 State Farm Faculty Fellows Award & Grant.

Academics
• Concordia University Chicago offers more than 60 majors through its College of Arts and Sciences, College of Business, College of Education and College of Graduate and Innovative Programs.
• To date, 12 Concordia alumni have been honored by the Golden Apple Foundation. The Golden Apple award is presented annually to "recognize outstanding teaching and to promote teacher recruitment."
• Among private colleges in Illinois, Concordia University Chicago educates more public school teachers than any other private college.

College Fast Facts

Four Year, Private, Suburban, Founded: 1864

Affiliation: The Lutheran Church–Missouri Synod (LCMS)

Web site: www.CUChicago.edu

Student Profile: Enrollment (Fall Term 2007) Undergraduate: 1,121. Female: 62%, Male: 38%. 40 states and a dozen countries represented, 30% of students are from states other than Illinois.

Faculty Profile: Student-to-Faculty Ratio: 17:1. Average Class Size: 20.

Athletics: NCAA Division III. Concordia University Chicago is a charter member of the Northern Athletics Conference (NAC). The NAC is made up of 12 private institutions from Illinois and Wisconsin.

Costs and Aid: 2008–2009: Tuition: $21,950, Room and Board: $7,350, Technology Fee: $200, Student Activity Fee: $240.

Admissions

Concordia University Chicago
Undergraduate Admission
7400 Augusta Street
River Forest, Illinois 60305-1499
Phone: 1 (877) CUChicago
(1-877-262-4422)
Email: admission@cuchicago.edu
www.CUChicago.edu

Service-Learning

Academic Service Learning
Alannah Ari Hernandez
Director of Academic
Service-Learning
Phone: 708-209-3633
Alannah.Hernandez@CUChicago.edu

DePaul University

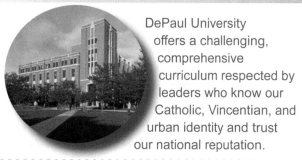

DePaul University offers a challenging, comprehensive curriculum respected by leaders who know our Catholic, Vincentian, and urban identity and trust our national reputation.

Flagship Programs

The Steans Center for Community-based Service Learning develops mutually beneficial, reciprocal relationships with community organizations in order to develop a sense of social agency in students through enrollment in CbSL courses, community internships and placements, and community-based student employment.

Community Service Studies

Community Service Studies is an interdisciplinary academic minor that offers students a context for critically reflecting upon and engaging in service and volunteerism. It is part of a university-wide effort to extend opportunities for learning through practice into multiple curricula at DePaul.

McCormick Tribune Community Internships

Through the support of the McCormick Tribune Foundation, DePaul undergraduates from all disciplines participate in paid, advanced internships that apply their knowledge and skills to benefit an organization while simultaneously gaining valuable work experience.

Community Service Scholarships

This program seeks incoming freshman who have demonstrated an exceptional record of community service. The Steans Center provides mentoring throughout their college career and connects them to community service and academic programs through the minor in Community Service Studies. Scholars receive an annual scholarship of $8,500.

Course Snapshot

SPN 125: Intermediate Spanish - Intercambio

Students exchange English and Spanish conversation with ESL students and community organizations. "The program encourages students to go way beyond a book in their learning," said Dr. Susana Martinez, who teaches the course. "It's about using language in an important context. The program creates a peer environment at the sites where the experience helps them build on the basics for class, like vocabulary and verb tense."

Academics

Our highly ranked service-learning program integrates the service concept into our curriculum and inspires students to make a lifelong commitment to service and social justice. Courses include:

Anthropology
Art and Art History
Computer Science
Finance
Geography
International Studies
Journalism
Latin American and Latino Studies
Spanish
Marketing
Management
Nursing
Political Science
Psychology
Public Policy Studies
Religious Studies
Sociology
Women's and Gender Studies
Writing, Rhetoric and Discourse

"This kind of class really challenges you to go beyond a typical college class. It's not just about working in a community—it's about understanding it."

~ Lauren Vinopal, DePaul Undergraduate

Check out all majors at:
www.depaul.edu/academics/index.asp

Awards and Recognition
Service-Learning

• One of only 62 schools in the nation – only one in Illinois – recognized in the highest distinction category of new Carnegie Foundation for the Advancement of Teaching classification in community engagement.

• Named one of the nation's top service learning programs by *U.S.News & World Report* every year since 2004.

• Recognized as one of the country's best for social responsibility and public service in 2005 guidebook "Colleges with a Conscience: 81 Great Schools with Outstanding Community Involvement."

• President's Higher Education Community Service Honor Roll with Distinction 2006-2007.

Academics

• Doctoral program faculty recognized as most productive in the country among universities with fewer than 15 doctoral programs by national Faculty Scholarly Productivity Index 2007.

• Evening MBA program ranked 6th in the nation by *U.S.News & World Report*.

• Graduate entrepreneur program ranked 2nd and undergraduate program 3rd in 2006 Entrepreneur magazine/Princeton Review rankings.

• College of Law ranked among the 100 best law schools in the nation by *U.S.News & World Report*. The college's intellectual property program ranked 11th; health law program ranked 14th.

College Fast Facts
Web site: www.depaul.edu

Student Profile: 15,024 undergraduate students (44% male,56% female);
Faculty Profile: 850 full-time faculty (plus 1,500 part-time and adjunct professionals who bring real-world experience into the classroom); 85 % hold terminal degrees; 16:1 student/faculty ratio; 68% of all classes have fewer than 30 students

Athletics: NCAA Division 1; BIG EAST Conference, 15 sports. Over the past six years, more than half of DePaul's athletic teams have represented the Blue Demons in NCAA postseason tournament play.

Costs and Aid: 2008-2009 tuition is $25,490 for most programs. About 68% of undergraduate students received some type of financial aid.

Admission
DePaul University
Office of Admission
1 E. Jackson Blvd.
Chicago, IL 60604
Phone: (312) 362-8300 (in Illinois);
1-800-4-DEPAUL (outside Illinois)

Service-Learning
Howard Rosing, Ph.D.
Executive Director
Steans Center for Community-Based Service Learning
Phone: (773) 325-7463
Email: hrosing@depaul.edu

Loyola University Chicago

As the nation's largest Jesuit, Catholic University, we are a diverse community seeking God in all things and working to expand knowledge in the service of humanity through learning, justice and faith.

Flagship Programs

Service-Learning National and Global Immersions

In collaboration with University Ministry, nearly 20 local, national and international trips are organized annually through alternative break immersion trips. Each immersion includes about 10 student participants with faculty/staff advisors and service connected to course content. Immersions vary to the Appalachian region, Washington D.C., New Orleans, and Latin America.

Loyola Community Literacy Center

The Literacy Center serves disadvantaged populations, such as the refugee population, to support basic literacy skills from all language groups. Students enrolled in a number of English courses serve as supervised tutors working with individuals. The Loyola Community Literacy Center is supported by the College of Arts and Sciences of Loyola University Chicago.

Community Health Outreach in Nursing

In the School of Nursing, students under the supervision of faculty provide over 1,000 home visits each year to chronically ill adults. Students also provide health education to community groups including classrooms of children enrolled in Chicago's public and private schools, residents of local shelters, and program participants at social service agencies.

Course Snapshot

UNIV 290: Seminar in Community-based Service and Leadership A student reflected: "The difference at [my service-learning site] is that they actually need people to do these tasks. My time volunteering is simple: an engaged citizen can make a difference." Another student reflected on an immersion experience in Alabama: "I am having an incredible experience! We really are building a home, not just a house, and the students have been so inspiring and wonderful. The homeowners are building alongside us, so we have gotten to know them and how incredibly deserving they are of this opportunity." It is through service-learning experiences like this that students at Loyola University Chicago recognize the opportunity they have to meaningfully contribute to their communities and the world in which they live.

Academics

Service-learning provides Loyola University Chicago students the opportunity to increase awareness of community issues, engage in social justice issues, enhance civic engagement, and foster career development.

Biology
Business
Chemistry
Communication
Education
English
Health Systems Management
History
International Studies
Journalism
Mathematics
Nursing
Philosophy
Psychology
Sociology
Social Work
Spanish
Theology

"Faith, knowledge and service are not three separate and independent aspects of education, but rather dynamically related, and any one term is incomplete without the other two. This integral philosophy of education is what makes Loyola truly distinctive."

–Dan Hartnett, S.J., Ph.D., Professor of Philosophy

Check out all majors at www.luc.edu

Awards and Recognition

• Offer more than 25 service-learning courses each semester, in addition to multiple academic internship courses, field work courses in the community, co-curricular service opportunities, and alternative break immersions.

• Recipient of several Illinois Campus Compact awards for civic engagement, including Raise Your Voice Fellowships for Loyola students and the Presidential Civic Engagement Fellowship for Rev. Michael J. Garanzini, S.J., President of Loyola University Chicago.

• Loyola University Chicago is the largest Catholic Research (high) institution in the nation.

• Recognizing Loyola's excellence in education, *U.S.News & World Report* has ranked Loyola consistently among the "top national universities," and named the University a "best value" in its 2008 rankings.

• One of only 8 percent of all American colleges and universities to have a Phi Beta Kappa honor society chapter.

• The University has four campuses: three in the greater Chicago area and one in Rome, Italy. Loyola also serves as the U.S. host university to The Beijing Center for Chinese Studies in Beijing, China.

• Loyola's ten schools and colleges include arts and sciences, business administration, communication, education, graduate studies, law, medicine, nursing, continuing and professional studies, and social work.

• Loyola offers 71 undergraduate majors, 85 master's degrees, and 31 doctoral degrees.

College Fast Facts

Four Year, Private, Urban, Founded: 1870

Web site: www.luc.edu

Student Profile: 9,729 undergraduate students; 33% minority, 15,545 total enrollment from 50 states and territories and 82 countries

Faculty Profile: 1,100 full-time faculty; 96% hold a terminal degree in their field. 13:1 student/faculty ratio.

Athletics: NCAA Division I Basketball, Loyola University Chicago Ramblers

Costs and Aid: 2008-2009: $42,846.00 comprehensive ($28,700.00 tuition). 91% of students receive some form of financial aid.

Admissions

Loyola University Chicago
Undergraduate Admission Office
820 N. Michigan Avenue
Chicago, Illinois 60611
Phone: (800) 262-2373
Email: admission@luc.edu
www.LUC.edu/undergrad

Service-Learning

Center for Experiential Learning
Patrick M. Green, Ed.D., Director
Sullivan Center
6525 N. Sheridan Rd.
Chicago, IL 60626
Phone: (773) 508-3366
E-mail: experiential@luc.edu
www.LUC.edu/experiential

Roosevelt University

Roosevelt University, a national leader in educating socially conscious citizens, is a private university founded on the principles of inclusion and social justice.

Service learning is a critical component of Roosevelt University's social justice mission. At Roosevelt, service learning is defined as an educational philosophy and pedagogical method of experiential learning that embraces ethical and socially responsible participation in structured learning activities. Service learning experiences enhance Roosevelt's connection to the communities it serves.

Flagship Programs

New Deal Service Day

Roosevelt University students, faculty, and staff gather annually two days in April to give back to communities where they live and work. This year's event had 315 participants, who lent talents to seven sites in Chicago and five locations in the northwest suburbs.

Service Learning Through Science

The faculty in the department of Biological, Chemical and Physical Sciences include themes of social awareness and community engagement in the curriculum. The efforts are coordinated through participation in the national initiative, Science Education for New Civic Engagements and Responsibilities (SENCER).

Social Justice High School

In 2006, RU offered Social Justice High School (located in Chicago's Little Village neighborhood) a life-changing opportunity for its students. All academically qualified students graduating from SJHS in 2009 and 2010 can attend RU for free for four years.

Course Snapshot

PSYC 383: Seminar: Controversial Issues

Undergraduates participate in community research and action to improve the lives of children who experience risk and adversity in Chicago. Students research specific issues that affect the lives of children who reside in lower socioeconomic neighborhoods. Students will learn how city government and other stake-holders respond to social challenges by attending City Council meetings and speaking with representatives from the Chicago Public Schools and the Chicago Housing Authority, as well as city and state legislators, to develop and promote a child advocacy agenda.

Academics

At Roosevelt University, balance is given to both "service" and "learning" that embraces ethical and social responsibility in structured activities. Some programs that incorporate service learning are:

African and Afro American Studies
Art
Biology
Chemistry
Counseling and Human Services
Early Childhood Education
Economics
Elementary Education
English Language Program
English
Environmental Science
First Year Seminar
Honors Program
Journalism
Mathematics
Public Administration
Philosophy
Political Science
Psychology
Language and Literacy
Sociology
Social Justice
Special Education

"The service learning piece is the most powerful aspect of the courses I teach, because the experience allows students to see social inequities so they can become catalysts for change."

--Steven Meyer
professor of psychology and 2007 Illinois Professor of the Year

Check out all majors at:
www.roosevelt.edu/academics/default.htm

Awards and Recognition

Academics

• Roosevelt University offers more than 60 undergraduate majors and pre-professional programs, 40 master's degree programs, and selected doctoral programs at campuses in downtown Chicago and northwest suburban Schaumburg.

• In 2008, Roosevelt University was honored by the American Immigration Law Foundation with its Distinguished Public Service Award, recognizing Roosevelt's strong support of immigrants, including making undocumented students eligible for full-tuition assistance and voicing public support of progressive federal immigration legislation.

• According to a New York Times study on diversity of undergraduate students, Roosevelt University ranks 10th in private institutions nationwide.

Service-Learning

• President's Higher Education Community Service Honor Roll

• Roosevelt's Initiative for Child and Family Studies participates in the President's Volunteer Service Award program as a Certifying Organization.

College Fast Facts

Four Year, Private, Urban/Suburban

Founded: 1945

Web Site: www.roosevelt.edu

Student Profile: 3973 undergraduate students (32% male, 68% female); 3190 graduate/doctoral students, 48 states and territories, 26 countries; 35% minority, 4 % international.

Faculty Profile: 216 full-time faculty. 84% hold a terminal degree in their field. 13:1 student/faculty ratio. Average class size is 19.

Costs and Aid: 2007–2008: ($16,680 tuition). 85% of students receive some financial aid.

Admissions
Office of Undergraduate Admission
430 S. Michigan Avenue
Chicago, IL 60605
Phone: (312) 341-3500
1-877-APPLY-RU
Email: applyRU@roosevelt.edu

Service-Learning
Pamela Robert, PhD
Associate Professor of Sociology
Roosevelt University
430 S. Michigan Avenue
Chicago, IL 60605
Phone: (312) 341-3737
Email: probert@roosevelt.edu

Franklin College

Franklin College is a personal, participatory, values-focused, career-sensitive, liberal arts teaching and learning undergraduate community.

Flagship Programs

FOCUS or Franklin Offering the Community Unselfish Service

During their first day on campus, new students join faculty, staff and student leaders in small groups for a day of service projects conducted throughout the community. This leadership-centered event sets the tone for an education emphasizing civic engagement.

Habitat for Humanity

Franklin College students orchestrated the creation of the county Habitat affiliate, permanently housed on our campus. This partnership provides service-learning, AmeriCorps, internship, volunteer and board of director opportunities for students. Over 15 percent of our students build with Habitat each year.

New Student Leadership Seminar

Every new student learns about the values, mission and culture of their new campus community in order to maximize their potential for participation and contributions. A strong service-learning component allows students to develop collaborative leadership skills.

Course Snapshot

LA 112A – Leadership in Inner-City Missions

Students gain exposure to the subculture of urban homelessness in our society by working and living in Indianapolis homeless shelters and missions. One student noted: "This class was a life-changing experience for me. I am more aware. I am aware of what my life could very easily have been. I am aware of other people's struggles. Most importantly, I am aware of my and society's responsibility to help."

Academics

Service-learning at Franklin College motivates and prepares graduates for productive and satisfying lives of excellence, leadership and service. Through the liberal arts curriculum, every Franklin College student completes two required courses with strong service-learning components. Additionally, the following departments offer service-learning courses:

Economics, Business & Accounting
Fine Arts
Journalism
Leadership
Mathematical & Computing Sciences
Modern Languages
Philosophy & Religion
Psychology
Sociology

"Through hands-on experiences students learn in a matter of minutes what might take several semesters in a classroom setting."

~ Dedaimia Whitney, Professor of English

Check out all of our majors & programs at: www.franklincollege.edu/majorsminors/

Awards and Recognition

Service-Learning
• President's Higher Education Community Service Honor Roll with Distinction

Academics
• Franklin College offers more than 50 areas of undergraduate study.
• Students score in the top 5% annually on the National College Business Exam.
• 100% acceptance rate into grad school for athletic training majors who apply.
• 95% job placement rate for education majors.
• 90% of journalism majors are employed or in graduate school within six months of commencement.
• 83% of chemistry and biology students who apply to medical school are accepted.
• In a survey of all 179 '07 graduates six months post-commencement, 74.9% were already employed full-time and 14% were in graduate school.
• In September 2006, *Golf Digest* named Franklin College among the top 50 schools nationwide that provide "the absolute best education and an opportunity to play competitive golf."

College Fast Facts

Four Year, Private Suburban, Founded: 1834

Web site: www.franklincollege.edu

Student Profile: Undergraduate students (50% male, 50% female); 14 states and territories, 3 countries

Faculty Profile: 65 full-time faculty. 12:1 student/faculty ratio. Average class size is 15.

Athletics: NCAA Division III, HCAC Athletic Conference, 16 varsity sports. Approximately 35% of our students compete in varsity athletics.

Costs and Aid: 2007-2008: $27,540 comprehensive ($21,150 tuition). 97% of students receive some form of financial aid.

Admissions

Franklin College
Office of Admissions
101 Branigin Boulevard
Franklin, IN 46131-2623
Phone: (317) 738-8062; (800) 852-0232
Email: admissions@franklincollege.edu

Service-Learning

Ruth Lilly Leadership Center
Doug Grant
Service Learning Coordinator
Phone: (317) 738-8762
Email: dgrant@franklincollege.edu

Goshen College

A four-year, Christian, liberal arts college established in 1894, Goshen College has an impressive history and offers student access to a unique international education program. Goshen is committed to graduating students prepared to make positive contributions to their communities, their churches, and to the world.

Flagship Program

Study-Service Term

SST allows the opportunity for students to become immersed in a culture significantly different from that of the United States. Goshen College's goals for each student are to develop intercultural openness, communication in a variety of forms, thinking that is active and reflective, and understanding of self and others.

The first six weeks of the term are spent studying the language and culture of the host country. The faculty leader uses local resources to support a largely experience-based learning program: home stays, lectures, discussion, field trips, journal writing, readings, special projects and examinations.

During the last six weeks of the term, students work in a field/service-learning assignment, usually in a rural area. In this second half of SST, students gain profound insights into the host culture—and the different meanings of service. No longer is it simply accomplishing a task, but service can be as simple and profound as listening to the life experiences of others.

"It was on service that a family received me as a complete stranger and, more than anyone I've ever met, taught me the meanings of hospitality, generosity and unselfishness." –Danny King '05, Germany SST

"SST has made me a more independent, socially improved person: both things that I wanted in myself. For my service project I spent time researching the effects of the community development initiatives of Church World Service. Working with CWS and hearing the stories of poverty straight from the poor blew my mind and taught me skills and understandings that I still have trouble articulating, but that I know will help me in future life moments." –Kelli Yoder, '08, Cambodia SST

Academics

As an exceptional Christian liberal arts institution, part of Goshen's mission is to inspire its students to be passionate learners, global citizens, compassionate peacemakers, servent leaders and Christ-centered.

Check out all programs at:

www.goshen.edu/academics/major_minor.php

"Study-Service Term does not change people: people change people. SST offers an opportunity for change. By removing myself from the majority of my identity, SST gave me ample space for self-exploration. It tore down my realities and forced me to make a new one. That new reality consisted of nothingness. It was when I realized that what is important to me is not really important to others that I began to explore my priorities. It is at our lowest points that we can begin to rebuild— that is what I did."

Adam Nafziger - Ivory Coast SST

God and Rythmic Dust: an SST Journal was published in 1998

Awards and Recognition

Academics

• In the 2007 *U.S.News & World Report* "America's Best Colleges," Goshen College again placed high in the third tier of the category of Best Liberal Arts Colleges for the sixth straight year.

• *The Princeton Review* named Goshen College as a Best Midwestern College in 2004.

• *Barron's* "Best Buys in College Education", which profiles colleges and universities offering first-rate educations at a reasonable price, included Goshen College in its ninth edition.

• In a 2005 edition of "Entrepreneurship Magazine", Goshen College's entrepreneurship program ranked as one of the best programs in the country.

College Fast Facts

Four Year, Private, Christian

Web site: www.goshen.edu

Student Profile: 947 undergraduate students (45% male, 55% female); 3.6% African American, 81.3% Caucasian, 6% Hispanic, 6% international.

Faculty Profile: 64 full-time faculty, 13:1 student/faculty ratio. Average class size is 20.

Athletics: NAIA, Mid-Central College Conference; baseball, basketball, cross country, soccer, golf, tennis, track and field, softball, volleyball.

Costs and Aid: 2008–2009: $22,300 tuition, 7,500 room and board. 98% of students receive some financial aid.

Admissions

Goshen College
1700 South Main Street
Goshen, IN 46526
Phone: (800) 348-7422 or
(574) 535-7535
Email: admission@goshen.edu

Indiana State University

Indiana State University is a four-year public university that embraces its mission to educate the leaders of tomorrow. With focus on research, experiential learning, and civic engagement, Indiana State is committed to providing students with the academic foundation they need to succeed.

Flagship Programs

Sycamore Service Corps
The AmeriCorps Sycamore Service Corps and the Citizen-Scholar Fellowship are programs of our nation's domestic service corps that address community needs in education, public safety, human services, and the environment while allowing volunteers to earn compensation and an educational award.

University Honors Program: Leadership and Civic Engagement Track
The Leadership and Civic Engagement Track of the University Honors Program is centered on application of theory to real problems and preparation of future leaders. Students complete core honors courses and civic leadership coursework, research projects, and field experiences.

American Humanics
The American Humanics Certificate Program in Nonprofit Organization Management provides students with the skills and knowledge they need to become professional managers in nonprofit organizations. American Humanics students get hands-on experience through several service-learning opportunities and an internship.

Course Snapshot

RCSM 485 Community Development in Nonprofit Organization

This course explores how nonprofit organizations work to address social, economic, and environmental challenges in local communities in various regions of the United States. This is a service-learning course which provides student an opportunity to study a social, economic, or environmental issue in-depth and then provide a week of direct service in conjunction with a nonprofit organization to address the issue. Students participate in the Alternative Spring Break program in conjunction with enrollment in the course.

Academics
Through service-learning activities, Indiana State students, faculty and staff learn the importance of community while gaining knowledge and developing leadership skills.

Biology
Communication
Criminology and Criminal Justice
Economics
Family and Consumer Sciences
Geography
History
Political Science
Psychology
Social Work
Social Studies Education
Science Education
Theater

Management
Management Information Systems
Education
Nursing
Athletic Training
Exercise science
Physical Education
Health Sciences
Recreation and Sport Management
Early Childhood Education
Elementary Education
Special Education
Speech-Language Pathology

Learn about all of our majors at:
www.indstate.edu/academic/undergrad.htm

"Service learning develops critical thinkers and passionate citizens by joining academic theory to human needs and situations." ~ Professor Gregory Bierly, Director, University Honors Program

Awards and Recognition

Service-Learning
• Carnegie Community Engagement Classification.
• For the second straight year. Indiana State was named to the President's Higher Education Community Service Honor Roll.
• AmeriCorps Grant.

Academics
• Indiana State was the first university in Indiana to become a laptop institution.
• For the fourth straight year, the Princeton Review has recognized Indiana State University as one of the best colleges and universities its 2008 list of the "Best Midwestern Colleges.
• Indiana State's Dewey Institute was awarded a $100,000 grant from the Bernard Osher Foundation to become the first and only Osher Lifelong Learning Institute in the state of Indiana.

College Fast Facts

Student Profile: Total enrollment: 10,543 (47% male, 53% female); Undergraduate: 8,493, Graduate: 2,050; In-state: 79%, Out-of-state: 17%, International: 4. Indiana State hosts students from all 92 Indiana counties, 53 states and U.S. territories and 65 countries.

Faculty Profile: 446 full-time faculty, 17.4:1 student/faculty ratio.

Costs and Aid: For academic fee information, go to:
www.indstate.edu/controller/bursar/academic_fees.htm
ISU recognizes academic excellence by awarding over $1 million each year in merit-based scholarships to deserving students. These renewable scholarships range from $1,100 a year to the full costs of in-state tuition, housing, and books.

Admissions
Indiana State University
Office of Admissions
218 North Sixth Street
Terre Haute, Indiana, USA
47809-1904
Phone: 1-800-GO-TO-ISU
Email: admissions@indstate.edu

Service-Learning
Nancy Brattain Rogers
Director of the Center
for Public Service
and Community Engagement
Tirey Hall, room 134A
Indiana State University
Terre Haute, IN 47809
Phone: 812-237-2334
Fax: 812-237-2525
Email: cpsce@indstate.edu

Indiana University-Purdue University Indianapolis

Indiana University-Purdue University Indianapolis is an urban research and academic health sciences campus, with 22 schools and academic units which grant degrees in over 200 programs from both Indiana University and Purdue University.

Flagship Programs

Sam H. Jones Service Scholarship Program

This service scholarship program is one of the largest in the nation and has been named after Sam H. Jones to honor his memory and deeds as a dedicated public servant and Chief Executive Officer of the Indianapolis Urban League for 36 years. Sam Jones built bridges between races and genders, advocated for social change to assure equal access to education, housing, healthcare, and contributed to improving the quality of life for many people in Central Indiana. Last academic year, IUPUI, through the Center for Service and Learning, awarded nearly $468,000 in service scholarships to 313 students.

Child Welfare Program

The IU School of Social Work recently initiated a Child Welfare certificate program to respond to the state's need for trained child welfare social workers. All of the courses in the certificate program integrate service-learning through student placements at state, local, and non-profit child welfare agencies.

Course Snapshot

To Mexico with Love

This program is a Summer term immersion experience in language and culture. It also includes a service learning component where students apply their academic discipline within a community agency, serving Mexican residents in their communities. In addition to the language, cultural, service and preparatory components of the program, students expand their knowledge and understanding of Mexican culture and history through weekend excursions to various sites in Mexico and by living with a Mexican host family. Excursions tentatively planned include art, governmental, and museum locations in Mexico City; pyramid sites, churches and an optional weekend in Acapulco.

Academics

Service-learning courses in the major help students at IUPUI develop a lifelong commitment to service and civic engagement, not only as individuals, but as civic-minded professionals.

Programs of Study include:

Anthropology	Engineering and Technology
Biology	English
Business	Geography
Communication Studies	Geology
Computer and Information Technology	History
Criminal Justice	Law
Dentistry	Medicine
Education	Museum Studies

Check out all majors at: http://csl.iupui.edu

"Service learning and civic engagement increasingly need to be seen as necessary, core components of both undergraduate and graduate education."

– David Strong, Faculty Member and Coordinator of the Sociology Department's Engaged Department Initiative

Awards and Recognition

Service-Learning

• *U.S.News & World Report*: For the fifth year in a row, U.S.News & World Report recognized IUPUI as having one of the best service learning programs in the nation.

• Saviors of Our Cities: Dr. Evan Dobelle, president of the New England Board of Higher Education released a report titled "Saviors of Our Cities," which ranked universities on the basis of the contributions they make to their home cities. IUPUI was ranked number 4 and was the first public university listed in the rankings.

• IUPUI was one of only three universities to be honored with the President's Award for Community Service in Higher Education, a presidential honor presented by the Corporation for National and Community Service.

• "Colleges with a Conscience," awarded by Princeton Review and Campus Compact.

• IUPUI was one of 62 campuses classified by the Carnegie Foundation for Community Engagement in both categories of Curricular Engagement and Outreach and Partnerships.

College Fast Facts

Four Year, Public Research University, Urban, Founded: 1969

Web site: www.iupui.edu

Student Profile: 21,202 undergraduate students (58% female, 42% male); 50 states and territories; 122 countries; 15% minority; 4% international.

Faculty Profile: 2,205 full-time faculty. 90% hold a terminal degree in their field. 10:1 student/faculty ratio.

Costs and Aid: $6,850 in-state tuition. $18,904 out-of-state tuition. 55% of students receive financial aid. Average Award is $7,664.

Admissions

IUPUI Enrollment Center
Cavanaugh Hall 129
425 University Blvd.
Indianapolis, IN 46202
Phone: (317) 274-4591
Web: http://enroll.iupui.edu/request_information.shtml

Service-Learning

Center for Service and Learning
Dr. Steven G. Jones, Coordinator
Office of Service Learning
801 W. Michigan St., BS 2010
Indianapolis, IN 46202
Phone: (317) 278-2539
Email: jonessg@iupui.edu
Web: http://csl.iupui.edu

Purdue University

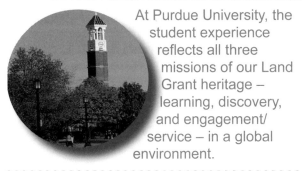

At Purdue University, the student experience reflects all three missions of our Land Grant heritage – learning, discovery, and engagement/ service – in a global environment.

Flagship Programs

EPICS (Engineering Projects in Community Service) is a unique program in which teams of undergraduates are designing, building, and deploying real systems to solve engineering-based problems for community organizations. Projects are in four broad areas: human services, access and abilities, education and outreach, and the environment.

Students in Professor Kim Wilson's **Landscape Architecture Design Studio Course, LA326 – Community Planning and Design,** worked in teams with community partners to formulate development plans that are based on a described vision of what could be, grounded in a thorough understanding of their assets, and incorporating current design principles, and industry practices and development strategies.

Nursing 404, a required nursing leadership course, helps senior students develop leadership capabilities while applying their nursing skills. Of seven projects to choose from, one involves working with Gulf Coast ambulatory  clinics in Biloxi, Mississippi, assisting and/or temporarily relieving nursing staff severely overtaxed since the Katrina catastrophe.

Course Snapshot

Students get to choose among seven service-learning projects in this course. By far the most popular projects are the nationally affiliated KYSS (Keep Your Children Safe and Secure) Walk, and the Biloxi Project Reach Out. Biloxi has been a long-term service-learning project, visited multiple times by teams of Purdue students. One student told me, "Volunteering here in Biloxi has given me a vision of how I want to use my nursing career. I now know what I want to do - and that is to work with low-income families."

- Professor Julie Novak (**NUR 404 : Nursing Leadership**)

Academics

Purdue has a campus-wide definition for service-learning which guides faculty as they design, implement and assess courses. Students can choose from more than 150 service-learning courses in 2008, up from 33 in 2002. Service-learning courses are offered across campus during any given school term in the colleges of:

Agriculture
Consumer and Family Sciences
Education
Engineering
Liberal Arts
Management
Pharmacy, Health Sciences, Nursing
Science
Technology
Veterinary Medicine

"By choosing their own not-for-profit agency to evaluate, students ... find their learning so compelling that many continue volunteering for the agency long after the class has ended."

~ Professor Charles Calahan, CDFS 515: Approaches to Research in Child and Family Programs

Check out all majors at: www.purdue.edu/Admissions/Undergrad/

Awards and Recognition

Service-Learning

• President's Higher Education Community Service Honor Roll with Distinction, 2006.
• Indiana Campus Compact Service Engagement Infrastructure Award, 2007.

General Awards and Recognitions (selected list):
• Number 24 ranking by *U.S.News & World Report*, America's Best Public Universities (undergraduate), 2007.
• Number 9 ranking by *U.S.News & World Report* of Purdue's undergraduate engineering program (among doctoral-granting public universities), 2007.
• Number 12 ranking by *U.S.News & World Report*, America's Best Engineering Graduate Schools, 2007.
• Number 1 ranking for Speech and Hearing Science program, 2007.
• Number 21 ranking for Purdue's Krannert School of Management's undergraduate program overall among doctoral-granting universities and was ranked 8th among public universities according to *U.S.News & World Report*, 2007.
• Number 2 ranking in the nation in *Design Magazine's* survey of recruiters ranked Purdue's Landscape Architecture undergraduate program, 2005.
• Number 1 ranking for the The Hospitality & Tourism Management program in the U.S. by the *Journal of Hospitality & Tourism Education*, 2002.

College Fast Facts

Ph.D Degree Granting Institution, Public, Urban, Founded: 1869

Student Profile: Undergraduate Enrollment for the 2007-08 school year was 31,186; 79.8% Undergraduate students (58.1% male, 41.9% female); 13.4% minority, 6.5% international. 50 states and 3 territories represented.

Faculty Profile: Full-time faculty 97.5%, part-time faculty 2.5%. 100% of faculty hold a terminal degree in their field. Student/Faculty ratio 13.8 to 1. Average Class size is 42.79 per class hour for Fall 2007 semester.

Athletics: NCAA Division 1. Conference: Big Ten. Number of Varsity Sports: 9 men and 9 women for a total of 18.

Costs and Aid: Indiana Resident: Tuition/Fees = $7,750, Total Costs = $18,800. Nonresident: Tuition/Fees = $23,224, Total Costs = $34,444. 79.2% of students received some financial aid.

Admissions

Purdue University
Office of Admissions
Schleman Hall of Student
 Services
475 Stadium Mall Drive
West Lafayette, IN 47907-0544
Phone: (765) 494-1776
TTY: (765) 496-1373
Email: admissions@purdue.edu
www.purdue.edu/Admissions/Undergrad/

Service-Learning

Marne Helgesen, Ph.D., Director
Center for Instructional Excellence
Phone: (765) 496-6424
Email: helgesen@purdue.edu
http://servicelearning.ics.purdue.edu/

University of Dubuque

The University of Dubuque is a small, private university affiliated with the Presbyterian Church (USA) offering undergraduate, graduate, and theological seminary programs. The University is comprised of individuals from the region, the nation, and the world.

Flagship Programs

World View Seminars

First Year students take part in a large-scale service project within a local nature reserve. In the second year, classes research a local charitable organization and develop and carry out a project to assist the organization's needs.

E.C.H.O. Project (Engaging the Community by Helping Others)

Each year, every floor within the residence halls adopts a local agency and works with that agency throughout the school year. Examples include hosting holiday celebrations for children with Big Brothers Big Sisters, and serving meals at a local shelter.

Wendt Character Scholars

All of the fifty Wendt Character Scholars participate in service projects as part of their required co-curricular scholarship program. The scholars work with local mentoring services, teach responsibility in the elementary schools, and participate in many other local projects.

Course Snapshot

First-Year English

In Jessica Schreyer's first-year English class, students used writing, oral communication, time management, organization, and planning skills by participating in "Lots of Socks." They collected over 500 pairs of new socks, gloves, and hats for needy children in the Dubuque Community School District.

Academics

The Service-Learning programs at the University of Dubuque are designed to provide students opportunities to use the skills they learn in the classroom to meet real needs in the community. Service-Learning provides UD students the opportunity to use the skills that they are learning to make a difference in their world.

Programs include:
Computer Graphics
Biology
Business
Education
English
Environmental Science
Health, Physical Education & Recreation
Nursing
Sociology

Check out all majors at:
www.dbq.edu/academics/academics.cfm

"Students are able to develop questions about themselves, their community, and how the world influences their lives. They, themselves, become better people by serving one another and the global community and by developing a sense of citizenship, social values, and character." ~ Kim Hilby

Awards and Recognition
Service-Learning
• President's Higher Education Community Service Honor Roll.

College Fast Facts

Four Year, Private, Urban, Founded: 1852

Affiliation: Presbyterian

Web site: www.dbq.edu

Student Profile: 1,285 undergraduate students (56% male, 44% female); 35 states and territories, 20 countries; 18% minority, 3% international.

Faculty Profile: 70 full-time faculty. 70% hold a terminal degree in their field. 13 :1 student/faculty ratio. Average class size is 20.

Athletics: NCAA Division III, Iowa Conference. 19 varsity sports.

Costs and Aid: 2007-2008: $26,810 comprehensive ($19,600 tuition). 95% of students receive some form of financial aid.

Admissions
University of Dubuque
Office of Admission
2000 University Ave.
Dubuque, IA 52001
Phone: (563) 589-3000
(800) 722-5583
Email: admssns@dbq.edu

Service-Learning
Office of Service-Learning
Mark Smith
Coordinator of Service-Learning
Phone: (563) 589-3127
Email: mwsmith@dbq.edu

Wartburg College

Wartburg College is a selective liberal arts college of the Lutheran church (ELCA), nationally recognized for community engagement, and is dedicated to challenging and nurturing students for lives of leadership and service as a spirited expression of their faith and learning.

Flagship Programs

Service Trips

Wartburg students participate in nation-wide service trips during college breaks. Students are engaged in action and reflection on some of the most important social problems today, including homelessness and affordable housing, urban community development, hunger, and the environment.

Service Learning

In the past year, Wartburg offers 70 courses involving 47% of students in community-based learning, such as ID 315, Leadership Theories and Practice, where students participate in the Community Builders program that brings together sixth-grade students, college students and community volunteers to participate in community service. Sixteen majors include and over 60 faculty have taught community-based courses.

Volunteer Action Center

The Volunteer Action Center is a student-run volunteer clearinghouse that connects students with community and campus service organizations. Service opportunities include monthly service days, Wartburg's collegiate Habitat for Humanity chapter and other special service opportunities as well as individual volunteer placements.

Course Snapshot

The Leadership Certificate Program

The Leadership Certificate Program (LCP) provides opportunities for Wartburg College students to demonstrate the Wartburg definition of leadership. The service-learning component requires that the students engage in a project that is consistent with the Wartburg College mission of "taking responsibility for our communities and making them better through public action." ID 315, Leadership Theories and Practice, offers critical reflection on theories of leadership and civic responsibility within the context of different disciplinary backgrounds and their application to community service projects.

Academics

Wartburg College actively connects students with the community in valuable service-learning partnerships. The College's Center for Community Engagement is a hub for experiential learning activities. In 2007, Wartburg was recognized as one of 106 colleges in the nation on the President's Higher Education Community Service Honor Roll.

Service-learning courses connect students and classroom learning to real life situations through participation in a service project, readings, and classroom discussions. Academic programs with service-learning courses include:

Accounting	Individualized Major
Biology	Interdepartmental Major
Business Administration	Leadership Certification
Church Music	Music Therapy
Communication Arts	Nursing
Communication Design	Physical Education
Computer Science	Political Science
Community Sociology	Religion
Economics	Social Work
Education	Writing
History	

"Wartburg offers more than 50 academic majors in the liberal arts and in professional areas.."

Check out all majors at: www.wartburg.edu/academics/majors.html

Awards and Recognition

• Among 109 schools named "with distinction" to the President's Higher Education Community Service Honor Roll, recognizing volunteer service by Wartburg students.

• Nationally classified by the Carnegie Foundation for the Advancement of Teaching as one of 62 colleges that foster community engagement in the curriculum and through community outreach and partnerships.

• Collaborating with Franklin Pierce University in New Hampshire on "Engaging Students: First in the Nation," a project encouraging student participation in the 2008 presidential election.

• Students in top 10% of high school class – 31%.

• Job and graduate school placement rate – 99%.

• Retention rate – 86%.

• Wartburg is the only private college in Iowa offering a major in music therapy.

• Warturg's social work program is the oldest undergraduate program of its kind in Iowa.

College Fast Facts

Four Year, Private Rural, Year Founded: 1852

Affiliation: Evangelical Lutheran Church in America (ELCA)

Web site: www.wartburg.edu

Student Profile: 1810 Undergraduate students (48% male, 52% female); 24 states and territories, 43 countries; 7% minority, 6 % international.

Faculty Profile: 107 full-time faculty. 97% hold a terminal degree in their field. 12 :1 student/faculty ratio. Average class size is 22.

Athletics: NCAA Division III, Conference IIAC. 19 varsity sports. "The Athletic department seeks to provide a meaningful and positive experience for serious student-athletes."

Cost and Aid: 2008-2009: $33,415 comprehensive ($25,360 tuition). 99% of students receive some financial aid.

Admissions

Wartburg College
100 Wartburg Blvd.
Waverly, IA 50677
Phone: (800) 772-2085

Fort Hays State University

Fort Hays State University, a regional liberal arts university in western Kansas, is dedicated to providing instruction within a computerized environment.

Flagship Programs

Collaborative Service-Learning in Agriculture

Students in four agricultural courses at Fort Hays State University hosted "Make Every Water Drop Count," a Soil Conservation and Water Quality Workshop for producers and citizens that care about natural resources in Kansas.

Ben Franklin Papers

The Ben Franklin Papers is an annual collaborative effort between the Center for Civic Leadership and Social Studies Methods course each fall. Students in this course create and facilitate curriculum to 500 local fifth and eighth graders. Original letters handwritten by Franklin are also viewed.

Annual Campus-Community Service Fair

FHSU students, faculty and staff have the opportunity each fall to create partnerships with local non-profit agencies at the annual campus-community service fair. The networking at the fair enhances service-learning partnerships between the campus and community.

Course Snapshot

LDRS 310--Fieldwork in Leadership Studies

As part of the Department of Leadership Studies program, students participate in a fieldwork class. Students learn leadership by doing it in the context of a required community project. The semester long project actively engages students in collaborative learning about the concept of "civic leadership" through service-learning. A few community organizations that students have worked with include American Red Cross, the Downtown Hays Development Corporation, Habitat for Humanity, Humane Society, and YouthFriends.

Academics

Through service-learning courses FHSU students have the opportunity to learn course content through practice, and also develop a lifelong commitment to civic engagement. FHSU offers more than 60 areas of undergraduate study and master's degrees on campus.

Programs include:

Art
Communication Studies
English
Geosciences
History
Information Networking and Telecommunications
Political Science
Psychology
Sociology and Social Work
Accounting and Information Systems
Leadership Studies
Management and Marketing
Special Education
Teacher Education
Technology Studies
Agriculture
Allied Health
Biological Sciences
Communication Disorders
Health and Human Performance
Nursing

"Service-learning participation increases civic awareness, enhances community involvement, and enriches experiences with children, teachers, families, and local organizations encouraging students to grow personally and professionally."

-Dr. Debbie Mercer, Dean, College of Education and Technology

Check out all majors at:
www.fhsu.edu/academics

Awards and Recognition

• President's Higher Education Community Service Honor Roll

• FHSU participates in the national AASCU project, American Democracy Project which encourages civic participation in students.

• Accredited by the Higher Learning Commission of the North Central Association of Colleges and Schools

• FHSU's Virtual College offers 12 bachelor's degree programs, 9 master's degree programs, and numerous certificates and endorsements.

• FHSU has the lowest tuition rate among four-year universities in the state of Kansas.

• FHSU is home to the Center for Civic Leadership (www.fhsu.edu/ccl) and the Docking Institute for Public Affairs (www.fhsu.edu/docking).

College Fast Facts

Four Year, Public, Rural: Founded 1902

Web site: www.fhsu.edu

Student Profile: 9,588 undergraduate and graduate students (42% male, 58% female); 50 states and territories; 7.5% minority, 27% international.

Faculty Profile: 295 full-time faculty; 17:1 student/faculty ratio.

Athletics: NCAA Division II; Men's sports: baseball, basketball, cross country, football, golf, track and field, wrestling, and yell leading; Women's sports: basketball, cheerleading, cross country, softball, tennis, track and field, and volleyball.

Costs and Aid: 2007–2008: $10,206.50 in-state comprehensive ($ 3,355.50 tuition); $11,502.80 contiguous-state comprehensive ($4,651.80 tuition); $17,394.50 out of state comprehensive ($10,543.50 tuition); 52% of students receive some financial aid.

Admissions

Fort Hays State University, Office of Admissions
600 Park Street, Hays, KS 67601
Phone: (800) 628-FHSU
Email: admissions@fhsu.edu
www.fhsu.edu

Service-Learning
Center for Civic Leadership, Fort Hays State University
600 Park Street
Hays, KS 67601
Phone: (785) 628-5592; (800) 628-FHSU
Email: ccl@fhsu.edu
www.fhsu.edu/ccl/service-learning

Kansas State University

Kansas State University is a land-grant, public research university, committed to teaching and learning, research, and service to the people of Kansas, the nation, and the world.

Flagship Programs

Leadership Studies and Programs is a value-centered learning community that supports curricular studies and co-curricular service, integrating thought and action. The interdisciplinary Leadership Studies minor combines a theoretical focus with an emphasis on personal leadership development and practical experience. It is the largest academic program on campus, enrolling over 1,500 students representing every college.

International Service Teams
International Teams serve developing communities during the summer break. Interdisciplinary student teams complete a 3-credit preparation course and work with the community to plan and implement service projects. Over the past 15 years, international teams have served communities worldwide by creating community-specific plans and projects focused on health, education, environmental concerns and other development issues.

Drama Therapy at K-State incorporates service-learning throughout the curriculum. Partnering with local schools, development centers and retirement communities, students use drama therapy's active,

experiential approach to provide participants with the means to explore their inner experience and to enhance interpersonal relationships.

Course Snapshot

CE 690: Natural Resources & Environmental Sciences Capstone Course
Professor Alok Bhandari reflected: "Service learning gives students a context for real world learning. Only after I tried it did I realize the true value for students and the community."

Students in the class conducted a hydrologic assessment of K-State's Campus Creek for their service-learning project. The class studied the creek's water capacity during storm flows and analyzed the quality of the water. The class then shared their results and recommendations with KSU's Department of Environmental Health and Safety.

Academics

Service-learning at K-State is part of a strong commitment to engagement, central to our identity as a land-grant institution. Engagement occurs when collaborative partners – from campus and community - work together to address a public need in a way that is both reciprocal and mutually beneficial. Service-learning at K-State links community service with structured reflection to promote academic learning and foster civic responsibility. Some courses include:

Accounting
Agricultural Economics
Agronomy
Anthropology
Architectural Engineering
Architecture
Art
Civil Engineering
Dietetics
Family Studies and Human Services
Geography
Gerontology
History
Human Nutrition
Hotel and Restaurant Management
Interior Design

Leadership Studies and Programs
Management
Marketing
Mass Communications
Natural Resources and Environmental -Sciences
Political Science
Regional and Community Planning
Secondary Education
Social Work
Sociology
Special Education
Speech
Theatre
Women's Studies

Check out all courses & majors at: www.k-state.edu

Awards and Recognition

• K-State ranks first nationally among state universities in its total of Rhodes, Marshall, Truman, Goldwater, and Udall scholars since 1986. Ranked #6 among ALL universities in national scholars.

• One of America's "best value" public colleges: Ranked #5 by Princeton Review and #16 by Consumers Digest.

• Top 25: American's best "cutting-edge schools." (2008)

• Listed among the nation's top colleges in *Princeton Review: Best 361 Colleges* and is listed as one of the "Best in the West" regional rankings.

• Rated Best Opportunity to Maximize Your Education by *Rugg's Recommendations on the Colleges (2003).*

College Fast Facts

Four Year, Public, Suburban: Founded: 1863

Web site: www.k-state.edu

Student Profile: 18,545 undergraduate students (50% male, 50% female); 49 states, 109 countries; 12% minority, 5.2% international.

Faculty Profile: 1,242 full-time faculty, 17:1 student/faculty ratio, average undergraduate class size ranges from 26-28.

Athletics: NCAA Division 1, Big Twelve Conference, 15 varsity sports. Intramural facilities: playing fields and gyms; basketball, tennis, volleyball, and racquetball courts; golf courses; swimming pools; indoor running tracks; and weight rooms

Costs and Aid: 2007-2008: $16,568 in-state comprehensive ($6,036 tuition). $25,654 out-of-state comprehensive ($15,122 tuition). 73% of students receive some financial aid.

Admissions

Office of Admissions
Kansas State University
119 Anderson Hall
Manhattan, KS 66506-0102
Phone: 1-800-432-8270;
785-532-6250
Fax: 785-532-6393
Email: k-state@k-state.edu

Service-Learning

Civic Leadership
Mary Hale Tolar
Associate Director
Leadership Studies and Programs
Phone: (785) 532-5701
Email: mtolar@k-state.edu

Southwestern College

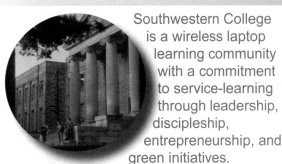

Southwestern College is a wireless laptop learning community with a commitment to service-learning through leadership, discipleship, entrepreneurship, and green initiatives.

Flagship Programs

Leadership Southwestern

The flagship service-learning program at Southwestern College, Leadership Southwestern involves students committed to changing themselves and the world around themselves through servant leadership. As a team, they are committed to making a positive difference and to leaving an impacting legacy.

Discipleship Southwestern

exists to encourage college students as they begin, or continue, the journey of becoming mature disciples of Jesus Christ at home, work, church, and the world. The Discipleship program engages the whole person and challenges students to think about their callings beyond college.

Students in Free Enterprise (SIFE) is a service-learning organization that promotes and teaches the importance of free enterprise in the community. By addressing the needs of their community, students are able to come up with creative projects that teach the principles of free enterprise.

Course Snapshot

Leadership, Discipleship, and Green team program participants can work toward academic minors in these program areas. A class included in each of the minors is **SOCS 101 Introduction to Leadership**. An introduction to leadership theory begins the class. Analysis of historical leaders, contemporary leaders, and self as leader follows. Students end the class with a service learning experience designed to foster collaboration among the team.

Academics

Service-learning is an integral part of Southwestern College's vision and mission. Development of "leadership through service in a world without boundaries" has led to award-winning co-curricular programs across academic disciplines. Service-learning at Southwestern exposes students to real world experiences—travel, community engagement, and other avenues of making a difference in the world.

Service-learning courses include:
Religion and Philosophy
Leadership*
Business

* Courses with a required service-learning component.

Check out all majors at: www.sckans.edu/admissions

"Service learning helps students learn through the vehicle of service as an alternative to learning through lecture or laboratory activity. Students prepare for service through study and after completing the service experience, participate in reflection through a variety of means such as journaling, group discussion, or reflective writing." ~ Dr. Cheryl Rude

Awards and Recognition

- President's Higher Education Community Service Honor Roll 2007.
- Association of Leadership Educators Best Leadership Program in the Nation 1997.
- John Templeton Foundation Exemplary Leadership Recognition 2000.
- Kansas Volunteer Commission "You Make a Difference Award" 2004.
- The Robert Wood Johnson Foundation Grant, 2001.
- Kansas Department of Health and Environment Grant, 2002.
- Kansas Health Foundation Grants, 2002 and 2003.
- Kansas Learn and Serve Program Grants, 2001, 2002, and 2003.
- AmeriCorps M3C Program 2006 and 2007.
- AmeriCorps VISTA 2007.
- General Board of Global Ministries Grant, 2003, 2004, and 2005.
- Foundation for Evangelism Grant, 2005, 2006, and 2007.
- Moody Memorial Fund, 2006 and 2007.
- SIFE National Market Economics Competition Finalist 2006.
- SIFE Regional Competition Champion 2005, 2006, and 2007.
- SIFE National Business Ethics Competition Finalist 2006.
- SIFE USA Regional Competition First Runner-Up 2004.
- SIFE Rookie of the Year USA Regional Competition 2004.
- SIFE National Entrepreneurship Competition Finalist.

College Fast Facts

Four Year, Private, Suburban, Founded: 1885

Affiliation: United Methodist

Web site: www.sckans.edu

Student Profile: 567 undergraduate students (44% male, 56% female); 24 states and territories, 12 countries; 17% minority, 4% international.

Faculty Profile: 48 full-time faculty. 58% hold a terminal degree in their field. 12:1 student/faculty ratio.

Athletics: NAIA, Kansas Collegiate Athletic Conference. 15 varsity sports

Costs and Aid: 2007-2008: $23,442 comprehensive ($17,720 tuition). 99% of students receive some form of financial aid.

Admissions

Southwestern College
Office of Admissions
100 College St.
Winfield, KS 67156-2499
Phone: (620) 229-6236
E-mail: scadmit@sckans.edu

Service-Learning

Dr. Cheryl Rude
Director of
Leadership Southwestern
Cheryl.Rude@sckans.edu

Berea College

Berea College promotes understanding and kinship among all people, service to communities in Appalachia and beyond, and sustainable living practices.

Service-Learning Focus

Through service-learning, Berea College students develop skills and knowledge, on their way to becoming service-oriented leaders for Appalachia and beyond.

Flagship Programs

Hispanic Outreach Project (HOP)
Building bridges between Spanish-speaking and English-speaking communities, the Hispanic Outreach Project (HOP) provides Berea College Spanish students with service-learning opportunities, including tutoring, teaching English as a Second Language (ESL) classes, and translating documents for community organizations.

Mental Health Awareness Fairs
Abnormal Psychology and Child Psychopathology courses use theoretical knowledge of psychological and developmental issues to educate others and to dispel myths about mental health, by planning and hosting Mental Health Awareness Fairs for local elementary to high-school-aged students.

Entrepreneurship for the Public Good (EPG)
Berea College students participate in the two-summer EPG program by taking courses in entrepreneurship and leadership, while participating in service-learning projects focused on organizational development and program implementation, in partnership with community-based organizations in the Appalachian region.

Course Snapshot

HIS 386: Civil Rights Movement in America

BC history majors partnered with local Black churches to conduct oral history interviews, during which community partners discussed personal experiences and events related to Civil Rights in Berea's Black community. The interviews were recorded and transcribed and will be preserved at the churches and at the Berea College archives.

Academics

African and African American Studies
Agriculture and Natural Resources
Appalachian Studies
Child and Family Studies
Computer Science
Economics and Business
Education Studies
English
General Studies
History
Nursing
Peace and Social Justice Studies
Physical Education and Health
Political Science
Psychology
Religion
Sociology
Spanish
Speech Communication
Sustainability and Environmental Studies
Technology and Industrial Arts
Theatre
Women's Studies

Learn More About All Classes! www.berea.edu/academics/
Service-Learning: www.berea.edu/celts/servicelearning/

Awards and Recognition
Service-Learning
• Recipient of two Learn and Serve America awards, to fund service-learning programming
• Endowed Bonner Scholars Program
• President's Higher Education Community Service Honor Roll, 2007

Academics
• Charges no tuition and only serves students with financial need.
• Nationally recognized labor program in which all students participate.

College Fast Facts
Four Year, Private, Rural: Founded 1855

Web site: www.berea.edu

Student Profile: 1514 undergraduate (40% male, 60% female); 40 states and territories, 71 countries; 22% minority, 7% international.

Faculty Profile: 131 full-time faculty. 91% hold a terminal degree in their field. 10:1 student/faculty ratio. Average class size is 16.

Athletics: National Association of Intercollegiate Athletics (NAIA), Kentucky Intercollegiate Athletic Conference (KIAC). 16 varsity sports.

Costs and Aid : 2007–2008: $6,282 comprehensive ($0 tuition). 100% of students receive some financial aid. Average award: The equivalent of a four-year scholarship, up to $85,000.

Admissions
Berea College, Office of Admissions
CPO 2220
Berea, KY 40404
Phone: (859) 985-3500; (800) 326-5948
Email: askadmissions@berea.edu

Service-Learning
Center for Excellence in Learning Through Service (CELTS)
Meta Mendel-Reyes, Ph.D.
Director, CPO 2170
Berea, KY 40404
Phone: (859) 985-3940
Email: Meta_mendel-reyes@berea.edu
www.berea.edu/celts/servicelearning/

Northern Kentucky University

Northern Kentucky University is a regional, metropolitan university focused on learner-centered teaching, excellence, access with the opportunity to succeed, public engagement, intellectual freedom, multiculturalism, innovation and creativity, collegiality and collaboration.

Service-Learning Focus

Service Learning is a course-based, credit-bearing educational experience in which students participate in an organized service activity that meets a community need and reflect on their service activity as a means of gaining a deeper understanding of course content, a broader appreciation of the discipline, an enhanced sense of appreciation of the discipline, an enhanced sense of civic responsibility, and/or greater interest in and understanding of community life.

Flagship Programs

Mayerson Student Philanthropy Project

Students in disciplines ranging from art to public administration and social work to business have the opportunity to learn their academic content through the grant making process. Students request and review grant proposals and recommend funding for local nonprofit agencies each semester.

Disaster Relief and Preparation

Through course work and alternative break trips students have the chance to learn about different steps to prepare for and respond to the disasters that are facing many of our communities today.

Course Snapshot

ENG 101/UNV 101/HIS 103 Learning Community

Students in this first year learning community were able to combine lessons from their English, History and College Orientation Seminar into a powerful service learning opportunity with senior citizens in the region. NKU students met with the seniors several times and created short oral histories or "story boards" about significant events in the seniors' lives. The posters were shared with the university and local community as well as family members during an art gallery display of the students' work at the end of the semester.

Academics

Students can find service learning opportunities in a number of different departments on campus. These classes give students a chance to combine their academic interests with community based projects.

Service-learning classes are available in many of our departments including:

- Accountancy
- Art
- Biological Sciences
- Business Informatics
- Chemistry
- Communication
- Computer Science
- Construction Management &
- Organizational Leadership
- Counseling, Human Services &
- Social Work
- First Year Programs/NKU Academy
- History & Geography
- Honors
- Kinesiology, Health & Educational Foundations
- Learning Assistance Program
- Liberal Studies
- Literature & Language
- Management & Marketing
- Mathematics
- Music
- Nursing & Health Professions
- Physics & Geology
- Political Science & Criminal Justice
- Psychology
- Sociology, Anthropology, Philosophy
- Social Work
- Teacher Education & School
- Leadership
- Theatre and Dance

Check out all majors at: www.nku.edu/academics.php

"I feel like I actually made a positive impact on the community and the project made me care about class and doing well in it. It was a great way to teach course concepts using real life situations. I would definitely recommend the class to anyone." ~ NKU Student

Awards and Recognition

- Carnegie Classification for Outreach and Engagement.
- Learn and Serve Grantee.
- US Election Assistance Commission Grant for Recruiting College Students to be Pollworkers.
- President's Higher Education Community Service Honor Roll, 2007

College Fast Facts

Web site: www.nku.edu

Student Profile: 12,647 undergraduate students (5350=42.3% male, 7297=57.7% female); 42 states and territories, 91 countries; 1462=11.6% minority, 175=1.4% international.

Faculty Profile: 608 full-time faculty. 75% hold a terminal degree in their field. 14:1 student/faculty ratio. Average class size is 24.

Athletics: NCAA Division 2, Great Lakes Valley Conference. 10 varsity sports.

Costs and Aid: 2007-2008: KY Resident: ($2,976/semester for undergraduate tuition). Non-KY Resident ($5,388/semester for undergraduate tuition). 73% of students receive some financial aid. Average award for full time student: $8,010.00.

Admissions

Northern Kentucky University
Office of Admissions
LAC 400
Nunn Drive
Highland Heights, KY 41099
Phone: (859) 572-5220
1-800-637-9948 (toll free)
Email: admitnku@nku.edu
http://www.nku.edu/~admitnku/

Service-Learning

Northern Kentucky University
Scripps Howard Center for Civic Engagement
FH 536
Nunn Drive
Highland Heights, KY 41099
Phone: (859) 572-1448
Email: civicengage@nku.edu
http://civicengagement.nku.edu/

University of Kentucky

One of the primary tenets of our land-grant mission is service. The University of Kentucky, as Kentucky's flagship university, is firmly committed to serving and engaging the entire Commonwealth of Kentucky. UK is devoted to applying, sharing, and disseminating knowledge across Kentucky and beyond, as we work to make the Commonwealth a better place to live and learn.

Flagship Programs

HP 613 Historical Structural Systems

Students taught an intensive four-day workshop (endorsed by the Kentucky Heritage Council) providing preservation and trades education to staff of the Pine Mountain Settlement School and local volunteer maintenance crews. Students gained greater insight into the historic building process and restoration work by performing masonry repair of the historic Pine Mountain Settlement School.

LA 975, Advanced Landscape Architecture Design Studio

Students work hand-in-hand with Kentucky communities to generate solutions to real problems regarding unplanned development. Students meet with stakeholders at public meetings, develop a vision statement, assemble and analyze data, and provide a written report of findings and recommendations and a series of story boards for use in furthering community support.

Course Snapshot

S. Nah, Spring 2007
CLD 440 Community Processes and Communication

This project paid particular attention to the role of Web sites developed by nonprofit organizations as communication tools with community and general public. Student groups worked in collaboration with the UK Nonprofit Leadership Initiative to choose a Lexington nonprofit organization. They collected information about the organization and its methods of communication, conducted analysis of its Web site, and provided a final report recommending improvements and effective use of its site for communication.

Academics

The service-learning program at UK provides opportunity for faculty and students to engage with the greater community and provides a mechanism to blend scholarship with authentic experience and service.

Anthropology
Biological Sciences
Clinical Sciences
Community Leadership
Economics
English
Entomology
Forestry
Freshman Discovery Seminar
Hispanic Studies
Historical Preservation
Journalism

Landscape Architecture
Medicine
Music
Nursing
Nutrition Sciences
Pharmacy
Physical Therapy
Sociology
Social Work
Special Education & Rehab.
Theatre

For a complete listing of department and major requirements go to:
www.uky.edu/Registrar/Major-Sheets/

"You don't always know what's going to happen in a service-learning course, but when you take chances you allow for the most amazing things to happen." ~ Gail Hoyt, PhD, Professor of Economics

Awards and Recognition

Service-Learning
Kentucky Campus Compact
Carnegie Classification: Outreach and Partnerships
Academics
• *U.S.News & World Report* Rankings-- College of Pharmacy – 5th (public and private); College of Medicine, family medicine -- 16th; College of Nursing – 18th (public), 26th (public and private); College of Medicine, rural health program -- 18th; Markey Cancer Center, cancer care -- 19th; College of Health Sciences, physician assistant studies program -- 25th; College of Arts & Sciences, clinical psychology -- 27th (public), 33rd (overall); College of Health Sciences, physical therapy program - 35th; College of Social Work -- 38th;
• National Science Foundation ranks UK 34th (public) and 52nd (public and private) in research expenditures.
• For 2007-2008, UK boasts 5 Fulbright Scholars, 2 faculty Guggenheim Fellows, 2 Beckman Scholars, 1 Goldwater Scholar, 1 Udall Scholar, and 1 Astronaut Scholarship Foundation recipient. During Fall 2007, 348 Governors Scholars and School for the Arts participants enrolled at UK.
•The Kentucky Kernel, the student-run newspaper, won the 2006 Pacemaker Award, considered the Pulitzer of college journalism.

College Fast Facts

Four Year, Public, Urban, Founded: 1865

Web site: www.uky.edu

Student Profile: Undergraduate students (48% male, 52% female); 50 states and territories, 117 countries; 9.1% minority, 4.8% international.

Faculty Profile: 2,028 full-time faculty.

Athletics: NCAA Division One Conference. Southeastern Conference.

Costs and Aid: 2007-2008: $3,651 tuition per semester (resident). $7,547 tuition per semester (out-of-state; non-resident).

Admissions

100 Funkhouser Bldg.
University of Kentucky
Lexington, KY 40506-0054
Phone: 859.257.2000
Fax: 859.257.3823
www.uky.edu/visitorcenter

Service-Learning
Esther Livingston
Assistant Director
Experiential Education
and Career Services
University of Kentucky
Phone: 859.257.1564

Katherine McCormick, Ph.D.
Stuckert Endowed
Professor in Service-Learning
and Associate Professor
College of Education
University of Kentucky
Phone: 859.257.9573

Western Kentucky University

Western Kentucky University prepares students to be productive, engaged, and socially responsible citizen-leaders in a global society.

Service-learning at WKU brings faculty, staff and students together with community partners in order to tackle issues affecting individuals or communities within our reach. The ALIVE Center coordinates student learning opportunities at WKU, linking them to our regional stewardship priorities and initiatives.

Flagship Programs

Women and Children Learning Together (WKLT)
WKLT focuses on education, the arts, physical and emotional wellness to improve the lives of low-income women and their children. WKU students, faculty and community leaders help participants explore self-expression and engage in new learning experiences. Creative activities encourage participants' children to express themselves in positive, healthy ways.

Rural Health Development and Research (IRHDR)

The CEC and IRHDR are community-university partnerships that enhance learning opportunities for students in the education and health and professions while serving the needs of the region. Students and faculty mentors provide a suite of services that increase the health status, quality of life, and educational awareness of individuals and families with disabilities as well as the medically under-served and uninsured in our region.

Community Development in Kenya
In partnership with the University of Nairobi, WKU students are working with a local community in southeastern Kenya to improve their economic opportunities and quality of life. Students in biology, sociology, photojournalism, and business are collaborating to develop ecotourism opportunities, find markets for baskets produced by the local women's cooperative, and enhance medical services available to the community.

Course Snapshot

American Humanics (Nonprofit Administration) Minor

American Humanics (AH) at WKU prepares students to work in the nonprofit sector through educational and experiential activities. As part of an annual community service partnership, AH students solicit proposals for project partnerships from local nonprofit organizations. In 2007-08, AH worked with Friends of the Lost River, Inc. on the first phase of a project to build community awareness, enhance fundraising efforts and design protocols for removal of invasive plant species and maintaining native seedbeds.

Academics

Service-learning courses combine meaningful community service with sound instruction and reflection, enhancing students' professional knowledge and skills while strengthening communities and developing individual social responsibility.

Service-learning opportunities are available in programs from each of our seven degree-granting colleges:

Bowling Green Community College
College of Education and Behavioral Sciences
College of Health and Human Services
Gordon Ford College of Business
Ogden College of Science and Engineering
Potter College of Arts and Letters
University College

"At WKU these days we are about identifying and solving problems that affect people within our reach."

– President Gary Ransdell

Check out all majors at: www.wku.edu/academics.html

Awards and Recognition

Service-Learning

• In 2007, The Corporation for National and Community Service recognized WKU with inclusion on the President's Higher Education Community Service Honor Roll with Distinction

• WKU was among the first 62 schools in the nation to receive the Carnegie Elective Classification in Community Engagement in both Curricular Engagement as well as Outreach and Partnerships categories

• In 2007, Provost Barbara Burch received the William Plater Award for Leadership in Civic Engagement from the American Association of State Colleges and Universities

• The ONE Campaign selected WKU as the best of over 1500 colleges and universities competing in the first ONE Campaign Challenge to raise awareness about the effects of global poverty.

Academics

• WKU was included in the Top 25 Public Universities – Master's South classification, ranking 13th in 2008.

• WKU is a first-tier university in the *U.S. News & World Report*'s *America's Best Colleges 2006 Edition* among Universities – Masters South.

College Fast Facts

Four Year, Public, Suburban, Founded in 1906

Web Site: www.wku.edu

Student Profile: 16,508 undergraduate students (43% male, 57% female); 47 states and territories, 55 countries; 19% minority, 3% international.

Faculty Profile: 726 full-time faculty. 97.4% hold a terminal degree in their field. 18:1 student/faculty ratio.

Athletics: NCAA Division I, Sun Belt Conference. 17 varsity sports.

Costs and Aid: 2007–2008: $12,056 in-state comprehensive ($6,416 tuition); $21,110 out-of-state comprehensive ($15,470 tuition) 92% of students receive some financial aid.

Admissions

Western Kentucky University
Office of Admissions
1906 College Heights Boulevard 11020
Bowling Green, KY 42101-1020
Phone: (270) 745-2551
Email: admissions@wku.edu

Service-Learning

Cheryl Kirby-Stokes
Service Learning and Volunteer Coordinator
ALIVE Center for Community Partnerships
1818 31-W Bypass
Bowling Green, KY 42101
Phone: (626) 782-0020
Email: cheryl.kirby-stokes@wku.edu

Nicholls State University

Nicholls State University, a comprehensive, regional institution, provides a unique blend of excellent academic programs with a personal touch.

Flagship Programs

Spring-Break Nursing Mission

Nursing students embark on a week-long medical mission trip during spring break to deliver care, hope, and goodwill at clinics and orphanages in an especially poor community within a developing nation. The lives of the students and those they served have been touched and changed forever by the experiences in this Nursing course.

Project Le Cirque

Students in Family and Consumer Sciences participate in the Le Cirque program which provides services for children and their families in 212-unit federal housing development. Students are engaged in crisis intervention, juvenile diversion, prevention of long term mental illness and school-based services through this service-learning opportunity.

Sociology Students Preserve History

Nicholls Sociology students partner with community agencies for the historical preservation and physical restoration of an abandoned African-American church. Students engage in applied research in site preservation techniques, retrieval of archived documents, research methods and documentation of cultural history, and the collection/

Course Snapshot

ART 456 (Campaigns) incorporates service learning by pairing each student with a different non-profit organization. This designer/client relationship lasts the entire semester. Students are expected to design 5-6 pieces for their clients. Clients participate in approximately 4-5 class meetings to provide feedback for students. Past clients include: Bayou Area Habitat for Humanity, Thibodaux Chamber of Commerce, BREC BMX Raceway, Bayou Country Children's Museum, Thibodaux Playhouse, Chauvin Sculpture Garden, Friends of Ellender Memorial Library, and HOPE for Animals.

Academics

Service--learning in the academic curriculum enhances student learning and curriculum integration through student engagement in our local and global communities. The combination of community service and course work engages students in real-life problem-solving activities, increases their critical thinking and reflection, and fosters their civic and personal responsibility.

Service-learning programs offer Nicholls students opportunities to make a difference throughout the world while enhancing their skills and abilities.

Some courses with service-learning components:
Art 451 Graphic Design III
Art 454 New Media Design
Biology 326 Comparative Physiology
Biology 332 Developmental Biology
Culinary Arts 279 Cajun & Creole Cuisine
Dietetics 390 Community Nutrition
English 310 Business Communications
English 467 Writing for the Web
Family and Consumer Science 431
Fine Arts 105 Arts in Education
History 371 History of Louisiana
History 421 Civil War in Louisiana
Marketing 485 Marketing Research
Marketing 450 Advertising
Music 193, Music 393 Nicholls Concert Choir
Nicholls Players Theater Productions
Nursing 385 Global Health Nursing

"Higher education today must not only provide students with a competitive academic experience, we also must ensure that students led by their own faculty will link classroom experiences with meaningful opportunities to serve. The result is an improved society and a better educated student"

~ UL System President Sally Clausen.

Check out all majors at: www.nicholls.edu/programs/

Awards and Recognition
Service-Learning
• 2006 President's Higher Education Community Service Honor Roll.
• 2007 President's Higher Education Community Service Honor Roll.
• Awarded numerous grants by the University of Louisiana System Service Learning Projects Grants.
• Nicholls student Olinda Ricard recipient of Gulf Summit 2007 Student of the Year for Service-Learning.

College Fast Facts
Four Year, Public, Rural, Founded: 1948

Web site: www.nicholls.edu

Student Profile: Undergraduate students (37.8% male, 62.2% female); 33 states and territories, 40 countries; 24.4% minority, 1.3% international.

Faculty Profile: Full-time faculty. 54.9% hold a terminal degree in their field. 19.68:1 student/faculty ratio. Average class size is 22.

Athletics: NCAA Division 1, Southland Conference. 6 varsity sports for men and 8 for women.

Costs and Aid: 2007-2008: $3,623 in state comprehensive ($2,231 tuition); $9,071 out of state comprehensive ($7,679 tuition).

Admissions
Nicholls State University, Office of Admissions
Phone: 1-877-Nicholls
www.nicholls.edu/request_info/

Service-Learning
Laynie Barrilleaux, Ph.D.
Assistant VP for Academic Affairs
Phone: (985)448-4174)
Email: laynie@nicholls.edu

Morris Coats, Ph.D.
Chair, Nicholls Service Learning Committee
Phone: (985)448-4237)
Email: morris.coats@nicholls.edu

Tulane University

The inauguration of the Center for Public Service reflects Tulane University's renewed sense of purpose within a city and region rising from devastation. Recognizing that active, civic engagement builds strong, healthy communities and responsible citizens, the Center for Public Service merges academic inquiry with sustained civic engagement. Tulane is the first Carnegie ranked Research University to implement an undergraduate public service graduation requirement and is being closely watched by the higher education community as a potential model for others to follow.

Flagship Programs

Academic Service Learning is an educational experience based upon a collaborative partnership between the university and the community. "Learning by doing" enables students to apply academic knowledge and critical thinking skills to meet genuine community needs. Through reflection and assessment, students gain deeper understanding of course content and the importance of civic engagement.

Fellows Program

The CPS Service-Learning Fellows Program allows students to work with faculty members to coordinate service learning projects, promoting active learning while modeling engaged citizenship. The Fellows program provides students with an opportunity to develop leadership, managerial, and organizational skills while working closely with faculty members and community partners.

Semester in NOLA

Focused on assisting with New Orleans rebuilding and renewal, Semester in NOLA is a 6-credit academic internship experience for students from both Tulane and other colleges. Students participate in a five-week internship with local organizations, including an interdisciplinary course focusing on the city's culture, history and environment as sources both of strength and contention. Students also explore the physical and social roots and consequences of the racial and class divisions frequently addressed in media broadcasts since the storm.

Course Snapshot

WMST 351-01: Feminist Ideas and Praxis, Women of the Storm
"Service learning has given me the opportunity to feel like I am truly contributing to the rebuilding and renewal of New Orleans. Working with Women of the Storm, I have met amazing people, who have inspired and taught me the importance of educating and enlightening not only our fellow New Orleanians, but the nation of our situation."

-Savannah Moon
School of Liberal Arts, '08, Pre-Med and Women's Studies

Academics

Programs of study with service-learning components include:

African Studies
Anthropology
Art History
Biomedical Engineering
Business
Cell and Molecular Biology
Chemistry
Communication
Dance
Ecology and Evolutionary Biology
Engineering Science
English
Environmental Biology
Environmental Science
Environmental Studies
French
Geology
History
International Development

Latin American Studies
Law
Literature
Music
Neuroscience
Philosophy
Physics
Political Economy
Political Science
Psychology
Psychology and Early Childhood Development
Public Health
Sociology
Spanish
Strategy and Entrepreneurship
Theatre
Urban Studies
Women's Studies

Check out all majors at:
www2.tulane.edu/academics_dept.cfm

Awards and Recognition

• President's Higher Education Community Service Honor Roll with Distinction, 2007

• President's Higher Education Community Service Honor Roll for Hurricane Relief Service Winner, 2006

• President's Higher Education Community Service Honor Roll for Excellence in General Community Service Finalist, 2006

• Kaplan/Newsweek's college guide named Tulane one of the nine "Hot Schools" in 2002 and 2007.

• Ranked 44th among *U.S.News & World Report's* top 50 national universities, 2006.

• The A.B. Freeman School of Business has been highly ranked by Forbes magazine (MBA program, 33rd); London's Financial Times (EMBA program, 54th; MBA, 73rd internationally and 46th nationally); *U.S.News & World Report* (MBA, 45th); America Economia (EMBA program, 32nd internationally); and Entrepreneur magazine (13th in graduate programs for entrepreneurs). In addition, London's Financial Times ranked the finance department of the A.B. Freeman School of Business sixth in the world.

College Fast Facts

Four Year, Private, City; Founded 1834

Web site: www.tulane.edu

Student Profile: 6,533 undergraduate students, 46 states and territories, 21 countries, 9:1 Student/faculty ratio.

Faculty Profile: 1,112 full-time faculty. Average class size is 22 students with 25% of classes under 10 students. 97% hold a terminal degree in their field.

Athletics: NCAA Division 1-A Conference USA, 16 varsity sports.

Costs and Aid: 2007–2008: $45,550 comprehensive ($36,610 tuition). 79% of students receive some financial aid. Average award: $25,224.

Admissions

Office of Undergraduate Admission
210 Gibson Hall
6823 St. Charles Ave
New Orleans, LA 70118
Phone: (800) 873-9283
Fax: (504) 862-8715
undergrad.admission@tulane.edu

Service-Learning

Center for Public Service
327 Gibson Hall
6823 St. Charles Ave.
New Orleans, LA 70118-5665
Phone: (504) 862-8060
Fax: (504) 862-8061
http://cps.tulane.edu

Xavier University of Louisiana

Xavier University of Louisiana is the nation's only Historically Black and Catholic institution of higher learning. Reaffirming its African American heritage and its Catholic tradition for more than eight decades, Xavier continues to offer a variety of opportunities in education and leadership development to the descendants of those historically denied the liberation of learning.

Service-Learning Focus

Xavier University of Louisiana views service-learning as an experiential educational teaching method that integrates academic course work with practical application in communities. As an educational method, service learning provides students with fertile ground on which to test theories acquired in the classroom and to concretize abstract thought.

Flagship Programs

College of Pharmacy teaching healthy living
The XU College of Pharmacy 1st year students taught lessons on nutrition and exercise to middle school students to challenge them to make healthy food choices and to maintain a regular exercise regimen. COP students learned skills and attributes necessary for competent pharmacists.

Cultural Appreciation in secondary schools
The cultural exchange program, designed to foster appreciation of African & Native American cultures, allows college students to facilitate workshops on their cultures at partnering K-12 schools. Students gain appreciation for their culture and become engrossed in the landscape, history, and customs of the visited area.

Course Snapshot

WRITING FOR PUBLIC RELATIONS and WRITING FOR PRINT MEDIA

Students organized a national campaign to bring in volunteers from HBCU's to help rebuild New Orleans during the month of March (spring break). This is framed as the "2nd freedom rides." The service-learning class distributed PSA's, and newspaper articles across the country and recruited more than 4000 volunteers to assist in rebuilding efforts in New Orleans. This program has blossomed and now recruits volunteers nationally for year round assistance in New Orleans. It also has sparked Xavier University to use a vacant residence hall to house volunteers who come to assist in rebuilding efforts.

Academics

Students receive an opportunity to achieve academically, apply their knowledge and gain knowledge from service that addresses immediate and long-term community needs.

Programs include:
Art
Business
Communications
Education
English
Math
Sociology
Political Science
Psychology
Theology
College of Pharmacy

"Service-learning makes the course objectives come alive. It helps to demonstrate through theory, practice, and interaction. What we're doing in class has real implications for what students are going to do one day do in the field"

— a Xavier University Service-Learning Faculty

Check out all majors at:
www.xula.edu

Awards and Recognition

Service-Learning
• Campus Compact's Indicators of Engagement Project – Model Institution
• President's Higher Education Community Service Honor Roll with Distinction
• President's Higher Education Community Service Honor Roll - 2006 Katrina Compassion Award for Excellence in Hurricane Relief

Academics
• According to the U.S. Department of Education, Xavier continues to rank first nationally in the number of African American students earning undergraduate degrees in both the biological/life sciences and the physical sciences.
• The American Institute of Physics (AIP) reports that Xavier is first nationally in awarding physics BS degrees to African-Americans.
• Xavier is first in the nation in placing African American students into medical schools, where it has been ranked for the past 13 years.
• The College of Pharmacy, one of only two pharmacy schools in Louisiana, is among the nation's top three producers of African American Doctor of Pharmacy degree recipients.
• *U.S.News & World Report's 2008 Best Colleges*

College Fast Facts

Four Year, Private, Urban, Founded in 1925

Web Site: www.xula.edu

Affiliation: Roman Catholic

Student Profile: 3,100 undergraduate, graduate and pharmacy (73% female); 38 states; 72% African American.

Faculty Profile: 132 full-time faculty; 15-1 student/faculty ratio.

Athletics: NAIA Division I; Men's and Women's Sports: Basketball, Cross Country and Tennis.

Costs and Aid: 2007–2008: $13,700 Arts and Sciences; $18,400 College of Pharmacy. 75% of students receive some financial aid.

Admissions
Xavier University of Louisiana
Office of Admissions
1 Drexel Drive
New Orleans, LA 70119
Phone: (504) 520-7388;
1-877-XavierU
Email: apply@xula.edu

Service-Learning
Nedra J. Alcorn
Associate Vice-President
Student Services/Dean of Students
Phone: (504) 520-7357
Email: nalcorn@xula.edu

Typhanie J. Butler
Service-Learning Site Coordinator
Phone: (504) 520-5133
Email: ttjasper@xula.edu

Unity College

Unity College is a small private college in rural Maine that provides dedicated, engaged students with a liberal arts education which emphasizes the environment and natural resources.

Service-learning at Unity College empowers students to become environmental stewards, effective leaders and responsible citizens.

Flagship Programs

Preservation of Working Landscapes

Students from the landscape horticulture, ecology, natural resource policy, forestry, and environmental science classes partner with local and regional environmental organizations to help preserve working farms, woodlands, and area wetlands by conducting field research, assessment, consulting, advocacy work, and public education.

Vibrant Community Project

This campus-community collaboration provides direct opportunities for student action research, problem-based analysis, policy assessment, and advocacy work.

" I am most proud of the fact that I researched and gathered fisheries data that will be used by Friends of Unity Wetlands. My project experience forced me to learn how to communicate with the community and to organize and evaluate data in new ways."

An example includes participation in the research and development of a local food guide that highlights local producers, makers of value-added products, farmers' markets and promotes opportunities to buy locally.

Youth Aspirations

Unity students in freshwater ecology, biology, wildlife, and chemistry classes provide laboratory science experiences for K-6 local elementary students. Environmental writing classes participate in literacy mentoring through creation of a young author's creative writing program and a school environmental newsletter.

Academics

All majors at Unity include opportunities to participate in hands-on service-learning.

Adventure Education and Leadership
Adventure Therapy
Aquaculture and Fisheries
Conservation Law Enforcement
Ecology
Environmental Analysis
Environmental Biology
Environmental Education
Environmental Humanities
Environmental Policy
Environmental Science
Environmental Writing
Forestry
Landscape Horticulture
Marine Biology
Parks, Recreation, and Ecotourism
Sustainable Design and Technology (Fall 2008)
Sustainable Food and Agriculture (Fall 2008)
Wildlife
Wildlife Biology
Wildlife Care and Education
Wildlife Conservation

America's Environmental College

College Fast Facts

Web site: www.unity.edu

Student Profile: 550 undergraduate students (1.5:1 male to female ratio) 70% of students live on campus; 30 states represented

Faculty Profile: 31 fulltime faculty; 68% hold terminal degrees; 14:1 student to faculty ratio

Distinctive Programs: Women's Environmental Leadership Program, Internship Program, Learning Resource Center

Athletics: USCAA and YSCAC, 7 intercollegiate and 10 club sports

Unique Campus Facilities: Adirondack Shelter, Computer Labs with GIS technology, Eco Cottage, Fisheries Boats, Indoor Archery Ranges, Maple Sugar Shack, Nature and Cross-Country Trails, Organic Community Garden, Woodsmen's Field

Cost and Aid: 2007-2008; $26,950 comprehensive ($18,630 tuition); 66% of students receive need-based institutional aid.

Course Snapshot

OS3132 Community Practices:

Students in this service-learning course have worked within the community to build hiking trails, monitor water quality, provide search and rescue training, develop interpretive media for wetlands education, provide youth leadership and diversity training, support an animal rehabilitation facility, and establish a community land trust.

Admissions
Unity College
Admissions Office
PO Box 532
Unity, ME 04988-0532
Toll-Free: (800) 624-1024
Phone: (207) 948-3131

Service-Learning and Community-Based Learning
Jennifer Olin
Community Service-Learning Coordinator
Phone: (207) 948-3131 ext 273
Email: jolin@unity.edu

Assumption College

Assumption College, a Catholic liberal arts and professional studies college, strives to form graduates known for critical intelligence, thoughtful citizenship, and compassionate service.

Service-Learning Focus

The CSL Program supports the mission of the college by promoting reflection, analysis and discipline-based learning embedded in a reciprocal relationship of service between the college and the community.

Flagship Programs

V.I.T.A. (Voluntary Income Tax Assistance)
Accounting students enrolled in IDS 250, Individual Tax Assistance, combine the study of low-income taxpayers with community service. In addition to studying sociological issues and researching individual tax credits, they become proficient with tax software. Each year the class works with a low-income community residential program as a community partner.

JA Academy (Junior Achievement of Central Massachusetts)
This is a program for college access and success coordinated with Junior Achievement of Central Massachusetts, employee volunteers from an insurance agency, and CSL minors. High school juniors and seniors spend two years in an after-school mentoring program that focuses on both business simulation and college preparedness.

English Major Concentration in Writing and Mass Communications
Students may take ENG 202, Introduction to Journalism, which combines academic classroom learning and experiential learning in the community. Each student arranges a service placement in a human service agency or non-profit organization.

Course Snapshot

ENG/SOC 225: Literature of Social Responsibility

The introductory course to the CSL minor is an interdisciplinary course which illuminates the social issue of shelter and homelessness from the perspective of literature and social science theory and research. One student reports:
"Doing community service put the books into reality and social responsibility has taken on a new perspective. I feel as though I am now responsible for doing things in society because I know what should be done."

Academics
The collaboration of literature and community service in action puts a revolutionary spin on learning.

Departments include:

Art, Music and Theatre
Business Studies
Economics
Education
English
Global Studies
History
Human Services and Rehabilitation Studies
Latin American Studies
Mathematics and Computer Science
Modern and Classical Languages and Cultures
Natural Sciences
Philosophy
Political Science
Psychology
Sociology and Anthropology
Theology

"CSL is an effective way to build a bridge between the theoretical and textbook knowledge that one acquires in the classroom and the real life application of those theories and practices."

– CSL Student, '06.

Check out all majors at: www. assumption.edu/acad

Awards and Recognition
Academics
• Assumption offers more than 35 areas of undergraduate study and 5 joint master's degree programs.

• Assumption is included in the top tier of *U.S.News & World Report's America's Best Colleges 2008 edition North-Universities Master's classification.*

• "Best in the Northeast" distinction in the 2008 edition of *The Princeton Review Best Northeastern Colleges.*

• Assumption is one of 247 colleges nationwide to be honored as a "Best Value" in higher education in *Barron's Best Buys in College Education.*

• Since 2001 Assumption has produced eight Fulbright scholars.

• Assumption ranks eighth nationally in NCAA Division II postgraduate scholarships.

College Fast Facts
Web site: www.assumption.edu

Affiliation: Catholic

Service-Learning Facts: 25% of students took a service-learning course last year (06-07). 38% of departments offer at least one service-learning course *Service-learning courses and credit-earning experiences are integrated into:* General education and/or core curriculum, Senior capstones or other culminating experience, Undergraduate research programs, Independent study, International study.

Student Profile: 2,125 undergraduate students (40% male, 60% female); 25 states and territories, 8 countries; 6% minority & international.

Faculty Profile: 143 full-time faculty. 91% hold a terminal degree in their field. 12:1 student/faculty ratio. Average class size is 20.

Athletics: NCAA Division II, Northeast-10 Conference.

Costs and Aid: 2007–2008: $36,977 comprehensive ($27,320 tuition). 96% of students receive financial aid. Merit Scholarships up to $20,000 per year.

Admissions
Assumption College, Office of Undergraduate Admissions
500 Salisbury Street, Worcester, MA 01609
Phone: (866) 477-7776
Email: admiss@assumption.edu

Service-Learning
Community Service Learning Program
Susan Perschbacher Melia, Ph.D., Director
Professor of Sociology
Email: smelia@assumption.edu

Babson College

At Babson, you will discover your strengths, pursue your passions, and create your own path to success.

Service-Learning Focus

Service learning infuses the community by raising the awareness and importance of civic engagement. We challenge our students to react to social injustice issues as social entrepreneurs. Service experiences are embedded in academic classes to move students through a continuum from a reflection/charity model to an analysis/social justice model.

Flagship Programs

Foundations of Management & Entrepreneurship

FME is a year-long immersion into the world of business for first-year students. Teams of students work together to develop, launch, and manage a business. The group is given $3,000 in start up money, with any profits made donated to a community service project. Since 1999, students have donated almost $250,000 and contributed over 30,000 volunteer hours to over 50 organizations.

Management Consulting Field Experience (MCFE)

The program strengthens and develops relationships with Boston area non-profit organizations by offering undergraduate students the opportunity to work with local companies as consultants. By helping a nonprofit company reach its goals, the students also give back to the community and gain valuable insight on how nonprofit organizations take on social responsibility. MCFE provides students with first-hand experience which will put them steps ahead in the competitive business world.

Course Snapshot

Ghana: Culture, Society & Entrepreneurship In a Developing Economy

Community members spend winter break in Ghana, Africa, teaching entrepreneurship and business to high school students and adult learners to boost business development opportunities in the area. Students are split into 12 teams to teach local high school students during the day and at night teach local business community members. In addition to receiving computers/laptops, textbooks and supplies provided by the Babson volunteers, the week culminates with a regional business plan competition and the three winning schools win cash prizes.

Academics

Service-learning at Babson is an educational experience that enhances classroom learning and allows students to make a difference in the world – as part of a team or individually. Some courses include:

Approaches to Human Rights
Foundations of Management and Entrepreneurship *
Joint Service-Learning Course with Stellenbosch University in South Africa*
Leadership
Management Consulting Field Experience
Ghana: Culture, Society & Entrepreneurship In a Developing Economy *
Social Entrepreneurship
Uganda: Culture, Society & Entrepreneurship In a Developing Economy *

* Courses with a required service-learning component.

Check out all majors at: www.babson.edu/academicservices

"Whether participating with Habitat or teaching business to middle school students, Babson is extremely dedicated to social responsibility." ~ Liz Allen, Class of 2008

Awards and Recognition

Service-Learning
• President's Higher Education Community Service Honor Roll (2006 & 2007).
• One of 18 institutions selected to comprise the Core Commitments Leadership Consortium by AAC&U.
• Recognized as a top producing Fulbright U.S. Student Program Institution.

Academics
• In entrepreneurship, ranked #1 by *U.S.News & World Report* for 13 straight years and #1 by Entrepreneur magazine.
• In International Business , ranked #17 by U.S. News.
• Named "Hottest College for Business" by *Newsweek/Kaplan*.
• Received A+ in teaching quality, A+ in facilities and services and A in Job Placement by *BusinessWeek*.
• Rated the #21 ROI among private colleges in BusinessWeek magazine.
• In BusinessWeek's specialty rankings, were voted #3 for Macro- and Micro-economics; #3 for Corporate Strategy; #6 for Financial Management; #7 for Marketing ; #10 for Accounting.

College Fast Facts

Four Year, Private, Suburban

Web site: www.babson.edu

Student Profile: 1799 undergraduate students (59% male, 41% female); 43 states and territories, 59 countries; 25% minority, 18% international.

Faculty Profile: 157 full-time faculty. 90% hold a terminal degree in their field. 14:1 student/faculty ratio. Average class size is 29.

Athletics: NCAA Division III, NEWMAC, ECAC and Pilgrim Conferences. 22 varsity sports.

Costs and Aid: 2007-2008: $45,782 comprehensive ($34,112 tuition). 48% of students receive some form of financial aid.

Admissions	Service-Learning
Babson College	Lisa Hellmuth Thomas
Lunder Undergraduate Admission Center	Manger
Babson Park, MA 02457-0310	Community Engagement
Phone: 781-239-5522	Volunteer Programs
800-488-3696	Phone: 781-239-5354
Email: ugradadmission@babson.edu	Email: thomasl@babson.edu
www.babson.edu/ug	

Bentley College

Bentley is a leader in business education offering a curriculum that combines deep business knowledge with the richness of a liberal arts education.

Flagship Programs

The Bentley Consumer Action Line (BCAL), a 15 year

partnership between the Massachusetts Attorney General's Office, Bentley Law Department, and BSLC, is the only consumer protection office in Massachusetts staffed by undergraduate college students. Offering students hands-on experience mediating disputes between consumers and businesses, it has recovered more $600,000 for consumers.

2+2=5: The Power of Teamwork

Created by one of the BSLC's student leaders, 2+2=5: The Power of Teamwork, encourages an understanding of and appreciation for the importance of teamwork in elementary school students by helping them develop a wide range of interpersonal skills. The 2+2=5

model has recently been replicated beyond Bentley.

Course Snapshot

INT 298 --

NGOs and Development in Ghana: Mmofra Trom Center

This course examines the role of NGOs in the context of developing countries using Ghana, and specifically the Mmofra Trom Center in Ghana, as experiential learning sites. As part of this course, Bentley students travel to Mmofra Trom, a resource center devoted to the education and care of AIDS orphans, and work on projects that will help the Center become self-sustaining by creating sources of income to increase the children's opportunities for education, healthcare, and a job to support themselves.

"Business can mean working in the accounting profession, working with financial markets and at the same time it can also mean changing lives. Bentley's partnership with Mmofra Trom has made business' ability to change lives a reality for me and has changed the course of my life."
~ Bentley student Jonathan Tetrault

Academics

Ethics and social responsibility are integral to Bentley's core mission and are woven throughout the curriculum. The service-learning program was developed to enhance that focus and to develop highly educated professionals and civically responsible individuals. Academic departments that offer service-learning in their courses are:

Accountancy	Law, Taxation and Financial Planning
Computer Information Systems	Management
Economics	Marketing
English	Mathematical Sciences
Finance	Modern Languages
History	Natural and Applied Sciences
Information Design & Corporate Communication	Philosophy
International Studies	Sociology

Check out all majors at: www.bentley.edu

"Students who aspire to lead in the private sector also need experience in addressing public problems."
~Professor Edward Zlotkowski (EXP101 & 201)

Awards and Recognition
Service-Learning
• The Corporation for National and Community Service named Bentley College to the 2007 President's Higher Education Community Service Honor Roll for exemplary service efforts and service to disadvantaged youth.
• *U.S.News & World Report* - Best Academic Programs for Service Learning.
• 2005 Random House/Princeton Review book, *Colleges with a Conscience: 81 Great Schools with Outstanding Community Involvement.*
Academics
• *U.S.News & World Report's 2008 America's Best Colleges*: Top 10 Undergraduate College: National Universities-Masters, North (#6); Top 50 Undergraduate Business Programs (#48); #15 in Management Information Systems nationally; #2 in New England.
• *BusinessWeek* ranks Bentley among the top 30 undergraduate business programs in the nation.
• Beyond Grey Pinstripes, a biennial survey and alternative ranking of business schools by the Aspen Institute, has named the Bentley McCallum Graduate School to its Global 100 list.
• Bentley entered the rankings at #55 and ranked 2nd in the Northeast in faculty research. *The Princeton Review* names Bentley one of "Best Colleges & Universities," in 2008 and one of "Best Colleges in the Northeast."

College Fast Facts
Four Year, Private, Suburban, Founded: 1917

Web site: www.bentley.edu

Student Profile: Undergraduate students (60% male, 40 % female); 42 states and territories, 71 countries; 27% minority, 7% international.

Faculty Profile: 267 full-time faculty. 84% hold a terminal degree in their field. 12:1 student/faculty ratio. Average class size is 23.88.

Athletics: NCAA Division II, Northeast-10 Conference. 21 varsity sports.

Costs and Aid: 2007-2008: $43,900 comprehensive ($31,450 tuition). 72% of students receive some financial aid.

Admissions
Office of Undergraduate Admission
Phone: (800) 523-2354
or (781) 891-2244
Email: ugadmission@bentley.edu

Service-Learning
Franklyn P. Salimbene, JD, LLM
Director
Bentley Service-Learning Center
Morison 101
Bentley College
175 Forest Street
Waltham, MA 02452-4705
Phone: (781) 891-2170
Fax: (781) 891-3410
service-learning@bentley.edu

Bristol Community College

Bristol Community College is a comprehensive, multi-campus public college serving more than 25,000 students enrolled in credit and noncredit courses.

Flagship Programs

BE ENRICHED After School Program

BCC students in Education, Math, ESL Advanced Conversation, Deaf Studies, Theatre and Psychology courses teach enrichment courses in their areas of expertise to 180 students at a local elementary school. Classes include American Sign Language, Computers, Crafts, Drawing, German, Japanese, Music, Portuguese, Statistics/Probability, and Theatre.

K-12 Computing Career Academy

Each year, 750 middle school students visit BCC to do computer programming using a 3-D graphics application to create an animated 3-D video. About 150 students from 4 high schools participate in two programming contests for which they solve problems through programming and create web sites.

Healthcare Career Day

Each spring, 100 students considering healthcare careers from 4 area high schools attend Career Day Programs at BCC. The students rotate through stations performing "hands on" lab testing activities that Medical Assisting students designed and present five times each career day.

Course Snapshot

DHG 44 Community Dental Health/ Dental Hygiene Program

Students in BCC's Dental Hygiene Program provide dental care at several area dental clinics. They treat children and adult patients with special needs, the elderly, and veterans including those returning from Iraq. In addition, the students learn how patient records are entered into the computer. In all of the above assignments, the students encounter many new experiences and they also learn about the different medications that are used with the population they are treating.

Academics

BCC's SERVE, LEARN, LEAD Program engages the intellectual and emotional life of each student through dialogue, action and reflection that nurtures a lifelong commitment to community service and leadership.

Accounting	History
Art*	Honors Program
Astronomy	Human Services*
Biology	Leisure Service Management
Chemistry	Medical Assisting*
Computer Information Systems	Nursing*
Culinary Arts	Office Administration
Dental Hygiene*	Philosophy
Deaf Studies*	Psychology
Early Childhood Education	Science
English	Sociology

* Courses with a required service-learning component

Check out all academic programs at: www.bristolcc.edu/Catalog/

"Students reported that their experience opened their eyes to challenges the elderly face and enhanced their personal growth." ~ Melane Paranzino, Professor of Nursing

Awards and Recognition

Service-Learning
• Recipient of Carnegie Classification of Community Engagement for both Curricular Engagement and Outreach & Partnerships categories.
• President's Higher Education Community Service Honor Roll for (2005-2006) and (2006-2007).

Academics
• BCC has more than 120 programs of study that lead to an associate degree in science, associate degree in arts, associate degree in applied science, or a certificate.
• 2007 Association for Career & Technical Education (ACTE), Region 1 – Innovative Vocational/Technical Program Award to Junior Apprentice Program in Massachusetts.
• 2006/2007 League for Innovation in the Community College – Innovation of the Year Award.
• 2005 ACTE--Innovative Vocational/Technical Program Award to Women In Technology.
• 2004 Women in Engineering Program (WEPAN) – Award for Women In Technology.
• 2002 Bellwether Award in Workforce Development for Women In Technology sponsored by Community College Futures.

College Fast Facts

Two Year, Public, Urban, Founded: 1965

Web site: www.bristolcc.edu

Student Profile: 9,680 undergraduate students (36.9% male, 63.1% female); 5 states and territories, 37 countries, 12% minority, 0.5% international.

Faculty Profile: 102 full-time faculty with 17 Doctorates, 81 Master's, and 4 Bachelor's degrees. 17:1 student/faculty ratio. Average class size is 18.

Costs and Aid: 2007-2008: Annual in-state tuition $3,120. Annual out-of-state tuition $8,064; 40.44% of students receive some form of financial aid.

Admissions

Bristol Community College
Office of Admissions,
Room G 128
777 Elsbree Street
Fall River, MA 02720
Phone: (508) 678-2811 ext. 2177
Email: admissions@bristolcc.edu

Service-Learning

Mary Zahm, Ph.D.
Director of Civic Engagement
Phone: (508) 678-2811 ext. 2579
Email: mary.zahm@bristolcc.edu

College of the Holy Cross

Holy Cross is renowned for its academic excellence and mentoring-based, liberal arts education in the Jesuit tradition.

Flagship Programs

Through many of our multidisciplinary concentration programs, students have direct experiences with real-life issues. These programs include Women's and Gender Studies, Environmental Studies, Africana Studies, Latin American and Latino Studies, Gerontology, Deaf Studies, and Peace and Conflict Studies, each of which integrate community-based learning into their courses of study.

Holy Cross partnerships with Latino organizations in Worcester provide learning opportunities for our undergraduates in courses on Spanish language, culture and history. Specifically, our students work with Latino children and adults at the Nativity School—a middle school for boys from Worcester—as well as the Latino Education Institute and Centró las Americas—two non-profit organizations serving Worcester's Spanish-speaking community.

Collaborative research courses are an important dimension of community-based learning at Holy Cross. These projects are designed to address local problems and issues of concern. For example, in Urban Politics, students work with the Worcester Regional Research Bureau and neighborhood residents to systematically identify and categorize neighborhood problems, as well as help the City of Worcester prioritize budget outlays for neighborhood improvement.

Course Snapshot

Worcester and Its People

In this team-taught course, faculty from history and other disciplines address the past, present and future of the city of Worcester. They consider ethnicity and race, religion, culture, work technology, the built environment, the natural environment, and politics, all in association with the various ethnic neighborhoods of the city. Students are required to participate in a community-based learning project that focuses on some dimension of Worcester's history, culture, and current economic and socio-political context.

Academics

Across the disciplines, students live out the College's commitment to service and social justice by integrating theory with practice. Community based learning invites participants to engage questions of moral, ethical, and civic responsibility.

List of academic programs with community-based learning:

Africana Studies
Biology
Classics
Deaf Studies
Economics
Education
Interdisciplinary and Special Studies
Gerontology Studies
History
Latin American & Latino Studies
Mathematics
Political Science
Psychology
Religious Studies
Sociology and Anthropology
Spanish
Women's and Gender Studies

"The Jesuit call to be "men and women for others" is not a casual idea at Holy Cross. It is a continuing commitment made by students, faculty and staff alike."

– Rev. Michael C. McFarland, S.J., President

Check out all majors at: www.holycross.edu/academics/

Awards and Recognition

• 2006 President's Higher Education Community Service Honor Roll

• In the top 3% of four-year colleges in the number of students going on to earn doctorates.

• Graduates admitted to medical school at rates better than twice the national average.

• Among the nation's 50 most competitive colleges and universities as ranked by *Barron's Profiles in American Colleges.*

• Highest rank of the 28 U.S. Jesuit colleges and universities in the percentage of graduates who go on to serve in the Jesuit Volunteer Corps.

• Among top 10 undergraduate schools nationwide in the number of American Chemical Society-certified chemistry majors.

College Fast Facts

Four Year, Private, Founded: 1843

Web site: www.holycross.edu

Affiliation: Catholic

Student Profile: 2790 undergraduate students (45% male, 55% female); 46 states and territories, 13 countries; 15% minority, 62% out of state.

Faculty Profile: 239 full-time faculty. 95% hold a terminal degree in their field. 1:11 student/faculty ratio.

Athletics: NCAA Division I. 27 varsity sports. Member of the Patriot League.

Costs and Aid: 2007-2008: $42,893 comprehensive ($32,820 tuition); 59% of students receive some financial aid.

Admissions

Admissions Office
Fenwick Hall, Room 105
One College Street
Worcester, Massachusetts 01610
Phone: (800) 442-2421; (508) 793-2443
Email: admissions@holycross.edu

Service Learning

Donelan Office of Community-based Learning
Margaret A. Post
Smith Hall, Room 332
Phone: (508) 793-3009
Email: mapost@holycross.edu

Emmanuel College

Emmanuel College is a coed, residential, Catholic liberal arts and sciences college located on 17 acres in the middle of the excitement, resources and culture of the city of Boston.

Course Snapshots

Chemistry of Boston Waterways

The course will provide opportunities for students to conduct environmental research projects on the water, soil and air quality of historical Fenway, as well as fully evaluate the impact of people on the environment. The results will be reported to local environmental organizations with suggestions for the most effective means of reducing pollutants. The students will also have the option of presenting this information on the state of the environment to local schools and communities. Students will complete about 30 hours of service work in the areas of environmental conservation, activism, or education. As a wrap up to the course, they will participate in annual Muddy River clean up event honoring Earth Day.

Spanish at Work in the Community

This is an upper-level language course that will promote linguistic fluency and better cultural understanding of the Spanish-American and Latino communities in the United States. Course's content will focus on Hispanic immigration, emphasizing the experiences of Spanish-speaking communities in the United States. Students are required to provide three weekly hours of service to Hispanic non-profit organizations with the Boston area, where they will use their language skills while assisting Spanish-speakers.

Catholic Social Teaching

This course will provide an introduction to over 100 years of Catholic social teaching, using Papal documents and documents from the U.S. Catholic Conference of Bishops primarily. Analysis of the documents and critiques of the teachings will also be used. The course will introduce students to the broad concept of social teaching as it exists in many religious traditions and will be focused on the particular teachings of the Catholic tradition. Each of the documents will be grounded in its sociological, political, economic and religious context. Students will do monthly service at various non-profit agencies such as St. Francis House, Rosie's Place and Haley House.

Academics

Service learning builds bridges between commitment and action. Emmanuel students are encouraged to articulate their social consciousness.

Art
Biology
Chemistry
Education
Global Studies
Management and Economics
Political Science
Psychology
Religious Studies
Sociology

Check out all majors at:
www.emmanuel.edu/academics

"Students thoroughly enjoy applying classroom concepts to the real world while giving back to the community!"

-Dr. Patricia Rissmeyer, Vice President of Student Affairs

Awards and Recognition

• Emmanuel offers opportunities in the pursuit of learning, teaching, exploration, and research in more than 25 areas of study.

• Emmanuel College's unique location allows student and faculty the opportunities to explore real world experiences through internships, research and strategic partnerships within the Longwood Medical area and the city of Boston, our extended classroom

•The National Academic Advising Association honored Emmanuel's Academic Advising Program (AAP) with an award in 2006. Emmanuel's AAP functions as integral part of the academic affairs of the College and has established strong links with offices throughout the institution.

College Fast Facts

Four Year, Private Urban, Founded: 1919

Affiliation: Catholic

Web site: www.emmanuel.edu

Student Profile: 1,750 undergraduate students (30% male, 70% female); 32 states and territories, 24 countries; 14% minority, 3% international.

Faculty Profile: 86 full-time faculty; 79% hold a terminal degree in their field. 15:1 student/faculty ratio. Average class size is 20.

Athletics: NCAA Division III, GNAC Conference. 14 varsity sports. Emmanuel's NCAA Division III athletics program gives every recruit a chance to make his or her mark.

Costs and Aid: 2008-2009: $40,000 comprehensive ($28,200 tuition).

Admissions

Emmanuel College
Office of Admissions
400 The Fenway
Boston, MA 02115-9911
Phone: (617) 735-9715
Fax: (617) 735-9801
Email: enroll@emmanuel.edu

Service-Learning

Deirdre Bradley-Turner
Associate Director of Community Service and Service Learning
Emmanuel College
400 The Fenway
Boston, MA 02115
Phone: 617-735-9753

Pine Manor College

Pine Manor College educates women for inclusive leadership and social responsibility in their workplaces, families and communities, celebrating diversity and respecting the common good.

Flagship Program

Inclusive Leadership and Social Responsibility (ilsr) Certificate Program

The ilsr Certificate Program combines a number of meaningful curricular and co-curricular experiences, including service-learning, which reflect the Mission of the College and enhance participants' understanding of and connection to inclusive leadership and social responsibility through engaged learning and mentoring.

Course Snapshots

AH (Art History) 235: Latin American Art

In this course, Pine Manor College students educated students in a high school studio art class about murals, by researching and preparing a series of oral presentations on twentieth-century Mexican mural art for the high school students, who were in the process of designing their own mural at their high school.

SPS (Social and Political Systems) 381: Methods of Social Research

This course had a tripartite role and worked on three premises: learning by doing, building social skills, and providing mutual support for community organizations (Brookline, MA, Police Department Domestic Violence Unit and Museum of African American History). Apart from the core learning objectives of research, e.g. formulating questions, analyzing evidence and creating action plans, students gained collaborative problem-solving skills not typical of a college classroom. These skills included sharing, trust, accountability, honesty, patience, and communication.

IDS 250(Interdisciplinary): Inclusive Leadership and Social Responsibility (ilsr)—Community Applications

In IDS 250, students work the entire semester in small groups with a community partner to define, plan and implement projects that meet an identified need of the community. Students in this class have worked with middle and high schools, an English as a Second Language program, a domestic violence assistance program, and a

college scholarship fund for low-income students. Students apply the concepts of ilsr as they work collaboratively with their community partner and with their group members.

Academics

Service-learning is an extremely effective way to educate women for inclusive leadership and social responsibility. Guided by the pursuit of the common good, Pine Manor is about innovative, relationship-based learning and embraces the idea that truly impactful learning experiences often happen outside of the lecture hall, while engaged with a community partner.

Service-learning courses give students the opportunity to present their research and learning in a real-life context with a community partner.

Some programs of study with service-learning components are:

Art History
Biology
Dance
Education
English
First-Year Seminars
Psychology
Social and Political Systems

View information about our full academic offerings at: www.pmc.edu/academics/index.htm.

"Effective education involves teaching and learning outside of the classroom within local and global communities."

-Pine Manor College

Awards and Recognition

• Selected as a host institution for a 2008-2009 AmeriCorps*VISTA by the Massachusetts Campus Compact, to support service-learning initiatives.

• For the past five years *U.S.News & World Report* has ranked Pine Manor at or near the top of the list of the most diverse private colleges in the country.

• Pine Manor was highlighted in the June 2005 issue of Black Issues in Higher Education for achieving such tremendous diversity at a private college.

College Fast Facts

Four Year, Private, Suburban; Founded 1911

Web site: www.pmc.edu

Student Profile: 500 undergraduate students (100% female); 28 states and territories, 31 countries; 62% minority, 7% international.

Faculty Profile: 29 full-time faculty. 75% hold a terminal degree in their field. 10:1 student/faculty ratio. Average class size is 14.

Athletics: NCAA Division III, GNAC Conference. 7 varsity sports.

Costs and Aid: 2007–2008: $30,072 comprehensive ($18,957 tuition). 91% of students receive some financial aid.

Admissions
Office of Admissions
400 Heath Street
Chestnut Hill, MA 02467
Phone: (800) PMC-1357
www.pmc.edu

Service-Learning
Center for Inclusive Leadership and Social Responsibility
Whitney Retallic, Director
Email: retalliw@pmc.edu or inclusive@pmc.edu
Phone: (617) 731-7620

Simmons College

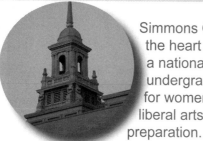

Simmons College, located in the heart of Boston, offers a nationally distinguished undergraduate program for women that combines liberal arts with career preparation.

Guide to Service-Learning Colleges & Universities

Building upon a long tradition of service to Boston, the college, through the Scott/Ross Center for Community Service, works closely with over forty community partners and offers a wide range of service learning and co-curricular opportunities that emphasize direct service, advocacy and social justice.

Flagship Programs

Farragut Elementary School Partnership

Over 100 Simmons students volunteer in seven programs at the Farragut Elementary, an underserved Boston public school. Programs take place from early morning until evening and include afternoon and morning programs, America Reads/Counts and assistance in the school library.

Social Justice Minor

This interdisciplinary minor provides an integration of academic study and community based learning in which students gain theoretical, historical, and practical backgrounds that assist them in advancing progressive social change. The community based courses provide opportunities for advocacy and social justice work.

Student Service Learning Assistants (SSLAs)

Our SSLA program is a unique undergraduate leadership opportunity. This program trains students to work as colleagues with professors in a specific service learning course, assisting students with site placement, designing questions, commenting on reflection journals, and leading class discussions. Students have presented our model at two national conferences.

Course Snapshot

Sociology 267: Globalization

In this course, the professor and her students partner with English language learners who have immigrated to the US. Through regular meetings, Simmons students and their partners meet to practice English conversation and share the immigration stories that add a personal/micro-level picture to the macro-level issues they examine. As highlighted in the Boston Globe, in addition to students learning about specific countries and moments in history from their partners, one student also said, "I learned not to assume that people are ordinary."

Academics

Over 600 undergraduates participate in service-learning each year in approximately 35 classes, representing a range of topics in 12 different departments.

Participating Departments:

Biology, Communications, Economics, Education,* Honors Program,* Interdisciplinary Studies, Multidisciplinary Core Course, Management,* Philosophy, Psychology, Social Justice,* and Sociology
* Departments with a required service-learning component.

Some participating courses are:

BIOL-109: Biology of Women
COMM-124: Media, Messages & Society
COMM-181: Public Speaking - & Group Discussion
COMM-390: Studio 5
ECON-100: Principles of Microeconomics
ECON-101: Principles of Macroeconomics
IDS 228: Service Learning in Nicaragua
MCC: Achievement or Opportunity Gap
MCC: Equal Education: A Reality?
MCC: Food, Glorious Food
MCC: My Space, Your Space
MGMT-100: Introduction to Management
MGMT-224: Socially-Minded Leadership
PHIL-139: Environmental Ethics
SJ-220: Working for Social Justice
SJ-222: Organizing for Social Change
SOCI-263: Sociology of Education
SOCI-266: Sociology of Sports

Check out all majors at: www.simmons.edu

"[Boston] is a city full of interesting people…. Instead of reading about immigration in a book, why not leave the confines of the school and talk to people who have migrated here? I wanted my students to understand that globalization was more than numbers and economic indicators."
~ Assistant Professor of Sociology Anna Sandoval

Awards and Recognition
Service-Learning
- Alumnae Association Centennial Grant 2006-2007.
- AmeriCorps Student Leaders In Service 2005-2007.
- Clowes Fund Grant 2006-2009.
- Jumpstart Site Affiliate Grant 2004-2008.
- Massachusetts Campus Compact AmeriCorps*VISTA Grant 2002-2008.
- Massachusetts Campus Compact/Rhode Island Campus Compact Curriculum Innovation Fellowship 2006-2007.
- Massachusetts Campus Compact Student College Access Fellowship 2007.
- President's Higher Education Community Service Honor Roll with Distinction, 2006-2007.
- Pottruck Family Foundation Summer Internship.
- Teacher Education Initiative 2005-2007.

Academics
- U.S.News & World Report: America's Best Colleges, 2008.
- Princeton Review: Best 366 Colleges, 2008.
- Highlighted in the 2008 Kaplan college guidebook as on of "25 cutting-edge schools with an eye toward the future."

College Fast Facts
Four Year, Private, Urban, Founded in 1899

Web site: www.simmons.edu

Student Profile: 2,072 undergraduate students (100% female); 40 states and territories, 39 countries (optional); 23% minority, 6% international

Faculty Profile: 236 full-time faculty. 12:1 student/faculty ratio.

Costs and Aid: 2007-2008: $38,606 comprehensive ($27,468 tuition). 80% of students receive financial aid

Admissions
Undergraduate Admissions
300 The Fenway
Simmons College
Boston MA 02115
Phone: (617) 521-2051
Fax: 617-521-3190
Email: ugadm@simmons.edu

Service-Learning
Scott/Ross Center for Community Service
Dr. Stephen London
Director
Phone: (617) 521-2590
Email: stephen.london@simmons.edu
www.simmons.edu/communityservice

Stonehill College

Stonehill is a selective Catholic college where many minds gather for one purpose-to educate students for lives that make a difference.

Service-Learning Focus

Integrated into the academic experience, Stonehill's community-based learning enhances the educational experience of our students. Stonehill's mission is to educate the whole person so that each graduate thinks, acts, and leads with courage toward creating a more just and compassionate world.

Flagship Programs

Through the Looking Glass Students challenge prevailing societal views of the disadvantaged in this Learning Community. Integrating the disciplines of sociology and computer science, students research and debate social policy. Community service enables students to see the relevance of the course content and make connections between public policy and personal lives.

Children as Urban Ecologists Exploring tidal pools on Cape Cod, inner city children use scientific observation and reasoning skills to understand the environment. Guided by Stonehill students enrolled in a Learning Community that links education and science, children in grades pre-K through 3 learn by doing, creating learning that lasts.

Course Snapshot

Photography/Multimedia Outreach: Mentoring Through Art

This program is an exciting collaboration involving Stonehill, the Plymouth County District Attorney's Office, the Brockton Police Department and a local elementary school. Serving as mentors, Stonehill students collaborate with their mentees through photography and visual arts. The program helps children overcome their negative environmental influences by providing them with positive role models. In existence since 1998, the program is directed toward fourth, fifth, and sixth grade high-risk children. More than 200 children have been mentored by 215 Stonehill students.

Academics

Community-based learning forces students out of their comfort zones to confront difference, "otherness." It's where true learning takes place. Programs of study include:

Business Administration
Communication
Computer Science
Criminology
Fine Arts
Education Studies
Environmental Studies
Health Care Administration
Psychology
Religious Studies
Sociology

"Community-based learning is like a four-legged stool, with benefits for students, community partners, faculty, and the institution."

–*Associate Vice President for Academic Affairs, Joseph Favazza*

Check out all majors at: www.stonehill.edu

Awards and Recognition
Service-Learning

• The 2007 President's Higher Education Community Service Honor Roll; finalist with Distinction for exemplary service efforts and service to disadvantaged youth.

• The 2006 President's Higher Education Community Service Honor Roll; finalist in general community service category; distinction for Hurricane Relief Services.

Academics

• Stonehill was named the 2007 Private College of the Year by The Washington Center for Internships and Academic Seminars.

• *U.S. News & World Report* ranked Stonehill number one for six consecutive years in the Best Comprehensive Colleges – Bachelor's (North) (2001–2006).

• The 2006 edition of *The Best Northeastern Colleges*, published by *The Princeton Review*, includes Stonehill in its list of select schools.

• *The Colleges of Distinction* guide has identified Stonehill as one of the "best bets" in American higher education.

• Stonehill ranks No. 4 on a list of top academic/athletic colleges in NCAA Division II, according to the latest National Collegiate Scouting Association's Power Rankings.

• According to NSSE, National Survey of Student Engagement, 2005 results, Stonehill ranks among the top 10% of all NSSE institutions on the enriching educational experiences benchmark.

College Fast Facts
Four Year, Private Suburban, Year Founded: 1948

Web site: www.stonehill.edu

Student Profile: 2,440 undergraduate students, (40% male, 60% female).

Faculty Profile: 145 full-time faculty; 13:1 student/faculty ratio; Average class size: 19.8; 81% faculty hold a terminal degree in their field.

Athletics: NCAA Division II, Northeast -10 Conference; 20 varsity sports.

Cost and Aid: As of 2007-2008: $28,440 (tuition); $11,430 (room and board); no comprehensive fees. 87.5% of students receive some financial aid.

Admissions

320 Washington Street
Easton, MA 02357
Phone: 508-565-1373
Fax: 508-565-1545
Email: admissions@stonehill.edu

Service-Learning

Office of Community Service & Volunteerism
Nuala Boyle
320 Washington Street
Easton, MA 02357
Phone: (508) 565-1067
Email: nboyle@stonehill.edu

Suffolk University

Suffolk University is a private, comprehensive, urban university. It's mission is to provide quality education at a reasonable cost for students of all ages and backgrounds with strong emphasis on diversity.

Flagship Programs

CJN 315 Media Writing: Service
Learning is incorporated into this class by asking students to write a five-minute script for a video that can be used to solve a communication problem that a non-profit organization currently faces. The script written in CJN 315 is later produced by a Media Production class and given to the non- profit.

JUMPSTART brings at-risk preschool children together with caring adults in one-to-one relationships that focus on language and literacy development along with social and emotional readiness. Jumpstart Boston at Suffolk University has taken part in innovative pilot programs including the "School Readiness for All" initiative in Roxbury. This initiative is a collaborative partnership between Suffolk and two other leading higher education institutions in Boston with strong civic engagement missions (Northeastern University and Wheelock College) and Jumpstart. The efforts of this initiative are specifically focused on the community of Roxbury in Boston, a community rich with culture, diversity and history, and yet one in which 1,649 children live in households below the federal poverty level.

S.O.U.L.S. Community Service and Service-Learning Center
The Center engages Suffolk University students, faculty, staff and alumni in a variety of meaningful service opportunities designed to strengthen communities and improve the quality of life for individuals. Service opportunities are developed that:enhance classroom learning through practical experience in community, offer participants a greater understanding of social justice and support their advocacy for social change, help participants establish an ethic of service, a sense of personal growth, and opportunities for leadership development, and express and promote the value and acceptance of diversity in our communities.

Course Snapshot

SF-202-B Media Literacy: A freshmen seminar course, explores the cultural and social functions of the media with an emphasis on learning how to critically evaluate media content. The service component of this course is 10 hours of required service at local non-profits to introduce students to unprivileged populations in Boston. Students will reflect upon their experience through a short, 5 minute documentary video that explores their understanding social issues and civic responsibility.

Academics
Through service-learning courses, classroom learning is enhanced through practical experience in the community, and students are offered a greater understanding of social justice to support their advocacy for social change.

Programs of study include:

Business
Communications
Education and Human Services
Philosophy
Psychology
Sociology
Spanish
Chemistry
Physics
Government
Environmental Science

"Service-learning work develops a passion for learning that is deeper and more profound than any other way I have seen during my 15 years of teaching. It is easy to teach course material didactically when students are yearning to learn more about the topic because they want to use the ideas immediately or they want to test the ideas out in the real world."

– Dr. Debra Harkins, Associate Professor of Psychology

Check out all majors at: www.suffolk.edu/academics/index.html

Awards and Recognition
• Suffolk rated among the best by Princeton Review for third year in a row.
• *U.S.News & World Report* ranks Suffolk in top tier of "Best Universities—Masters" in the North for 2007.
• Suffolk Among Top 100 Campuses for LGBT Students.
• Suffolk University Cited Among Best 361 Colleges.
• Suffolk chosen by *The Princeton Review* as one of the "Top 25 Most Connected Campuses."
• *U.S.News & World Report* 2005 rankings list Suffolk among first tier of "Best Universities-Master's" in the North.
• 2005 Massachusetts Professor of the Year.
• Suffolk recognized by NAFSA for achieving high level of internationalization.
• *The Princeton Review* has selected Suffolk as one of the "Best Northeastern Colleges."
• Suffolk praised in Barron's Best Buys in College Education.
• Suffolk included among "The Best 201 Colleges for the Real World."

College Fast Facts
Four-Year, Private, Urban, Founded: 1906

Web site: www.suffolk.edu

Student Profile: 5,196 undergraduate; 2,016 graduate; 1,546 degrees conferred annually; 948 international students from 95 countries.

Faculty Profile: 91% hold Ph.D. degrees; 1:12 Faculty/student ratio (undergraduate); 1:21 Faculty/student ratio (law school).

Athletics: Division 3, GNAC Conference.

Costs and Aid: 2007-2008; $24,170 (undergraduate) $35,948 (law school); $54,673,740 Financial Aid avalaible for the College of Arts & Sciences and Sawyer Business School (awarded to 50% of students); $50,020,842 Financial Aid for Suffolk Law School (awarded to 88% of students).

Admissions
73 Tremont St, 6th Floor
Boston, MA 02108
Phone: (617) 573-8460 or 1-800-6SUFFOL(k)
Email: admission@suffolk.edu

Service-Learning
Carolina Garcia
Director of Service Learning
Phone: (617) 305-6306
Email: Cgarcia@suffolk.edu

Tufts University

Tufts offers a premier liberal arts college within a leading research university. Undergraduate Schools of Arts and Sciences and of Engineering educate students for transformational leadership in communities around the world.

Flagship Programs

Jonathan M. Tisch College of Citizenship & Public Service

Tisch College is unique because it gives students across all disciplines and schools at Tufts opportunities to develop their potential to contribute to the greater world. Many universities have created separate schools or programs that focus public service toward a narrow group of students. In contrast, Tisch College breaks through barriers among schools and infuses active citizenship throughout the entire University.

Citizenship and Public Service Scholars Program

"Scholars encourage community building, forge relationships with our host communities based on service, educate others on the importance of active citizenship, and incorporate public service into our lifestyle" (Scholar Program Mission Statement). They take a foundation course – Education for Active Citizenship – and become part of the Scholar community, undertaking progressively more complex social change initiatives, with advice and support from Tisch College staff, advisors and community partners.

Media and Public Service (MPS) provides students the media tools and resources that will prepare them for lifetimes of active citizenship. The Program blends the capabilities of a university-wide civic education initiative and a robust undergraduate media studies program. MPS reaches across the campus bringing Tufts faculty and students together with community members and activists.

Course Snapshot

ANW 153 – Ghana Gold: A Corporate Social Responsibility Tour

Led by Political Science Associate Professor Pearl Robinson, a group of students and one alumnus, spent two weeks traveling around Ghana in a mini-bus, meeting with artists, educators, government officials and leaders from Ghana's gold industry. The trip provided an inside and inter-disciplinary look at the economic and social impact of gold—a major Ghanaian export. The trip was followed by an academic colloquium, to wrap the experience in theory and study.

Academics

Students can get started in education for active citizenship right away by enrolling in one of the more than one hundred Tisch courses designated as part of the Education for Active Citizenship curriculum and offered by virtually every school and department at Tufts. Tufts' focus on the outcome – building civic skills and habits among all its students – means that our designation of active citizenship embraces every department – and is not restricted to courses or programs that require community engagement. Opportunities appear in many areas:

Civil and Environmental Engineering
American Studies
Community Health
Drama / Dance
Active Citizenship in an Urban Community
Biological Anthropology
Community Health Internship Seminar
Education for Active Citizenship
Experiments in Ecology
Global Cities
Internships in Social Change - Organizations

Introduction to Hazardous Materials - Management
Occupational & Environmental Health Seminar in Environmental - Preservation and Improvement
Social Change & Community - Organizing
Tourism & Social Justice
Tropical Ecology/Conservation
Urban Borderlands
Wealth, Poverty & Inequality

Check out all majors at: www.tufts.edu/home/admissions

Awards and Recognition

Community Engagement
• Carnegie Elective Classification for both Curricular Engagement and Outreach & Partnerships
• Co-Convener of the Research Universities and Civic Engagement Network
• Founding member, Campus Compact; Host, Massachusetts Campus Compact

Academics
• Tufts offers undergraduate and graduate programs in the schools of Arts & Sciences, Engineering as well as graduate and professional programs at schools of Law & Diplomacy, Medicine, Dental Medicine, Nutrition and Veterinary Medicine. Also offers dual degree programs with the New England Conservatory and the School of the Museum of fine Arts.
• Top 30 of *U.S.News & World Report's 2008 America's Best Colleges.*
• *The Princeton Review* included Tufts in Colleges with a Conscience and Best Colleges in the Northeast.

College Fast Facts

Four Year, Private, Suburban, Founded: 1852

Web site: www.tufts.edu

Student Profile: 4,997 undergraduate students (49% male, 51% female); 53 states and territories, 67 countries; 45% minority, 6.0% international.

Faculty Profile: 411 full-time faculty (229 part-time).100% hold a terminal degree in their field.

Athletics: NCAA Division III, NESCAC Conference. 31 varsity sports.

Costs and Aid: 2008-2009: $51,400 comprehensive ($38,840 tuition). 48% received some kind of financial aid.

Service-Learning/Civic Engagement

Jonathan M. Tisch College of Citizenship & Public Service
Lincoln Filene Hall
Tufts University
Medford, MA 02155

Nancy E. Wilson
Director & Associate Dean
Phone: (617) 627-3453
Email: Nancy.wilson@tufts.edu

University of Massachusetts Lowell

UMass Lowell is a comprehensive University committed to educating students for lifelong success in a diverse world, while conducting research and sustainable outreach activities.

Flagship Programs

SLICE (Service-Learning Integrated throughout a College of Engineering)

Every semester students have service-learning projects in core required courses in five engineering undergraduate degree programs. Over 35 faculty members in over 40 courses engage 700 students each year, serving local and international communities, with a blend of required and elective service-learning projects.

Village Empowerment Project

Twice annually since 1998 students travel to remote Andean villages in Peru to install student-designed projects as part of over 20 courses, with and for the villagers, providing telecommunication, light, water... Participants' majors include Engineering, Nursing, Physical Therapy, English, History, and more!

Assistive Technology Program

Through required senior capstone design projects, and lower level coursework, students interact directly with clients to propose, design, construct and deliver devices to improve the functional capabilities or lifestyles of individuals with disabilities. The vast number and range of community partners include Helping Hands – Monkey Helpers.

Course Snapshot

10.304 Heat Transfer

Fundamental principles of heat transmission by conduction, convection, radiation, and mass transfer are applied in an energy conservation service-learning project. For example, the Merrimack Valley Food Bank occupies a warehouse in a historic Lowell building. Three student groups analyzed heat losses in the wintertime and heat gains in the summertime, applied course concepts and equations, proposed and presented three options in alterations to the warehouse, requiring a minimum amount of capital investment, in order to reduce energy consumption.

Academics

At UML service-learning is a hands-on approach in which students achieve academic objectives in a credit-bearing course by meeting real community needs.

"Your projects have saved many lives." ~ *doctor in Peru*

Art	Gender Studies
Biomedical Engineering and Biotechnology	History
Business Administration	Mathematical Sciences
Chemical Engineering (BS*)	Mechanical Engineering (BS*)
Civil Engineering (BS*)	Medical Technology *
Clinical Science	Music
Community Health Education *	Nursing *
Computer Engineering (BS*)	Nutrition *
Computer Science	Philosophy
Education (M.Ed.) *	Plastics Engineering (BS*)
Electrical Engineering (BS*)	Political Science
Energy Engineering (Solar option*)	Psychology
English	Regional Economic &
Environmental, Earth and Atmospheric Sciences	Social Development
Exercise Physiology (Physical Therapy *)	Sociology

* Courses with a required service-learning component.

UML Colleges & Departments:
www.uml.edu/collegesdept/collegesdeptinterimpage.html

Awards and Recognition

National Rankings
- Carnegie Foundation: Doctoral Research University - Intensive.
- American Association of University Professors: Category I.
- *Princeton Review*: Best Northeastern Colleges.
- U.S. HUD selection for "Best Practices" in Community Outreach Partnerships.

Service-Learning
- Major grant from NSF for SLICE (Service-Learning Integrated throughout a College of Engineering).
- The Carter Partnership award for Campus-Community Collaboration – finalist 2007 in MA - Village Empowerment Program.
- Boston Celtics Heroes Among Us Award 2007 – Village Empowerment

College Fast Facts

Four Year, Public, Urban, Founded: 1890's

Web site: www.uml.edu

Student Profile: 8,879 undergraduate students - 6,063 FTEs - (59.8 % male, 40.2 % female); 7.5% out of state, 19% minority, 1% international.

2,756 graduate students - 1,660 FTEs - (52.5% male, 47.5% female); 32.6% out of state, 11.9 % minority,15.3 % international.

Faculty Profile: 684 faculty. 94% hold a terminal degree in their field. 14:1 student/faculty ratio. 56% Classes with fewer than 20 students; 4% Classes with 50 or more students.

Athletics: NCAA Division II program with NCAA Division I ice hockey, 16 varsity sports, in Hockey East and the Northeast 10 Athletic Conference.

Costs and Aid: 2007–2008: $15,709 in-state comprehensive ($8,731 tuition & fees); $27,362 out-of-state comprehensive ($20,384 tuition & fees). 73% of students receive some form of financial aid. UML awarded more than $50 million in aid.

Admissions

UML Undergraduate Admissions
883 Broadway Street, Suite 110
Lowell, MA 01854-3931
Phone: 978-934-3931

Service-Learning

Linda Barrington
Engineering S-L Coordinator
One University Avenue
Lowell, MA 01854
978-934-2627
Linda_Barrington@uml.edu

Paul Marion, Executive Director
Office of Outreach
UMass Lowell
978-934-3107
paul_marion@uml.edu

Wentworth Institute of Technology

Wentworth Institute of Technology is a leader in providing career-focused education in engineering, technology and design. Our education model combines classroom work, hands-on practice in state-of-the-art labs and studios, and professional experience gained through our co-op programs.

Flagship Programs

Certificate for Community Learning

This program provides students with resources and support to set a path for engaging in service learning throughout their college career. Completed with a optional senior capstone project, participating students graduate with distinction and the skills to engage their profession and society.

Digital Divide Initiative

Students from computer science, networking, engineering and management work together through classes, work study, and co-op as a consulting team. This team works to develop innovative technology solutions for a wide range of not-for-profit organizations and public agencies.

Community Cooperative Education

At Wentworth, all students work in a cooperative education position for at least two semesters in a firm or agency associated with their field of study. Included in this program are opportunities to work for not-for-profit and social-enterprise organizations. These positions provide an unparalleled level of responsibility and opportunity for hands-on learning while making a difference.

Course Snapshot

Housing & Community Design Studio

This studio for upperclassman provides architecture students the opportunity to collaborate with community-based organizations on design and development initiatives/projects that maintain a community focus. Students meet with clients and partners and present at public meetings that are attended by local officials and community and business leaders. Students gain a keen understanding of how fresh ideas and theory meet the complex processes required to take a design from concept to reality. Students develop and apply their professional visions while contributing to real world concerns.

Academics

Through service-learning courses Wentworth students apply theoretical and practical knowledge to community-identified issues such as the Digital Divide, Sustainable Design, and Social Entrepreneurship. Unique to Wentworth, BOTH faculty and students are supported in initiating and executing service learning ideas inside and outside of the classroom.

Classroom and out-of-the-classroom service-learning opportunities are available in every academic department at Wentworth.

Departments:
Applied Mathematics and Sciences
Architecture
Civil, Construction and Environment
Computer Science and Systems
Design and Facilities
Electronics and Mechanical
Humanities, Social Sciences, and Management

Information on all majors at Wentworth can be found at:
www.wit.edu/prospective/academics/overview.html

"With service-learning I have gained professional confidence to work with clients, but also to understand how design affects the community." ~ Jennifer Fruscillo, Interior Design Class of 2008

Awards and Recognition

• President's Higher Education Community Service Honor Roll with Distinction 2007.

• President's Higher Education Community Service Honor Roll 2006.

• Jimmy & Rosyln Carter Campus-Community Partnership Award Finalist 2005.

• *Princeton Review*: Best Northeastern College.

• Students are recognized in many competitions across all academic disciplines.

College Fast Facts

Four Year, Private, Urban, Founded: 1904

Web site: www.wit.edu

Student Profile: 3,412 undergraduate students (80% male, 20% female); 37 states and territories, 50 countries; 15% minority, 5% international.

Faculty Profile: 15:1 student/faculty ratio.

Athletics: NCAA Division III, CCC, ECAC. 15 varsity sports. 15 varsity teams, variety of sports clubs & co-ed intramural program

Cost and Aid: 2007-2008 academic year: tuition, $20,150; typical room and board, $9,650. More than 75 percent of Wentworth students receive financial aid.

Admissions

Admissions Office
Wentworth Institute of Technology
550 Huntington Avenue
Boston, Massachusetts 02115-5998
Phone: (800) 556-0610 or (617) 989-4000
Fax: (617) 989.4010
Email: admissions@wit.edu
www.wit.edu

Service-Learning

Center for Community & Learning Partnerships
Sean P. Bender
Director
Phone: (617) 989-4992
Email: benders@wit.edu

Central Michigan University

CMU is a nationally distinguished institution of higher education offering more than 200 academic programs at the bachelor's, masters, specialists, and doctoral levels.

Flagship Programs

Michigan Service Scholars Student Teaching Program

CMU student teachers do a service-learning project with their class as part of the student teaching requirement. The project started as a pilot program in 1993 with about 18 students. Now approximately 40% of CMU student teachers carry out service-learning projects within their host schools in communities all around the state. The directly affects thousands of students, educators, and community members each semester.

Alternative Breaks

The Alternative Breaks program provides students the opportunity to participate in a week-long service project experience. Students can participate in projects relating to hunger, homelessness, animal endangerment, urban renewal, terminally ill, sexual abuse, elderly, and many more. Participants are educated on their issue, given the opportunity to serve and reflect on their service, and are encouraged to continue working toward social change.

Course Snapshot

RPL 552: Environmental Interpretation

Students work in groups with a community organization to develop self-guided interpretative trails for nature areas. All of the projects are based on the goals of the agency. Each agency gets a photo-copy ready final brochure that goes with the interpretative trail that they can then copy and use. The agency is invited to the final presentation in the class.

Academics

As part of CMU's 2010 Vision the campus has reasserted its priority to serve the public good by merging theory and practice.

Anthropology
Business Information Systems
Communications & Dramatic Arts
Communication Disorders
Human Environmental Studies
Mathematics
Recreation, Parks
and Leisure Services Administration
Social Work
Sociology

"Service projects provide students with a real-world authentic learning experience that allows them to practically apply the theory and concepts we've worked on in the classroom."

~ Professor Lynn Dominguez (RPL 552 Environmental Interpretation)

Check out all majors at:
www.cmich.edu/directories/academic-deans.asp

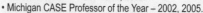

Awards and Recognition

Service-Learning
- President's Honor Roll – 2006, 2007.
- Michigan CASE Professor of the Year – 2002, 2005.
- One of 9 universities nationwide to receive the Katrina Compassion Award for Excellence in Hurricane Relief Service.
- Central Michigan University has the second largest Special Olympics program in the nation.
- CMU's Alternative Breaks program was named the recipient of the national Break Away Program of the Year award. This is the first such award given by the organization since 1998.

Academics
- Performs in the top 17% of all national universities for graduation rate performance.
- Fourth largest enrollment - 27,768 - among Michigan's 15 public universities.
- BCA program is one of only two nationwide to win National Broadcasting Society production competition grand prizes in six or more categories.
- Entrepreneurship program is ranked in *Entrepreneurship magazine's* "Top 26."
- Eighty nine percent of employed CMU graduates are employed in a job related to their field or degree of choice.

College Fast Facts

Four Year, Public, Suburban, Founded: 1892

Web site: www.cmich.edu

Student Profile: 20,078 undergraduate students (44% male, 56% female) 16% minority, 3% international.

Faculty Profile: 704 full-time faculty, 82% hold a terminal degree in their field. 22:1 student/faculty ratio. Average class size is 20-29 students.

Athletics: NCAA Division 1, Mid-American Conference. 14 varsity sports. CMU athletics offers every student the chance to get involved in sports or fitness on campus.

Costs and Aid: 2007–2008: $9,120 in-state comprehensive ($7,343 tuition); $21,210 out-of-state comprehensive ($17,078 tuition) 80% of students receive some financial aid.

Admissions

Central Michigan University
Admissions Office
Warriner Hall
Mount Pleasant, MI 48859
Phone: 888-292-5366 (toll-free)
(989) 774-3076
Email: cmuadmit@cmich.edu

Service-Learning

Todd Zakrajsek, Ph.D.
Director Faculty Center
for Innovative Teaching
Email: zakra1t@cmich.edu

Volunteer Center
Shawna K. Ross
Coordinator of Volunteer Center
Email: ross1sk@cmich.edu

Madonna University

Madonna University is a private, Catholic university where dedicated faculty and staff deliver a quality liberal arts education combined with career preparation and public service.

Flagship Programs

Certificate Program in Community Leadership

Students enrolled in this program travel to the Gulf Coast over Spring Break to rebuild homes and provide needed social support to residents affected by Hurricanes Katrina and Rita. At the same time they are introduced to the concepts and tools necessary to become successful community leaders and social entrepreneurs.

Improve STATUS (Systems, Training, Applications, Tools and Utilities for Service)

Masters of Business Administration (MBA), Nursing and Graphic Design students provide technical assistance to grass-roots organizations and schools in the Detroit area through this program sponsored by the 3M Corporation. Projects include web site and data-base development, marketing and business planning, and community health education.

Community Based Research: Southwest Detroit

Students conduct focus groups, ethnographic observations, and face-to-face interviews to support the work of non-profits building healthy neighborhoods in Southwest Detroit. Courses involved in the research include SOC 1010: Introduction to Sociology and Cultural Anthropology, SOC 4900: Research Methods, NUR 3310: Family Health Promotion across the Life Span and NUR 4750: Community Health Nursing Roles.

Course Snapshot

English 1010
with Professor Neal Haldane

Blog entry regarding Habitat for Humanity project:

"What sticks in my mind is the fact that in the midst of all this work, I ended up interacting with other students from the class. I feel that whatever kind of work we did, we did it for the good of the community and for the benefit of the new homeowners."
~ Christopher Din

Academics

Many Madonna service-learning projects employ sophisticated data collection strategies, instruments and computer technology in the field. Students also discuss the moral and political issues associated with the service they provide.

Service-learning courses include:
Allied Health Administration
Art
Broadcast and Cinema Arts
Business
Child Development*
Education
English
History
Management
Management Information Systems
Marketing
Music
Nursing*
Nutrition
Psychology
Reading
Social Work*
Sociology
Spanish

"The Carnegie Community Engagement classification commends the University's work to address community-identified needs and enhance community well-being, while deepening the civic and academic learning of its students and enriching the scholarship of its faculty,"

~ Ernest Nolan, vice president for academic administration

* Programs with a required service-learning component.

View our degree offerings: http://cms.madonna.edu/pages/academics

Awards and Recognition
Service-Learning and Community Engagement
• Recognized by the Carnegie Foundation for the Advancement of Teaching for "Curricular Engagement" and "Outreach and Partnerships"-2006 to present.
• Winner of the Jimmy and Rosalyn Carter Partnership Award for Campus-Community Collaboration-2007.
• Selected for the President's Higher Education Community Service Honor Roll -2007.
• Learn and Serve Grant recipient, 2007.
• 20 community engagement grants received in the past 10 years.
• Member Campus of the Campus Community Partnership for Health (CCPH).
Academics
• MU offers more than 75 undergraduate and 27 graduate programs of study and soon will offer a doctor of nursing practice program.
• *U.S.News & World Report's 2007 America's Best Colleges* – master's classification.

College Fast Facts
Four Year, Private, Suburban, Founded: 1937

Affiliation: Catholic

Web site: http://cms.madonna.edu/

Student Profile: 3,264 undergraduate students (22.4% male,77.6% female); 38 states and territories, 45 countries; 17.4% minority, 1% international.

Faculty Profile: 108 full-time faculty. 53% hold a Ph.D. in their field.13:1 student/faculty ratio. Average class size is 15.

Athletics: Division NAIA, Wolverine-Hoosier Athletic Conference WHAC Conference. 11 men's and women's varsity sports. Coaches and athletes demonstrate the Champions of Character values:, Respect, Responsibility, Integrity, Servant Leadership and Sportsmanship.

Costs and Aid: 2007-2008: $6,092 comprehensive ($2,700 tuition). 74% of students receive some financial aid.

Admissions
Mike Quattro
Director of Admissions
36600 Schoolcraft Road
Livonia, MI 48150-1176
Phone: 734-432-5341
800-852-4951 ext. 5341
Email: mquattro@madonna.edu

Service-Learning
Kevin West
Director
Office of Service-Learning
Phone: 734-432-5704
Fax: 734-532-5634
Email: kwest@madonna.edu.

Michigan State University

Michigan State University is a public university with a global reach, dedicated to advancing knowledge and transforming lives through innovative teaching, research and outreach.

Flagship Programs

C.S.L.C.E. (Center for Service-Learning and Civic)

The Center for Service-Learning and Civic Engagement (CSLCE) at MSU assists faculty by helping to integrate service-learning into courses; students by linking them with appropriate placements; and community partners by working with them to establish and enhance placement opportunities..

Integrated Studies in Social Sciences

ISS courses increase student awareness of the contemporary world, methods of objective inquiry, and means of making a difference personally and for human-kind. Examples of service-learning courses include social differentiation and inequality; power, authority and exchange; and global diversity and independence.

Alternative Spring Break (ASB)@ MSU

ASB provides a unique living and working experience for students looking for a service opportunity during spring break. Students confront a variety of social issues such as poverty, homelessness, substance abuse, physical and mental disabilities, education, and hunger in stateside and international locations.

Course Snapshot

WRA 135 - Writing: Public Life in America

This course unites challenging intellectual content, writing instruction, and community-based service-learning writing projects into an innovative educational experience. Readings, writing assignments, discussions, student-organized public forums, and actual public service placements confront students with basic questions about the struggle for a revitalized public sphere. Students discuss, debate, evaluate, and write about such questions with the help of diverse readings, assignments, and research resources.

Academics

Academic service-learning involves students in organized service that addresses community-based needs while developing academic skills, civic responsibility and commitment to community.

Academics list of programs::

College of Agriculture and Natural Resources: Bailey Scholars *
College of Arts and Letters : Writing, Rhetoric and American Cultures *
College of Education: Counseling, Educational Psychology and Special Education *, Teacher Education *
College of Engineering: Mechanical Engineering *
James Madison College *
College of Social Science: Family and Child Ecology *, Social Work *, Urban and Regional Planning Program *
Residential College in the Arts and Humanities*
* designates required service-learning

More info on Academics:
Academic Units by College:
www.msu.edu/common/academic/units.html
Academic Programs & Areas of Study:
www.msu.edu/common/academic/areas.html

"The Small Town Design Initiative (STDI) provides an excellent service-learning opportunity and capstone experience for MSU landscape architecture students, allowing for research opportunities in the area of community participation."

– Professor Warren Rauhe

Awards and Recognition

• 2006 President's Higher Education Community Service Honor Roll With Distinctions for General Community Service and Hurricane Relief Service

• 2007 President's Higher Education Community Service Honor Roll With Distinctions

• 2006 Carnegie Engagement Elective Classification: Curricular Engagement and Outreach & Partnerships

• *Colleges with a Conscience*, The Princeton Review 2005

• 2007 *U.S.News & World Report*-Best Colleges and Best Service Learning Academic Programs

• Ranked the top public university for study abroad in the nation by the Institute of International Education.

College Fast Facts
Four Year, Public, Suburban: Founded 1855

Web Site: www.msu.edu

Student Profile: 35,821 undergraduate students (45% male, 55% female); 50 states, 150 countries; 18% minority, 7.5% international.

Faculty Profile: 4148 full-time faculty. 14:1 student/faculty ratio. Average undergraduate class size ranges from 34-47.

Athletics: NCAA Division 1, Big Ten Conference. 25 varsity sports. Intramural facilities: playing fields and gyms; ice arena; basketball, tennis, volleyball, and racquetball courts; golf courses; swimming pools; indoor running tracks; and weight rooms

Costs and Aid: 2007–2008: $18,876 in-state comprehensive ($8,672 tuition). $32,678 out-of state comprehensive (22,474 tuition) 73% of students receive some financial aid. Average award: $10,925

Admissions

Office of Admissions, Michigan State University
250 Hannah Administration Building
East Lansing, Michigan 48824-0590
Phone: (517) 355-8332

Service-Learning

Center for Service-Learning and Civic Engagement
27 Student Services Building
East Lansing, MI 48824-1113
Phone: (517) 353-4400
Email: servlrn@msu.edu
www.servicelearning.msu.edu

Northern Michigan University

Northern Michigan University is a comprehensive university where faculty and staff not only know your name but actively participate in helping you achieve your goals.

Flagship Programs

Student Leader Fellowship Program

Fifty NMU students are selected annually into this nationally recognized leadership program. The two-year commitment involves examining and developing one's leadership skills. Students must complete an extensive (usually yearlong) community service internship of their choosing for the second year.

Superior Edge

The motto: "Learning to live a life that matters." Each of Superior Edge program's four "edges" – citizenship, diversity, leadership and real world – requires 100 hours of activity chosen by the student during his/her college career. Students can choose to complete some or all edges.

Course Snapshot

PS 301 - Seminar in Public Policy Analysis

"We were required to volunteer 20 hours with a government or non-profit community organization in my Public Policy Analysis class. I chose the Medical Care Access Coalition and worked as an enrollment counselor. At first, I viewed it as just one more thing to do for school. However, during the experience I really began to understand the purpose of academic service learning. We had talked about the health care crisis in class, but until saw the number of people without health care, I didn't understand the scope of the issue. I have continued to volunteer with MCAC because I find it so rewarding."
~ Brianne Rogers, NMU student

Academics

Through service-learning courses, NMU students develop awareness that their actions, application of learning and commitment make a difference in the world. Programs offering academic service-learning courses include:

Art and Design	History
Art and Design Education	Hospitality Management
Computer Science	Management
Construction Management	Management of Health and Fitness
Criminal Justice	Marketing
Earth Science	Media Production and New Technology
Ecology	Nursing
Economics	Outdoor Recreation Leadership and
Elementary Education	--Management
English	Physical Education
English/Graduate Bound	Political Science
Entertainment and Sports Promotion	Psychology
Environmental Conservation	Public Administration
Environmental Science	Public Relations
French	Secondary Education
Geographic Information Science	Ski Area Business Management
Geography - Human	Social Work
Geography - Physical	Technology and Applied Sciences

"Academic service learning is an opportunity for faculty to showcase student growth. It highlights what our students have learned." ~ *Professor Robert Kulisheck, Political Science*

Check out all 180 + majors at: www.nmu.edu/majors

Awards and Recognition
Service-Learning

• NMU Student Leader Fellowship Program and use of community mentors included in New Directions for Student Services (2002).

• SLFP cited in The Templeton Guide: Colleges That Encourage Character Development.

• SLFP named finalist for 2008 Carter Award, recognizing outstanding campus and community partnerships.

• Superior Edge cited in Programming, magazine of National Association of Campus Activities.

Academics

• NMU offers more than 180 academic programs that range from diploma/certificate, associate, bachelor's and master's levels.

College Fast Facts
Four Year, Public, Small Town Setting: Founded 1899

Web site: www.nmu.edu

Student Profile: 8,488 undergraduate students (47% male; 53% female); 48 states states and territories, 7% minority, 1% international.

Faculty Profile: 322 full-time faculty. 77% hold a terminal degree in their field. 23:1 student/faculty ratio. Average class size is 28.

Athletics: NCAA Division II, except men's ice hockey, Division I Conference. Great Lakes Intercollegiate Athletic Conference; men's ice hockey - Central College Hockey Association. 5 men's and 8 women's teams. NMU has some of the best sports facilities in Division II. National championships in football, men's ice hockey, women's volleyball (2).

Costs and Aid: 2007-2008: $13,704 in-state comprehensive ($6,144 tuition). $17,804 out-of-state comprehensive ($10,080 tuition). 80% of students receive financial aid packages, average award $7,300.

Admissions
Admissions Office
Northern Michigan University
1401 Presque Isle Avenue
Marquette, MI 49855
Phone: 906-227-2650
Email: admiss@nmu.edu

Service-Learning
Center for Student Enrichment
Dave Bonsall, Director
Phone: 906-227-2439
Email: dbonsall@nmu.edu

Augsburg College

Augsburg students don't just learn in the classroom.

They serve, work, and learn everywhere they go.

Flagship Programs

City Service Day

Through their Augsburg Seminar (AugSem) courses, first-year students participate in the City Service Day project. On the day before fall term classes begin, students, faculty, and staff go out into the community to plant trees, paint walls, clean up near the Mississippi River — or go wherever Auggies are needed.

Campus Kitchens at Augsburg College (CKAC)

Campus Kitchens is a student-led program. Food donations from campus food service and local food banks are used to prepare meals that are delivered to after-school programs, homeless shelters, elderly and disabled individuals, and low-income people. Student, staff, and faculty volunteers prepare and serve about 1,500 meals each month.

Environmental Studies Major/Minor

This interdisciplinary program teaches students not only to be informed about environmental issues, but also how to make an impact on their world. As a class project, students in the Environmental Connections course designed and built three rain gardens on campus.

Course Snapshot

HIS 316: Environmental History

Too often, historians overlook the crucial role played by the physical world in the human past. Last fall, students in "Environmental History" (HIS 316) not only learned about the significance of nature in U.S. history, but also applied new perspectives and questions to a semester-long project on the environmental history of Augsburg College.

Academics

Through service-learning courses, students are given opportunities for direct involvement with the community, firsthand discovery, self-awareness through reflection, exploration of vocation, and learning that is life-long.

Accounting
American Indian Studies
Art
Biology
Business Administration
Chemistry
Clinical Laboratory Science
Communication Studies
Computer Science
Economics
Education
Engineering
English
Environmental Studies
Film
Finance
Health Education
History
International Relations

Management Information Systems
Marketing
Mathematics
Medieval Studies
Metro-Urban Studies
Modern Languages
Music
Nordic Area Studies
Nursing
Philosophy
Physical Education
Physics
Political Science
Psychology
Religion
Social Work
Sociology
Theater Arts
Women's Studies

"This experience has really opened my eyes to other paths I could take." --Augsburg Student

Check out all majors at: www.augsburg.edu/academics/

Awards and Recognition
• *U.S.News & World Report* - In the top 25 college for Best Academic Programs for Service Learning.
• President's Higher Education Community Service Honor Roll with Distinction for 2006 and 2007.
• One of 81 schools in *The Princeton's Review: Colleges with a Conscience.*

College Fast Facts
Four Year, Private, Urban, Founded:1869
Affiliation: The Evangelical Lutheran Church in America (ELCA)
Web site: www.augsburg.edu
Student Profile: 1911 undergraduate students (50% male, 50% female) 42 states, 40 countries, 21.7% students of color,72 international students.
Faculty Profile: 185 full-time faculty,15:1 student/faculty ratio, Average class size is 13-17.
Athletics: NCAA Division III, Minnesota Intercollegiate Athletic Conference (MIAC). 18 of varsity sports (9 men's, 9 women's).
Costs and Aid: 2007-2008 comprehensive tuition: $24,046. More than 80% of students receive some sort of financial aid.

Admissions
Office of Undergraduate Admissions (Day College)
Phone: (800) 788-5676
Email: admissons@augsburg.edu

Weekend and Graduate Admissions
Phone: (612) 330-1101
Email: wecinfo@augsburg.edu

Service-Learning
Center for Service, Work, and Learning (CSWL)
Phone: (612) 330-1148
Email: careers@augsburg.edu
www.augsburg.edu/cswl/

Century College

Century College is a learning-centered community committed to providing quality lifelong educational opportunities for a diverse citizenry.

Flagship Programs

RN Program Students in all semesters participate in service learning through one-on-one elder matches, HeadStart programming, assisting with educational health screenings, and learning about vulnerable populations. These experiences develop therapeutic communication skills and reinforce the need for professional boundaries.

Interior Design students apply techniques and concepts, such as function, style, physical and social environment, by drafting floor plans for elderly clients who are downsizing to apartments or assisted-living facilities. Students hold a series of meetings with seniors over the course of the semester, providing an outlet for the clients at what is likely a stressful time in their life. At the end of the project, the client is presented with two alternative floors plans for the new space utilizing existing furniture and decor. This design service is one that many clients would not otherwise be able to afford.

Juvenile Justice Students work with juveniles and administrators involved in the criminal justice system. Students gain valuable experience with agencies such as community corrections, substance abuse courts, correctional facilities, and court administrations.

Course Snapshot

Biology students assist a local nature center and neighborhood preserve by implementing community rain gardens, reinforcing creek beds, identifying plants, seeding and planting native prairie grasses, removing the noxious weed buckthorn, as well as maintaining the trails and outdoor space. These students work as a class alongside other community volunteers, including elementary school groups and Scout troops.

The students and these projects are vital to the work of the nature center, an organization that depends on contributions from the community.

Academics

Service learning is a type of experiential learning that engages students in service with the community as an integrated aspect of a course. This method of teaching and learning has students in community organizations addressing needs while increasing understanding of discipline specific content and promoting social responsibility.

Biology	Kitchen & Bath Design
Chemical Dependency	Micro Computer Support Technology
Communication*	Medical Assisting*
Cosmetology*	Nursing*
Criminal Justice Science*	Orthotics Practioner
Dental Hygiene	Political Science
Education	Radiologic Technology
English	Sociology
Engineering	Spanish
Interior Design	Visual Communications Technology

* Courses with a required service-learning component.

Check out all majors and programs at: www.century.edu

Century College Service Learning web site:
www.CenturyServiceLearning.project.mnscu.edu

"I never imagined what a profound effect service learning would have on my overall character."

Awards and Recognition
Service-Learning
• Century College's partnership with Bruce F. Vento Elementary was named a Certified Carter Partnership and was recognized as a 2006 finalist for the Carter Partnership Award for Campus-Community Collaboration.

• For the second year in a row, the Corporation for National and Community Service named Century College to the President's Higher Education Community Service Honor Roll for exemplary service efforts and service to disadvantaged youth. The Honor Roll is the highest federal recognition a school can achieve for its commitment to service learning and civic engagement.

• Service Learning Director, Tracey Wyman, received the 2002 Sister Pat Kowalski Leadership Award presented by MN Campus Compact.

• Century College President Larry Litecky received the President's Award for outstanding leadership from the National Council of Staff, Professional and Organizational Development (NCSPOD)

• Century College was awarded the Minnesota College Personnel Association's Innovations in Student Development Award for the GPS LifePlan, the online planning tool that helps students connect their educational goals with their career goals.

College Fast Facts
Affiliation: Century College is a member of the Minnesota State Colleges and Universities System. The Minnesota State Colleges and Universities system comprises 32 colleges and universities, including 25 two-year colleges and seven state universities.

Web site: www.century.edu

Student Profile: 8,828 students, 43% male, 57% female, 24% students of color.

Faculty Profile: 169 full-time faculty, student/faculty ratio 24 to 1.

Costs and Aid: Tuition and fees this year is $146.99/credit. A full-time student taking 15 credits Fall and Spring (total 30 credits for the year) would be charged $4,409.70.

Admissions
Century College,
Admissions Office
3300 Century Avenue North
White Bear Lake,
Minnesota 55110
Phone: 651-773-1700
800-228-1978 ext. 1700
Email: admissions@century.edu

Service-Learning
Tracey Wyman
Director of Service Learning and International Education
Phone: 651-748-2602
Email:
tracey.wyman@century.edu

College of Saint Benedict and Saint John's University

College of Saint Benedict and Saint John's University foster exceptional leadership for change and wisdom for a lifetime.

The Liemandt Family Service-Learning Program at the College of Saint Benedict and Saint John's University models Benedictine values by providing education and support to faculty, students, and the community through service experiences in order to strengthen communities, integrate theory and praxis, and foster active citizenship.

Flagship Programs

Teaching in a Diverse World

Annually, more than 160 CSB/SJU students encounter underserved youth while serving 30+ hours at local schools, Boys & Girls Clubs, and after school programs. CSB/SJU students provide tutoring and 1:1 attention while gaining valuable practical experience.

Empty Bowls

Advanced Ceramics students create more than 200 bowls and artistic pieces for a silent auction and staff a community event that raises funds and awareness surrounding hunger in the St. Cloud Area. Students come to realize a connection between art and social justice and civic responsibility.

Habitat for Humanity

Service-Learning has established an ongoing partnership with Habitat for Humanity. Students enrolled in Organizational Communication serve at Habitat for Humanity each semester, gaining firsthand insight into the daily operations of a nonprofit organization, while utilizing their skills and talents to increase the impact of the organization.

Course Snapshot

PSYCH 360: Developmental Psychology

"I believe that Service-Learning is important because it allows a person to give back to the community in a way that directly affects the people that are being helped. I learned that the person doing the service benefits just as much as the one receiving the service being done." -CSB/SJU student

Students engage in a variety of projects, from playing educational games with children at a ReachUP/HeadStart program to engaging in a conversation with an elderly resident at a long term care facility, allowing students to bring their community experience into the class.

Academics

Central to the learning goals of CSB/SJU, students gain academic credit while developing leadership, an increased understanding of the human condition, and a sense of civic responsibility.

Art
Communication
Economics
Education*
English
Gender & Women's Studies
German
Honors
Management
Nutrition
Peace Studies
Psychology
Social Work*
Sociology
Spanish
Theology

"Service-Learning challenges students' preconceived notions about the world more effectively than course readings. In my course, the Service-Learning focuses on the character of poverty and poor people. Whether students begin with liberal or conservative assumptions working directly with poor people challenges them to move to a more realistic picture of the situation."

-Professor Dan Finn

Check out all academic offerings:
www.csbsju.edu/academics/programs.htm

Awards and Recognition

Academics

• CSB, for women, and SJU, for men, are two of *U.S.News & World Report* top three Catholic colleges in the nation.

• Saint Ben's and Saint John's, together, are the largest of the nation's liberal arts colleges.

• 81 percent of CSB/SJU students complete their degree; 90 percent of those graduates finish within four years. Nationally, the six-year completion rate is 58 percent of all private college students and 36 percent of public college students.

• CSB and SJU rank first nationally in semester-long study abroad participation and fourth among baccalaureate institutions for total number of study abroad students according to Open Doors 2007, published by the Institute of International Education (IIE).

College Fast Facts

Four Year, Private, Rural

Web site: www.csbsju.edu

Student Profile: 3,928 undergraduates (52% women, 48% men); 40% of states represented, 17% from outside Minnesota; 3.8% multicultural; 3.8% international.

Faculty Profile: 294 full-time; 65 part-time. 80 percent of full-time faculty have the highest degree in their field. 100 percent of classes are taught by faculty members. Student/faculty ratio is: 13:1, average class size is 21.

Athletics: NCAA Division III, MIAC Conference; Varsity sports: 11 at CSB, 12 at SJU; 21 club sports; 10-15 intramural sports.

Costs and Aid: 2007–2008 Tuition & Fees: $28,668, Room & board: $7,959. 92% of students receives some financial aid.

Admissions

Office of Admission
College of Saint Benedict
Saint John's University
PO Box 7155
Collegeville, MN 56321
Phone: (800) 544-1489
(320) 363-2196
(320) 363-2750 (fax)

Service-Learning

Marah Jacobson-Schulte
Service-Learning Coordinator
Email: mjacobsonsc@csbsju.edu
Phone: (320) 363-5117

College of St. Catherine

Educating women to lead and influence, the College of St. Catherine is the nation's largest women's college.

St. Kate's partners with schools, agencies and non-profits for community work and learning opportunities. Students apply their education to contribute more fully to their communities and the world.

Flagship Programs

Service-Learning Partnerships

St. Kate's service-learning partnerships include nursing students collaborating with community organizations to meet the health needs of at risk and vulnerable populations, including a three-year project to assess, pilot and implement a program to assist a homeless shelter's clients.

Community-Based Research

Graduate nursing students study theories of community-based and participatory action research methods.

Community projects include the effect of racism and cultural misunderstanding on the health of women and girls of color with a multi-cultural wellness center.

Multi-Cultural Education

Students engage in trans-cultural education by tutoring children in multi-cultural reading programs. They also help younger students become more engaged in science, technology, engineering and mathematics during Science Saturday, a Centers of Excellence for Women, Science and Technology education event.

Course Snapshot

Critical Studies of Race and Ethnicity

Critical Studies of Race and Ethnicity (CRST) is an interdisciplinary program that has a strong basis in the sociology department and involves many other departments. This major/minor provides students with a framework for understanding race and ethnicity in historical and contemporary, national and global contexts. Course work will engage students to analyze issues of racial and ethnic identity and perspective. They will learn to more effectively communicate across lines of differences and engage in strategizing for social change.

Academics

Through community work and learning, St. Kate's students learn and reflect on civic, social and cultural issues and build critical thinking and leadership skills to serve their community over a lifetime.

List of programs:
American Sign Language
Associate Program Core Curriculum
Biology
Core Curriculum
Communication Studies
Family, Consumer and Nutritional Sciences
Education
English
Master of Library and Information Sciences
Nursing
Occupational Therapy Assistant
Radiography
Doctor of Physical Therapy
Sociology
Spanish

Check out all majors at:
www.stkate.edu/catalog

St. Kate's focus on academic excellence prepares students to be engaged citizens who encounter confounding complexity with poise, purpose and a full backpack of values, skills and creativity.

Andrea J. Lee, IHM
President of the College of St. Catherine

Awards and Recognition

• St. Catherine's was the first Catholic college in America to be awarded a chapter of Phi Beta Kappa for academic excellence in 1937.

• In 2006, St. Kate's ranking went from 17th to 13th among 140 in the *U.S.News & World Report*'s *America's Best Colleges* in the Midwest Universities-Master's category.

• The College formed a School of Health to graduate leaders with an interdisciplinary, team approach who can integrate technology with exceptional patient care.

• 20 service-learning courses offered during 2006–2007.

• 269 students worked 3,007 hours at service-learning sites during the 2006–2007 academic year.

College Fast Facts

Four Year, Private, Urban: Founded 1905

Web site: www.stkate.edu

Student Profile: 3,811 undergraduate students (96.6% female, 3.4% male); 37 states, 38 countries; 23.3% minority/international.

Faculty Profile: 261 full-time faculty. 11:1 student/faculty ratio. Average class size is 13. 82% hold a terminal degree in their field.

Athletics: NCAA Division III, MN Intercollegiate Athletic Conference, 9 varsity sports. The MIAC is one of the strongest NCAA divisions attracting many nationally ranked student athletes.

Costs and Aid: 2007–2008: $25,942 comprehensive ($802 per credit tuition). 90% of students receive some financial aid. Average award: $8,800.

Admissions
College of St. Catherine
Office of Admissions
2004 Randolph Avenue, F -02
St. Paul, MN 55105
Phone: (651) 690-8850
(800) 656-KATE
Email: admissions@stkate.edu

Service-Learning
Community Work and Learning
College of St. Catherine
2004 Randolph Avenue #4252
St. Paul, MN 55105
Phone: (651) 690-6842
Email: communitywork@stkate.edu

Macalester College

Macalester College is an urban liberal arts college with a commitment to rigorous learning that prepares students for lives as effective and ethical global citizens.

Flagship Programs

Lives of Commitment

LOC is a year-long program, which engages a select group of first-year students in intentional reflection on issues of social justice, ethical commitments, and meaningful work. Students participate in weekly service, visit communities in the Twin Cities, and gather for discussions and activities.

Community-Based Learning Employment Options

Students can earn their financial aid award working 10 hours a week with a local nonprofit organization and meeting monthly for discussion and further learning on social change issues. Paid opportunities for nonprofit internships and community-based research, while living in community on campus, are also popular summer options.

Academic Concentrations

Macalester offers several interdepartmental concentrations, which support global citizenship and community engagement. These involve 5-8 courses from various departments linked by a theme. Students can graduate with a concentration in Global Citizenship, Human Rights, Community and Global Health or Urban Studies.

Course Snapshot

HiSP 307-2: Introduction to the Literary Analysis of Hispanic Texts offered by the Hispanic and Latino Studies Department

In this course, students engaged Spanish-language texts, while completing oral history interviews with senior citizens at Centro, a Minneapolis nonprofit. Students filmed the interviews and compiled the transcribed interviews into a booklet, which they presented to the senior citizens. Through this project, students developed their Spanish skills and strengthened their connection to the local Latino community. Students and seniors also shared a meal together on campus and met in the community. Students have other opportunities to work with Centro's preschool, youth programs, and English-language trainings.

Academics

Community-based learning and research allows students to connect their classroom theory with direct applications, which fuels their passion for learning and engagement.

American Studies*
Anthropology
Art
Biology
Economics
Educational Studies*
English
Environmental Studies*
Geography*
Hispanic and Latin American Studies

History
Humanities and Media and Cultural Studies
Philosophy
Political Science*
Psychology
Religious Studies
Sociology
Theater and Dance
Women's, Gender, and Sexuality Studies

* Departments with a required civic engagement requirement.
Check out majors at: www.macalester.edu/admissions/academics/

"Through community engagement, students connect academic interests with local environmental initiatives that address global challenges." ~ Roopali Phadke, Environmental Studies Professor

Awards and Recognition

Service-Learning
• President's Higher Education Community Service Honor Roll with Distinction.
• Inaugural member of Project Pericles.
• Campus Compact Member and recognized by National Campus Compact for Exemplary Partnerships.
• Featured in *Colleges with a Conscience, Princeton Review.*
• Bonner Scholar/Leader School.
• Bonner Community-Based Research School.
• Each semester, more than half of our students engage in local community work through a community-based course, applied research, off-campus work-study, community service or a civic leadership program. Over 90% are active in our urban community before graduating.
• Nationally recognized Off-Campus Work-Study Program.

Academics
• 36 majors, 35 minors; over 700 classes offered; Students who study abroad for a semester or more: 62% in more than 65 countries.
• *U.S.News:* 5th for international student presence on campus, 26 overall and 14th for academic reputation among the 266 national liberal arts colleges, 9th on academic quality and the net cost for a student receiving the average level of financial aid, listed as one of 25 "New Ivies."
• 12th for percentage of students from liberal arts colleges who go on to serve in the Peace Corp and 11th for those who go on for PhD's.

College Fast Facts

Private, Urban, Founded: 1874

Web site: www.macalester.edu

Student Profile: 1920 undergraduate students (42% male, 58% female); 48 states and territories, 75 countries; 18 % minority, 12 % international.

Faculty Profile: 157 full-time faculty. 94% hold a terminal degree in their field. 10:1 student/faculty ratio. Average class size is 17.

Athletics: NCAA Division III, MN Intercollegiate Conference. 21 varsity sports.

Costs and Aid: 2007-2008: $41,914 comprehensive ($33,694 tuition). 66% of students receive some financial aid. Average first year need based award: $28,298, The average financial aid package includes the following: Grant 85%, Loan 9%, Work 6%.

Admissions
Admissions Office
1600 Grand Avenue
St. Paul, MN 55105-1899
Phone: (651) 696-6357
Toll Free: (800) 231-7974
admissions@macalester.edu

Service-Learning
Community-Based Learning
Karin Trail-Johnson, Associate Dean
Institute for Global Citizenship
Director, Civic Engagement Center
Phone: (651) 696-6040
Email: trailjohnson@macalester.edu
Dept Email: cec@macalester.edu
www.macalester.edu/cec
www.macalester.edu/globalcitizenship

Winona State University

Winona State University has built a true community of learners improving our world by integrating meaningful service-learning experiences with challenging academic opportunities.

Flagship Programs

Center for Mississippi River Studies

WSU's Center for Mississippi River Studies creates greater under-standing of the multi-faceted nature of the Mississippi River and the people and places it touches. The center builds greater knowledge of the history, environment, literature, natural and social sciences, folklore, visual and performing arts, and economics of the Mississippi through research, teaching, service-learning, and outreach. Its goal is to expand knowledge and deepen relationships with the river.

Caribbean Island Culture and Environment - St. Croix, U.S. Virgin Islands

This travel-study and service-learning course provides students with diverse perspectives on how gender, race, and class intersect in a culture with similarities to American culture, yet with a different political, economic, and cultural context. Students learn first-hand from men and women who are involved in struggles for social change.

Computer Technology Minor

The CT Minor covers fundamentals of computer tech-nology and develops students' confidence in applying technology to problems relevant to their own majors. For the capstone experience, over half of the students take CS 395: Community-Based Computer Technology Project.

Course Snapshot

Amistad Project

As part of an education class, and in partnership with Big Brothers Big Sisters of Winona, WSU students mentor K-12 Latino students in a neighboring, rural town. Once a week, WSU students travel to St. Charles, Minn. to interact with their "Littles." And once a month, the Latino students spend time on campus in Winona with their "Bigs." Amistad means friendship in Spanish. That is exactly what is being formed between these students from different cultures.

Academics

Service-learning and civic-engagement opportunities at WSU come in all shapes and sizes.

Programs of study include:
- Art (ART)
- Biology (BIOL)
- Business Administration (BUSA)
- Child Advocacy Studies (CAST)
- Communications Studies (CMST)
- Computer Science (CS)
- Education (EDUC)
- English (ENG)
- Geoscience (GEOS)
- Global Studies (GS)
- Health, Exercise and Rehabilitation Sciences (HERS)
- History (HIST)
- Mass Communication (MCOMM)
- Management Information Systems and Operations (MISO)
- Nursing (NURS)
- Political Science and Public Administration (POLS)
- Psychology (PSY)
- Social Work (SOCW)
- Sociology (SOC)
- Women's and Gender Studies (WAGS)

"He expressed how our group, and the other college groups, give him hope in the future of our country."

~ New Orleans store owner, RESC 150 – Insights and Implications: New Orleans after Katrina

Check out all majors at: www.winona.edu/academics

Awards and Recognition

Service-Learning
- Recipient of State of Minnesota "Community Service-Learning & Campus-Community Collaboration Initiative Grant" for 2008-09.
- Carnegie Classification: Community Engagement – Curricular Engagement and Outreach & Partnerships (www.carnegiefoundation.org).
- Leadership Circle member of the American College and University Presidents Climate Commitment (www.presidentsclimatecommitment.org).

Academics
- WSU offers 65 undergraduate and 15 graduate, pre-professional and licensure programs.
- Named one of America's Best Colleges 2008 by *U.S.News & World Report.*
- Designated a Best Midwestern College by *The Princeton Review.*

College Fast Facts

Four-Year, Public, Rural, Founded: 1858

Web site: www.winona.edu

Student Profile: 7,693 undergraduate students (40% male, 60% female); 34 states and territories, 54 countries; 5% minority, 25% international.

Faculty Profile: 382 full-time faculty; 70% hold a terminal degree in their field; 21:1 student/faculty ratio; Average class size is 24.

Athletics: NCAA II, NSIC Conference. 15 varsity sports; Male Programs: Football, Basketball, Baseball, Cross Country, Golf, Tennis; Women Programs: Gymnastics, Volleyball, Basketball, Softball, Tennis, Golf, Cross Country, Track & Field, Soccer.

Costs and Aid: 2007-2008: $12,710 comprehensive ($5,600 tuition/$6,110 housing/1,000 laptop) $17,180 out of state comprehensive ($10,070 tuition/$6,110 housing/$1,000 laptop). 70% of students receive some financial aid.

Admissions

Winona State University
Admissions Office
P.O. Box 5838
Winona, MN 55987
Phone: 800-DIAL-WSU ext. 5100
(507) 457-5100
Email: Admissions@winona.edu
www.winona.edu/admissions

Service-Learning

Center for Engaged Teaching and Scholarship
Joan Francioni, Ph.D.
Director
Phone: (507) 457-2336
Email: jfrancioni@winona.edu
www.winona.edu/ets

Tougaloo College

Tougaloo College "…prepares students to be imaginative, self-directed, lifelong learners and mindful thinkers, committed to leadership and services in a global society by offering a high quality liberal studies program."

Flagship Programs

Higher Education National Community-Based Research Networking Initiative

This is a Learn and Serve America program, administered by Princeton University and the Bonner Foundation, designed to spread the practice of CBR by students, faculty, and community partners.

Bonner Leaders Program

We have recently developed a Bonner Leaders program in a relationship with the Bonner Foundation, and are recruiting students to serve with community-based organizations.

Course Snapshot

PSB 327: Topics in Psychology

Students in this course on Health Psychology research mental and physical health issues of the homeless in Jackson, Mississippi, in collaboration with the Country Oaks Recovery Center. The students searched the Internet and libraries for information on the homeless prior to doing interviews with Country Oaks clients. After they analyzed the data they collected from clients during interviews, they made recommendations for action to help the homeless.

Academics

Founded in 2004, the Center for Civic Engagement & Social Responsibility is engaged in activities designed to empower Tougaloo College students so that they become active participants in the life of their communities. The center administers the sixty-hour student community service requirement, service-learning, and community-based research. It has also collaborated with the HBCU Faculty Development Network to work with historically black colleges and universities, other institutions, community organizations, and government agencies to host conferences, workshops, and summer institutes, including summer institutes on "Civic Engagement & Social Justice" and "Community-Based Participatory Research: A Pathway to Sustainable Partnerships;" a symposium on "Response to Community Crisis: Lessons from Recent Hurricanes;" and a community capacity workshop on "Building Community-Campus Partnerships for Healthy Communities: Continuing the Dialogue."

Departments with service-learning or community-based research activities:
Art
Biology
Honors Program
Mass Communications
Physics
Psychology
Sociology/Social Work
Speech

Check out all majors at:
www.tougaloo.edu/academics

Awards and Recognition
Service-Learning

• The Mississippi Higher Education Consortium Mississippi Lighthouse Service Learning Program: "Most Outstanding Historically Black College" award to Tougaloo College "In Appreciation of its designation as an Innovator of Community Service Learning and Civic Engagement."

• President's Higher Education Community Service Honor Roll, 2007

Academics

• Highest Ranking HBCU in Mississippi (*U.S. News & World Report*).

• One of Best Colleges and Universities in the Southeast (*Princeton Review*).

College Fast Facts
Web site: www.tougaloo.edu
Affiliation: United Church of Christ and the Disciples of Christ
Student Profile: 913 undergraduate students (31% male, 69% female), 24 states, 2 foreign countries; 99% African-American; less than 1% international.
Faculty Profile: 77 full-time faculty; 60% hold a terminal degree in their field. 1:12 student/faculty ratio.
Athletics: Tougaloo College is a member of the Gulf Coast Athletic Conference (GCAC) and the National Association of Intercollegiate Athletics (NAIA).
Costs and Aid: $16,525 comprehensive ($9,900 tuition).
97% of students receive some financial aid. Average award: $7,000.

Admissions
Tougaloo College, Office of Admissions
500 W. County Line Rd. Tougaloo, MS 39174
Phone: (601) 977-7772
Email: jjacobs@tougaloo.edu

Service-Learning
Center for Civic Engagement & Social Responsibility
Director Stephen L. Rozman
Phone: (601)977-4460
Email: srozman@tougaloo.edu

Kansas City Art Institute

The Kansas City Art Institute, founded in 1885, is a private four-year college of art and design. KCAI is accredited by the Higher Learning Commission and National Association of Schools of Art and Design.

Flagship Programs

Community Arts and Service-Learning Certificate Program

The CASL certificate program is a 15-hour course of study that directs the students' academic experiences, studio and liberal arts, toward engagement with communities of need and interaction with community groups as clients. The certificate curriculum includes two required courses - the Artist's Role in Society and Collaborative Art Practices - an internship and two electives. Electives are offered through all of the fine art departments, graphic design and liberal arts.

Toward a Green Sculpture

KCAI sculpture Associate Professor Karen McCoy has created a series of service-learning courses under the title Toward a Green Sculpture. Intended as an exploration of the possibilities for making sculpture in ways that are not harmful to humans or the rest of the ecosystem, recent TGS courses have included collaboration with Native American scholars, artists, reservation leaders and residents to share stories and make art to bridge the distance between two cultures.

Internship Program: Accessible Arts

CASL collaborates with Kansas City's Accessible Arts, a not-for profit organization that exists to "unlock the arts for children with disabilities." KCAI interns at Accessible Arts helped establish a ceramics program for blind children. They taught students to successfully center and throw pots on a wheel, to do hand building and glazing. One intern praised the opportunity she had, saying "(Working with blind kids,) I learned a language of interpreting how ceramic work is done, which has started my education in becoming a teacher of this art."

Academics

At KCAI, service-learning is a part of the academic program that creates opportunities for faculty and students to explore the role of the artist in society. The Community Arts and Service-Learning program is not a volunteer program, although voluntary service is an important element of its philosophy. Rather, CASL exists to build relationships between the community and the college and to promote the art students' and artists' successful, lifelong engagement in community and civic life.

KCAI's service-learning program is driven by faculty and managed by the career services department. Therefore, students see civic engagement modeled by their professors and come to think of it as a means of professional development.

School of Fine Arts
Ceramics
Fiber
Painting
Print Making
Interdisciplinary Arts
Sculpture
Photography
Digital Film
School of Design
Graphic Design
Animation
School of Liberal Arts
Art History
Studio Art In Creative Writing

"Community and New Genre artists create strategies, not objects, they leave the participating community with processes and systems for social change."

~ Hugh Merrill. Professor, Printmaking

Check out all majors at:
www.kcai.edu/majors

Course Snapshot

Experimental Documentary

Assistant Professor Dwight Frizzell's class formed an art and production team to develop and produce an original documentary. Students shot footage of people and places involved with scrap metal reclamation. They interviewed individuals working in the local industry and those who push a cart collecting and selling discarded metal to maintain their subsistence living. In their completed documentary, "Scrap," students investigated America's "throw away" goods and "throw away" people, both kept on the margins of the city and its consciousness.

College Fast Facts

Four Year, Private College of Art & Design, Urban, Founded: 1885

Web site: www.kcai.edu

Student Profile: 676 undergraduate students (49% male, 51% female); 26 states and territories, 8 countries; 15% minority, 2% international.

Faculty Profile: 50 full-time faculty. 15:1 student/faculty ratio. Average class size is 15.

Costs and Aid: 2007-2008: $25,680 tuition. 99% of students receive financial aid.

Admissions

Kansas City Art Institute
Office of Admissions
4415 Warwick Boulevard
Phone: (816) 802-3300; (800) 522-5224
Email: admiss@kcai.edu
www.kcai.edu

Service-Learning

Community Arts and Service Learning
Julie Metzler, Director
Career Services and CASL
Phone: (816) 802-3357

Missouri State University

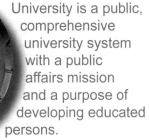

Missouri State University is a public, comprehensive university system with a public affairs mission and a purpose of developing educated persons.

Flagship Programs

BIO 369

In General Ecology, students may choose service-learning as part of their program. One of their community partner options is the Dickerson Park Zoo, where they learn firsthand about the relationship between humans and animals. Classroom knowledge is supported by their experiences.

CSC 450

Students in Introduction of Software Engineering assisted the local USDA-NRCS South Missouri Water Quality Project by applying their expertise to a digital photo storage organization problem. Their "PhotoStore" software was released to NRCS offices nationwide.

Public Service Tax Clinic

Students in the Public Service Tax Clinic and community volunteers assisted low-income, English as second language, disabled and Older Adult individuals with over 18,000 federal tax returns. Over $6 million in tax refunds were received due to this volunteer work. Additionally, students conducted 34 financial literacy and tax issue workshops and resolved 44 tax controversy cases.

Course Snapshot

NUR 482: Leadership and Management

Dr. Susan Sims-Giddens' nursing students learn that being an effective leader means service. Her students founded The Coalition for Healthy Communities—a nursing center without walls. The purpose is serving and assisting populations that do not have access to consistent health care. Those served include K-12 schools, shelters for homeless youth and men, hospices, county health departments, health and dental clinics for homeless and low-income, and facilities for mentally ill and disabled citizens.

Academics

Through service-learning experiences, Missouri State University students cultivate skills and the perspective that encourages continued learning and engaged citizenship. Programs of study include:

Accountancy
Agriculture
Art & Design
Biology
Biomedical Sciences
Chemistry
Childhood Education & Family Studies
Communication
Communication Sciences & Disorders
Computer Science
Counseling, Leadership & Special Education
English
Fashion & Interior Design
Finance & General Business
Geography, Geology & Planning
Health, Physical Education & Recreation

Hospitality & Restaurant Administration
Industrial Management
Management
Marketing
Mathematics
Media, Journalism & Film
Modern & Classical Languages
Music
Nursing
Physical Therapy
Political Science
Psychology
Reading, Foundations & Technology
Social Work
Sociology, Anthropology & Criminology
Theatre & Dance

Check out all majors at: www.missouristate.edu/majors

"You gain valuable knowledge by working closely with those who have been in the field." ~ Wendy Phiropoulos, SWK 205—Human Diversity

Awards and Recognition

Service-Learning

• President's Higher Education Community Service Honor Roll.

• The only school in Missouri included in the *Princeton Review—Colleges with a Conscience: 81 Great Schools with Outstanding Community Involvement.*

• In 2007-2008, Service-Learning students (1,770) provided 45,520 hours of service, generating $733,782 worth of service to the community.

• Included in *The Templeton Guide: Colleges that Encourage Character Development.*

Academics

• Missouri State offers more than 150 undergraduate majors and 48 graduate programs, including 3 doctorate degrees.

• Approximately 200 students per year participate in Study Abroad Programs.

• American Democracy Project Leader.

• The University's Annual Public Affairs Conference brings significant leaders, both domestic and international, from a variety of disciplines and backgrounds to campus for dialogues about topics relevant for a 21st century democracy. Community members, students, faculty and staff benefit from the conference which is intended to nurture and stimulate conversation and thinking among informed, engaged citizens.

College Fast Facts

Four Year, Public, Urban, Founded: 1905
Web site: www.missouristate.edu

Student Profile: 14,709 undergraduate students; 56% female; 44% male; 81 countries.

Faculty Profile: 718 full-time faculty.

Athletics: 16 varsity sports; since moving to Division I, Missouri State teams have made 40 NCAA championship appearances.

Costs and Aid: 2008-2009: $11,922 in-state comprehensive ($6,256 tuition); $17,202 out-of-state comprehensive ($11,536 tuition); 58% of students receiving some financial aid.

Admissions

Missouri State University
Office of Admissions
901 South National Avenue
Springfield, MO 65897
Phone: 417-836-5517
Toll Free: 800-492-7900
info@missouristate.edu

Service-Learning

Citizenship & Service-Learning
Elizabeth Carmichael Burton
Associate Director
Phone: 417-836-5774
ServiceLearning@missouristate.edu

Rockhurst University

Rockhurst University exists to transform lives and form leaders through learning, leadership and service in the Catholic, Jesuit tradition.

Flagship Programs

Rockhurst Modern Languages Service-Learning
Students taking advanced courses in Spanish and French participate in various service-learning projects that allow them to practice their language skills while helping others.

Nonprofit Leadership Studies Service-Learning
Students in the Nonprofit Leadership Studies have a variety of opportunities for real-world experiences. Through service-learning, students apply theories

learned in class to help nonprofit organizations and the clients they serve. In return, they learn about issues of social justice and best practices from the community.

Service-Learning Studies
Rockhurst supports students who want to become leaders in service through Service-Learning Studies seminars and practica. By teaching students peer facilitation techniques and teaming them with faculty members, advanced service-learning students lead projects and group reflection.

Course Snapshot

PL 1100:
Reality and Human Existence
In Dr. Robert Vigliotti's philosophy course, Rockhurst students are introduced to the discipline of philosophy. Based on the premise that individuals cannot know about happiness in isolation, Vigliotti's class tutors youth in after-school elementary programs. Students connect their community work with class by reflecting on the meaning of happiness and how individual happiness depends on the state of the community.

Academics
The Jesuit tradition ensures that Rockhurst graduates are prepared to lead, shape and change the world. Service-learning is an integral part of the student experience. Rockhurst graduates leave with a commitment to lead and serve others with a greater social conscience.

American Humanics
Biology
Chemistry
Communication
Communication Sciences & Disorders
English
French
History
Management
Nonprofit Leadership Studies
Occupational Therapy
Philosophy
Physical Therapy
Physics
Psychology
Spanish
Theater Arts

"Service-learning students engage social issues, perform meaningful research, and take ownership of their own learning."

-- Daniel J. Martin, Ph.D., Associate Professor of English and Director of Honors Program

For a complete list of academics programs, visit:

www.rockhurst.edu

Students can choose from programs in the humanities, health professions, sciences, education, pre-professional and business fields designed to meet the needs of contemporary society.

Awards and Recognition
• Recent surveys show that Rockhurst students rank their educational satisfaction among the highest in the nation.

• In 2006, the Carnegie Foundation selected Rockhurst as one of 12 colleges and universities to lead an effort to improve teaching in higher education.

• Rockhurst University is ranked among the top master's universities in the Midwest by *U.S.News & World Report*.

• Intel has ranked Rockhurst University one of the nation's top wireless college campuses.

• Service-Learning Studies offers two service-learning leadership seminars and a variety of associated practicum courses. This program combines learning, leadership and service, all of which are important to the Jesuit tradition of education.

President's Higher Education Community Service Honor Roll, 2007

College Fast Facts
Four Year, Private, Urban: Founded 1910

Web site: www.rockhurst.edu

Student Profile: 1,528 undergraduate students (41% male, 59% female); 26 states and 1 territory, 8 countries; 16% minority, 1% international.

Faculty Profile: 125 full-time faculty. 11:1 student/faculty ratio. Average class size is 21. 87% hold a terminal degree in their field.

Cost and Aid: 2007-2008: $22,000 tuition. 98% of students receive financial aid including scholarship, grants and loans. Average award: $17,500.

Service-Learning Facts
• 38 service-learning courses offered during last year (06-07).

• 6% of total courses are service-learning courses.

• 31% of students took a service-learning course last year (06-07).

• 55% of departments offer at least one service-learning course.

Admissions
Admission Office
Rockhurst University
1100 Rockhurst Rd
Kansas City, MO 64110
Phone: (816) 501-4100 or
(800) 842-8776
Email: admission@rockhurst.edu

Service-Learning
Center for Service Learning
Julia Vargas, Director
Phone: (816) 501-4545
Email: julia.vargas@rockhurst.edu

Truman State University

As the state of Missouri's designated undergraduate liberal arts and sciences university, Truman State University embraces its mission to provide professionals and leaders in a knowledge-based society who can contribute to their community.

Civic Engagement through service-learning and other experiential learning augments the study of liberal arts and sciences at Truman State University with experiences in community that link imagination, knowledge and service.

Flagship Programs

Service-Learning Advantage

Whether their courses include service-learning or not, students at Truman State can do service-learning through clubs via Service-Learning Advantage. Project planning and reflection opportunities tie club efforts to learning goals so students are able to take their volunteer agenda to the next level – the service-learning level.

Undergraduate Research

Faculty from the sciences and the humanities sponsor undergraduate research opportunities, including grant-funded summer projects. Over 290 students presented at the last Student Research Conference Day.

Missouri Government Internship

This program offers a unique opportunity for junior/senior students to intern with a legislator, public official or state agency. The program provides interested students an inside look at state government and the political process.

Course Snapshot

HLH 362
Environmental Health

This course actively involves the student in the determination of environmental health concerns. Students examine the impact of the individual on the environment, the environment on individual and population health, Healthy People 2010 objectives for environmental health, and the sources/etiology, effects, and control measures for selected environmental and personal safety hazards. Integrated service learning is a vital component of this course.

Academics

In all forms available on campus, service-learning at Truman helps students take leadership of their intellectual and civic growth.
Courses of Study include: (courses with required service-learning component)*

Agricultural Science	Math and Computer Science
Anthropology/Geography/Sociology	Nursing*
Biology	Political Science
Business and Accountancy	Psychology
Classical and Modern Languages	Theater
Communication Disorders*	
Education*	A complete listing of all undergraduate areas of study is here:
Environmental Studies	http://admissions.truman.edu/academics/
Health and Exercise Science*	majors.asp
History	

"The students' high-energy and enthusiasm for the project is what propels me forward in the semester and pushes me to ensure excellence in the classroom so that each student realizes their maximum positive impact outside of the classroom."

Assistant Professor Teak Nelson (NU 311 Human Nutrition)

Awards and Recognition

Service-Learning

• Member, Missouri Campus Compact. 4-year recipient of Missouri Campus Compact grant funding.

• Recipient, Corporation for National Service VISTA grant.

• 60% of departments offer at least one service-learning course

Academics

• #1 public university in the Midwest among master's-level institutions for 11 years running – *U.S.News & World Report*'s "America's Best Colleges"

• Highlighted as having an excellent Undergraduate Research/Creative Projects Program – *U.S.News & World Report*

• #2 public college value in the nation – *The Princeton Review*'s 2008 edition of "America's Best Value Colleges"

• 8th in the nation among master's-level universities for the number of students studying abroad – Open Doors

• 25th among medium-sized schools based upon production of Peace Corps volunteers – "Peace Corps Top Colleges 2007"

College Fast Facts

Four Year, Public, Rural: Founded 1867

Web site: www.truman.edu

Student Profile: 5,608 undergraduates (43% male, 57% female); 9.8% minority, 4.2% international.

Faculty Profile: 344 full-time faculty, 83% hold a terminal degree in their field. 16:1 student/faculty ratio.

Athletics: NCAA Division II, Mid-America Intercollegiate Athletics Association (MIAA) Conference. 21 varsity sports. Truman offers more varsity sports than any other university in the conference.

Costs and Aid: 2007–2008: $12,247 in-state comprehensive ($6,210 in-state tuition); $16,857 out-of-state comprehensive ($10,820 out-of-state tuition). 96% of students receive some financial aid.

Admissions
Truman State University
Office of Admission
100 East Normal
Kirksville, MO 63501
Phone: (800) 892-7792
Email: admissions@truman.edu

Service-Learning
The Center for Teaching and Learning
Julie Lochbaum, Ph.D.
Director
Phone: (660) 785-4391
Email: ctl@truman.edu

William Jewell College

William Jewell College promises students an outstanding liberal arts education that cultivates leadership, service, and spiritual growth within a community inspired by Christian ideals and committed to open, rigorous intellectual pursuits.

Flagship Programs

Leadership Legacy Project

WJC nursing students identify a specific area of interest, and then develop and implement a leadership legacy project. Students conduct a literature review indicating the need for the project. The project also requires students to complete a service to either the community or the nursing department.

The Department of Languages

The WJC Language Department includes service-learning as part of course objectives and requirements. Last year students served and learned by tutoring, running a basketball clinic, assisting at a citizenship workshop, assisting with art lessons and helping with church services.

C.L.I.C.K. (Community Leaders Introduction To Computer Knowledge (SIFE project)

SIFE students delivered training workshops on software capabilities to enhance work productivity through technology for leaders in non-profit organizations. The sessions were utilizing Microsoft Productivity tools, Word, and Excel.

Course Snapshot

SVL 301: Service-Learning Internship

This internship allows students to become engaged in community service pertaining to a social concern of their own choice. Interns work directly with a non-profit agency or organization toward fulfilling defined learning competencies.

Corrine Cooper '06 reflects on her internship at Harvesters through SVL 301. "My overall experience at Harvesters was extremely positive. I feel incredibly fortunate to have been a part of a well-organized team of people dedicated to alleviating hunger in the community and seeing how practical measures were taken to do so."

Academics

At Jewell, service-learning is not only service to the community, but includes a learning component so that specific coursework is incorporated into the service and supplemented with ongoing reflection.

Programs of study include:

Applied Critical Thought and Inquiry (ACT-In)
Business Administration (BUSAD)
Christian Related Vocation (CRV)
Communication (COM)
History
Languages
Nonprofit Leadership
Nursing
Political Science
Psychology

Check out all majors at: www.jewell.edu

"In each S-L course students encounter human needs, analyze the conditions creating problematic situations, perform actual service, and evaluate the service activity."

Awards and Recognition

Service-Learning

• President's Higher Education Community Service Honor Roll.

• Students contributed more than 25,000 hours of service learning and community service in 2006-07.

Academics

• *U.S.News & World Report* included William Jewell among the top 184 national liberal arts colleges in its 2008 edition of "America's Best Colleges."

• Jewell was named by *The Princeton Review* as one of "The Best 366 Colleges" in its 2008 edition.

• In 2006-07, the college claimed a Fulbright Scholar, a Goldwater Scholar, two Rhodes Scholar national finalists, a Truman Scholar, a National Institute of Health Fellow, a Council of Independent Colleges American Graduate Fellowship finalist, and a Point Foundation Scholar.

• Among the first-year class entering in 2007, 55% graduated in the top 25% of their class.

College Fast Facts

Four-Year, Private, Suburban, Founded: 1849

Web site: www.jewell.edu

Student Profile: 1,329 undergraduate students (40% male, 60% female); 10.8% minority

Faculty Profile: 78 full-time faculty; 84.5% hold a terminal degree in their field; 14:1 student/faculty ratio; average class size: 19.

Athletics: NAIA; 15 varsity sports.

Costs and Aid: 2007-2008: $27,240 comprehensive ($21,400 tuition). 99% of students receive some form of financial aid.

Admissions

William Jewell College
Office of Admission
500 College Hill, Liberty, MO 64068
Phone: (816) 415-7511; (888) 2-JEWELL (253-9355)
Email: admission@william.jewell.edu

Service-Learning

Phone: (816) 415-7504
Email: servicelearning@william.jewell.edu

University of Montana Missoula

At The University of Montana in Missoula, students have the opportunity to learn, live, and work in the middle of western Montana's stunning natural landscape.

Flagship Programs

Missoula Flagship After-School Program

Students from various departments at UM teach lessons and create semester-long interdisciplinary curricula for public schools. Examples include drama/dance students designing arts classes and chemistry students teaching science to public school classes using creative and innovative techniques.

International Service-Learning

Students may participate in a service-learning/study-abroad program consisting of a semester-long academic course paired with a 3-week travel component to Vietnam and either Cambodia or Laos. The course offers students the unusual prospect of working and traveling in a Communist state in which freedom of movement and speech is sometimes restricted.

Watershed Education Network: Water Explorations

UM students coordinate "Water Explorations" projects

with high schools in Missoula by facilitating field trips to local streams. Activities include water montoring, fish counts, aquatic insect sampling, journal writing and fly-fishing.

Course Snapshot

Program in Ecological Agriculture and Society (PEAS)

Through the Environmental Studies department, students research and analyze the nature of the contemporary food system. PEAS provides hands-on learning about organic farming practices and teaches students the value of helping those in need while providing locally grown food to low-income individuals.

Over the past 10 years, literally hundreds of UM students have gained invaluable hands-on knowledge through this course.

Academics

Accounting
Art
Dance
Drama
Environmental Studies
Health and Human Performance
Honors College
International Studies
Liberal Arts
Management
Pharmacy

The University of Montana also offers students the chance to apply their academic learning in a real-world setting through Internship Services and Career Services.

At The University of Montana, service learning courses are designated in the Course Offering Directory and on student transcripts.

Check out all majors at:
http://umtedu/academicindex/

"Record numbers of University students are volunteering their time as mentors, tutors, or class instructors through the Flagship Program. This not only benefits the young people they are working with, but also enhances their own education by allowing them to apply what they are learning in their University classes."

~ Rosalie Buzzas, Director, The Flagship Program

Awards and Recognition

Service-Learning

• Named to the Washington Monthly's Top 100 Colleges, which emphasizes service and civic engagement.
• President's Higher Education Community Service Honor Roll with Distinction in 2007.
• Named to the Princeton Review's "Colleges with a Conscience."
• AmeriCorps grantee.
• No. 10 on the Peace Corps' list of "Top Producing Colleges and Universities."

Institutional

• "Most scenic campus in America"—Rolling Stone magazine.
• Rated among the top 10 by Outside Magazine for combining academic quality and outdoor recreation.
• Among the top "schools with the most beautiful campus in an urban setting" by Kaplan's "Unofficial, Unbiased Guide to the 328 Most Interesting Colleges."
• Princeton Review's 150 best-value undergraduate institutions.
• America's Best 100 College Buys and Barron's Best Buys in College Education.
• Sports Illustrated On Campus ranked UM on its top 25 list of best college sports towns. UM is the only I-AA school on the list.

College Fast Facts

Four Year, Public, Mid-town campus with a rural backyard: Founded 1893

Web site: www.umt.edu

Student Profile: 11,841 undergraduate students (46% male, 54% female); 68% in-state, 32% out of state.

Faculty Profile: 588 full-time faculty (73 percent), 221 part-time (27 percent) 19:1 student-faculty ratio.

Athletics: Football Championship Subdivision (FCS), Big Sky Conference.

Costs and Aid: 2007–2008: $5,849 in state comprehensive ($2,494 tuition), $10,602 out-of-state comprehensive ($7,247 tuition). 67% of students receive some financial aid.

Admissions

Enrollment Services
Lommasson Center
The University of Montana
32 Campus Drive
Missoula, MT 59812
http://admissions.umt.edu
Phone: (406) 243-6266
E-mail: admiss@umontana.edu

Service-Learning

Andrea Vernon, Ed D.
Office for Civic Engagement
Davidson Honors College 015
Missoula, MT 59812
Phone: (406) 243-5159
E-mail: andrea.vernon@mso.umt.edu

Creighton University

Creighton University is a Catholic and Jesuit university committed to excellence in its undergraduate, graduate, and professional programs.

Academics

Service-learning courses provide Creighton students a unique opportunity for personal growth, shared reflection, and moral and social responsibility. Service-learning courses and other educational opportunities are found throughout Creighton's Colleges and Schools:

College of Arts and Sciences
College of Business Administration
School of Dentistry
School of Law
School of Medicine
School of Nursing
School of Pharmacy and Health Professions
Graduate School

"I've had the privilege to serve. . .I feel called to be an advocate and a voice for the voiceless."

-Patrick Chee, 3rd year law student

Creighton offers 50+ majors and 20+ graduate and professional programs.

Check out all majors at:
www2. creighton.edu/academics

Flagship Programs

Encuentro Dominicano

Encuentro Dominicano is an undergraduate, academic, living-learning program integrating community-based learning in a cross-cultural immersion in the Dominican Republic. Students balance traditional coursework with immersions, service-site work, and retreats as they grow in their appreciation of ethnic and cultural diversity, a faith that promotes justice, and service to others.

Cortina Community

Cortina Community is a sophomore living-learning community dedicated to the four pillars of community, service, faith, and justice. Community members together complete service-learning within courses offered by the departments of Communication Studies, Philosophy, Political Science, Sociology and Anthropology, and Theology.

OISSE (Office of Interprofessional Scholarship, Service, and Education)

OISSE offers health professional students opportunities to engage in community activities that provide authentic learning experiences while making an impact in underserved local, rural, and international communities.

Awards and Recognition

Service-Learning

• President's Higher Education Community Service Honor Roll, with Distinction.

• Midwest Consortium on Service Learning in Higher Education 2007 Awards for Faculty Researcher and Student Commendation in Service Learning.

• 68,000 student service hours annually.

• 200+ students take Spring Break Service Trips.

• Saviors of Our Cities "best-neighbor" urban university Top 25 in the nation.

• Omaha is rated 4th in the nation for volunteerism by the Corporation for National and Community Service.

Academics

• Creighton's Freshman Academic Profile places us in the Nation's Top 45 Private Universities (4,000+ Enrollment).

• Creighton University cited as an outstanding value by publications such as Money and Kiplinger's Personal Finance.

• #5 Most Wired College by PC Magazine.

College Fast Facts

Four Year, Private, Founded 1878

Web site: www.creighton.edu

Student Profile: 4104 undergraduate students (40% male, 60% female); 49 states and 2 territories, 33 countries; 15.5% minority, 1.8% international

Faculty Profile: 501 full-time faculty. 87% hold a terminal degree in their field. 12:1 student/faculty ratio. Average class size is 22.

Athletics: NCAA Division I, Missouri Valley Conference. 14 varsity sports. With a 95% graduation rate for student-athletes, Creighton is tied for 15th among all Division I Universities.

Costs and Aid: 2008-2009: $28,542 comprehensive ($27,282 tuition). Room and board, $8,516. 86% of students receive some financial aid. Average award: $21,260.

Admissions

Creighton University, Office of Undergraduate Admissions
2500 California Plaza
Omaha, NE 68178
Phone: (402) 280-2703; toll-free (800) 282-5835
Email: admissions@creighton.edu
http://admissions.creighton.edu

Service-Learning

Mary Ann Danielson, Ph.D.
Associate Vice President for Academic Excellence and Assessment
Phone: (402) 280-2535
Email: maddam@creighton.edu

Course Snapshot

ACCT 521: Advanced Accounting

Accounting majors are offered the opportunity to participate in a service-learning project designed to incorporate their knowledge of financial accounting in assisting a local non-profit organization. Working in pairs or teams, the students apply current accounting pronouncements while utilizing critical thinking and problem solving skills. Additionally, students are offered the opportunity to voluntarily increase their spiritual awareness through guided reflections, journal writing, and service projects.

University of Nebraska at Kearney

The University of Nebraska at Kearney is a public, residential university that provides a multidimensional learning environment, engagement with community and public interests, and preparation of students to lead responsible and productive lives in a democratic, multicultural society.

Flagship Programs

Service-Learning in Teacher Education

Service-learning has been a core component of the undergraduate Teacher Education program for the past 17 years, and is required for all students entering the certification program for Teacher Education. Each year, approximately 300 students are placed in 45 different community agencies and programs, in which they give of their time and skills to meet specific community needs. Students work with before/after-school programs, persons with disabilities, youth rehabilitation centers, service organizations and elder care facilities. They tutor, plan and implement recreational activities, and lead additional service-learning projects with youth.

Communication's Capstones: In the Multi-Media Capstone and Advanced Advertising Campaign classes, students work with authentic clients from the off-campus nonprofit world, who have needs for complete, professional web sites and advertising campaign materials they can officially enact. Formed into teams, the students work directly with the clients throughout the semester. They conduct research, determine challenges and target audiences; design logos, campaign slogans and build complete web sites; and develop brochures, ads, programs, billboards, video clips, radio and TV spots. Complete packages are formally presented to the clients(often at the Board of Directors level) with management instruction manuals and prototypes.

Course Snapshot

Dancing with Cranes

Our Geography Water Sources course works with Rowe Sanctuary, a nonprofit community organization located on the banks of the Platte River, performing crucial water tests that guide Rowe on their programming and wildlife preservation efforts. The Sanctuary and the students learn about the impact of the famous Sand Hills Cranes that have taken annual spring residence in this area for thousands of years, as well as gain an understanding of the relationship between the River and wildlife. Students then share their analyses at the subsequent service-learning conference.

Academics

Service-learning classes are offered in each of the four colleges at UNK, including: Business and Technology, Education, Fine Arts & Humanities and Natural & Social Sciences. UNK advocates service-learning as a means to its mission of teaching students the value of being civically-engaged in lifelong involvement in the community. Service-learning courses and components are offered in the following disciplines:

Accounting
Art & Art History
Biology
Business
Communications
Communication Disorders
Computer Science & Information Systems
Criminal Justice
Economics
Teacher Education*
English
English as a Second Language

Geography
Health & Physical Education
History
Industrial Technology
Marketing & Management
Music
Nursing
Political Science
Psychology
Social Work
Sociology

* Courses with a required service-learning component.

Check out all majors at: **www.unk.edu**

"Students and teachers alike would benefit through service-learning. Learning does not happen 8am-4pm, 5 days a week, in a school building. Genuine learning comes from the outside world." ~ UNK Service-Learning Student

Awards and Recognition

• UNK has been recognized as one of the top 15 public universities in the Midwest region at the Master's Level, according to the 2008 edition of *U.S. News & World Report*'s annual America's Best Colleges rankings.

• In 2005, UNK Director of the Office for Service-Learning received the Midwest Consortium Voyager Award for a Scholarly Practitioner of Service-Learning.

• UNK was selected as the site for the 2007 Midwest Consortium for Service-learning in Higher Education Fourth Annual Conference.

College Fast Facts

Founded: 1905

Web site: www.unk.edu

Student Profile: 5000+ undergraduate, 1000+ graduate, nearly 500 international students; 44 states and territories, 54 countries.

Faculty Profile: 17:1 student/faculty ratio.

Athletics: NCAA Division II, UNK athletic teams have won 11 consecutive Rocky Mountain Athletic Conference all-sports championships and consistently have placed in the top 20 overall programs nationally.

Costs and Aid: $129.50/credit hour/resident; $265.25/credit hour/resident. More than two-thirds of UNK students receive some form of financial assistance through scholarships, grants, loans, and work-study programs.

Admissions

Dusty Newton, Director
University of Nebraska at Kearney
905 West 25th Street, Kearney, NE 68849
Phone: (308) 865-8702;
1-800-KEARNEY (532-7639)
Email: newtond@unk.edu

Service-Learning

Geraldine Stirtz, Director
B185 College of Education
Phone: (308) 865-8957
Email: stirtzg@unk.edu

University of Nebraska at Omaha

UNO is located in the heart of Nebraska's largest city, and is proud to serve as the state's metropolitan university.

Service-Learning Focus

Service-Learning at UNO builds bridges between the campus and the community. Students not only address community needs but also enrich their own education by experiencing the real-world application of academic subjects and developing the habit of active citizenship.

Flagship Programs

Seven Days of Service

Seven Days of Service has evolved from a small collaborative program between UNO and local nonprofit agencies during spring break four years ago to an annual celebration of volunteerism. More than 500 students in 2007 renovated homes for low-income families.

K-16 Initiative

At UNO, the K-16 Initiative focuses on increasing the college going rate and creating a future community of active citizens. K-16 projects both send students out to schools and community groups and bring members of the community to campus.

American Humanics

Devoted to preparing students for careers in youth and human service organizations, the UNO American Humanics program creates tomorrow's nonprofit leaders. Students apply their classroom learning by serving at agencies and organizations that serve the community.

Course Snapshot

MGMT 4000:

As a student reflected: "The further we advanced into this project, the less I worried about a grade and the more I worried about creating a result that could really make a difference. I have never in my entire educational 'career' felt anywhere near that level of pride in what I was doing." As a result of this service learning project, UNO undergraduate business majors helped a non-profit community skating rink build a comprehensive job-skills training program for economically-disadvantaged youth.

Academics

Service-learning addresses UNO's outreach mission as a metropolitan institution. It is an effective teaching strategy that increases faculty/student contact while contributing to student development.

Programs of study include:
Black Studies
Communications
Construction Systems
Criminal Justice
English
Foreign Languages
Gerontology
Goodrich Scholars Program
Health, Physical Education and Recreation
History
Information Systems and Quantitative Analysis
Journalism
Latino/Latin American Studies
Marketing and Management
Music
Philosophy and Religion
Political Science
Psychology
Public Administration
Social Work
Sociology
Special Education and Communication Disorders
Teacher Education
Theatre

"Students are given the opportunity to apply what they've learned to address community issues and help community organizations."

--Associate Professor David Ogden, recipient of the 2007 UNO Outstanding Service-Learning Faculty Award

Check out all majors at:
www.unomaha.edu/colleges.php

Awards and Recognition

Service-Learning
* 2006 President's Higher Education Community Service Honor Roll
* *U.S.News & World Report* recognized UNO's Service Learning as "an Academic Program to Look for" among 42 programs listed nationally.

Academics
* UNO listed in *U.S.News America's Best Colleges* 2007 rankings
* UNO received a top schools ranking for the Universities–Master's Midwest.
* UNO is listed in the top 150 ranked undergraduate business programs.
* UNO ranks among the top 10 in the Entrepreneurial Colleges in the limited curriculum category, which included more than 120 colleges and universities.
* UNO is one of only six Nebraska institutions receiving a listing in *Princeton Review's Best Midwestern College Guide 2007*.
* In *U.S News America's Best Graduate Schools 2007*, Public Affairs ties for 26th overall and ranks 18th nationally among public institutions.

College Fast Facts

Four Year, Public, Urban; Founded 1908

Web site: www.unomaha.edu

Student Profile: 11,929 undergraduate students (50.1% male,49.9% female); more than 91% from Nebraska, students from 111 countries attend UNO; 13 % of all students are minority or international students.

Faculty Profile: 499 full-time faculty. 18:1 Student/Faculty ratio. Class sizes are small - 63% are under 30 students

Athletics: NCAA Division II, North Central Conference (joining MIAA in 2008-09). 15 varsity sports.

Costs and Aid: 2007–2008: Resident: $10,620 w/parent; $15,200 - $15,230 (tuition/fees $4,430.) Non-resident: $17,680 w/parent; $22,260 - $22,290 (tuition/fees $11,490.) About 70% of students receive some financial aid. Average award: $1,500 (estimated per semester for undergraduate State of Nebraska residents.)

Admissions

University of Nebraska at Omaha, Undergraduate Admissions
6001 Dodge Street, EAB Room 103
Omaha, NE 68182-0286
Email: dcicotello@mail.unomaha.edu

Service-Learning
Service-Learning Academy
Paul Sather
Director of Service-Learning Academy & American Humanics
Phone: (402) 554-3196
Email: psather@mail.unomaha.edu

Montclair State University

Montclair State University offers all the advantages of a large university — a wide range of excellent undergraduate and graduate programs, a diverse faculty and student body — combined with the individual attention of a small college.

Service-Learning Focus

The Service-Learning Program at MSU focuses on several issue areas as a way to build and sustain reciprocal community partnerships. We also believe the social issues addressed by our community partners are best attended to by a variety of disciplines and specialties working together in partnership.

Flagship Programs

Emerging Leaders Learning Community
One hundred freshman student leaders in this program serve as mentors to area middle school students. The primary goals of the ELLC are to expose students to leaders; to help the students develop their own personal styles of leadership; to provide contact with MSU students who maintain healthy lifestyles; to build a secure support network, and; to acquaint students with leaders from different cultures and backgrounds.

STARS Program
Each semester approximately 100 service-learning students are assigned to 11 school and community sites as part of the STARS program. Service-Learning students serve 2-4 hours a week providing academic support to approximately 125 low- performing students in grades 1-5. The goal of STARS is to provide more opportunities for STARS children to have a literacy experience with a caring adult who can model good reading behavior; engage children in fun literacy activities that help improve important literacy skills such as fluency and comprehension; cultivate a love for books; and foster much-needed literacy development in children that will enhance overall academic achievement.

Course Snapshot

Introduction to Gerontology: This course introduces students to a broad based, integrated approach to understanding aging. It focuses on theory and the interrelatedness of social, psychological, economic, ethnic, biological, legal, cultural, political, spiritual, and health issues. It is open to students in all majors who want to increase their knowledge of aging, career paths in gerontology, and services for older adults and their families. Students provide 2-3 hours of service each week as they work with well, frail or institutionalized older adults in one of MSU's partner organizations.

"I loved my service experience and it helped me explore career opportunities. Everyone should take a service-learning course!
- Marissa Bednar, 2007

Academics

Service-Learning is a course-based, credit bearing educational experience in which students participate in an organized community-based service activity. This activity meets identified community needs, and provides a student with sufficient time to reflect on the service activity in such a way as to gain a greater understanding of course content and an enhanced sense of civic responsibility.

Business
Communications
Curriculum and Teaching
English
Justice Studies
Anthropology
Psychology
Family and Child Studies
New Student Experience
Theater and Dance
Earth and Environmental Studies

"Service-Learning made me realize that democracy does not take care of itself and I have developed an understanding that we all have a responsibility to serve our community"

Jordan Fullam
MSU Service-Learning Leader, 2005

Check out all majors at: www.montclair.edu/academics.html

Awards and Recognition
Service-Learning
• In 1997, The MSU Service-Learning Program was awarded a three-year, $105,000 Learn and Serve America Higher Education grant.

• In 2001, The MSU Service-Learning Program was awarded a three-year, $400,000 Community Outreach Partnership (COPC) grant from the US Department of Housing and Urban Development.

• In 2007, The MSU Service-Learning Program was awarded a two-year, $90,000 Bringing Theory to Practice Demonstration Site grant from the Charles Engelhard Foundation and the Association of American Colleges and Universities.

• In 2008 the MSU Service-Learning Fellows Program was awarded the TIAA-CREF Theodore M. Hesburgh Certificate of Excellence.

Academics
• MSU offers over 250 majors, minors and concentrations, through its five Colleges and Schools.

• MSU has the nation's only doctorate in pedagogy.

• *U.S.News & World Report* ranked MSU among the top tier of Northern Regional Universities.

• Celebrating 100 years of higher education in 2008.

College Fast Facts
Four Year, Public, Suburban, Founded in 1908

Web site: www.montclair.edu

Student Profile: 13,017 undergraduate students (38% male, 62% female); 36% minority, 5% international.

Faculty Profile: 491 full-time faculty (706 PT Faculty). 95% of FT faculty hold a terminal degree in their field. 17:1 student/faculty ratio. Average class size is 24.

Athletics: MSU participates in 17 varsity sports that compete on the intercollegiate level. The Red Hawks compete on the National Collegiate Athletic Association (NCAA) Division III level, and are also members of the Eastern College Athletic Conference and the New Jersey Athletic Conference.

Costs and Aid: 2007–2008: $23,709 comprehensive ($8,908 tuition). $24,491 out-of-state comprehensive ($14,690 tuition). 57% of students receives some financial aid.

Admissions
Montclair State University
Center for Career Services
and Community-based
Learning
Morehead Hall, Rm. 334
1 Normal Avenue
Montclair, NJ 07043

Service-Learning
Bryan Murdock
Director of Experiential Education
Phone: (973) 544-6831
Email: bmurdockb@mail.montclair.edu

Rider University

At Rider, we offer experiences that are relevant to you today and to your future. Rider helps you create meaningful linkages between the classroom and a variety of other learning experiences that will help you build leadership skills and achieve success in life and work.

Flagship Programs

Rider Community Scholars/ Bonner Leaders

Students in RCS commit to doing 300 hours of community service per academic year, through 7 partner agencies, using a team based model. Students receive training and enrichment as part of this four-year developmental program modeled by the Bonner Foundation in Princeton, New Jersey.

Minding Our Business (M.O.B.)

M.O.B. is a community outreach project that seeks to advance the development of youth in Trenton, New Jersey through entrepreneurship, education and mentoring. M.O.B.'s mentoring relationships and active-learning curriculum support the development of life skills, positive attitudes toward school and learning, and students' self-esteem. M.O.B. has three components: the Spring Program, the Summer Program, and the Advanced Program.

Special Olympics Bowling

This group of students bowl on a "Unified" Special Olympics team. A Unified Team pairs special needs athletes with Rider student partners in a year-long commitment. The special needs athletes are teens and young adults from the Mercer County area, mostly from West Windsor-Plainsboro high school.

Course Snapshot

IND 210-02 Global Encounters

A student reflected: "It has been said that the greatest resource of a country is its people. I learned to admire the Jamaican people who possess a deep strength in their country that is oftentimes overlooked." As a result of this service-learning course, undergraduate students are able to integrate curricular goals with community needs in the rural provinces of Jamaica.

Academics

In omnia paratus is Rider's Latin motto which means "in all things prepared." Our goal is to prepare you—for a life of success and a life of significance. We'll help you to find powerful connections in a variety of disciplines between the classroom and experiential learning to help you build leadership skills and much more.

Accounting
American Studies
Baccalaureate Honors
Biochemistry
Biology
Biopsychology
Business Policy and Environment
Communications and Journalism
Economics
Education
English Literature and Writing

Fine Arts (THE, ART, MUS)
Foreign Languages
Geological, Environmental, and Marine Sciences
Global and Multinational Studies
Law and Justice
Leadership Development Program
Multicultural Studies
Psychology
Political Science
Social Work

Check out all majors at: www.rider.edu/academics

"What service-learning really does for a student is increase the potential for a love of learning. My classroom teaching was confirmed when I saw the look of passion and understanding in the child my student was tutoring."

~ Professor Don Brown (IND 210-02 Global Encounters MCS 110 Multicultural Studies, Race, Class, Gender and Ethnicity)

Awards and Recognition
U.S.News & World Report; Princeton Review.

Accreditations
Association to Advance Collegiate Schools of Business (AACSB), National Council for the Accreditation of Teacher Education (NCATE), Council for Accreditation of Counseling and Related Educational Programs (CACREP), National Association of State Directors of Teacher Education and Certification (NASDTEC), Educational Leadership Constituent Council (ELCC), National Association of Schools of Music (NASM).

College Fast Facts
Four Year, Private, Suburban, Founded: 1865

Web site: www.rider.edu

Student Profile: 4,733 undergraduate students (40% male, 60% female); 35 states, 50 countries; 17% minority, 3% international, 23% out of state.

Faculty Profile: 244 full time faculty, 96.3% have a terminal degree; 301 part time faculty, 66.8% have a terminal degree.13.5:1 student/faculty ratio. Average class size is 27.

Athletics: NCAA Division I, MACC Conference. 10 varsity men's sports, 10 varsity women's sports.

Costs and Aid: 2007-2008 tuition = $25,650, room = $5,640, board = $4,140, required fees = $580. 63.8% of full time undergraduate students receive some form of financial aid.

Admissions
Rider University, Office of Undergraduate Admissions
2083 Lawrenceville Rd.
Lawrenceville, NJ 08648
Phone: 609-896-50402 or 800-257-9026
Email: admissions@rider.edu

Service-Learning
Bart Luedeke Center, Student Affairs
Phone: 609-896-5247

Seton Hall University

Seton Hall is a Catholic university founded in 1856. For over 150 years, it has been a "home for the mind, the heart and the spirit."

Flagship Programs

Journey of the Transformation

First-year students explore how to answer the call to service and leadership by discerning their skills through readings, discussions and a weekend retreat. Students are immersed into servant leadership, and get to know their community neighbors as part of this new core curriculum course.

Center for Community Research and Engagement

The CCRE develops partnerships that connect Seton Hall students, faculty, staff and neighboring communities through service learning opportunities and community-based research. Service learning is integrated into classes and provides opportunities for students to serve and broaden their understanding of nearby communities.

Major in Environmental Studies

The Environmental Studies major prepares students to be global servant leaders who build an environmentally, economically and socially sustainable society, one that balances the needs of people today with those of future generations. Among other things, students participate in town-wide clean-up and beautification efforts.

Course Snapshot

Community Health Perspectives

In Community Health Perspectives, senior nursing students complete community assessment and intervention service learning projects, which involve collaboration with nursing and other disciplines.  Service learning experiences focus on nursing students, agency partners, community members and faculty collaborating to assess the health needs of high risk populations, planning, implementing and evaluating interventions that address health needs.

Academics

At Seton Hall, developing servant leaders who will make a difference in the world is a priority. That's why students take classes in ethics and learn in a community informed by Catholic ideals and universal values. Students learn the importance of possessing integrity, compassion and a commitment to others. Twenty-four courses incorporate service learning into their curriculum utilizing classroom work and community engagement to introduce students to social and community issues.

Service-learning areas include:
Nursing
Marketing
Entrepreneurship
Business
Non-profit Studies
Physical Therapy
Financial and Fundraising Management
Educational Studies
English
Biology
Modern Languages
Art and Music

"Students and agency partners all benefit from collaborating on service learning projects. Students increased knowledge and critical thinking skills, while agencies decreased community health problems."

~ Kathleen Sternas, PhD, RN
Associate Professor, College of Nursing

Check out all majors at: www.shu.edu/academics/index.cfm

Awards and Recognition

Service-Learning
• *Templeton Guide: Colleges that Encourage Character Building.*

Academics
• Seton Hall's Nonprofit Management Program is ranked in the Top 10 nationally by *U.S. News & World Report.*

• The Stillman School, which is AASCB accredited, was included in the Princeton Review's 2008 Edition of *Best 290 Business Schools.*

• Seton Hall's Health-Law Program is ranked 4th in the country by *U.S.News & World Report.*

• The Whitehead School of Diplomacy and International Relations is one of approximately 30 professional schools of International Relations in the U.S. and is the only school in the country that is affiliated with the U.S. United Nations Association in New York.

• *U.S.News & World Report* ranked The Stillman School of Business in the Top 100 of College Business Programs in the U.S. and in the Top 10 of Catholic universities.

• Seton Hall is home to the oldest College of Nursing in New Jersey.

• Named one of the "most wired" universities by Yahoo! Internet Life magazine.

College Fast Facts

Four Year, Private, Suburban, Founded: 1856

Web site: www.shu.edu

Affiliation: Catholic

Student Profile: 8,400 undergraduate and graduate students (46% male, 54% female); 50 states and territories, 74 countries.

Faculty Profile: 860 full-time faculty. 92% hold a terminal degree in their field. 14:1 student/faculty ratio. Average class size is 25.

Athletics: NCAA Division I, BIG EAST Conference. 17 varsity sports.

Costs and Aid: 2007-2008: $37,860 comprehensive ($28,150 tuition). 90% of students receive some form of financial aid.

Admissions

Seton Hall University
Office of Undergraduate Admissions
400 South Orange Ave.
South Orange, NJ 07079
Phone: (973) 761-9000
Email: admissions@shu.edu

The College of New Jersey

The College of New Jersey (TCNJ) is a public comprehensive, highly selective, residential institution recognized nationally for its commitment to excellence.

Flagship Programs

Community Engaged Learning at TCNJ

At TCNJ, all 1300 first year students complete at least eight hours of structured community engaged learning (CEL) activities. Starting with the class of 2011, most of the students will participate in a second CEL experience (10 to 15 additional hours). While participating in upper level courses, they will apply knowledge and skills they gain to unmet needs of the region and state.

The Bonner Community Scholars Corps

TCNJ has a diverse team of 60 students who receive four-year service learning and leadership based scholarships. These students take classes together (e.g., a seminar on poverty), join one of twelve issue based teams that focus on specific

community issues in collaboration with a non-profit partner organization, and complete 300 hours of community engaged learning activities annually in the Trenton area. These teams also work with the Bonner Center staff to create and supervise first year students as they complete their required Community Engaged Learning experience.

Course Snapshot

Professor Beth Paul's Psychology students formed a **Community Based Research Corps** and produced a report for the city of Trenton's Youth Service Commission. Using surveys, interviews and GIS mapping, they found inconsistencies among the number of young residents and the existence of after-school programs serving their needs.

A member of the Mayor's staff said,

"this campus-community partnership shows how professors and students can play critical roles in enhancing the capacity of non-profit organizations to make informed and strategic decisions."

Academics

TCNJ seeks to be a national exemplar in the education of those who sustain and advance the communities in which they live.

Business	First Seminar Courses, including
Education*	Living in a Virtual World*
Engineering	American Masculinities*
English	Race, History & the Fictive Imagination*
Journalism	Video Games: Issues & Influences*
Nursing	Income Inequality*
Political Science	Urban Parks*
Psychology	Human Abilities Unplugged*
Sociology	Deconstructing Autism*
Women & Gender Studies*	

* Courses with a required community engagement component.

Check out all majors at: www.tcnj.edu/~bulletin/degree.html

"Some students told me this was the most meaningful learning they've ever experienced!" ~ Janet Mazur, First-Year Seminar Professor

Awards and Recognition

• Placed on the President's Higher Education Community Service Honor Roll With Distinction, awarded by the Corporation for National and Community Service.

• Featured in AACU's Diversity Digest (Volume 10, Number 1, 2006).

• National Resource Center for First-Year Experience: Program Director awarded Outstanding First-Year Student Advocate (2007)

• Recognized in Civic Engagement in the First Year of College, jointly published by The New York Times and The National Resource Center for the First-Year Experience, 2008 (forthcoming).

• Recognized for excellence in first-year and service programming in the *Templeton Guide to Colleges that Encourage Character Development*.

• *Baron's*: TCNJ is one of only five public institutions identified as "Most Selective" among their list of the top 75 colleges and universities nationwide.

• *US News and World Report*: TCNJ is consistently identified as the top masters-level public institution in their northern category.

• *Kiplinger's Personal Finance* rates TCNJ as the 5th best value in public higher education nationally for out of state students and the 23rd best value for in-state students in 2008—significantly higher than any other New Jersey school.

College Fast Facts

Four Year, Public Suburban, Year Founded: 1855

Web site: www.tcnj.edu

Student Profile: Undergraduate students (42% male, 58% female); 19 states and territories, 12 countries; 22% minority, 4% international.

Faculty Profile: Full-time faculty, 335; 88% hold a terminal degree in their field; student/faculty ratio is 13/1; average class size is 21.

Athletics: NCAA Division: III; Conferences: New Jersey Athletic Conference, Eastern Collegiate Athletic Conference, Metropolitan Conference; 20 intercollegiate sports teams (both men and women).

Costs and Aid: 2007-2008: $20,549 in-state comprehensive ($8,072 tuition). 56% of students receive some financial aid. 2007–2008: $27,772 out-of-state comprehensive ($15,295 tuition).

Admissions

The College of New Jersey
Office of Admissions
Paul Loser Hall, Room 228
2000 Pennington Road
P.O. Box 7718
Ewing, NJ 08628-0718
Phone: (609) 771-2131

Community Engagement

Patrick Donohue
Director
Bonner Center for Civic
& Community Engagement
Phone: (609) 771-2548
Email: bonner@tcnj.edu

Buffalo State College

Our goal is to inspire a lifelong passion for learning and to empower a diverse population of students to succeed as citizens of a challenging world.

Flagship Programs

Volunteer and Service-Learning Center

The Volunteer and Service-Learning Center (VSLC) leads efforts to integrate service with learning in departments across campus while improving the success of local agencies and schools in meeting the needs of community residents

The VSLC was created to address the following objectives:
• To encourage and assist faculty members to integrate service-learning into course curricula.
• To make information about service-learning opportunities available to students.
• To broaden communication and relationships between the campus and community-based organizations in order to meet identified community needs.
• To connect students with volunteer opportunities in the community.

Last year Buffalo State College students contributed over 23,000 hours of service through 57 service-learning courses and 2 volunteer events.

West Side Community Collaborative (WSCC) Partnership
The college's official service-learning partnership began with the WSCC, and has grown to include over 100 partners throughout western New York. The WSCC is a collaboration of over 30 non-profit, community, and faith-based organizations; along with public and private schools located on the west side of Buffalo. This successful partnership brings hundreds of students each semester into this ethnically diverse, low income neighborhood adjacent to campus to work on issues ranging from refugee resettlement to economic development.

Course Snapshot

ENG 354:
Ethnic American Literature

A community-based experience in Dr. Barbara Bontempo's service-learning course deepens students' learning and helps them to more fully understand and appreciate the kinds of issues, struggles, and joys akin to those experienced by people they had "met" in the literature. Interacting with children and adults from diverse backgrounds brings a very personal dimension to their coursework.

Academics

Linking classroom learning with service is an effective strategy for enhancing student learning, improving educational experience and fostering civic engagement. The following departments have included a service-learning component into existing courses:

School of Arts and Humanities
Art Education
Communication
English
Fine Arts
Interior Design
Modern and Classical Languages
Music
Theater
School of the Professions
Business
Computer Information Systems
Creative Studies
Hospitality and Tourism
Social Work
Student Personnel Administration

School of Natural and Social Sciences
Chemistry
Economics and Finance
Geography and Planning
History and Social Studies
Mathematics
Political Science
Sociology
School of Education
Educational Foundations
Elementary Education and Reading
Exceptional Education
University College
Foundations of Inquiry
Learning Communities

Check out all majors at: www.buffalostate.edu/academics

"As much as I value the contribution service-learning has lent to my success academically, I value even more the resulting feeling of connection to my school and to my community. There is a sense of empowerment in that connection as well as a sense of responsibility." ~ Sarah Smith, Sociology student

Awards and Recognition
Service-Learning
• President's Higher Education Community Service Honor Roll, 2007 and 2008.
• SUNY Outstanding Student Affairs Program for Civic Engagement, 2007.
• Demonstrated distinctiveness for service-learning on the 2006 National Survey of Student Engagement (NSEE).
• Learn and Serve awardee (2003-2006).
• Recipient of 4 AmeriCorps VISTA volunteers (2005-2008).

College Fast Facts
Four Year, Public, Urban, Founded: 1871
Affiliation: Nondenominational State University College

Student Profile: 41% Male, 59% Female, 20% minorities. Total undergraduate students 9,314. 30 states are represented at BSC with .01 % international students.

Faculty Profile: Full-time 416, part-time 339, total faculty 755, 44% hold terminal degrees,16:1 student/faculty ratio.

Athletics: NCAA Division III, ECAC SUNYAC Conference, 14 varsity sports.

Costs and Aid: In State: $8,700/yr; Out of State: 21,220/yr comprehensive (Room and Board): $8,514. 69% of students receive some financial aid.

• 136 undergraduate programs with 11 honors options.

• 63 graduate programs, including 18 postbaccalaureate teacher certification programs.

• Five schools: School of Arts and Humanities; School of Education; School of Natural and Social Sciences; School of the Professions; The Graduate School.

• Programs not available at any other SUNY institution: Adult Education; Applied Economics; Art Conservation; Creative Studies; Engineering Technology; Fashion and Textile Technology; Forensic Chemistry; Industrial Technology; Student Personnel Administration.

Admissions
Admissions Office
Buffalo State College
Moot Hall 110
1300 Elmwood Avenue
Buffalo, NY 14222
Phone: (716) 878-4017
Email: admissions@buffalostate.edu

Service-Learning
Volunteer and
Service-Learning Center
Buffalo State College
Clev. 306, 1300 Elmwood Avenue
Buffalo, NY 14222
Phone: (716) 878-5811
Email: vslc@buffalostate.edu

Canisius College

Canisius College is proud to share in the Jesuit heritage, which offers students a highly personalized education solidly based in the liberal arts that emphasizes the development of the whole person.

Service-Learning Focus

Service-Learning at Canisius College promotes the development of an enhanced learning process by incorporating community service within academic courses, together with structured reflection upon that experience in the context of the course. As a Jesuit college, Canisius adheres to the precepts expressed by Peter-Hans Kolvenback, S.J., Superior General of the Society of Jesus, *"Our purpose in education is to form men and women 'for others.' The Society of Jesus has always sought to imbue students with values that transcend the goals of money, fame, and success. We want graduates who will be leaders concerned about society and the world in which they live. We want our graduates to be leaders in service."*

Flagship Program

SIFE (Students in Free Enterprise)
Canisius College participates in SIFE (Students in Free Enterprise), a global not-for-profit organization of 1600 college teams in more than 40 countries. Designed to assist others in improving their economic well-being, SIFE creates and implements educational projects in entrepreneurship, market economics, financial literacy, business ethics, and personal success skills.

SIFE projects are both extracurricular and incorporated within economics courses. As part of their ECO 101 (Principles of Macroeconomics) and ECO 255 (Business Statistics I) courses, Canisius students teach Play-Dough Economics, a SIFE project, in area elementary schools. Play-Dough Economics consists of 15 economics lessons taught to children through the use of Play-Dough. Children use the dough to make tangible representations of the concepts they are learning. Canisius students keep statistics on the progress of the

Play-Dough Economics

elementary school children and at the same time reinforce their own understanding of basic economic principles.

Academics

Service-learning is incorporated into certain courses in every academic division. Service-Learning Courses included in:

Biology
Communications/Digital Media Arts
Criminal Justice
Economics
Education & Physical Education
English
Entrepreneurship
Fine Arts
History
Information Systems
Linguistics
Management/Marketing
Modern Languages
Philosophy
Religious Studies
Sociology
Women's Studies

One Canisius student comments, "My service was valuable because, in transcending boundaries of social class and location, I saw that people can be deeply connected when judgment is not passed and blame is not placed."

Canisius College offers more than 70 distinct majors, minors, and special programs.

Check out all of the undergraduate programs at:
www.canisius.edu/academics/undergrad_az.asp

Course Snapshot

ENG 210 Mothers in Literature and Film
In conjunction with this course, students volunteer at service sites that provide aid to mothers and children, such as Haven House, a shelter for victims of domestic violence, and Refugee Services of Catholic Charities. Service-learning brings literature alive as students reflect on the joys and challenges of motherhood and its meaning in contemporary society.

Awards and Recognition
• Consistently ranked in the top tier of *U.S.News & World Report* - America's Best Colleges, Northern Universities – Master's
• #12 in *U.S.News & World Report* - Great Schools, Great Prices
• Listed in *Barron's Best Buys in College Education*
• Listed in *Rugg's Recommendations on the Colleges*

College Fast Facts
Four Year, Private, Catholic, Urban; Founded 1870
Web site: www.canisius.edu
Student Profile: 3,233 undergraduate students (45.6% male, 55.4% female).
Faculty Profile: 215 full-time faculty. More than 95% hold a terminal degree in their field. Average class size is 17. Student:Faculty Ratio is 12:1
Athletics: NCAA Division I, MAAC Conference, 16 varsity sports (8 men, 8 women).
Costs and Aid: 2007-2008: $25,370 annual tuition. 98% of students in the class of 2011 receive some financial aid.

Admissions
Office of Undergraduate Admissions
2001 Main St., Buffalo, NY 14208
Phone: (716) 888-2200 or
1 (800) 843-1517
admissions@canisius.edu

Service-learning
Sr. Patricia Brady, SSMN
Director of Service-Learning
Phone: (716) 888-2177
bradyp@canisius.edu

Colgate University

Colgate University is a residential liberal arts college for men and women of talent who are preparing for lives of leadership and productive citizenship.

Flagship Programs

Upstate Institute

The Upstate Institute establishes meaningful links between Colgate and the upstate New York region by collaborating on community-based projects related to the economy, culture, and social fabric of the area. The Institute brings together students, faculty, area residents, and nonprofit leaders. Initiatives include: * The Upstate Institute Field School - During the summer, the Field School places more than 20 students in full-time paid internships to conduct research projects for community organizations.

The Center for Outreach, Volunteerism, and Education (COVE)

The COVE is Colgate's center for service, citizenships, and community building. The COVE sponsors about 35 student-led, community-based teams supporting a wide variety of local needs: after-school programs, tutoring, support for local senior citizens, and community services. Initiatives include: *Emergency responder volunteers - A dedicated group of students volunteer with fire departments and ambulance corps in the surrounding communities.

Course Snapshot

GEOG 318:
International Migration, U.S. Immigration, and Immigrants

Ellen Percy Kraly, geography professor

This course introduces students to international migration, immigrant assimilation and adjustment, and immigration policy formation. As part of their learning and research, students assist staff of a local refugee center by providing valuable assistance to families who often arrive in the U.S. without household possessions. Colgate students provide tutoring, English language training, and preparation for citizenship tests to immigrants from more than 30 countries.

Academics

Through service-learning initiatives, Colgate students test their knowledge in real world settings, become engaged in the community and develop an awareness and appreciation for something larger than themselves

Art and Art History
Biology
Computer Science
Economics
Educational Studies
English
Environmental Studies
French
Geography
Geology

German
History
Music
Peace and Conflict Studies
Physics
Psychology
Social Sciences
Sociology and Anthropology
Spanish

To see majors and minors, go to: www.colgate.edu

"Our energy – in and out of the classroom – goes toward preparing students to make effective and meaningful contributions to communities."

~ Ellen Kraly, geography professor and Upstate Institute director

Awards and Recognition

• Colgate was awarded the second annual Senator Paul Simon Award for Campus Internationalization, given by NAFSA: Association of International Educators.

• *Kaplan* and *Newsweek* listed Colgate as one of the 25 "New Ivies."

• Colgate has been recognized as one of the top producers of Peace Corps volunteers.

• Colgate is regularly recognized as one of the nation's "best buys" in higher education, thanks to its generous financial aid packages.

• Colgate is the 2006 winner of the National Arts Club's Medal of Honor.

College Fast Facts

Four Year, Private, Rural, Founded: 1819

Web site: www.colgate.edu

Student Profile: 2800 undergraduate students (48% male, 52% female); 35 countries; 22% identify themselves as students of color.

Faculty Profile: 277 full-time faculty. 96% hold a terminal degree in their field. 10:1 student/faculty ratio. Average class size is 18.

Athletics: 25 NCAA Division I teams. 23 intramural sports. 30+ club sports.

Costs and Aid: 2007–2008: $ 46,830 tuition and fees. 39% of students receive some financial aid.

Admissions

Colgate University Office of Admission
13 Oak Dr.
Hamilton, NY 13346
Phone: (315) 228-7401
Email: admission@colgate.edu

Service-Learning

Upstate Institute
Ellen Kraly, Director
Phone: (315) 228-6623
Email: ekraly@colgate.edu

The Center for Outreach,
Volunteerism,
and Education (COVE)
Ingrid Hale, Director
Phone: (315) 228-6880
Email: ihale@colgate.edu

Daemen College

Daemen College is a private college grounded in the liberal arts and known for exceptional professional degree programs.

Flagship Programs

Dominican Republic Health Clinic

Each year, through the student-run volunteer organization Students Without Borders, Daemen students, faculty, and alumni gather donations and travel to the Dominican Republic to provide medical care to residents of Progresso Dos, an impoverished and neglected barrios in the city of San Pedro DeMarcoris, Dominican Republic.

Seneca Babcock

Daemen College students from various majors including Social Work, Political Science, and Health Care Studies work together with Daemen's Center for Sustainable Communities to provide services to low-income residents. The Drama Club is a favorite of the children.

West Side Partnership

Students from Daemen work on projects including afterschool tutoring, civic-engagement workshops with area youth, assisting voters on Election day, coaching a team of students to compete in a Mock Trial, and encouraging students to see college life first hand.

Course Snapshot

IND 209-Campus Environmental Service Learning

In this course, students design and implement the campus Ecotrail which integrates art, science and nature appreciation. Recycled building materials have been used to make benches, stream crossings and a display building. Students have developed signage and hands-on exercises for K-12 students to use in their visits to the Ecotrail. Invasive plants have been removed and native plants as well as a living roof on the building have been incorporated into the trail.

Academics

Daemen believes in "learning through service." Students from every major and class level participate as individuals or groups. Throughout the city, and across the world, students are involved in environmental organizations, nursing homes, hospitals, clinics, and mentoring in schools, just to name a few of the hundreds of possibilities.

Hands on experience and civic engagement provide students with a service learning experience that develops habits to enrich their lives and their communities long after they graduate from Daemen. Some courses include:

Accounting	Mathematics
Art	Natural Sciences
Biology	Nursing
Biochemistry	Physical Therapy
Business Administration	Physician Assistant
Education	Political Science
English	Psychology
French	Religious Studies
Health Care Studies	Social Work
History &Government	Spanish

Check out all majors at: www.daemen.edu

"Service learning is an educational experience that goes beyond volunteering- it connects students to the community by integrating academic curriculum with active participation in service." ~ Dr. Edwin Clausen, Vice President for Academic Affairs and Dean

Awards and Recognition

Over the years, Daemen has received over 95 awards. Among them are:
• The Presidential Points of Light National Service Award for students' volunteer work and service learning activities.
• The New York State Governors Service to the Community Award
• The JC Penney/United Way Golden Rule Award – for Outstanding Service to the Community.
• March of Dimes Hero for Babies Award.
• Amherst Museum Service Appreciation Award.
• Weinburg Campus Service Appreciation Award.
• President's Higher Education Community Service Honor Roll Member.
Accomplishments
• Daemen is co-founder and headquarters for the Western New York Service Learning Coalition.
• Daemen founded and operates the Center for Sustainable Communities and Civic Engagement.
• Daemen has received numerous grants for service-learning, including two grants from Youth Service America through their Red, White and Green Program to fund the energy-efficiency projects.
• More Daemen seniors reported being involved in community-based projects as part of a regular course than did their peers at other institutions as reported in the National Survey of Student Engagement.

College Fast Facts

Four Year, Private, Suburban, Founded: 1947
Web site: www.daemen.edu

Student Profile: 1,705 undergraduate students.

Faculty Profile: 102 full-time faculty; 15:1 student/faculty ratio.

Athletics: NAIA Division, American Mideast Conference. 5 varsity sports. Men: Basketball, Cross Country, Soccer, Golf, Women: Basketball, Cross Country, Volleyball, Soccer. Plus many club sports. Casual athletes take part in intramural sports and keep fit in the exercise and weight rooms.

Costs and Aid: 2008-2009 $19,870 comprehensive ($19,400 tuition). 96% of students receive some form of financial aid.

Admissions

Daemen College
4380 Main Street
Amherst, NY 14226-3592
Phone: (716) 839-8225
1 (800) 462-7652
Email: www.daemen.edu/admissions
admissions@daemen.edu

Fordham University

Fordham University, the Jesuit University of New York, is committed to the discovery of Wisdom and the transmission of Learning, through research and through undergraduate, graduate and professional education of the highest quality. Guided by its Catholic and Jesuit traditions, Fordham fosters the intellectual, moral and religious development of its students and prepares them for leadership in a global society.

Flagship Programs

Interdisciplinary Seminar Program

In this student-initiated program, a student can earn one additional academic credit by meaningfully connecting a service experience to a particular academic course. To enroll in the program, students must complete 30 hours of service with an agency in the community, two integrative essays outside of additional course requirements, attend five seminars facilitated by the Community Service Program (CSP) and submit weekly reflections via e-mail.

Integrated Service-Learning

In this form of service-learning, a professor chooses to integrate community work as a learning resource for the course. Service is a requirement of these courses, so reflection and integration take place within the classroom. Faculty members work closely with CSP in finding appropriate local agencies for their students to work with, and CSP continues to provide support to faculty, students and the agency throughout the semester.

Course Snapshot

SPRU 2640 Spanish & New York City

This course is an advanced language course that examines the Latino experience in the United States while also promoting community engagement, greater linguistic fluency and cultural understanding of the Spanish-speaking world. Special attention is paid to the diverse history of Spanish-speaking populations in NY, emphasizing the specific cultural and linguistic practices of these communities. We will have several fieldtrips to different Spanish-speaking areas and cultural institutions in NY. The service-learning component of this course treats the topic of Hispanic migration as a contemporary — not just historical — occurrence. Students will work in the community every week using their Spanish and improving their language skills in a highly contextualized environment unmatched by the classroom experience. At the same time, they will gain first-hand knowledge about the immigrant experience while seeing real-world applications for their language skills.

Academics

Service Learning at Fordham

As a living-learning initiative, service-learning offers students an opportunity to expand their academic experience by bringing together service in the community with the learning resources of a course. The central idea with service-learning is that students are testing the concepts of their courses (e.g. in the humanities) or practicing the skills of a course (e.g. languages or sciences) through experience in the community. This experience is in service to an underrepresented or marginalized group. Thus, service-learning aims to benefit both the student who learns course materials through additional methods, exposure and experience, and the community agency where the student volunteers his/her time.

Following is a listing of some of our Service-Learning courses:

Art&Ecology	Religionin Public Life
Community Service&Social Action	Spanish&New York City
Feminist Theories in Inter-Cultural Context	Sustainability&Process
Films of Moral Struggle	The African City
Global Governance	Understanding the Global Economy
Intro to Sociology	Work and Family
Politics in Film	

Check out all majors & programs at: www.fordham.edu/comm_serv

Awards and Recognition
Community Engagement
• The Community Service Program was awarded three (3) grants (06-08)of $25,000 from the Teagle Foundation to run an academic summer program for local high school students called the History Makers Program.This project is a collaborative effort between Fordham and the Citizens Advice Bureau.
• Fordham University's Bronx African American History Project (BAAHP) has received an $18,000 grant (08) from the New York Council for the Humanities to support a series of public programs on the hisory of New York's most under-represented borough.This is a joint project with the Bronx County Historical Society to document the rich history of the borough's 500,000 residents of African descent.

Academics
• Fordham offers more than 65 academic programs in 11 colleges and schools.
• In 2008, *U.S.News & World Report*, ranked Fordham 67th among national universities in the United States.
• The undergraduate College of Business Administration was ranked 27th nationally in *Business Week* in 2008.
• Fordham University has been chosen as one of the "25 Hottest Schools in America " by the editors of *Kaplan/Newsweek's How to Get Into College Guide.*

Carnegie Classification
Research University (High Research Activity). This classification is based on number of doctoral degrees awarded, research expenditures, and numbers of research staff. Fordham is one of about 277 universities in the US that is classified as a research university.

College Fast Facts
Four Year, Private, Urban, Founded: 1841

Web site: www.fordham.edu

Student Profile: 7,652 undergraduate students (57% F, 43% M) 24.6% Students of Color; 48 states, PR, Guam, The Virgin Islands and 58 countries.

Faculty Profile: 667 Full-time instructors (60% M; 40% F; Faculty of Color 16%). Student/faculty ratio: 11.9:1, Average class size: 22.

Athletics: Athletics: NCAA Division I, A-10 (Football: Patriot League, I-AA)

Costs and Aid: Costs & Aid: $31,800 (most programs). 83.7% of the class of 2011 received financial aid.

Admissions
Office of Undergraduate Admission
Duane Library
441 East Fordham Road
Bronx, NY 10458-5191

Service-Learning
Community Service Program
101 McGinley Hall
441 East Fordham Rd.
Bronx, NY 10458-5191
www.fordham.edu/comm_serv
csprh@fordham.edu

Hobart and William Smith Colleges

Hobart and William Smith Colleges are liberal arts colleges dedicated to producing graduates with worlds of experience who will lead lives of consequence.

Flagship Programs

HWS Responds

In response to Hurricane Katrina, HWS fundraises, sponsors service trips with reflection tied to academic credit,

and participates in the Gulf Coast Civic Works Project Network, raising awareness and advocating legislation to help rebuild the Gulf Coast.

HWS Compass

Combining opportunities in community service, civic engagement/service-learning and civic leadership, HWS Compass is the model the Center for Community Engagement and Service-Learning uses to guide students toward a life of engaged citizenship. By following a path of learning and leadership through service they more deeply understand the complex issues that shape our world.

America Reads

Nearly 100 HWS students tutor children in reading at six different schools. Tutors gain experience working one to one

with elementary-aged children and also tackle the policy issues related to literacy. Children benefit from the individual attention and show real improvement in their reading levels.

Course Snapshot

FYSM 061: The Politics of Disaster

Students in Professor Cedric Johnson's seminar not only read about the response to Hurricane Katrina, they live it. Through a service trip, students participate in reconstruction efforts and speak with homeowners, and meet iwth area experts. "Since returning I have used examples from the trip in a number of my classes… The trip helped me to connect with the information that I learned…The information and experiences that I had over the course of my trip are something that could never be learned in a classroom."

-Ryan Conley, Hobart '10

Academics

Service-learning courses engage students through real community needs allowing them to gain new insights on the academic content while developing citizenship skills and making a material change in the community.

Service-Learning classes in the following areas:

- Africana Studies
- Anthropology and Sociology
- Architectural Studies
- Arts and Education
- Chemistry
- Dance
- Economics
- Education
- Environmental Studies
- Geosciences
- History
- Holocaust Studies
- Individual majors
- Media and Society
- Peer Education in Human Relations
- Philosophy
- Political Science
- Psychology
- Public Policy
- Study Abroad
- Urban Studies
- Women's Studies

"The Colleges have long been committed to service-learning and global studies, so with a president who was Director of the Peace Corps, it was natural that those programs would grow even stronger."

-Teresa Amott
Provost and Dean of Faculty

Check out all majors at:
www.hws.edu/academics

Awards and Recognition

- *Colleges With a Conscience, The Princeton Review*, 2005, 2007
- 2006 President's Higher Education Community Service Honor Roll With Distinctions for General Community Service and Hurricane Katrina Relief.
- Bonner Leader College
- Top 30 of *Washington Monthly*'s 2007 College Rankings of liberal arts colleges based on service to society.
- Founding Member, NY Campus Compact
- Minor in Public Service
- Phi Beta Kappa Chapter
- Economics Professor Jo Beth Mertens named Carnegie Foundation NYS Professor of the Year, 2005
- Rhodes, Fulbright, Goldwater and Gates Cambridge Scholarships awarded to graduates since 2004

College Fast Facts

Four Year, Private, Rural; Founded 1822 (Hobart), 1908 (William Smith)

Web site: www.hws.edu

Student Profile: 2,000 undergraduate students (47% male, 53% female); 39 states and territories, 20 countries.

Faculty Profile: 207 full-time faculty. 96% hold a terminal degree in their field. 11:1 student/faculty ratio. Average class size is 18.

Athletics: NCAA Division III (D-I for Men's Lacrosse), Liberty League, ECAC, ISCA, MAISA Conference. 22 varsity sports. HWS athletes have garnered numerous league championships and All-America honors. Each team completes a service project through HWS Athletes for Geneva's Youth.

Costs and Aid: 2007-2008: $47,768 comprehensive ($36,718 tuition); 77% of students receive some financial aid.

Admissions

Office of Admissions
629 South Main Street
Geneva, NY 14456
Phone: (800) 852-2256; (315) 781-3622
Email: admissions@hws.edu

Service-Learning

W. Averell H. Bauder
Director, Center for Community Engagement and Service-Learning
Phone: (315) 781-3825
Email: bauder@hws.edu

Nazareth College

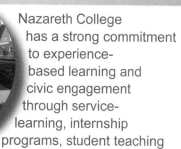

Nazareth College has a strong commitment to experience-based learning and civic engagement through service-learning, internship programs, student teaching opportunities, curriculum-based field experience and community service.

Flagship Programs

INAD 640: Transition Planning for Students with Disabilities
Students work one-on-one with youth at OCFS Industry Residential Center facilitating the development of the youths Transition Plans for transitioning from incarceration to employment, educational/vocational school, post-secondary ed/training, and independent living.

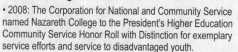

Freshman Seminar

At Freshman Seminar, students come together for three small-group service projects, each working with groups of youth who attend after-school programs. Examples include projects at Rochester City Rec Centers, and working with youth affected by AIDS and HIV. After working closely with the youth over 6 weeks, students learned about social, cultural, class and racial differences and commonalities across the borders between communities. They also build cultural competency skills, and gained confidence in working in difficult settings.

Chamber Players

Students perform recitals for special populations in the community, which requires students to coalesce and use the results of their daily practice, weekly lessons and weekly ensemble class for the benefit of others. While strengthening their performance skills, they experience the power of musical performance to communicate and affect others leadership, presentation and verbal communication skills.

Course Snapshot

"..At the settlement house I was a mentor with the kids. I listened to them talk about their day, I helped them with their homework, and sometimes we just sat and laughed about nothing.

Yes, service-learning is a different way of meeting class requirements, and yes, .. the time was worth it. I know I changed as my stereotypes and prejudices of others and at the same time, I helped as well."

Academics

Service-learning provides students, faculty and community members an opportunity to engage with each other and work together through meaningful service. While addressing course content, service-learning brings to life "theory" with "practice" as students reflect upon the connection between their in-class and out-of-class learning. The mission of Nazareth College's Center for Service- Learning is to facilitate the use of service-learning to achieve student learning outcomes by integrating reflective academic study with community experiences of services.

Service-learning is a pedagogical strategy that can be embedded within any academic area at Nazareth.

Colleges and Schools include:

College of Arts and Sciences
School of Management
School of Health and Human Services
School of Education
Freshmen Seminar

"The core curriculum exposed me to so many different disciplines – literature, philosophy, math, the sciences, arts, history and religious studies – but I was able to still focus on the subjects that interested me the most."

- Emily Cannon '08
Mathematics and Inclusive Education Major

View all majors and programs on the web at:
www.naz.edu/dept/admissions/consider/academics/index.cfm

Awards and Recognition
Service-Learning

• 2008: The Corporation for National and Community Service named Nazareth College to the President's Higher Education Community Service Honor Roll with Distinction for exemplary service efforts and service to disadvantaged youth.

• 2007: Nazareth named to the President's Higher Education Community Service Honor Roll; 2008 Nazareth was awarded with distinction (versus just plain awarded in 2007)

Academics

▪ *U.S.News & World Report:* College survey for 2008 ranks Nazareth in the top tier for the category of "Universities-Masters, North Region"

▪ *U.S.News & World Report:* Nazareth has been included in the "Great Schools at Great Prices" list.

▪ *Princeton Review:* Included in the upcoming "The Best 368 Colleges: 2009 Edition" guide. Nazareth is one of only four U.S. colleges added for the 2009 edition, and only 10% of all U.S. colleges are named to this list.

▪ *Princeton Review:* Features a two-page profile of Nazareth in its annual guide, "The Best Northeastern Colleges."

▪ *Princeton Review:* Awarded Nazareth College a 97 score in the category of Quality of Campus Life.

▪ During the past decade 2 Nazareth graduates were been awarded the Pickering Foreign Affairs Fellowships.

College Fast Facts
Four Year, Private, Suburban, Founded 1924

Web site: www.naz.edu

Student Profile: 2167 undergraduate students (25% male, 75% female); 24 states and territories; 10% minority, 1.6% international.

Faculty Profile: 24 full-time faculty. 90.1% hold a terminal degree in their field. 12 :1 student/faculty ratio.

Athletics: NCAA Division III, Empire 8 Conference. 23 varsity sports.

Costs and Aid: 2007–2008: $35,412 comprehensive ($23,046 tuition). 96% of students receives some financial aid.

Admissions

Nazareth College of Rochester
Office of Admissions
4245 East Avenue
Rochester, New York 14618-3790
Email: admissions@naz.edu
Phone: (585) 389-2860
Toll-free: 1-800-462-3944
Fax: (585) 389-2826

Service-Learning

Center for Service-Learning
Dr. Marie Watkins, Ph.D., M.S.W., M.S.
Associate Professor
Director, Center for Service-Learning
Director, Community-Based Youth Development Minor
Email: mwatkin2@naz.edu
Phone: (585) 389-2748

Niagara University

Niagara University is a comprehensive university which strives to educate its students through programs in the liberal arts and career preparation informed by the Catholic and Vincentian traditions.

Flagship Programs

Students in the College of Education and other majors tutor elementary and secondary students at 50 school and after-school sites in Western New York and the Canadian Province of Ontario. In the academic year 2006-2007, approximately 1000 Niagara University students tutored over 1000 elementary and secondary students providing over 30,000 hours of service.

Introduction to Social Work (SWK 100)

An introduction to the profession and general social work practice. The values, knowledge, and skills necessary for practice will be critically examined and discussed, along with social problems of concern to the profession. Students are required to engage in twenty-five hours of service-learning experience.

Marketing Research (MGK 311)

Students in this marketing research class study contemporary research methods used to provide information for solving marketing problems. Topics include market-research design and ethics. Students in this course work with high school students through Junior Achievement. Each Niagara University participates in twenty hours of service-learning.

Course Snapshot

ACC 223 – Intermediate Accounting I

Niagara University students were recruited and trained to participate in the Tax Counseling for the Elderly Program. The program was coordinated by the course professor in accordance with the terms and conditions specified in the Cooperative Agreement. The program was administered by Professor Oddo with assistance from other Niagara University faculty and was coordinated with the Upstate New York SPEC office to ensure compliance with administrative rules and guidelines. Our 75 volunteers worked a total of 750 hours, assisting 1,142 taxpayers with tax returns and other assistance. All of the 646 federal tax returns we prepared were e-filed, for an e-file percentage of 100%. Taxpayers received total federal refunds of $531,570, which includes $140,719 of earned income credits. Assistance consisted of preparation of Federal and State tax returns, and other assistance such as answering tax questions and W-4 assistance.

Academics

Through service-learning, Niagara University hopes to inspire its students to serve all members of society, especially the poor and oppressed, in local communities and throughout the larger world.

Accounting
Biology *
Commerce
Communication Studies *
Education *
English
History
Hospitality and Tourism Management *
Math
Nursing *
Philosophy
Political Science
Psychology *
Sociology *
Social Work *
Spanish
Theater*

"In keeping with our Catholic and Vincentian identity, we encourage students to assist others who are in need, and our students respond by providing thousands of hours of service annually in a variety of settings"

~ Rev. Joseph L. Levesque, C.M. President

* Courses with a required service-learning component.

Check out all majors at: www.niagara.edu

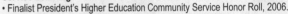
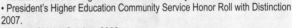

Awards and Recognition

Service-Learning
• Finalist President's Higher Education Community Service Honor Roll, 2006.
• President's Higher Education Community Service Honor Roll with Distinction 2007.
• Points of Light, October 2002.

Academics
• Niagara University offers more than 50 undergraduate majors, seven professional options and several five-year combined master's programs. Master's degrees in Education, Criminal Justice, Interdisciplinary Studies and an M.B.A.
• *U.S.News & World Report*'s 2007 ranks Niagara University in the category Best Universities – Masters in the North.
• *The Princeton Review* designated Niagara University as one of its select colleges and universities in the Northeast.
• Niagara University is one of 250 institutions nationwide selected as a member of the *Colleges of Distinction*.

College Fast Facts

Four Year, Private, Suburban, Founded: 1856

Web site: www.niagara.edu

Student Profile: 2800 undergraduate students (40% male, 60% female); 31 states and territories; 8% minority, 12% international.

Faculty Profile: 150 full-time faculty, 92% hold a terminal degree in their field. 14:1 student/faculty ratio. Average class size is 25.

Athletics: NCAA Division I, MAAC Conference. 17 varsity sports.

Costs and Aid: 2007-2008: $30,700 comprehensive ($21,000 tuition). 98% of students receive some form of financial aid.

Admissions

Niagara University
Office of Admissions
PO Box 2011
Niagara University, NY 14109
Phone: (716) 286-8700
(800) 462-2111
Email: admissions@niagara.edu

Service-Learning

Marilynn P. Fleckenstein, Ph.D.
Associate Vice President
for Academic Affairs
Phone: (716) 286-8750
Email: mpf@niagara.edu

College of Environmental Science and Forestry

SUNY-ESF is a small and selective public college with 50 academic programs focused on our environment and natural resources.

Service-Learning Focus

Students at the State University of New York's College of Environmental Science and Forestry (SUNY-ESF) enroll in service-learning courses that provide real world experience, college credits, and the satisfaction of helping others while solving environmental problems.

Flagship Programs

Service-Learning on a tropical island
Students in ESF's Tropical Ecology class recently traveled to the Island of Dominica and built a micro-hydro turbine to replace a diesel generator at a tropical research station. A running stream was diverted to turn the turbine and to generate electricity.

Helping high school students and the local environment
ESF students work on many projects to introduce local high school students to environmental problem-solving. A summer 2007 project helped to restore an inland salt marsh to control runoff and create a wildlife habitat at a polluted industrial site.

Service-learning in Landscape Architecture
Community projects provide rich learning opportunities for studio courses in ESF's top ranked Landscape Architecture program.

Course Snapshot

LSA 470 Advanced Site Design Studio

Community members from Fayetteville (NY) and landscape architecture students from SUNY-ESF worked together to develop design ideas for a Canal Landing Park located in the historic center of the village. This class provided an opportunity for students to learn how to involve community members in the design process, and to apply their design and graphics skills.
You can see the students' work at:
www.esf.edu/la/ccdr/projects/CanalLandingPark.htm

Academics

Service-Learning at ESF combines community service with academic instruction and focuses on critical, reflective thinking and civic responsibility. Programs of study include:

Aquatic and Fisheries Science
Bioprocess Engineering
Biotechnology
Chemistry
Conservation Biology
Construction Management
Environmental Biology
Environmental Resources and
    Forest Engineering
Environmental Science
Environmental Studies

Forest Ecosystem Science
Forest Health
Forest Resources Management
Landscape Architecture
Natural History and Interpretation
Natural Resources Management
Paper Engineering
Paper Science
Wildlife Science
Wood Products Engineering

ESF is ranked among the nation's top universities for value, small classes, and student engagement in learning...

Check out all majors at:
www.esf.edu/admissions/programs.htm

Awards and Recognition
•Ranked #33 among "Top 50 Best Buys" by *U.S.News*
•Ranked #38 among "Top 50 Public Universities" by *U.S.News*
•Ranked #85 among "Best National Universities" by *U.S.News*
•Ranked one of 25 "Cutting Edge Schools" in *Kaplan's College Guide*
•Ranked in *Peterson's 440 Colleges for Top Students*
•One of only 250 colleges in *Barron's Best Buys in College Education*
•Listed on President's Higher Education Community Service Honor Roll
•One of 71 Making a Difference Colleges (SageWorks Press, 2008)
•Ranked among the nation's top colleges for scholarly work (Academic Analytics, Inc.)
•ESF Alumnus Dr. Ronald Eby won a National Medal of Technology (2007)
•Rated higher than peer universities for "Enriching Experiences" in the 2007 National Survey of Student Engagement

College Fast Facts
Four Year, Public, Urban; Founded 1911
Web site: www.esf.edu
Student Profile: Of undergraduate students 60% male, 40% female, 24 states and territories, 7 countries; 9% minority, 1% international.
Faculty Profile: 136 full-time faculty; 90% hold a terminal degree in their field; 12:1 student/faculty ratio. Average class size is 20.
Athletics: ESF students compete on intercollegiate club sports teams sponsored by the College and by Syracuse University.
Costs and Aid: 2007–2008: $18,670 in-state comprehensive ($4,350 tuition); $24,930 out-of-state comprehensive ($10,610 tuition). 85% of students receive some financial aid.

Admissions
SUNY-ESF, Office of Undergraduate Admissions
1 Forestry Drive, Syracuse, NY 13210
Phone: (315) 470-6600; (800) 777-7373
Email: esfinfo@esf.edu

Service-Learning
Associate Dean for Student Life and Experiential Learning
1 Forestry Drive, Syracuse, NY 13210
Phone: (315) 470-6658

State University of New York at Oswego

SUNY Oswego contributes to the common good by empowering women and men to pursue meaningful lives as productive, responsible citizens.

Service-learning at SUNY Oswego promotes student growth and social change through directed civic engagement. Active engagement, learning by doing and involvement in the community are the hallmarks of education at SUNY Oswego.

Flagship Programs

Adopt-a-Grandparent

Oswego's Adopt-a-Grandparent Program pairs students with senior adults in the community through such activities as crafts, games and parties. Each week students visit local nursing homes to spend time with residents talking, sharing stories and participating in the planned activity.

Mentor Oswego

Mentor Oswego connects college students with children and adolescents in the Oswego community. They act as role models while providing fun activities and companionship to local youth through after-school programs, homework and lunch groups, and one-on-one mentoring.

Service-Learning Group Leaders

Service-Learning Group Leaders are students placed in leadership roles at numerous community sites. The group leaders lead reflection sessions with service-learning students and act as liaison between SUNY Oswego, the community site and the service-learning students. This program incorporates students of all academic majors.

Course Snapshot

COM 490: Communication and Service Learning
Students in Dr. Nola Heidlebaugh's senior capstone course are required to complete 20 hours of service through the semester at sites such as nursing homes, after-school programs and soup kitchens. The course is designed to integrate and apply students' knowledge through service to the community and seminar study.

"Through service, students discovered how applicable their communication major was to filling real-world needs."

~ Professor Nola J. Heidlebaugh

Academics

Through service-learning courses SUNY Oswego students are able to apply what they have learned in their courses to their service experiences.

Programs of study include:
Art
Communications
Education
English
Honors
Human Development
Human Resource Management
Management
Math
Psychology
Public Justice
Sociology
Spanish

Check out all majors at:
www.oswego.edu/academics/majors_list/
SUNY Oswego offers more than 110 academic programs for undergraduate and graduate study.

Awards and Recognition

Service-Learning
• President's Higher Education Community Service Honor Roll
• Founding institution, New York State Campus Compact

Academics
• SUNY Oswego is included in U.S. News' *America's Best Colleges* and Princeton Review's *Best Northeastern Colleges*.
• Oswego's School of Business has appeared in Princeton Review's *Best Business Schools* every year.
• Oswego's School of Business is accredited by the Association to Advance Collegiate Schools of Business International.
• Oswego's School of Education is accredited by the National Council for the Accreditation of Teacher Education (NCATE).
• *Hispanic Outlook* magazine lists SUNY Oswego among its "Publisher's Picks" every year for "offering Hispanic students a solid chance of academic success."

College Fast Facts

Four Year, Public, Small-city environment; Founded 1861
Web site: www.oswego.edu
Student Profile: 6,669 undergraduate students (47% male, 53% female); 18 states and territories, 30 countries; 12% minority, 2% international.
Faculty Profile: 326 full-time faculty. 83% hold a terminal degree in their field. 18:1 student/faculty ratio. Average class size is 24.
Athletics: NCAA Division III, State University of New York Athletic Conference. 24 varsity sports.
Costs and Aid: 2007–2008: $14,904 in-state comprehensive ($4,350 tuition); $20,080 out-of-state comprehensive ($10,610 tuition). 64% receive aid. Average award: $8,596.

Admissions

State University of New York at Oswego
Office of Admissions
229 Sheldon Hall
Oswego NY, 13126
Phone: 315-312-2250, Fax: 315-312-3260
Email: admiss@oswego.edu
www.oswego.edu/admissions

Service-Learning

State University of New York at Oswego
Center for Service Learning and Community Service
142 Campus Center
Oswego, NY 13126
Phone: 315-312-2505, Fax: 315-312-5406
Email: service@oswego.edu
www.oswego.edu/commserv

Syracuse University

SU Photo & Imaging Center

Syracuse University's vision of Scholarship in Action can change lives, neighborhoods, cities, regions and the world.

Flagship Programs

The Syracuse University Literacy Corps (SULC), an AmericaReads program founded in 1997, is a service-learning experience that mobilizes SU students to tutor at elementary and secondary schools and community based organizations working in partnership with the Syracuse community toward improved literacy.

Photo Credit: Stephen Mahan

Under the auspices of the **Partnership for a Better Education,** Art, Literacy and Technology is a collaborative photography and writing initiative that involves high school students from the Syracuse City School District, SU's College of Visual and Performing Arts (CVPA), Light Work, and the Creative Writing Program in the College of Arts & Sciences (A&S). High School students work with SU students and faculty to photograph scenes from their lives then use these images as catalysts for verbal and written expression.

Public Affairs Program (PAF) at the Maxwell School applies a problem-solving model to social issues through understanding the implementation of public policy as well as the challenges and importance of gathering information/data in a variety of ways. Students in the Community Benchmarks Program, a PAF core course, provide research support to local governments and nonprofits using comparative measures which is part of a continuous improvement effort by the clients.

Course Snapshot

WRT 205: Critical Research: Writing with the Community: Critically Researched Perspective on Disability Arts, History, and Culture.

The role of the student is to capture the imagination of the participants (developmentally challenged adults) and to creatively form a text depicting the emotions and thoughts of the participants as they theatrically transform into the idol or, role model of their choosing. The extended goal is to have the journal published with professional photos of the participants in character followed by the text that the students and participants penned. The finished service-learning project will be showcased at Syracuse University Bird Library.

Academics

Service-learning/research courses at Syracuse University address real community-identified needs, involve reciprocal relationships with community partners, include reflective components offering students opportunities to process their experiences within the construct of their curriculum.

Service-learning opportunities are offered in the following schools and colleges:
School of Architecture
The College of Arts & Sciences
School of Education
College of Human Ecology
School of Information Studies
LC Smith College of Engineering & Computer Science
Martin J. Whitman School of Management
Maxwell School of Citizenship & Public Affairs
S.I. Newhouse School of Public Communications
College of Visual and Performing Arts
University College (SU's College of Continuing Education)

Check out all majors at:
www.students.syr.edu/cpcs/course_listing.html
www.compact.org/carnegie/applications/full_text/syracuse

"For someone like me, who had never tutored anyone, let alone a refugee from Somalia, my service-learning experience was 100% unique and equally rewarding."

~ Service-Learning Student, A&S '11 WRT 301: Civic Writing

Awards and Recognition

• Carnegie Community Engagement Classification in Curricular & Outreach Partnerships 2006.
• President's Higher Education Community Service Honor Roll Awardee: Special Focus Area, "Youth from Disadvantaged Circumstances" 2007.
• President's Higher Education Honor Roll with Distinction for Community Service and Hurricane Relief 2006.
• *Princeton Review: Colleges with a Conscience* 2005.
• Maxwell School named #1 Graduate School of Public Affairs by *U.S.News & World Report* 2008.
• International Reading Association, Central New York Council, Honor for Exemplary Service and Promotion of Literacy.
• Westside Learning Center Community Education Award.
• United Way of Central New York 2005 Spirit of Caring: Professional Service Award.
• The Salvation Army National Salvation Army Week "Can-Do Awards" 2008.
• Syracuse City School District Certificate of Recognition for the SU Literacy Corps.

College Fast Facts

Four Year, Private, Urban, Founded: 1870

Affiliation: Nondenominational

Web site: www.syr.edu

Student Profile: Undergraduate students 12,491, 44% male, 56% female; 50 states and territories, 115 countries, 29% minority, 4% international.

Faculty Profile: 909 full time faculty, 106 part-time, 447 adjunct. Of the full time faculty, approximately 88% have earned Ph.D or professional degrees.

Athletics: NCAA Division 1 Conference: Big East.

Costs and Aid: 2007-2008 tuition - $ 30,470. Approximately 64% of all undergraduate students receive need-based financial aid from Syracuse University and other sources. Overall, 79% receive some form of financial support, including assistance from institutional, federal, state, or private sources.

Service-Learning

Pamela Kirwin Heintz, Director
Syracuse University
Mary Ann Shaw Center for Public & Community Service (CPCS)
237 Schine Student Center
Syracuse, NY 13244
Phone: 315-443-3051; (Fax) 315-443-3365
Email: pkheintz@syr.edu

University of Rochester

The University of Rochester, founded in 1850, is one of the nation's leading private universities. With just over 4,500 undergraduates, Rochester is one of the smallest and most collegiate in character among the top research universities.

Flagship Programs

Wilson Day was a first of its kind orientation activity which sends new students out into the community during their first days at college. Over its ten year history, it has been featured in The New York Times, Time, The Chronicle of Higher Education, and last year won the prestigious Georgen award for its distinctive contributions to learning. Through Wilson Day, the University of Rochester hopes to instill an idea of service into all of its students.

Residential Life
• The Tiernan Project was founded in 1978 as the first community service special interest living center in the country.
• The Community Learning Center, a 25-member house dedicated to the exploration of service and social justice issues.

Portable Research Grants
The goal of the Portable Research Grant is to get undergraduate students involved in experiential activities that stimulate your mind, broaden your perspectives, expand your intellectual and social networking, and strengthen your connections to the University community, as well as the research and creative communities throughout the world. Portable Research grants provide funding of up to $3,000 for undergraduate students working with a faculty sponsor. Students awarded a Portable Research Grant who are also hired for an unpaid and non-credit bearing community service internship or service learning position can be compensated with the grant.

Course Snapshot

CAS 385: Leader to Leader

Leader to Leader will provide students with an opportunity to learn about leadership history, theory, and practice. It is not a leadership workshop, but rather a means through which students can better grasp the nuances of a complex and multi-faceted idea. Leadership discussions and guest speakers on the topics of leadership history, the influence of culture, gender, race, and ethnicity, negative and charismatic leadership, emerging leadership models, leaders within government, business, community development, education, and religion.

Academics

The Rochester Curriculum encourages students to take responsibility for their learning and for where they live. Students learn best when they learn what they love and communities are strongest when members get involved. Rochester students are therefore encouraged to become involved community members and to act as leaders who give shape and direction to the world around them by committing of their time, learning, talents energy and resources.

African and African-American Studies, American Sign Language, Anthropology, Art & Art History, Economics, English, History, Political Science, Engineering

Check out all majors at:
www.rochester.edu/college/academics
www.rochester.edu/college/rccl/academics/courses/

"Entering a new environment and interacting with diverse people may be daunting, but if we are open to new ideas, flexible, and willing to communicate and make an effort, this situation can be extremely positive. Service often helps students learn more about the wider world and shape their views, and may give us an idea of what we want to do in the future." ~ Meghan Ochal, Anthropology '05

Awards and Recognition
• *U.S.News & World Report 2008* ranked the University of Rochester 35th among top national universities.
• The University of Rochester was one of only 25 schools named a "New Ivy" in the 2007 *Kaplan/Newsweek* "How to Get into College Guide."
• In 2006 the University of Rochester placed 21st on The Washington Monthly College Rankings list of schools that are "benefiting the country."
• The University of Rochester ranked in the top 25 among U.S. universities by the Times of London.
• Top 15 colleges in service activity by Who Cares magazine.
• President's Higher Education Community Service Honor Roll, 2007

College Fast Facts
Four Year, Private, Suburban, Founded: 1850

Web site: www.rochester.edu

Student Profile: Undergraduates (49% male, 51% female), 50 states; 52 countries; 44% undergraduates from out of state, 18% if you choose to count Asian/Pacific Islander); 8% international.

Faculty Profile: 515 full-time faculty; 88% hold a terminal degree in their field; 9:1 student/faculty ratio; Average class size: 30 (Arts & Sciences), 28 (Engineering).

Athletics: NCAA Division III; UAA, Liberty League; 22 varsity sports.

Costs and Aid: 2007-08: $45,830 comprehensive ($34,380 tuition); 87% receive some financial aid.

Admissions
University of Rochester
Office of Undergraduate
Admissions
P.O. Box 270251
Rochester, NY 14627-0251
Phone: (585) 275-3221 or
Toll Free: (888) 822-2256
Website: www.enrollment.rochester.edu/admissions
Email: admit@admissions.rochester.edu

Service-Learning
Rochester Center for Community Leadership
Phone: (585) 276-3278
Fax: (585) 276-0151
Website: www.rochester.edu/College/rccl/
Email: csn@ur.rochester.edu

Appalachian State University

Appalachian State University is a comprehensive, public university committed to academic excellence, teaching, scholarship and transformative co-curricular experiences for students.

Flagship Programs

20/20 Program: Bringing Community Issues Into Focus!

ASU's Elementary Education program involves students in service-learning and teaches them how to incorporate it into their future classrooms. Projects range from working with poverty to disabilities to immigration, and prepare teachers for dealing with social issues that affect children.

International Service-Learning

Students travel to Latin America, Africa, India or Britain and serve a variety of populations and social issues. These courses/trips range in length from 1-6 credits and 8 to 30 days, and are offered over winter/spring break and summer.

Public Service Research Program

Provides students two opportunities for community-based research. Lower-level students can work on a multidisciplinary research project (currently trail use conflicts).

Upper-level students can work on independent research with community partners for their senior honor's thesis or independent study.

What our Students Say

Nearly 89% of students told us that their involvement in service-learning gave them a better understanding of how their course-work relates to "real world" situations.

Nearly 79% found that the academic projects combined with their service-learning experience helped them more effectively learn and retain course material.

Almost 89% of students told us that service-learning broadened their understanding of social issues that affect their community.

Academics

Increase your knowledge about crucial social/environmental concerns, research solutions to these systemic problems, and gain the necessary skills to become a global citizen! Some courses include:

Art	Interior Design*
Chemistry	Language, Reading, &
Communication	Exceptionalities
Communication Disorders*	Management*
Curriculum & Instruction*	Music
English	Political Science
Family & Consumer Sciences*	Recreation Management*
German	Social Work*
Health Education	Sociology
Health Promotions	Spanish
Human Development & Psychological Counseling	Special Education
Interdisciplinary Studies	Technology
	Theatre & Dance

* Majors with a required service-learning component.

Check out all majors at: www.web.appstate.edu/academics/

"This class has forced me to think critically about myself, my world view, and the difference between my words and my actions." ~ April Eichmiller, ASU student

Awards and Recognition

General/Academic
• *U.S.News & World Report's 2008 America's Best Colleges* Guide.
• *The Princeton Review*'s 2008 edition of "America's Best Values in Colleges."
• *Consumers Digest* magazine's listing of the top 50 best values for public colleges and universities.
• *Kiplinger's Personal Finance* magazine's "100 Best Values in Public Colleges."

Service
• Recognized by the *U.S.News & World Report* as having a strong academic service-learning program.
• Recognized on the President's Higher Education Honor Roll for our work with hurricane relief efforts in 2006.
• Recognized with distinction on the President's Higher Education Honor Roll, with a focus on outreach to disadvantaged youth in 2007.
• Charter and very active member of North Carolina Campus Compact.
• Applying for Carnegie Classification of Community Engagement in 2008.

College Fast Facts

Four Year, Public, Rural, Founded: 1899

Web site: www.appstate.edu

Student Profile: 13,997 undergraduate students (52.7% male, 47.3% female); 10 % minority, 1% international; 1,327 out-of-state.

Faculty Profile: 710 full-time faculty, 77% hold a terminal degree in their field. 1:17 student/faculty ratio. Average class size is 24.

Athletics: NCAA Division 1-A . Southern Conference. 20 varsity sports. Also offer 19 club sports and more than 60 intramural sports.

Costs and Aid: 2007-2008: $9,894.00 in-state comprehensive ($4,534 tuition); $19,954 out-of-state comprehensive ($14,594 tuition). 59% of students receive some form of financial aid.

Admissions
Appalachian State University
Office of Admissions
John E. Thomas Hall
Boone, NC 28608
Phone: (828) 262-2120
Email: admissions@appstate.edu
www.appstate.edu

Service-Learning
Shari Galiardi
Director of Service-Learning
University College/ACT Program
Phone: (828) 262-8211
Email: galiardisl@appstate.edu
www.act.appstate.edu

Duke University

Duke offers rigorous academics with a strong interdisciplinary focus, a spirited community, and an emphasis on broad-based civic engagement.

Flagship Programs

DukeEngage

Duke's newest service-based initiative is DukeEngage, a program launched in 2007 which provides full funding for Duke undergraduates who wish to pursue an immersive civic engagement experience anywhere in the world. Through DukeEngage, students apply what they have learned in the classroom to address societal issues at home or abroad.

The Hart Leadership Program

The Hart Leadership Program within the Sanford Institute for Public Policy provides Duke undergraduates with an opportunity to practice the art of leadership in public life. Courses give students analytical frameworks for grappling with problems facing our global community. Immersion experiences help them see how policy works in the real world.

The Duke University Community Service Center (CSC)

strives to engage members of the Duke community in thoughtful collective action, enrich the educational experience of students, and assist our home city of Durham, North Carolina.

Course Snapshot

PUBPOL 109: Natural Catastrophes – Rebuilding

Students will conduct a life cycle analysis of natural disasters. Invited experts will discuss meteorologic, hydrologic, and geologic factors that cause disasters; explore how societies plan and/or respond to the immediate and long-term physical, social, emotional and spiritual issues associated with survival; and present case studies of response, recovery and reconstruction efforts. Students will carry out response activities over Spring Break in an area ravaged by a natural disaster. They will keep a journal of their activities, write a brief synopsis, and make a group oral presentation of their findings following their return. They will also submit a hypothetical research proposal for a project which might stem from the course and their experiences.

Academics

Service-learning at Duke links classroom learning with service to local and global communities. Developed through collaboration among faculty, students, and individuals and organizations, service placements are designed to enhance the educational goals of a course and to serve the public good by providing a needed service to individuals, organizations, schools, or other entities. Students at Duke are challenged to translate knowledge gained in the classroom into service to communities across the globe.

Art
Cultural Anthropology
Documentary Studies
Education
Engineering
Environmental Studies
History
Human Development
Psychology
Public Policy *
Sociology
Spanish

"Duke provided structure and resources to translate my curiosity about the world into action...you do not have to wait until the "real world" to start getting involved."

-Sara Jewett Nieuwoudt, '00

* Courses with a required service-learning component.

Check out all majors at: www.duke.edu/academics.html

Awards and Recognition

Service-Learning
• *U.S.News & World Report* - 38 Best Academic Programs for Service Learning.
• President's Higher Education Community Service Honor Roll with Distinction.

Academics
• Top 10 of *U.S.News & World Report's* 2008 America's Best National Colleges and Universities.

College Fast Facts

Four Year, Private, Suburban

Web site: www.duke.edu

Student Profile: 6197 undergraduate students (51% male, 49% female); 49 states and territories, 41 countries; 46% minority, 6% international.

Faculty Profile: 787 full-time faculty; 8:1 student/faculty ratio. Average class size is 22.

Athletics: NCAA Division 1, ACC Conference. 24 varsity sports. Multiple Duke athletics programs are nationally ranked. Men's basketball is consistently ranked in the top 10 programs annualy.

Costs and Aid: 2007-2008: $45,091 comprehensive ($35,856 tuition). 40% of students receive some financial aid.

Admissions

Duke University , Office of Undergraduate Admissions
2138 Campus Drive
Box 90586
Durham, NC 27708
Phone: (919) 684-3214

Civic Engagement

Duke Center for Civic Engagement / DukeEngage
Eric Mlyn, Ph.D.
Director
Phone: (919) 668-1724
Email: eric.mlyn@duke.edu

Mars Hill College

Mars Hill College is committed to character development, to service, and to responsible citizenship in the community, region, and world.

Flagship Programs

The Bonner Scholars Program

Bonner Scholars gain access to affordable education and opportunities to serve in a wide range of community engagement activities. Bonner Scholars participate in 140 hours of service and reflection activities each semester, as well as two full-time summers of service.

The LifeWorks Civic Engagement Certificate

Students in the LifeWorks Civic Engagement program engage in weekly service and participate in weekly team-building and leadership development seminars over 6 semesters. The seminars are designed to cultivate knowledge, skills, and dispositions for lifelong contributions to the common good.

The Appalachian College and Community Economic Development Project (ACCEDP)

In a collaboration with Mountain Bizworks, a local microenterprise incubator, Mars Hill students gain experience in entrepreneurship and microenterprise. ACCEDP fosters community-based research focusing on three areas of potential growth in our county: niche agriculture, the craft industry, and housing/construction.

Course Snapshot

LAA121: Character (General Education, taught by faculty from across the disciplines)

This is the second in the sequence of five interdisciplinary Commons courses that all MHC students take. In this course, students read a variety of texts answering the question "what makes a good person?" Additionally, each student chooses one area of community engagement as their own personal "life text" and connects the world of experience with the world of ideas, using each as a lens to examine the other. Service-oriented experiences are encouraged, but not required, for the life text.

Academics

MHC offers service-learning in general education and major courses, with community-based research, field education and service-oriented internships in many departments.

Art
Business
General Education
History
Religion and Philosophy
Social Work
Sociology
Teacher Education
Theatre
Women's Studies

Check out all majors at: www.mhc.edu/academics.asp

"The two most important things students learn in college are who they are and what they love. Service-learning is a great vehicle for discovering both."

–Professor Kathy Meacham (Religion and Philosophy)

Awards and Recognition

Service-Learning
• Bonner Scholars Program
• President's Higher Education Community Service Honor Roll
• Learn and Serve America grantee
• Ford Foundation Difficult Dialogues grantee
• FIPSE Civic Engagement grantee
• Council for Independent Colleges Campuses and Communities grantee

Academics
• MHC offers 31 majors in 18 academic disciplines
• Accredited pre-professional programs in Teacher Education, Social Work, Music, Theatre, and Athletic Training
• National Endowment for the Humanities grantee
• U.S Department of Education Title III grantee
• Participant in American Association of Colleges and Universities Greater Expectations program

College Fast Facts

Four Year, Public, Rural, Founded: 1856

Affiliation: Baptist

Web site: www.mhc.edu

Student Profile: Undergraduate students (51% male, 49% female); 34 states and territories, 21 countries; 22% minority, 8 % international.

Faculty Profile: 81 full-time faculty. 58% hold a terminal degree in their field. 14:1 student/faculty ratio. Average class size is 15 -22.

Athletics: NCAA Division II South Atlantic Conference. 20 varsity sports.

Costs and Aid: 2007–2008: $26,785 comprehensive ($19,984 tuition). 96% of students receives some financial aid.

Admissions

Mars Hill College Admissions Department
PO Box 370 Mars Hill, NC 28754
Phone: (866) MHC-4-YOU
Email: admissions@mhc.edu

Service-Learning

Stan Dotson
Dean of LifeWorks
Phone: (828) 689-1161
Email: sdotson@mhc.edu

North Carolina State University

NC State is a comprehensive land-grant university globally recognized for its leadership in education and research, especially in science, technology, engineering, and mathematics.

Flagship Programs

Center for Excellence in Curricular Engagement:
From one-time immersions, to semester-long activities, to capstones, to course sequences, our goal is the integration of academic learning with civic learning and personal growth through critical reflection. We approach service-learning developmentally, co-creating with students opportunities for ever-higher levels of responsibility, leadership, and learning.

Co-curricular Service-Learning:
The Shelton Leadership Challenge Institute enables youth to practice leading their peers through leadership development activities, service, and reflection integrating a 3-tier inter-generational staffing model. The Alternative Service Break (ASB) program provides a service-learning experience in which students engage in direct service to a community (in the US or abroad), while being immersed in the culture and customs of that community.

Nonprofit Studies Minor:
Students in any major can enroll in this minor to learn about, experience, and reflect on the challenges facing leaders (broadly defined) in the nonprofit sector. Service-learning runs throughout the minor, from an introductory survey course, through core courses in the history of nonprofits and organizational leadership, to an internship and a capstone.

Course Snapshot

One of our longest running service-learning enhanced courses is **"Recreation Programming Planning,"** in the Department of Parks, Recreation, and Tourism Management. Working in teams, students engage in direct service with people ranging from children at community centers to older adults at community senior centers and use that interaction and their course material to design, implement, and assess two recreational events at their partner organization. Students reflect not only on the challenges of recreation programming but also on the civic purposes of their profession, including its role in enhancing quality of life and building community.

Academics

Our goal is that students will become increasingly responsible for their own learning, skilled at critical thinking, and able to connect academic and community knowledge in the search for solutions to the challenges of the 21st century. Courses across campus integrate service-learning, from the first year through graduate school, in general education and in the major. Some students design their own capstone service-learning projects as independent studies or honors projects, often including a research component. Every College offers community-based learning opportunities in its curriculum.

*"We have to keep striving, not only towards fulfilling the **hope** that all students will **become** active citizens, but the **intention** that they will **be** active citizens: that they will be engaged **while they are here** on our campus, that they will be committed to changing their own lives and the lives of those around them, both now and in the future."*

~ Erin Possiel – Class of 2005 and 2007

Check out degrees and programs at:
www.ncsu.edu/academics/degrees-programs/index.php

Awards and Recognition
Academics
• NC State offers bachelor's degrees in 110 fields, master's degrees in 110 fields, and doctorates in 61 fields.
NC State Recognitions
• President's Higher Education Community Service Honor Roll with Distinction (2008).
• Invited to contribute a student co-authored book chapter to Higher Education and Civic Engagement – International Perspectives (2007).
• Carnegie Classification for Community Engagement (2006).
• Princeton Review ranked NC State as the second-best value among public colleges and universities (2006).
• One of 19 service-learning programs across the US featured for its student leadership roles in Students as Colleagues: Expanding the Circle of Service-Learning Leadership (2006).
• One of 81 universities and colleges across the US featured in *Colleges with a Conscience* (2005).

College Fast Facts
Four Year, Public, Urban, Founded: 1887
Web site: www.ncsu.edu
Student Profile: 24,145 undergraduate students (55.8 % male, 44.2% female); 100 countries; 20% minority.
Faculty Profile: 1939 total faculty population. 90.7% hold a terminal degree in their field. 16:1 student/faculty ratio. Average class size is 35.
Athletics: NCAA Division I. Atlantic Coast Conference.
Costs and Aid: 2007-2008: $5,117.00 in-state comprehensive ($3,760.00 tuition); $17,315.00 out-of-state comprehensive ($15,958.00 tuition). 25% of students receive some form of financial aid.

Admissions
Office of Undergraduate Admissions
203 Peele Hall, Campus Box 7103
Raleigh, NC 27695-7103
Phone: (919) 515-2434; Fax: (919) 515-5039
Email: undergrad_admissions@ncsu.edu
http://admissions.ncsu.edu

Service-Learning
Center for Excellence in Curricular Engagement
Office of the Provost and Executive Vice Chancellor
NC State University
Box 7119
Raleigh, NC 27695
Phone: (919) 513-0650
Fax: (919) 513-0679
Email: curricular_engagement@ncsu.edu

University of North Carolina at Chapel Hill

Through its teaching, research and engagement, the University of North Carolina at Chapel Hill serves as an educational and economic beacon for the people of North Carolina and beyond.

Flagship Programs

Service-Learning Courses

Service-learning courses integrate community-based service into the course curricula. Students take abstract theories from the classroom and put them into practice through service to the community. Students complete a minimum of 30 hours of service during the semester at community partner sites.

Alternative Break Programs

Alternative Fall and Spring Break programs provide an avenue for students to perform service activities across North Carolina, the Southeast, and the Mid-Atlantic. Each experience offers academic learning and service engagement around particular social issues ranging from urban poverty and immigration to the environment and civil rights.

Global Service-Learning

The Global Service-Learning Program offers undergraduate students a unique opportunity to work with global and local immigrant communities, while uniting academic coursework with substantive volunteer service. In the semester after their return, students participate in a reflection seminar and engage in a local service project with immigrant youth. The seminar focuses on establishing connections between the lives of immigrants in their origin countries and their new communities. Themes related to global migration and migration transitions, as well as health, education and social justice are central to the seminar.

Course Snapshot

SOCI 068, (Section 001)
 "Immigration in Contemporary America" Jacqueline Hagan

Contemporary international migration is transforming politics, economics, social relations, and ethnic identities in societies throughout the world. This first-year seminar course is designed to introduce students to the fascinating and ever-changing study of immigration in contemporary America. As a part of this service-learning course, students volunteer with organizations that serve immigrant populations or address immigration issues.

Academics

Service-learning focuses on the connection made between service in the community and what one learns in an academic setting. A sampling of departments APPLES works with are listed below:

Department of African Studies
-and Afro-American Studies
Department of Anthropology
Department of Astronomy
Department of Biology
Department of Biomedical Engineering
Department of Chemistry
Department of Communication Studies
Department of Computer Science
Department of Comparative Literature
Environmental Science and Studies
Department of Geography
Department of Philosophy
Department of Psychology
Department of Romance Languages
Department of Sociology

"APPLES enables me to construct a course which I believe is the ideal learning experience. It allows me to merge a reciprocally beneficial mix of cognitive-based classroom learning and experiential-based learning in the community."

~ Dr. Joel Schwartz, Political Science

View information on all academic programs at:
www.unc.edu/ugradbulletin/

Awards and Recognition
• UNC is recognized by the Carnegie Foundation as "A Community Engaged University."

U.S.News & World Report
• 5th among public national universities (August 2007).
• 28th among national universities.
• 1st among publics, 9th overall in "Great Schools, Great Prices."
• 14th "least student indebtedness" among national universities.
• 5th (tied) "best undergraduate business program."

Princeton Review
• One of the best college values in the nation (April 2005).
• 3rd for the Daily Tar Heel student newspaper (September 2005).
• 5th for fan loyalty (September 2005).
• 8th for happiest students.
• 16th in popularity of both intramural and intercollegiate sports.

Princeton Review and Forbes.com
• 1st in Entrepreneurship (October 2004).

Kiplinger's Personal Finance
• "Best value" among public universities for the sixth consecutive time (February 2007).

College Fast Facts
Four Year, Public, Founded: 1789

Web site: www.unc.edu

Student Profile: 28.18% minority, 3.9% international, 80.4% North Carolina residents, 19.6% residents of other states and countries.

Faculty Profile: 3200 full-time faculty, 90% hold a terminal degree in their field. 14 :1 student/faculty ratio. 50% of classes have 20 or fewer students, 70% of classes have fewer than 30 students.

Athletics: NCAA Division I, Conference ACC.

Costs and Aid: 2007–2008: $15,796 in state comprehensive ($3,705 tuition). $32,004 out of state comprehensive ($19,353 tuituion). Carolina meets 100% of demonstrated need through federal, state, and University grants; scholarships; and loans.

Admissions
Office of Undergraduate Admissions
University of North Carolina
at Chapel Hill, CB #2200
Jackson Hall
Chapel Hill, NC 27599-2200
Phone: (919) 966-3621
Fax: (919) 962-3045
Email: unchelp@admissions.unc.edu
www.unc.edu/admissions

Service-Learning
APPLES
Service-Learning Program
University of North Carolina
at Chapel Hill, CB #5210
Chapel Hill, NC 27599-5210
Phone: (919) 962-0902
Fax: (919) 843-9685
Email: apples@unc.edu
www.unc.edu/apples

Warren Wilson College

Warren Wilson College combines liberal arts study, work, and service with a strong commitment to environmental responsibility and opportunities for cross-cultural understanding.

Flagship Programs

Developmental Psychology Series: Infant, Child, Adolescent, and Adult

Students enrolled in this four-part series of courses are given the opportunity to volunteer in a variety of agencies that serve the relevant target population. Students enrolled in Adult Development, for instance, dedicated ten hours to interviewing residents of a center for adults with developmental disabilities.

Human Behavior and the Social Environment

These two-part Social Work courses provide practical experience to students by engaging them in various community-based initiatives. For example, students formed a small task force and volunteered time participating in a local drug and alcohol rehabilitation program.

Warren Wilson College First Year Experience Program

All students enrolled in the College's First Year Seminar program engage in service during their initial semester. Many of these service opportunities make a connection between the Seminar's course content and the volunteer work. For example, several Seminar service projects strive to provide education and exposure to important local issues such as affordable housing, water quality, diversity, and homelessness.

Course Snapshot

First Year Seminar #107: Information Matters

A first-year student reflected: "I found a great connection between my tutoring and mentoring and the content of the Seminar. I have come to the understanding that education is the most important defense. To become a part of a child's life early in their education is the best way...I can extend my talents into the community and help out."

Academics

Art
Biology
Business Administration & Economics
Chemistry
Creative Writing
English
Environmental Studies
History & Political Science
Global Studies
Humanities
Integrative Studies
Mathematics
Outdoor Leadership*
Philosophy
Psychology*
Religious Studies
Social Work*
Sociology/Anthropology
Spanish
Women's Studies
* indicates a required service-learning component

"I experienced a lot of 'Aha!' moments relating the course's theory to practice."

--*Warren Wilson student enrolled in*

EDU 93 : Explorations in Science Education

Check out all majors at:
www.warren-wilson.edu/academics/

Awards and Recognition

Service-Learning

• *U.S.News & World Report*: For five consecutive years, one of only 25 schools nationwide listed in the "Service Learning" category of "Programs to Look For" in choosing a college

• Bonner Scholars College

• Charter campus, North Carolina Campus Compact

Academic Distinctions

• #1 in the number of students over the years who have won North Carolina Academy of Science awards for their research.

• Only work college that also has a service-learning program in which all students are required to participate in order to graduate.

• #1 in the Southeast on *Outside Magazine*'s list of "40 schools that turn out smart grads with top-notch academic credentials, a healthy environmental ethos, and an A+ sense of adventure."

• #1 in receiving the national 2006 Campus Sustainability Achievement Award from the Association for the Advancement of Sustainability in Higher Education, in the category of four-year schools with fewer than 1,000 students.

• #1 in its selection by the organization Sustainable North Carolina as recipient of the 2006 N.C. Sustainability Award, in the Environmental Stewardship category.

College Fast Facts

Four Year, Private, Rural: Founded 1894

Web site: www.warren-wilson.edu

Student Profile: 868 students (38% male, 62% female); 44 states and territories; 5% minority, 4% international.

Faculty Profile: 62 full-time faculty. 12:1 student/faculty ratio. Average class size is 16.

Athletics: United States Collegiate Athletic Association. 12 varsity sports (6 men's: basketball, soccer, cross-country, mountain biking, canoe & kayak, swimming; 6 women's: basketball, soccer, cross-country, mountain biking, swimming), 3 club sports, and other intramurals.

Costs and Aid: 2007–2008: $25,384 comprehensive ($21,384 tuition). 90% of students receive some financial aid. Average award: $12,374.

Admissions

Office of Admissions
P.O. Box 9000
Asheville, NC 28815-9000
Phone: 800-934-3536
Local: 828-771-2073
Email: admit@warren-wilson.edu

Service-Learning

Carolyn Wallace
Dean of Service-Learning
Phone: 828-771-3015
Email: cwallace@warren-wilson.edu
service@warren-wilson.edu

Western Carolina University

A campus of the University of North Carolina, Western prepares graduates to lead and succeed in the communities they serve.

Flagship Programs

Medford Scholars

This program awards scholarships to five undergraduates who have demonstrated their commitment to community service and academic achievement. Winners serve as peer mentors and reflection leaders in the service-learning program. Scholarships are announced during the annual Service-Learning Awards Ceremony honoring students, faculty, staff and community partners for their achievements.

Faculty Fellows

Fellows serve as consultants and mentors, assisting the Center for Service Learning by providing resources and support to their colleagues in order to make service learning an integral part of their teaching, research and professional service. Each Fellow represents a college of the university and receives a three-credit-hour course release.

Civic Place

The Civic Place program offers seminars, workshops, a film series, community service projects and academic support. Students participate in a living-learning community where they can develop interpersonal, team-building, civic leadership and communications skills; connect with community agencies; experience personal, social and intellectual growth; and cultivate long-lasting friendships.

Course Snapshot

RTH 360: Recreation Therapy
Students, who provide recreational therapy interventions to residents of the Alzheimer's unit at a local nursing home as part of their coursework, coordinated an evening of dining, dancing and socializing, patterned after traditional high school prom nights.

"We wanted to give them an opportunity to have fun. It was good for us, too. You can sit in a lecture all day long, but it is important to get experience so you'll be ready for your career." – Laura Corriher, Recreation Therapy major

Academics

Service learning enables students to learn at a deeper level and apply their discipline-specific knowledge to community and workplace issues.

Progams of Study include:

Art	Physical Therapy
Business Administration	Psychology
Communication	Public Relations
Computer Information Systems	Social Work
Education	Sociology
English	Spanish
History	Sport Management
Interior Design	Theatre in Education

Check out all majors and programs of study at:
www.wcu.edu/studentd/29.asp

"Service learning can change one's life for the better and make our communities stronger." ~ Garrett Richardson, political science student

Awards and Recognition

• An education writer for the Washington Post listed WCU as a "hidden gem" among "the top 100 outstanding but underappreciated colleges" in the nation.
• Learn & Serve America gave WCU a three-year, $7,500 grant – one of only 11 awarded nationally in 2007 – to help the town of Canton develop a comprehensive plan to recover from recent severe flooding and to serve as a model for other towns.
• WCU student Katherine "Katie" Graunke was named a finalist for the National Campus Compact's Howard R. Swearer Humanitarian Award.
• The American Association of State Colleges and Universities selected WCU for the prestigious Christa McAuliffe Award of Excellence in Teacher Education in 2007.
• President's Higher Education Community Service Honor Roll, 2007

College Fast Facts
Four Year, Public, Rural: Founded 1889

Web site: www.wcu.edu

Student Profile: 8,665 total; 7,403 undergraduate; 1,263 graduate students (46% male, 54% female); 46 states and territories, 39 countries; 13.3% minority, 3.6% international

Faculty Profile: 457 full-time faculty; 74% hold terminal degrees in their fields; 14:1 student/faculty ratio; average freshman class size: 23.

Athletics: NCAA Division I, Southern Conference, 12 varsity sports. Student-athletes at Western strive for winning programs, academic achievement, exceptional sportsmanship and integrity. Go CATS!

Costs and Aid: $13,630 in-state comprehensive ($4,871 tuition); $23,767 out-of-state comprehensive ($14,454 tuition); 74% of students receive some financial aid; average award is $7,500.

Admissions
WCU Admissions
Phone: 1 (828) 227-7317
Toll free: 1 (877) WCU-4YOU (877-928-4968)
Email: admiss@wcu.edu

Center for Service Learning
Glenn Bowen, Ph.D.
Center for Service Learning
Phone: 1 (828) 227-2643
Email: gbowen@email.wcu.edu

Defiance College

Defiance College is a nationally recognized liberal arts college educating students for leadership and service in a democratic society.

Using knowledge they have gained in the classroom, Defiance College students are empowered to apply their learning to real-world settings, creating a better quality of life within their community. One way that students integrate community engagement with leadership development is through participation in AmericaReads, providing supplemental academic support within local schools.

Flagship Programs

Student Ernest Clover with youngsters during project in Cambodia.

McMaster School

The McMaster School for Advancing Humanity prepares students to examine the root causes of human suffering in the world and take measured action to alleviate it. Its scholars and fellows program sends Defiance students and faculty all over the world for research, service, and leadership through collaboration. Students have studied and researched in such places as Belize, Cambodia, Guatemala, and Jamaica.

Citizen Leaders

Defiance College Citizen Leader Program provides $2,000 tuition scholarships for new students who demonstrate a record of service in their communities. Citizen Leaders participate in unique and exciting programs that develop their leadership skills and strengthen their individual career interests. Leaders also have opportunities for domestic and international travel.

Bonner Leaders

Citizen Leaders who distinguish themselves as emerging leaders are invited to become Bonner Leaders. This 1-3 year leadership program provides Defiance College students with opportunities to professionalize their leadership skills, strengthen their resumes, and deepen their understanding and practice of community engagement and democratic practice.

Course Snapshot

OS3132 Community Practices:

For students who participate, an international McMaster Scholar experience becomes a life-shaping event. As a faculty member and McMaster Fellow to Cambodia, social work professor Jeff Weaner has watched the student transformation: "They are called upon to act. They are galvanized in their academic study with the real world."

Academics

There is no better way to truly understand a subject than by taking what is learned in the classroom and applying it out in the world. Because the learning done by Defiance College students includes service to others, they are not just theorizing about improving the world. They are making it happen, reshaping lives through their efforts.

Service-learning is offered as a component of 130 courses. By the time they graduate, nearly all students at Defiance College have had both a structured service-learning component within a course and a capstone experience linking their academic learning to community needs.

Awards and Recognition

• *U.S.News & World Report* named Defiance College as one of the top schools in the nation for its service-learning program. *U.S.News & World Report* also named Defiance among the top tier of comprehensive colleges in the Midwest.

• Defiance is featured for excellence in blending academics with community work by *The Princeton Review* in its Colleges with a Conscience: 81 Great Schools with Outstanding Community Involvement.

• The John Templeton Foundation's Honor Roll for Character-Building Colleges recognized Defiance for its first-year, second-year, civic education, and volunteer service programs.

• Defiance College was named to the President's Higher Education Community Service Honor Roll with Distinction for its commitment to community service and Hurricane Katrina relief efforts.

Service-Learning Fast Facts

• All freshmen participate in Freshman Service Day, volunteering at one of four sites with a follow-up week, guided readings, and written reflections.

• All intercollegiate student-athletes participate in service projects with their teammates. In the 2007-08 academic year, more than 2,500 hours of service were performed by DC student-athletes.

• This year more than 50 students will travel internationally on academic-based service projects. There is no additional cost to the student to participate.

• The teacher education program requires teacher interns to use service learning as pedagogy during their internship semester in classes at all grade levels and in all disciplines.

• A service learning component is incorporated into the senior field placement for all social work majors.

College Fast Facts

Four Year, Private, Small Town, Founded: 1850

Web site: www.defiance.edu

Student Profile: 1,000 undergraduate and graduate students; 50% women and 50% men among full-time students; 66% of traditional students live on campus.

Faculty Profile: Average class size is 15 students; student/faculty ratio is 12:1. Nearly half of full-time faculty participate in international projects, most of them partnering with students for collaborative research and service.

Athletics: NCAA Division III, 18 intercollegiate sports competing in the Heartland Collegiate Athletic Conference.

Costs and Aid: 2008-2009, $10,655 tuition per semester; 99 percent of full-time students receive some form of financial aid.

Admissions

Defiance College, Office of Admissions
701 N. Clinton St., Defiance, OH 43512
Phone: (419) 783-2359; (800) 520-GO DC (4632)
Email: admissions@defiance.edu

Service-Learning

Dr. Laurie Worrall
Dean, McMaster School for Advancing Humanity
Phone: (419) 783-2553
Email: lworrall@defiance.edu

John Carroll University

As a Jesuit Catholic university, John Carroll inspires individuals to excel in learning, leadership, and service in the region and in the world.

Flagship Programs

Cultivating Community

The Cultivating Community class focuses on learning about Cleveland neighborhoods through multiple disciplinary lenses. Students learn the history of Cleveland and tour those historic sites, they learn about the governing system of the city by visiting City Hall to meet with the Mayor and a City Councilperson, or meeting with residents of a neighborhood to learn about their lives and community. The class culminates in a day long service project in which 250 John Carroll students, faculty, staff and alumni join with the residents to clean, paint, and plant. All participants share a meal at the conclusion of the work day.

Arrupe Scholars Program for Social Action

Students applying to the university are selected based on their application essays. Over the course of their four years at John Carroll, Arrupe Scholars deepen their understanding of the inequities in society and engage in positive actions to effect change. This unique scholarship program integrates the curricular and co-curricular experience to develop students who are committed to social action.

Course Snapshot

In **Honors 168, The Border/La Frontera,** John Carroll students study about Tijuana and border issues between Mexico and the U.S. Students then travel to Tijuana, Mexico to work with the Los Niños Community Development Program. Working side-by-side with members of local communities, JCU students learn about and give back to the vibrant communities of the U.S.-Mexican border.

Academics

Once faculty members have the students asking questions about social inequities, particularly in the classroom, we begin the process of bringing about change. Faculty members are teaching them to identify problems, use theory and data to analyze these realities, and develop strategies to effect change. We are suggesting that their intellectual life informs their lived reality; that with the gift of education comes the responsibility to reach out to those in need. Whether a student chooses business, science, the humanities, or social science, a university education means each one has the obligation to work for the common good.

"When the heart is touched by direct experience, the mind may be challenged to change." --- Peter-Hans Kolvenbach, SJ

Departments that offer service-learning courses:
Arts and Sciences, Biology, Communication and Theatre Arts, Education and Allied Studies, First Year Seminar, Physical Education, Philosophy, Political Science, Psychology, Religious Studies, Sociology, and Spanish.

Check out all majors at: www.jcu.edu/academics/

Awards and Recognition
• *U.S.News & World Report*: John Carroll University ranks among the top 10 universities in the Midwest that grant master's degrees.
• *U.S.News & World Report*: Ranked second in graduation rate.
• *U.S.News & World Report*: 12th overall among universities selected in the "Great Schools, Great Prices."
• *The Princeton Review* cited the Boler School of Business in its Best 282 Business Schools for 2007.
• Twice within the last five years John Carroll has placed in the top three nationally in passing percentage of the CPA exam for first-time test takers.
• 92% of our graduates are employed full-time or in full-time graduate programs within 9 months of graduation.
• *The Carroll News* was awarded second place in the region by the Society of Professional Journalists for all-around weekly newspapers.
• JCU Student: 2007 Howard R. Swearer Student Humanitarian Award.
• JCU Student: 2007 Charles J. Ping Student Community Service Award.
• 2007 President's Higher Education Community Service Honor Roll.
• JCU students perform more than 27,000 hours of community service during the school year.
• More than 100 students participate in immersion trips annually.
• 1,300 members of the JCU community participated in some form of

College Fast Facts
Four Year, Private, Suburban, Founded: 1886
Affiliation: Jesuit, Catholic
Web site: www.jcu.edu
Costs and Aid: 2007–2008: $34,934 comprehensive ($26,144 tuition). 98% of students receives some financial aid

Admissions
John Carroll University
Office of Undergraduate Admission
20700 North Park Blvd.
University Heights, OH 44118
Phone: (216) 397-4294; (888) 335-6800
Email: admission@jcu.edu

Service-Learning
Dr. Peggy Finucane, Interim Director
Center for Service and Social Action
Phone: (216) 397-1780
Email: mfinucane@jcu.edu

Oberlin College

Oberlin is a four-year, highly selective liberal arts college that is also home to a world-renowned Conservatory of Music.

Service-Learning Focus

Ranked among the nation's top liberal arts schools, Oberlin College is committed to academic rigor, artistic and musical excellence, and social justice. Learning through direct interaction with society enriches the educational process, and a wide spectrum of curricular and co-curricular programs supports a culture of social engagement.

Flagship Programs

Cole Scholars Program

Oberlin students are intensely interested in the electoral process. The Cole Scholars Program prepares students for careers as elected public officials. Each year, 15 sophomores and juniors are selected for a paid summer internship; the following fall, they enroll in a seminar in which they relate their experiences to wider issues of electoral politics. **http://www.oberlin.edu/politics/initiative.htm**

SITES (Spanish In The Elementary Schools)

Oberlin students can improve their Spanish while exploring a career path in teaching through the SITES program (Spanish In The Elementary Schools). Student tutors meet with the program coordinator twice weekly through a practicum course (EDUA 010), that covers professional issues related to language teaching. **http://www.oberlin.edu/SITES/about.htm**

Course Snapshot

POLT 411: Practicum in Policy Evaluation & Applied Research, Professor Eve Sandberg

In this upper-level Politics course, students serve as consultants to a variety of civic institutions, many devoted to social action and policy-making. In the past, students have worked with City Year - Cleveland, Ohio Legislative Black Caucus, Save Our Children, Policy Matters Ohio, and the Oberlin City Council. Students write grants, provide information to lobbyists, and fulfill the research needs of many local organizations. Professor Sandberg hopes to teach students pre-professional skills in consulting and research design, as well as provide students with the tools to apply what they learn to contribute to their community.

Academics

Oberlin students have multiple opportunities for community service integrated with academically rigorous, credit-bearing courses through over 25 service-learning courses per year, in which faculty and students apply knowledge beyond the classroom setting to make a positive difference in society.

College of Arts & Sciences:

African American Studies	Hispanic Studies
Anthropology	History
Art	Psychology
Biology	Religion
Comparative American Studies	Rhetoric & Composition
East Asian Studies	Sociology
English	Theater & Dance
Environmental Studies	
First-Year Seminar Program	**Conservatory:**
Gender & Women's Studies	Music Education

Check out all majors at: www.oberlin.edu/nav/majors_dept.html

Students synthesize their own intellectual and artistic experiences with knowledge from many academic disciplines.

Awards and Recognition
Service-Learning

• Recognized for a culture of civic engagement through inclusion in The Princeton Review's publication *Colleges with a Conscience: 81 Great Schools with Outstanding Community Involvement*. The 2005 publication features Oberlin for its record of excellent service-learning programs and for blending academics with community work.

• Listed on the President's Higher Education Community Service Honor Roll with Distinction in both 2006 and 2007.

• Invited by the Bonner Foundation to engage in endowment process of existing Bonner Scholars Program.

Academics

• Oberlin offers 47 academic majors and 42 minors and areas of concentration.

• Top 20 of *U.S.News & World Report*'s 2007 America's Best Liberal Arts Colleges.

• Ranked 13th in the Washington Monthly 2006 college guide, which tracks schools on how well they perform as engines of social mobility, produce academic minds and scientific research, and encourage an ethic of service.

• Oberlin was listed in the top 30 of Black Enterprise's "50 Top Colleges for African Americans" in 2006.

College Fast Facts
Founded: 1833
Web site: www.oberlin.edu

Student Profile: 2,800 undergraduate students (45% male, 55% female); 19% minority, 6% international, 9% in-state, 85% out-of-state, 6% from abroad.

Faculty Profile: 274 full-time faculty, 95% hold a terminal degree in their field. The student-faculty ratio in the College of Arts and Sciences is 11:1 and in the Conservatory of Music the ratio is 8:1. Average class size is 18.

Athletics: NCAA Division III, North Coast Athletic Conference (NCAC). 22 varsity sports.

Costs and Aid: 2008–2009: $48,150 comprehensive ($38,012 tuition). 70% of students receive some form of financial aid. Average award: $25,000.

Admissions
Oberlin College of Arts and Sciences
101 N. Professor St.
Oberlin, OH 44074
Phone: 800-622-6243 or 440-775-8411
Email: college.admissions@oberlin.edu
Fax: 440-775-6905

Oberlin Conservatory of Music
39 W. College St. Oberlin, OH 44074
conservatory.admissions@oberlin.edu
Phone: 440-775-8413

Service-Learning
Bonner Center for Service & Learning
Beth Blissman, Ph.D., Director
68 S. Professor St.,
Oberlin, OH 44074
Phone: 440-775-8055
beth.blissman@oberlin.edu
www.oberlin.edu/csl

Otterbein College

Founded in 1847, Otterbein is a private, coeducational comprehensive liberal arts college, located in the heart of central Ohio.

Flagship Programs

youthLEAD at Otterbein

Otterbein offers seventeen service-learning programs where students work side-by-side with our community's urban youth to solve community problems and address local issues. We have made a commitment to move beyond a youth-as-beneficiary model to a community-building model, where students and "at-promise" youth are working together to strengthen their communities through service, research, and direct volunteerism.

The Genoa Creative Literacy Alliance

The GCLA is a Poet-in-Residence collaboration with Genoa Middle School that provides creative literacy experiences for middle school youth. College students in English 375 are trained in the art of teaching literacy through poetry and theater strategies.

Plan-it EARTH

This CardinalCorps organization takes an activist approach to address environmental issues and promote awareness about our ecological footprints. Plan-It Earth plans activities that encourage and challenge Otterbein students to make steps to reduce, re-use, and recycle.

Course Snapshot

SYE 473: AFRICA

Why is the birthplace of humanity, on one hand, a continent rich with beauty and resources and, on the other hand, wracked with conflict and disaster? Students of Dr. Glenna Jackson and Dr. Simon Lawrance experience, explore, and impact Rwanda. After attending class sessions covering introduction to African cultures, students fly to Rwanda. During their two-week stay, they live in African communities, visit the mountains where the Karisoke Research Centre in the Parc National des Volcans is located, and provide direct service in orphanages, schools, and other community resource organizations.

Academics

At Otterbein we are educating citizens for a global community. Learning at Otterbein moves beyond the classroom and into the community through experiential, hands-on, real-life opportunities in one of Ohio's greatest cities and across the globe.

Otterbein students apply their academic skills in communities by addressing the literacy, social, economic, and health needs of our local and global neighbors. Otterbein offers service-learning in 18 different disciplines, including:

Business	Integrated Studies
Chemistry	Journalism
Communication	Life Sciences
Computer Science	Math
Education	Music
English	Nursing
Equine Science	Political Science
Foreign Languages	Psychology
Health and Sport Sciences	Senior Year Experience
History	Sociology

Check out all majors at: www.otterbein.edu/academics/majors.asp

"Students gain a greater understanding of the challenges faced by our communities as they become more informed and better prepared global citizens."

Awards and Recognition

General/Academic
• Otterbein has consistently placed high among peer institutions in *U.S.News & World Report*'s "Guide to America's Best Colleges" for over a decade.
• Otterbein is currently ranked 15th among its 140 peers in the University-Master's (Midwest) category.
• The Westerville Education Association and Westerville Chamber of Commerce recognized Otterbein College as Business Partner of the Year.

Service
• President's Higher Education Community Service Honor Roll: Winner in the General Community Service Category.
• Center for Community Engagement Director Melissa Kesler Gilbert was named National Civic Scholar by Campus Compact.
• Otterbein serves as the lead institution for the Learn and Serve Great Cities ~ Great Service Consortium, mobilizing 13 institutions of higher education to serve their cities through course-based programs for urban youth.

College Fast Facts

Four Year, Private, Suburban, Founded: 1847

Affiliation: United Methodist

Web site: www.otterbein.edu

Student Profile: 3,100 full and part time graduate and undergraduate students; 35 states and territories, 11 countries; 10% minority, 1% international.

Faculty Profile: 162 full-time faculty; 91% hold a terminal degree in their field. 13:1 student/faculty ratio.

Athletics: NCAA Division III, Ohio Athletic Conference. 18 varsity sports.

Costs and Aid: 2008-2009: $26,319 tuition. 95% of students receive some form of financial aid.

Admissions

Office of Admissions
One Otterbein College
Westerville, OH 43081
Phone: (800) 488-8144
Email: uotterb@otterbein.edu
www.otterbein.edu/
admission/index.asp

Service-Learning

Center for Community Engagement
Melissa Kesler Gilbert Director
One Otterbein College
Westerville, OH 43081
Phone: (614) 823-1270
www.otterbein.edu/cce

Xavier University, Ohio

At Xavier, a liberal arts university, learning often goes beyond the classroom to enrich your academic experience and deepen your personal development.

Service-Learning Focus

Service learning at Xavier challenges students to develop a deeper, more compassionate world view, and to integrate the intellectual, moral and spiritual aspects of life. Xavier's Jesuit tradition inspires students to be men and women for others, and will prepare you to go into the world to make a real difference.

Flagship Programs

Academic Service-Learning Semester Programs

Academic study and service while living in Ghana, Nicaragua, India or urban Cincinnati introduces you to the local culture and society through the lens of social justice and the perspective of the economically poor.

Alternative Breaks

The Alternative Breaks program provides service, education and immersion opportunities for 250+ students, faculty and staff each year through 17 domestic and five international trips. Student leaders provide pre- and post-trip orientation and design opportunities for learning and reflection.

Summer Service Internship

Focused on providing service in the greater Cincinnati area, this program aims to develop "people for others" who will continue to make service an integral part of their lives. Students also develop their own community through sharing and reflecting on their experiences.

Course Snapshot

ACCT 312 (Accounting) Volunteer Income Tax Assistance

This service-learning course focuses on study of federal and state income tax topics, marketing and administration of tax preparation services, and preparation of federal and state income tax returns for low-income and elderly taxpayers.

Academics

Xavier teaches students how to think and communicate effectively, and fosters lifelong learning and a commitment to serving others.

Service-learning requirements in various courses enable students to apply classroom learning to real-world experiences.

Accounting
Business Administration (graduate program)
Business Law
Criminal Justice *
Economics
Education *
English
Entrepreneurial Studies
Human Resources
Information Systems
Marketing
Management
Nursing *
Occupational Therapy
Political Science
Social Work *
Spanish
Theology

* Courses with a required service-learning component.

Check out all majors at: www.xavier.edu/academics

Awards and Recognition

Academics

• Xavier offers 74 undergraduate majors and concentrations, 43 undergraduate minors, 11 graduate programs, and 1 doctorate.

• *U.S.News & World Report* and *The Princeton Review* rate Xavier as one of the best colleges in America.

College Fast Facts

Four Year, Private, Urban, Founded: 1831

Affiliation: Catholic, Jesuit

Web site: www.xavier.edu

Student Profile: Undergraduate students (46% male, 54% female); 30 states and territories, 38 countries; 18% students of color, inclusive of both minority and international.

Faculty Profile: 289 full-time faculty. 90% hold a terminal degree in their field. 13:1 student/faculty ratio. Average class size is 22.

Athletics: NCAA Division I, Atlantic 10 Conference, 16 varsity sports. Three fully funded sports: men's and women's basketball; women's volleyball.

Costs and Aid: 2007-2008: $34,000 comprehensive ($24,000 tuition). 95% of students receive some form of financial aid.

Admissions

Office of Admissions
Xavier University
3800 Victory Parkway
Cincinnati, OH 45207-5311
Phone: 513-745-3301; 877-XUADMIT
E-mail: xuadmit@xavier.edu

Service-Learning

Academic Service-Learning Semester Programs
Irene B. Hodgson, Ph.D., Interim Director
Phone: 513-745-3541
E-mail: hodgson@xavier.edu

Oklahoma City University

Oklahoma City University. Preparing Servant Leaders for Today and Tomorrow.

Service-learning at Oklahoma City University gives students opportunities to apply what they are learning in the classroom through service in a community-based setting. Every student at Oklahoma City University takes at least one service-learning course before graduating.

Flagship Programs

OIKOS Scholars Program

The Oikos (Greek for house) Scholars program prepares students to engage in lives of social and ecological responsibility. Oikos scholars participate in service-learning projects, complete courses addressing issues of peace, justice, and ecological sustainability, and participate in at least one international education experience.

OCUServes

Oklahoma City University's general education service-learning program gives students across all disciplines the opportunity to participate in at least one service-learning experience.

OCULeads

OCULeads is a program designed to honor and develop leadership skills of freshman students who have already demonstrated these abilities through various social, academic, and volunteer organizations during high school.

Course Snapshot

ENGL 113H: Honors Composition I: Students collaborate with the Oklahoma City National Bombing Memorial curators, survivors, and others directly affected by the bombing to research and create digital museum exhibits. Exhibits are displayed in the "Virtual Archives" kiosk in the museum and in Teaching trunks" distributed to elementary schools nationwide.

"After teaching service-learning for many years I find that the hidden, or not-so-hidden, gift of this pedagogy is that it brings my students and me closer together as researchers and as colleagues."

~ H. Brooke Hessler, Associate Professor of English, Oklahoma City University

Academics

Service-Learning at OCU always relates to the content of the course, thereby enhancing the educational experience for each student. These include:

Accounting (ACCT)
Art (ART)
Biology (BIOL)
Computer Science (CSCI)
Dance (AMGT)
Chemistry (CHEM)
Criminal Justice (CJ)
Economics (ECON)
Education (EDUC)
English (ENGL)
Environmental Science (BIO)
Mass Communications (MSBC)
Management (MGMT)
Music (MUS)
Nursing (NURS)
Philosophy (PHIL)
Psychology (PSYC)
Social Work (SOC)
Spanish (SPAN)
Theatre (THRE)

"Service-learning taught me how to take classroom theory and make it practical and relevant."

– Mike Slack, Oklahoma City University Religion Student

Note: All undergraduates must complete at least one service-learning course.

Check out all majors at: www.okcu.edu/academics

Awards and Recognition
Service-Learning
• Kerr Foundation Service Learning Grant
Academics
• OCU offers more than 60 areas of undergraduate study, and 13 master's degree programs.
• Listed in the top tier of *U.S.News & World Report's* 2008 America's Best Colleges Western-Universities Master's classifi cation, ranking 23rd.
• Among the Princeton Review's 2008 Best in the West colleges.
• Named one of America's 100 Best College Buys.
• Named one of America's Best Christian Colleges.

College Fast Facts
Four year private university founded in 1904

Web site: www.okcu.edu

Affiliation: United Methodist

Student Profile: 1,726 undergraduate students (45% male, 55% female); from 46 states and 56 foreign countries; 17% minority, 27% international

Faculty Profile: 156 full-time faculty and 142 part-time faculty; Over 79% hold a terminal degree in their fi eld. 14-to-1 student/faculty ratio. Average class size for freshmen: 17; Average class size for upperclassmen: 13.

Athletics: NAIA: 10 varsity sports.

Costs and Aid: 2007–2008: $30,900 comprehensive with average room and board, books and fees per year ($19,600 tuition per year). 96% of freshmen receive some financial aid.

Service-Learning Facts:

3% of total courses are service-learning courses.

26.7% of students took a service-learning course last year (06-07).

54% of departments offer at least one service-learning course.

Service-learning courses and credit-earning experiences are integrated into:

Freshman orientation, Freshman seminar or other fi rst-year experience, General education and/or core curriculum, Senior capstones or other culminating experience, Independent study, International study.

Admissions	Service-Learning
Office of Undergraduate Admissions	Mark Davies, Ph.D.
2501 N. Blackwelder	Dean
Oklahoma City, OK 73106	Wimberly School of Religion
Email: uadmissions@okcu.edu	Email: mdavies@okcu.edu
	Phone: (405) 208-5284

Portland State University

Portland State University is a comprehensive, public university dedicated to enhancing the intellectual, social, cultural, and economic qualities of urban life.

Flagship Programs

Office of Community-University Partnerships (CUP)

CUP facilitates partnerships that engage faculty and students from the disciplines in meaningful, course-based learning opportunities that link them with community partners and track relationships on the Community-University Partnership Map. Explore hundreds of PSU's local, national, and international partnerships at http://partner.pdx.edu.

University Studies-Capstone Program

Senior Capstone is the culminating course in University Studies, PSU's required undergraduate studies program. Capstone courses take students from a variety of majors into the field to work on community projects. Students, faculty, and community leaders collaborate to complete projects that address community issues.

Student Leaders for Service (SLS)

SLS is a civic engagement and leadership development program that helps students develop as civic leaders by serving at Portland-area community-based organizations. Students serve 5-10 hours a week, attend a weekly leadership and civic engagement skill-building course, and lead service projects that engage the entire campus community.

Course Snapshot

UNST 421, Grant Writing for Community Change

This class pairs students with a local non-profit organization to research likely funders and prepare grant proposals based on research and lessons learned in class. Students learn to research different funding options, assess the organization's needs, and write effective grant proposals, while providing a crucial service to community-based nonprofit organizations.

Academics

Through service-learning, PSU educates responsible global citizens and fosters actions, programs, and scholarship that will lead to a sustainable future.

University Studies, undergraduate education program
School of Business Administration
Graduate School of Education
College of Urban & Public Affairs
The Maseeh College Of Engineering & Computer Science
School of Fine & Performing Arts
College of Liberal Arts & Sciences
School of Social Work
School of Extended Studies

Check out all majors at:
http://pdx.edu/programs.html

"PSU graduates come out ready to contribute; the high-tech industry doesn't have to spend years training them."

–Dr. Youssef El-Mansy
Vice President,
Intel Corporation

Awards and Recognition

Service-Learning

• For the fifth consecutive year, *U.S.News & World Report* ranked PSU among the Best Academic Programs for First-Year Experiences, Service-Learning, Internships/Co-ops, Learning Communities, and Senior Capstone Courses.

• One of 62 schools to receive two Carnegie Classifications for Community Engagement: Curricular Engagement and Outreach and Partnership.

• Listed in Princeton Review's *Colleges with a Conscience: 81 Great Schools* for outstanding involvement for service-learning programs and blending academics with community work.

• One of 141 schools to be honored with the President's Higher Education Community Service Honor Roll, an award for civic engagement.

• One of 25 considered "Saviors of Our Schools" by the New England Board of Higher Education.

• Association of American Colleges and Universities report recognized PSU as a leader in the area of fostering civic, intercultural, and ethical learning.

• President's Higher Education Community Service Honor Roll

College Fast Facts

Web site: http://pdx.edu

Service-Learning Facts: 464 service-learning courses offered ('06-07); 59% of students took a service-learning course ('06-07); 100% of departments offer at least one service-learning course.
Service-learning courses and credit-earning experiences are integrated into: general education and/or core curriculum, senior capstones or other culminating experience, undergraduate research programs, independent study, international study, Civic Leadership Minor, Freshman orientation, Freshmen seminar or other first-year experience.

Student Profile: 16,980 undergraduate students (46.8 % male, 53.1% female); 82.1 % in-state, 17.9% out of state; 24 % minority, 3.9 % international.

Faculty Profile: 648 full-time faculty; 563 hold a terminal degree in their field; 23:1 student/faculty ratio; Average class size is 23 .

Athletics: NCAA Division I Conference; Big Sky Conference; 14 varsity sports.

Costs and Aid: 2007–2008: Resident, $18,777 comprehensive ($5,229 tuition). 52.99% of students receive some financial aid. 2007–2008: Non-resident, $31,017 comprehensive ($16,617 tuition).

Admissions

Portland State University
Admissions
P.O. Box 751
Portland, OR 97207-0751
Phone: 503-725-3511 or
800-547-8887, extension 5-3511

Service-Learning

Office of Community-University Partnerships
Center for Academic Excellence
PO Box 751
Portland, OR 97207
Phone: 503-725-5642
Email: cae@pdx.edu

University of Portland

Devoted to a mission with three central tenets--teaching, faith, and service--the University of Portland believes that an education is complete when it combines heart, mind and hands.

Flagship Programs

Bridgebuilders is a local organization for African-American males in grades 9-12 (referred to in the program as "Prospective Gents"). Partnering with U. of P.'s School of Education, Bridgebuilders provides social, emotional and academic support for its members and fosters cultural pride and awareness through communal study of Black history. Among the volunteer community leaders who serve as mentors for the youth are African American teachers, engineers, carpenters and school counselors. They share a vision of nurturing youth into strong, healthy and respected Black manhood. More than a thousand young African-American men from Portland have prepared for college and life with mentoring from University faculty and students, and more than 97 percent have gone on to college.

The Social Justice Program instills in students a commitment to work for justice and peace and for an approach to life that promotes social integrity, economic prosperity and defense of human rights for all. The service dimension of learning is expressed in a unique and effective way within the Social Justice Program. It challenges students to place their personal development and career choices into an ethical world view within an interdisciplinary context. Students in the program prepare themselves to challenge unjust systems and become leaders who will create a better world. Social Justice Studies draws from diverse disciplines like business, education, english, fine arts, history, mathematics, philosophy, political science, psychology, sociology, and theology.

Course Snapshot

Foundations of Education aims to increase understanding of the interactions between education, schools, and society. Service-learning serves as an additional text for the course—an experiential one that enhances major concepts, themes, and questions. The primary goal is not new instructional techniques or classroom ideas, but much broader: to gain a better understanding of the ways in which the lives and structures outside of school affect what goes on inside schools. Students also gain a better sense of how U.S. society and its educational institutions work, particularly for those who are disadvantaged.

Academics

"The University takes very seriously its role as intellectual, cultural, scholarly, creative, artistic, and spiritual resource center for city, state, region, and nation – come see for yourself why we are ranked among the very best Catholic universities in the West." -Brother Donald Stabrowski, C.S.C., Provost and Professor of Political Science.

Some study areas which incorporate service-learning are:

Biology
Chemistry
Communication
Drama
Environmental Ethics and Policy
Environmental Science
History
Life Science
Mathematics
Organizational Communication
Political Science
Psychology
Social Work
Sociology
Criminal Justice
Spanish
Marketing and Management
Elementary Education
Theology

"Dr. Karen Eifler in the School of Education varies her reflective techniques, eliciting unexpected insights, honoring her students' unique gifts and experiences, and reinforcing and deepening their understanding of course content."

-(from text honoring the 2006 Oregon Campus Compact Service Learning Professor of the Year)

Check out all academic offerings at:
www.up.edu/academics

Awards and Recognition

• *U.S.News & World Report* named the University one of the top five Western regional universities. The University has been named a top ten regional university for 13 years.

• *U.S.News & World Report* has also ranked the University as an educational "best buy," recognizing it for providing an excellent education at a reasonable cost.

• President's Higher Education Community Service Honor Roll, 2006 and 2007.

• In 2005, Washington Monthly ranked the University of Portland first among all the nation's colleges and universities for national service.

• Four recipients of the Carnegie Foundation's Oregon Professor of the Year award since 1997, including National Professor of the Year.

College Fast Facts

Four Year, Founded: 1901

Affiliation: Catholic, Congregation of Holy Cross

Web site: www.up.edu

Student Profile: 2,849 undergraduate students (37% male, 63% female); 40 states and territories; 15% minority, 1% international.

Faculty Profile: 197 full-time faculty, 119 part-time faculty. 12:1 student/faculty ratio. Average class size 25.

Athletics: NCAA Division I, West Coast Conference. 16 varsity sports (8 men's: baseball,basketball, cross-country, golf, soccer, tennis, indoor & outdoor track; 8 women's: basketball,cross-country,golf,soccer,tennis,indoor & outdoor track, volleyball); misc.club sports, and intramurals.

Costs and Aid: 2007-2008: $35,800 comprehensive ($27,500 tuition). Nearly 94% of students receive some financial aid. Average freshman award: $20,356 in 2005-2006.

Admissions

Admissions Office
University of Portland
5000 N. Willamette Blvd.
Portland, OR 97203
Phone: (503) 943-7147

Service-Learning

Moreau Center for Service and Leadership
University of Portland
5000 N. Willamette Blvd.
Portland, OR 97203
Phone: (503) 943-7132
Email: moreaucenter@up.edu

Alvernia College

Alvernia College is a private Franciscan College, rooted in the Catholic and liberal arts traditions, founded by the Bernardine Franciscan Sisters in 1958.

Flagship Programs

Center For Community Engagement's South Reading Youth Initiative

Alvernia students in Education, Psychology, Social Work and Nursing bring cultural awareness, health and wellness and literacy activities to this after school program serving the needs of underserved students in an inner city neighborhood. Together with partnerships from multiple non-profit arts, music, and service agencies, grade school students are encouraged to stay in school and make healthy choices.

First Year Seminar FYS

This course introduces all 300 incoming freshman along with faculty, staff and student leaders to service during New Student Orientation. Seventeen FYS classes volunteer throughout the local community completing service at local senior centers, the Police Athletics League, the local homeless shelter, food bank and more. Continued projects throughout the semester emphasize service learning and leadership development in the college career.

COM 251 Broadcasting and Electronic Media

The course is offered at a local cable station. Students learn the basics of broadcasting and have completed service-learning projects including:
• An educational video on ovarian cancer for an area hospital.
• Behind-the-scenes documentaries on Skate America, an international figure skating competition.
• Promotional videos for many campus groups such as Sigma Delta Tau (English honor society), Intramural Sporting Events, the International Club, the First Year Seminar Program, and the College Bookstore.

Course Snapshot

THE 390 Immersion Experience in Santo Domingo, Dominican Republic

Course covers theology and social justice topics as they relate to service in the developing world. Explores a theology of liberation for the poor, Catholic social teaching and advocacy methods. Service includes running an elementary school classroom for one week, (English lessons, educational projects, field day) and includes a building project within the community.

Academics

Alvernia College strives to strengthen student learning by making the community an important part of the curriculum; at the same time, further strengthening the quality of life in its communities. While especially attuned to the needs of Greater Reading, the College seeks to foster in our graduates and all at Alvernia a life-long commitment to service and to the responsibilities of national and global citizenship.

Alvernia students gain an understanding of their community, locally, regionally and globally by committing to service learning. Participating in these experiences develops a lifelong affinity to helping others and making a difference.

Art
Business
Communications
Criminal Justice
Education
English
Music
Nursing
Occupational Therapy
Psychology
Social Work

Check out all majors at:
www.alvernia.edu/ academics/academics2.htm

"Students here are often exposed to different ways of looking at things than they might have experienced in the past. We emphasize open discussion and looking at all sides of an issue."

– Donna Yarri, M.Div., Ph.D., Associate Professor of Theology

Awards and Recognition

Service-Learning
• Alvernia was named to the Templeton Guide for Colleges that Encourage Character Development.
• President's Higher Education Community Service Honor Roll.

Academics
• Alvernia offers more than 50 areas of undergraduate study, 6 master's degrees, and 1 doctorate.

College Fast Facts

Four Year, Private, Suburban: Founded 1958

Affiliation: Catholic

Web site: www.alvernia.edu

Student Profile: 2,038 undergraduate students (31% male, 69% female); 11 states and territories 16 countries; 19% minority, 1% international.

Faculty Profile: 81 full-time faculty. 62% hold a terminal degree in their field. 15:1 student/faculty ratio.

Athletics: NCAA Division III, Conference. MAC (Fall 2008). 15 varsity sports and 3 Club sports.

Costs and Aid: 2008-2009: $31,688 comprehensive ($22,800 tuition). 99% of students receive some type of financial aid, including scholarships, grants, loans and work-study.

Admissions	Service-Learning
Office of Admission	Ginny Hand
400 Saint Bernardine Street	Director
Reading, PA 19607	Center for Community Engagement
Phone: 1-888-ALVERNIA	540 Upland Avenue
(1-888-258-3764)	Reading PA 19611
Fax: 1-610-790-2873	Phone: 1-888-ALVERNIA
Email: admissions@alvernia.edu	Email: ginny.hand@alvernia.edu

Cabrini College

Students do extraordinary things at Cabrini College, a comprehensive, residential Catholic college committed to vision, respect, community, and excellence.

Flagship Programs

Engagements in the Common Good (ECG)

This series of four service-learning courses, taken in each year of study, develops students' participation in social justice. Students have powerful experiences serving in the community, moving from observation and reflection, to participation and reflection, and to research and advocacy with a community partner.

Youth Empowerment Program

Cabrini works with potential first-generation college students from a local high school, providing academic enrichment, career exploration, health and wellness services, and cultural enrichment. Cabrini students from a wide variety of majors participate, providing workshops, activities, and mentoring.

Partnership with Catholic Relief Services

Cabrini was the first college to partner with Catholic Relief Services (CRS). CRS provides speakers from projects around the world, discussing issues of development and advocacy.

Course Snapshot

ECG 300: Community-based Research and Advocacy

Students in this course explore issues of writing, speaking, and organizing for change; organizational dynamics and capacity-building; and utilizing personal strengths and teamwork in the process of creating justice. Sample projects include classes partnering with prison inmates to design reentry programs, working with juvenile court and high school students to create a truancy resource guide for families, and collaborating with a domestic violence shelter to educate and advocate against domestic and dating violence.

Academics

Service-learning is the central unifying experience of a Cabrini education. Each year, students at Cabrini take courses that develop a deepening understanding of social justice and experience of service-learning. Cabrini promotes an "education of the heart," providing experiences to guide our students as they pursue lives of purpose and meaning.

Through service-learning courses, Cabrini students will demonstrate a sustained commitment to the practice of social justice. Departments that incorporate service-learning include:

Communications	
English	Religion
Business	Social Work
Biology	Sociology
Health Science and Health Promotion	Education
Psychology	Philosophy
History	Romance Languages
	Graphic Design

Learn more about academic programs at: www.cabrini.edu/academics

"I am called to serve. I see what is happening in the world, and I know it is my responsibility to change what I know is wrong."
~ Meghan Hurley, '07

Awards and Recognition

• 2006 and 2007 President's Higher Education Community Service Honor Roll with Distinction.

• Dr. Jeffery Gingerich named 2007 finalist for Ehrlich Faculty Award for Service Learning.

• Dr. Jerry Zurek named 2005 Pennsylvania Professor of the Year by the Council for the Advancement and Support of Education.

• 1997 John Templeton Foundation's Honor Roll of Character-Building Colleges.

• First college to partner with Catholic Relief Services.

• On the Collegiate Learning Assessment, Cabrini is in the top 20%, providing a "value-added" education.

• One of 25 Colleges and Universities to receive a federal Youth Empowerment Program grant.

• The Loquitur named finalist by Associated Collegiate Press as the best college newspaper in the country.

College Fast Facts

Four Year, Private Suburban

Web site: www.cabrini.edu

Student Profile: 1,600 undergraduate students, 37% out of state

Faculty Profile: 66 full-time faculty, 16:1 student/faculty ratio. Average class size is 18.

Athletics: NCAA DivisionThree; 18 varsity sports.

Costs and Aid: 2007-2008: $38,530 comprehensive ($27,200 tuition). 97% of students receive some form of financial aid.

Admissions

610 King of Prussia Road
Radnor, PA 19087
Phone: 800-848-1003;
610-902-8552
Email: admit@cabrini.edu
www.cabrini.edu/admissions

Service-Learning

The Wolfington Center
610 King of Prussia Road
Radnor, PA 19087
Phone: 610-902-8431
Email: wolfington@cabrini.edu
www.cabrini.edu/wolfington

Messiah College

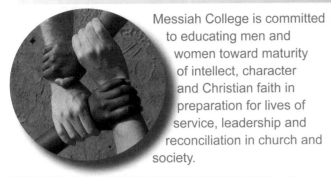

Messiah College is committed to educating men and women toward maturity of intellect, character and Christian faith in preparation for lives of service, leadership and reconciliation in church and society.

Flagship Programs

Taking Psychology Outside The Classroom

Reflecting on her service-learning experiences at a local long-term care facility, a student in Dr. Seegobin's Abormal Psychology class wrote, "The residents at Paxton (Ministries) are truly a gift from God. Going into this experience, it was my hope that I would be a blessing to these people. But after spending several months, I knew that the residents were blessing me just as much, if not more. One word sums up these amazing people – love."

Using Sign to Service

Describing how sign language can be a form of service to older adults, one student reflected on a recent conversation saying, "I sat with Lou at dinner that evening, chatting with my hands and feeling surprisingly useful. He was patient when I had to fingerspell words I couldn't remember the signs for, and my grammar was atrocious, but the conversation managed to cover sports, how he liked life at Paxton Street, and international politics. Lou had read reports about what was happening in Darfur, and he made the signs for my heart is hurting. "You have a good heart, then," I signed back, smiling. His response was complicated; I had to ask him to repeat some of the signs. It seemed that he was saying, what human heart would not hurt?

Course Snapshot

At Messiah College, students permitted to enroll in the **Agape Center's Foundations for Service, Mission and Social Change course (SERV 231 & 232)** not only engage in learning beyond the traditional classroom and local community setting, but also receive significant scholarships for their proposed 6-8 week summer service experiences. As Richard Hughes, senior Boyer fellow says, "If Messiah College were a one-dimensional institution--if, for example, we cared only about the life of the mind--it would be so much easier to achieve the excellence we seek. But Messiah College combines a passion for the minds of our students with a comparable passion for their hearts and their hands. We seek to nurture in our students a spirit of wonder and curiosity, the ability to think critically, and a commitment to raise serious and probing questions about the world in which they live."

Academics

Service-learning meets both educational and community objectives through mutually designed experiences that have measurable goals and meaningful outcomes.

Visual Arts
Education
Human Development and Family Science
Psychology
Sociology
Biology
Communications
Management and Business
General Education
Latin American Studies CCCU Study Abroad Program
Uganda CCCU Study Abroad Program

"Through out the curriculum, service has become a distinctive way of teaching and learning at Messiah College."

Check out our majors at:
www.messiah.edu/academics/catalog

Awards and Recognition

• Founder and host of the nationally recognized Faith-Based Service-Learning Conference.

• 2008 President's Higher Education Community Service Honor Roll with Distinction.

• Institute for International Education ranked Messiah College's study abroad program 9th in the nation.

• Achieved a 100% pass rate on the National Council Licensure Exams (NCLEX), one of only three nursing programs in Pennsylvania to do so (Class of 2006).

• Ranked number one in Pennsylvania and seventh in the nation by the National Association of State Boards of Accountancy for percentage of students passing the CPA exam on the first attempt (2004).

• Internationally recognized scholarship of School of the Humanities faculty, students, and alumni, including a Rhodes Scholar, Marshall Scholar, Truman Scholar, and several Fulbright Fellowships and awards.

• Messiah is consistently named by *U.S. News & World Report* as one of the top five "Best Colleges" for comprehensive bachelor's colleges in the North and by *The Princeton Review* as a Best Northeastern College.

College Fast Facts

Four Year, Private Suburban, Founded: 1909

Affiliation: Brethren In Christ

Web site: www.messiah.edu

Student Profile: 2,837 undergraduate students (36% male, 64% female); 46% out of state, 37 states and territories, 23 countries; 6.5% minority, 1.8 % international.

Faculty Profile: 172 full-time faculty. 79% hold a terminal degree in their field. 3:1 student/faculty ratio.

Athletics: NCAA Division III, Conference. MAC, 21 varsity sports.

Costs and Aid: 2007-2008: $31,760 comprehensive ($23,710 tution). 97% of students receive some form of financial aid.

Admissions	Service-Learning
Admissions Office	Agape Center for
Messiah College	Service and Learning
One College Ave.	Chad Frey, Director
Grantham, PA 17027	One College Ave. Box 3027
Phone: (717) 691-6000	Grantham, PA 17027
Email: admiss@messiah.edu	Phone: (717) 796-1800 ext. 7255

Rosemont College

Rosemont College, located in suburban Philadelphia, offers undivided attention and unlimited opportunities that will truly amaze you.

Service-Learning Focus

Rosemont knows how much employers and graduate schools value practical experience. That's why students are required to complete at least one internship, study abroad, or Service-Learning opportunity during their time at Rosemont.

By incorporating Service-Learning into their classes, Rosemont's faculty helps students to develop contacts with community organizations allowing for a truly interactive learning experience.

Flagship Programs

Women in Politics

From the classroom, to the halls of Congress, students discover what life is like as a public figure by engaging in off-campus activities that connect them with women who work in the political sphere.

Elections

Students will gain first hand knowledge of politics and elections by participating in grassroots campaign work with a candidate of their choosing and help to organize an on-campus voter registration drive registration drive.

Course Snapshot

PSC-0276 Elections

A student's reflection on the on-campus voter registration drive, "In the spirit of bipartisanship, we're encouraging students to register to vote. While I'd rather see democrats win in the upcoming election, that isn't as important to me as getting students to participate in the political process."

Academics

Rosemont's first-class faculty members demand and encourage their students to value the diversity of human culture and experience through service learning. *Programs of study include:*

Biology
Business
-Accounting Track
-Management Track
-International Business Track
Chemistry
Communication
Economics
Education Certification with Co-liberal Arts
-Elementary Education Certification
-Secondary Education Certification
-Early Childhood Education Certification
English Literature
French
Health Science
History of Art
History

Humanities
Italian Studies
Philosophy
Political Science*
-Pre-Law Track
Psychology
Studio Art and Design
Religious Studies*
Women's Studies
Social Science
Sociology
-Forensic Sociology and Criminology Track
-Applied Sociology and Sociology Practices Track
-Deaf Studies (Teacher Certification) Track
Spanish*

Check out all majors at:
http://www.rosemont.edu/uwc/academics/programs.php

"I've become more open-minded…more outgoing… more independent as a young woman."

-Kristen Reilly, Class of 2008, French major

Awards and Recognition

• John Templeton Foundation's Honor Roll for "character building colleges"

• The second most diverse liberal arts college in the nation according to U.S.News & World Report (2007)

• Included among The Princeton Review's list of "best northeastern colleges"

• Among only a few schools in the Philadelphia region that has annually earned top rankings from U.S. New and World Report for nearly 20 years.

College Fast Facts

Four Year, Private, Catholic, Suburban; Founded 1921

Web site: www.rosemont.edu

Student Profile: 371 undergraduate students (0% male, 100% female), 13 states and territories, 8 countries; 51% minority, 3.1% international.

Faculty Profile: 31 full-time faculty. 90% hold a terminal degree in their field. 8:1 student/faculty ratio. Average class size is 12.

Athletics: NCAA Division III, PAC Conference, 6 varsity sports.

Costs and Aid: 2007–2008: $31,735 comprehensive ($21,630 tuition). 79% of students receives some financial aid.

Admissions

Rosemont College
Office of Admissions
1400 Montgomery Ave
Rosemont, Pennsylvania 19010
Phone: (610) 526-2966
Email: admissions@rosemont.edu

Service-Learning

Lezlie McCabe
Coordinator of Experiential Learning
Phone: (610) 527-0200, ext. 2389
Email: lmccabe@rosemont.edu

Saint Joseph's University

Saint Joseph's University provides a rigorous Jesuit liberal arts education demanding high achievement and deepened understanding, while developing moral and spiritual character and imparting enduring pride.

Flagship Programs

Freshmen Service-Learning
The Saint Joseph's University offers six year-long freshmen service-learning courses. Courses are limited to 20 students, build a sense of community in the classroom, and provide volunteer opportunities for the academic year. Reflection is integrated into class discussions and written assignments.

Service Scholars
Service Scholars are student employees hired after their year-long freshmen service-learning course. Scholars hold the position for the following three years and work within a faith-based community. They act as peer liaisons in service-learning classes and

facilitate classroom discussions, read and respond to students' volunteer journals and address placement concerns.

Service-Learning Site Assistants

Covenant House of Pennsylvania and SJU Site Assistants collaborate in hopes of encouraging continued education for Covenant House youth and offering a sustained service experience for SAs. For 3 years, SAs volunteer weekly and organize on-campus programs for Covenant House youth and SAs to attend.

Course Snapshot

ENG 1011-SL2, The Craft of Language, Dr. Owen Gillman

"This course is all about writing. As you work through the various assignments semester, and as you engage young students over at Samuel Gompers Elementary School, you will want to think of yourself as a writer. Writers have curiosity....Writers look to know more... The more you know, the more you have to say—and the more reason you have to write. Your experiences in service-learning will contribute much new knowledge, about which you will write often."

Academics

Service-Learning courses challenge students to engage in and integrate rigorous academic inquiry and relationship-based service work to develop the whole person with a commitment to social justice.

Courses of Study include:

Accounting	Interdisciplinary Health Services
Biology	Pharmaceutical Marketing
Chemistry	Philosophy
Education	Psychology
English	Sociology
Fine and Performing Arts	Theology
Food Marketing	
Foreign Languages & Literatures	

Check out all majors at:
www.sju.edu/sju/academics.html

Awards and Recognition

Service-Learning
- President's Higher Education Community Service Honor Roll with Distinction
- 2005-2006 National Service-Learning Conference model site
- Recipient of Learn and Serve grants

Academics
- SJU offers 40 undergraduate majors, 10 additional special-study options, 23 study abroad programs, 53 graduate study areas, and an Ed.D. in Educational Leadership.
- *U.S.News & World Report*'s 2008 "America's Best Colleges" edition ranked Saint Joseph's as tied for eighth in the category Best Universities-Master's (North).
- This ranking marks the fifth time in the past seven years that SJU has attained Top 10 status in its U.S. News cohort.
- This school is one of the 222 colleges named a Best Northeastern College by *The Princeton Review*.
- The Erivan K. Haub School of Business at Saint Joseph's University was recognized by *U.S.News & World Report* as having the No. 1 part-time M.B.A. program in Pennsylvania.

College Fast Facts

Four Year, Private, Urban: Founded 1851

Web site: www.sju.edu

Student Profile: 4150 undergraduate students (49% male, 51% female); 36 states and territories, 40 countries; 8.6% minority.

Faculty Profile: 281 full-time faculty, 381 part-time faculty. 98% hold a terminal degree in their field. 1:15 student/faculty ratio.

Athletics: NCAA Division 1 Conference: Atlantic 10. Athletics and Recreation at SJU is a major rallying point among students. Almost 70% of our overall student body participates in some way: 20 varsity sports; 16 club sports; 6 intramural sports for men, women or coed teams; fitness programs; outdoor trips and other instructional programs.

Costs and Aid: 2008–2009: $46,260 comprehensive ($32,710 tuition). 85% of students receives some financial aid.

Admissions

Undergraduate Admissions
Bronstein Hall
Saint Joseph's University
5600 City Avenue
Philadelphia, PA 19131-1395
Phone: (610) 660-1300
1 (888) BE-A-HAWK (toll-free)
Email: admit@sju.edu

Service-Learning

The Faith-Justice Institute
Ann Marie Jursca, MSW
Assistant Director
Phone: (610) 660-1337
Email: ajursca@sju.edu

Slippery Rock University

Slippery Rock University is Pennsylvania's premier public residential university. SRU provides students with a comprehensive experience that combines academic instruction with enhanced learning opportunities.

Flagship Programs

I CARE House

SRU's I CARE House provides services to 100 children and more than 20 mature adults monthly. SRU students and AmeriCorps members lead 15 programs for children and youth. Children's services include tutoring, art, recreation, music and newspaper clubs.

The Connector Corps/AmeriCorps program at Slippery Rock University

SRU student AmeriCorps members from all academic areas mobilize volunteers to enhance the quality of life of children, youth, families, mature adults and other underserved populations. English majors provide literacy tutoring. Sport management students lead basketball and soccer camps.

Care Breaks

Since 1994, students have spent their spring breaks providing flood relief, tutoring children, completing environmental projects and building houses in communities nationwide. Students provided aid in New Orleans following Hurricane Katrina.

Course Snapshot

COMMUNITY CHANGE AND DEVELOPMENT

Students partner with local communities to assess community needs and assets. They interview residents, association members, organizational staff and local government leaders and recommend strategies that will ensure voice of all parties and enhance quality of life.

Academics

SRU sponsors more than 30 service-learning programs that put theory into action. Students lead after-school programs, help the homeless, spend time with hospitalized veterans and provide disaster relief locally and nationally. They volunteer with community, faith-based and non-profit organizations.

Service learning is a core component of SRU's mission to creating a caring community connecting with the world. Through service-learning students become more engaged citizens.

Art
Business
Communication
English
Elementary Education *
Environmental Education *
Exercise and Rehabilitative Sciences
Criminology
Health and Safety
Parks and Recreation/Environmental Education
Professional Studies
Psychology
Special Education *
Sport Management *
Secondary Education *

"We're training people who will make contributions in their academic field and in the lives of their communities, families and schools."

~ Alice Kaiser-Drobney, SRU director of The Institute for Community, Service-Learning and Nonprofit Leadership

* Courses with a required service-learning component.

For more information on academics, visit:
www.sru.edu/pages/5152.asp

Awards and Recognition

• Institutional accreditation by Middle States Association of Colleges and Schools. 35-program specific earned accreditations.
• *Consumers Digest* ranked SRU as one of the "Top 5 Best Values Among Public Colleges and Universities" in the nation.
• *Princeton Review* included SRU in its "Best Northeastern Colleges" 2008 edition
• Results from the National Survey of Student Engagement show that SRU students rate their experience at SRU higher than do students attending peer institutions.
• Nearly 85 percent of students report that SRU is their first college choice.

College Fast Facts

Four-year, Public, Coeducational

Web site: www.sru.edu

Student Profile: 8,325 students (4,749 female, 3,576 male).

Faculty Profile: 331 full-time faculty, 39 part-time faculty; Student/faculty ratio. 20:1.

Athletics: NCAA Division II, **P**ennsylvania State Athletic Conference. 18 varsity sports. 7 men's teams, 11 women's teams. www.rockathletics.com

Costs and Aid: Full-time In-State tuition $5,178, Full-time out-of-state tuition $7,766, Room/board: $7,862, Mandatory fees: In-state/$1,492 Out-of-state/$1,582. Students receiving need-based aid whose need was fully met: 46%.

Admissions

Slippery Rock University
Office of Admissions
1 Morrow Way
Slippery Rock, Pa. 16057
Phone: 1 (800) 929-4778

Service-Learning

The Institute for Community, Service-Learning, and Nonprofit Leadership
Slippery Rock University
Robert A. Lowry Center
Slippery Rock, PA 16057
Phone: (724) 738-CARE
Email: theinstitute@sru.edu
Director: Alice Kaiser-Drobney

University of Scranton

Founded in 1888, The University of Scranton is a comprehensive Jesuit institution known for the outstanding success of its graduates.

Service-Learning Focus

Service to others is a vital component of a Jesuit education at Scranton. Service that is connected to learning affirms the value of human life and enhances a lifelong commitment to justice, social responsibility, and citizenship. All students of the University's Panuska College of Professional Studies participate in service learning.

Flagship Programs

Clinic for the Uninsured: A Cooperative Project

The Edward R. Leahy Jr. Center Clinic for the Uninsured is a rich collaboration with the Lackawanna Medical Society and other community partners and the students, faculty and staff of The University of Scranton that meets a critical healthcare need.

After School Program for English Language Learners

The Leahy Community Health and Family Center, with the support of community partners and student volunteers, piloted an after school tutorial program to improve reading and language development of 6 to 10-year old children whose first language is not English.

The Edward R. Leahy Jr. Center Clinic for the Uninsured

"I am very grateful for the opportunity to serve at the Leahy Clinic. This is an eye-opening experience that I have not had elsewhere. The Leahy Clinic has proven to fulfill a great need within our community." ~ Ellie Judge, senior, nursing

Course Snapshot

"During our community health/home-care rotation at the Leahy Clinic, in just two days, I was able to take patients in from the waiting room, take vital signs, do a full history, respond to questions, be present for the full doctor's examination, give shots, fill prescriptions and even give a patient an eye exam. These are all imperative nursing care duties that we must know before graduation. We saw the elderly, young people and children." ~ Genna Frappaolo, senior, nursing

Academics

The Service-Learning Program is grounded in developing men and women who actively and reflectively seek to make a difference.

Early Childhood Education/Special Education
Elementary Education/Early Childhood Education
Elementary Education/Special Education
Secondary Education
Exercise Science
Health Administration
Human Resource Studies
Nursing
Health Sciences
Occupational Therapy
Physical Therapy
Pre-Health professions

Scranton students demonstrate a deep commitment and passion for service informed by St. Ignatius Loyola.

Each PCPS department determines which of their courses are suitable for service experiences. Students are expected to follow their department's recommendations for curriculum and service opportunities.
All PCPS students must complete service learning as a requirement for graduation.

Check out all majors at: www.scranton.edu/academics

Awards and Recognition

Service-Learning
• President's Higher Education Community Service Honor Roll.
• More than 2,400 students perform well over 165,000 service hours each year.
• Templeton Foundation's Honor Roll of Character-Building Colleges.

Academics
• 117 Fulbright and other prestigious international fellowships since 1972.
• Four Truman Scholarships and six Goldwater Scholarships in the past five years.
• Of the 319 senior applicants to medical schools over the last eight years, an average of 81% were accepted.
• For the 14th consecutive year, among the 10 top master's universities in the north by *U.S. News & World Report* and for the fourth consecutive year, among the "Great Schools at a Great Price" and the "Best Graduation Rates."
• Kiplinger's "Best Values in Private Universities."
• For the past six years, among *The Princeton Review's 366 Best Colleges.*

College Fast Facts

Four Year, Private, Urban, Founded: 1888

Web site: www.scranton.edu

Affiliation: Catholic, Jesuit University

Student Profile: 4,083 undergraduate students (43% male, 57% female); 25 states and territories, 18 countries; 9% minority, 1% international.

Faculty Profile: 267 full-time faculty. 82% hold a terminal degree in their field. 11:1 student/faculty ratio. Average class size is 23.

Athletics: NCAA Division III, Landmark Conference. 19 varsity sports. Student-Athlete Achievement: 50 All-Americans, 21 Academic All-Americans and 13 NCAA Post-Graduate Scholars.

Costs and Aid: 2007-2008: $37,782 comprehensive ($28,458 tuition). 82% of students receive some form of financial aid.

Admissions

Office of Admissions
800 Linden Street
Scranton, PA 18510-4699
Phone: 1-888-SCRANTON or
570-941-7540
http://matrix.scranton.edu/
academics/ac.shtml

Providence College

Reflecting Providence College's Catholic and Dominican tradition, which recognizes the dignity of all God's people, and Alan Shawn Feinstein's vision of educating youth for community service, the Feinstein Institute for Public Service offers numerous service learning opportunities, preparing students to become builders of human communities and transformers of society.

Flagship Programs

Major in Public and Community Service Studies

Providence College was the first college to offer this major, with service-learning at the center. The major involves a systematic and rigorous study of the conceptual themes of community, service, and democracy in the context of diversity and social justice and is enriched by integrating academic coursework and community service.

Community Input

Community leaders worked closely with the development of the Feinstein Institute and its academic major and minor. Now, some community partners also serve as Community Faculty, co-teaching Department courses with Public Service faculty, bringing their expertise and knowledge of the community into the classroom.

Practicum in Public and Community Service

This two semester course for Public Service majors provides the practical skills necessary for developing leadership, facilitating reflection, and strengthening communication, team building, management, and problem-solving skills. Serving as Community Assistants, students are paired with a community partner site and facilitate the service learning experience of other Providence College students.

Course Snapshot

PSP 101:
Introduction to Service in Democratic Communities

"This class and my service at an urban farm helped me to realize the importance of community and the individual. Injustice plagues the world, and I must do my part for the community to replace it with justice. If I want to see change in the world, I must work with my community to bring this about for a better world."

Academics

The Feinstein Institute for Public Service focuses on building and nurturing community-based relationships. Community Partners, representatives of local organizations, work closely with the Feinstein Institute to ensure that service experiences meet real community needs and provide deep learning for students. Through service and reflection in courses, students develop the knowledge, values, and skills to become active members of their communities committed to social justice and the dignity of all people.

Service learning is at the center of the Public and Community Service major. The major involves a systematic and rigorous study of the conceptual themes of community, service, and democracy in the context of diversity and social justice and is enriched by integrating academic coursework and community service.

Some of the departments that incorporate service-learning include:
Department of Public and Community Service Studies
Education
Global Studies
Management
Marketing
Philosophy
Political Science
Psychology
Social Work
Spanish
Theater, Dance and Film
Theology

Check out all majors at: www.providence.edu/academics

"At the Feinstein Institute, the classroom is transformed into an active, supportive, and democratic community, empowering students, faculty, and community partners to come together to engage one another in learning about complex issues of community, service, and social change." ~ Angela Kelly, Class of 2004

Awards and Recognition

• Prof. Rick Battistoni was awarded major funding through the Pew Charitable Trusts to lead Project 540, a national high school civic engagement initiative.

• *U.S.News & World Report* ranks Providence College as one of the top institutions in the nation in the service learning category - which lists "outstanding examples of academic programs that are believed to lead to student success."

• Providence College ranked #2 among master's level universities in the North region.

• PC's 85% average graduation rate is the highest among 557 master's level universities nationwide.

• The College is ranked among the top 15 schools in the "Great Schools, Great Prices" category -- which relates academic quality to the net cost of

College Fast Facts

Four Year, Private, Urban, Founded: 1917

Web site: www.providence.edu

Student Profile: 3,850 undergraduate students (43% male,57% female); 42 states and territories, 17 countries; 9% minority, 2% international.

Faculty Profile: 295 full-time faculty. 91% hold a terminal degree in their field. 12:1 student/faculty ratio. Average class size is 22.

Athletics: NCAA Division 1, Big East, Hockey East and Metro Atlantic Conferences. 19 varsity sports. The Department of Intramural and Recreational Sports also supports numerous club sports.

Costs and Aid: 2007-2008: $39,255 comprehensive ($28,920 tuition). 59% of students receive some financial aid. Average award: $20,470.

Admissions	Service-Learning
Providence College	Providence College
Office of Admission	Feinstein Institute for Public Service
Harkins Hall 222	Phone: (401) 865-2786
549 River Ave.	Email: fips@providence.edu
Providence, RI 02918	www.providence.edu/feinstein
Phone: (401) 865-2535	
Email: pcadmiss@providence.edu	

Benedict College

"Learning to Be the Best: A Power for Good in the Twenty-First Century" characterizes Benedict College's commitment to community

Flagship Programs

Leadership Development Institute (LDI) at BC

LDI is designed to provide students with a foundation for developing or furthering their potential as servant leaders. LDI students establish and implement campus and community centered projects as well as local, national, and international alternative Spring Break service opportunities.

P.L.U.S. Day (Preparation for Leadership and Unity through Service)

This annual event was established in 1995 to allow students from area K-12 schools, colleges, and universities to serve collaboratively with the Benedict College family. Participants provide a variety of services to help improve communities in the Columbia area.

Saturday Academy

Male Teacher Education majors serve as lead facilitators of the Saturday Academy Program. The Program is a series of enrichment activities designed to expose community children to an array of diverse academic, social, and cultural experiences.

Course Snapshot

CHEM 148: General Principles of Chemistry

Science, Technology, Engineering, and Mathematics (STEM) majors enrolled in this course facilitate science labs for the Harambee Children's Village. This is an annual event first started in 1989 for community children of all ages. Under the supervision of College faculty and students, participating children engage in mini-lab experiments which expose them to hands-on scientific experiences and generate future interest in the STEM career fields.

Academics

"While they learn and serve, Benedict students provide incredible resources to help address important social and community issues."
-Dr. David H. Swinton, President Benedict College

• English, Foreign Languages and Mass Communication
• Fine Arts
• Social Sciences and Criminal Justice
• Education, Child, and Family Studies
• Health, Physical Education and Recreation
• Social Work
• Military Science
• Biology, Chemistry, and Environmental Health Science
• Physics and Engineering
• Mathematics and Computer Science
• Business Administration, Management, and Marketing
• Economics, Finance, and Accounting

Check out all majors at: www.benedict.edu

Service-Learning teaches students to take ownership and think in terms of "us" and "we" rather than "them" and "they."

- Dr. David H. Swinton, President Benedict College

Awards and Recognition

Awards
• South Carolina Commission on Higher Education – Commendation of Excellence for Service-Learning.
• Partner in Education Award – Richland County Public School District Two.

Recognitions in National Publications
• A Gallery of Portraits in Service-Learning - Action Research in Teacher Education.
• One with the Community - Indicators of Engagement at Minority Serving Institutions (Campus Compact).
• Studying Service-Learning Innovations in Education Research Methodology.
• Service-Learning in Higher Education: A Portrait of Five Institutions (video).

Academics
• BC is the 4th largest private HBCU in the US.
• Ranked #2 in the nation for producing African-Americans with an undergraduate degree in Physics.

Nationally Accredited Programs
• Teacher Education (NCATE)
• Social Work (CSWE)
• Environmental Health Science Program (EHAC)
• Child Development Center (NAEYC)
• Recreation and Leisure Services (NRPA)

College Fast Facts

Four Year, Private, Urban, Founded: 1870

Web site: www.benedict.edu

Affiliation: Baptist

Faculty Profile: 117 full-time faculty. 65% hold a terminal degree in their field. 19:1 student/faculty ratio.

Costs and Aid: 2007–2008: $20,454 comprehensive ($12,516 tuition). 95% of students receive some financial aid.

Admissions

Benedict College
Office of Admissions
and Student Marketing
1600 Harden Street
Columbia, SC 29204
Phone: (803) 705-4491;
(800) 868-6598

Service-Learning

Tondaleya Green Jackson, M.Ed.
Director of Service-Learning
Phone: (803) 705-4726
Email: jacksont@benedict.edu

Clemson University

Clemson University, one of the country's top public universities, combines the best of small-college teaching and big-time science, engineering, and technology.

Flagship Programs

Creative Inquiry
Creative Inquiry is a faculty mentored multi-semester commitment to a team-based undergraduate research project. The project's "Partnerships to Create Landscapes for Water Quality," engaged Clemson Horticulture and other interested students with a local non-profit organization dedicated to preserving water quality.

Joseph F. Sullivan Academic Nursing Center
A community clinical research facility, Sullivan Center partners with academic disciplines across Clemson University to provide unique, real-life, hands-on, inter-disciplinary learning experiences enhancing student in-class education. From 2002 to 2006, 1,233 students rotated through the Center logging 25,239 clinical/field service hours.

Clemson Client-Based Writing Program
The Advanced Writing Program offers practical learning experiences through Client-Based Projects. Business and technical writing students help non-profit groups improve their organizations. From creating volunteer manuals to updating websites, students put writing and analytical abilities to use in the community.

Course Snapshot

CLEMSON
Performing Arts

Performing Arts 401/402
The Department of Performing Arts Capstone Service-Learning course requires senior music, theatre, and audio students to collaborate on a project each year. The project not only must better their community, but also must introduce artistic endeavor to populations lacking opportunities to participate in cultural activities. Students imaginatively conceive the project and learn the challenges of effective communication within a collaborative process. Students take ownership of every aspect of the event, including planning, advertising, finding venues, determining audiences, performing, and assessing impact.

Academics

Clemson's goal is to develop students' communication and critical-thinking skills, ethical judgment, global awareness, and scientific and technological knowledge.
Programs of Study include:

- Agricultural Education
- Architecture
- Bioengineering
- Biological Sciences
- Chemistry
- Communication Studies
- Construction Science and Management
- Education
- English
- Environmental Science & Policy
- Experimental Statistics
- Food Science & Human Nutrition
- Horticulture
- Industrial Engineering
- Landscape Architecture
- Languages
- Management
- Marketing
- Nursing
- Parks, Recreation and Tourism Management
- Performing Arts
- Public Health Sciences
- Rural Sociology
- Sociology

Check out all majors at: www.clemson.edu/futurestudents/majors.html

"Through teaching elementary school students, students learned about community involvement and communicating to non-scientific audiences." ~ John Kaup (CH152 Chemistry Communication I)

Awards and Recognition
Service-Learning
- President's Higher Education Community Service Honor Roll with Distinction.
- Included in 2005 "Colleges with a Conscience; Engaged Student's Guide to College" (Campus Compact/Princeton Review Publication).
- Winner 2005, Innovision Technology Award for Community Service for iCARE program involving Clemson Business students.

Academics
- Named *TIME Magazine*'s Public College of the Year, 2001.
- Top 30 of *U.S.News & World Report's* 2007 America's Best Colleges National Public Universities.
- Ranked 29th by *Kiplinger* magazine as one of top educational buys in the nation.

College Fast Facts
Four Year, Public, Suburban: Founded: 1855

Web site: www.clemson.edu

Student Profile: 14,069 undergraduate students (54% male, 46% female); 50 states and territories, 53 countries (undergraduate); 10% minority, . 5% international.

Faculty Profile: 1,246 full-time faculty; 86% hold a terminal degree in their field. 14:1 student/faculty ratio. Average class size is 31.

Athletics: NCAA Division 1, ACC Conference. 19 varsity sports. Clemson Athletics provides a comprehensive community service program targeting opportunities for student-athlete involvement with community.

Costs and Aid: $16,592 in-state comprehensive ($9,870 tuition). $28,522 out-of-state comprehensive ($21,800 tuition), 72% of students receive some financial aid. Average award: $11,123.

Admissions
Clemson University
Office of Undergraduate Admissions
105 Sikes Hall Box 345124
Clemson. SC 29634-5124
www.clemson.edu/futurestudents/contactus.html

Service-Learning
Kathy Woodard, Director
Community Engagement and Service-learning Education
214 Barre Hall
Phone: (864) 656-0205
Email: ckathy@clemson.edu

University of South Carolina

The University of South Carolina commits to providing the knowledge, skills, and values necessary for success in a changing world.

Flagship Programs

Carolina Service-Learning Initiative

At USC students can engage in service-learning through a variety of classes and also through community service programs. The Center for Teaching Excellence, South Carolina Honors College, and Division of Student Affairs and Department of Academic Support provide professional development and support for faculty and staff to integrate service-learning principles into discipline specific courses through workshops and grant programs.

University 101

Since the mid-1990s, students enrolled in our nationally recognized first-year seminar program, University 101, have fulfilled a ten-hour service requirement through a variety of experiences, such as youth mentoring, that help students make meaning of transition in a broader context.

Service Saturdays

Community Service Programs provides transportation and lunch to Carolina students who participate in monthly, half-day service opportunities in the Columbia community. In the

fall of 2007, more than 850 participants donated an estimated 4,250 hours of volunteer service.

Course Snapshot

Community Psychology Practicum

Students in Dr. Brad Smith's "Community Psychology Practicum" have a service-learning experience in the after-school Challenging Horizons Program (CHP). Students in the CHP provide interventions, such as tutoring and behavior management, for youth with learning or behavior problems. Throughout the semester, PSYC 489 students discuss the psychological basis for these interventions and how to improve their performance through better understanding of intervention science. This service-learning experience allows students to strengthen their professional backgrounds and clarify their research interests.

Academics

The University of South Carolina seeks to engage students, faculty, and community organizations in service-learning partnerships to foster and encourage collaborative learning, academic achievement, humanitarian service, global citizenship, and moral, ethical, and spiritual development. Students learn through service to critically think about and act on issues that affect local and global communities.

South Carolina Honors College
University 101
Moore School of Business
College of Journalism and Mass Communications
• College of Mass Communications and Information Studies
College of Arts and Sciences
• Department of Psychology
• Department of History
• Department of Languages, Literature, and Cultures
• German
• Spanish
• Arts: Media Arts
• Women's Studies
College of Engineering and Computing
College of Hospitality, Retail, and Sport Management
College of Education
• Early Childhood
• Exceptional Children

Check out all majors at: www.sc.edu/bulletin/ugrad/index.html

"Students working in our Green Quad Community Garden get their hands dirty while learning about sustainability."

~ Dr. David Whiteman, Associate Professor and Principal of the Green Quad Learning Community.

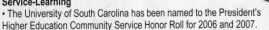

Awards and Recognition

Service-Learning
• The University of South Carolina has been named to the President's Higher Education Community Service Honor Roll for 2006 and 2007.
• The Office of Community Service Programs was designated as a Target Corporation Grant Recipient for the Service Saturday Program in 2005 and 2006.
• The Salvation Army of the Midlands distinguished partnership award was given to the Office of Community Service Programs in 2006 and 2007.

Academics
• Highest research designation awarded by the Carnegie Foundation.
• International business program ranked best in the nation in *U.S.News and World Report's Best Colleges 2006* rankings.
• The School of Hotel, Restaurant, and Tourism Management is ranked in the Top 10 nationally.
• The South Carolina Honors College has been lauded as one of the best in the nation.
• The University of South Carolina was one of eight U.S. flagship universities featured for rising academic quality in a November 2006 article in The Wall Street Journal.

College Fast Facts

Four Year, Public, Urban, Founded: 1801

Web site: www.sc.edu

Student Profile: Undergraduate: 18,827. 45% male/ 55% female. 17.75% minority.

Faculty Profile: 88.46% of faculty hold a Ph.D.

Costs and Aid: Academic year (undergraduate) $7,946 in-state (approx.) $21,232 out-of-state (approx.). Room & board for the academic year $6,946 (approx.). 94% of new freshmen received some form of financial aid.

Admissions

University of South Carolina
Office of Undergraduate Admissions
Lieber College
Columbia, SC 29208
Phone: (803)777-7700
(800)868-5872
Email: admissions-ugrad@sc.edu

Service-Learning

Jimmie Gahagan
Assistant Vice Provost
for Student Engagement
gahagan@sc.edu
Phone: (803) 777-1445

Wofford College

Committed to a philosophy of "access to education and opportunities for service," Wofford is a Phi Beta Kappa liberal arts college related to the United Methodist Church.

Flagship Programs

The Bonner Scholars Program
Begun in 1991 at Wofford, the BSP is a community of sixty students dedicated to personal and communal transformation through service learning, civic engagement, and social justice. Bonner Scholars serve in the community, reflect in group settings, create community on the Wofford campus, and develop an understanding of their life's calling. **http://www.wofford.edu/bonnerScholars.**

Interim
The Interim permits students and professors to concentrate for a month on a single study project of his or her choosing. Because interim projects are designed to move beyond traditional classroom courses and teaching methods, study projects regularly include service learning in the local community, around the country, and abroad. **http://www.wofford.edu/interim/.**

Alternative Break Experiences
Alternative break trips are designed to broaden the experience of students by providing diverse opportunities for understanding and appreciating the earth, its inhabitants, and their needs. Recent experiences include a Borderlinks project on the Arizona-Mexico border and a Habitat project on the island of Eleuthera in The Bahamas.

Course Snapshot

Spanish 303: Advanced Spanish
Matt Lowe, Class of 2009, reflected: "The greatest aspects of the class were not only learning about Hispanic culture and serving the Latino community but also having the opportunity to actually experience Hispanic life and meet so many different people,

each with a different story to tell." Students participate in Latino community life by serving as mentors, classroom helpers, and tutors to school children each week and by reflecting together as a class about the challenges and triumphs of the growing immigrant population in the Carolinas.

Academics

Courses with a strong service-learning component at Wofford shape students into life-long learners committed to civic engagement and social justice.

Academics list of programs:

Accounting
Biology
Chemistry
Computer Science
Education
English
Finance
Mathematics
Philosophy
Psychology
Sociology
Spanish
Theater

"Service learning adds a depth of understanding and appreciation for a topic beyond the typical classroom experience. "

– Dr. Kara Bopp, Professor of Psychology

Check out all majors at: www.wofford.edu/academics/

Awards and Recognition
Service-Learning
• Bonner Scholars Program (since 1991)
• President's Honor Roll for Community Service, 2006

Academics
• Phi Beta Kappa liberal arts college offering bachelor's degrees in 25 majors, plus pre-professional programs in health care, law, and the ministry.
• Benchmark campus in the book Student Success in College, based on survey results from the National Study of Student Engagement (NSSE).
• One of the nation's top five in student participation in studies abroad (annual Open Doors Report).
• Profiled in the major guides to selective colleges and universities (*Princeton Review, Fiske, the Insider's Guide*, etc.)

College Fast Facts
Web site: www.wofford.edu
Affiliation: Methodist
Student Profile: 1260 undergraduate students (52% male,48 % female);32 states and territories, 10 countries (optional); 11% minority, Less than 1% international.
Faculty Profile: 98 full-time faculty. 92% hold a terminal degree in their field. 1:11 student/faculty ratio. Average class size is 13.
Athletics: NCAA Division I, Southern Conference. 18(#) varsity sports. (May include 15 word phrase about Athletics)—Home to the Carolina Panthers summer training camp, Wofford is the smallest college or university fielding a Division I football program. 2003 Southern Conference Champions in football; 2007 Southern Conference Tournament Champions in baseball.
Costs and Aid: 2007–2008: $35,535 comprehensive ($27,830 tuition). 86.9% of students receive some financial aid. Average award: $22,889

Admissions
Wofford College, Office of Admissions
429 North Church Street Spartanburg, SC 29303-3663
Telephone: (864) 597-4130
admissions@wofford.edu

Service Learning
Corella Bonner Service Learning Center
Lyn Pace, MDIV
Director
Phone: (864) 597-4402
Email: pacepl@wofford.edu

South Dakota State University

As a land-grant university, SDSU prides itself in excellence in education, innovation and new knowledge creation, and community outreach.

Flagship Programs

International Partnership for Service-Learning and Leadership

Through the Lakota Nation program of the IPSL (**www.ipsl.org**), students earn up to 15 credits from SDSU over 13 weeks living and serving on an American Indian reservation while studying the history, culture, issues and concerns of the Indians of the Northern Plains.

Leadership and Management of Nonprofit Organizations

Students pursuing this interdisciplinary minor have partnered with a community development agency to plan and implement an annual downtown street festival, coordinating vendors, entertainment, fundraising, and volunteers.

Students can receive national certification in LMNO through a service internship.

The American Humanics Program connects students with local nonprofits. Through service-learning and co-curricular activities, students gain experience in the competencies of a nonprofit professional while addressing identified needs of the nonprofit organization and the clients they serve.

Course Snapshot

SPAN 492: Service-Learning in Spanish

This class allows students to put their Spanish skills to the test and learn about the culture first hand. While studying immigration issues, students work with native speakers teaching ESL to dairy farm workers, or tutoring and mentoring Spanish-speaking students in the public schools. A student in the class reflected, "Mexican culture is no longer an idea or a story, but something living and real. This has been a magnificent experience. I will never forget these girls and this class."

Academics

Faculty members and community partners design service-learning projects to meet specific learning goals and to advance student understanding of course content. Participating departments include:

American Indian Studies
Apparel Merchandising
Communication Studies
Counseling and Human Resource Development
Early Childhood Education
English
Gerontology
Health, Physical Education, and Recreation
Health Science
Leadership and Management of Nonprofit Organizations

Mass Communications
Media Production
Modern Languages
Nursing
Pharmacy
Political Science
Sociology
Teacher Education
Visual Arts

View all majors at:
www3.sdstate.edu/Admissions/MajorsandMinorsListing/

"Service-learning gets me excited about my academic work, my role as a citizen, and also as a future nonprofit professional. It helps tie the information I learn in my classes to the real world."

Awards and Recognition

• More than 200 majors, minors and options are available with more than 6,000 course offerings. Master's degrees are offered in more than thirty areas, and doctorates are available in eight fields.
• National Research Doctoral Granting Institution; *U.S.News & World Report* Level III.
• Geographic Information Science Center of Excellence (partnership with the EROS Data Center).
• Enterprise Institute encourages and assists new businesses in the region.
• National Children's Study South Dakota/Minnesota site leader.
• Innovation Campus research park under development.
• Research advances in aviation grade ethanol, renewable fuels, and wind power.
• 2005 Secretary of Defense Employer Support Freedom Award.
• 2004 Pro Patria Award for outstanding support to SDSU students and employees in the National Guard and the Reserves.

College Fast Facts

Four Year, Public, Rural, Founded: 1881

Web site: www3.sdstate.edu/

Student Profile: 10,332 undergraduate students (47% male, 53% female); 50 states and territories, 47 countries; 6% minority, 3% international.

Faculty Profile: 522 full-time faculty; 77% hold a terminal degree in their field; 17:1 student/faculty ratio; 25-30 average class size.

Athletics: NCAA Division 1, Mid-Continent Conference. 21 varsity sports.

Costs and Aid: 2007-2008: $11,126 in-state comprehensive ($1,328 tuition); $12,438 out-of-state comprehensive ($1,984 tuition). 87% of students receive some financial aid.

Admissions

Undergraduate Admissions
South Dakota State University
Admissions Office
Box 2201
Brookings, SD 57007
Phone: (605) 688-4121
(800) 952-3541(toll-free)
FAX: (605) 688-6891
Email: SDSU.Admissions@sdstate.edu

Service-Learning

Dianne Nagy
Office for Diversity Enhancement
Box 550
Brookings, SD 57007
Phone: (605) 688-6004
FAX: (605) 688-6900

East Tennessee State University

Our Appalachian Mountains inspire the campus community as citizen leaders for our region and world.

The Office of Service-Learning at ETSU strives to make service an integral part of students' education by providing hands-on learning opportunities, and creating an expectation of service as an intentional part of the collegiate experience.

Flagship Programs

Migrant Education
Applied Spanish Minor courses: Introduction to the Spanish Speaking Communities; Translation/ Interpretation; The Migrant Experience; Summer Migrant Education

Program, a supplementary educational experience for at-risk migrant children. Students tutor Hispanic children, teach Spanish in elementary schools, translate articles for an ETSU/ community bilingual newspaper in conjunction with the ETSU Communication Department.

America Reads Challenge Program
The ETSU America Reads Challenge Program has recruited, trained and placed over 500 students at partnering schools and community centers, providing reading instruction to nearly 3,000 children while promoting confidence and encouragement. ETSU students realize that they have responsibility beyond their own school work.

PASTA
Providing Area Schools with Technical Assistance (PASTA) was conceived in 1999 when a faculty member in computer science began assisting his wife, a 5th grade teacher, with her classroom computers. PASTA is now a capstone service-learning course for seniors. Students pair with area schools to act as a "help desk" for a semester. Each student spends 75 hours providing technical assistance. As ETSU computers are replaced, students sanitize them, reinstall software, and donate them to local schools.

Course Snapshot

SRVL-1020: Introduction to Service-Learning
The Introduction to Service-Learning course offers students a more in-depth look at community needs by providing a variety of service placements such as tutoring school children, building

community gardens, providing care or companionship to the elderly and providing community education on issues such as drug and alcohol awareness.

Academics

At ETSU service-learning reflects the belief that education must be linked to social responsibility and that the most effective learning is not only active but is connected to experience in a meaningful way.

Art
Computer Science
Criminal Justice
History
College of Education
English
Environmental Studies
Family & Consumer Sciences
Journalism
Nursing
Public Administration
Service-Learning
Sociology
Social Work
Spanish
Theatre

"The experiential component is a crucial part of the class. Students are able to make important connections to course content and often report personal growth through the experience."

-SPED Instructor

Check out all majors at:
www.etsu.edu/etsu/academics.asp

Awards and Recognition

Service-Learning
• 2 Daily Point of Light Awards
• State of TN Love Community Service Award
• Awarded 2 Learn & Serve Grants
• Veterans History Project Recognition
• President's High Education Community Service Honor Roll with Distinction

Academics
• ETSU has been honored as one of the South's best regional universities based on quality and cost.
• ETSU offers the variety of courses, field experiences, and stellar out-of-classroom activities often associated primarily with much larger universities
• Included in "America's Best Graduate Schools" *U.S. News & World Report*
• Included as Best Value College by Princeton Review.

College Fast Facts

College Website: www.etsu.edu

University Profile: Overall enrollment 13,300 plus; ETSU is accredited by the Commission on Colleges of the Southern Association of Colleges and Schools to award Certificate, Associate, Bachelor's, Master's, Educational Specialist, Doctor of Education, Ph.D, and M.D. degrees. Attracting students from all 50 of the United States and over 60 countries, ETSU is comprised of 11 colleges and schools: Arts and Sciences, Business and Technology, Clinical and Rehabilitative Health Sciences, Education, Honors, Medicine, Nursing, Pharmacy, Public Health, School of Continuing Studies, and School of Graduate Studies.

Athletics: NCAA Division I, Atlantic Sun Conference; 17 varsity sports. ETSU Athletics is extremely proud that 100% of students and coaches participate in community service events.

Costs and Aid: 2007–2008: $16,929 in state comprehensive ($4,887tuition); $27,205 out of state comprehensive ($4,887 tuition); 74% of students receive some financial aid; average award: $10,907

Service-Learning Facts
Service-Learning courses and credit earning experiences are integrated into: General Education and core curriculum, Undergraduate research programs, Capstone courses, Independent study.

Admissions

East Tennessee State University
Office of Undergraduate Admissions
P.O. Box 70731
Johnson City, TN 37614
Phone: (423) 439-4213;
1-800-GO2-ETSU
E-mail: GO2ETSU@etsu.edu

Service-Learning

Teresa Brooks Taylor
Assistant Director Service-Learning
Phone: (423) 439-5675
E-mail: taylort@etsu.edu

Lee University

Lee University's foundational purpose is to develop students for responsible Christian living in a complex world.

Service-Learning Focus

Students engaging in service-learning at Lee University should:

• Understand the biblical mandate for service.
• Recognize that service to others is part of God's purpose for them.
• Have insight into appropriate service and its impact.
• Understand how vocation can be used in service to God and others.

Flagship Programs

RELG 200 is a required sophomore-level course that focuses on the biblical and theological foundations for benevolence and service. Students reflect on course material and service projects which are often completed in the inner-city housing projects of Atlanta.

Nursing Home Visits

During fall new student orientation, all new students, faculty members, and peer leaders visit nursing homes. Students participate in activity therapy experiences, engage residents in conversation, assist residents with their meals, and gather with residents to sing together.

Cross-Cultural Experience

Students are required to complete a cross-cultural experience. Oftentimes these trips integrate service. The more popular trips have been to Peru, Nicaragua, Honduras, and Guatemala. The Peru trip included building an open-air church with villagers.

Course Snapshot

TCOM 495: Christianity and the Media

This course featured a project called Heritage Videos. The students visited local nursing homes to complete videotaped interviews with residents. These projects chronicled the family history of the residents to be persevered for future generations. The students edited and produced the interviews, creating a number of DVDs for each family. The residents and their family members were invited to campus to share a meal and screen the videos.

Academics

Lee University students learn to use their gifts to meet the world's needs and to develop this as a lifestyle. All students must complete 80 hours of service-learning and approved reflection as a graduation requirement.

• Vocal Music
• Instrumental Music
• Early Childhood, Elementary, and Special Education
• Health, Exercise Science, and Secondary Education
• Christian Ministries
• Theology
• Behavioral and Social Sciences
• Business
• Communication and the Arts
• English and Modern Foreign Languages
• History and Political Science
• Natural Sciences and Mathematics

Check out all majors at: www.leeuniversity.edu/academics/

"Service-learning helped students enhance their learning and place it in the context of community needs." -Dr. Mike Hayes

Awards and Recognition

Service-Learning

• President's Higher Education Community Service Honor Roll with Distinction (2006 and 2007).
• President's Higher Education Community Service Honor Roll with Distinction for 2006 Special Focus Area (Hurricane Relief).
• Awarded two AmeriCorps VISTA workers through Tennessee Campus Compact in 2007.

Academics

• Top Tier in *U.S.News & World Report* – Universities-Master's (South).
• Listed in the *Princeton Review* ranking of "best colleges" in the South.
• Ranked in Open Doors 2007 as first in the country among the top 20 baccalaureate institutions in the percentage of undergraduates receiving credit for studying abroad.
• Recipient of two grants from Lilly Endowment, Inc., for the theological exploration of vocation.

College Fast Facts

Four Year, Private Suburban, Founded: 1918

Affiliation: Church of God (Cleveland, TN)

Web site: www.leeuniversity.edu

Student Profile: 3,789 undergraduate students (43.6% male, 56.4% female), 48 states and territories, 41 countries, 13% minority, 5.4% international.

Faculty Profile: 167 full-time faculty, 79% hold a terminal degree in their field, 16:1 student/faculty ratio. Average class size is 22.

Athletics: NAIA Division 1; Southern States Athletic Conference; 12 varsity sports

Costs and Aid: 2007-2008: comprehensive - $16,460 (tuition - $10,392). 85.5% of students receive some financial aid.

Admissions

Lee University
Office of Admissions
P.O. Box 3450
Cleveland, TN 37320-3450
Phone: (800) 533-9930 or (423) 614-8500
Email: admissions@leeuniversity.edu

Service-Learning

Mike Hayes, Ed.D.
Assistant Vice President for Student Life
P.O. Box 3450
Cleveland, TN 37320-3450
Phone: (423) 614-8406
Email: mhayes@leeuniversity.edu

Lipscomb University

Lipscomb University is a Christian community of scholars, dedicated to excellence in learning, leading and serving.

Flagship Programs

Law, Justice and Society Program
Students within the Law, Justice and Society major participate in service-learning throughout their four year academic career. Service-learning experiences in this program take place in class, internship and research experiences where students partner with agencies to address the social issues. Law, Justice and Society graduates are prepared for work in the legal profession, nonprofit or governmental careers.

Lipscomb Engineering Projects in Central America
Engineering students at Lipscomb have the opportunity to utilize their skills and abilities to make a difference in communities in Guatemala and Honduras. Week-long service-learning trips allow students to design and implement necessary engineering projects such as constructing a suspension bridge that increases accessibility to main roads and increasing a community's ability to store clean drinking water.

Strategic Planning for Nonprofit Organizations
The capstone course in Lipscomb's undergraduate business program, Business Policy and Strategy, allows students to

hone their professional skills and contribute to the effectiveness of local nonprofit organizations. In this course, students form consulting teams and work with nonprofit agencies to perform a strategic audit to increase organization effectiveness.

Course Snapshot

SW 4523: Applied Social Work Research Methods
As a result of research completed through this service-learning course, Lipscomb Social Work students provided nonprofit organization Choral Arts Link, Inc. with resources and information that allowed the agency to move forward with funding opportunities that will provide for growth for their programs. One student reflected: "The research project that we did for CAL, Inc., was one of the most rewarding projects I have ever been apart of. We were able to give the agency some great information which will help them receive grant money and recognition."

Academics

Service-Learning experiences at Lipscomb include both curricular and co-curricular opportunities. A sample of academic departments supporting service-learning include:

Bible
Biology
Management*
Marketing
Education
English
Engineering
First Year Seminar
History
Kinesiology
Law, Justice and Society
Nursing
Nutrition
Premed
Social Work
Spanish

*Courses with a required service-learning component.

Check out all majors at: http://academics.lipscomb.edu

Awards and Recognition

Service-Learning

• Students at Lipscomb complete two types of service-learning experiences before graduating as a part of an academic service-learning graduation requirement.

President's Higher Education Community Service Honor Roll, 2007

Academics

• Top 25 of *U.S News & World Report's 2007 America's Best Colleges Southern*—Universities Master's classification

• Lipscomb University offers more than 130 programs of study in 47 majors, 12 Master's degrees and, beginning in 2008, a doctoral degree in pharmacy with a focus on community responsibility.

• Over 90% of Lipscomb graduates report job placement within 6 months of graduation.

• The new Institute for Sustainable Practice at Lipscomb University offers a bachelor's degree in sustainability where students learn how to integrate ecological, social and economic awareness into the day-to-day decision-making process of a career in business or public service.

College Fast Facts

Liberal Arts University Founded in 1891 Offering both Undergraduate and Graduate Degrees.

Web site: www.lipscomb.edu

Affiliation: Church of Christ

Student Profile: Undergraduate students (47% male, 53% female); 43 states and territories, 18 countries; 13% minority, 8% international.

Faculty Profile: 43 full-time faculty 83% hold a terminal degree in their field. 14:1 student/faculty ratio. Average class size is 22.

Athletics: NCAA Division 1, Atlantic Sun Conference. 17 varsity sports. Lipscomb University will host the Atlantic Sun Conference men's and women's basketball championships in 2008 and 2009.

Costs and Aid: 2007–2008: $24,457 comprehensive ($15,986 tuition). 97% of students receive some financial aid.

Admissions

Lipscomb University, Office of Undergraduate Admissions
One University Park Drive
Nashville, Tennessee 37204
Phone: (877) LU-BISON (582-4766)
Email: www.golipscomb.com

Service-Learning
The SALT Center
Christin Shatzer, MPA
Director of Service-Learning
Phone: (615) 966-7225
Email: christin.shatzer@lipscomb.edu

Tennessee State University

Tennessee State University is a comprehensive land-grant university committed to life-long learning, service, and scholarly inquiry. Graduates embody the university's motto: "Think. Work. Serve."

Flagship Programs

TN State University Students Help Katrina Victims

Following Hurricane Katrina, 33 TN State University students and 3 faculty traveled to New Orleans to lead a free 4-week camp for 250 children whose lives were disrupted by the hurricane. "Camp Supercharge" provided these young hurricane victims with high quality learning activities, arts and crafts, science projects, games, field trips, and mentoring in a safe and engaging environment. Through a blend of academics and fun, TSU students helped these children cope with the devastation of their lives while catching up on their learning.

TSU becomes the lead institution in establishing the TN Campus Compact (TNCC)

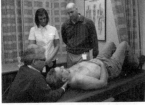

As the host site for TNCC and an AmeriCorps* VISTA Project, TSU is at the forefront of service-learning and civic engagement in the state. "We are delighted to welcome TN Campus Compact as our 33rd state office," notes national Campus Compact president Maureen F. Curley. "The office will be a huge resource in building state capacity for campus-based civic engagement through partnerships, research, training, and development of best practices."

Course Snapshot

Physical Therapy 5580 Physical Agents

Physical Therapy students learn physical therapy skills such as massage, ultrasound, heat or Cryotherapy as they apply the skills with patients at Siloam Family Health Center, a faith-based family clinic that serves Nashville's refugee population. These TSU students work with Siloam to provide quality health care for families, some of whom have fled war-torn homelands and lived in refugee camps in extremely poor living conditions. Through this service-learning experience, students work with highly qualified staff to provide the best services to those in need while learning their course content in a real world setting.

Academics

Students participating in service learning understand the relevance of academic study to the "real" world while developing a sense of civic responsibility to their community.

Africana Studies
Art
Biological Sciences
Business
Chemistry
Communications
Consumer Sciences
Cooperative Extension
Counseling Psychology
Dental Hygiene
Education
Educational Administration
Family and Consumer Sciences

"Students in my Urban Geography course learned how to convey relatively complex geographic information systems (GIS) methods in ways that community activists might easily understand and use for neighborhood asset mapping efforts."

~ *Professor David Padgett (GEOG 4850)*

All offered majors can be found at: www.tnstate.edu

Awards and Recognition

• The Center for Service-Learning and Civic Engagement has more than $1,900,000 in grant funds to build service initiatives.

• A $584,119 Housing and Urban Development grant is being used to upgrade facilities at 3 community partner sites.

• Tennessee State University is home to the 2007 National Honda-All Star Championship team.

• The Office of Business and Economic Research secured $2.25 million to fund the Pilot Center of Academic Excellence in Intelligence Studies.

• The National Science Foundation has awarded TSU a $2.5 million grant for Science, Technology, Engineering, and Mathematics research.

• Tennessee State University was selected as one of five finalists for the 2008 C. Peter Magrath University Community Engagement Award. TSU captured the 1890/1994 Land-Grants Award for Think, Work, Serve: Outreach & Engagement at Tennessee State University. TSU serves as a bridge, connecting the needs and assets of the community with the resources of the university.

College Fast Facts

Four Year, Public, Urban, Founded: 1912

Web site: www.tnstate.edu

Student Profile: 7,132 undergraduate students (36% male, 64% female); 42 states and territories, 78% minority, 1% international.

Faculty Profile: 421 full-time faculty, 80% hold a terminal degree in their field, 22:1 student/faculty ratio. Average class size is 19.

Athletics: NCAA Division 1, Conference: Ohio Valley. 15 Varsity sports, (8 women teams, 7men teams). Over 250 TSU athletes participate in broad-based programs of intercollegiate athletics which are inextricably linked to the university's academic mission.

Costs and Aid: 2007-2008: $4886 in-state comprehensive ($2,243 tuition); $15,162 out-of-state comprehensive ($7,581 tuition).

Admissions

Tennessee State University, Office of Admission and Records
PO Box 9609
3500 John A. Merritt Blvd.
Nashville, TN. 37209-1561
Phone: (615) 963-5105; 1(888) 463-6878

Service-Learning

Center for Service Learning and Civic Engagement
Deena Sue Fuller, Ph. D.
Director of Service Learning
Phone: (615)963-5383
www.tnstate.edu/servicelearning

Union University

Union University is a Christian university characterized by rigorous academics and Christian commitment involving the head, heart and hands.

Flagship Programs

JUST Jackson Union Sculpture Tour
This five-year partnership initiated by art students with the city of Jackson, Tennessee, establishes permanent urban sculpture displays. Students research and invite sculptors, make shipping and installation arrangements, develop the tour's accompanying public relations campaign and serve on the judging panel to select the piece purchased annually.

Green Chemistry Laboratory Manuals
As an undergraduate research project, chemistry students produced green chemistry laboratory manuals for use by high school students and by non-science majors in regular and web-based college courses. These manuals are used in high schools throughout the United States.

The First Job
In high school, teenagers often seek their first part-time job. Union's business students teamed up with J-Crib Urban Ministries – an outreach program for at-risk teens. Students presented workshops that taught these teens important skills: interviewing, filling out applications, dressing for success and managing money.

Course Snapshot

SW 315: Foundations for Social Work Practice applies learned skills through the Memory Book Project, which matches students with elder resident volunteers in nursing homes, assisted living facilities and retirement villages. The elder person collaborates with the student in the making of their memory book, saying what stories, photos and items they wish to be included. Together they collect an heirloom of memories and memorabilia into a masterfully constructed scrapbook which is a gift to the resident. Both student and elder learn, laugh, listen and gain from the semester-long experience.

Academics

Currently Union University's service-learning initiatives either originate with individual faculty or through department-based or university-wide service projects.

College of Arts and Sciences
Art
Chemistry
Communication Arts
Engineering
History
Language Studies
Psychology
Family Studies
McAfee School of Business Administration
SIFE
School of Christian Studies
Christian Ministries Mentorship
School of Education and Human Studies
Education
Social Work

"Service-learning greatly matures a student. That student gains an exposure to the professional world not possible in the classroom."

~ Aaron Lee Benson, M.F.A.,
Union University Professor of Art

Find out more about our programs of study at:
www.uu.edu/academics/

Awards and Recognition

Service-Learning
• President's Higher Education Community Service Honor Roll.
• "Best BSW Student Project" in the Influencing State Policy National Contest.
• Union University's Student Affiliate Chapter of the American. Chemical Society (SAACS) received the American Chemical Society (ACS) grant 4 years in a row.

Academics
• Union students choose majors from among more than 100 programs of study. Bachelors, masters and doctorate degrees are offered.
• *U.S.News & World Report* has ranked Union in the top tier of either "Baccalaureate Colleges" or more recently "Best Universities–Master's" for more than a decade.
• *Princeton Review* names Union among 100 Best Colleges in the Southeast.

College Fast Facts

Four Year, Private, Suburban, Founded: 1823

Web site: www.uu.edu

Affiliation: Tennessee Baptist Convention

Student Profile: 2,383 undergraduate students (40% male, 60% female); 41 states and 35 countries; 15% minority, 1% international.

Faculty Profile: 178 full-time faculty. 83% hold a terminal degree in their field. 11:1 student/faculty ratio.

Athletics: NAIA Division I, TranSouth Conference. 12 varsity sports. Union has a tradition of strong intercollegiate sports teams. We also enjoy a vibrant intramural program.

Costs and Aid: 2008-2009: $26,870 comprehensive ($18,980 tuition). More than 90% of students receive some financial aid.

Admissions

Union University
Office of Undergraduate Admissions
1050 Union University Drive, Jackson, TN 38305
Phone: 1(800-)33-UNION (731) 661-5100
Email: info@uu.edu

Service-Learning

Melinda Clarke, Ed.D.
Associate Professor of Education,
Director of the Center for Educational Practice and Director of Ed.D.
Phone: (731) 661-5379
Email: mclarke@uu.edu

Abilene Christian University

Outstanding academics and bold Christian faith are the two leading characteristics that define Abilene Christian University.

Flagship Programs

Volunteer and Service-Learning Center (VSLC)

Students at ACU have countless opportunities to develop their hearts for a lifestyle of service through volunteering, service events, and service-learning. The VSLC collaborates with faculty to design meaningful service-learning experiences, connects students with appropriate placements, and engages community partners as participants in the learning process.

Study Abroad Service-Learning

The goal of the international service-learning course, conducted in Oxford, England and Montevideo, Uruguay, is to engage students with local society and institutions so that "study abroad" becomes an experiential activity more than a "consumption" activity, giving students a more realistic global view.

Spring Break Campaigns

For the past 32 years, over 400 ACU students travel during spring break to approximately 25 locations in North, Central and South America. Students raise their own support to do everything from building churches to teaching children to feeding the homeless.

Course Snapshot

ENGL 326 – Business and Professional Writing
Students in this service-learning course partner their growing knowledge of professional writing skills with real needs of our community partners. From preparing annual reports to developing web sites to writing grants, the products developed from this course have come to be a valued and reliable annual resource for many of our partner agencies, including revenue acquired from grants. While perfecting their writing ability, students experience nontraditional ways of serving, gaining an understanding of community needs and getting a rare look at nonprofit management issues. Students also have actually produced and distributed writing samples to include in their

Academics

Service-learning experiences show ACU students the reality of local and global social issues while instilling in them a lifelong desire to change the world.
Programs of Study include:

General Educ (U100)
Bible
Biology
Business-Management
Communications
Communication Sciences and Disorders
English
Exercise Science and Health
Honors
Political Science
Psychology
Social Work
Spanish
Study Abroad

"We love ACU students. The university is helping the students receive hands-on experience which is the single most important quality to have when one enters the work force."

– Agency service-learning

Check out all majors at: www.acu.edu/academics

Service-Learning Focus

Service-learning at ACU is grounded in our university mission, "to educate students for Christian service and leadership throughout the world." Students engage in activities such as writing the annual report for a nonprofit agency, teaching Junior Achievement modules, feeding the homeless, or countless other experiences.

College Fast Facts

Four-Year, Private, Suburban

Web site: www.acu.edu

Affiliation: Churches of Christ

Student Profile: About 4700 undergraduate students (45% male, 55% female); 50 states and territories, 60 countries; 16% minority, 4% international.

Faculty Profile: More than 200 full-time faculty. 95% hold a terminal degree in their field. 17:1 student/faculty ratio. Average class size is 17.

Athletics: NCAA Division II, Lone Star Conference. 14 varsity sports.

Costs and Aid: 2007–2008: $25,265 for tuition, fees, room and board, plus approximately $800 for textbooks and supplies. 90% of students receive some financial aid.

Admissions
ACU Box 29000
Abilene, Texas 79699-9000
Phone: (325)674-2650;
1 (800) 460-6228
Email: info@admissions.acu.edu
www.acu.edu/admissions

Service-Learning
Volunteer and
Service-Learning Center
Nancy Coburn
Director
Phone: (325) 674-2932
Email: vslc@acu.edu

Texas Christian University

~ TCU Center for Community Involvement & Service-Learning ~
involved.
Effecting Change Through Service

Texas Christian University (TCU) delivers a world-class, values-centered university experience, educating individuals to think and act as ethical leaders and responsible citizens in the global community.

Flagship Programs

Planting the Seeds for Public Health

As part of two practicum courses in Nutritional Sciences and Nursing, TCU students partner with a social services agency to work side by side with local residents to build a community garden and help them achieve health benefits from gardening.

Research Apprentices in Physics Program (RAPP)

Through RAPP, graduate and undergraduate students in the TCU Department of Physics and Astronomy become mentors to high school students; with the lab as their classroom, TCU students learn by teaching their apprentices to appreciate science.

International Service-Learning

During a TCU summer Social Work course in Mexico, TCU students study Spanish, experience Mexican culture, conduct needs assessments to explore community strengths and challenges, and volunteer with social service agencies, learning to work with others across borders and create collaborative solutions to community problems.

Course Snapshot

Practicum: Community Health Nursing (N40882)

"We spent months involving and investing ourselves in this community, which resulted in a very personal feeling of pride regarding the success of the emergency preparedness fair... only a service-learning project can offer a college student that kind of satisfaction."

"We were able to sharpen other skills such as resourcefulness, organizational thinking and communication. Most importantly, service-learning gave us a personalized opportunity to see how our hard work and dedication served and impacted our community."

Academics

Through service-learning courses, TCU students contribute to the community while gaining valuable interpersonal and professional skills to become agents of change locally, nationally and globally. Below is a partial list of departments/schools in which service-learning can be found:

Business
Communication Studies
Economics
Education
Engineering
Environmental Sciences
English
French
Geology
Journalism
Nursing
Nutritional Sciences
Physics and Astronomy
Political Science
Religion
Social Work
Sociology
Spanish
Theater

"Service-Learning affords students the opportunity to integrate theory with practice... providing opportunities for the development of a mutually beneficial relationship between the university and the community."

~ Dr. Amiso George, Journalism, Writing for Public Relations/Advertising (JOUR 30803)

Check out all majors at:
www.catalog.tcu.edu/

Awards and Recognition

• Dr. Mary McKinney selected as a Campus Compact Faculty Fellow for her work in service-learning.

• Recognized by the Fort Worth Chamber of Commerce, TCU received its prestigious Spirit of Enterprise Award. The honor recognizes unique contributions to the city. TCU is the only college or university in Fort Worth to have ever won the award.

• The Pre-health Professions Program for prospective doctors, dentists and veterinarians enjoys an acceptance rate at professional schools that is approximately twice the national average.

• The pass rate for TCU students on the Texas state teachers' exam typically exceeds 98 percent and has reached 100 percent in two of the past three years.

• The long-term commitment of the Neeley School of Business to diversity has resulted in its inclusion among the Best Business Schools for Hispanics by Hispanic Magazine.

• In 2007, the Society of Professional Journalists ranked *Image* as the No. 1 U.S. college magazine.

• The TCU ad campaigns team placed eighth in the country in the 2007 National Student Advertising Campaign for Coca-Cola and first in regional competition.

College Fast Facts

Four Year, Private, Urban, Founded: 1873

Affiliation: Christian Church (Disciples of Christ)

Web site: www.tcu.edu

Student Profile: Undergraduate students (42% male, 58% female); 15% minority, 5% international. 85 countries represented.

Faculty Profile: 465 full-time faculty. 90% hold a terminal degree in their field. 14:1 student/faculty ratio. Average class size is 27.

Athletics: NCAA Division I-A, Mountain West Conference. 19 varsity sports. More than half of TCU's student-athletes achieved GPAs of 3.0 or better during the spring 2006 semester.

Costs and Aid: 2007-2008: $33,918 comprehensive ($24,868 tuition). 70% of students receive some form of financial aid.

Admissions

Texas Christian University
Office of Undergraduate
  Admissions
Saddler Hall 112
Fort Worth, TX 76129
Phone: (817) 257-7490

Service-Learning

Rosangela Boyd, Ph.D.
Director, Center for Community
Involvement and Service-Learning
Phone: (817) 257-5356
Email: r.boyd@tcu.edu

The University of Texas at Arlington

The University of Texas at Arlington is a public university with a commitment to life-enhancing research, teaching excellence and service to the larger community.

Flagship Programs

Alternative Spring Break

Students participate in a service project and learn about issues such as literacy, poverty, racism, hunger, homelessness and the environment. The objective is to involve college students in community-based service projects and to offer them an opportunity to learn about the problems faced by members of communities with whom they otherwise may have had little or no direct contact.

Service-Learning Collaboration Project

The University of Texas at Arlington has initiated a service-learning collaboration among university, community college, and school district faculty. This interdisciplinary collaboration creates an environment of learning content and working for the common good in contexts of service to the community.

The Innocence Project

As part of the Innocence Project of Texas, our Department of Criminology and Criminal Justice students devote time to investigating inmates' claims of actual innocence and work toward freedom for the wrongfully-convicted, who would otherwise become lost in the criminal justice system.

Course Snapshot

KINE 4320: Teaching Secondary Physical Education

University Kinesiology students organized a youth leadership program that emphasized social support, self-respect, and personal responsibility through an outdoor activities service-learning class assignment. Each semester these university students mentor middle school students, including special groups, such as the Hurricane Katrina students. The activities focus on meeting new people, supporting teammates, and realizing strengths and limitations through a variety of physical challenges that include a significant level of perceived risk (e.g., rock-climbing, zip-line, etc.). Class celebrations include a BBQ and a Dallas Mavericks home game.

Academics

Service-Learning is learning in the real world, taking risks; developing critical, reflective thinking; and strategies that increase both academic understanding and responsibility to others.

School of Architecture
College of Business Administration
College of Education
College of Engineering
Honors College
College of Liberal Arts
School of Nursing
College of Science
School of Social Work
School of Urban & Public Affairs

"I have always appreciated the fact that education doesn't give us all the answers; in fact, it sometimes means we have more questions because we see how much bigger the world is than our own experiences."

-Jim Spaniolo, President
University of Texas at Arlington

Check out all majors at:
www.uta.edu/uta/academics

Awards and Recognition

- President's Higher Education Community Service Honor Roll with Distinction 2006 and 2007.
- 2005 *U.S. News & World Report* -School of Urban and Public Affairs listed as one of the best Graduate Schools in Public Affairs.
- College of Business Administration has largest executive Masters of Business Administration graduate school in China.
- 2008 $9.8 million Civil Engineering Laboratory Building (CELB)
- 2007 The School of Nursing is one of the 20 largest schools of nursing in the United States.
- 2007 School of Nursing's Smart Hospital – First in the nation!
- 2007 Mind, Brain Education Council in the College of Education.

College Fast Facts

Web site: www.uta.edu

Student Profile: Undergraduate students (48% male, 52% female); 48 states and territories; 130 countries; 32.85% minority,10.8% international.

Faculty Profile: 1100 full-time faculty; 85% hold a terminal degree in their field. 20:1 student/faculty ratio; average class size is 25.

Athletics: NCAA Division Conference. Men/Women Basketball, Women's Volleyball.

Costs and Aid: 55% of students receive some form of financial aid.

Admissions

University of Texas at Arlington
Office of Admissions, Recruitment & Orientation
Box 19111
Arlington, Texas 76019-0111
Phone: (817) 272-6287 (MAVS)
Fax: (817) 272-3435

Service-Learning

Center for Community Service Learning
Shirley Theriot, Ph.D.
Director
Phone: (817) 272-2124
Email: theriot@uta.edu
www.uta.edu/ccsl/

Salt Lake Community College

Salt Lake Community College is a multi-campus college serving more than 60,000 students through credit and non-credit courses and workshops each year.

College-wide student learning outcomes at Salt Lake Community College state that graduates will be critical thinkers who are civically engaged. Service-learning courses focus on personal ethics and global civic responsibility.

Flagship Programs

Faculty Development Initiatives
SLCC offers programs for faculty to deepen their skills as service-learning practitioners, including a Research Fellows program, a prestigious Service-Learning Faculty Mentorship, interdisciplinary project-based cohorts, course development grants, and training opportunities tailored for beginning, intermediate, and advanced practitioners, including a podcast series and online courses.

Partners in Service & Learning
Created in 2004 by SLCC and the University of Utah, Partners in Service & Learning is a coalition of four colleges/universities and a K-12 institution. PSL plans biannual training events for community organizations across the Salt Lake Valley and is guided by a committee of community representatives.

Civically-Engaged Scholars
This program combines academic service-learning, co-curricular service, a foundation class on civic participation, a capstone project, and a final portfolio. After completing the program, students graduate with distinction, receiving special recognition at Commencement and on their transcripts.

Course Snapshot

BUS 2200: Business Communications
Students learn business communication skills through a mix of theory and practice.

For example, one student team raised money to fund six micro-credit loans for cell phones in African villages, and collected over 400 books for Books for Africa.

Student Mary Lindsay reflected: "I learned that the best way to provide service is to follow my passion. This revelation has shown me how I can continue to be involved as a citizen in the future."

Academics

Salt Lake Community College institutionalized official criteria for service-learning course designation in April 2004. The Service-Learning Advisory Board approves all service-learning curricula. These include courses in the following departments:

Art	Health Science
Barbering & Cosmetology	Learning Essentials
Business	Management
Education	Math
English	Nursing
Environmental Technology	Occupational Therapy Assistant
Geography	Political Science
History	Sociology

SLCC offers more than 120 programs for students pursuing Associate degrees, apprenticeships, certificates, or continuing education.

For a complete listing visit: www.slcc.edu/areasofstudy
For more infomation on service-learning courses visit: www.slcc.edu/thaynecenter

"The longer I practice service-learning pedagogy, the greater my enthusiasm for teaching."
~ Associate Professor Elisa Stone, English

Awards and Recognition
• Learn and Serve America Grantee (2003-2006).
• President's Higher Education Community Service Honor Roll (2006 and 2007).
• Grantee and mentor institution with the American Association of Community Colleges' national project, *Community Colleges Broadening Horizons through Service Learning* (2006-2009).
• Among the 1,200 community colleges in the nation, SLCC ranks 5th in the number of Associate degrees awarded.
• SLCC has fourteen locations and an eCampus for distance learning.

College Fast Facts
Community College, Public, Urban: Founded 1948
Web site: www.slcc.edu
Student Profile: 23,822 students in credit-seeking programs (51% male, 49% female); 50 countries; 14% minority, 1% international.
Faculty Profile: 352 full-time faculty. 20:1 student/faculty ratio. Average class size is 18.
Costs and Aid: 2007-2008: $2,534 in-state tuition (12-18 credits); $7,954 out-of-state tuition (12-18 credits). 65% of students receive some financial aid. Average award: $2,990.
In 2007-2008, SLCC offered 156 service-learning courses.
Over 2,600 students take service-learning courses each year.

Admissions
Salt Lake Community College Enrollment Services
PO Box 30808
Salt Lake City, UT 84130-0808
Phone: (801) 957-4298
Email: futurestudents@slcc.edu

Thayne Center for Service & Learning
Betsy Ward
Director
Phone: (801) 957-4689
Email: betsy.ward@slcc.edu
Gail Jessen
Service-Learning Coordinator
Phone: (801) 957-4688
Email: gail.jessen@slcc.edu

Service-Learning Advisory Board raking leaves for senior citizens during an annual service project.

Johnson State College

At JSC, we believe in higher education's power to transform lives and are committed to helping students achieve their dreams. We challenge you to "Change Your World."

Flagship Programs

Break Away JSC students plan and participate in year-long education and service locally, nationally and globally in this award-winning alternative break program.
Intensive service trips occur over school breaks focusing on issues such as the environment, affordable housing, disaster relief, and hunger and homelessness.

Bonner Leader Program
Bonner Leaders engage in intensive, sustained service internships at local community organizations while participating in ongoing leadership training on topics including project management, goal setting, and public education and advocacy. This two-year commitment includes scholarship support and federal work-study.

Our **CSLocal program,** based in the Center for Service-Learning, engages student leaders in meaningful local service opportunities in the beautiful Lamoille Valley. Service projects are organized and led by student leaders, and matched with issue-based education opportunities.

Course Snapshot

Advanced Photography/Fine and Performing Arts (John Miller):

Students in Advanced Photography partnered with a senior center. Weekly interaction with elders helped students understand the nature of aging.

During the time students were at the Center, they photographed residents individually, in groups, and documented various aspects of their lives. This led to the final component of the servicelearning endeavor: a framed, traveling exhibition, accompanied by reflective statements written by the students as the project progressed.

Academics
JSC promotes service learning to link faculty, students, and community to work together to change our world and to find solutions to society's problems.

Programs of Study include:
Fine and Performing Arts
Behavioral Sciences
Business / Economics
Education
English
Environmental and Health Sciences
Dance
Fine and Performing Arts
Humanities
Journalism
Music
Nonprofit Management Studies
Outdoor Education
Psychology
Writing and Literature

Check out all majors at: www.jsc.edu/Academics

"Students were actually interacting with individuals with disabilities, giving real meaning to the issues discussed in our class."

~ Assistant Professor Jean Haigh, Special Education

Awards and Recognition
Service-Learning
• Title III grant (2005-2008)-supporting extended classroom experiences, including service learning.
• Bonner Leader Program (2005).
• Learn and Serve Grantee (2004-2006): supporting faculty development for service-learning.
• National Alternative Break Program of the Year (1995).
Academics
• JSC offers more than 25 majors, as well as teacher licensure programs, and certificate programs in nonprofit management and small business management.
• JSC is the only college in Vermont to participate in the National Student Exchange program.
• The college offers more than 30 student clubs and organizations, community service organizations, student leadership programs, and 25 intramural athletic activities.
• JSC students can take advantage of the Babcock Nature Preserve, a 1,030- acre tract of forest owned and maintained by the college.

College Fast Facts
Four-Year, Public, Rural

Web site: www.jsc.edu

Student Profile: 1,934 students (undergraduate-1,554, graduate -201, non-degree-179); 50% male, 50% female; 25 states and territories; 67% In-State; 33% Out-of-State.

Faculty Profile: 54 full-time faculty; 83 part-time faculty; 17:1 student/faculty ratio; average class size:17.

Athletics: NCAA Division III, North Atlantic Conference; 12 varsity sports; JSC's athletic philosophy supports students balance of athletics, academics, and giving back to local community.

Costs and Aid: 2008–2009: $15,694 in-state comprehensive ($7,488 tuition); $24,348 out-of-state comprehensive ($16,152 tuition); New England Regional Program Students: $19,414. 80% of students receive some financial aid.

Admissions
337 College Hill
Johnson, Vermont 05656
Main Number: 802-635-1219
Toll Free: 1-800-635-2356
www.jsc.edu/AdmissionsAndAid

Service-Learning
Ellen Hill
Director, Experiential Learning
Phone: 802-635-1339
Email: ellen.hill@jsc.edu
www.jsc.edu/changeyourworld

Southern Vermont College

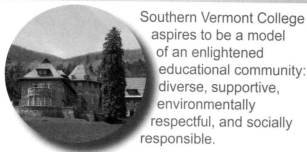

Southern Vermont College aspires to be a model of an enlightened educational community: diverse, supportive, environmentally respectful, and socially responsible.

Flagship Programs

Quest for Success

Students in our award-winning "Quest for Success" first-year course have multiple choices to engage in community-based projects ranging from developing a book of interviews with war veterans to clearing valuable land from invasive species for environmental protection and human utilization.

Creative Writing for Local Youth

Our Creative Writing courses enable students to work with younger children in local elementary schools on creative writing projects, drawing forward their spirit, energies and creative self-expression, and leading ultimately to a public presentation of their creations at the College.

Community Service Program Participation

In introductory psychology, students develop healthy and engaging friendships with local children through one of several community service programs. Our campus then serves as a resource to support these relationships and to provide additional instruction on a practical, human level.

Course Snapshot

CM 304 Communications: Advertising

"By working with an actual nonprofit organization, I was able to take concepts taught in the textbook and apply it to a real advertising campaign, with radio spots, signage, TV commercials, being generated by Big Brothers/Big Sisters for their annual fund-raising event. It was really successful. And in addition, as a result, I now have an excellent item for my portfolio that I can use as a centerpiece in furthering my career."

Matt McGetrick '08, a Communications/English major, commenting on the service-learning component of his communications course in which students provided media assistance to a local nonprofit.

Academics

Service-learning and civic engagement experiences are central to the College's curriculum and its sense of community and social responsibility. Our service-learning model endeavors to transform students into engaged citizens with a broad perspective of our ever-changing society. We immerse students in the concept of becoming lifelong and dynamic learners. Through service-learning focused courses and learning experiences, SVC students develop personal commitments to civic engagement -- locally, nationally, and globally.

Business
Business Administration/Management
Business Administration/Nonprofit Management
Business Administration/Sports Management
Communications
Creative Writing
Criminal Justice
English
History and Politics
Human Services
Liberal Arts
Liberal Arts/Management
Nursing
Professional Studies
Psychology
Radiologic Technology

"Students become more deeply engaged learners as they experience real-world educational opportunities in community-based organizations."

~ Daniel Cantor Yalowitz, Ed.D. Course Administrator for FY 100,

Check out all majors and more academic information at:
www.svc.edu/academics/divisions

Awards and Recognition
Service-Learning
• 2008 Semifinalist First-Year Experience Award, National Resource Center for the First-year Experience and Students in Transition, University of South Carolina.
• 2008 Finalist for Campus Leadership for Civic Engagement from Vermont Campus Compact.
• 2006-2007 Vermont Service-Learning Award given to SVC junior by Vermont Campus Compact.
• SVC President Karen Gross joins Executive Committee of Vermont Campus Compact board.
• SVC President Karen Gross delivers address on service-learning at VCC annual meeting.
Academics
• SVC offers a service-learning based course to all entering students.
• 35% of full-time and adjunct faculty utilize service-learning projects in one or more of their undergraduate courses.
• The majority of courses at SVC offers civic engagement and hands-on learning opportunities to students based on content area and students' level of interest and readiness.
• Several SVC core faculty are trained in and trainers for service-learning leadership and pedagogy.
• Build the Enterprise program offers students an opportunity to invent, manage and profit from their own business.

College Fast Facts
Four Year, Private, Rural, Founded: 1926
Affiliation: Nondenominational
Web site: www.svc.edu

Student Profile: 450 undergraduates, 36% male, 64% female. 22 states, 5 foreign countries, 9% minority.

Faculty Profile: 19 full-time, 16% hold a terminal degree, 16:1 student/faculty ratio. Average class size: 13.

Athletics: NCAA Division III, NECC Conference. 12 Intercollegiate Sports Teams.

Costs and Aid: 2008-2009: $26,460 comprehensive ($17,960 tuition). 73% of students receive some financial aid.

Admissions
Office of Admissions
Southern Vermont College
982 Mansion Drive
Bennington VT 05201-6002
802-447-6304
800-378-2782
E-mail: admis@svc.edu

Service-Learning
Daniel Cantor Yalowitz, Ed.D.
Associate Dean for Special Projects
dyalowitz@svc.edu
802-447-6351

Eastern Mennonite University

Eastern Mennonite University is a Christian college guided by a commitment to non-violent peacemaking, social justice, and love of neighbor.

Flagship Programs

Cross-Cultural Study: Required

Academic study, home stays, and service in a new culture -- it's a graduation requirement at EMU. Time and again, it is life-changing. While in other cultures, students reflect on the forces that shape any society—religious, economic, social, artistic, geographic, historic.

Community Learning Component

More intense than a lecture, more motivating than a field trip, Community Learning teams students, professors and local organizations together. Students deepen their academic learning, test classroom material, consider creative ways of addressing real community needs, and explore their personal vocation.

Community Service Through the Arts

Music students serve the community through performances for residents at area retirement centers, in the county jail and at a school for the deaf and blind. Literature students gather life stories of local seniors. Visual arts students produce documentaries on topics such as the local Kurdish community.

Course Snapshot

LANG 201: Advanced Writing
A student reflected: "I remember after interviews when I felt energized and inspired by the life lessons I learned. [This project] has given me perspective that I badly needed as a college student." Students interviewed nursing home residents and journaled about the exchange. At the semester's end, students hosted a reception and presented residents with their memoirs, preserving their oral histories. Students applied their writing ability to an unfamiliar genre for a specific audience for whom they learned to care.

Academics

Community Learning is an integral part of EMU's general education curriculum; all students are required to take Community Learning courses.

Programs of study include:
Applied sociology
Biblical studies
Business administration
Computer information systems
Culture, mission and religion
Digital media
Environmental science
Justice, peace and conflict studies
International business
Philosophy and theology
Photography
Political studies
Pre-law
Pre-engineering
Pre-professional health sciences
Socio-economic development
Teaching English as a second language

"Poverty has touched all of us here... I've started wondering if there's more I can do to help at home.

~ Joe Horst, India cross-cultural program

EMU offers 39 undergraduate degrees with emphasis on integrity and just relationships woven into every program.

Check out all majors at: http://emu.edu/academics

Awards and Recognition

• EMU was one of the first colleges in the country to require cross-cultural study for graduation beginning in the mid 1980s.

• In the late 40s, EMU tied with University of Arkansas as the first college in the south to admit black students.

• Enrollment of non-white students at EMU in 2006-07 was 22%; independent colleges in Virginia averaged 12% in 2006.

• The Center for Justice and Peacebuilding is known worldwide in the restorative justice field.

• The STAR program, began after 9-11, teaches trauma healing skills.

• The Summer Peacebuilding Institute brings hundreds of people from nearly 50 countries to study peacebuilding each summer.

• Many students spend a full semester abroad. Interaction with community members, mentoring with professors, classroom conversation all prepare students to live in a global context and walk boldly in Christ's way of non-violence and peace.

College Fast Facts
Four Year, Private, Suburban; Founded 1917

Web site: www.emu.edu

Student Profile: 916 undergraduate students (40% male, 60% female), 19.9% ethnic/international enrollment.

Faculty Profile: 60 full-time faculty. 12:1 student/faculty ratio.

Athletics: NCAA Division III, Old-Dominion Athletic Conference, 15 varsity sports. EMU athletics provides students the chance to integrate personal growth, athletic skills, wholesome attitudes and spiritual understanding.

Costs and Aid: 2007–2008: $21,860 tuition and fees. 97% of students receive some financial aid.

Admissions

Eastern Mennonite University , Office of Undergraduate Admissions
1200 Park Road, Harrisonburg VA 22802
Phone: (540) 432-2665; (800) EMU-COOL
Email: admiss@emu.edu

Service-Learning

EMU Community Learning
www.emu.edu/communitylearning
Phone: (540) 432-4912

Mary Baldwin College

Mary Baldwin College is a dynamic liberal arts college primarily for women dedicated to developing civically and globally engaged citizens.

Flagship Programs

The Spencer Center for Civic and Global Engagement

Facilitated by the Spencer Center, the world becomes the community and the community becomes the classroom. Through service-learning projects, students apply academic knowledge to real life situations while helping others. Such experiences help students grow to become engaged citizens in their communities, nations, and the world.

Virginia Women's Institute for Leadership (VWIL)

VWIL students learn competence and build character as they live and learn in a demanding environment where honor, integrity, and excellence are governing standards. A weekend of community service is required each semester.

Ida B. Wells Living Learning Community

This unique academic residential program addresses the transitional needs of African-American first-year students. Through events and projects, students are equipped with tools for college success, self-discovery, service learning, wellness, and leadership development.

Alternative Spring Break and May Term Trips

Students can choose to spend the week of Spring Break or the three-week May Term participating in one of several organized service learning or community service trips—from working at a girls' home in central Kentucky to doing hurricane relief in the Gulf Coast. Students can initiate ideas for trips, and many options offer credit.

Course Snapshot

PHIL 140 Community and Service Learning

In Professor Rod Owen's PHIL 140 – "Community and Service Learning" course, students meet practical community needs and goals while developing skills in critical thinking and problem solving. This combined course and internship includes hands-on experiences in an approved community agency, religious or humanitarian organization, as well as critical reading and written reflection about service work. Past community partners have included the local women's shelter, the homeless shelter, nursing homes, and after school programs for youth.

Academics

Service-learning courses at MBC help students to be engaged citizens who are committed throughout their lives to making a difference locally and globally.

Biology (BIOL)
Chemistry (CHEM)
Communication (COMM)
Economics (ECON)
Education (ED)
English (ENG)
Health Care Administration (HCA)
History (HIST)
Philosophy (PHIL)
Political Science (POLS)
Psychology (PSYC)
Religion (REL)
Social Work (SOWK)
Sociology (SOC)
Spanish (SPAN)

"The synergy created by combining community-service and international programs at the Spencer Center has given MBC students a greater sense of agency and of their place in the world."

–Professor Bruce Dorries, Ph.D. and Asst. Professor of Communication

Check out all majors at: www.mbc.edu/about/academics.asp

Awards and Recognition

Service-Learning
• President's Honor Roll of Service Learning Colleges and Universities
• Clinton Global Initiative University Inaugural Member

Academic
• *U.S. News & World Report*'s Best Colleges - Top 25 Master's Universities in the South, ranking 23rd
• *Barron's Best Buys in College Education*
• *Colleges of Distinction* (organized by Student Horizons)
• *Princeton Review's Best Colleges in the Southeast*

College Fast Facts

Four-Year, Private, Founded: 1842

Affiliation: Presbyterian

Web site: www.mbc.edu

Student Profile: Residential College for Women, undergraduate students 100% female; 35 states and territories, 4 countries; 33% minority, 2% international.

Faculty Profile: 97% hold a terminal degree in their field. 10:1 student/faculty ratio. Average class size is 16.8.

Athletics: NCAA Division 3, USA South Conference. 6 varsity sports.

Costs and Aid: 2007–2008: $29,200 comprehensive ($22,530 tuition). 98% of students receive some financial aid.

Admissions

Mary Baldwin College, Admissions
Staunton, VA 24401
Main Phone: (540) 887-7019
Phone: (800) 468-2262
Fax: (540) 887-7292
Email: admit@mbc.edu

Service-Learning
Julie Shepherd
Director of Civic Engagement
Phone: (540) 887-7181
Email: civicengagement@mbc.edu

Norfolk State University

Norfolk State is a comprehensive four-year institution committed to providing an affordable high-quality education for an ethnically and culturally diverse student

NSU encourages students to actualize leadership in all components of their educational experiences. As students apply what they have learned in the classroom within the context of addressing real community needs, they increase their commitment to civic engagement and social justice.

Flagship Programs

Department of Nursing

The nursing curriculum at NSU culminates with a service-learning course allowing students to develop and deliver a mental health workshop. Through the workshop, students educate the community about the well-documented disparity in recognition and treatment of mental illness in the African-American community.

Challenge Day

The School of Education Professor, Dr. Norma W. Brumage, coordinated graduate students' participation in the Challenge program sponsored by Norfolk Public Schools. Graduate candidates facilitated small group discussions between students, and helped students review safety methods for urban school settings while discussing bully solutions, gang involvement and awareness, self-esteem, and appropriate decision making for life skills development.

The Ethelyn R. Strong School of Social Work

In one of several service-learning projects, students use advocacy, empowerment, and planning skills to enhance the quality of life of the residents at a health care facility. By using skills learned in social work courses, students gain real-world experience they can use after graduation and beyond.

Course Snapshot

Professional and Technical Writing 303

Professor Michael J. Cotter's class helps students apply business skills to achieve a philanthropic endeavor. In each class students are presented with opportunities to conduct fundraisers for a charity of their choice. Operation Smile recently commended students for their financial donation of more than $1,300. Students' work on abstracts, feasibility reports memos, cover letters and résumés affirms practical expectations for students post-graduation.

Academics

NSU works to equip our diverse student population with the capability to become productive citizens. As a public university, Norfolk State believes it must provide public service and that education should develop social responsibility and involvement in society. One of the University's main goals is to improve understanding of social and public policy problems, contribute to their solution, and recommend preventive strategies. Several courses developed academically-based service and civic projects to build successful student outcomes, enhance critical thinking skills, career explorations, and promote community engagement, traditionally inherent in Historically Black Colleges and Universities.

Some examples of courses with a service-learning component are:

NUR 485-01 Nursing	SWK 312, Social Work
Eed102H Honors English	Spn.111, Intro Spanish
Hum 210,211,212 Humanities	UAF Urban Community placement
HSM 300, Health Management System	POS 180 Political Science
GST 345-1 Honors Seminar	ENT 387-01 Entrepreneurship
INT 387-1 Interdisciplinary Studies	UED 793, Internship inn School Counseling
BIO 100, Biology	Vocal Jazz Ensemble
CPS 895-1 Psychology	SPE 497H Honors Senior Community Serv. Seminar
IMT 205.01/Industrial Safety Management	OEN 200/201 Geometrics, Physical and
MCM 493-01 WSNB Practicum	Instrumentation Engineering

Check out all NSU majors at:
www.nsu.edu/academics

View more service-learning programs at:
www.nsu.edu/servicelearning

Awards and Recognition

Service-Learning

• Listed in the 2007 President's Higher Education Community Service National Honor Roll

• Third place awards in all three categories for the American Association of State Colleges and Universities ADP South Regional Conference on Civic Engagement

• One of three institutions to initiate the Virginia Tidewater Consortium Service-Learning and Civic Engagement Committee comprised of 13 Institutions in South Hampton Roads, Va., 2007

• Appreciation Plaque for Leadership in Community activities: United Way of South Hampton Roads

• Certificate of Appreciation for Students as service facilitators: Eastside Community Development Corporation

• First Place : 2006/7 Students In Free Enterprise(SIFE) Business Entrepreneurs Regional Service-Learning Competition

• NSU Coordinator, Dr. Ross-Hammond, recognized as one of the Authors for Campus Compact's 20th Anniversary Summit, Visioning papers, 2006

• Certificates of Appreciation to NSU Students for Leadership and Service: Annual Youth Skills and Career Building Day Workshops, 2008

College Fast Facts

Four Year, Public, Urban, Founded: 1935

Web site: www.nsu.edu

Student Profile: 6,250 total, including graduate (38% male, 62% female); 1% international, 31% out of state, 92% African american.

Faculty Profile: 314 full-time faculty. 16:1 student/faculty ratio. Most frequent class size is 10-19. 46% of full/part time faculty have Ph.D.'s.

Costs and Aid: 2007-2008: $1,658 in-state tuition, $10,065 out-of-state tuition. $5,588 room and board. 64% of students receive some financial aid.

Admissions
Norfolk State University
700 Park Avenue
Norfolk, VA 23504
Phone: (757) 823-8396

Service-Learning
Service-Learning and Civic Engagement Program
Dr. Amelia Ross-Hammond
Chair, Dept. of Music, and Coordinator
Phone: (757) 823-8568

The College of William and Mary

Our college experience is more than classrooms and books. Rather, it's application. We learn through immersion.

-Allison Anoll, Class of 09

Flagship Programs

Sharpe Community Scholars Program

William & Mary invites every entering freshman to apply and selects approximately 75 highly motivated students who want to connect their academic studies to community activism and participation to live and learn together, engaged in yearlong community-based research projects.

Community Scholars House

The Community Scholars House (CSH) is an interdisciplinary residence hall with an emphasis on integrating civic and service involvement with academic coursework. CSH offers upper level students the opportunity to experience service-learning with a residential option beyond the freshman year.

Student Organization for Medical Outreach and Sustainability (SOMOS)

SOMOS offers unique opportunities for W&M Students, Faculty, and Alumni to engage in service-learning, contribute to an on-going service project, and invest in peaceful, positive change. The team facilitates an annual clinic and engages indigenous knowledge to create shared ownership of local health initiatives in Paraiso, in the Dominican Republic.

Course Snapshot

Citizenship and the Community

Capped at fifteen students, Citizenship and the Community is a reading intensive class exploring competing theories of American democracy. Students are expected to debate and discuss civic engagement and participatory democracy in order to produce a better understanding of American citizenship. These methods of engagement are then transferred into a community project of forum building. Whether in schools, the community, or on the college campus, students facilitate the creation and sustainability of deliberative forums which explore pertinent

Academics

Service-learning at William & Mary provides structured opportunities for people to reflect critically on service experiences; maintains academic rigor; recognizes that the community's definition of its needs is critical to the method's success; strives to build capacity in the community; includes support and evaluation to meet service and learning goals.

Service-learning projects emphasize student development toward community-based research and leadership, in partnership with domestic and international nonprofit and government agencies.

American Studies	Interdisciplinary Studies
Education	• Environmental Studies
English	• Public Health (self-designed)
Global Studies	• Women's Studies
Government	Psychology
Hispanic Studies	Sociology
History	Theatre, Speech, and Dance

For more information about these and other majors, go to: www.wm.edu/academics

Awards and Recognition
Service-Learning
• President's Higher Education Community Service Honor Roll with Distinction.
• WM offers more international service trips than any member of Breakaway, the national alternative breaks organization (2007).

Academics
U.S.News & World Report
• WM ranked sixth among all public universities (2008).
• WM ranked the top public institution in the nation in terms of commitment to teaching.
Newsweek
• Named WM "hottest small-state university" (2006).
Fiske Guide to Colleges (2005)
• WM given the highest rating of academics--five stars.
• WM designated a "Best Buy" because of its combination of quality and cost.
Princeton Review: Best 361 Colleges (2007)
• WM named a "Best in the Southeast" school.
Washington Monthly (2006)
• Washington Monthly rankings, the D.C.-based magazine listed William and Mary as 23rd in the country – second in terms of the percentage of students who go on to serve in the Peace Corps.
• WM ranked 19th nationally (the highest of any Virginia college or university).

College Fast Facts
Four Year, Public, Suburban, Founded: 1693

Web site: www.wm.edu

Student Profile: 5,703 undergraduate students (46% male, 54% female); 52 states and territories, 43 countries; 24% Asian, African-American, Latino/ Hispanic or Native students.

Faculty Profile: 596 full-time faculty. 12:1 student/faculty ratio.

Costs and Aid: 2007-2008: In-state Students: $4,582 comprehensive ($2,774.50 tuition), Out-of-state: $13,467 comprehensive ($11,555 tuition). 85% of students receive financial aid.

Admissions
The College of William and Mary
Undergraduate Admission
P.O. Box 8795
Williamsburg, VA 23187-8795
Office Location: 116 Jamestown Road
Phone: (757) 221-4223
Fax: (757) 221-1242
Email: admission@wm.edu

Service-Learning
Monica Griffin, Ph.D.
Director
Sharpe Community
Scholars Program
Phone: (757) 221-2495
Email: mdgrif@wm.edu

Gonzaga University

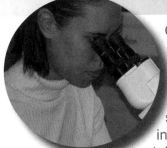

Gonzaga's educational philosophy is based on the Ignatian model and aims to educate the mind, body and spirit through an integration of science, art, faith, reason, action and contemplation.

Flagship Programs

Service-Learning and Mentoring

Gonzaga's Service-Learning program encourages students to serve as mentors. GU students are paired with local school children by one of GU's five different mentoring programs. These programs reach 370-400 of Spokane's neediest elementary and middle school students. Through these offerings, Gonzaga students can discover the importance of developing community locally and serving as ambassadors for life-long learning and service.

Service-Learning in Zambia

Gonzaga offers Service-Learning in Zambia programs for select students. These month-long programs are an opportunity for students to become culturally immersed through service and community development. The Zambia program serves to promote global community development, cultural growth, and broadens a student's understanding of the reality in which they exist.

Faculty Development Grants are awarded to faculty with innovative service-learning course proposals. Annual grants of $700 are given to support course development. Examples of courses developed: Strategies for Dance Instruction, Ecological Thought and Politics, and the Environmental Education Program. These grants allow the integration of the Jesuit mission into the daily lives of students. Theses courses show that living a life of servant leadership contributes to our global community in many unique and valuable ways.

Course Snapshot

PHIL 201: Philosophy of Human Nature

Through working with homeless, disabled and marginalized populations Philosophy of Human Nature students explore the human experience. The Service-Learning project challenges students' assumptions and reveals the complexities of the human condition.

Academics

In accordance with its Jesuit mission to educate men and women for others, Gonzaga University encourages students to deepen their understanding of community and social justice through exploring links between service and academic work. Through interactions with diverse communities, we learn to be effective agents of social change.

The academic focus of Gonzaga University serves to bolster a student's ability to think critically, act ethically, lead justly, and serve purely. The strength of varied course offerings with a focus on servant leadership provides the catalyst for personal growth and a lifetime spent pursuing further opportunities to serve others.

Accounting
Art
Biology
Civil Engineering
Communication Arts:
- Applied Communication Studies
Comprehensive Leadership Program
Exercise Science*
History
Public Relations*

Honors Program*
Law
MA in Teaching English as a Second
- Language
Nursing*
Organizational Leadership
Philosophy
Political Science
Psychology

* Programs with a required service-learning component.

Check out all majors & programs at: www.gonzaga.edu/Admissions/ Undergraduate-Admissions/Academic-Majors-and-Programs.asp

"Service-Learning is an integral part to forming leaders for the common good." ~ Fr. Robert J. Spitzer, S.J. President, Gonzaga University

Awards and Recognition
Academics

• Gonzaga University has been ranked among the best comprehensive regional universities in the Western United States for 16 of the last 19 years by *U.S.News & World Report.*

• *The Princeton Review* has consistently placed Gonzaga among the nation's best colleges.

• Gonzaga is rated #34 out of the top 100 private colleges and universities by Kiplinger for Best Value in Private Education.

College Fast Facts
Four Year, Private, Urban, Founded: 1887

Affiliation: Jesuit Catholic

Web site: www.gonzaga.edu

Student Profile: Undergraduate enrollment 4,385; 46% male, 54% female.

Faculty Profile: Full-time faculty 325; 100% of classes taught by professors. Student-faculty ratio 11:1; average class size 22.

Athletics: NCAA Division I West Coast Conference; baseball, m/w basketball, m/w cross-country, m/w golf, m/w soccer, m/w tennis, m/w track, w volleyball.

Costs and Aid: Tuition $13,910/semester, room & board $7,600 (Double Occupancy w/ Gold Meal Plan). 98% of students receive financial aid.

Admissions

Gonzaga University
Office of Admission
502 E. Boone Avenue
Spokane, WA 99258
Phone: (509) 323-6572; 1(800) 322-2584
Email: mcculloh@gu.gonzaga.edu
www.gonzaga.edu

Service-Learning

Center for Community Action and Service-Learning
Sima Thorpe, Director
Phone: (509) 323-6856, ext. 6856
Email: thorpe@gu.gonzaga.edu

Bethany College

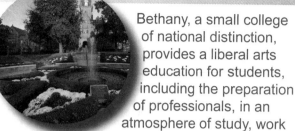

Bethany, a small college of national distinction, provides a liberal arts education for students, including the preparation of professionals, in an atmosphere of study, work and service.

Flagship Programs

Kalon Scholar Service Program

Each spring semester, up to 15 incoming first-year students are awarded a Kalon Scholar Leadership scholarship. Recipients are selected on their ability to become leaders while at Bethany. During the interview process of the scholarship competition, students are queried about their leadership plans and the development of service-learning projects.

In the first year, each recipient is paired with a faculty mentor and then proceeds to develop and provide the service project. Some scholars continue with this project over the following three years, while others change from one year to the next. Upperclass scholars also serve as mentors and one junior or senior is selected to serve as co-advisor to the group each year. Scholars are expected to provide a minimum of 30 service hours per year.

Junior Bison Club

A group activity for local children to experience the joys and benefits of athletic participation. Elementary and middle school children are invited to attend home games for football, basketball, soccer and baseball. The children have an opportunity to meet the players before the game and practice skill development following.

Foreign Language Speak Out Day

Each spring a Kalon Scholar and the World Languages and Cultures Department sponsors a Speak Out Day, where students, faculty and community members speak or sing for 15-minute intervals in a world language other than English.

Relay for Life

Kalon Scholars have helped to organize and direct the campus Relay for Life fundraiser for the American Cancer Society, raising thousands of dollars each year during fall semester.

Academics

Service-learning at Bethany College enhances classroom learning by encouraging students to apply their knowledge and skills to making improvements and providing support services to the local and surrounding communities. As a result, students and residents alike are transformed by the experiences. Working closely with a faculty mentor, students also develop a sense of commitment to community service and professional identity in their chosen field.

The Kalon Scholar Program provides the foundation for service-learning at the College, however a large number of courses also provide substantive opportunities for service-learning. **Service-learning opportunities are available in the following areas:**

English
Social Work
Education
Communication
Psychology
Theatre
Music
Visual Arts
Biology
Chemistry
Environmental Studies
Equine Studies
Physical Education
World Languages and Cultures

"Students and faculty alike benefit greatly from the service-learning experience. For the student the benefit comes from application of learning. For the faculty mentor the experience provides an opportunity to continue to explore an area of interest. Lifetime friendships are forged during the provision of service."

~ Katherine Shelek-Furbee, Social Work

Check out all majors at:
www.bethanywv.edu/academics

College Fast Facts

Four Year, Private, Rural, Founded 1840

Affiliation: Disciples of Christ

Web site: www.bethanywv.edu

Student Profile: 815 undergraduate students (45% male, 55% female); 37 states and territories, 6 countries; 5% minority, 2% international.

Faculty Profile: 57 full-time faculty. 67% hold a terminal degree in their field. 14:1 student/faculty ratio.

Athletics: NCAA Division III, Presidents' Athletic Conference. 20 varsity sports.

Costs and Aid: 2007–2008: $29,800 comprehensive ($18,695 tuition). 90% of students receive some financial aid.

Course Snapshot

SOSC 100: Service-Learning

This course is an experiential learning activity in a social welfare agency or academic setting supervised by a professional. Each student selects from a list of designated settings in an area of interest. To earn credit for the course, a student must complete a minimum of 30 hours of activity and observation in the designated setting; and complete reading assignments, maintain journals, and write an analysis of the experience. The course is designed to provide experience in a practice area such as school social work or elementary education to assist students in making decisions about majors, or to enable students to develop experience-based resumes.

Admissions
Bethany College
Office of Admission
Bethany, West Virginia 26032
Phone: (304) 829-7000
www.bethanywv.edu/admission

Service-Learning
Professor Katherine Shelek-Furbee
Kalon Scholar Advisor and
Chair of Social Work
Phone: (304) 829-7189
Email: kfurbee@bethanywv.edu

Marquette University

Marquette University—where students learn values that last a lifetime—delivers nationally known programs for undergraduates, graduate students and working professionals in the Catholic, Jesuit tradition.

Flagship Programs

South Africa Service-Learning Program
www.marquette.edu/safrica/

Students spend a semester in Cape Town, taking courses through the University of Western Cape and the Desmond Tutu Peace Centre. Students work two days a week for non-governmental organizations in the Cape Town area and participate in many other educational experiences and reflections.

Service-Learning in Spanish

Students in a variety of Spanish classes (e.g. composition, conversation, literature, contemporary issues, business, health professions) provide needed assistance to adults, youth and children in Milwaukee's Spanish-speaking community. About 10% of the service learners each semester come from Spanish courses.

Student Leaders in Service-Learning

The Service-Learning Program staff includes 15 students who work with service learners, faculty and community partners to set up, maintain and evaluate service learning placements and projects. They play a major role in conducting six themed reflections for service learners throughout each semester.

Course Snapshot

PSYC 175: Health Psychology: Using the "Presentation Plus" model of service learning (one of five models practiced at Marquette), Dr. Astrida Kaugars' students worked in groups to design and conduct a Wellness Day (health fair) for students at Our Next Generation after-school program. More than 80 children learned about stress and coping, body image, exercise, nutrition, and self-efficacy. Other courses did similar presentations at the school the same week, which then was dubbed, "MU WEEK AT ONG."

"Our partnership with a community agency to prepare and present the Wellness Day program provides a way of connecting individuals and institutions to teach and learn from one another."
~ Dr. Astrida Kauger

Academics

Following in the Jesuit tradition of faithful service, the Service-Learning Program at Marquette University facilitates student academic learning through meaningful service experiences, which encourage and enable faculty and students to positively impact the community. Service-Learning at Marquette is an academic, course-based program. Courses across the curriculum incorporate a service-learning component.

College of Arts and Sciences: Anthropology, Criminology and Law Studies, English, Foreign Languages and Literature, History, Honors Program, Mathematics and Computer Science, Philosophy, Physics, Political Science, Psychology, Sociology, Social Welfare and Justice, Theology.
College of Business Administration: Economics, Entrepreneurship, Management, Real Estate.
College of Communication: Advertising and Public Relations, Broadcast and Electronic Communication, Communication Studies.
College of Professional Studies: Leadership Studies, Public Service.
School of Education: Counseling, Counseling Psychology, Education, Educational Policy and Leadership.
College of Engineering: Biomedical Engineering, Civil and Environmental Engineering, Electrical and Computer Engineering.
College of Health Sciences: Biomedical Sciences, Exercise Science, Program in Physical Therapy, Speech Pathology and Audiology.

Check out all majors at: www.marquette.edu/student/ugrad/majors

"Family life and stressors become real to them and family communication principles are animated—not simply words in a book." ~ Lynn Turner, Professor of Communication Studies

Awards and Recognition
Service-Learning
• *U.S.News & World Report* recognizes Marquette as one of the best examples of service-learning in a feature characterizing Catholic, Jesuit education as one "that translates into granting students more than just degrees; it means, in the Jesuit tradition, no less than shaping the moral and spiritual character of young men and women."

Academics
• Rigorous programs in 100 undergraduate majors, 36 master's programs, 16 doctoral programs, 10 certificates and nine joint master's programs.
• Home to the state's only dental school and a Law School with a reputation as a forum for public policy debate.
• *U.S.News & World Report* ranks Marquette 81st among the nation's top 100 universities in the 2007 edition of America's Best Colleges and highlights the programs in dispute resolution, biomedical engineering and education.
• *BusinessWeek* ranks the College of Business Administration among the top 50 undergraduate business schools in the nation.

College Fast Facts
Four Year, Private, Urban, Founded: 1881

Affiliation: Roman Catholic - Jesuit

Web site: www.marquette.edu

Student Profile: 7,923 undergraduate students; 11,470 total students (including dental, graduate and law schools); all states and more than 80 countries represented in student population; more than 200 student organizations.

Faculty Profile: 15 to 1 student to faculty ratio; average lower-division class size: 31; average upper-division class size: 25.

Athletics: NCAA Division 1, Big East Conference.

Costs and Aid: 2007-2008 year: $26,270 tuition, $8,590 typical room and board, all families encouraged to file a FAFSA.

Admissions
Roby Blust
Dean of
Undergraduate Admissions
PO Box 1881
Milwaukee, WI 53201-1881
Phone: (414) 288-7302
Email: admissions@marquette.edu

Service-Learning
Bobbi Timberlake
Director, Service-Learning Program
Email:
bobbi.timberlake@marquette.edu
Phone: (414) 288-3261

Ripon College

Ripon College prepares students of diverse interests for lives of productive, socially responsible citizenship.

Flagship Programs

Leadership Studies 100

Students draw on their coursework in group leadership skills and group dynamics as they select and organize a major community program. Projects range from organizing an annual community-wide half-marathon to collecting thousands of books for low-income children.

Creative Enterprise Center

Students in upper-level business administration courses apply their skills as consultants for local nonprofit organizations. Students work individually with a faculty advisor to write business plans, conduct background research, and develop marketing programs that provide dramatic benefits to local agencies.

Applied Spanish

Ripon students personalize their studies in Spanish through a major service-learning project with the Ripon School District. Students study translation by creating documents, practice their communication skills by teaching after-school enrichment courses, and promote literacy by reading aloud bilingual books.

Course Snapshot

SPANISH 541: Applied Spanish

A senior Spanish major and her advisor developed an individualized program to teach Spanish to elementary school students. "I felt that I was really achieving something important," the student reflected. "I got to tackle the real-life challenges of teaching and I ended the project feeling more confident in my skills than I ever expected." As one of several personalized service-learning projects in the course, this student's efforts helped the college win a major award from a regional agency that serves English Language Learners.

Academics

Ripon College students use service-learning to develop as responsible and engaged citizens in our diverse, complex and global community. Our rigorous programs are carefully structured to promote academic enrichment while they provide genuine community benefits. Service-learning provides students a chance to genuinely engage the community, while giving them the skills to be lifelong citizens and leaders.

Anthropology
Art
Biology
Business Administration
Chemistry
Communication*
Educational Studies*
Environmental Studies
Exercise Science

History
Interdisciplinary Studies
Leadership Studies*
Philosophy
Religion
Romance and Classical Languages
Sociology
Spanish

* Courses with a required service-learning component.

Check out all majors at: www.ripon.edu/academics/

"I see such growth in every student involved in these projects... They transform from students into young professionals."

~ Jody Roy, professor of communication

Awards and Recognition

Service-Learning

• President's Higher Education Community Service Honor Roll.

• *Princeton Review's Best 366 Colleges* named Ripon fourth in the nation for positive town-gown relations, in large part because of our strong service-learning program.

• *The Washington Monthly* ranked Ripon among the top 50 colleges for service in 2008, using factors like the number of alumni who join the Peace Corps and the percentage of work-study funds spent on service.

College Fast Facts
Four Year, Private, Rural, Founded: 1851

Web site: www.ripon.edu

Student Profile: 1000 undergraduate students (52% male, 48% female); 34 states and territories, 14 countries; 9% minority, 2% international.

Faculty Profile: 81 full-time faculty. 97% hold a terminal degree in their field. 15:1 student/faculty ratio. Average class size is 20.

Athletics: NCAA Division III, Midwest Conference. 21 varsity sports.

Costs and Aid: 2007-2008: $29,733 comprehensive ($23,048 tuition). 90% of students receive some financial aid.

Admissions
Office of Admission
Ripon College
PO Box 248
Ripon, WI 54971-0248
Phone: (920) 748-8114; (800) 947-4766
Email: adminfo@ripon.edu

Service-Learning
Deano Pape
Director
Office of Community
Engagement
paped@ripon.edu
Phone: (920) 748-8152

University of Wisconsin - Eau Claire

UW-Eau Claire a top Midwest public university with small classes led by talented professors, providing hands-on research and cutting-edge programs.

Flagship Programs

Jumpstart-Eau Claire
a literacy program working toward school preparedness, pairs college students with preschool children for amazing

one on one experiences in area Head Start centers. All children in the centers benefit when Jumpstart works in classrooms improving teacher-child ratios.

Community Leadership Class
This experiential course gives students a better understanding of what it means to be a community leader. Students work with community organizations on a semester-long project. Projects present students with real life challenges and opportunities to develop leadership skills.

Opera On Wheels
The touring outreach arm of the Opera Workshop Ensemble. Its mission is to create enriching, high-energy opera experiences for elementary age children throughout Western Wisconsin. Over the past ten years, Opera On Wheels has performed for over 30,000 elementary school students.

Course Snapshot

IS 460: Seminar in Information Systems
In their last semester, IS seniors develop complete information systems for community clients. Supervised by department chair Tom Hilton, teams serve organizations such as the United Way, YMCA, Boys & Girls Clubs of America, Epilepsy Foundation, and National Alliance for the Mentally Ill. They develop Web sites, databases, and computer networks. They do software maintenance and training. And they learn both professional ethics and personal caring as they awaken to their crucial role in improving the world.

Academics
The University of Wisconsin-Eau Claire commits to educating students for full participation in society by fostering habits of public engagement.
Academics list of programs:

Art & Art History
Biology
Communication Sciences & Disorders
Elementary Education
Environmental Public Health
Health Care Administration
History
Nursing
Secondary Education
Social Work
Special Education

Check out all majors at:
www.uwec.edu/sl/guidebook.htm

Awards and Recognition
Service-Learning
• President's Higher Education Community Service Honor Roll with Distinction for General Community Service 2006 and 2007.
• *U.S.News & World Report* – recognized as one of 38 "Programs to Look For" in Service Learning in 2008.
• Founding member of Wisconsin Campus Compact 2002.

Academics
• Top five of *U.S. News & World Report's 2008 America's Best Colleges* regional public universities in Midwest, ranking 5th and 26th among all private and public institutions in the Midwest.
• *The Princeton Review* designated UW-Eau Claire among one of 161 colleges in Best Midwestern College category.
• *The Princeton Review's 2008 edition of "America's Best Value Colleges* named UW-Eau Claire one of the nation's best-value undergraduate institutions.
• Listed as one of 21 institutions included in the master's institution category on the Fulbright Program's list of colleges and universities that produce the most U.S. Fulbright Fellows.

College Fast Facts
Web site: www.uwec.edu

Student Profile: 10,096 undergraduates; 59% women and 41% men; 5.7% international students; 43 countries.

Faculty Profile: 412 full-time faculty; 84% hold Ph.D. or other terminal degree; 19 to 1 student to faculty ratio (undergraduate).

Athletics: NCAA Division III, 20 intercollegiate sports, UW-Eau Claire has placed first in Women's Conference All Sports Competition seven times in the last 14 years; 6 national team titles; 63 national champions; 27 Academic All-American awards.

Costs and Aid: 2007-2008: $10,465 in-state comprehensive ($5,845 tuition); $10,859 reciprocity with Minnesota ($6,239 tuition); $18,038 out-of-state comprehensive ($7,842). 65 percent of students receive financial aid, including grants, loans, scholarships and/or on-campus employment.

Admissions
UW-Eau Claire, Office of Admissions
Schofield Hall, Room 112
112 Eau Claire, WI 54702-4004
Phone: (715) 836-5415
Email: admissions@uwec.edu

Service-Learning
Center for Service Learning
Donald Mowry, Ph.D., Director
Human Sciences & Services, Room 205
Phone: (715) 836-4649
Email: srvlearn@uwec.edu

The University of Ottawa

The University of Ottawa is a multicultural and officially bilingual institution offering students the opportunity to study – and live – in both French or English.

Flagship Programs

Holocaust Memory Project
Jewish Studies students travel to either Montreal or Toronto for a multi-day experience to visit several cultural centers and to interview Holocaust survivors for individual projects, as well as to contribute to a larger, national initiative to preserve survivor stories.

Science Travels
Science and Engineering students travel to remote communities stretching from North Bay to James Bay to engage high school and Aboriginal youth with fascinating and interactive experiences to prompt them

to consider studies in science and high technology, areas in which they traditionally have very low participation rates.

First Nations Experience
Students in several History and Aboriginal Studies courses partake in a multi-day placement on a first-nation's reserve where they participate in a program that includes volunteerism, cultural events, and lectures from tribal elders.

Course Snapshot

HSS 4324 Community Health Practicum
Health Sciences students travel to Northern Ontario, by Lake Temiskaming, for a month long placement with grass roots organizations, particularly those helping children and the elderly in areas that include nutritional and recreational programs. They also interact with several community groups that teach them about life and society in Canada's north.

"This wonderful experience enabled us not only to expand our knowledge of physical activities for the elderly, but also to introduce us …to the world of community health."

-Isabelle Laplante and Selina Bertuzzo, Students in Nursing

Academics
With the participation of over 120 professors, service-learning at the University of Ottawa is embedded within scores of courses, deepening student engagement, understanding of course theory, and commitment to improving civil society.

Programs of Study include:

Aboriginal Studies	History
Civil Law	Human Kinetics
Common Law	Institute of Canadian Studies
Communications	Management
Criminology	Music
Economics	Philosophy
Education	Political Science
Engineering	Psychology
English	Rehabilitation Science
Environmental Studies	Second Language Institute
Executive MBA	Social Work
Geography	Sociology
	Women's Studies

Check out all majors at:
www.uottawa.ca/academics

"True education includes not only outstanding academic and professional programs, but also the goal of instilling ethics. Community Service Learning benefits us all: it builds a better university, better citizens, and a better society."

-- Gilles Patry, President, University of Ottawa

Awards and Recognition
Service-Learning
• Among university faculty is one of North America's leading theorists on Service Learning, Prof. Joel Westheimer, recently named as a John Glenn Scholar in Service Learning.
• Students receive one free Co-Curricular Record each year listing, describing and quantifying their volunteer service, both course based and non-course based.
• Recipient of a $1 million grant from the J.W. McConnell Family Foundation.
• Recognized by United Way/Centraide Ottawa as a community builder.
• Nearly 1500 students participating in Community Service Leaning per year.
• Selected as the first university outside the United States to host the International Conference on Service-Learning and Community Engagement (2009).

College Fast Facts

Four-Year, Public, Suburban: Founded 1848

Web Site: www.uOttawa.ca

Student Profile: 30,283 undergraduate students (39.4 % male, 60.6% female)

Faculty Profile: 1063 full-time faculty

Costs and Aid: Non-exempt International Students - 2006-2007: $13,701.13 to $21,702.13 (Tuition and incidental fees for undergraduate students, fall-winter, depending on the program of study). Canadian Citizens, Permanent Residents, Exempted International Students – 2006-2007: $4,770.15 to $9,089.13 (Tuition and incidental fees for undergraduate students, fall-winter, depending on the program of study). 35.8% of students receive some financial aid.

Admissions
Undergraduate Admission
Infoservice
Tabaret Hall
75 Laurier Av. E.
Ottawa, Ontario, Canada
K1N 6N5
Toll-free: 1-877-868-8292
Email: infoserv@uOttawa.ca

International Admissions
General inquiries
Email: eureka@uOttawa.ca

Service-Learning
Experiential Learning Service
Professor Jeff Keshen, Manager
100 Marie-Curie, Suite 341
University of Ottawa
Ottawa, Ontario, Canada
K1H 5Y7
Toll-free: 1-877-868-8292, ext. 1287
Email: keshen@uOttawa.ca

notes

notes

notes

index